ABOUT
CRIMINALS

2 Edition

I am very pleased to dedicate this book to Letty Cotton Pogrebin, the most talented writer in our family. With love and respect.

2 Edition

ABOUT
CRIMINALS

A View of the Offenders' World

EDITED BY

MARK R. POGREBIN

University of Colorado at Denver

Los Angeles | London | New Delhi
Singapore | Washington DC

Los Angeles | London | New Delhi
Singapore | Washington DC

FOR INFORMATION:

SAGE Publications, Inc.
2455 Teller Road
Thousand Oaks, California 91320
E-mail: order@sagepub.com

SAGE Publications Ltd.
1 Oliver's Yard
55 City Road
London EC1Y 1SP
United Kingdom

SAGE Publications India Pvt. Ltd.
B 1/I 1 Mohan Cooperative Industrial Area
Mathura Road, New Delhi 110 044
India

SAGE Publications Asia-Pacific Pte. Ltd.
33 Pekin Street #02-01
Far East Square
Singapore 048763

Acquisitions Editor: Jerry Westby
Editorial Assistant: Erim Sarbuland
Production Editor: Karen Wiley
Copy Editor: Amy Rosenstein
Typesetter: C&M Digitals (P) Ltd.
Proofreader: Laura Webb
Indexer: Jennifer Pairan
Cover Designer: Michael Dubowe
Marketing Manager: Erica DeLuca
Permissions Editor: Karen Ehrmann

Copyright © 2012 by SAGE Publications, Inc.

Printed in the United States of America

Library of Congress Cataloging-in-Publication Data

About criminals : a view of the offenders' world/editor,
Mark R. Pogrebin.—2nd ed.

p. cm.
Includes bibliographical references and index.

ISBN 978-1-4129-9944-1 (pbk. : acid-free paper)

1. Criminals—United States. 2. Criminal behavior—United States.
3. Crime—United States. I. Pogrebin, Mark.

HV6789.A3442 2012
364.30973—dc23   2011033239

This book is printed on acid-free paper.

11 12 13 14 15 10 9 8 7 6 5 4 3 2 1

CONTENTS

PREFACE

The purpose of this book is to present students with recent and important research on criminal behavior. The methodological approach taken is termed naturalistic, one that allows criminals to discuss their offenses and lifestyles from their perspective. Having offenders' voices heard along with the researchers' analyses offers students a real-life view of what, how, and why various criminals behave the way they do. In short, the field studies conducted by the authors for all the articles in this anthology should provide the reader with a realistic portrayal of just what actual offenders say about crime and their participation in it.

In this anthology, I have chosen a collection of readings that highlight criminological concepts that are extremely relevant to the study of crime and criminals. The articles explore a wide array of specific types of criminal behavior, covering the majority of topics on criminal types found in almost every standard criminological text. This book is unique because each type of crime is arranged under a particular subject, with different perspectives discussed for similar types of criminal behavior.

In this second edition of *About Criminals*, I have kept the organization of the subject topics the same while adding a new section on "support systems and crime," an important subject that has been neglected by many anthologies on crime and criminals. Although I have shortened the actual number of articles from four to three per section, I have expanded the readings to reflect the issues and changes that have occurred in the world of criminals. The study of crime and those who participate in its various offender activities is not static, but rather fluid and ever-changing, which accounts for the majority of the new articles in the second edition. Some of the articles included in this new edition were published some years ago because of their classic nature. However, most of the selections are more recent and offer some new perspective on offense types considered new research, conducted by social scientists of a more recent era. Many new criminology researchers are using a qualitative approach to relate the offenders' perspective as the major focus of their studies.

The readings feature field study research on property crimes, violent crimes, sex crimes, white-collar crimes, gangs and crime, drugs and crime, gender and crime, support systems, and a final section on desistance from crime. Along with the articles, I introduce each category of crime and describe each article's contents. These introductions are meant to help students understand the method that each researcher used to conduct the study as well as to provide an overall description of the study's general contents.

It is my belief that the naturalistic approach using field studies will assist students in gaining a more in-depth understanding of how criminological theories of crime causation actually relate to real-world examples of criminal behavior. I have found from years in the college classroom that the real-world accounts of offenders for their criminality facilitate active learning and tend to motivate student participation in a more meaningful way by connecting abstract theoretical concepts to the real-life experiences of criminals.

About Criminals: A View of the Offender's World can be used in courses as a supplemental anthology in criminology courses and as a separate text for those courses taught from a criminal behavior systems approach. Either way this book is used, it should aid students in providing an analytical perspective on the various motivations and explanations for types of criminal behavior. Perhaps being introduced to the different types of criminal offenses and offenders throughout this book may dispel many of the myths or stereotypes we tend to believe about criminals based on images we receive from movies, media outlets, and television. We may then develop a more realistic understanding of why and how offenders commit particular crimes and how they account for their involvement in such a deviant lifestyle.

ACKNOWLEDGMENTS

First, I would like to thank the authors who wrote the articles that make up this anthology. Some written in past years, and others more recently, are representative of high-caliber research on crime and criminals.

Jerry Westby, criminal justice editor at SAGE, deserves my gratitude for his belief in this project and his encouragement to produce this second edition. Jerry's suggestions for ways to improve the book were most helpful. My thanks to Erim Sarbuland, editorial assistant, for help with all of the important logistics that were necessary to get this book produced and published. A very special thanks to my student assistant Alexander Dahl, for all of his help throughout these past months with every aspect of the book's production, not to mention his patience and positive attitude. A very special thank-you to copy editor Amy Rosenstein for finding numerous errors in the manuscript that needed correction. I would like to the thank the following reviewers for their feedback on the first edition from which I and the book benefited: Lawrence Bench, University of Utah; Peter English, California State University, Fresno; Robert Lombardo, Loyola University, Chicago; Gina Respass, Old Dominion University; Gerald R. Venor; Colorado State University; and Volkan Topalli; Georgia State University. I would also like to thank the following reviewers for the second edition: Angela Butts, Rutgers the State University of New Jersey, New Brunswick; Philip Davis, Georgia State University; Walter S. DeKeseredy, University of Ontario Institute of Technology; Heather Griffiths, Fayetteville State University; Stephen Hagan, Southern Illinois University; Charles Hanna, Duquesne University; Angie Henderson, University of Northern Colorado, Greeley; Robert J. Homant, University of Detroit Mercy; Lutz Kaelber, University of Vermont, Burlington; Chad Kimmel, Shippensburg University of Pennsylvania; Brenda Lauts, University of New Mexico; Gina Luby, Depaul University Chicago; Kate Luther, Pacific Lutheran University; Michelle Mackinem, Claflin University; Michael Massoglia, Pennsylvania State University; James D. Orcutt, Florida State University, Tallahassee; Pete A. Padilla, University of Colorado Denver; Victor Shaw, California State University, Northridge; Melissa Thompson, Portland State University; Janelle Wilson, University of Minnesota; and Edward F. Vacha, Gonzaga University.

Last, but not least, a special thanks to Howard Eiden, close friend, retired probation officer who was forced to listen to my numerous discussions about my ideas for this book for too many months.

ABOUT THE EDITOR

Mark R. Pogrebin is a professor of criminal justice in the school of public affairs at the University of Colorado at Denver. He has conducted numerous field studies in the areas of police undercover work, police and tragic events, African-American policewomen, emotion management, women jailers, psychotherapists' deviant behavior with clients, women in prison and on parole, the strategic uses of humor among police, ex-prisoners' reentry problems, and elite high school students' academic dishonesty. He has published six books, the most recent being a coauthored monograph *Guns, Violence and Criminal Behavior,* and numerous journal articles and has had more than 30 of his publications reprinted in anthologies.

INTRODUCTION

The vast majority of criminology textbooks break particular types of crimes into groupings or classifications, such as white-collar or property offenses and so on, for the purposes of describing and analyzing multiple variations of criminal behavior. Grouping or typifying certain categories of offenses and offenders may serve to highlight types of criminal behavior and allow for systematic study. This anthology attempts to do just that. Its purpose is to provide students with a more in-depth understanding of the types of criminality by using studies that not only break down particular crimes into specific categories, but that also include the offenders' self-explanations or accounts for their criminal activities and lifestyles.

Some years ago, Clinard and Quinney (1973) attempted to define or distinguish types of criminality because they believed that putting particular crimes into categories allowed for a level of commonality for comparative and systematic analysis. Scarpitti and Nielson (1999, p. 318) note, "It has been shown that criminal typologies are helpful in allowing us to understand the nature of criminal offenses." According to Meier (1989), behavior system typologies can be used for organizing data about offenders and are used by researchers to break crimes into smaller, more meaningful categories.

The historical argument for the limitations of approaching the study of crime by looking at separate types of criminal offenses is understood. There is an awareness that most offenders do not generally specialize in a particular type of criminal activity, but rather participate in a variety of offenses. In short, criminals are versatile, not specialized, because the majority of their crimes are not planned, but rather are opportunistic in nature. However, adult criminals are more likely to specialize in a particular type of crime than are juveniles (Kempf, 1987), especially if they are actively participating in ongoing criminal activities.

I am cognizant of the debate, pros and cons, strengths and weaknesses, for studying crime typologies. What I am attempting to accomplish with the production of this anthology is to offer criminology students the opportunity to gain insight into crime and criminals by offering them research on actual offenders who, throughout the majority of the pages in this book, actually discuss and provide details of offending behavior and reasons for their participation in crime. That is, their motivations, descriptions of how they operate, their thoughts about victims, and a whole host of "thick" descriptive analysis about their unlawful lifestyles are discussed. The objective is to provide students with the opportunity to draw their own conclusions about crime and criminals based on the interviews and observations of offenders portrayed in the 26 selected studies published in this book.

The ultimate value for the naturalistic use of field studies with criminals is best said by Miethe and McCorkle (2001, p. 17) in their discussion of the importance of letting offenders relate their personal experiences and rationale for their behavior:

> One of the most important but often neglected sources of data about crime is offenders' own accounts. Perpetrators of crimes are in the unique position of being able to describe, in their own words, the motivations and causes of crime, the level and nature of crime calculus, and the perceived effectiveness of crime control activities in detecting crime. Narrative accounts by offenders also provide the rich details about the situational dynamics of crime and target selection process.

The articles selected in this book of readings offer a naturalistic method for the study of various types of crimes and offenses. Every article used a fieldwork perspective, which stresses interpretive, ethnographic methods that attempt to provide insightful knowledge at a close range (Daly & Chesney-Lind, 1988) and, further, expose parts of the criminal's social world that often remain hidden by more traditional methodological techniques (Caulfield & Wonders, 1994). The selected studies attempt to have offenders explain how they make sense of the world in which they live (Spradley, 1980).

Any book of readings attempts to offer a comprehensive view of the subject matter's contents. However, it would be prohibitive to select articles that cover every type of crime. Therefore, as author, I purposely based my selection of writings on two major criteria; the first being the perceived interests to students, coupled with my subjective thoughts on the quality and relevance for each study chosen, and the second, the availability of naturalistic, qualitative type articles for particular categories of crime. To my surprise, there remains a genuine void of naturalistic materials for some criminal types, and as a result, there is a bit of overlap between a few categories. It is my belief that this publication will bring to life the world of crime and criminals for students who are striving for a connection between theory and reality.

REFERENCES

Caulfield, S., & Wonders, N. (1994). Gender and justice: Feminist contributions to criminology. In G. Barak (Ed.), *Varieties of criminology* (pp. 213–229). Westport, CT: Prager.

Clinard, M., & Quinney, R. (1973). *Criminal behavior systems.* New York: Holt, Rinehart, and Winston.

Daly, K., & Chesney-Lind, M. (1988). Feminism and criminology. *Justice Quarterly, 5,* 497–535.

Kempf, K. (1987). Specialization and the criminal career. *Criminology, 25,* 399–420.

Meier, R. (1989). *Crime and society.* Boston: Allyn & Bacon.

Miethe, T., & McCorkle, R. (2001). *Crime profiles.* Los Angeles: Roxbury Publishing.

Scarpitti, F., & Nielsen, A. (1999). *Crime and criminals.* Los Angeles: Roxbury Publishing.

Spradley, J. (1980). *Participant observation.* New York: Hold, Rinehart, and Winston.

PART I

PROPERTY CRIMES

Property crimes are the most frequent type of offenses committed in the United States. As distinguished from violent offenses, property crimes most often do not have a confrontational interaction between offenders and victims. According to the Uniform Crime Reports list of property index crimes, burglary, larceny-theft, motor vehicle theft, and arson are considered the most serious property offenses. However, vandalism, receiving stolen property, shoplifting, and destructive acts against property are included under the definition of property offenses.

From the following section of readings, readers can see that property crimes are committed by males and females, adults and adolescents. Decision-making and motivations for committing these crimes are explored. I have attempted to provide an introspective view of various property crimes. Although far from being comprehensive of every type of crime that comes under this offense category, the readings will offer some insight into those law violators who commit these crimes as well as the rationale they provide for their offenses.

The first chapter, by Vera Lopez, uses symbolic interactionist and cultural perspectives to explain male adolescent property offenders' involvement in committing property crimes. Lopez sought to understand what youthful persons were thinking and feeling during the unlawful event, and what their motivations were at that time. Lopez further studied how the adolescent offenders would interpret and formulate meaning in relation to the delinquent act.

The issue of participation in streetlife as it relates to auto theft was explored by Heith Copes. Here, the author examined the offenders' perceived rewards within the street-life subculture for committing this particular property crime. Copes focuses on criminal decision-making and the extensive values street-life culture imposes on those auto thieves who perceive themselves to be active participants in this type of lifestyle.

Christopher W. Mullins and Richard Wright explored and analyzed how gender structures the crime of residential burglary and, further, how it affects criminal opportunities and perceptions of meanings for both male and female participants. The comparisons between man and woman property offenders are examined together with how these gender-based social networks, which play such an important role in the street-life subculture, affect and influence the actual commission of burglary for both participating sexes.

1

UNDERSTANDING ADOLESCENT PROPERTY CRIME USING A DELINQUENT EVENTS PERSPECTIVE

VERA LOPEZ

The perceptions of adolescent offenders' involvement in property crimes are the focus of this paper. These youthful teenagers provided information regarding the various situations in which they committed their criminal activity, and their thoughts and emotions during the property offense itself. Multiple motives and interactions that were related to the youthful offenders' interpretive meaning for their involvement in property crimes was explored.

INTRODUCTION

Property crimes committed by adolescents represent a significant economic and societal problem in the United States. Indeed, although Property Crime Index arrest rates, which include burglary, larceny-theft, auto theft, vandalism, shoplifting, and arson, have been declining in recent years (Snyder 2004), adolescents still continue to commit property crimes more often than any other types of crimes (Klaus 2006). To the extent that adolescent offenders choose to engage in property crime, it becomes important to examine the events and conditions leading up to the decision to commit crime as well as the subjective (offenders' perceptions) and objective (e.g., presence of peers, drug/alcohol use) characteristics associated with the offending situation, otherwise known as the "immediate setting" in which criminal behavior takes place (Birkbeck and LaFree 1993:115). Ultimately, such offender-based and offense-specific explanations can play a significant role in the development of crime theory and prevention.

APPROACHES FOR STUDYING CRIME FROM A SITUATIONAL PERSPECTIVE

Criminal or Delinquent Events Perspective

Researchers have, in recent years, begun to adopt a more integrated approach for the study of crime situations resulting in the development of the criminal events perspective (CEP) (Meier et al. 2001; Sacco and Kennedy 2002). The CEP challenges the offender-based focus of most criminological theories in favor of an integrated perspective, which includes simultaneously examining the offenders' perceptions and characteristics, the victim, and the situational correlates and context of specific offenses associated with the criminal event, or what I refer to as the "delinquent event" in the current study.

Criminal and delinquent events, unlike criminal acts, involve a beginning, middle, and an end (Kazemian and LeBlanc 2004; Sacco and Kennedy 2002), and have been alternatively referred to as the precursor, transaction, and aftermath phases (Sherley 2004). The beginning or precursor phase involves what was going on prior to the commission of the crime and includes an examination of the preexisting offender—victim relationship, interactions with peers, and emotional and cognitive states. The transaction phase, in turn, involves examining what occurred during the commission of the crime. Understanding the interactions as how these interactions are influenced by contextual and situational dynamics is crucial at this stage. Finally, the aftermath phase involves what happened after the crime, including what the offender did afterward as well as any resulting short-term and long-term legal or social consequences.

STUDY PURPOSE

The purpose of the present study was to expand on the situational crime literature by using the criminal events perspective (Meier et al. 2001; Sacco and Kennedy 2002) to guide an examination of male adolescents' subjective interpretations of delinquent events characterized by the commission of property crimes. Symbolic interactionism in conjunction with a cultural studies approach (Dotter 2004) provided the theoretical backdrop for the study. Although the major focus of this study was to explore how male adolescents define, interpret, and justify their actions within criminal offending situations and how cognitions and emotions influence decisions to commit property crimes, it was also recognized that their narratives represented

idealized accounts, which in turn were shaped and influenced by larger cultural idealizations centered on youth, offenders, gender, and in some cases, race and ethnicity. Finally, it should be noted that my interpretation of the adolescents' narratives were also influenced and shaped by larger cultural idealizations and discourses pertaining to offenders, youth, gender, and race/ethnicity. In particular, social science research, most notably dominant criminological theories steeped in modernist traditions, influenced my own thinking about the adolescents' narratives. Thus, when appropriate, I refer to, and ultimately critique these theoretical approaches when discussing the narratives.

METHODS

Study Participants and Recruitment

Twenty-four male adolescent offenders, ages 14–20, participated in this study. All youths were under the supervision of the state juvenile correction agency. Eleven of the youths were Mexican American; five were white; and eight were African American. Eighty-five percent came from midsized or larger cities, and 15 reported a previous gang affiliation.

In an attempt to maximize the number of accounts and variation in responses, youths were recruited from two settings: a residential treatment home and a halfway home. Youths across the two settings differed with regard to length of stay. Residential treatment youths had completed half their stay whereas the halfway home youths were in the process of being transitioned into the community. Despite this, youths across both settings were similar in terms of age, race/ethnicity, inner-city background, and gang affiliation.

Data Collection

A semistructured interview was used to obtain information about each adolescent's perceptions of his delinquent acts. All interviews were tape recorded and transcribed in a private setting; therefore, only the participant and I were present during the interview.

Although information was obtained on other types of crimes, this study specifically focused on delinquent events characterized by the commission of property crimes. To accomplish this, I asked each adolescent to discuss all crimes that he could remember committing in his lifetime. I then asked each adolescent to:

Think back to a time when you committed a crime. Can you remember that time? Okay, now I'd like you to tell me a story about that time. I want you to tell me everything you can remember beginning with what you were doing several hours before, during, and after the crime. I also want you to tell me what you were thinking and feeling at each of these points, just as if you were telling me a story about what happened that day.

ANALYSIS

Working inductively, I coded each delinquent event according to what I though was the primary motivation as well as the participant's thoughts and feelings prior to, during, and after the commission of a property crime. Additionally, I coded for the degree and presence of planning, peer involvement, and drug/alcohol use. I focused on these three aspects of the delinquent events accounts for two reasons. First, most of the adolescents mentioned these three components in their narratives. Thus I wanted to determine if, from the adolescents' perspectives, these three aspects influenced how they viewed their participation within the delinquent event. Second, previous delinquent events research suggests that planning, peers, and drug/alcohol use play a prominent role in the commission of delinquent acts (see Kazemian and LeBlanc 2004). Finally, I developed codes focused on feelings of remorse and regret as they related to the victim as well as whether thoughts about getting caught influenced the decision to commit a property crime. However, because the majority of the adolescents failed to discuss any feelings of remorse/regret, I was only able to code whether they expressed remorse/regret or not. A colleague independently coded the transcripts based on my previously established coding categories. We cross-classified our results and found substantial reliability in our categorization of these events.

RESULTS

The sample of 24 adolescents described 60 delinquent events characterized by the commission of a property crime. Property crimes included any act of destroying or stealing property even when the primary motive was to "get back"[1] at an actual person(s). Examples of such crimes included thief, shoplifting, auto theft, arson, burglaries, vandalism, and drive-bys (only when directed against property, without the specific intent to directly harm someone).

Four motive/interpretive strategies emerged as a result of the data analysis. That is, each motive was associated with a certain set of events and conditions, which served as cues to guide the adolescents' interpretive process and eventual meaning construction. Put another way, motive/interpretive strategies were closely associated with the situational context. Qualitative accounts of each delinquent event context, as characterized by one of these motives—thrill seeking, coping, defending the gang's honor and obtaining material goods—are presented in what follows. However, because delinquent events are characterized by complex interactions between individual offenders and situational contexts and dynamics, I present only the most "popular" scenarios, that is, those that were most often reported, for each motive-driven crime type.

CRIME MOTIVES

In Search of Thrills

Thirty-one (52%) of the 60 delinquent acts involving property offenses were committed primarily for "kicks," "fun," or "thrills." Different property crimes, including theft, shoplifting, burglary, vandalism, and auto theft characterized this type of delinquent event. Although most of the crimes in this category were committed in the presence of peers, some youths also reported committing crimes alone. The most salient aspect of these events, irrespective of whether only one youth or more than one youth participated, was the degree of risk involved: the higher the risk, the more attractive the crime. Despite these similarities, delinquent events characterized by a group of offenders versus a solo-offender were distinct on a number of qualitative dimensions.

Group Crimes. Twenty-one delinquent events were committed either in pairs or in groups of three or more adolescents. The following example demonstrates a delinquent event characterized by the search for thrills and the presence of "co-conspirators," as narrated by an 18-year-old African-American male:

> . . . We had just come back from a party . . . and everybody was real hungry. So they said, "Let's go to Denny's and run out." We all went to Denny's. I didn't order a whole lot. I didn't want them [Denny's employees] to get suspicious. If we ordered all this food,

---

[1]Throughout the text, I use quotation marks to signify the participants' words to distinguish them from my own.

they might get suspicious. But my friends ordered a lot of desserts and stuff. Then the lady brought us the ticket. All my friends, they walked to the car. I played it off like they was giving me money for the meal. So I walked up to the counter and they [friends] were already in the car. And told the person [Denny's employees], "I need to ask my friends something." And she said, "Hold on sir." I ran out, went through two doors, and jumped in the car and took off. It was a thrill.

This account provides an illustration of a crime that was committed with a high risk of getting caught. That is, the youth was readily identifiable to many witnesses and the crime was in a public setting. Nevertheless, the youth decided to participate, indicating that the crime would not have been "as fun" had there not been at least "some possibility" of getting caught. Despite this, the youth acknowledged that he was not "overly concerned" with getting caught because he figured he could "outrun the lady [Denny's employee]."

Other adolescents also reported committing property crimes primarily for fun. A 19-year-old Mexican-American male described how he and his friends broke into a neighborhood "mom and pop" store. According to this adolescent, he was feeling bored when he and his friends came across a store that had an unlit storefront on the way home from a night of "drinking and partying." When asked why he committed the crime, the youth responded, "I didn't break in the store for money. I had a pocketful of money. I was bored. I did it just for the fun of it, the excitement I guess."

At other times, adolescents admitted that they were motivated by both a desire to obtain stolen goods and to "put excitement in [their] day." However, their accounts of these delinquent events tended to focus primarily on the fun they had while committing the crimes, as opposed to their ill-begotten material goods, as illustrated by the following account from an 18-year-old white male:

... We robbed this dude's house. And we found a little ounce of weed underneath his bed in a little tin tray and a little bong, a green one. It was tight. We hit it hard ... put a porno flick on the TV ... had a good time ...

Although the youth initially decided to break into the house to steal, it became clear that he also enjoyed the process of committing the burglary. Again, the high-risk nature of the crime, as indicated by the youth staying in the home and "smoking [a] bong" and watching

TV may have added to the dangerous allure of the delinquent experience.

As the previous narratives illustrate, group crimes, at least from the perspective of adolescents, are often characterized by a sense of risk-taking and camaraderie. Indeed, peers played a number of salient roles in these delinquent events dramas. They served as "co-conspirators" who not only participated in the decision to commit the crime, but also helped carry it out by partaking in a number of supporting roles ranging from decoy to lookout. Additionally, they served as audience members to the individual offenders antics. And, of course, they always stayed to celebrate the successful completion of the crime, as illustrated by a 16-year-old Mexican-American male who described what happened after the commission of a group theft:

When we was done and at the house, we were mostly ragging on [friend's name] for going down the candy aisle and almost getting us busted right then and there. We were laughing at him and laughing at us, saying, "Yeah, we got away!" even though we tipped the sensor off!

Another youth, a 15-year-old African-American male, described what happened after participating in a joint shoplifting spree with peers:

We ran out to the car, and almost got caught; it was a close call. But we made it. We all ran out, drove off in our cars, and met up at the school. We got out, jumped up and down, hollering, just acting a fool, clowning, and laughing ... cheering like we'd just accomplished something good.

Not surprisingly, alcohol (and more rarely marijuana) played an important role in postcrime celebrations with groups of young men often meeting up afterward to drink and laugh about their close calls. Sometimes, as in the case with the store theft described earlier, youths reported drinking or smoking marijuana prior to committing the crime. However, what was absent from these accounts was any insight into the role that drugs/alcohol might have played in their decision to commit crimes. Although the youths generally acknowledged that the alcohol or drugs (usually marijuana) made them feel good, rarely did they report a belief that drugs/alcohol influenced their decisions.

As the aforementioned narratives illustrate, adolescent offenders like other groups of offenders commit crimes for fun and thrills (Copes 2003; Hochstetler 2002; Jacobs et al. 2003; Katz 1988) with little precrime planning beyond an agreed upon decision to commit the offense (Kazemian and LeBlance 2004). The intent was to engage in a group crime for the primary benefit of having fun in a highly risky context (Copes 2003; Katz 1988; Jacobs et al. 2003; Jacobs and Wright 1999). Thus, from an interpretive perspective, the adolescents approached and continued to view their participation in these delinquent events as inconsequential, harmless fun. They did not express remorse or regret and did not view their participation as problematic from a personal viewpoint even if they did acknowledge that it was problematic from a legal standpoint.

Solo-Crimes. Ten thrill crimes were committed alone. A 16-year-old white male provided an example of a solo-crime committed for thrills:

> ... The best house I ever broke into? It was this security guard's house. ... I know 'cause he had his uniform in there. I went in and checked under the bed first to see if he had guns or anything. And I opened up some drawers and he had stacks about this high (holds hand about 2 feet off the ground) of *Playboys* and *Penthouse* and I flipped through them. ... I then started looking through other drawers and stuff and I found a .22, an old-fashioned .22, yeah! And I also found a Crown Royal bag and it was just like a Christmas present. I opened it up. It was a chrome .25 and I was feeling powerful. Like I had some power. ... That was my best house!

Although the youth clearly enjoyed the items he stole, his reaction to the guns went beyond a utilitarian desire for money. An 18-year-old white male described a similar depiction; he also compared the process of committing burglary to Christmas:

> It does give you a rush. ... Once you crack that window and you're inside the house, it's like Christmas Day. Anything in this house is yours and you never know what you are going to find. Guns, jewelry. ... You always gonna find jewelry. Anything you see. It's just like Christmas. That's the best I can explain it. It's yours.

Solo-crimes lacked the celebratory component associated with the group thrill crimes. Instead, adolescents derived their enjoyment primarily from the "power" they felt when sorting through other people's belongings. This was particularly evident with burglaries, as illustrated in the aforementioned narrative. The youths also seemed to be very in-tuned to the material objects they accrued, as illustrated by the second example. The stolen goods represented objects of affection as opposed to generic items that could be easily pawned for money and drugs (Katz 1988). Such

a relationship between the offender and the stolen goods was not evident in the group crime situations.

Coping With Frustration, Anger, and Hopelessness

In 10 (17%) of the 60 property crime delinquent events, adolescents committed acts of vandalism, theft, and arson primarily out of an extreme state of frustration, anger, or hopelessness stemming from what they perceived as an injustice done to them by another. In each instance, the adolescent reported either trying to initially address the perceived injustice in a conventional manner, only to be met with failure, or he reported a belief that alternative noncrime means for solving the problem would most likely meet with failure. As a result, these adolescents coped with their feelings of frustration and anger by taking matters into their own hands. In seven instances, they reported destroying or, less commonly, stealing the property of their perceived perpetrator(s). Alternatively, in three instances, they destroyed property that was somehow associated with the perceived perpetrator, as illustrated by the following narrative from a 17-year-old Mexican-American male who described how a school fight led to a negative encounter with the school principal, which in turn, precipitated the destruction of school property.

> And the principal started taking his side. He [the principal] started raggin' on me and talking all this mess about my negative attitude and stuff that already had happened in the past. He suspended me! I didn't start the fight, the other dude did and he didn't get nothing. ... I was so mad, mad that the principal and the teachers always blame everything on me. That's why I went back after school and busted up all the windows with a baseball bat. I made sure to especially get the principal's office windows. I didn't think it was fair what he did to me. And I showed him what I thought of it ...

As this narrative illustrates, the youth did not believe that the school principal had treated him fairly. Thus, he decided to take matters in his own hands by committing a property crime characterized by aggression. He planned when and where to commit the crime and waited until after school to carry out his plan. Thus, this crime instance was not an impulsive response, but rather one that was thought out. The school represented a symbolic representation of the principal, thus making it the ideal target for the youth to release his pent-up frustration and anger at a perceived injustice. Not surprisingly, instead of feeling remorse or regret, the youth instead reported a "feeling of accomplishment" and a belief that justice had been established, or in his own words that the "the principal and the teachers got what they deserved."

In another example, a 17-year-old white male, described why he decided to steal from an ex-girl-friend:

I went to her [ex-girlfriend] house . . . and I asked her if she wanted to come drink with me . . . and she was like, "Nah." So I was like, "Then, can I get a cup of ice?" She gave me the ice and I went back drinking. I wasn't even buzzing, but I went back to her house and told her can I get another cup of ice and she had this attitude with me and I was like, "Whatever." And then she said, "Is that all you come to my house for is a cup of ice? All you doing is coming up to my house for a cup of ice, you don't even want to talk to me." I was like, "Man, whatever, fuck you bitch! I don't give a fuck!" And I just left. And I knew where she kept her key, she kept it under the stairs . . . so like a couple of weeks later l told my homeboy [peer's name], "know this really easy hit we can pull fool, make some easy money. Buy some dope . . . ."And we just broke in. I stole money out of her room. I think 20 out of her sister's room. I stole all her mom's jewelry.

When asked if he was trying to get back at his ex-girl-friend for slighting him, the youth at first responded, "It was all about easy money." But then he went on to state:

I didn't really care about the bitch anymore. I was happy when I did it. I just didn't give a fuck about her anymore. She was getting a funky ass little attitude with me, talking trash and stuff. And she slammed the door on my face. I was like, "Fuck that bitch if she wants to be a stuck up little bitch!" I don't care.

Although he professed that the crime was "all about easy money," it was clear that his ex-girlfriend was tar-geted in large part because she had displayed an "atti-tude" and had slammed the door in the youth's face.

Some youths indicated that they participated in property crimes as a way to cope with life stressors. However, they spoke in general terms as opposed to describing specific delinquent events. Nevertheless, their narratives provide further insight into the link between coping and property crimes as indicated by the following passage from a 16-year-old Mexican-American male:

My life was fucked up. . . . We didn't have no food, never had nothing nice like other people have. Shit. . . . Life

was just totally fucked up. Ever since we were growing we lived in shelters and all that shit. That shit was stressful. . . . You didn't know what the fuck to do. . . . So whenever we got the chance to get away and have fun, we did crime. We stole things, destroyed things. . . . That was just something to do to get our minds off things.

Although youths sometimes used drugs/alcohol as a means for coping with life stressors, such usage was not consistently associated with coping crimes. Only 4 of the 10 coping crimes involved drug/alcohol use at some point in time. These data, although limited in scope, indicate that committing crimes served as a way to deal with problematic situations above and beyond the use of drugs/alcohol.

From an interactionist perspective, adolescents mentally processed problematic situations and arrived at the conclusion that they themselves were the true victims. As a result of their interpretations, they became angry and incensed. To cope and deal with these feelings, they engaged in an emblematic attack against their perceived oppressor characterized by either destroying or stealing his or her property. Such an interpretive outlook is consistent with Agnew's (1992, 2001) General Strain Theory (GST), which refers to strains as "relationships in which others are not treating the individual as he or she would like to be treated" (Agnew 1992:48). Under such circumstances, according to Brezina (1996), strains or stressors increase the likelihood of negative emotions like anger and frustration, which in turn create pressures for "corrective action," with crime being a particularly appealing coping response for some individuals. However, unlike Agnew's GST, an interpretive frame-work emphasizes how the offender's interpretation of the situation results in his decision to engage in the delinquent act. In this respect, the individual is an actor with agency, not just a person who reacts to a problematic situation with anger. Additionally, a cul-tural studies perspective would take this analysis one step further by asking why these adolescent males interpreted the event in the way that they did and why they ultimately decided to participate in the emblem-atic attack against their victim.

Defending the Gang

I coded six (10%) of the 60 property crime delin-quent events as gang crimes committed because the individual believed that his gang had been affronted in some way. Two types of property crimes, vandalism and drive-by shootings, typified this context. Precrime feeling of "nervous energy" and "adrenaline highs" along with negative thoughts about the victim[2] (i.e., victim as the oppressor) characterized these crime contexts. Other characteristics included the presence of "co-conspirators," drug/alcohol use, and the use of weapons, as illustrated by the following narrative:

> . . . Me and a bunch of my homeboys
> found out this [rival gang name] was talking noise
> about jumping [fellow gang member's name] so we was
> upset so we went and got a bunch of zay, you know,
> embalming fluid on weed . . . and we smoked to curb
> those feelings . . . it [zay] made us even more crazier.
> Psyched us up and we planned it out. We got together
> and we drove by the house and shot it up and then we
> took the back streets until we hit [name of freeway] to
> [name of club]. If the police come around . . . they
> [owners] would say, "Hey, they were here the whole
> night. And they never left."

When asked to state the primary reason why he engaged in the drive-by, the youth indicated, "Because I wanted to hurt or scare him [enemy] for what he did to [gang member's name] and to show him up for messing with [gang name]."

Youths also reported tagging over other gang members' markings or tagging in a rival gang's territory as a way to display dominance, as indicated by the following quote from a 16-year-old Mexican-American male: "We do it to mark our territory . . . we mark out other gang signs and write ours. We show them what's up, let them know we mean business."

As the previous example illustrates, peer solidarity represented an enduring facet of gang crime. Indeed, many of the gang members reported that "being down" for their "homeboys" was of utmost importance to gang life. When describing gang crimes, the youths often emphasized the importance and value of their friendships, as illustrated by the following quote from a 16-year-old Mexican-American male:

> I ain't no faith in God's ass. I ain't got no faith. I mean I
> can't trust Him . . . you can't see the motherfucker. I can
> see my OG over there, if I need help, he gonna pull me
> off the ground. He can reach out and pull me up and I
> can see him do it. Can't see God doing that for me. I can
> see them walking down the street. They see me on the
> ground with no money in my pocket. They gonna give
> me some money. I can see that. I have faith in that.
> Maybe one day . . . they say faith is the size of a mustard
> seed, I ain't even got that. It shouldn't be that way, but I

got no faith. I got no faith in God, but I got my faith in my people.

Despite exulting their peers, youths still tended to downplay their influence, as indicated by the following quote from a 16-year-old African-American male:

> I ain't got friends that try to peer pressure you. You don't
> want to do it [commit crime]. They ain't actually going
> to make you do it if you don't want to. You don't want to
> do it; you don't do it.

Yet, another youth, a 16-year-old white male, discussed the ramifications of refusing to follow peer-initiated gang directives:

> We'd have our meetings. . . . We ask you to do something
> and you want to be down with us, we expect you to do
> them. Shit it'd be like that. You ain't got to do it you
> know. . . . It's just when you violate our [gang] laws, then
> we do something to you. But then, shit, it's cool. It's like
> unity. We're all together. There ain't no reason to go
> against each other. We got loyalty. You just know who is
> the leader and who is not and you respect them
> [leaders] for that. . . . I mean if you're asked to do
> something and it's in the law, you do it.

As this quote indicates, youths, at least on the surface, are pressured to act in accordance with gang rules and norms. Failing to do so results in a number of social consequences, including decreased status in the gang. Despite this, the youths still presented their narratives in such a way as to indicate that they bought into the gang rules and norms. That is, when faced with conflict with rival gang members, they interpreted the situation through the lens of existing gang rules and norms. Thus, from a cultural perspective, subcultural values and norms have a tremendous influence on the individual gang member's interpretive process and eventual meaning construction with respect to those situations involving conflict with a rival gang or its members. A number of theoretical frameworks, most notable Anderson's (1994, 1997) discussion of the "code of the streets" and the gender role strain-conflict model (O'Neil et al. 1995) provide a useful backdrop from which to speculate about these findings. According to such perspectives, when inner-city males are unable to live in accordance with idealized conceptions of masculinity, they may suffer from psychological problems or strain, which leads them to partake in "codes" or "dark

---

[2]The author uses the term "victim"; the adolescents did not.

behaviors" of masculinity such as aggression and violence, behaviors that are valued within certain cultural contexts and settings (Anderson 1994, 1997; Brooks and Silverstein 1995). That is, in certain situations males may. Engage in delinquent or criminal behavior as a mechanism for demonstrating their masculinity (Copes and Hochstetler 2003; Messerschmidt 1993).

Going After Money, Goods, and Drugs

Thirteen (22%) of the property crime delinquent events were committed primarily to accrue some material benefit, usually to obtain money for drugs. Crimes in this category included a wide array of property thefts characterized by some degree of planning. Furthermore, adolescents sought to minimize risk, and peers when present operated as "co-conspirators" only. The intent was to commit the crime and reap its benefits, not to have fun. For example, an 18-year-old African-American male described how he would steal jerseys and then sell them to an "established customer":

> Some guy that lived in my apartments.... I'd steal jerseys for him and he'd pay me. And so I went to the mall to Champs where they had jerseys for his kids. And I'd steal them.

A 17-year-old white male provided another example of this type of delinquent event, only this time the youth confided that he wanted to steal in order to sell the stolen goods for drug money.

> I was at my house and it was around Thanksgiving and I wanted some drugs and I didn't have no money so I ran over to this house and I broke into my neighbor's house. I just walked into her house and robbed her.

A 16-year-old white male also described burglarizing a house in order to obtain material goods, which could then be sold for drug money:

> We took the microwave, the stereo, the black-and-white TV. We took whatever we could get. These people, they didn't live in no good neighborhood, so we didn't get no good stuff.

When asked what he was feeling during the burglary, the youth responded:

> I was nervous. I don't know about the other dudes, but I was nervous. We didn't have a good time, we didn't sit on the couch and smoke, we done stuff like that at other times ... but not this time. We didn't have a good time.

> For one, what we needed wasn't there. We wasn't getting no money off no microwave, a black-and-white TV and a little stereo. So wasn't no good time.

As this example illustrates, youths who participated in economically driven crimes tended to report being "nervous" and "scared" during the commission of these crimes. They were concerned with getting caught and wanted to be as covert as possible. Youth who committed burglaries were particularly nervous about owners walking in on them, as illustrated by the following narrative from a 17-year-old African-American male:

> ... Somebody could be in the room and we don't even know about it. Somebody could shoot you. It's like you're scared, you're creeping up to the room. Like a book will fall, and you'd just have a heart attack ....

Because adolescents approached these crimes with the intent to accrue material goods, planning beyond an initial decision to carry out the crime characterized these delinquent events, as illustrated by the following quote from an 18-year-old African-American male:

> I was thinking about exactly what I was going to need to do to get the jerseys. Watch the store to see who all was watching. See if it was busy or not. And just walk up to the store and get what I needed. To play it off, I'd ask them a question. Ask them if they had something I knew they didn't sell. They would tell me they didn't have it and I'd say thank you and move on. I'd say [for example], "Do you have such and such whatever?" And they'd say "no" and I'd say "All right." And I'd walk out the store.

Similarly, a 16-year-old white male described a ploy he would use to burglarize homes:

> I knock on the door on a street that don't have many cars on it ... streets that don't got that crime watch and all that. And I knock on the door and if somebody answers, I say, "Is James Epstein here?" I try to be very sincere ... Like a nerdy kid.... That's the kind of image I try to portray to people. I'll say "Is James Epstein here?" If they say, "Nah," I act like I'm looking at something. "Oh I must have the wrong address!" Just go on about my business. If they [homeowners] ain't there, I go to the back. Check the windows first. If the windows are open, I just go through them or break them.

The decision to include peers as "co-conspirators" was also influenced by the desire to minimize the possibility of getting caught. Indeed several youths stated that they would prefer to "work alone" because they were afraid that the peers would "snitch" if they "got caught." For example, a 17-year-old Mexican-American male stated:

> I commit most of my [crimes] by myself. Because if I go alone . . . with some other person and we get caught, they will snitch. And if he gets caught, he'll snitch on me and then me and him will go down for it so I'd rather just go by myself.

This is not to say that youths never included peers in economic crimes, but rather that they recognized the potential for problems if they did so. For example, one youth who involved a peer later came to regret his decision:

> I grabbed some CDs and I walked out and I stuck them in my pocket. And the damn beeper thing went off. And he [co-conspirator] was right behind me and I just broke off and I was already gone. And I was waiting for him down the road, but he stayed there. The big dummy. . . . I don't know what was up with him. He stayed there. And his parents got called and all this other stuff. And he told on me . . . and it was my mistake for trusting him . . . should have never trusted him in the first place.

In terms of drug/alcohol use, most youths agreed that it was not a "good idea" to be under the influence while committing economically driven property crimes. Indeed, several adolescents noted that they intentionally stayed away from drugs or alcohol because "you get so messed up you don't know what you're doing and sometimes you get caught. . . ." On the other hand, one youth described both advantages and disadvantages to using drugs when committing property crimes:

> It's better not to do them [crimes] at all. But if you do, it's better not to [do drugs] so that you can know what you are doing. On the other hand, when you high, you don't think about it as much. It don't ride your mind as much.

Despite this, most youths reported that they were not under the influence when committing economically driven crimes. On the other hand, most also acknowledged that they were committing property crimes in order to obtain stolen goods that could then be sold for money to support a drug habit. Thus, the role of drug/alcohol use appeared to take on a different form for economically driven property crimes than it did for thrill crimes. In economically driven crimes, the goal was to obtain money to supply a drug habit whereas in thrill crimes, drugs/alcohol use served primarily to enhance the celebratory nature associated with carrying out the crime.

In contrast to crimes committed for other reasons, youths sometimes expressed remorse or regret for their delinquent actions. However, the only time youths tended to express guilt or remorse was when they broke into someone's house and were confronted with pictures and deeply personal objects belonging to their victims. Nevertheless, even in these instances, the youths tended to quickly displace these unpleasant feelings with a "fuck it who cares" attitude, as illustrated by the following example narrated by a 16-year-old white male:

> Seeing the pictures [after breaking into a house]. Yeah it does kind of bother me, but you know how I used to feel, I didn't care about nobody else but myself and or my homeboys or my family or whatever. That's just how I felt, so didn't let it bother me too much. That was just me . . . .

A 16-year-old Mexican-American male also shared how he felt remorse/regret after a burglary, only to quickly displace these feelings:

> I felt bad this one time . . . we saw this lady's graduation ring and I felt bad about it. And then we drank a 40 and I was thinking, "Man, I'm going to leave this [graduation ring] on her [lady's] doorstep. Then I said, "Fuck the bitch!" and threw it in the bayou.

Youths also rarely expressed concern for getting caught prior to committing their offenses. Again, however, the exception to this was when the youths were committing economically driven crimes. In these instances, youths reported that they did not want to get caught, they just wanted "To get the job done." However, at other times, youths reported that it was unlikely that they would get caught. For example, an 18-year-old African-American male stated this when asked if he had thought about the possibility of getting caught after shoplifting:

> No. I guess I didn't even think about it. I had done it so many times and had never gotten caught. I was at the point where I couldn't believe that I would get caught.

At other times, youths expressed a lack of concern for getting caught:

> There wasn't a lot going through my mind. I knew that I had gotten caught. I wasn't too concerned about it. They would just take me to juvenile and I would end up going home anyway so I wasn't too concerned. It was just another day.

Crimes committed primarily to obtain money, material goods, or drugs provided the most clear-cut examples of delinquent events that I studied. Economically motivated crimes generally involved fewer co-offenders, planning, and a tendency to select anonymous victims (Kazemian and LeBlanc 2004). Adolescents approached these crimes in a rational manner, considering the costs and benefits, with an intent on minimizing the possibility of getting caught (Clarke and Cornish 1985; Cornish and Clarke 1986). In contrast to crimes committed for thrills, youths were usually not on drugs/alcohol during the commission of economically driven crimes.

SUMMARY AND DISCUSSION

An integrated symbolic interactionist and cultural studies approach (Dotter 2004) was used as the overarching framework of this study. This theoretical approach, with its underlying postulation that actors construct meaning through an interpretative process based on their interaction with others as well as their position within the larger society, was particularly relevant to an explanation of adolescent involvement in delinquent events.

Stories specific to each of the four motive/interpretive strategies were presented in different ways. For example, when discussing stories centered on fun and postcrime celebrations, the adolescents tended to emphasize the thrills and adventurous nature present throughout the delinquent events, often laughing and smiling as they recalled and shared their exploits. They did not express remorse or regret, except fleetingly, nor did they discuss any negative aspects related to their participation in those scenarios characterized by a desire for thrills. Overall, their stories suggest that crime, in some instances, serves as a means for adolescent males to engage in a mutually satisfying and shared experience. In contrast, their portrayals of the economic crimes were much different. The adolescent cast himself in the more serious role of the economically driven thief, an individual who was not interested in fun and games, only in obtaining the economic benefits of the crime.

Another aspect that the adolescents tended to emphasize, irrespective of the specific motive/interpretative strategy used, was the saliency of their involvement in comparison to their peers and in relation to drugs/alcohol. They were the "stars" of their dramatizations, whereas their peers, when present, served as a supporting cast. As such, they did not rely on peer pressure as an explanation for their involvement nor did they blame their involvement on drugs/alcohol.

Again, their willingness to place themselves front and center may have had to do with the degree to which they believed me to be a sympathetic listener with no vested interest or power to harm them. Some aspects of their stories might have differed had they been forced to share them with police or other authority figures. In particular, they might have been tempted to downplay their own role while simultaneously enhancing the role that peers and drugs/alcohol played. On the other hand, they might have been more open to sharing different, perhaps less appealing aspects of the delinquent event, with a trusted friend than they were with me. This is not to say that any of these possible versions represent the absolute truth or even that an absolute truth, at least as represented by postevent narratives, is possible, but rather to emphasize that adolescents, like all individuals, construct meaning within interactions with others.

Understanding the adolescent's perspective is crucial if we are to gain a more balanced view of the delinquent event. Social science interviews, because of their supposed nonjudgmental nature, offer one stage upon which the individual can share his story without threat of repercussion. In such settings, the adolescent's voice is valued and he is allowed to speak for himself, to share his interpretations of the delinquent event. This is essential given that the adolescent offender, as a consequence of his age, gender, and perhaps, race/ethnicity, is not often afforded such opportunities. Thus, the current study represents an attempt to provide such a platform. Nevertheless, the delinquent event's meaning, despite its concrete aspects, cannot be understood from one view alone. Hence, it's essential that future researchers consider a number of voices and perspectives when examining the delinquent event. Dotter's (2004) use of the "meaning scenario" as a way of describing and critiquing mediated meaning-generation processes represents one avenue for engaging in such work. In short, Dotter proposes that an examination of the links between deviant events, media reconstruction, and the "stigma movie" is necessary in order to understand the multilayered meaning construction process. Stated another way, multiple perspectives, including those of the actors involved in the original event in addition to journalists and other meaning constructors, must be accounted for, with an emphasis on understanding how this process leads to the deviance label and the distancing of society from those who engage in deviant acts. Although this process initially seems best suited for highly publicized deviant events, it can be applied, in part, to any delinquent event for which the offender has been caught. Doing so would entail conducting multiple interviews with actors, reading police reports and court transcripts, talking to lawyers and judges, and reading existing newspaper accounts. This process would allow the researcher to gain access to various viewpoints and ultimately be able to understand the delinquent event at multiple levels of meaning construction.

In sum, the current study utilized a symbolic interactionist/cultural studied framework to further understand why and how adolescents commit property crimes. The unique contribution of the current study is that it provides insight into a number of different motive/interpretative strategies used by adolescents when faced with certain situations, thus allowing for a deeper understanding of how adolescents interpret and construct meaning in relation to the delinquent event. Finally, this study recognized that the adolescent offender constructs meaning in relation to the larger culture. However, the larger culture as represented by popular media and discourses often does not consider the adolescent offender's perspective in turn (Young 1996). Thus, it is recommended that future researchers interested in delinquent events research and meaning construction consider the adolescent offender's perspective in addition to those of the other actors and the media. Doing so would lead to a more balanced meaning construction process that is based on all voices and interpretations.

REFERENCES

Agnew, Robert. 1990.

——. 1992. "Foundation for a General Strain Theory of Crime and Delinquency." *Criminology* 30:47–48.

——. 2001. "Building on the Foundation of General Strain Theory: Specifying the Types of Strain Most Likely to Lead to Crime and Delinquency." *Journal of Research in Crime and Delinquency* 38:319–361.

Anderson, Elijah. 1994. "The Code of the Streets." *Atlantic Monthly* 5:81–94.

——. 1997. "Violence and the Inner-City Street Code." Pp. 1–30. *In Violence and Children in the Inner City*, edited by Joan McCord. New York: Cambridge University Press.

——. 1997. *Violent Criminal Acts and Actors Revisited.* Chicago: University of Illinois Press.

Birkbeck, Christopher and Gary LaFree. 1993. "The Situational Analysis of Crime and Deviance." *Annual Review of Sociology* 19:113–137.

Brezina, Timothy. 1996. "Adapting to Strain: An Examination of Delinquent Coping Responses." *Criminology* 34:39–60.

Brooks, Gary and Louise Silverstein. 1995. "Understanding the Dark Side of Masculinity: An Interactive Systems Model." Pp. 280–333. *In A New Psychology of Men*, edited by Ronald Levant and William Pollack. New York: Basic Books.

Clarke, Ronald and Derek Cornish. 1985. "Modeling Offender's Decisions: A Framework for Research and policy." Pp. 147–185. *In Crime and Justice: An Annual Review of Research, Volume 6*, edited by Michael Tonry and Norval Morris. Chicago: University of Chicago Press.

Copes, Heith. 2003. "Streetlife and the Rewards of Autotheft." *Deviant Behavior* 24:309–332.

—— and Andy Hochstetler. 2003. "Situational Construction of Masculinity Among Male Street Thieves." *Journal of Contemporary Ethnography* 32:279–304.

Cornish, Derek and Ronald Clarke. 1986. *The Reasoning Criminal: Rational Choice Perspectives on Offending.* New York: Springer-Verlag.

Dotter, Daniel. 2004. *Creating Deviance. An Interactionist Approach.* Walnut Creek, CA: AltaMira Press.

Hochstetler, Andy. 2001. "Opportunities and Decisions: Interactional Dynamics in Robbery and Burglary Groups." *Criminology* 39:737–763.

Jacobs, Bruce, Volkan, Topalli, and Richard Wright. 2003. "Carjacking, Streetlife, and Offender Motivation," *British Journal of Criminology* 43:673–688.

—— and Richard Wright. 1999. "Stick-up, Street Culture, and Offender Motivation." *Criminology* 37:149–173.

Katz, Jack. 1988. *Seductions of Crime.* New York: Basic Books.

Kazemian, Lila and Marc LeBlanc. 2004. "Exploring Patterns of Perpetration of Crime Across the Life Course." *Journal of Contemporary Criminal Justice* 20:393–415.

Klaus, Patsy. 2006. "National Crime Victimization Survey—Crime and the Nation's Households, 2004." (pp. 1–4). *Bureau of Justice Statistics.*

LeBlanc, Marcel and Marc Frechette. 1989. *Male Criminal Activity from Childhood Through Youth: Multilevel and Developmental Perspectives.* New York: Springer-Verlag.

Meier, Robert, Leslie Kennedy, and Vincent Sacco. 2001. *The Process and Structure of Crime.* New Brunswick, NJ: Transaction.

Messerschmidt, James. 1993. *Masculinities and Crime.* Lanham, MD: Rowman and Littlefield.

O'Neil, James, Glenn Good, and Sarah Holmes. 1995. "Fifteen Years of Theory and Research on Men's Gender Role Conflict: New Paradigms for Empirical Research." Pp. 164–206. *In A New Psychology of Men*, edited by Ronald Levant and William Pollack. New York: Basic Books.

Sacco, Vincent and Leslie Kennedy. 2002. *The Criminal Event.* Belmont, CA: Wadsworth.

Sherley, Alison. 2004. "Contextualizing the Sexual Assault Event: Images from Police Files." *Deviant Behavior* 26:87–108.

Snyder, Howard. 2004. "Juvenile Arrests 2002." Juvenile Justice Bulletin. Washington, DC: U.S. Department of Justice, Office of Justice Programs, Office of Juvenile Justice and Delinquency Prevention.

Wright, Richard and Scott Decker. 1994. *Burglars on the Job: Streetlife and Residential Break-ins.* Boston: Northeastern University Press.

2

Streetlife and the Rewards of Auto Theft

Heith Copes

An offender's decision-making process includes the assessments of pains and plea-sures of crime within the context of their lives. This article analyzes the perceptions of auto thieves within the context of street-life culture. The rewards and risks for committing this type of crime are explored in order to understand the role that street-life culture plays in shaping the motivations for auto theft.

Understanding the process by which offenders choose crime is critical as it has important implications for both theory and policy. The bulk of research on criminal decision-making is grounded in rational choice theory and assumes that offenders rationally measure the potential penalties of crime against its anticipated rewards (Becker 1968; Cornish and Clarke 1986). Individuals are thought to pursue goals reflecting their self-interest and purposively choose to commit crime if the expected benefits of illegal behavior exceed the benefits of engaging in legitimate activity. Conversely, the decision to forgo criminal behavior may be based on the individual's perception that the benefits have diminished or the risk of detection and subsequent cost is too great. In other words, individuals explore their options and choose the alternative that provides the highest expected gain.

Numerous qualitative studies have elaborated on the indulgent lifestyles that many offenders live (e.g., Fleisher 1995; Hagan and McCarthy 1992, 1997; Jacobs and Wright 1999; Shover 1996). What can be synthe-sized from this literature is that persistent offenders emphasize the "enjoyment of good times" (Shover 1996:94) at the expense of all else. They live in a social world that emphasizes "partying" and fast living where they are frequently "caught up in a cycle of expensive, self-indulgent habits" (Jacobs and Wright 1999:163). Offenders quickly erode any legitimate resources for obtaining money to support their lifestyle, making criminal behavior appear more rewarding.

Participation in street culture constrains individu-als' subjective assessments of the risks and rewards of crime. The paltry financial rewards of most street crimes would not encourage most members of the middle class to pursue this life. Yet, these rewards when coupled with other intrinsic rewards of crime, such as status, autonomy, and action, are enough to turn the heads of many toward street crime. Researchers have explored the role of streetlife on decision-making for a variety of crimes, including burglary, robbery, carjacking, and drug dealing (Jacobs 1999; Jacobs et al. 2003; Shover 1996; Wright and Decker 1994, 1997). Absent from this list is an in-depth exploration of the relationship between streetlife and motor vehicle theft.

There has been relatively little research on auto theft (Clarke and Harris 1992a), especially using qualitative methods (notable exceptions include, Fleming 2003 and Spencer 1992). This is surprising considering the symbolic importance of automobiles to Americans and the prevalence and cost of auto theft to the public (Freund and Martin 1993). According to current data from the Federal Bureau of Investigation (FBI 2002), approximately 1.2 million cars were illegally taken from their owners in 2001. It is not surprising that the result of motor vehicle theft causes an enormous financial loss. In 2001 alone, the loss due to motor vehicle theft was estimated to be over $8.2 billion, averaging $6,646 per vehicle (FBI 2002). This is much larger than the estimated loss from burglary ($3.3 billion).

Because of the prevalence and high cost of motor vehicle theft and its neglect by researchers, there is a need to understand the criminal decision-making of auto thieves. The current study examines offenders' perceptions of the rewards of auto theft within the sociocultural context of streetlife. It relies on semistructured interviews with auto thieves to determine how participation in streetlife facilitates offenders' decisions to engage in motor vehicle theft by providing the motivations for their behaviors. The results of this endeavor will increase our understanding of motor vehicle theft and will add to our understanding of criminal decision-making in general.

METHODS

Criminal decision-making by street offenders has been the focus of substantial research over the past two decades. What distinguishes this research from other methodological approaches to crime is the emphasis on using interviews and other ethnographic techniques to explore the perspectives, social organization, and behavior of offenders. Use of qualitative research methods has demonstrated value for permitting investigators to get close to their subject matter. Personal interviews with offenders can inform researchers and policy makers about the motives and rationalizations that facilitate and impede crime. If we are to substantially increase and improve our understanding of auto theft, clearly there is both rationale and precedent for using qualitative methods.

Data for this study are drawn from semi-structured interviews with 45 individuals on community supervision in one metropolitan area in Tennessee. All respondents were under probation or parole following convictions for various property crimes and had committed at least one motor vehicle theft. The Tennessee Board of Probation and Parole granted access to parolees' and probationers' files, which included enough information to locate and contact offenders. Pre-sentence investigation reports (PSIs) were used as the primary source of data for finding and contacting suitable persons to interview. The PSIs contained addresses and phone numbers, if available, of offenders who met the requirements for inclusion in the study. The PSIs also contain official lists of previous arrests, an unofficial list of previous arrests as well as an unofficial list of prior arrests as stated by the offender. If respondents had a motor vehicle theft in their prior record, official or unofficial, it was included in the study sample. Offenders who fit the criteria were solicited for participation by a letter and by phone. To provided additional encouragement for participation, those who appeared for the interview were paid $10.

Interviews for this study focused on a range of decision-making topics, including offenders' motivations to commit motor vehicle theft, their target selection process, the perceived risks and rewards of participating in motor vehicle theft, and the techniques and skills used to accomplish their tasks. To determine self-defined motives or rewards for auto theft, offenders were asked why they stole cars and what they saw as the major rewards of auto theft. Typically, offenders described the motives for their most recent thefts. After offenders gave their initial responses they were then asked about other possible motivations for this and any other auto theft. The participants also were asked about whether their motives changed as they became more experienced. Additionally, respondents were asked about their educational backgrounds, families, occupations, criminal histories, drug use, and other aspects of their lives. It was during this phase that characteristics of offenders' lifestyles were explored. The interviews were tape recorded and transcribed. They were then analyzed with a software package designed to code and organize textual data.

Investigations of street crime using samples of known offenders have produced detailed, accurate, and useful data on a variety of topics (e.g., Athens 1997; Hochstetler 2001; Maruna 2000; Nee and Taylor 2000; Rengert and Wasilchick 2000; Shover 1996). There is little reason to believe that the results of these studies contradict or are inconsistent with what has been learned from studies using active offenders. Despite misgivings about using offenders known to criminal justice agencies, there is little hard evidence that these offenders think, act, or report information differently than active offenders contacted independent of criminal justice sources. In fact, a recent study examining target selection of burglars found a "striking similarity" between studies using free-ranging and prison-based samples (Nee and Taylor 2000:45). This combined with its cost-effectiveness warrants the use of a sample of auto thieves under state supervision.

STREETLIFE AND MOTIVATIONS FOR AUTO THEFT

Previous studies have described the indulgent lifestyles that many offenders live and have shown how this lifestyle impacts offenders' decisions to engage in crime (e.g., Fleisher 1995; Hagan and McCarthy 1992, 1997; Jacobs and Wright 1999; Shover 1996; Shover and Honaker 1992; Wright and Decker 1997). These studies suggest that the defining characteristic of streetlife is the quest to lead "a life of desperate partying" (Wright and Decker 1997:35). As Shover (1996) states, "The hallmark of life as party is enjoyment of 'good times' with minimal concerns for obligations and commitments external to the person's immediate social setting" (p. 93). It is a lifestyle that encourages the hedonistic pursuit of sensory stimulation, lack of future orientation, and neglect of responsibility (Fleisher 1995). Continuing the good times takes precedent over all else. This emphasis on partying is illustrated in the writings of Jackson (1969):

> [The life] is mostly a party. I don't think people understand that it's quite like that, but it is. In other words, you don't work. . . . When you get your money, you usually get it real fast and you have a lot of time to spend it. You can sleep all day if you want to and you can go out and get drunk, get high—you don't have to get up the next morning to go to work (pp. 146–7).

In this context crime can emerge without warning to continue the good times or to forestall circumstances that are perceived to be unpleasant.

Making Money

This lifestyle of "ostentatious consumption" (Shover 1996:94) entails major expenses. The material excess that is promoted in this lifestyle, especially when it comes to drug use and personal style, dictated that the proceeds from crime be spent quickly. Offenders in the criminal lifestyle spend the spoils of their criminal

ventures with seeming abandon, in part because money acquired illegally holds less intrinsic value than income earned through hard work. As one auto thief said, "I don't treasure the money I make. I don't even try to save it. All down in the end I know I won't be able to save it anyway." The income from the minimum-wage jobs that characterize the employment possibilities of people in their social position are woefully inadequate to support this fast lifestyle. Even those with employable skills are left with empty pockets. As one unusually skilled offender explained:

> Well, it's hard to go to work and work 12 hours a day when you got a two hundred dollar drug habit a day. You only make two hundred dollars a day at best, you know. That's at 16 or 17 dollars an hour, when I went to industrial carpentry. You still can't support a drug habit and a family.

Auto theft affords offenders the luxury of living their chosen lifestyle by providing a viable source of income. Seventeen offenders said they stole cars to profit financially from the sale of stolen vehicles. Auto theft can be a profitable business if one has the proper skills and connections. Auto thieves can earn anywhere from $500 to $5,000 per car, depending on their position in the chop shop hierarchy and the type of vehicles stolen. Many are aware that they can potentially make a great deal of money by selling stolen cars. In fact, the perceived ease at making fast money persuaded one offender to quit the "drug game" and begin a career in stealing cars. In his words:

> I was selling drugs and got tired of selling drugs. A friend of mine, he told me I could make more money and it would be because I'm a good mechanic. There ain't nothing I can't do to a car . . . I come from maybe, I wouldn't say a big time drug dealer but maybe a second class drug dealer making maybe two thousand to three thousand dollars a day. It was just so hectic so I stopped selling drugs to steal cars because it was easier. The money come quicker.

While knowledge of chop shops secured higher payoffs, offenders without these connections could still profit from auto theft by stripping cars and selling the parts in a loosely structured network of friends and acquaintances (Fleming 2003). Six offenders stripped stolen cars to sell individual parts. As one offender said:

> Sometimes [we] sold the parts, sometimes [we] just put it on our car. But most time we'll strip the car all

the way down to the engine and sell the engine, you know what I'm saying. When we didn't know about going to sell the cars [to chop shops], that's what we were doing. We were selling body parts . . . We'd sell parts all day.

Even for those who do possess the necessary skills to obtain economically satisfying employment, streetlife makes it nearly impossible to keep the job for any extended amount of time. The resentment of authority and disdain for conventional employment all but prohibits these offenders from maintaining stable employment. Thus, most persistent offenders choose not to work, preferring instead to lead a more autonomous life—a life where they are free from the constraints of the working stiffs nine-to-five world (Akerstrom 1985, 2003). Mac Isaac (1968:69), an ex-thief, illustrates this belief, "I was always quite candid in admitting that I participated in their parties by providing the necessary financial resources and by allowing them to travel when the desire arises." When asked if he worked before his arrest one offender replied, "What I need a job for? I make my money with them cars. I got everything I need right here."

Looking Good and Being Seen

Offenders living "life in the fast lane" (Gibbs and Shelley 1982) spend and exorbitant amount of money buying clothes and other items in an attempt to "keep up appearances" (Wright and Decker 1997:40; see also McCall 1994; Shover and Honaker 1992). By spending money conspicuously offenders can "create a look of cool transcendence" and show others that they are "members of the aristocracy of the streets" (Wright and Decker 1997:40). As one offender explained when asked what he did with the money, "Parlay, you know, go buy a new fix [drugs] and shit. Take care of a bill or something like that. Mostly, just to dress with." Another offender replied, "I like lavish clothes. I like to go out to clubs. I had a lot of girlfriends—when you living that lifestyle you going to spend the money, you know." Offenders spend without thinking in order to create an "impression of affluence" (Wright and Decker 1994). On the streets, the image projected is critical and those in "the game" must visually play the role. This includes dressing well and driving the right car.

Offenders often value nice cars and hope to garner the respect of others in their community by "flossing,"[1] and a large proportion of auto thieves steal cars to cruise around in or joyride. Typically, they only keep the car for a short time, usually under three days, but they try to make the most of their time. When asked why he stole cars, one young auto thief replied, "I never wanted anything out of the cars, man. I was only interested in the car. I loved riding. Always did, always will. I liked riding." These auto thieves use the stolen vehicle to continue the good times by visiting friends, picking up girls, or just being seen.

For a significant number of offenders who were intent on cruising around in a stolen car, stealing a suitable one was a prerequisite. They searched for vehicles that fit the style and image they wished to project. For instance, one auto thief said:

> I was very choicey. I used to go and look at them. Let me give you an example. If I had a choice between this car and that car. This one here looks more sporty because the windows are dark. I would get that car. [I went for] sportier cars. The girls will go for that one more than the other one because that one there is too plain. This one there is really nice. I had to have something real beautiful sporty because of my taste. I had good taste.

Some avoided stealing cars that were wrecked or too old. Some would not break the windows of the car because they saw no point in cruising in a car that did not look good or that was obviously stolen. As one offender stated, "I would try not to break no window getting in. Who wants to ride around in a car with a broken window?"

Auto thieves want to look good by driving the right car but some recognize that trying to sport a stolen car as their own is too risky. To overcome this risk, they use the spoils of auto theft, by stripping stolen cars and keeping the desirable parts for themselves, or by stealing the exact vehicle they wanted and keeping it intact. As one offender explains, "I took a car and demolished it to build up my car, you know what I'm saying. I never did steal a car to sell or anything. It was always for my use." Another explained:

> I got a Pontiac and I see you got a Pontiac, and my fenders are bent up. I'll take your car and take the fenders off and put it on my car. Do the paint up real quick and go ditch yours. Nothing might be wrong with yours. Yours might be brand new. Mine is second hand. But I'd jack your car to take the body parts to put on mine. Make my shit look good. And just ditch yours off.

---

[1]Flossing is a slang term meaning "to show off." It is frequently used in the context of driving a nice vehicle.

Stereos rank high on the list of sought-after accessories. When the beats (stereos) are loud they draw the attention of others, thus, offenders are not only heard they are seen. One car thief stated that his primary motive for the car thief was to take out the stereo. "Sometimes we would jack them just for the music. Sometimes we'd jack a car, take the music out [and] hook our car up with the music." As one joyrider stated, "Every now and then I might take a little radio or some music out of them. Keep a little music or whatever."

Despite the high number of offenders who sold cars to chop shops, it was rare for auto thieves to steal cars to permanently keep for themselves. In fact, only two offenders stated they did so. One offender stole a car for his brother to keep:

> [My brother's] car broke down and couldn't be fixed. It was through. We didn't have no more money . . . We saw a car that looked just like my brother's. So we waited until everybody went into the store, got in the car and took off . . . He's still got it. It's legal now.

The other offender stole a motorcycle to keep for himself. He claimed he had always wanted a motorcycle and when the opportunity to steal one presented itself, he took it. In his words, "I took a motorcycle—a little blue Honda motorcycle. It had 'for sale' on it. God knows I didn't have the money to buy no machine like that."

Auto theft provides offenders with the opportunity to cruise in stylish cars. However, if one wants to truly stand out he or she must be "seen" in their car. One technique for being seen is to develop a distinctive driving style. Evidence that stylistic driving is a means to gain status is illustrated in the following description: "I wouldn't just sit up and drive, because after I had learned how to drive real well from stealing so many vehicles, I used to like to lean." This style of driving is frequently called a "gangsta lean" by those in the street.

Going Places

> I had went to a club. I was living with [my girl]. I got dropped off at the house and I didn't have the key. Or she wasn't there, or she kicked me out or something. I don't remember. But I was stuck way over here. It was like two in the morning. So, I'm drunk and I walk outside and I'm like damn. I didn't know no better. I wasn't even planning on stealing a car. All I knew I was stuck.

The previous quote perhaps best illustrates how some offenders find themselves in situations where they "desperately" need a ride. A hallmark of streetlife

is the desire to be up for anything, at any time, especially a party. This desire to party often leaves them stranded far from home with no means of getting back. Fourteen offenders stated they had stolen a car for the purpose of short-term transportation. Several auto thieves wanted to go to a party but had no ride there; others went to a party and were left by their friends. In his words, one auto thief explained:

> I remember one time I was stuck at these apartments. I just came from these girls' house and it was like ten or eleven o'clock and I had no ride to go across town. . . . I jumped into an old Toyota, and I took off with it.

Some just needed a ride after their domestic partners kicked them out of the house or took their car keys. One auto thief explained, "[I stole a car] because my girlfriend took my keys and I wanted to go out. I had to be from one point to another, like a 30-minute drive. And I seen [a car]. It was a spur of the moment thing I guess." One young man went out of town for a drug deal. When the deal went bad he was forced to abandon his car. He later stole a car just to get home:

> I was up there, and they had a dope deal went bad. I was about 16. So, the dope deal went bad, and we had to run. By the time [everything was over], I couldn't find [my car], you know. So, I had some money, but it wasn't enough money, you know what I'm saying. So, I saw a Lincoln on like a store lot. I just went over there. The door was open . . . So when I popped [the ignition], I turned the music on and I came straight home.

All of these offenders were faced with situational pressures that were the products of the party lifestyle. The desire to maintain or extend the party created a need to get out of town or to another part of town quickly. Thus, in a moment of self-defined desperation, they stole a car to get where they needed to go, so that they could continue their search for good times.

Living for the Moment

While impulsiveness is often portrayed as a psychological short-coming in the criminology literature (e.g., Gottfredson and Hirschi 1990), a measure of it and other indicators of a "devil may care" attitude are respectable in street-offenders' surroundings. Offenders, especially younger ones, are expected by peers to embrace and enjoy adventures ranging from street-fights, to heavy drug use binges, to commission of acquisitive felonies. Dozens of studies document the presence of what might be termed the cult of adventure and toughness among males in the lower tiers of the working class (Anderson 1999; Gibbs and Shelley 1982; Jacobs and Wright 1999; MacLeod 1987; Miller 1958). It is spontaneity and action, not reserve, that brings about "good times" for those immersed in this lifestyle. Thus, offenders seek out risky situations (Katz 1988). Many design their crimes with the intent of maximizing the risks so they can boost the level of excitement that crime creates. For instance, one car thief said, "Man, I done stole a fucking car with people right there in their window. I mean a big ole picture window and shit." The added risk was a source of pride and accomplishment for this offender as it was evidence of his ability to "face and overcome dangerous situations" (Jacobs et al. 2003).

Offenders can prove their willingness to engage in thrilling and exciting behavior by engaging in auto theft. This is evident by the choice of adjectives used to describe crimes. Words such as "fun," "thrilling," or a "high" are frequently used to explain the overriding emotions that auto theft elicits. One young auto thief said, "Well, a lot of people just do it to make money. I take them for the thrill, the adrenalin rushes." Similarly, another young car thief said, "It was fun because I was doing it so long it was just like I would get a little adrenalin rush off of it. It was just a thrill. Like a thrill." The experience associated with engaging in auto theft is often compared to the physical sensation of drug use. As one offender recalls, "Yeah, I mean it's like just about as good of a rush as snorting a foot-long line of cocaine." The thrill of auto theft is in offenders' abilities to "dance with danger" (Jacobs et al. 2003). This can be achieved by putting their physical safety and freedom on the line by driving dangerously, by being chased by police, or by simply doing things that most people do not have the nerve or cannot stomach.

Auto thieves' thirst for excitement is evidenced by their desire to stolen to race, test drive, tear up, or engage in dangerous car stunts. In other words, to "just raise hell." As one offender stated, "We actually played quite a dangerous game of bumper cars if we got two or more in one night."

Another stated, "When I was younger, [we stole them] for joyrides, demolition derbies. Steal a car and tear it up." Just how much wear some put on these cars is best illustrated by one young car thief:

> There was a Porsche [we stole] that had the front
> wheel ripped off it completely. In some of the [cars],
> the radiator would be busted and before we knew it
> there would be steam coming out and we had to ditch
> it because the block was about to crack.

Driving chaotically not only threatens offenders' physical safety but it also increases their chances of coming into contact with agents of the law. Few activities can generate the excitement and the ability to prove one's reckless abandon like fleeing from police in a stolen car. Four offenders claimed they stole cars with the deliberate intention of getting chased by police. When asked what motivated him to steal cars, one auto thief stated:

> It wasn't the thrill of stealing the vehicle itself—it was
> the thrill of being in a stolen vehicle and cops behind
> you. I don't too much do drugs. It's pretty high. It's pretty
> awesome. You getting behind a vehicle, behind the wheel
> of a stolen vehicle, and you run this truck that you have
> no idea what it's capable of doing. You don't know if
> you'll be able to escape from them, how fast it can go,
> how slow it will go, you know. So, you just shaking.
> [Your] nerves are wrecked.

This same belief was reflected in the words of another offender:

> The fun part about it is. . . . If the police get after us we
> going to get in a police chase. That was the excitement
> you know . . . That was the fun part.

A major component of the motivation to commit auto theft and part of its inherent thrill is the pleasurable feelings that come with doing the act and being successful, or "getting away with it" (Frazier and Meisenhelder 1985). To many offenders, being successful at crime provides a sense of accomplishment (Gibbens 1958). By getting away with crime they are able to accomplish things most people could not. This is illustrated by the following offenders:

> But, man really though, it was like, it was more of like, a
> thrilling thing to me. To be able to get away with it. I
> mean, it would just give me goose pimples. Man I
> mean, it was like I pulled this off and I made this, you
> know. How I mean I would manage to keep from
> getting caught.

For offenders who stole high-end cars equipped with alarms and other security devices, a feeling of accomplishment was especially prevalent. One experienced car thief said:

> I just liked to steal the cars, you know. I used to pride
> myself on which car I could steal. You know, the harder
> and more mysterious it was, the more I wanted to get it.
> So, it's harder to steal the Porsches. All right, I'm going to

go get one . . . I take the pride in the knowledge of how to beat the system. It's just like them hackers. Sometimes I just amaze myself.

Getting Even

Justice on the streets seldom involves the criminal justice system. The "code of the street" demands that problems be taken care of informally, thus making street justice a common practice (Anderson 1999). Often offenders steal the property of others as a form of social control; so what may seem as an unprovoked theft is really a response to the perceived misconduct of the victim (Black 1998, 1983; see Jacobs 2000; Jacobs et al. 2003). Offenders exact revenge or retribution on those who, in their opinions, deserve it. For example, over one-third of the burglaries in New York resulting in arrest involve grievances between the burglar and victim (Vera Institute 1977). Seven auto thieves said that they had stolen cars because of spite or revenge. For these men, car theft is a way to express their dislike for another person. Auto theft is chosen as a method of revenge because these offenders possess the necessary skills to do so. Those auto thieves motivated by revenge were experienced car thieves, some stealing as many 200 cars in their lifetimes. These skills as car thieves translated into a natural means of exacting revenge or retribution on "deserving" others.

Car thieves who steal for revenge give several reasons for their "moralistic concerns" (Jacobs 2000:33). Being disrespected or unfairly treated by the victim was the primary reason for "punishing" them. But even these insults must be interpreted within the context of streetlife. The "sins" of the victims are often minor transgressions but are interpreted as threats to the offenders' identity as being a legitimate player of the streets. One man described a situation where he was publically humiliated and decided to get back at the instigator. When asked why he stole the particular car in question he responded, "This dude was drinking and kept on putting me down." Another offender was upset with a drug dealer because the dealer refused to provide him with drugs at no cost.

I always wanted to get some dope from this one dude. All my other little partners he would front them dope and stuff like this. But, we damn near stayed at the same house, but every time I come to get drugs I had to buy it from him. So, I was like fuck him I'm get me something else. I just took his car.

Sometimes car thieves had long-standing feuds with the people whose car they stole. One offender

resorted to auto theft in an attempt to get back at the person who shot at him. "The last one, I stole it because the nigger had tried to shoot at me."

Some of the victims highly coveted their cars, often more than any other possession, making it the most obvious way for the offender to exact revenge. One offender believed that his victim "flossed" too much so he took it upon himself to put the braggart in his place.

[What happened was] one day me and one of my friends—you know we used to be friends back in the day—we got into it. We used to fight about girls and stuff. Well he had a nice car. He used to always come in my neighborhood late at night playing his music loud, loud, loud. Boom, boom, boom! He had like four 18-inch punchers in the back. Nice amps, speakers all over. Bumping. He thought he was bigger than everybody else, you know. Nobody had more sound than him. We used to always fight. I said I'm going to fix him. I'm going to show him. He had nice rims. Nice, nice rims. . . . I showed him a thing or two.

For some offenders retribution is a secondary motive for the auto theft. These offenders were determined to steal a car for any number of reasons. It was when they began searching for a suitable target that they decided to steal from those people whom they saw as deserving. One younger offender wanted to show his friends that he was "man enough" to steal a car. He described why he chose this particular car:

I stole [this lady's] Lincoln. This lady, she used to come ride around. She was mean. That lady was mean. One time I asked her to go cut her grass, she ain't never looked at me. She never answered me, just rolled her eyes. So, [I thought] I'm going to fix you. I was going to do something to her dogs. Throw them a pill in a burger or something and give it to them. But I never did it. Then one night I wanted to go riding. I was like I wonder if I can [steal a car.] I know I can do it. I bet you I can show them I can [steal a car], you know.

Staying Low

Individuals embedded in street culture engaged in a wide range of illicit behaviors. The desire to avoid being identified when committing other crimes leads them to steal cars to use as get away vehicles. Since most cannot find people willing to loan a car to them, some offenders turn to auto theft to ensure their anonymity. By stealing a car, offenders fulfill the practical need to moving around town while simultaneously concealing their identities. When asked if he ever stole a car to commit another crime, one offender stated:

> A few. Maybe like for a drive-by, or something like that. We did that a few times, you know. If it was like some situation like that. Don't let the mother fucker know what I got. If it's something like that in the "hood." See like if I'm in my neighborhood and some mother fucker be done got down bad, and I know he know what I'm driving. [Then] I might go get something from somewhere else and handle up on our business. Because I know if I come by in my shit they know what I'm riding in, so. Like a few times, see like [we stole a] pick-up truck and put a few mother fuckers in the back. They don't know who it is passing through. And we handle our business and we gone, shit. Keep shit down cool like that.

This is perhaps the rarest form of motor vehicle theft (McCaghy et al. 1977). Only four offenders stated they stole cars for the purpose of concealing their identity.

DISCUSSION AND CONCLUSION

Before concluding, a caveat is in order about auto theft typologies. Others have developed motivational typologies of auto theft (e.g., Challinger 1987; Clarke and Harris 1992a; McCaghy et al. 1977). They have even used these typologies to explain the type and frequency of cars stolen (Clarke and Harris 1992b; Tremblay et al. 1994). It is possible to use the date presented to construct a motivational typology, however, doing so may be inappropriate. Typologies imply exclusivity and stability; they are based on the idea that offenders in one group are qualitatively different from the offenders in the other group. Based on the current data, this portrayal does not accurately represent auto thieves because the motivational categories are not mutually exclusive. It is common for car thieves to have multiple motivations over their careers and for a single theft. This progression is illustrated in the words of one offender:

> Just getting somewhere, trying to move, you know. Just being seen mainly. To get different places. You know if you got a car and shit you ride around, you can get with the girls and shit, you know. I mean that's basically what it's about then, you know. It wasn't about no money and shit then, back that early. As time went on and shit, I went to stealing them for like the rims, the tires, or the sound system and shit like that out of them. And me

dealing with body shops, I might get it for a different body part that might cost a whole lot, you know. Like one shop I was working with we used to take the cars, say you got a car that is wrecked on the front, we'll go steal another one like it and cut in half and weld that shit back together. They would make like ten or fifteen G [thousand]—Depends on how much damage the insurance company paid for, you know. So I mean, it got to be to a different level as time progressed.

The fluid nature of offender's motivations suggests that typologies may obscure auto theft more than they illuminate it.

The motivations to engage in auto theft are a product of the hedonistic culture of the street. This is a lifestyle that encourages the enjoyment of good times and the dismissal of all that is restrictive. Those embedded in streetlife paint themselves as autonomous, action-adventurers who cannot be held back by the rigid life of the "working stiff" (Akerstrom 1985). They "relish the independence and autonomy to structure time and daily routines as they wish" (Shover 1996:95). But enjoyment of this life often comes at a major expense, financially and socially, and participants often find themselves "strapped for cash." Faced with eroding legitimate resources, the high cost of the lifestyle makes criminal behavior all the more enticing. Offender's accounts of their crimes reveal that money is typically the primary motive for their crimes (Feeney 1986; Tunnell 1992). This desire for money instigates many auto thefts. The sale of stolen cars goes a long way in filling the pockets of offenders. If auto thieves have the necessary skills and proper connections, they can easily bankroll their lifestyle.

Offenders are motivated by other things besides money. Auto theft is uniquely suited to support streetlife in ways other than financially. First, it gives offenders the ability to make their parties mobile. If their current location becomes boring or is uncomfortable they can "hot wire" a car and travel to more thrilling locations. The automobile allows them to move the party off the stoop and travel of places where they imagine real hustlers, party-goers, and girl-getters to be. No other crime affords offenders with this degree of geographic mobility. Second, in the world of the street, appearance is everything. One's style should be reflected in everything they do, including the type of car they drive. Auto theft provides a direct means of acquiring high-end car accessories like stereos and rims. If an offender wants drugs they can rob drug dealers or pharmacies (Jacobs 2000). If they want cash, they can engage in armed robbery or check forgery (Lemert 1985; Wright and Decker 1997). If they want to travel in stylish vehicles, they can steal cars. Third, auto theft fuels the desire for action more than most other crimes. Interviews with robbers shows that they often experience thrills and rushes while they are committing the robbery. But the actual act of robbery lasts a short time, usually under a minute or two. The excitement of auto theft can last for hours and even days, depending on how long offenders want to push their luck and drive in a "hot car."

Finally, and perhaps most importantly, auto theft carries with it symbolic importance. Driving the right car can do more to tell others about themselves than any other activity or personal item. Automobiles project a sense of power, prestige, and status, especially in many urban subcultures (Bright 1998). Displaying material items shows that they are "someone who has overcome—if only temporarily—the financial difficulties faced by others on the street corner." (Wright and Decker 1997:40). Thus, the ability to drive around, or "floss," in a car is important for many male youths because it allows them to literally cruise past the poverty and despair of the street.

Recent efforts to understand the criminal calculus using qualitative methods has provided much insight into the process by which offenders weigh the costs and benefits of crime, however, there is still more to learn. If decision-making research is to progress, investigators must explore how gender, age, criminal experience, and other characteristics of offenders shape their assessments of the costs and benefits of crime within their given lifestyle. Doing so would allow for a better understanding of criminal behavior and, consequently, lead to more efficient crime control policies.

References

Akerstrom, Malin. 1985. *Crooks and Squares: Lifestyles of Thieves and Addicts in Comparison to Conventional People.* New Brunswick, NJ: Transaction.
——. 2003. "Looking at the Squares: Comparisons with the Square John." Pp. 51–9 in Their Own Words: *Criminals on Crime,* 3rd edition, edited by Paul Cromwell. Los Angeles: Roxbury.
Anderson, Elijah. 1999. *Code of the Street: Decency, Violence and the moral Life of the Inner City.* New York: W. W. Norton.
Athens, Lonnie. 1997. *Violent Criminal Acts and Actors* Revisited. Urbana, IL: University of Illinois Press.
Black, Donald. 1983. "Crime as Social Control." *American Sociological Review* 48:3–45.
——. 1998. *The Social Structure of Right and Wrong.* San Diego CA: Academic.
Bright, Brenda. 1998. "Heart Like a Car: Hispano/Chicano Culture in Northern New Mexico." *American Ethologist* 25:583–609.

Challinger, Dennis. 1987. "Car Security Hardware—How Good is it?" In *Car Theft: Putting on the Brakes, Proceedings of Seminar on Car Theft,* May 21. Sydney, Australia: National Road and Motorists' Association and the Australian Institute of Criminology.
Clarke, Ronald and Patricia Harris. 1992a. "Auto Theft and its Prevention." Pp. 1–54 in *Crime and Justice:* A Review of Research (Vol. 16), edited by Michael Tonry. Chicago: University of Chicago Press.
——. 1992b. "A Rational Choice Perspective on the Target of Auto Theft." *Criminal Behavior and Mental Health* 2:25–42.
Federal Bureau of Investigation. 2002. Uniform Crime Reports: *Crime in the United States.* Washington, DC: U.S. Department of Justice.
Feeney, Floyd 1986. "Robbers as Decision Makers." Pp. 53–71 in *The Reasoning Criminal:* Rational Choice Perspectives on Offending, edited by Derek Cornish and Richard Clarke. New York: Springer-Verlag.
Fleisher, Mark S. 1995. *Beggars and Thieves: Lives of Urban Street Criminals.* Madison, WI: University of Wisconsin Press.
Fleming, Zachary. 2003. "The Thrill of it All: Youthful Offenders and Auto Theft." Pp. 99–170. In *In Their Own Words,* 3rd ed., edited by Paul Cromwell. Los Angeles: Roxbury.
Frazier, Charles and Thomas Meisenhelder. 1985. "Exploratory Notes on Criminality and Emotional Ambivalence." *Qualitative Sociology* 8:266–84.
Freund, Peter and George Martin. 1993. *The Ecology of the Automobile.* Montreal, Canada: Black Rose Books.
Gibbens, Thomas. 1958. "Car Thieves." *British Journal of Delinquency* 8:257–65.
Gibbs, John and Peggy Shelly. 1982. "Life in the Fast-Lane: A Retrospective View by Commercial Thieves." *Journal of Research in Crime and Delinquency* 19:299–330.
Gottfredson, Michael and Travis Hirschi. 1990. *A General Theory of Crime.* Stanford, CA: Stanford University Press.
Hagan, John and Bill McCarthy. 1992. "Street Life and Delinquency." *British Journal of Sociology* 43:533–61.
——. 1997. *Mean Streets: Youth Crime and Homelessness.* Cambridge, MA: Cambridge University Press.
Hochstetler, Andy. 2001. "Opportunities and Decisions: Interactional Dynamics in Robbery and Burglary Groups." *Criminology* 39:737–63.
Jackson, Bruce. 1969. *A Thief's Primer.* New York: Macmillan
Jacobs, Bruce. 1999. *Dealing Crack: The Social World of Streetcorner Selling.* Boston, MA: Northeastern University Press.
——. 2000. *Robbing Drug Dealers: Violence Beyond the Law.* New York: Aldine de Gruyter.
Jacobs, Bruce, Volkan Topalli, and Richard Wright. 2003. "Carjacking, Streetlife, and Offender Motivation." *British Journal of Criminology* 43:673–88.
Jacobs, Bruce and Richard Wright. 1999. "Strick-Up, Street Culture, and Offender Motivation." *Criminology* 37:149–73.
Katz, Jack. 1988. *Seductions of Crime.* New York: Basic.

Lemert, Edwin. 1958. "The Behavior of the Systematic Check Forger." *Social Problems* 6:141–9.

Mac Isaac, John. 1968. *Half the Fun Was Getting There.* Englewood Cliffs, NJ: Prentice-Hall.

MacLeod, Jay. 1987. *Ain't No Making It: Aspirations and Attainment in Low-Income Neighborhood.* Boulder, CO: Westview.

Maruna, Shadd. 2002. *Making Good: How Ex-Convicts Reform and Rebuild Their Lives.* Washington, DC: American Psychological Association.

McCaghy, Charles, Peggy Giordano, and Trudy Henson. 1977. "Auto Theft: Offender and Offense Characteristics." *Criminology* 15:367–85.

McCall, Nathan. 1994. *Make Me Wanna Holler: A Young Black Man in America.* New York: Random House.

Miller, Walter. 1958. "Lower-Class Culture as a Generating Milieu of Gang Delinquency." *Journal of Social Issues* 14:5–19.

Nee, Claire and Max Taylor. 2000. "Examining Burglars' Target selection: Interview, Experiment of Ethnomethodology?" *Psychology, Crime & Law* 6:45–59.

Rengert, George and John Wasilchick. 2000. *Suburban Burglary: A Tale of Two Suburbs,* 2nd ed. Springfield, IL: Charles C. Thomsa.

Shover, Neal. 1996. *Great Pretenders: Pursuits and Careers of Persistent Thieves.* Boulder, CO: Westview.

Shover, Neal and David Honaker. 1992. "The Socially Bounded Decision Making of Persistent Property Offenders." *Howard Journal of Criminal Justice* 31:276–93.

Spencer, Eileen. 1992. *Car Crime and Young People on a Sunderland Housing Estate.* Crime Prevention Unit Series Paper 40. London: Home Office.

Tremblay Pierre, Yvan Clermont, and Maurice Cusson. 1994. "Jockeys and Joyriders. Changing Patterns in Car Theft Opportunity Structures." *British Journal of Criminology* 34:307–21.

Tunnell, Kenneth. 1992. *Choosing Crime: The Criminal Calculus of Property Offenders.* Chicago: Nelson Hall.

Vera Institute. 1977. *Felony Arrests: Their Prosecution and Disposition in New York City's courts.* New York: Vera Institute of Justice.

Wright, Richard and Scott Decker. 1994. *Burglars on the Job: Street Life and Residential Break-Ins.* Boston: Northeastern University Press.

——. 1997. *Armed Robbers in Action.* Boston: Northeastern University Press.

3

GENDER, SOCIAL NETWORKS, AND RESIDENTIAL BURGLARY

CHRISTOPHER W. MULLINS AND RICHARD WRIGHT

Residential burglary is a crime that is characterized by good network connections. These social networks most often are influenced by gender-based relationships. This research study utilizes burglary offenders who are active participants in committing these crimes to explore the various ways in which gender relationships provide access to, and participation in, this type of offense. The examination of gender stereotypes reveals how criminal networks influence the life experiences of men and women who commit burglary.

Criminological researchers have devoted substantial attention to the dynamics of residential burglary in both Great Britain (e.g., Bennett and Wright, 1984; Maguire and Bennett, 1982) and the United States (e.g., Cromwell et al., 1991; Wright and Decker, 1994). Taken as a whole, their research has established that residential burglary is a prototypically social offense, shaped by ongoing relationships and interactions set in the broader world of streetlife. For example, residential burglars typically offend in groups, routinely use inside information fathered during their daily rounds to select promising targets, and frequently dispose of stolen goods through established networks of buyers (Wright and Decker, 1994; see also Steffensmeier, 1983). As Shover (1972, 1973) has observed, one of the key characteristics of the "good burglar" is an ability to get along well with others.

Given the highly social nature of residential burglary, it is striking that the potential role played by gender in shaping commission of the offense has received little attention from researchers. Feminist ethnographers have documented the fact that streetlife is highly gendered and that this often serves to marginalize women's access to, and participation in criminal networks (see, e.g., Laidler and Hunt, 2001; Maher, 1997; Maher and Curtis, 1992; Maher and Daly, 1996; 1996; Maher et al., 1996; Miller, 1998, 2001; Phoenix, 2000). It is only reasonable to assume that residential burglary is not immune to these patriarchal forces. Indeed, Alarid et al. (1996) found that women who engaged in serious street crimes, including burglary, tended to do so within the context of predominately male offending groups (see also English, 1993; Haynie, 2002).

Source: From Gender, Social Networks, and Residential Burglary by C. W. Mullins & R. Wright, *Criminology, 41*(3). ©2003. Reprinted with permission from the American Society of Criminology.

The paucity of research on gender and residential burglary is all the more striking because the proportion of female arrests for this offense exceeds that for any other Index crime except larceny/theft (Steffensmeier, 1995; Uniform Crime Reports, 2001). Having risen from about 8% of all burglary arrests in 1991 to almost 15% in 2000 (Uniform Crime Reports 1992, 2001). Thus, a full understanding of the potentially important role of gender in facilitating and constraining participation in, and accomplishment of, such offenses.

In the only large-scale study to look directly at women involved in committing residential burglary, Decker et al. (1993) compared the offending styles and criminal histories of currently active male and female burglars. They also looked at the work roles typically adopted by the female burglars during the commission of their residential break-ins. Drawing on a typology developed by Ward et al. (1979), Decker et al. identified two distinct work roles played by the female burglars in their sample: accomplice and partner. Accomplices were clearly subservient to others—usually men— during their burglaries, whereas partners participated as equals in their offenses. However, Decker et al. did not examine the range of work roles adopted by the *male* burglars in their sample, so it is difficult to assess the extent to which gender situates and shapes the accomplishment of residential burglaries. Perhaps men also frequently play submissive or accomplice roles in such offenses; without an explicit comparison, this remains a matter of speculation. Furthermore, Decker et al. did not explore paths of initiation into, or continued involvement with, burglary crews. Because such crews emerge out of social networks that appear to be heavily gender stratified, it is likely that gender also influences factors other than work roles.

This study explores how gender structures residential burglary networks, opportunities, and meanings, using in-depth interview data, to make direct comparisons between male and female offenders. It seeks an insider's understanding of how the gendered social networks characteristic of streetlife influence male and female participation in, and accomplishment of, residential burglary. We begin by providing a brief overview of research into female participation in offending groups and male attitudes toward female participation in such groups, establishing the patriarchal nature of criminal networks. We then discuss recent feminist work that addresses issues of agency and "doing gender," thereby laying the groundwork for later discussions of the ways in which men and women negotiate the gendered structures inherent in criminal networks. Next we present our findings, concentrating on how patriarchal attitudes and

behaviors frame initiation into, participation in, and potential desistance from, residential burglary. We conclude with a discussion of the ways in which gender differentially structures experiences for men and women in *both* criminal and non-criminal social networks. Our overall aim, following Miller (1998:42), is to advance the ongoing debate "about women's place in the contemporary urban street world."

GENDER AND CRIME

Early work on female criminality linked offending by women to their broader social network relationships. Pollak (1950), for example, explained females' law-breaking in terms of their relationships with men, while Cameron (1964) explored the ways in which women's in-group relationships functioned to deter recidivism. More recent work on female criminality had emphasized women's marginalized status in street crime networks. While this marginalization has been shown often to push women into female-dominated crimes (see Daly, 1989; Maher, 1997), it is clear that some women do manage to penetrate male-dominated streetlife networks. Where this occurs, researchers have pointed to the strong overlap between community social structures and the structures of criminal networks located in these communities (see Maher, 1997; Miller, 2001). Thus, a fuller understanding of female criminality requires an examination of the ways in which gendered structures in the broader community— especially those involving peers and family—shape women's (and men's) entry into, and participation in, offender networks.

Steffensmeier (1983:1012) attributes the marginalization of women in street crime networks to the masculinized homosocial reproduction of deviant peer groups, observing that women "are more likely to be solo perpetrators or part of small, relatively non-permanent crime groups." In a study based on interviews with 49 male offenders, Steffensmeier and Terry (1986:306) also found that "the large majority of thieves had, at one time or another, committed crimes with women ... [although] their involvement with women was sporadic and situational" and when men did work with women, the women were either romantic partners or acquaintances used temporarily for a specific crime. While this work called needed attention to the gendered nature of criminal social networks, it did not consider how female offenders themselves perceive their place and participation within such networks.

GENDER AND AGENCY

Feminist scholars have long recognized that gender is accomplished and reinforced through socially situated behaviors and interactions (West and Fenstermaker, 1995; West and Zimmerman, 1987). In carrying out even the most mundane daily activities, men and women "do gender by taking account of, and orienting their conduct with reference to, prevailing normative beliefs about masculinity and femininity. This, in turn, serves to perpetuate a highly gendered status quo dominated by patriarchal notions of appropriate masculine and feminine behavior that can constrain the range of opportunities available to both sexes, but especially to women." As Miller (2002) has pointed out, however, gender-situated behavior need not *necessarily* be limited to the fulfillment of traditional role expectations; for some women it also can be called upon as a resource to negotiate patriarchal social networks in pursuit of decidedly non-traditional activities such as street crime.

Social actors seldom remain passive in the face of constrained opportunities, but rather actively work within and around structural and cultural constraints in a dialectical attempt to achieve desired goals. Feminist criminologists have explored how women negotiate gender constraints in the context of female criminality. Research on the role of agency in female criminality has tended toward one of two general interpretations: (1) women are dependent upon men and are only involved in crime due to their connections with men (e.g., Pollak, 1950); or (2) women are wholly in control of their offending opportunities and actions (e.g., Adler, 1975). According to Maher (1997:1), this tendency to "dichotomize agency" either "denies women any agency" or else "over-endows then with it." We too see these approaches as reductionistic in so far as we can understand much of female (and male) offending as the action of an individual attempting to meet personal short-term goals and, in the process, capitalizing on available resources. In two recent studies, for example, Miller (1998, 2001) has carefully documented the ways in which women involved in robbery or gang delinquency operate within the broader constraints of male-dominated streetlife. Her research highlights both the women's awareness of these pervasive constraints and their ingenuity in surmounting them. Previous research on female participation in property crime has not fully explored how gender both constrains and, via the exercise of personal agency, facilitates opportunities for females and males involved in committing residential burglaries. This paper examines how gender structures women's—and men's—perceptions and expectations of their co-offenders, especially focusing on how female offenders negotiate the patriarchal perceptions of their male co-offenders (as well as those of their non-criminal peers) and, in doing so, expands our understanding of these important processes.

DATA AND METHOD

The data for our study were drawn from a larger sample of 105 active residential burglars—18 females and 87 males—interviewed by Wright and Decker (1994). From this larger sample, we extracted all 18 of the female offenders and 36 of the males, matched approximately on age. To avoid sampling bias, the males were chosen as follows: both the males and females were grouped into three broad age categories: 17 and under, 18 to 25, and 26 and over. Within each of these categories, a random number generator was used to select twice as many males as females. The offenders included in our final sample ranged in age from 15 to 51, with a mean age of 25. Half of the female offenders were African-American, with the other half being non-Latina whites. Twenty-six of the males (72%) were African-American, and the remaining 10 were non-Latino whites.

The active residential burglars included in our sample were recruited in the early 1990s on the streets of St. Louis, Missouri. They were located through the use of a snowball sampling technique, whereby an initial respondent was asked to refer others who, in turn, provided further contacts, and so on. The recruitment process was initiated by a specially trained field ethnographer, an ex-offender who retained close ties to the St. Louis underworld. Trading on his connections, the field ethnographer began by approaching former criminal associates and expanded his network of referrals outward from there. He explained the research to potential interviewees, stressing that it was confidential and that the police were not involved. He also told them that eligible participants would be paid $25 for their time. If they agreed to take part, he scheduled an interview and, when the time came, accompanied them to the research site (see Wright et al., 1992 for a full description of the snowball sampling procedure).

In order to be considered an active residential burglar, potential interviewees had to meet three basic inclusion criteria. First, they had to have committed a residential burglary in the recent past, typically within the two-week period prior to being interviewed. Second, they had to define themselves as currently active. Third, they had to be regarded as active by other offenders in their social circle. Virtually all of the interviewees reported that they had committed crimes other than residential burglary at some point in their lives, and many had done so in the recent past. These offenses included, among others, robbery, assault, drug selling, and auto theft. Thus, while it may be convenient to think of the offenders as "residential burglars" for the purposes of the present study, it is important to remember that they—males and females alike—are more criminally versatile than such a label implies (for more on this issue, see Wright and Decker, 1994).

The representativeness of a sample drawn from criminals at large in the community can never be determined conclusively because the parameters of the total population are unknown (Glassner and Carpenter, 1985). But as Miller (1998:43) has noted, studying active offenders "overcomes many of the shortcomings associated with interviewing ex-offenders or offenders who are incarcerated." The fact that Wright and Decker purposely had over-sampled female residential burglars (that is, made a special effort to recruit as many women offenders as possible rather than trying simply to construct a sample that reflected the gender composition of local burglary arrest statistics) was crucial to the success of our research; it ensured sufficient cases for comparison with the males.

The racial make-up of our sample—64.8% African-American and 35.2% white—mirrors the population of arrested burglary suspects for the City of St. Louis at the time the data were collected. The St. Louis Metropolitan Police Department's Annual Report for 1989, for example, reveals that 64% of burglary arrestees were African-American and 36% were white. Remember, however, that the racial composition of our female and male samples varied somewhat, and that this represents a potentially important—if unavoidable—limitation of the present research. Overall, the African-American offenders were more criminally involved than their white counterparts. African-American men were more likely than white males to report drug sales activity, and African-American women were more likely than white females to report having committed serious violent crimes such as armed robbery.

The interviews, which were tape-recorded by mutual consent and transcribed verbatim, were semi-structured and conducted in an informal manner, thereby allowing offenders to speak freely using their own concepts and terminology. The offenders were asked to report as much as they could about their most recent residential burglary. Throughout their description of the offense, they were prompted with further

questions centering on its temporally sequential stages: motivation, target selection, gaining entry to the dwelling, and searching for valuables. For each of these stages, the offenders were asked whether it was "typical" of the way they committed their residential burglaries. If they answered that it was not, the offenders were requested to describe a more typical situation. The aim was to get a richly detailed overview of how the offenders carried out their break-ins. In addition, the offenders were questioned about broader matters concerning their initiation into, and hypothetical desistance from, residential burglary. Finally, the offenders were asked directly about matters relevant to gender and crime, such as their experience of committing residential burglaries with members of the opposite sex, and/or their attitudes to doing so (for a comprehensive discussion of the interview process, including matters related to internal validity, see Wright and Decker, 1994).

FINDINGS

Initiation

Most of the offenders in our sample, male or female, were initiated into residential burglary via interaction in intimate groups. With few exceptions, they committed their first burglary with older friends, family members, or street associates.

> [M]e and my brother, we wanted, you know, he came and got me and say he know where a house at to break into. And, uh, we go there and uh, we just do it . . . me and my brother, he and some more friends. (Jeffery Moore)

> A couple of friends of mine, we had been drinking some beer and we decided we needed some money. A couple of friends of mine said well, come on let's go break in this house . . . I said well, I'm a try it. (Robert Johnson)

> I was young and a guy I knew sold weed. He had been in the [target's] house before and we knew the guy very well and knew that he left his back door open because he didn't have a lock on it. We was young and he didn't give us much. He just said I'll give you a few joints if you go in there and get his stereo system. (Andre Neal)

But there was one key difference between the male and female offenders: the men typically were introduced to burglary through same-sex peers, whereas the women often came to the offense through their boyfriends (see also Alarid et al., 1996).

> Okay, [on my first burglary] me and my boyfriend, my kids' father, we was together and he was way older than I was anyway. He was into breaking into houses and stuff so it was me, him and his brother. (Sharon Adams)

Many of the women said they were coerced by a boyfriend into their first, and sometimes their subsequent, residential burglaries.

> Well, it was one like, 'If you love me, you'll do it' . . . He was saying, 'If you love me, you'll do it.' So I was really in love with him, so that's how it really got started. (Nicole)

> I had to go by his rules cause I was living with him. He told me if I wouldn't do it that he would do something to me. I guess drug me up or something. (Yolanda Williams)

Some of the female offenders claimed not even to know that their boyfriends were planning to do a burglary until they arrived at the would-be crime scene—when it was difficult to back out.

> I was living with my boyfriend. He didn't exactly tell me we was going to do a burglary, he told me that we was going somewhere. So next thing I know, he just broke into the house and he told me to come with him and take things out. (Yolanda Williams)

> Well I met this guy and he was doing it and, the first time, it was him and his friend and they came and picked me up with a stolen automobile . . . We went out there to this house and they got out . . . didn't know what was going on at first . . . one of the men came back out and told me to come in and keep an eye out to see if anybody was coming . . . I'm not stupid, so I put two and two together . . . I was scared. As a matter of fact we got in a big argument . . . I made a big scene, but I went in anyway. (Tammy Smith)

Males, by and large, act as gatekeepers to the social world of residential burglary. Reflecting the gender segregation that characterizes much of day-to-day streetlife, they bring male peers and family members into their offending networks, while remaining generally resistant to including women in their residential break-ins, save for the rare exception of a girlfriend or female relative (for a general overview, see Warr, 2002). Even when they *do* include women in such offenses, they tend to marginalize them and to limit their participation to secondary or subservient roles.

Motivation

In her study of active robbers, Miller (1998:44) found that the reasons such offenders give for committing their stick-ups represent similar motivations between the male and female burglars in our sample when it came to the reasons they offered for their offenses. Most said that they committed residential break-ins to finance a "party" lifestyle centered on illicit drug use, and incorporating the ostentatious display of various status-enhancing items like designer clothing and jewelry.

> It's usually, say we'll be doing some coke and then you really want more, so we'll go and do [a burglary] and get some money. (Sasha Williams)

> [I commit burglaries mainly] to get high. And buy clothes, buy me two buttons of heroin and one button of girl (cocaine). When I get high off that, I go buy me some clothes. (Jon Monroe)

> [I spend the money from my burglaries on] odds and ends, sometimes I get clothes or something real fancy. [But drugs], That's my first stop. (Karen Green)

Despite this overall similarity, there were a few notable differences in the reasons that the men and women gave for their burglaries. For example, a number of the males reported using some of the proceeds from their break-ins to pursue sexual conquests while, perhaps not surprisingly, none of the female burglars did so. By contrast, the female burglars were far more likely than their male counterparts to say that they used a portion of the money from their break-ins to buy necessities for their children (see also Daly, 1989).

> I needed money, cause I needed a roof over my head, food to eat and things for my baby . . . cause I needed diapers and I was broke and, you know, my hours had been cut and I didn't have the money to pay rent plus to get the baby what it needed. You know, it's gonna be cold soon, I need winter clothes for my kid, I need clothes. (Lynn)

Although a few of the men also mentioned using some of the money from their burglaries for child support, most emphasized the need to protect their status by looking after their *own* needs.

> I like to stand on my own two feet as a man, you know what I'm sayin? I like to pay my way and I don't like to ask nobody for nothin.' Don't want nobody talkin' about

me like I won't pay my way. I ain't freeloadin' off nobody. I'm a man, so I take care of myself. (Jeffery Moore)

Taken as a whole, the differences outlined above offer considerable insight into the gendered nature of streetlife in socio-economically disadvantaged areas. The neighborhoods from which the offenders in our sample were recruited contain an extremely high proportion of female-headed households in which women bear sole or primary responsibility for supporting their children. Men in these neighborhoods are expected to look after themselves and, as a consequence, often come to place a premium on maintaining their independence and autonomy (see Shover, 1996: Ch. 2). As Miller (1998:45) has observed: "Masculine street identity is tied to the ability to have and spend money, and included in this is the appearance of economic self-sufficiency." In such circumstances, men and women are largely isolated from one another and, for this and a host of other reasons, often find it difficult to form stable, mutually supportive relationships (see Anderson, 1990). This seems to be particularly true in disadvantaged African-American neighborhoods (see, e.g., Wilson, 1987). Indeed, we found only one thing to distinguish the African-American and white offenders in terms of the ways in which gender shapes their participation in residential burglary: African-American men were less likely than their white counterparts to report ever having committed a residential burglary with female co-offenders (see Anderson, 1989 for more on sex roles and attitudes among African-American males).

Target Selection

When asked what they were looking for in a prospective residential burglary target, the male and female offenders expressed similar preferences; both wanted to find a dwelling that was (a) unoccupied, and (b) contained something of value (see Wright and Decker, 1994: Ch. 3 for a comprehensive discussion of the situational factors that influence offenders' choice of targets). Breaking into a residence while the occupants were at home was almost universally regarded as being too risky, and no level of risk was acceptable in the absence of a compensating reward (see also Bennett and Wright, 1984). Accordingly, neither the men nor the women were willing to burglarize a residence without first knowing something about the people who lived there (especially their day-to-day routine) and the kinds of things it contained.

Some clear gender differences exist in the strategies the offenders used to obtain such information. A number of the male offenders, for instance, had legitimate jobs as home remodelers, cable television installers, or gardeners that allowed them to scout potential burglary targets without attracting undue suspicion. None of the female burglars had a licit job that gave her access to a comparably wide range of residences. Thus, while some of the male offenders could identify promising burglary targets in the course of their work, the female offenders could not. As a result, the women in our sample often had to rely on information generated by the men in their immediate criminal social network. This strategy is exemplified by Stacey Jones, who explained to us that she let her boyfriend select their burglary targets because " he works in construction . . . so he goes all over and sees all different houses and stuff."

Although the legitimate jobs realistically available to the female burglars offered little scope for gathering information about promising targets, a few of the women found a way around this problem by using sex or the appearance of sexual availability to gain access to the homes of gullible men

I was with my lady friend and we was coming up on this liquor store. This fellah started talking to us. He was asking us did we want to go over his house. He wanted to date. Her. So while they was in the back. I took his door key he had sittin' in the front room. So after I got the door key I was sittin' in the front room drinkin' beer. So when they got through, they came out and we left and I had the door key. The next day we went back by his house and did [the burglary]. (Janet Wilson)

[Our burglaries] are usually set up or it usually by a guy that we've met or something like that. Then we stick around with him for about a week. Then slip his key off his ring. That's how we do it . . . Most of the time we like, one without the other, then we not going. So a guy see us, he's like, "Wow! I'm getting' me a treat, two of them." They'll fall for that. See what I'm saying? (Karen Green)

These women were capitalizing on their femininity and sexuality to exploit opportunities available to them in a gendered social structure (also see Maher, 1997). We can see women using sex to gain access to targets as a rather straightforward use of available resources in the face of constraint. Alternatively, we can follow Emirbayer and Mische (1998) in speculating that this strategy arises from the contradictions inherent in border crossing activities—those without highly developed practical-evaluative skills will tend to deal with problematic situations by falling back on deeply held, traditional schemas. The fact that Karen Green and her partner refused to work alone (e.g., "We like, one without the other, then we not going") highlights the tension and uncertainty in the activity.

The effectiveness of strategies based on the appearance of sexual availability is attested to by the fact that some mixed-gender burglary crews employed them as a means of luring men out of their residences so that they could be burglarized. The difference is that, in these cases, the female offender charged with getting the man out of his dwelling was not in full control of the operation and thus risked being exploited by more dominant male members of the crew.

My guy knew what girl to pick to go over there [and get the potential victim out of his residence] . . . She was supposed to do her thing . . . to get in the car and give him head and drop him off. That's what she was told to do. She said she did it, but our guy could care less because she got him out of the house one way or the other and he didn't throw a fit about it. (Candy Johnson)

A male burglar described a similar situation.

We were over to this guy's house, me and this other person. She went in the house. She knew the person better than I did. She had been going to see him quite often. So she told me what was in the house. We decided that she go in first and talk to him and just leave the door open . . . So during the time she was distracting him, I was taking stuff out of the house . . . she still knows him and she goes to see him all the time. (Maurice Ross)

The male burglars' answers to questions about the strategies women typically use to choose targets brought the gendered nature of streetlife into sharp relief. Although a few of the women in our sample *did* sometimes rely on sex or the appearance of sexual availability to gather information about potential targets, to hear the male offenders talk one might conclude that they used this strategy much more often than was actually the case. Far more men than women mentioned the use of sex as a way in which female burglars located potential targets and, in doing so, they made broad generalizations rooted in traditional beliefs about feminine deviousness and sexuality.

They (women) get in the house and then say, "Hey, I'll have sex with you." Then once they get in the house they check everything out and then they find out what's going on and then if they know that person is going to

leave or something like that they find out where the keys are and get the extra set or take the set that the people have . . . a few of them call they male friends and say, 'Come on with the car.' (Maurice Ross)

See what they (women) do, I've seen 'em do it lots of times, what they do is they'll be talking to this guy and they'll say, "Let's go to your place," you know and get them all drugged, put a few tablets in the drinks, you know, they'll pass out, they'll take the stuff and they're out. I've seen them do it about four or five times. (Dan Ford)

Taking traditional notions of femininity a step further, one male burglar insisted that female offenders had little choice but to use their sexuality to gain access to potential targets because they were too weak to break into buildings.

They (female burglars) ain't got the strength to do that (kick in windows). They probably meet an old man or something and lonely and then go kick it (party) with him while he there they take what they want and be gone and he subject not to see them no more. You know how women is man, they up with you and beat you. (James West)

These male understandings of female criminality reflect the misogynistic prism through which femininity is refracted so as to reduce women's participation in crime to stereotypically sexualized roles.

Although both the male and female residential burglars wanted to ensure that prospective targets were unoccupied and contained items worth stealing, they frequently adopted different strategies to obtain this information: men capitalizing on gender-specific employment opportunities or social network connections with other men involved in streetlife and women capitalizing on the appearance of, or actual, sexual availability. In doing so, the men and women were exploiting the divergent pools of potential resources inherent in a gendered social structure that favors males in the realm of legitimate employment and females in the realm of informal interaction. Further, in mixed-gender crews, men and women freely drew on the others' advantages in information gathering and target selection. A similar process can be seen in the commission of residential burglary.

Commission

While some of the men in our sample claimed that they preferred to commit residential burglaries by themselves, mostly because they did not trust their colleagues and were unwilling to share the proceeds, none of the women expressed a desire to work alone. The female burglars, even those working in all-female crews, routinely reported that they lacked the knowledge or skills needed to break into a dwelling on their own. Perhaps for this reason, the women were much less likely than their male counterparts to dwell on the negative aspects of working with others.

In a sense, the fact that the women appeared to find working with others to be less problematic than did the males is surprising because our data indicate that females often are limited to secondary or subservient roes in mixed-gender burglary crews (also see Decker et al., 1993). They seldom participate in planning the crime, and frequently do not even enter the residence, acting as lookout or driver instead.

> All I had to do, all I ever do, is drive. I just go, like he'll (her boyfriend) go, him and his friend . . . during the day and he'll look at a house and he'll find one and then he'll tell me about where the house is and stuff, and all I have to do is drive to the place and wait for them to start bringing the stuff out and then drive off. (Stacey Jones)

That said, some of the women *did* enter dwellings to unlock a door for their male co-offenders, but from then on their participation in the offense was limited.

> I'm mostly the helper because I'm small enough to get in places and I'm light on my feet. I can't be heard easily . . . Either I'm looking out or they (her co-offenders) are looking out . . . but by me being the lighter and the shorter, it's easier for me to get in. (Jade)

Although it is stereotypical to focus on issues of size (or strength), the fact remains that when women such as Jade discussed being the first person in her crew to enter the residence they specifically attributed this assignment to their smaller and slighter physique. This represents yet another example of women capitalizing on limited resources at their disposal. Thus, although not all women are small, those in our sample who were petite found this to be an advantage during offense commission, a fact reflected in their somewhat more central role in the activity, even in mixed-gender burglary crews.

A subtle division of labor emerged when the female burglars discussed the goods they focused on inside the house. Those women who typically entered a structure while working in mixed-gender crews claimed expertise in finding so-called women's items. One of these women described what happened when she and a girlfriend, accompanied by male co-offenders, entered a dwelling with no female resident.

> I didn't do nothing to this house at all. I just sat there and watched a video . . . It was mostly the guy's shit. We knew there was no girl there . . . me and a girlfriend of mine, we just sat there and watched a video, drank soda and that was it. (Candy Johnson)

Overall, then, the roles available to females during offense commission were limited, both by personal choice and by others in their crew.

Many of the men in our sample admitted to performing functions similar to women during their burglaries, but (a) not when female co-offenders were present, (b) typically of their own volition rather than at the behest of a more dominant co-offender, or (c) in the early stages of their burglary careers. There was no stigma attached to these roles in such situations, with the male offenders generally adopting the attitude that this was a necessary "apprenticeship" in their craft. This contrasts markedly with the situation that prevailed for the female burglars, who often were solely engaged in secondary roles. And there was quite a bit of disparity in how men and women perceived this division of labor. Many of the male burglars claimed that the exclusion of women was necessary because they were too soft and emotional to handle the pressures inherent in the offense.

> That's (burglary) something I never discussed in my life with any women I was involved with. I really wouldn't discuss it with a woman who told me she did a burglary. Cause I talk about that with a woman, I couldn't trust a woman . . . Wouldn't no matter how good she was, I wouldn't . . . I just have a certain feeling about women. Women break down under pressure. If we got into a certain situation, they probably wouldn't be able to handle it. (Eddie Cagen)

Even when men made statements that would seem to indicate egalitarian relationships and work roles, they quickly backed off of them.

> [Women] do just as much as you do. But really, a woman may normally match. Or y'all could be working at the same time. She'll go take care of this while you go down here you know. They specifin' in knowing what jewelry is and what things are being hid that a women would hide and stuff like that. (Andre Neal)

John Black's response betrays a similar sentiment: "[They do the] same things. She be a lookout sometimes.

Or she set the person up." While both Andre Neal and John Black initially claim that the roles played by female co-offenders are equal, the examples they offer clearly qualify this assertion. Indeed, it was rare to find women assuming true partner roles in burglary crews. Only in all female crews did they attain truly egalitarian status.

Within mixed-gender crews, some women appeared happy to accept marginal involvement in the offense, believing that this would mitigate their culpability in case they were caught.

> I guess we basically let him do all like the kickin' the window and all that kind of stuff. But it wasn't nothing that we couldn't have done on our own. I guess the fact was we thought, "Well, let him do it. If he's the one that does all that, should we get caught [he'll be the one who has to take the consequences]." (Bonnie Williams)

> I think down in my mind, when I first started doing burglary I saw a show and in it my mind, when I first started incompetent; that she'd been brainwashed. And I guess I felt like if we ever got caught that I could blame it on him. That's pretty shit attitude, but ... I don't know, I kind of feel like I'm smarter than they (the male burglars) are. (Darlene White)

Comments such as these indicate that female offenders are well aware of the fact that street crime is widely perceived as a masculine activity and believe that their femininity may offer them some protection from legal sanctions, especially if it appears that they were coerced by their male co-offenders (see also Laidler and Hunt. 2001; Miller, 2001).

> [If I got caught, all I need to say is], he made me do it, you know, I'm just a feeble little woman. He said he had to go in his friend's house for a minute. I don't know what he's doing, you know. I'm out here waiting for him ... They don't suspect women as much as men. If I was a black man or a white man it does not matter. If a man came running out of a house and a woman came running out of a house, someone might automatically think, "What's wrong with that woman? Did someone attack her? Is she okay?" A man comes running out of the house, what do you first think? "Hey man, what did you steal?" You know, that kind of thing. (Darlene White)

There may be some truth in this belief (see Simon and Landis, 1991). But as Wright and Decker (1994:152–153) have observed, it hardly matters whether the women are correct in believing that the criminal justice system operates in a chivalrous manner: "[T] he important point

is that [they are] convinced this is the case, and thus [are] able to mentally discount the threat of arrest and punishment."

Hypothetical Desistance

Because our study is based on interviews with male and female residential burglars who, at the time, considered themselves to be *currently active*, their responses to questions about desistance are necessarily hypothetical, and should be interpreted as such. But this does not mean that active offenders have nothing important to tell us about desistance (see, e.g., Maruna, 2001). They are the ones we are trying to persuade to desist, and their views about how this might best be accomplished are worthy of our consideration. Moreover, such information, though hypothetical, may offer insight into the ways in which gender mediates offenders' perceived attachments to the conventional moral and social order.

When asked what would have to happen to make them stop committing residential burglaries, both the men and the women identified imprisonment. Here, however, they were referring solely to the incapacitative effect of incarceration, not to its deterrent or rehabilitative potential. This answer failed to address the underlying issues that the question sought to tap, which had to do with the conditions that might make the offenders stop *wanting to commit* burglaries. When asked to speculate about that, the male and female offenders offered strikingly different responses.

Many of the male offenders claimed that a good job, by which they meant one that paid well and involved little or no disciplined subordination to authority, might cause them to reduce their offending or give it up altogether (for a detailed discussion of this issue, see Wright and Decker, 1994). Beyond rewarding employment, a majority of the men also identified a stable and supportive relationship as something that might convince them to stop committing crimes, speculating that they would probable give up burglary once they "settled down" and started a family (also see Shover, 1996). Indeed, many of the males claimed that they had stopped offending altogether during periods in the past when they were happily married.

> When I first got out of the service, I didn't do nothin' wrong cause I had money. Had a little job, plus I had a wife. You know, I didn't want to do nothing ... [But] after me and my wife broke up, hey, knock on your door and, if you don't answer, I'm comin' in. (Jon Monroe)

> I got into the Bible and stuff with my old lady ... My old lady is pretty religious and I started watching it with her

and I got interested. We got really close to God. So I quit doing all of that. I quit stealing,' didn't rob nobody . . . Then we split up for a while and I went back to doing it . . . I started drinking, smoking, stealing, robbing, burglaries, whatever. (Earl Martin)

One of the male burglars reported that his *current* girlfriend was trying to persuade him to give up crime, and that his upcoming marriage made it important for him to do so.

My girlfriend . . . is trying to get me to stop doing it. Sure, she would like to not have to pay for a box of soap, but she's a good girl, she don't like that . . . I mean, I'm supposed to get married soon and there ain't no way I'm going to make it doing stuff like that . . . It's not the way I want to live. It's not right, it's scary. (Matt Detteman)

Along with marriage, some of the men also felt that, as fathers, they should stop offending so as to provide a law-abiding role model for their children. One male burglar said that he currently was trying to give up crime and support his children "the right way."

I feel that now, since I have two kids, I'm more responsible to get out here and get me a job and hold up as a father. Provide for my kids the right way . . . I feel my obligation is to take care of [my daughter]. My responsibilities are to take care of her and see that she grows up the right way and not doin' nothing wrong. (Howard Ford)

Comments such as these demonstrate the powerful influence of gendered social structures on the male offenders' thinking about their eventual desistance from crime. They have incorporated the traditional male role of "breadwinner" as something to be accomplished through lawful employment. Enacting mainstream "head-of-the-household" masculinities, therefore, involves a retreat from deviant and criminal behaviors; adult masculinity (as opposed to adolescent masculinity) is actualized through legitimate work, not criminal activity.

Whereas the male burglars identified finding a rewarding relationship with a woman as something that might cause them to turn away from crime, the situation was quite different for the females; their offending was driven by ongoing relationships with the (mostly male) co-offenders who initially introduced them to residential burglary. Because burglary networks are dominated by men who, as a rule, are reluctant to co-offend with women, once those relationships broke down, it was unlikely that the females would

be initiated into another crew and, as a consequence, they refrained from committing further break-ins. Put more bluntly, the female burglars needed to sever their relationships with criminally involved males in order to reduce their offending. Tammy Smith, for example, was introduced to residential burglary by her boyfriend and committed all of her offenses with him. When asked why she had been able to go for substantial periods of time without offending, she explained: "[It's] times when I am away from [my boyfriend]. Since he has been arrested, I don't want to be a part of them. It's not a way of living, I'll tell you." Conversely, males were likely to find another group to offend with or to offend alone once their original burglary crew dissolved.

Many of the women in our sample expressed strong concerns about how their parents and other close family members might view their criminal behavior.

It's like my mama be making me feel guilty at times, you know. She be telling my kids, you know. She be getting old, I got enough stuff in my house that she ain't paid for and stuff like that, you know . . . She telling me to go talk to somebody, some psychiatrist or something. (Marie Spencer)

I was not scared of being in the house, but scared that somebody would find out in the family. I was [more] worried that somebody in our family would find out and we would be the black sheep of the family than [about] actually getting caught. (Darlene White)

I was worried about if I would be recognized. If I did get caught, how am I going to get up from under this? My most worry was my Mom. What would she say? Now that's the biggest hassle with anything I do. What would my mother say or what she thinks. So I learned a lesson from that, whatever I did I would always tell my mother. She's my best friend. She's my wife, my husband, my son, my daughter, but first and foremost, she's my worst nightmare. (Running Wolf Woods)

Men never expressed this form of guilt or concern about how family members might perceive their criminality. For instance, when asked what would happen if his parents discovered his involvement in crime, Anton White simply said, "Well, they'll just find out." One offender did say that, when he was much younger, he used to worry about the prospect of his parents finding out about his criminality, but only because he did not want to be punished.

I didn't want no one to tell on me because I knew I would get into more trouble if somebody told that I done it. Cause then, I wasn't raised to do this and I knew I would get in trouble. We was brought up as, if you did wrong, you got punished. Not no staying in no room and watching no TV, you got the strap put on you . . . Those whuppins just wasn't no fun cause not only did you get whupped by your parents, you had your uncle, your aunt, all of them. (Joe Outlaw)

Indeed, rather than worrying about what their families might think about their criminal activities, some men actually expressed contempt for their relatives' conformity. One of the male burglars cynically capitalized on his aunt's babysitting job as a way to gather information about potential targets without her knowledge.

My aunt keeps her (the would-be burglary victim's) little baby. We just dropped my aunt off. I had used the bathroom, so that's how I got a chance to see their house . . . I didn't take [the valuables] then because she kept the baby at night while they went out. If anything came up missing while they out, they would have though my aunt did it. Which now I don't give a shit about the bitch for real. (Charlie)

Taken as a whole, these data suggest that the female burglars are more sensitive than the males to conventional informal social control—especially potential and actual shaming and ostracism at the hands of their relatives (also see Decker et al., 1993). This is understandable in light of broader gender norms. Compared with men, women are socialized to pay substantially more attention to the maintenance of interpersonal relationships (Beutel and Marini, 1995; Broidy and Agnew, 1997; Hagan and Simpson, 1985; Kessler and McLeod, 1984), and this may be especially true in communities dominated by female-headed households. Most of the women in our sample were worried that knowledge of their lawbreaking would be a bitter disappointment to their mothers and other female relatives. If communities dominated by female-headed households truly are knit together by informal ties between women, then female offenders should be more conscious of their social position in relation to other women. The women interviewed here seemed aware that their criminal behavior could jeopardize their network of conventional social relationships. While this did not stop them from offending, it did produce a level of guilt and unease that far exceeded that expressed by the male residential burglars, and may help to explain why fewer women than men engage in predatory street crime in the first place.

DISCUSSION

Our findings demonstrate that residential burglary is a significantly gender-stratified offense; the processes of initiation, commission, and potential desistance are heavily structured by gender norms. Women engaged in residential burglaries do not confront all of the gender issues that females face in violent offending, especially with respect to face-to-face impression management with targets (see Miller, 1998), but they do have to negotiate male-dominated networks and landscapes in accomplishing their crimes. It seems to us that gender plays the strongest role in shaping opportunity (e.g., initiation) and the events leading up to residential burglaries (e.g., information gathering), while playing a lesser, but still important, role in molding actual offense commission.

The powerful sexism that structures streetlife serves to constrain the opportunities available for women to engage in residential burglary. Male offenders typically do not like to work with women, seeing them as physically and emotionally weak. This perceived weakness undermines women's potential utility in the eyes of their male co-offenders so that, when females *are* drawn into a male-dominated burglary crew, their participation often is limited to an accomplice role. Perhaps this helps to explain why females are much less likely than males to participate in residential burglary, and why those women who *do* participate appear to do so with less frequency (see English, 1993).

Once women successfully gain access to residential burglary networks, they tend to adopt accomplishment strategies very similar to their male counterparts and co-offenders. Whether this is due to the innate appeal of these strategies or to the socialization experiences of female offenders is impossible to determine from our data. However, it is significant that when offending in female-only groups, the women interviewed here discarded these strategies in favor of more gender-specific techniques that served to reduce the uncertainty inherent in residential burglary. By gaining access to male victims' residences via the appearance of sexual availability, the two all-female crews in our sample used potential targets' gendered blind spots (e.g., patriarchal attitudes that define women as sex objects) to gather inside information and thereby facilitate their offending. Thus, in their engagements with property crime, the women in our sample proved to be active negotiators operating in a constrained social environment.

As other feminist ethnographers have shown, social actors are not blindly internalizing and recapitulating gendered social structures (e.g., Maher, 1997; Miller, 1998). Both the men and women in our study were cognizant of prevailing gender norms. Men called upon them to cement their own positions in burglary crews, apparently freely using the advantages that women might bring to the enterprise, while limiting the overall level of participation and integration these women enjoyed within such crews. As seen in other studies (e.g., Laidler and Hunt, 2001; Maher, 1997; Miller, 1998, 2001), the women were well aware of the male-dominated nature of streetlife and attuned to their tenuous position within it. Most of the women took advantage of opportunities presented to them, while playing the significance of their gender up or down in a highly situational fashion. Whether motivated by the financial demands of heading a household or by their involvement in street-corner partying and drug use, the majority of the women were creatively operating within the constraints that those roles imposed upon them. Overall, we suggest that for female offenders the boundaries of traditional femininity represent both opportunities and limitations, which the women interviewed here experienced and negotiated to varying degrees. While such activities do not erase the powerful disempowerment women experience in streetlife, they do provide pathways through gender hierarchies that may allow them to accomplish their short-term goals.

In addition to negotiating male-dominated criminal networks, the women in our sample also had to be mindful of their position within female-dominated domestic networks. The neighborhoods from which most of our subjects were drawn exhibit distinctly overlapping social networks segregated along gender lines. Male-dominated criminal and party networks predominate as a key aspect of streelife. Adult men in these networks lead lives largely separate from adult women. Female-dominated social networks of friends and relatives comprise the core domestic space and activity for the women in these neighborhoods. While there is quite a bit of overlap between networks, they remain distinct social arenas (Anderson, 1990; Stack, 1974). Thus, for men, discovery of criminal activities by family and non-criminal peers caused little concern and probably did not jeopardize these already tenuous relationships. On the other hand, for women, such a revelation could generate substantial shame and potentially trigger outright ostracism. The risk of this happening clearly carried considerable emotional force for the female burglars in our sample, albeit not enough to deter their offending altogether.

Although unanswerable from our data, this raises broader questions about the nature of delinquent peer group participation for women. Involvement with criminally active men will not only increase women's exposure to criminal values, potential criminal opportunities,

and victimization, but may also become self-reinforcing, as engagement in streetlife networks serves to weaken ties to family groups—the set of peer influences available to the women most likely to promote criminal desistance. As other feminist ethnographers have concluded (e.g., Daly, 1992; Gilfus, 1992; Maher, 1997; Miller, 2001; Richie, 1996), female criminality arises out of a combination of romantic relationships, victimization, and streetlife connections. Such lived experiences dialectically engage each other, thereby serving to embed women in criminal networks. The women in our sample entered streetlife networks though their male associations, while those who lessened their involvement in streetlife did so through the severing of those same relationships, whether voluntarily or involuntarily.

Traditional gender norms constitute the foundation on which street-based social interactions occur. Those norms, however, are intensified, or refracted, through street networks so as to become almost caricatures of their mainstream counterparts. The male offenders, compared to the females, expressed far more antipathy toward conventional norms and values, which is hardly surprising given their deeper criminal embeddedness and stronger commitment to streetlife. This is why the female offenders believed that, in order to go straight, they first needed to sever ties with their male associates (see also Richie, 1996). Interestingly, it is only when speculating about the possibility of a law-abiding future that the males adopt a more traditional stance than the females do; they see their best hope of going straight as lying in the establishment of an enduring relationship with a "good" woman. Perhaps both the males and the females are essentially correct in their reform, but it is clear that they are working at cross purposes—the men talk about the need to *make* a tie, the women about the need to *break* one.

REFERENCES

Adler, Freda. 1975. *Sisters in Crime: The Rise of the New Female Criminal*. New York: New York University Press.

Alarid, Leanne, James Marquart, Velmer Burton Jr., Francis Cullen, and Steven Cuvelier. 1996. Women's roles in serious offenses: A study of adult felons. *Justice Quarterly* 13(3):431–454.

Anderson, Elijah. 1989. Sex codes and family life among poor inner-city youths. *Annals of the American Academy of Political and Social Science* 501:59–78.

——.1990 *Streetwise: Race, Class and Change in an Urban Community*. Chicago, IL: University of Chicago Press.

Bennett, Trevor and Richard Wright. 1984. *Burglars on Burglary: Prevention and the Offender*. Aldershot, England: Gower.

Beutel, Ann M. and Margaret Mooney Marini. 1995. Gender and values. *American Sociological Review* 60:436–448.

Broidy, Lisa and Robert Agnew. 1997. Gender and crime: A general strain theory perspective. *Journal of Research in Crime and Delinquency* 34:275–306.

Cameron, Mary. 1964. The *Booster and the Snitch: Department Store Shoplifting*. London: Free Press of Glencoe. Collier-Macmillan Ltd.

Cromwell, Paul, James Olson and D'Aunn Avery. 1991. *Breaking and Entering: An Ethnographic Analysis of Burglary*. Newbury Park, Calif.: Sage.

Daly, Kathleen. 1992. Women's pathways to felony court: Feminist theories of lawbreaking and problems of representation. *Southern California Review of Law and Women's Studies* 2(1):11–52.

——.1989. Gender and varieties of white-collar crime. *Criminology* 27(4):769–794.

Decker, Scott, Richard Wright, Allison Redfern, and Dietrich Smith. 1993. A woman's place is in the home: Females and residential burglary. *Justice Quarterly* 10:143–162.

Emirbayer, Mustafa and Ann Mische. 1998. What is agency? *American Journal of Sociology* 103:962–1023.

English, Kim. 1993. Self-reported crime rates of women prisoners. *Journal of Quantitative Criminology* 9(4):357–382.

Federal Bureau of Investigation. 2001. *Crime in the United States. 2000*. Washington, D.C.: U.S. Government Printing Office.

——.1996. *Crime in the United States. 1995*. Washington, D.C.: U.S Government Printing Office.

——.1992. *Crime in the United States. 1991*. Washington, D.C.: U.S Government Printing Office.

——.1991. *Crime in the United States. 1990*. Washington, D.C.: U.S Government Printing Office.

——.1986. *Crime in the United States. 1985*. Washington, D.C.: U.S Government Printing Office.

——.1981. *Crime in the United States. 1980*. Washington, D.C.: U.S Government Printing Office.

Gilfus, Mary. 1992. From victims to survivors to offenders: Women's routes of entry and immersion into street crime. *Women and Criminal Justice* 4:63–89.

Glassner, Barry and Cheryl Carpenter. 1985. *The feasibility of an ethnographic study of property offenders: A report prepared for the National Institute of Justice*. Mimeo. Washington, D.C.: National Institute of Justice.

Hagan, John, A.R. Gillis, and John Simpson. 1985. The class structure of gender and delinquency: Toward a power-control theory of common delinquent behavior. *American Journal of Sociology* 90:1151–1178.

Haynie, Dana. 2002. Friendship networks and delinquency: The relational nature of peer delinquency. *Journal of Quantitative Criminology* 18(2):99–134.

Jacobs, Bruce. 1999. *Dealing Crack: The Social World of Streetcorner Selling*. Boston, Mass.: Northeastern University Press.

Katz, Jack. 1988. *Seductions of Crime: Moral and Sensual Attractions in Doing Evil*. New York: Basic Books.

Kessler, Ronald and Jane McLeod. 1984. Sex differences in vulnerability to undesirable life events. *American Sociological Review* 49:620–631.

Laidler, Karen Joe and Geoffrey Hunt. 2001. Accomplishing femininity among the girls in the gang. *British Journal of Criminology* 41:656–678.

Maguire, Michael and Trevor Bennett. 1982. *Burglary in a Dwelling: The Offence, the Offender, and the Victim*. London: Heinemann.

Maher, Lisa. 1997. *Sexed Work: Gender, Race and Resistance in a Brooklyn Drug Market*. Oxford, England: Oxford University Press.

Maher, Lisa and Richard Curtis. 1992. Women on the edge of crime: Crack cocaine and the changing contexts of street-level sex work in New York City. *Crime, Law and Social Change* 18:221–258.

Maher, Lisa and Kathleen Daly. 1996. Women in the street-level drug economy: Continuity or change? *Criminology* 34:465–492.

Maher, Lisa, Eloise Dunlap, Bruce Johnson, and Ansley Hamid. 1996. Gender, power and alternative living arrangements in the inner-city crack culture. *The Journal of Research in Crime and Delinquency* 33:181–205.

Maruna, Shadd. 2001. *Making Good: How Ex-Convicts Reform and Rebuild Their Lives*. Washington, D.C.: American Psychological Association Press.

Miller, Jody. 2002. The strengths and limits of 'Doing Gender' for understanding street crime. *Theoretical Criminology* 6:433–460.

——.2001. *One of the Guys: Girls, Gangs and Gender*. New York: Oxford University Press.

——.1998. Up it up: Gender and the accomplishment of street robbery. *Criminology* 36:37–66.

Phoenix, Joanna. 2000. Prostitute identities. *British Journal of Criminology* 40:37–55.

Pollak, Otto. 1950. *The Criminality of Women*. Philadelphia: University of Pennsylvania Press.

Richie, Beth E. 1996. *Compelled to Crime: The Gender Entrapment of Battered Black Women*. New York: Routledge.

Shover, Neal. 1996. *Great Pretenders: Pursuits and Careers of Persistent Thieves*. Boulder. Colo.: Westview.

Shover, Neil. 1973. The social organization of burglary. *Social Problems* 20:499–514.

Shover, Neil. 1972. Structures and careers in burglary. *Journal of Criminal Law. Criminology and police Science* 63:540–549.

Simon, Rita and Jean Landis. 1991. *The Crimes Women Commit: The Punishments They Receive*. Lexington, Mass.: Heath.

Stack, Carol. 1974. *All Our Kin: Strategies for Survival in a Black Community*. New York: Harper and Row.

Steffensmeier, Darrell. 1995. Trends in female crime: It's still a man's world. In B. Price and N. Sokoloff (eds.). *The Criminal Justice System and Women: Offenders, Victims and Workers*. New York: McGraw Hill.

——.1983. Organization properties and sex-segregation in the underworld: Building a sociological theory of sex differences in crime. *Social Forces* 61:1010–32.

Steffensmeier, Darrell and Robert Terry. 1986. Institutional sexism in the underworld: A view from the inside. *Sociological Inquiry* 56:304–23.

St. Louis Metropolitan Police Department. 1997. *Annual Report*

——.1989. *Annual Report*

Ward, David. Maurice Jackson and Renee Ward. 1979. Crimes of violence by women. In Freda Adler and Rita Simons (eds.). *The Criminology of Deviant Women*. Boston: Houghton Mifflin.

Warr, Mark. *Companions in Crime: The Social Aspects of Criminal Conduct*. Cambridge, UK; New York: Cambridge University Press, 2002.

West, Candace and Sarah Fenstermaker. 1995. Doing difference. *Gender and Society* 9:3–37.

West, Candace and Don Zimmerman. 1987. Doing gender. *Gender and Society* 1:125–151.

Wilson, William J. *The Truly Disadvantaged:The Inner City, the Underclass, and Public Policy*. Chicago: University of Chicago Press. 1987.

Wright, Richard, Scott Decker, Allison Redfern, and Dietrich Smith. 1992. A snowball's chance in hell: Doing fieldwork with active residential burglars. *Journal of Research in Crime and Delinquency* 29:148–161.

Wright, Richard and Scott Decker. 1994. *Burglars on the Job: Streetlife and Residential Break-ins*. Boston, Mass.: Northeastern University Press.

PART II

Violent Crimes

Violent crimes include any illegal behavior that threatens to or actually does harm another through physical means. Such criminal acts include murder, robbery, rape, and assault. Violent acts are viewed as the most serious of crimes by our society and are punished more severely than any other type of criminal offense by our justice system.

Violent crime is more feared by the public than other types of crime and receives more mass media publicity than most other types. It is usually an urban problem, but does occur less frequently in nonurban areas. Crimes involving violence are most often committed by urban males, 15 to 24 years of age, who come from neighborhoods that can best be characterized as lower socioeconomic in nature and are located in the inner city with predominantly minority populations. Excluding robbery, most acts of violence can be described as crimes of passion that are motivated by people who are most often known to each other. Emotions play a big part in the occurrence of violent behavior, and offenders usually have a history of previous violence in their background.

In their study of the accounts of incarcerated prison inmates who used a firearm in the commission of a violent crime, Pogrebin, Stretesky, Unnithan, and Venor examined the violent encounters and explanations of both male and female offenders who were serving lengthy sentences for their gun-related violence. Their uses of accounts were attempts to explain the offenders' violent actions in conventional terms that would be acceptable to a particular audience.

Carjacking through violent means has become a more prevalent offense in recent years. Topalli and Wright discuss how the sensational nature of this violent offense increases communities' overall general fear of crime when law-abiding citizens can become so randomly victimized. The authors focus on the decision-making factors that precede the actual criminal activity and the situated interaction between particular sorts of perceived opportunities, needs, and desires of the offenders.

Through her exploration of 403 rap songs, Kubrin's content analysis explored their lyrics for the use of violence as a means of acceptable behavior when viewed in the context of the inner city street code. Violence found in the words of many rap songs serve the purpose of establishing a social identity and a violent reputation within an inner-city environment as normative behavior.

4

RETROSPECTIVE ACCOUNTS OF VIOLENT EVENTS BY GUN OFFENDERS

MARK R. POGREBIN, PAUL B. STRETESKY,
N. PRABHA UNNITHAN, AND GERALD VENOR

In this study, accounts are utilized to examine the narrative explanations gun offenders provide for engaging in their violent acts. These narrative accounts illustrate how gun offenders attempt to preserve a conventional sense of self through the use of multiple stories of violent acts by a sample of inmates serving time for violent offenses with a firearm. The results were drawn from observations based on in-depth interviews of offender accounts for their criminal behavior.

Scott and Lyman first introduced their concept of "accounts" in 1968. Since that time researchers have expanded on the sociology of accounts to produce an impressive body of research. Interest in the study of accounts is not surprising because it allows for understanding and "insight into the human experience [in order to] arrive at ... culturally embedded normative explanations" (Orbuch 1997:455). Studies of accounts are wide ranging and cover a variety of behaviors, including HIV risk-taking (Fontdevila, Bassel, and Gilbert 2005), Medicare/Medicaid fraud (Evans and Porche 2005), computer hacking (Turgeman-Goldschmidt 2005), intimate partner violence (Wood 2004), violent crime (Presser 2004), rape (Scully and Marolla 1984), child abandonment (Geiger and Fischer 2003), snitching (Pershing 2003), steroid use (Monaghan 2002), and

white-collar crime (Willott, Griffin, and Torrance 2001). Although studies of accounts are pervasive in the sociological literature, there has been little examination of the accounts presented by violent gun offenders. The purpose of this research, then, is to examine the types of accounts employed by violent gun users to gain insight into their construction of reality.

The data for this study come from intensive qualitative interviews with a random sample of individuals who are incarcerated for using firearms in the commission of a violent crime. The violent encounters our study participants were involved in lasted a very short period of time, but the interviews lasted much longer and provide offenders with an opportunity to reflect on their past gun-related violent behavior. One performance norm in personally discrediting encounters is

Source: Retrospective Accounts of Violent Events by Gun Offenders by Pogrebin, M. R., and Stretesky, P., Unnithan, N. P., & Venor, G. in *Deviant Behavior, 13*(3), pp. 229–252, http://www.informaworld.com. Reprinted with permission.

giving others the benefit of doubt by allowing them an opportunity to adopt conventional role behavior (Gross and Stone 1964). It is within this context that our subjects provided us with accounts of their untoward acts with a gun.

THEORETICAL PERSPECTIVE

Mills (1940:904) observes, "The differing reasons men give for their actions are not themselves without reasons." Mills draws a sharp distinction between "cause" and "explanation" or "account." He focuses not on the reasons for the actions of individuals but on the *reasons individuals give for their actions.* Mills (1940:906) views motive as "a complex of meaning, which appears to the actor himself or to the observer to be an adequate ground for his conduct." Yet, there is another dimension: the individual's perception of how the motive will appear to others. Mills argues that such motives express themselves in special vocabularies that must satisfactorily answer questions concerning both social and lingual conduct as well as account for past, present, or future behavior. According to Scott and Lyman (1968) accounts are socially approved vocabularies that serve as explanatory mechanisms for deviance. These linguistic devices attempt to shape others' attribution about the actor's intent or motivation, turning it away from imputations that are harmful (e.g., their personal devaluation, stigma, or imposition of negative sanctions).

It is no doubt true that, in many instances, being able to present accounts effectively will lessen the degree of one's moral responsibility. However, moral responsibility is rarely a present-or-absent attribution. Just as there are degrees of deviation from expected conduct of norms, there are probably types and degrees of accountability, as well as acceptability, to various audiences with respect to the accounts that individuals offer. "The variable is the accepted vocabulary of motives of each man's dominant group about whose opinion he cares" (Mills 1940:906).

Most people are able to draw from a repertoire of accounts in explaining their untoward acts. This is not to suggest that their reasons are either sincere or insincere. Nor does it deny the validity of their claims; they many well have committed the disapproved behavior for the very reasons that they give. However, what is important is that they require an appropriate vocabulary of motives to guide their presentation of self.

Accounts are, above all, a form of impression management that represents a mixture of fact and fantasy. Goffman (1959), for example, argues that social behavior involves a great deal of deliberate deception as self impressions are continually created, managed, and presented to others. In short, we "put on a face to meet the faces we meet." Since accounts are often judged by others for authenticity, determining if the mixture of fact and fantasy is functional can be difficult. That is, the accounts that a social actor presents cannot be interpreted by others as deceptive and must be judged as a sufficient indicator of intentions, motivations, beliefs, and values (i.e., one's character). In short, for a social interaction to be mutually successful each social actor must assume a degree of genuineness in appearances presented by the other, as well as be able to take for granted the concomitant meanings implicit in those appearances (Goffman 1959). As Gross and Stone (1964) point out, each participant in an interaction must present a construction of self that complements others engaged in that interaction.

An individual's commitment and performance of conventional roles are crucial for impression management. A portrayal of pro-social behavior when accounting for one's deviance may be interpreted as an attempt by the offender to reaffirm his or her commitment to conventional values and goals in order to win the acceptance of others (Tedeschi and Riordan 1981). The demonstration of shared standards of conduct may also be seen as consistent with the wish to redeem oneself in the eyes of another in order to preserve self-respect. The desire for self-validating approval becomes more important when circumstances threaten the individual's identity. In these circumstances a person will make self-presentations for purposes of securing feedback that will restore the perception of self by others (Prus 1975). As Jones and Pittman (1982:255–256) note, "To the extent that the threatened sustains his counteractive behavior or to the extent that the counteractive behavior involves effort and costly commitments, social confirmation will have the restorative power sought."

If an offender can maintain a normal presentation of self within an abnormal situation that offender may be successful in having her or his past criminal behavior perceived by others as atypical (i.e., it is not indicative of her or his true or real self). Therefore, the offender is allowed to accept the moral responsibility of her or his violent behavior without having to accept the associated deviant identity. Thus, Goffman (1959) contends that individuals are not concerned with questions of morality about their behavior as much as they are with the amoral issue of presenting a moral self. Individuals, then, are largely concerned with moral matters, but as performers they do not have a moral concern with it.

Even where no guilt or shame is consciously felt, Goffman (1959:251) argues that "one may offer accounts in the hope of lessening what could be, none the less, attributions of a deviant identity." When used convincingly accounts blur the distinction between "appearances and reality, truth and falsity, triviality and importance, accident and essence, coincidence and cause" (Garfinkel 1959:420). Thus, we believe that the offenders in our study are likely to provide us with accounts that most effectively counter their deviant identity.

METHODS

As previously noted, we seek to identify the accounts offenders offer for their gun-related violence. We draw on the classic work of Scott and Lyman (1968) to aid us in this endeavor. Scott and Lyman (1968) identify the kind of talk that is meant to explain the void between actions and societal expectations as an account for deviant behavior by a person who attempts to offer explanations for their untoward acts. Both justifications and excuses as accounts are an effort to reconstruct social perceptions of wrongful behavior. Justifications are "accounts in which one accepts responsibility for the act in question, but denies the pejorative quality associated with it" (Scott and Lyman 1968:47). Excuses are "socially approved vocabularies for mitigating or relieving responsibility when conduct is questioned" (Scott and Lyman 1968:47). In the current study we analyze accounts in terms of justifications and excuses (for a legal distinction between these two concepts; see Brody, Acker, and Logan 2001).

Our use of narrative accounts is a strategic method by which we ask our study participants to relate their violent past. Narrative analysis is often described as a successful approach that can be used to study controversial and difficult topics (Migliaccio 2002). A narrative format can provide rich and very detailed data that may lead to insights into the connections between life experiences with that of one's social environment (Pierce 2003). Narrative analysis, notes Pierce, explains how people strategize and act within the context of their past interpersonal experiences. Relating stories through narratives is a type of social interaction where the primary purpose is to construct and communicate meaning. Chase (1995:7) argues that such a forum "draws on and is constrained by the culture by which it is embedded." Walzer and Oles (2003) point out that explanations may reflect attempts to maintain face to convince our audience that we are okay by framing our actions in terms of what we perceive to be acceptable.

The data for this analysis are drawn from interviews with Colorado prison inmates who used a firearm in the commission of their most recent offense, and were

sentenced to the Colorado Department of Corrections (CDOC). We selected inmates to be interviewed with the help of the CDOC research staff. A total of 119 inmates from 11 different correctional facilities were randomly selected by means of a simple random sample from a list of all inmates incarcerated for a violent crime in which a firearm was involved. We sent letters to each inmate's correctional case worker. These letters (1) identified the inmates selected for inclusion in our study; (2) explained the nature of the study; and (3) stated that inmate participation in the study was voluntary. Correctional case workers were asked to provide inmates with information about the study, tell them that their participation was voluntary, and inform them of the dates that the researchers would be at the prison to conduct interviews. Of the 119 inmates selected into the sample, 73 (63% of the total sample) agreed to be interviewed. Our study participants were between 20 and 67 years of age and most were convicted of armed robbery, assault, murder, kidnapping, and attempted murder. The inmates in our sample were also more likely to have committed their crimes in relatively urban areas as compared to more rural or suburban areas. The sample was composed of 39.1% whites, 40.6% African Americans, 15.6% Hispanics, and 4.7% Asians and Middle Easterners. Eight percent of our subjects were female. The demographics of the inmates in our study correspond closely to the demographics of inmates incarcerated in Colorado prisons (see Colorado Department of Corrections 2005).

Interviews were conducted in the prison in private conference rooms, vacant staff offices, and empty visitation rooms. Each interview was tape recorded with the subjects' consent and lasted between 60 and 120 minutes. A semi-structured format was used, which relied on sequential probes to pursue leads provided by the inmates. This technique allowed subjects to identify and elaborate important domains they perceived to characterize their criminal life history. Generally, these included their engagement in violent encounters throughout their life including the most recent offense, and their involvement with a firearm in that situation. The interview tapes were transcribed for qualitative data analysis, which involves scanning and identifying general statements about relationships among categories of observations. As Schatzman and Strauss (1973:110) noted, "The most fundamental operation in the analysis of qualitative data is that of discovering significant classes of things, persons, and events and the properties which characterize them." We employed grounded theory techniques first advocated by Glaser and Strauss (1967) to categorize our subjects' accounts of their violent gun crimes into excuses and justifications.

Findings

We present our findings in the form of detailed inmate narratives. The inmate narratives presented here offer considerable insight into the types of accounts they offer for their gun-related violence. The drawback of our approach is that lengthy narratives cannot be used to efficiently enumerate every type of inmate account. Nevertheless, the inmate narratives we chose to include in this analysis are rich in description and representative of the most common types of accounts given by inmates. Thus, the inclusion of extra accounts is not likely to provide additional insight. In short, the inmate narratives provided are accurate in that they depict the most common types of accounts and therefore represent the way most violent gun users construct reality.

We discovered that accounts of gun-related violence mainly fall into two groups—those that rely on justifications and those that rely on excuses. The most common justification used by the inmates in our sample is the denial of victim. When a subject uses the denial of victim justification she/he implies that the victim deserved the injury under the circumstances (Sykes and Matza 1957). Excuses were also often offered as explanations of untoward acts. Specifically, many inmates presented accounts that draw on the excuse of defeasibility. Scott and Lyman (1968) point out that defeasibility is an excuse that claims an untoward act is the result of a lack of knowledge and will. Thus, an individual that uses defeasibility as an excuse is asserting that she/he is not completely free at the time of the untoward act. As demonstrated later, defeasibility was seldom used as the only account. In other words, defeasibility was often used as an excuse, but was also used together with other excuses and/or justifications.

Denial of Victim as Justification for Gun Use

The most common justification used by the gun offenders in our sample was the denial of victim. As previously stated, denial of victim implies that the victim deserved the injury. The four inmate narratives presented illustrate the diverse ways in which our subjects claim that the victim was responsible for their injury. In the first case the offender shot his supervisor for terminating his employment. In the second case the offender shot the victim for physically threatening him and stealing his drugs. In the third case the offender shot the victim for failing to play by the rules and acknowledge that guns are dangerous. In the fourth case the offender shot the victim to defend himself.

Story 1

I got tired; I had been working a long time for that company. Then one day one of the tenants had not paid their rent, so they decided to put their belongings on the street. So, we went with the Sheriff and started carrying chairs, tables, that kind of stuff. There were other people that were supposed to be helping me. That would be my supervisor and another maintenance guy. I told my supervisor—his name is Robert—"Aren't you supposed to be helping me man?" He put his face in front of mine and said, "You know what, you work for me!" He said, "You do not have to tell me what I have to do, okay?" So, I got very upset because nobody yells in my face like this before. So I point my finger close to his face and started laughing, you know. He said, "That's okay I will see you crying in five minutes." After that I went to clean the swimming pool. I got a call on my radio that told me to come to the office. Robert said, "Give me your keys, your radio, and the beeper." So when this happens he said, "Good luck"—meaning that I was fired. He fired me on the spot. I was very upset. The money I was making at the apartment complex was to help my family in Colombia. The guy had to pay for what he did. I wanted to explode you know. I had a .38 caliber gun in my car. When I grabbed the weapon I knew I was ready. When I approached him [Robert] I had a sport magazine and I covered the weapon with it. I was approaching him but the other maintenance man became suspicious. He said, "Robert, watch out!" When he said that, "Boom."—I shot him. I sat down and waited for the police. It was a relief for me. You felt rested.

This particular offender had no prior criminal history. The demeaning incident that led up to the shooting of his supervisor was associated with the humiliation he experienced by his supervisor's confrontational interaction. The subject noted two important occurrences that took place prior to the shooting. First, his supervisor talked harshly to him close to his face, thereby violating his personal space that should be respected by another during face-to-face interaction. Second, the supervisor abruptly fired the interviewee from his seven-year job.

The shooter appeared to feel a deep sense of anger over his two confrontations with his supervisor. He clearly discussed his anger and desire for retaliation when he made the point that he was so angry that he felt like he was going to explode. He noted that his supervisor would have to pay for his actions. It is at this point in the account that our subject justified his attempted murder. He also accounted for his actions by arguing that the loss of his job would adversely impact his family who still resided in Colombia. In short, from this offender's perspective, the victim was responsible for his injury.

After the shooting incident was over, the subject noted that he sat down and waited for the police. He expressed a sense of relief and claimed he felt rested. The actual retaliatory incident rapidly decreased his rage. He did what he had to do to vindicate the anger he experienced because of the victim. Nowhere in our interview did this particular participant make claims to the righteousness of his violent action, but instead laid claims and attempted to portray himself as a person who needed, at the time, to redeem his sense of self by causing pain and physical harm to the person who committed a terrible wrong against him.

Story 2

> I had a gun in my pocket and I told him, you know, "Why did you jack us?" And he [victim] tried to play it off like he didn't know what I was talking about. I says, "You owe me $18,000 or your gonna give me back my dope." And he says, "Hey, you come over here running your mouth again, I'll put a fucking hole in your head." So when he threatened me like that, I turned around pulled out my gun and walked right up to him and shot him in the head. When he hit the ground I shot him and shot him in the head. When he hit the ground I shot him 2 or 3 more times. . . . I was selling drugs, drugs was my life, and when he went in there and jacked us for dope he was taking away from how I made my living. Word gets back on the street that me and my partner had got jacked [and] everybody's waiting to see what we're going to do. If we didn't do nothing everybody else, everybody would come and rob us. It was like "Damn what am I gonna do?" Some of it did have to do with peer pressure, but they didn't make me do it. But, the man threatened my life and, you know, that's not good to threaten people's lives.

This subject was a gang member that was robbed of a considerable amount of drugs he was going to sell. He described his conflict of whether he should shoot the robber or not. But he accounted for his decision to get his drugs back or the money they were worth. By sharing his conflict with the interviewer, he reiterated his dilemma. The subject could either lose face as a gang member and drug dealer or do something to gain respect in the drug/gang community. In the gang environment our subject argued that he had no choice. He had to retaliate against that drug robber because the robber had threatened his livelihood and showed him a considerable amount of disrespect.

Our subject justified shooting the victim because he felt threatened. He accounted for his shooting the drug robber by arguing that "people should not threaten other people's lives." But, the shooter is also expressing his choices within a limited set of possible actions. He could lose face and have nothing left of his gang member identity or cause harm to the person who wronged him. Here, he presented a self that needed to maintain his street image. From the point of view of our subject there appeared to be no other alternative course of action than to shoot the victim.

Those African-American and Latino gang members in our study who were involved in violent gun encounters and imprisoned all expressed the importance of not losing face among their peers. The code of retaliation for both groups was sincerely believed to represent an ongoing presentation of self as tough and fearless. This image often leads to violent encounters using guns over the most incidental actions that are interpreted as disrespectful. Being disrespectful was often viewed as an act that deserved retaliation. This same presentation of self continues and is often exacerbated by gangs of all races and ethnicities within the prison.

In case after case we observed our subjects saying that if you carry a gun you must be willing to use it. These justifications were often also related to the denial of victim in which the subject admitted the commission of the untoward act but also argued that the victim caused the offender to use a gun. In other words, the injury would not have occurred but for the victims' actions. In the following account an offender used the denial of victim justification to explain his violent actions.

Story 3

> I guess there are loner criminals out there but for me there are two or three guys. I really didn't do a lot of crime by myself. We would need some money for whatever reason and then, you know, "Hey man," where can we get some money. We go rob it. We done convenience stores, liquor stores, any places we really thought had some decent money . . . well I get out of the military and me, my brother, a friend of mine, and a friend of his decided to do a robbery. We had an interaction with some other young people and we both stopped at a light. We got into an interaction and I pulled out my gun and shot the guy in the stomach. I was gonna fight him but I had a gun. Why fight, you know, when you have a gun? My brother looks at me and says, "Man, you're a real killer now, aren't you?" I says, "No, I'm not," but if you got a weapon you might as well use it to protect yourself. I still had a sense of trying to

do the right thing. I shot a warning shot up in the air to get him (victim) away from the car. He stood there. He started talking trash and I just jammed the gun into his belly and pulled the trigger. He fell to the ground. We drove off and went and pulled a robbery. I was arrested and I am doing time for attempted murder.

In his explanation of the events that transpired during the violent altercation our subject offered a self-perception of his integrity when he claimed he tried to do the "right thing" by firing a warning shot to let the victim know that he was serious in his demand to back down. In similar cases throughout our study we found numerous instances when victims threatened with a gun failed to comply with the warnings given by the shooter to retreat often ended up getting shot. This usually occurred when the perpetrator actually feared physical retaliation from the victim as was the case here. As our study participant noted—Why fight someone when you possess a gun? Or, when put another way, why take the chance of being overpowered physically and experiencing humiliation in front of your peers when you can avoid a physical encounter or a threatening situation by harming the aggressing victim before the harms you?

While relating his account of the events that led up to and after the violent encounter, the inmate offered two factors that tend to bolster his self image as a "bad ass" (Katz 1988). His younger brother's admiration of him as a "genuine killer" seems to have masked his feelings of cowardice by shooting the victim instead of physically fighting him when confronting an unarmed victim. The subject presented a self that is in control of his emotions as he goes on after the shooting to commit an armed robbery. In short, he did not allow the emotional response associated with a possible homicide interfere with his original mission to rob a business for money.

Story 4

I kept the gun in the house most of the time. But this night that this happened I had it in my car with me under the seat. On my way to work I'm driving through the middle of a black neighborhood and there's these three guys out on the street corner jumping out in the middle of the street throwing rocks at cars. So this guy jumps out in the street at me throwing a rock over the hood of my car. So right away I make a U-turn right in the middle of the street and I'm going back to confront him like, "What are you doing? Why are you guys out here yelling and all that?" His partner threw something else over the top of the car. I didn't see what it was—like

a rock or something. So I make another U-turn to where they were on the right side. I stopped the car and we got . . . got into this big argument and it escalates from there. I start to ask them why they are throwing rocks and stuff like that—jumping out into the middle of the street at cars—and they are acting all crazy and cussing at me. So, they start to approach the car and I pull out my gun. In my mind I'm figuring I'm going to scare them away. I never figured on shooting anybody. When I pulled out the gun one of them kinda backed up behind the bushes, but the other two were still standing kinda tough. The guy I ended up shooting, he was still talking to me this whole time, still cussing at me and called me racial names and that type of stuff. I had the gun out telling him to stop, you know "I'll shoot you, if you don't stop coming toward the car." He's like, "Well, if your gonna do it, just do it. If not just drive away." I'm sitting there all confused now because I'm like "this guy thinks he's Superman or something." I couldn't figure out why he wasn't scared of the gun. I looked back at him he jumped towards the car like I don't know if he was going to come through the window or open the door, and go for the gun. But, as I look he jumps toward me and I jerked the trigger one time and it ended up hitting him in the middle of the chest. I can see him grab himself and kind of start to go down. I drove off right away.

This subject is a 16-year-old Caucasian youth who was in a confrontation with three African-American teenagers. He confronted the rock throwing teenagers from the confines of his car. It is likely that he never would have driven back to the where the youth were had he not had a loaded gun in his possession that he could wield from the safety of his car.

The subject appeared to suggest that the firearm caused him to have a false sense of bravado and he implied that had he not taken his gun he would not have confronted the victim. The gun, as was true in many other cases in our study, allowed the instigator to have a self-perception as a powerful person. One who can pull the weapon out during a conflict and have a more physical, threatening individual back down. This sense of power over another was exemplified in this case study. The gun gives an advantage to the more vulnerable party, and more than evens the odds that there will be no physical threat to our subject. Yet, the threat of a weapon does not always provide the desired end result. This and other cases we analyzed sometimes saw the victim pursue the gun carrier despite the threat of severe physical harm or worse. Once the victim does not adhere to the gun carrier's threats, the self-perception of power on the part of the instigator immediately changes. He pointed to this feeling when he tells us that he could not understand why the threat of the pointing gun did not prevent the victim from leaving the scene afraid. At this point his account is formulated. This subject implied that if only the victim had reacted with fear when threatened with the gun, the shooting would never have occurred.

This particular inmate had no previous criminal history but seemed to be infatuated with his gun. In most circumstances where a person is outnumbered by those who threatened them, getting away would be the logical action to take. But here the possession of a firearm directly changed this inmate's self-perception to that of a person in control, a person not to be wronged. It is clear that his feared image of a confrontational person who was wronged was not effectively communicated to his victim. Our shooter miscued the victim's non-compliance, even after displaying his gun. He claimed he became the threatened party and had to shoot to protect himself.

APPEALS TO DEFEASIBILITY AS EXCUSE FOR GUN USE

Scott and Lyman (1968) stated that appeals to defeasibility are excuses that claim untoward behavior was the result of the lack of knowledge and will. In our sample, the subjects that used this excuse were essentially asserting that they were not completely free at the time they used a firearm in the commission of violent act. It is interesting to note that excuses of defeasibility were always accompanied by at least one other excuse or justification. The following three accounts illustrate appeals to defeasibility. In the first case a girl robs a convenience store to avoid losing her boyfriend. In the second case a young girl shoots her ex-boyfriend because she has temporarily lost her mind and because he rejected her. In the third case a young man shoots his stepfather because he was not thinking clearly and because he was encouraged to act violently toward his stepfather by a close friend.

The first account by the girlfriend in a boyfriend-girlfriend partnership illustrates both defeasibility and scapegoating as reasons for her violence. Scapegoating is the allegation that untoward behavior is a "response to the behavior or attitude of another" (Scott and Lyman 1968).

Story 5

> The boyfriend I had at the time I don't know, we were just kind of having fun that's how I looked at it. Not that the crimes that we committed were fun or anything. We partied a lot, did drugs and stuff, but more than that we were just having fun and living it up. Then in the summer in the period of a couple months we just went on a robbery spree.... It all started while we were watching the movie *Point Break*. He was sitting there saying, "We could do that." I was like, "Oh yeah, that is a great idea," and it just went on from there. I mean he could not stop talking about it ... thinking about it. Then, it kinda turned to a manipulation thing. He said, "I am serious about this and I could find another partner, but I really trust you, and if I have to I will." I was in love with this guy and thinking he is not really going to do this with anybody else. We were just being dumb. I don't think we considered that it was really a violent act. We did have a gun and we pulled it on someone when we walked into the store, but it wasn't like we ran in and roared. It was weird.... You cannot count how many people will be in the store, who the clerk is, what they are doing, unless you study them and we really didn't. It wasn't like some big planned thing, it was really spontaneous. We didn't know if we were going to do anything until we were there, then after go back to work [summer job] and do it again on another day.

The pair committed three armed robberies of large discount department stores in a short period of time. The subject's boyfriend insisted that she hide the gun that they procured for the crimes at her parent's house. After her boyfriend bragged to a few friends about their criminal acts, one of those friends informed the authorities who questioned the boyfriend about the incidents. The boyfriend told authorities where to find the gun and then became the State's lead witness against the girl. He received a court sentence to a drug treatment program and our interviewee received a 12-year sentence to prison.

The subject engaged in these robberies without ever thinking about the consequences of engaging in serious crime. Of course, she implied that if she would have thought about the consequences of her actions she would have never engaged in the robberies. She also noted that her affection for her boyfriend overcame her sensibilities and she argued that she had no choice but to go along with his wishes or possibly lose him. In this particular situation the girlfriend claims her motives were to maintain her romantic relationship. This account might also be viewed as a justification in the sense that it served the interests of another to which she has an "unbreakable allegiance of affection" had she not later argued that she was "manipulated" by her boyfriend. She implied that she never really thought they would commit the first robbery. However she subsequently engaged in multiple armed robberies prior to being apprehended by the police. Here, Hewitt and Stokes' (1975) thematic organization of meaning applies. It is based on interactions that most often are dependent on people's ability to interpret others' actions as types of particular identities. When events fail to fit themes in interaction, which appears to be the case here, identities may become problematic if the acts of others do not in reality appear sensible in light of his or her identity in the situation. Maybe her boyfriend is not who he appeared to be.

The boyfriend's fantasy-identity as a "bad guy" was not really who he was. For in reality he escaped any meaningful punishment, but instead when the seriousness of his criminal escapades as short lived as they were, forced him quickly to return to a conventional status he blamed our prison subject (also using the excuse of scapegoating) for his fantasized criminal identity. Certainly, she miscued the veracity of his claims to want to be an outlaw type. Instead, she became the person with the labeled identity and his excuse was accepted (i.e., he was perceived as the one who had been led astray and was sent to a drug rehabilitation program).

Scott and Lyman (1968) point out that a sad tale is a justification of an untoward act in terms of a bleak past. The following account by the girlfriend who uses a firearm to shoot her boyfriend illustrates the sad tale of justification combined with the excuse of defeasibility and denial of the victim.

Story 6

> I was going with my boyfriend who I felt I was totally in love with and I couldn't live without and all those things. He wanted to leave me and we played this game off and on for a month. He'd leave me and then come back. The last time I was like, "I can't take this anymore. I don't want to live anymore. I am going to kill myself." I asked my mom for a gun because Randy, who had lived with us, had saw me at the 7-11, and I am afraid of him. But I want to go out so she handed me the gun and I went out. I told my mom a lie. I wanted the gun to kill myself so I told her a different story. I went out to the country to an open field and I fired the gun to make sure I could because I am scared of guns, always have been. I stopped and said to myself, "I have to know what's wrong with me first. I need to know why he doesn't love me the way he said he did." I got back in the car and I drove to an outdoor party where I knew he was at. I told him I had to talk with him and we went and talked inside. I had put the gun in my jacket pocket after I shot it in the field. We talked for like an hour and we were walking back to the

car and he said something, I don't remember what, and I took the gun out and I shot him and I shot myself.

In this account our subject claimed she had no premeditated thoughts of harming her boyfriend. She began her account by referencing her mother's ex-boyfriend (who we learned about upon further questioning) was sexually abusive to her while he was residing with the family. She claimed that the end of her relationship with her boyfriend was simply too much for her to take. She then went on to portray herself as a person who only meant to harm herself but presented an excuse of not really being responsible for her violent actions toward her boyfriend. The events leading up to the actual shooting of her boyfriend and herself appear vague in description and rather coincidental in nature. She clearly claimed she was not aware of her actions at the time of the shooting as she could not even remember what her boyfriend said moments before she shot him. Did his final statement (whatever it was) provoke the murder? Or, was the intention always there to dramatically take both of their lives if she was unable to reconcile her relationship with her boyfriend? The fact that her boyfriend may have said something that was hurtful in those final moments prior to the shooting seemed to us as an attempt to leave open to interviewer interpretation that he deserved to be hurt for what he said—although this justification of denial is not likely to be very effective without her sad tale and appeal to defeasibility.

This study participant's accounts for her murder are related in such a way as to justify them in terms of a sad tale and then to attempt to excuse her violent actions as if the sequence of events that occurred prior to the shooting were scripted for her to follow and she had little control over the events that followed her procuring the gun from her mother. This is an account that offers indirectly the theme of this "wasn't the real me" who committed such a terrible crime.

In a few cases, generally dealing with abusive relationships, the subjects in our study drew on justifications and excuses. In the following scenario the subject clearly invoked the defeasibility excuse, but also justified his acts by arguing that his abusive stepfather deserved to be shot. He also presented an appeal to loyalties to his mother who he asserts he saved from death.

Story 7

> My stepfather would break my mom's jaw, break her nose. You know, he never broke anything on me. . . . I was 18, living on my own and I went to visit my mom. She was living in an apartment, but they weren't living together at

the time. She had a black eye so I called my step dad and told him, "I'm a grown man now. You hit her again and I'm coming after you." He said, "If I hit her again, I'll kill her and I'll end up killing you too." About three weeks later I saw leather indentations where she had been tied up. The morning of my 19th birthday I went out and shot him. When I decided that there was no alternative but, but to do what I did to my step dad, that's when I went and got a gun and used it. So it was like a 12-hour period of being angry and the person with me [subject's friend] was egging me on. He was having me go through every time I'd seen my step dad hit my mom and every time he hit me. Every time I started to cool down he would start in again. So he kept me pumped up ready to do this until the act occurred. I was totally disconnected from myself in the act. Once the act was complete, I saw somebody I didn't know shooting my step dad. Once the act was over, I'm back to myself, total rush, dizziness, everything was blurry, adrenaline rush, and he's still standing asking me why. I just freaked out.

Murdering his abusive stepfather was a release of pent-up emotions after years of physical abuse to his mother. Yet, he accounted for the decision to shoot his abusive stepparent only after his friend kept reminding him of all the terrible abusive incidents he had experienced over the years. He used, in part, his friend's persuasiveness to help justify the shooting. True, his stepfather was a long-time abuser, and needed to be stopped. However, the subject in this case indicated that he may not have shot his abusive stepdad had it not been for his friend's constant reminders of his past beatings at the hands of his stepfather.

Our subject related the feeling that after he actually shot the victim he experienced a disconnection from his physical person and noted that he visualized someone else doing the shooting. This indicated a presentation of self as a person who would not commit such a violent act. It was as if somebody other than himself did the shooting. His account has the objective of relating the real type of person he really is, one whose self-presentation consists of a nonviolent person who was overwhelmed by his circumstances. Further, he justified the shooting because of his responsibility to be his mother's protector. By including his mother to help justify his foreground thoughts of killing his stepfather, he offered an almost heroic self-image as the boy who is now a man, and therefore must confront the evil abuser. In reality it is difficult to discern if our study participant was getting even with the victim for his own years of abuse, or to rectify the years his mother experienced abuse. For this particular subject, protecting his mother heightened his image as a guardian of a weak person rather than that of an angry retaliator who was getting

back for his own abusive past. The justification for his action, although wrong, is perceived as necessary.

DISCUSSION

The consequences of deviant activity are often dependent on a given "definition of the situation." When a definition of a specific situation emerges, even though its dominance may be only temporary, individuals must adjust their behavior and views to it. Alternative definitions of problematic situations routinely arise and are usually subject to negotiation. Thus, it is incumbent upon convicted offenders to have their situation defined in ways most favorable to maintaining or advancing their own interests. When "transformations of identity" are at stake, such efforts become especially consequential (Strauss 1962). The rejection of a deviant identity has ramifications for the person's self-perception of who they are. As noted earlier, the negotiation of accounts is really a negotiation of identities. Accounts serve as a management technique, or "front," that minimizes the threat to identity (Goffman 1967). If the violent perpetrator can offer an acceptable account for his or her violent gun use, he or she increases the likelihood of restoring a cherished identity brought into question by their criminal behavior.

There is a close link between successfully conveying desired images to others and being made to incorporate them in one's own self-construction. When individuals offer accounts for their problematic actions, they are trying to ease their situation in two ways; by convincing others and by convincing themselves. An important function of accounts is to make an individual's transgressions intelligible to themselves and others. The gun users we interviewed sought to dispel the view that their deviation was a defining characteristic of who they really were. In short, they attempted to engage the centrality or primacy of a deviant role imputation. To accomplish this task they offered accounts that were mainly focused on the denial of victim and defeasibility. Their goal was to maintain or restore their own sense of personal worth notwithstanding their violent behavior. In a way, laying claim to a favorable image in spite of aberrant behavior means voiding an apparent moral reality that is apparent to the deviant.

Individuals seek a "common ground" in accounts of their deviant behavior, explaining their actions in conventional terms that are acceptable to a particular audience. It is important to point out that these accounts should not be viewed as mere rationalizations. Many offenders really believed in their accounts. Moreover, accounts do not themselves prove the cause of one's behavior. They do, however, provide contextually specific answers about the act in question and manifest a certain style of looking at the world.

Finally, it should be noted that, as retrospective interpretations, accounts often have little to do with the motives that existed at the time the criminal violence occurred. In this case, accounting for one's deviant behavior requires one to dissimulate, that is, to pretend to be what one is not or not to be what one is. Thus, it is not logically necessary that one agree with other's moral judgments in order to employ accounts. Even where no guilt or shame is consciously felt, one may offer accounts in the hope of lessening what could be, nonetheless, attributions of a deviant identity.

REFERENCES

Brody, David, James Acker, and Wayne Logan. 2001. *Criminal Law.* Gaithersburg, MA: Aspen.

Chase, Susan E. 1995. *Ambiguous Empowerment: The Work Narratives of Women School Superintendents.* Amherst, MA: University of Massachusetts Press.

Colorado Department of Corrections. 2005. *General Statistics.* Colorado Springs, CO. Colorado Department of Corrections, Retrieved September 14, 2005. Available at http://www.doc.state.co.us/Statistics/7GeneralStatistics.htm

Evans, Rhonda D. and Dianne A. Porche. 2005. "The Nature and Frequency of Medicare/Medicaid Fraud and Neutralization Techniques among Speech, Occupational, and Physical Therapists." *Deviant Behavior* 26(3):253–270.

Fontdevila, Jorge, Nabila El-Bassel, and Louisa Gilbert. 2005. "Accounting for HIV Risk among Men on Methadone." *Sex Roles* 52(9–10): 609–624.

Garfinkel, Harold. 1956. "Conditions of Successful Degradation Ceremonies." *American Journal of Sociology* 615(5):420–424.

Geiger, Brenda and Michael Fischer. 2003. "Female Repeat Offenders Negotiating Identity." *International Journal of Offender Therapy and Comparative Criminology* 47(5):496–515.

Glaser, Barney G. and Anselm L. Strauss. 1967. *The Discovery of Grounded Theory: Strategies for Qualitative Research.* New York: Aldine.

Goffman, Erving. 1959. *The Presentation of Self in Everyday Life.* Garden City, NY: Doubleday.

Goffman, Erving. 1967. *Interaction Ritual: Essays on Face-To-Face Behavior.* Chicago: Aldine.

Gross, Edward and Gregory P. Stone. 1964. "Embarrassment and the Analysis of Role Requirements." *American Journal of Sociology* 70(1): 1–15.

Hewitt, John P. and Randall Stokes. 1975. "Disclaimers." *American Sociological Review* 40(1):1–11.

Jones, Edward E. and Thane S. Pittman. 1982. "Toward a Theory of Strategic Self-Presentation." Volume 1, Pp. 231–262. *In Psychological Perspectives on the Self,* edited by Jerry Suls. Hillsdale, NJ: Lawrence Erlbaum.

Katz, Jack. 1988. *Seductions of Crime: Moral and Sensual Attractions in Doing Evil.* New York: Basic Books.

Migliaccio, Todd A. 2002. "Abused Husbands: A Narrative Analysis." *Journal of Family Issues* 23(1):26–52.

Mills, C. Wright. 1940. "Situated Actions and Vocabularies of Motive." *American Sociological Review* 5(6):904–913.

Monaghan Lee, F. 2002. "Vocabularies of Motive for Illicit Steroid Use among Bodybuilders." *Social Science and Medicine* 55(5):695–708.

Orbuch, Terri. 1997. "People's Accounts Count: The Sociology of Accounts." *Annual Review of Sociology* 23:455–478.

Pershing, Jana L. 2003. "To Snitch or Not to Snitch? Applying the Concept of neutralization Techniques to the Enforcement of Occupational Misconduct." *Sociological Perspectives* 46(2):149–178.

Pierce, Jennifer L. 2003. "Introduction to Special Issue." *Qualitative Sociology* 26(3):307–312.

Presser, Lois. 2004. "Violent Offenders, Moral Selves: Constructing Identities and Accounts in the Research Interview." *Social Problems* 51(1):82–101.

Prus, Robert C. 1975. "Resisting Designations: An Extension of Attribution Theory into a Negotiated Conflict." *Sociological Inquiry* 45(1):3–14.

Schatzman, Leonard and Anselm L Strauss. 1973. *Field Research: Strategies for Natural Sociology.* Englewood Cliffs, NJ: Prentice Hall.

Scott, Marvin B. and Stanford M. Lyman. 1968. "Accounts." *American Sociological Review* 33(1):46–61.

Scully, Diana and Joseph Marolla. 1984. "Convicted Rapists' Vocabulary of Motive: Excuses and Justifications." *Social Problems* 31(5): 530–544.

Strauss, Anselm. 1962. "Transformations of identity." Pp. 63–85. *In Human Behavior and Social Processes: An Interactionist Approach,* edited by Arnold M. Rose. London: Routledge and Kegan Paul.

Sykes, Gresham, and David Matza. 1957. "Techniques of Neutralization: A Theory of Delinquency." *American Sociological Review.* 22(6):664–670.

Tedeschi, James T. and Catherine A. Riordan. 1981. "Impression Management and Pro-social Behavior Following Transgression." Pp. 223–244. *In Impression Management Theory and Social Psychological Research,* edited by James T. Tedeschi. New York: Academic Press.

Turgeman-Goldschmidt, Orly. 2005. "Hackers' Accounts—Hacking as a Social Entertainment." *Social Science Computer Review* 23(1):8–23.

Walzer, Susan and Thomas P. Oles. 2003. "Managing Conflict after Marriage's End: A Qualitative Study of Narratives of Ex-spouses." *Families in Society* 84(2):192–200.

Willott, Sara, Christine Griffin, and Mark Torrance. 2001. "Snakes and Ladders: Upper-Middle Class Male Offenders Talk about Economic Crime." *Criminology* 39(2):441–466.

Wood, Julia T. 2004. "Monsters and Victims: Male Felons' Accounts of Intimate Partner Violence." *Journal of Social and Personal Relationships* 21(5):555–576.

5

DUBS AND DEES, BEATS AND RIMS

Carjackers and Urban Violence

VOLKAN TOPALLI AND RICHARD WRIGHT

In order to study carjacking as a violent crime, Topalli and Wright conducted a field study with 28 active carjackers. They focused their research on factors (opportunities, risks, rewards) that those offenders think about when contemplating carrying out their crimes. The authors were interested in carjackers' motivations, planning, execution, and postcrime activities. The authors analyzed the links between carjackers' lifestyles and the contextual situation in which offending decisions were made. They conclude that the decision to carjack is based on two important factors: perceived situational inducements and opportunity. Either one of these variables is sufficient to cause an offender to carjack. The degree of involvement in street crime culture also plays an important role in determining if an individual will commit a carjacking by lowering one's resistance to temptation.

With the exception of homicide, probably no offense is more symbolic of contemporary urban violence than carjacking. Carjacking, the taking of a motor vehicle by force or threat of force, has attained almost mythical status in the annals of urban violence and has played an undeniable role in fueling the fear of crime that keeps urban residents off of their own streets. What is more, carjacking has increased dramatically in recent years. According to a recent study (Bureau of Justice Statistics [BJS], 1999), an average of 49,000 carjackings were attempted each year between 1992–96, with about half

of those attempts being successful. This is up from an average of 35,000 attempted and completed carjackings between 1987–92—a 40 percent increase.

Although carjacking has been practiced for decades, the offense first made national headlines in 1992 when a badly botched carjacking in suburban Washington, D.C., ended in homicide. Pamela Basu was dropping her 22-month-old daughter at preschool when two men commandeered her BMW at a stop sign. In full view of neighborhood residents, municipal workers, and a school bus driver, the two men tossed her daughter (still strapped to her car

Source: Topalli, V. & Wright, R. (2004). Dubs, Dees, Beats, and Rims: Carjacking and Urban Violence, in D. Dabney (Ed.) *Criminal Behaviors: A Text Reader.* Belmont, CA: Wadsworth Publishing. Reprinted with permission.

seat) from the vehicle and attempted to drive off with Basu's arm tangled in the car seat belt. She was dragged over a mile to her death. This incident focused a nationwide spotlight on carjacking and legislative action soon followed with the passing of the Anti Car Theft Act of 1992. Carjacking was made a federal crime punishable by up to a 25-year term in prison or—if the victim is killed—by death.

Like other forms of robbery, carjacking bridges property and violent crimes. Although a manifestly violent activity, it appears often to retain elements of planning and calculation typically associated with instrumental property crimes such as burglary. Unlike most robberies, however, carjacking apparently is directed at an object rather than a subject.

Most of the research on carjackings is based on official police reports or large pre-existing data sets such as the National Crime Victimization Survey. From this research, we know that carjackings are highly concentrated in space and time, occurring in limited areas and at particular hours (Friday and Wellford, 1994). These studies also indicate that carjackers tend to target individuals comparable to themselves across demographic characteristics such as race, gender, and age (Armstrong, 1994; Friday and Wellford, 1994). We know that weapons are used in 66–78 percent of carjackings, and that weapon usage increases the chance that an offense will be successful (BJS 1999; Donahue, McLaughlin, and Damm 1994; Fisher, 1995; Rand, 1994). Finally, these studies suggest that carjacking is often a violent offense; approximately 24–38 percent of victims are injured during carjacking (BJS 1999; Fisher, 1995; Rand, 1994).

Despite these studies, much about carjacking remains poorly understood. By their very large-scale nature, such studies are incapable of providing insight into the interaction between motivational and situational characteristics that govern carjacking at the individual level. What is more, they overrepresent incidents in which the offenders and victims are strangers. Recent literature on the nature of acquaintance robbery (e.g., Felson, Baumer, and Messner, 2000) and drug robbery (see Jacobs, Topalli, and Wright, 2000; Topalli, Wright, and Fornango, 2002) suggests that this limitation may represent a crucial gap in our understanding of the social and perceptual dynamics associated with carjacking. If for example, offenders target victims who they know or "know of," the chance of serious injury or death may increase because within-offense resistance and post-offense retaliation both are more likely.

We conducted a field-based study of active carjackers, focusing on the situational and interactional factors (opportunities, risks, rewards) that carjackers take into account when contemplating and carrying out their crimes. Drawing on a tried and tested research strategy (Jacobs, 1999; Jacobs, Topalli, and Wright, 2000; Wright and Decker, 1994, 1997), we recruited 28 active offenders (with three asked back to participate in follow-ups) from the streets of St. Louis, Missouri, and interviewed them at length about their day-to-day activities, focusing on the motivations, planning, execution, and aftermath of carjackings. This methodological strategy allowed us to examine the perceptual links between offenders' lifestyles and the immediate situational context in which decisions to offend emerge, illuminating the contextual uses that mediate the carjacking decision. Interviews focused on two broad issues: (1) Motivation to carjack and vehicle/victim target selection, and (2) aftermath of carjacking offenses (including vehicle disposal, formal and informal sanction risk management, use of cash, etc.). The issue of how carjacking occurs (i.e., offense enactment) is covered across the discussion of these two broader themes, because enactment represents a behavioral bridge that unites them. Thus, the procedural characteristics of carjacking naturally emanated from discourse regarding motivation, target selection, and aftermath.

Motivation and Target Selection

In the area of motivation, our interviews focused on the situational and interactional factors that underlie the decision to commit a carjacking, and the transition from unmotivated states to those in which offenses are being contemplated. On its face carjacking seems risky. Why risk a personal confrontation with the vehicle owner when one could steal a parked car off the street? Respondents felt that car theft was more dangerous because they never knew if the vehicle's owner or law enforcement might surprise them.

> *Low-Down:* I done did that a couple of times too, but that ain't nothing I really want to do cause I might get in a car [parked on] the street and the motherfucker [the owner of the vehicle] might be sitting there and then it [might not] be running [any] ways. I done got caught like that before, got locked up, so I don't do that no more. I can't risk no motherfucking life just to get into a car and then the car don't start: That's a waste of time. I would rather catch somebody at a light [or] a restaurant drive-thru or something like that.

Throughout the interviews, two global factors emerged as governing motivation, planning, and target selection: the nature of a given carjacking *opportunity* (that is, its potential risks and rewards) and the level of *situational inducements* (such as peer pressure, need for cash or drugs, or revenge). When these factors, in some combination, reached a critical minimal level, the decision to carjack became certain.

Internal and External Pressures: Situational Inducements and Carjacking

Many of the offenders we spoke to indicated that their carjackings were guided by the power of immediate situational inducements. Such inducements could be internal (e.g., money, drugs, the avoidance of drug withdrawal, need to display a certain status level, desire for revenge, jealousy) or external (objective or subjective strains, such as pressure from family members to put food on the table, the need to have a vehicle for use in a subsequent crime). Situational inducements could be intensely compelling, pressing offenders to engage in carjacking even under unfavorable circumstances, where the risk of arrest, injury, or death was high or the potential reward was low. Here, the individuals' increased desperation caused them to target a vehicle or victim they would not otherwise consider (such as a substandard car, or one occupied by several passengers), initiate an offense at a time or location that was inherently more hazardous (e.g., daytime, at a busy intersection), or attempt a carjacking with no planning whatsoever.

Internal situational inducements usually were linked to the immediate need for cash. Most street offenders (including carjackers) are notoriously poor planners. They lead cash-intensive lifestyles in which money is spent as quickly as it is obtained (due to routine drug use, street gambling, acquisition of the latest fashions, heavy partying; see e.g., Jacobs, 1999; Wright and Decker, 1994, 1997; Shover, 1996). As a result, they rapidly run out of money, creating pressing fiscal crises, which then produce other internal situational inducements such as the need to feed oneself or to avoid drug withdrawal.

The sale of stolen vehicles and parts can be a lucrative endeavor. Experienced carjackers sometimes stripped the vehicles themselves (in an abandoned alley or remote lot) and sold the items on the street corner or delivered them to a chop shop owner with whom they had a working relationship. Of particular value were "portable" after-market items, such as gold or silver plated rims, hub caps, and expensive stereo components. Across our 28 respondents, profits from carjacking per offense ranged anywhere from $200 to $5,000, with the average running at $1,750. The cash obtained from carjacking served to alleviate ever emergent financial needs.

Little Rag, a diminutive teen-aged gang-banger, indicated that without cash the prospect of heroin withdrawal loomed ahead.

INT: So, why did you do that? Why did you jack that car?

Little Rag: For real? Cause it's the high, it's the way I live. I was broke. I was fiending [needed drugs]. I had to get off my scene real quick [wanted to get back on my feet]. I sold crack but I'd fallen off [ran out of money] and I had to go and get another lick [tempting crime target] or something to get back on the top. I blow it on weed, clothes, shoes, shit like that. Yeah, I truly fuck money up.

The need for drugs was a frequent topic in our discussions with carjackers. Even the youngest offenders had built up such tolerances to drugs like heroin and crack that they required fixes on a daily basis. Many were involved in drug dealing and had fallen into a well known trap; using their own supply. Whether they sold for themselves or in the service of someone else, the need for cash to replenish the supply or feed the habit was a powerful internal motivator. L-Dawg, a young drug dealer from the north side of St. Louis, also had developed a strong addiction to heroin. Only two days before his interview with us, he had taken a car from a man leaving a local night club.

L-Dawg: I didn't have no money and I was sick and due some heroin so I knew I had to do something. I was at my auntie's house [and] my stomach started cramping. I just had to kill this sickness, cause I can't stay sick. If I'd stayed sick I would [have to] do something worse. The worse I get sick, to me, the worse I'm going to do. That's how I feel. If I've got to wait on it a long time, the worse the crime may be. If it hadn't been him then I probably would have done a robbery. One way or another I was going to get me some money to take me off this sickness. I just seen him and I got it.

External situational inducements could be just as compelling. Pressures from friends, family, other criminal acquaintances, or even the threat of injury or death were capable of pushing offenders to carjacking. For example, C-Low described an incident that occurred while he was with a friend in New Orleans. The two were waiting in the reception room of a neighborhood dentist when a group of men hostile to C-Low's friend walked into the office.

C-Low: They knew him. I d idn't know them. It was something about some fake dope. I think it was some heroin. He got caught. We weren't strapped [armed] at the time. We booked out. We left. We just left cause he know this person's gonna be strapped, and I didn't know this, so my partner was like. "Man, just burn out man, just leave." So we was leaving and they was coming up behind us [and started] popping [shooting] at us just like that, popping at my partner, just started shooting at him, so my partner he was wounded.

We had no car or nothing so we were running through and the guy was popping at us. So, there was a lady getting out of her car, and he stole it. We had to take her car because we had no ride. She worked at the [dentist's]. She like a nurse or something. It was a nice little brand new car. Brand new, not the kind you sort of sport off in like. She saw I was running. She heard the gun shots. I know she heard them, but she didn't see the guy that was shooting at us though. She had the keys in her hand. She was getting out her car, locking her door, yeah. She had her purse and everything. [My partner] just came on her blind side, just grabbed her, hit her. She just looked like she was shocked, she was in a state of shock. She was really scared. And [we] took her car and we left. We could've got her purse and everything, but we were just trying to get away from the scene cause we had no strap and they were all shooting at us. We just burnt on out of there. Got away. But then [later that day] he got caught though ... some-body snitched on him and they told them [the police] that he had the car. He gave me the car but he got caught for it, they couldn't find the car cause I'd taken it to the chop shop. I sold the car for like twenty-seven hundred bucks and about 2 ounces of weed.

Similarly, Nicole, a seasoned car thief and some-times carjacker, described a harrowing spur-of-the-moment episode. She and a friend had been following a young couple from the drive-in, casually discussing the prospect of robbing them, when her partner suddenly stopped their vehicle, jumped out and initiated a carjacking without warning. Nicole was instantly drawn into abetting her partner in the commission of the offense.

Nicole: My partner just jumped out of the car. He jumped out of the car and right then when I seen him with the gun I [realized] what was happening. I had to move. Once he got the guy out of the car he told me, "Come get the car." The girl was already out of the car screaming, "Please don't kill me, please don't kill me!" She was afraid because [she could see] I was high. You do things [when] you high. She's running so I'm in the car waiting on him. He's saying, "Run bitch and don't look back." She just started running . . . across the parking lot. [At] the same time he made the guy get up and run. "Nigger you do something, you look back, I'm gonna kill your motherfucking ass." As he got up and run he shot him anyways.

Risks and Rewards: How Opportunity Drives Carjacking

Need was not the only factor implicated in carjacking. Some carjackers indicated that they were influenced by the appeal of targets that represented effortless or unique opportunities (e.g., isolated or weak victims, vehicles with exceptionally desirable options). Here, risks were so low or potential rewards so great that, even in the absence of substantive internal or external situational inducements, they decided to commit a carjacking. Such opportunities were simply too good to pass up.

Po-Po (short for "Piss Off the Police") described just such an opportunity-driven incident. She and her brother had spent the day successfully pickpocketing individuals at Union Station, a St. Louis mall complex. On their way out, she noticed an easy target, an isolated woman in the parking lot, preoccupied with the lock on her car door.

Po-Po: It was a fancy little car. I don't know too much about names of cars, I just know what I like. A little sporty little car like a Mercedes Benz like car. It was black and it was shiny and it looked good. I just had to joy ride it. She was a white lady. It looked like she worked for [a news station] or somebody. We just already pick pocket[ed] people down at Union Station, but fuck. So we just walked down stairs and [I] said, "You want to steal a car? Come on dude, let me get this car." I didn't have a gun on me. I just made her think I had a gun. I had a stick and I just ran up there to her and told her, "Don't move, don't breathe, don't do nothing. Give me the keys and ease your ass away from the car." I said, "You make one sound I'm going to blow your motherfucker head off and I'm not playing with you!" I said, "Just go on around the car, just scoot on around the car." Threw the keys to my little brother and told him go on and open the door. And she stood around there at the building like she waiting on the bus until we zoomed off. We got away real slow and easy.

Likewise, Kow, an older carjacker and sometimes street robber, was on his way to a friend's house to complete a potentially lucrative drug deal when he happened on an easy situation—a man sitting in a parked car, talking to someone on a pay phone at 2 A.M.

INT: What drew you to this guy? What were you doing? Why did you decide to do this guy?

Kow: Man, it ain't be no, "What you be doing?," [it's] just the thought that cross your mind be like, you need whatever it is you see, so you get it, you just get it. I was going to do something totally different [a drug deal] but along the way something totally different popped up so I just take it as it comes. I was like, "Whew! Get that!" I don't know man, your mind is a hell of thing. On our way to this other thing. It just something that just hit you, you know what I'm saying? Plus, [he looked like] a bitch. I don't know, it's just something, he look like a bitch, just like we could whip him, like a bitch, you know what I'm saying? Easy.

Not all irresistible opportunities were driven solely by the prospect of monetary gain. In a city the size of St. Louis, offenders run into one another all the time, at restaurants, malls, movie theaters, and nightclubs. As a result, individuals with shared histories often encounter unique chances for retaliation or personal satisfaction. Goldie emphasized how such opportunities could pop up at a moment's notice. While cruising the north side of St. Louis, he spotted an individual who had sexually assaulted one of his girlfriends.

Goldie: I did it on the humbug [spontaneously]. I peeped this dude, [saw that] he [was] pulling up at the liquor store. I'm tripping [excited] you know what I'm saying, [as I'm] walking there [towards the target]. You know, peep him out, you dig? He [was] reaching in the door to open the door. His handle outside must have been broke cause he had to reach in [the window] to open the door. And I just came around you know what I'm saying. [I] put it [the gun] to his head, "You want to give me them keys, brother?"

He's like, "No, I'm not givin' you these keys." I'm like, "You gonna give me them keys, brother. It's as simple as that!" Man, he's like, "Take these, motherfucker, fuck you and this car. Fuck you," I'm like, "Man, just go on and get your ass home" [Then I] kicked him in his ass, you know what I'm saying, and I was like, "Fuck that, as a matter of fact get on your knees. Get on your knees, mother-fucker ..." Then I seen this old lady right, that I know from around this neighborhood. I was like "Fuck!," jumped on in the car [and] rolled by I wanted to hit him but she was just standing there, just looking. That's the only thing what made me don't shoot him, know what I'm saying? Cause he's fucking with one of my little gals. Cause he fucked one of my little gals. Well, she was saying that he didn't really fuck her, you know, he took the pussy, you know what I'm saying? He got killed the next week so I didn't have to worry about him. Motherfuckers said they found him dead in the basement in a vacant house.

Alert and Motivated Opportunism

Offenses motivated purely by either irresistible opportunities or overwhelming situational inducements are relatively rare. Most carjackings occur between these extremes, where situational inducements merge with potential opportunities to create circumstances ripe for offending. What follows are descriptions of offenses spurred by the combination of internal or external situational inducements and acceptable (or near acceptable) levels of risk and reward. The degree to which a given situation was comprised of rewards and risk on the one hand and internal and external pressures on the other varied, but when the combination reached a certain critical level, a carjacking resulted.

Offenders often described situations in which inducements were present, but *not* pressing, where they had *some* money or *some* drugs on them, but realized that the supply of either or both was limited and would soon run out. In such cases, the carjackers engaged in a state of what Bennett and Wright (1984; see also, Feeney, 1986) refer to as *alert opportunism*. In other words, offenders are not desperate, but they anticipate need in the near term and become increasingly open to opportunities that may present themselves during the course of their day-to-day activities. Here, would-be carjackers prowled neighborhoods, monitoring their surroundings for good opportunities, allowing potential victims to present themselves.

Corleone, a 16-year-old with over a dozen carjackings under his belt, had been committing such offenses with his cousin since the age of 13. The two were walking the streets of St. Louis one afternoon looking for opportunities for quick cash when they saw a man walking out of a barbershop toward his parked car, keys in hand. Motivated by the obliviousness of their prey and the lightness of their wallets, they decided to take his car.

Corleone: It was down in the city on St. Louis Avenue. We was just walking around, you know. We just look for things to happen you see just to get money. We just walk around and just see something that's gonna make us money. We just happened to be going to the Chinaman [a restaurant] to get something to eat. [We had] about five or six dollars in our pocket which ain't nothing. It was this man driving a blue Cutlass. It has some chrome wheels on there. He just drove up and we was going to the Chinaman and . . . my cousin was like, "Look at that car, man, that's tough [nice]. I'm getting that. I want that." [I was] like, "Straight up, you want to do it?" He was like. "Yeah." He was all G[ood] for it. Then he [the victim] came out the barbershop. It was kind of crowded and we just did what we had to do. There was this little spot where [my cousin] stash[es] his money, drugs and all that type of stuff and then he got the gun [from the stash]. He got around the corner. He say, "Hey, hey." I asked him for a cigarette so he went to the passenger's side [of the vehicle to get one]. I ran on the driver's side with a gun. Put it to his head and told him to get out the car.

INT: Did you know that you were going to do carjacking or . . . ?

Corleone: No. Not necessarily. But since that was what came up, that's what we did.

No matter how alert one is, however, good opportunities do not always present themselves. Over the course of time, situational inducements mount (that is, supplies of money and drugs inevitably dry up), and the option of waiting for ideal opportunities correspondingly diminishes. Such conditions cause offenders to move from a "passive" state of alert opportunism to an "active" state of what could be referred to as *motivated opportunism* (creating opportunities where

none previously existed or modifying existing nonoptimal opportunities to make them less hazardous or more rewarding). Here, attention and openness to possibilities expands to allow offenders to tolerate more risk. Situations that previously seemed unsuitable start to look better.

Binge, a 45-year-old-veteran offender who had engaged in burglary, robbery, and carjacking for over 20 year, discussed his more recent decision to get a car on a wintry January day. He had been carrying a weapon (a 9mm Glock) since that morning, looking to commit a home invasion. After prowling the streets for hours and encountering few reasonable prospects, he happened on an easy opportunity—a man sitting parked in a car, its engine running, at a Metrolink (trolley) station.

Binge: Well, I was out hustling, trying to get me a little money and I was walking around. I was cold. I was frustrated. I couldn't get in [any] house[s] or nothing, so I say [to myself], "Well I'll try and get me a little car, and you know, just jam off the heat and shit that he [the vehicle's owner] got," you know? I was strapped [carrying a firearm] and all that, you know and I was worried about the police catching me, trying to pull my pistol off, and I see this guy. Well, he was at the Metrolink you know, nodding [falling asleep] in his car. So, I went up to the window. I just think that I just peeped it on [happened on the situation]. I was at the Metrolink you know, I was standing at the bus station trying to keep warm and so I just walked around with no houses to rob, and I seen this dude you know sitting in his car, you know, with the car running. And I said "Ah man, if I can get a wag at this [take advantage of this opportunity]," you know. It wasn't just an idea to keep warm or nothing like that. I can get away with it, and I just did it. I'd do anything man, I'd do anything. If I want something and I see I can get away with it I'm gonna do it. That's what I'm saying. That night I saw an opportunity and I took it, you know. It just occurred to me.

Just as compelling were instances where third parties placed demands on offenders. A number of our respondents indicated that they engaged in carjacking to fulfill specific orders or requests from chop shop owners or other individuals interested in a particular make and model of car or certain valuable car parts. The desire to fulfill such orders quickly created conditions ripe for motivated opportunism.

Goldie, for instance, was experiencing strong internal situational pressures (the need for cash) and external pressures (the demand for a particular vehicle by some of this criminal associates) combined with a moderately favorable opportunity (inside information on the driver of the wanted vehicle and its location):

Goldie: He's from my neighborhood. He's called Mucho. He's from the same neighborhood but like two streets over. Them two streets don't come over on our street. You know, we not allowed to over on they street. It was a nice car. The paint, the sound system in it, and the rims. [It] had some beats, rims. Rims cost about $3,000, some chrome Daytons, 100 spokes platinums.

INT: OK. That's a lot of money to be putting on a car. What does he do for a living?

Goldie: I don't know. I don't ask. What they told me was they wanted this car and they are going to give me a certain amount of money.

INT: You say they told you they wanted this car. You mean they told you they wanted his car or they wanted a car like that?

Goldie: His car. His car. They want [Mucho's] car. They said, "I need one of these, can you get it for me?" And they knew this guy. So now, I need that car. That car.

Low-Down also specialized in taking orders from chop shops.

Low-Down: What I do, I basically have me a customer before I even go do it. I ask a few guys that I know that fix up cars, you know what I'm saying, I ask them what they need then I take the car. But see, I basically really got a customer. I'm talking about this guy over in East St. Louis. Me and Bob, we real cool. He buy 'em cause he break 'em down, the whole car down and he got an autobody shop. He sell parts. He'll take the car and strip it down to the nitty gritty and sell the parts. He get more money out of selling it part by part than selling the car. And, before I get it I already set the price.

He also had a drug habit:

Low-Down: The main reason basically why I did it was I be messing with heroin, you know

what I'm saying, I be using buttons [heroin housed in pill-form]. I be snorting some, but I be snorting too much, you know? I got a habit for snorting cause I be snorting too much at a time, that's how I call it a habit. I probably drop about 5 or 6 [buttons] down first [thing in the morning]. [So] I was basically really sick and my daughter needed shoes and shit like that and my girlfriend was pressuring me about getting her some shoes. She had been pressing me about two or three days. Baby food and stuff like that. But the money I had, I had been trying to satisfy my habit with it. Basically I just thought it was a good thing to do. It was a good opportunity.

AFTERMATH

The second portion of our interviews with carjackers dealt with the aftermath of carjackings. Here, we were concerned with basic questions: What did they do with the vehicles? What did they do with their money? Given the propensity of many carjackers to target other offenders, how did they manage the threat of retaliation? The majority of our respondents immediately disposed of the vehicle, liquidating it for cash. As Corleone put it, "There's a possibility they report[ed] the car stolen and while I'm driving around the police [could] pull me over. I ain't got time to hop out [of the vehicle] and run with no gun. I just want to get the money that I wanted."

Although most of our respondents immediately delivered the vehicle to a chop shop or dismantled it themselves, a fair number of them chose to drive the vehicle around first, showing it off or "flossing" to other neighborhood residents and associates. Despite the possibility that the vehicle's owner or the police might catch up with them, they chose to floss.

INT: What do you like to do after a carjacking?

Binge: Well, what I like to do is just like to, see my friends. They don't give a damn either, I just go pick them up and ride around, smoke a little bit [of] weed, and get some gals, and to partying or something like that you know, I know it's taking a chance but, you know like I say, they don't give a damn.

INT: Is that what you did with the car that you took off the guy at the Metrolink?

Binge: Yeah. I was just riding around listening to the music, picked up a couple of friends of mine. We rode around. I told them it was a stolen car. It was a nice little car too. Black with a kind of rag top with the three windows on the side. The front and back ones had a little mirror and another window right in the roof. Oh yeah, oh yeah—[it had] nice sounds. I was chilling man, I was chilling, you know? I was driving along with the music playing up loud. He ha. You know I wasn't even worried. I was just feeling good. 'Cause I'm not used to driving that much you know cause I don't have a car you know. That's why when I do a carjacking I just play it off to the tee, run all the gas off, keep the sounds up as loud as I can, keep the heat on, you know just abuse the car you know. That's all about carjacking like that.

C-Low described his desire to floss as having to do with the ability to gain status in his neighborhood.

C-Low: Put it this way, you got people you know that's driving around. We just wanna know how it feels. Were young and we ain't doing shit else. So they [people from the neighborhood] see you driving the car, they gonna say, "Hey, there's C-Low!" and such and such. That makes us feel good cause we're riding, and then when we're done riding we wreck the car or give it to somebody else and let him ride. We took the car and drove around the hood, flossing everything. And then we wrecked it on purpose. We ran it into a ditch. I don't know, we were fucked up high, we were high man, just wild! Wrecked the thing.

But even for offenders like these, the prospect of getting caught and losing profits eventually began to outweigh the benefits of showing off.

INT: So how long did you drive around in the [Chevrolet] Suburban before you stripped it?

Loco: Oh, we was rolling that. We drove for a good thirty minutes, then I said that I want[ed] to get up out of it because they might report it stolen. We was [still driving] right there [near] the scene [of the crime] and they [the police] would have probably tried to flag me [pull me over]. And if they tried to flag me, I would [have to] have taken them through a high-speed chase. Fuck that.

Sleezee-E informed us (as did other respondents) that disposing of the vehicle quickly was the key to getting away with a carjacking. Indeed, almost all respondents were aware of the police department's "hot sheet" for stolen vehicles (although their estimations of how long it took for a vehicle to show up on the hot-sheet varied greatly, from as soon as the vehicle was reported stolen to 24 hours or even longer afterwards).

Sleezee-E: [People think that] the cops will wait 24 hours just to see what you are going to do with the car. Because some idiots, when they jack a car, they just drive it around and then they leave it someplace. I don't do that. That's how you get caught. Driving it around. You take that car right to the chop shop and let them cut that sucker up.

Once the vehicle was stripped, most carjackers disposed of the vehicle by destroying it somehow.

Little Rag: Cause it was hot man! It was too hot. All I [wanted] was to take the rims, take the beats, the equalizer, the detachable face. Got all that off then I just pour gas on it and burnt that motherfucker up. I had fingerprints [on it]. I didn't have no gloves on. I had my own hands on the steering wheel. I left my fingerprints.

Nicole and a boyfriend chose a less conventional method of getting rid of their stolen vehicle.

Nicole: We got rid of the car first. We drove the car two blocks and went back down a ways to the park. We drove the car up there, we parked right there and sat for about ten minutes, made sure how many cars come down this street before we can push it over there, It's a pond, like it's a lake out there with ducks and geeses in it.

Cash for Cars: Life as Party

While a few respondents reported that they used the proceeds from carjacking to pay for necessities or bills, the overwhelming majority indicated that they blew their cash indiscriminately on drugs, women, and gambling.

We had interviewed Tone on a number of previous occasions for his involvement in strong-arm drug robbery. Although robbery was his preferred crime, he engaged in carjacking occasionally (about once every two months) when easy opportunities presented themselves. During his most recent offense, he and three of his associates took a Cadillac from a neighborhood drug dealer and made $6000. When we asked what he did with his portion, he indicated that he, " . . . spent that shit in like, two days."

INT: You can go through $1500 in two days?

Tone: Shit, it probably wasn't even two days, it probably was a day, shit.

INT: What did you spend fifteen hundred on?

Tone: It ain't shit that you really want. Just got the money to blow so fuck it, blow it. Whatever, it don't even matter. Whatever you see you get, fuck it. Spend that shit. It wasn't yours from the getty-up, you know what I'm saying? You didn't have it from the jump so. . . . Can't act like you careful with it, it wasn't yours to care for. Easy come, easy go. The easy it came, it go even easier. Fuck that, fuck all that. I ain't trying to think about keeping nothing. You can get it again.

INT: So what does money mean to you?

Tone: What money mean? Shit, money just some shit everybody need, that's all. I mean, it ain't jack shit.

INT: Ok, so it's not really important to you?

Tone: Fuck no. Cause I told you, easy come, easy go.

Mo had taken a Monte Carlo from two men residing in another neighborhood. He had planned the offense over the course of a month and finally, posing as a street window cleaner, carjacked them as they exited a local restaurant. The vehicle's after-market items netted $5000 in cash.

INT: I'm just kind of curious how you spend like $5,000!

Mo: Just get high, get high. I just blow money. Money is not something that is going to achieve for nobody, you know what I'm saying? So everyday, there's not a promise that there'll be another [day] so I just spend it, you know what I'm saying? It ain't mine, you know what I'm saying, I just got it, it's just in my possession. This is mine now, so I'm gonna do what I've got to do. It's a lot of fun. At a job you've got to work a lot for it, you know what I'm saying? You got to punch the clock, do what somebody else tells you. I ain't got time for that. Oh yeah, there ain't nothing like getting high on $5000!

Binge and others confirmed that the proceeds from their illegal activities went to support this form of conspicuous consumption.

Binge: I just blowed it man. With the money me and my girlfriend went and did a bit of shopping, stuff for Christmas. But, the money I got from his wallet? I just blowed that, drinking and smoking marijuana.

For Corleone, the motivation to carjack was directly related to his desire to manage the impressions of others in his social milieu. His remarks served as a poignant comment on sociocultural and peer pressures experienced by many inner-city youths. The purpose of carjacking was to obtain the money he needed to purchase clothing and items that would improve his stature in the neighborhood.

Corleone: [$1500 is] a lot. [I bought] shoes, shoes, everything you need. Guys be styling around our neighborhood. The brand you wear, shoes cost $150 in my size. Air Jordans, everybody want those. Everybody have them. I see everybody wearing those in the neighborhood. I mean come on, let's go get a car. I'm getting those, too.

INT: How many pairs of sneakers have you got?

Corleone: Millions. I got, I got, I got a lot of shoes. Clothes, gotta get jackets.

INT: Well, why do you have to look good, what's so big about looking good?

Corleone: It's for the projects, man. You can't be dressing like no bum. I mean you can't, you can't go ask for no job looking like anything.

INT: So you're saying like if you don't look good, you can't get girls, if you don't have the nicest shoes?

Corleone: You can't. Not nowadays, not where I'm from. You try to walk up to a girl, boy, you got on some raggedy tore up, cut up shoes they're gonna spit on you or something. Look at you like you crazy. Let's say you walking with me. I got on creased up pants, nice shoes, nice shirt and you looking like a bum. Got on old jeans. And that dude, that dude, he clean as a motherfucker and you look like a bum.

INT: So you're competing with each other, too?

Corleone: Something like that. Something like a popularity contest.

INT: Well, you know, you can look nice and clean and not have to spend $150 bucks on shoes, you know.

Corleone: It's just this thing, it's a black thing. You ain't going [to] understand, you don't come from the projects.

The Hazards of Carjacking: Retaliation and the Spread of Violence

Interestingly, a sizable proportion of our respondents purposely targeted people who themselves were involved in crime. Such individuals make excellent targets. Their participation in street culture encourages the acquisition of vehicles most prized by carjackers (those with valuable, if often gaudy, after-market items). And, because they are involved in a number of illegal activities (such as drug selling), they cannot go to the police. As Mr. Dee put it:

Mr. Dee: You can't go to no police when you selling drugs to buy that car with your drug money. So, I wasn't really worried about that. If he would have went to the police he would have went to jail automatically cuz they would have been like, "Where'd you get this thousand dollar car from?" He put about $4,000 into the car. So, he ain't got no job, he ain't doin' it like that bro. He'd be goin' to the police station lookin' like a fool tellin' his story. I [could] see if he's workin' or something ... and slinging. It'd be different cause he could show them his check stub from work.

However, there is a considerable danger associated with targeting such individuals because, unable to report the robbery of illegal goods to the police, they have a strong incentive to engage in retaliation—those who fail to do so risk being perceived as soft or easy (see e.g., Topalli, Wright, and Fornango, 2002). This introduces the possibility that incidents of carjacking likely are substantially higher than officially reported.

When asked about the possibility of retaliation many of the carjackers, displaying typical street offender bravado, indicated that they had no fear. The need to see oneself as capable and tough was essential to respondents. Such self-beliefs served to create a sense of invulnerability that allowed carjackers to continue to engage in a crime considered by many to be hazardous. As Playboy put it, 'It [can't be] a fear thing. If you're gonna be scared then you shouldn't even go through with stuff like that [carjacking people].'

Likewise, Big-Mix expressed an almost complete disregard for the consequences of his actions. His comments confirm the short-term thinking characteristic of many street offenders. "I don't give a damn. I don't care what happens really. I don't care. That's how it always is. Whether they kill us or whether we kill them, same damn shit. Whatever. I don't fucking care." Pacman, a younger carjacker who worked exclusively with his brother-in-law, indicated that thinking about the possible negative consequences was detrimental to one's ability to execute an offense. When asked if he was worried about retaliation, he was dismissive.

Pacman: Yeah, you be pretty pissed. But like I say, I'm not looking over my back, you know what I'm saying? Because, I wouldn't be here for I wouldn't have lasted as long as I lasted. Because it would be too many motherfuckers [that I've victimized], you know what I'm saying, [for me to look] over my shoulder all the time. When I look what the fuck could I do anyhow? I could get a few of them, but it would take a lot of motherfucking looking over my shoulder. I try to avoid that altogether. I'm going to avoid all that.

Other carjackers relied on hypervigilance (obsessive attention to one's surroundings and to the behavior of others), or anonymity maintenance (e.g., targeting strangers, not talking about the crime, using of disguises, carjacking in areas away from one's home ground; see Jacobs, 2001; Jacobs, Topalli, and Wright, 2000) to minimize the possibility of payback. Sexy-Diva, a female carjacker who worked with Sleezee-E, often spent hours with potential victims at night clubs before taking their cars, "Just disguises myself, I change my hair ... my clothes. I change whatever location I was at. And then I don't even go to that area no more. They can't find me. No way, no how."

Nukie sacrificed a great deal of his day-to-day freedom by engaging in behaviors designed to anticipate and neutralize the threat of retaliation.

Nukie: That's why I don't go out. If I go somewhere to get me a beer, if I'm gonna get me some bud [marijuana] or something, I stay in the hood.

I don't go to the clubs. There's too many people going there at night, you know what I'm saying? I don't need to be spotted like that. That's why I keep on the DL [down-low, out of sight]. You see, I stay in the hood. [If] I be riding [in a car], while I'm riding I might have my cats [friends] with me, you know, no motherfucker's gonna try to fuck with us like that. Yeah, I be with some motherfucker most of the time. If we're [going] to do something, go get blowed [high]—see, we get blowed everyday—I be with people, shit.

Pookie chooses to employ similar preemptive tactics, but also emphasized the need to be proactive when dealing with the threat of retaliation, predicated on the philosophy that "the best defense is a good offense."

Pookie: Well, you know the best thing [to deal] with retaliation like this here, you know, in order for you to get some action you got to bring some action. If I see you coming at me and you don't look right then this is another story here. If you doing it like you're reaching for something, I'm gonna tear the top of your head off real quick, you know. I'm gonna be near you, where you're at because they ain't nothing but some punk-ass tires and rims that I took from you, that's all it is. What you gotta understand is that you worked hard for it, and I just came along and just took them, you know. You go back and get yourself another set son, cause if I like them then I'm gonna take them again.

In the end, there were no guarantees. No matter how many steps a carjacker took to prevent retaliation, the possibility of payback remained. As self-confidence bred the perception of security, so too did it breed overconfidence. This was true in the case of Goldie, whose motivation to carjack a known drug dealer named Mucho was described earlier. His attempt did not go planned.

Goldie: He was going to put up a fight trying to spin off with [the car]. I jumped in and threw it in park so now I'm tussling with him, "Give me this motherfucker!" He's trying to speed off. He got like in the middle of the intersection. I dropped my gun on the seat and he grabbed me like around here [the neck], trying to hold me down in the car; and throw it back in

drive, with me in the car, you dig? You know, I'm no, I ain't going for that shit. I had my feet up on the gear [shift], you know what I'm saying? He ain't tripping off the gun. He trying to hold me, "Nigger motherfucker, you ain't going to get this car! Punk-ass nigger! What the fuck wrong with you? What the fuck do you want my car for?" [I said], "Look boy, I don't want that punk ass shit dude! I'm getting this car. This is mine. Fuck you!" The gun flew on the passenger's seat. So I grabbed the gun and put it to his throat, "So what you gonna to do? Is you gonna die or give up this car?" [He replied], "Motherfucker, you're going to have to do what you are going to have to do." He don't want to give up his car, right? So I cocked it one time, you know, just to let him know I wasn't playing, you dig? But I ain't shoot him in his head, put it on his thigh. Boom! Shot him on his leg. He got to screaming and shit hollering, you know what I'm saying, "You shot me! You shot me! You shot me!" like a motherfucker gonna hear him or something. Cars just steady drive past and shit, you know what I'm saying. By this time I opened up the door, "Fuck you!" Forced his ass on up out of there. He laying on the ground talking about, "This motherfucker shot me! Help, help!" Hollering for help and shit. But before I drove off I backed up, ran over him I think on the ankles like. While he was laying on the street, after I shot him. Ran over his bottom of his feet of whatever, you know what I'm saying. Oh, yeah. I felt that. Yeah. Boom, boom. "Aaaah!" scream. I hear bones break, like all this down here was just crushed. I didn't give a fuck though. Sped off. Went and flossed for a minute.

INT: I don't know—two streets over and he sounds like he's pretty scandalous. You're not worried about him coming up on you for this?

Goldie: No. I pretty much left him not walking. And he don't know who I am. [Later on] I heard about that. [People were saying], "Motherfucker Mucho, he got knocked [attacked], motherfucker tried to knock him, took his car, you know what I'm saying, on the block." I'm like, "Yeah, I heard about that. You know what I'm saying, I wonder who did this shit."

Three months later, we spoke to Goldie from his hospital bed. Mucho had tracked him down and shot him in the back and stomach as he crossed the street to buy some marijuana.

Goldie: I call them a bad day . . . I got shot. I saw him [Mucho] drive by but I didn't think he seen me. He caught up to me later. [I got shot] in the abdomen (pointing at his stomach) . . . here's where they sewed me up. I had twenty staples.

INT: How did it go down?

Goldie: I wanted [to] stop on the North[side] and get me a bag of grass, grab me a bag of weed or something. So, [we were] going around to the set [the dealer's home turf] and I'm getting out, I see [Mucho's] car parked this time. He wasn't in it. I'm thinking in my mind like you know, "That's that puss ass." So I'm like, "Damn I'm having bad vibes already." So I instantly just turned around like, "Fuck it, I'll go somewhere else to get some grass." I'm walking [back] to [my] car and hear a gunshot. Jump in the car. You know . . . you [don't] feel it for a minute. [Then,] my side just start hurting, hurting bad you know what I'm saying? I'm like damn. Looked down, I'm in a puddle of blood, you know. She freaking out and screaming, "You shot! You shot!" and shit. [She] jumped out the car like she almost should be done with me, you know what I'm saying? So I had to immediately take myself to the hospital. [They] stuffed this tube all the way down my dick all the way to my stomach . . . fucking with my side, pushing all of it aside. [I was there] about a good week. I done lost about 15 or 20 pounds. That probably wouldn't have happened if I wouldn't have to go do that. Wanted some more grass. At the wrong spot at the wrong time.

Goldie made it clear during the interview that he felt the need to counter-retaliate to protect himself from future attack by maintaining a tough reputation, a valuable mechanism of deterrence.

INT: You don't feel like you all are even now? You shot him—he shot you. Why go after him?

Goldie: It's [about] retaliation. When I feel good is when he taken care of . . . and I don't have to worry about him no more. I mean my little BGs [Baby Gangsters, younger criminal protégées] look up to me. Me getting shot and not going and do [something about, it they would say], "Ah [Goldie's] a bitch. Aw, he's a fag." Now down there [in the neighborhood], when they hit you, you hit them back. You know, if someone shoot you, you gotta shoot them back. That's how it is down there or you'll be a bitch. Everybody will shoot you up, whoop your ass. Know what I'm saying? Treat you like a punk. It's just I got to do what I have to do, you know what I'm saying.

Many carjackers echoed such sentiments, indicating a common belief in the importance of following unwritten rules of conduct and behavior related to street offending, especially when they refer to matters of honor or reputation (see Anderson, 1999; Katz, 1988).

CONCLUSION

This chapter has demonstrated that the decision to commit a carjacking is governed by two things: perceived situational inducements and perceived opportunity (Loftin, 1969). Situational inducements involve immediate pressures on the would-be offender to act. They can be internal (e.g., the need for money or desire for revenge) or external (e.g., the peer pressure of co-offenders). Opportunities refer to risks and rewards ties to a particular crime target in its particular environmental setting. Figure [5.1] outlines how these forces lead individuals to decide to initiate a carjacking.

Carjackings occur when perceived situational inducements and a perceived opportunity, alone or in combination, reach a critical level, thereby triggering that criminogenic moment when an individual commits to the offense. It is important to reiterate that either a perceived opportunity or perceived situational inducement on its own may be sufficient to entice an individual to commit a carjacking. Numerous examples of this have been detailed throughout the first part of the chapter. It is also important to note that background and foreground factors (such as membership in a criminogenic street culture) can increase the chance that a carjacker will go alter a vehicle by lowering his/her capacity to resist the temptation to offend.

More often, carjackings were motivated through the combined influence of opportunity and inducement. The carjackers' response indicate that offenses triggered by *pure* opportunity or *pure* need are relatively rare. Most carjackings occur between the extremes, where opportunities and situational inducements overlap.

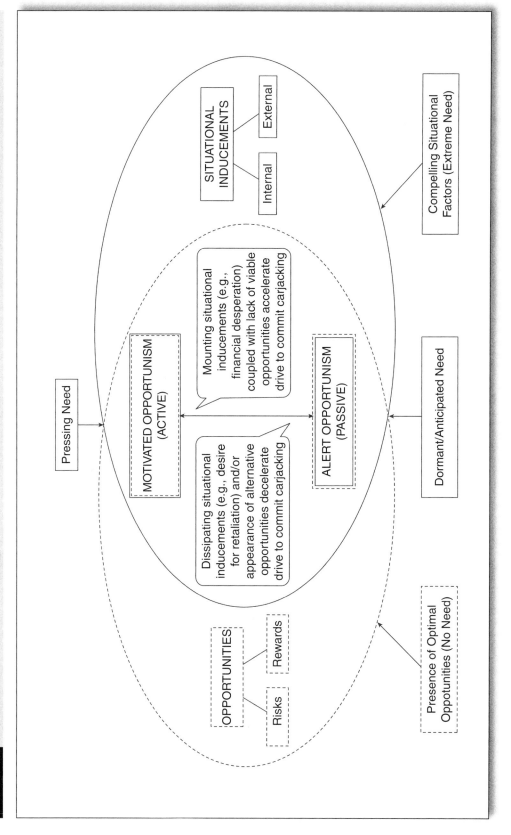

Figure 5.1 A model of decision-making in carjacking.

Owing to their precarious day-to-day existence—conditioned by risk factors such as persistent poverty, and exacerbated by "boom and bust" cycles of free-spending when money is available—carjackers are always under some degree of pressure and thus are encouraged to maintain a general openness to offending. During a "boom" period, carjackers anticipate future needs, but are not desperate to offend. This encourages Bennett and Wright's (1984) previously described notion of alert opportunism—a general willingness to offend if a particularly good opportunity presents itself.

But as time passes and no acceptable opportunities emerge, situational pressures to offend begin to mount in the face of diminishing resources. Approaching "bust" periods increasingly promote an active willingness to offend, driven by heightened situational inducements. Dormant or anticipated needs become pressing ones, moving carjackers from a state of alert opportunism to a state of motivated opportunism. As they continue to become more situationally desperate, their openness to offending expands to include opportunities perceived to have greater risk or lower reward (see Loftin, 1969). Targets that previously seemed unsuitable become increasingly attractive and permissible. The logical outcome is a carjacking triggered almost exclusively be pressing needs.

It is also possible for carjackers to move from a state of motivated opportunism to the lower state of alert opportunism, especially where the decision to commit such an offense is a driven desire for revenge. Retaliatory urges tend to be high initially, and then to dissipate over time. This is not to say, however, that the offended party has necessarily forgiven the offending party. They may simply be getting on with their lives, even as they keep their eyes open for the object of their wrath.

Although infrequent when compared to strong-arm robbery or drug robbery, carjacking's proportional impact on the spread of violence is probably more significant than has been suspected. When offenders themselves are targeted, carjacking, like other forms of violent crime, can produce retaliatory behavior patterns that serve to perpetuate and proliferate cycles of violence on the streets. In addition, their sensationalist nature increase the public's general fear of crime when law-abiding citizens are victimized. In either case, the preceding evidence and discussion indicate that carjacking is a unique and dynamic form of crime that probably deserves its own categorization (separate from robbery or auto theft) or, at the very least, further study and attention by those interested in criminal decision-making.

REFERENCES

Anderson, E. (1990). *Streetwise.* Chicago: University of Chicago Press.

Armstrong, L. (1994). Carjacking, District of Columbia (September, 1992-December, 1993; NCJRS, abstract data base).

Bennett, T. & Wright, R. (1984). *Burglars on burglary: Prevention and the offender.* Brookfield, VT: Gower.

Bureau of Justice Statistics (1994). *Carjacking: National Crime Victimization Survey* (Crime Date Brief).

Bureau of Justice Statistics (1999). *Carjacking: National Crime Victimization Survey* (Crime Date Brief).

Donahue, M., McLaughlin, C. & Damm, L. (1994). Accounting for carjackings: An analysis of police records in a Southeastern city (NCJRS, abstracts data base).

Feeney, F. (1986). Robbers as decision-makers. In R. Clarke and D. Cornish (Eds.), *The reasoning criminal.* New York: Springer-Verlag.

Felson, R., Baumer, E. & Messner, S. (2000), Acquaintance robbery. *Journal of Research in Crime and Delinquency* 37, 284–305.

Fisher, R. (1995). Carjackers: A study of forcible motor vehicle thieves among new commitments (National Institute of Justice/NCJRS abstracts data bases).

Friday, S. & Wellford, C. (1994). Carjacking: A descriptive analysis of carjacking in four states, preliminary report (National Institute of Justice/NCJRS abstracts data base).

Jacobs, B. A. (1999). *Dealing crack: The social world of streetcorner selling.* Boston: Northeastem University Press.

Jacobs, B. A. & Wright, R. (1999). Stick-up, street culture, and offender motivation. *Criminology, 37,* 149–173.

Jacobs, B. A., Topalli, V. & Wright, R. (2000). Managing retaliation: The cases of drug robbery. *Criminology, 38,* 171–198.

Katz, J. (1988). *Seductions of crime: Moral and sensual attractions in doing evil.* New York: Basic Books.

Loftin, C. (1985). Assaultive violence as a contagious social process. *Bulletin of the New York Academy of Medicine, 62,* 550–55.

Rand, M. (1994). Carjacking (Bureau of Justice Statistics/NCJRS abstracts data base).

Shover, N. (1996). *Great pretenders: Pursuits and careers of persistent thieves.* Boulder, CO: Westview.

Topalli, V., Wright, R. & Fornango, R. (2002). Drug dealers, robbery and retaliation: Vulnerability, deterrence, and the contagion of violence. *The British Journal of Criminology, 42,* (337–351).

Wright, R. & Bennett, T. (1990). Exploring the offender's perspective: Observing and interviewing criminals. In K. Kempf, *Measurement issues in criminology.* New York: Springer-Verlag.

Wright, R. & Decker, S. (1994). *Burglars on the job.* Boston: Northeastern University Press.

Wright, R. & Decker, S. (1997). *Armed robbers in action: Stickups and street culture.* Boston: Northeastern University Press.

6

Gangstas, Thugs, and Hustlas

Identity and the Code of the Street in Rap Music

Charis E. Kubrin

This study describes and analyzes how inner-city structural conditions have led to cultural adaptations that are integrated in a street code, which is characterized by an acceptance for the use of violence as normative behavior. The article focuses on the relationship between social identity, the street code, and rap music. A content analysis of how rappers' lyrics justify violence and provide for a violent identity as an integral part of the code of the street is provided.

Recent years have witnessed a resurgence of sociological research on identity, culture, and violence in inner-city black communities (Anderson 1999; Bruce, Roscigno, and McCall 1998; Fagan and Wilkinson 1998; Krivo and Peterson 1996: Kubrin and Wadsworth 2003; Kubrin and Weitzer 2003; Sampson and Wilson 1995). This work portrays a black youth culture or "Street code" that influences the identity and behavior of residents, particularly with respect to violence. Typically ethnographic in nature, this literature describes how the code supplies compelling elements of local culture, a culture of the streets in which violence is rendered accountable and even normative.

One complementary medium for studying these issues that has not been fully exploited is rap music, a genre consistently noted for its focus on masculinity, crime, and violence. An aspect of hip-hop culture (Guevara 1996:50; Kelley 1996:117; Keyes 2002:1; Krims 2000:12), "rap is a musical form that makes use of rhyme, rhythmic speech, and street vernacular, which is recited or loosely chanted over a musical soundtrack" (Keyes 200:1). Rap emerged from the streets of inner-city neighborhoods, ostensibly as a reflection of the hopes, concerns, and aspirations of urban black youth. When the genre first appeared in the 1970s, critics predicted a quick demise, but rap music flourished and has reshaped the terrain of American popular culture.

Rap music has undergone major transformations in the last two decades. One of the most significant occurred in the early 1990s with the emergence of "gangsta rap" the *St. James Encyclopedia of Popular*

Source: Gangstas, Thugs, and Hustlas: Identity and the Code of the Street in Rap Music by Kubrin, Charis E., *Social Problems, 52*(3), pp. 360–378. Reprinted with permission.

Culture identifies gangsta rap as the most controversial type of rap music, having received global attention for "its vivid sexist, misogynistic, and homophobic lyrics, as well as its violent depiction of urban ghetto life in America" (Abrams 2000:198). Its roots can be traced to early depictions of the hustler lifestyle and blaxploitation movies of the 1970s, which glorified blacks as criminals, pimps, pushers, prostitutes, and gangsters. Mainly associated with West Coast artists (Keyes 2002:4), gangsta rap is considered a product of the gang culture and street wars of South Central Los Angeles, Compton, and Long Beach, and the resurgence of the retromack culture (pimp attitude and style) of East Oakland (Perkins 1996:18). Since its early pioneers were gang members, gangsta rap relates to the life experiences of the rappers themselves, and its lyrics portray gang and ghetto life from a criminal's perspective (Krims 2000:70).

Gangsta rap departed from earlier rap forms, which were often characterized as socially conscious and more politically Afro-centric (Keyes 2002:88, 158–59; Martinez 1997; Perkins 1996:19). Even today, gangsta rap differs from other types of rap mainly in that it is the musical expression of ghettocentricity, an expression that engages the "black youth cultural imagination that cultivated varying ways of interpreting, representing, and understanding the shifting contours of ghetto dislocation" (Watkins 2001:389). Scholars agree that other rap forms reflect a generic concern for chronicling the "black" experience, while gangsta rap is specifically interested in the black underclass in the ghetto (Keyes 2002:122; Rose 1994:12, 114: Smith 1997:346). Today gangsta rap purportedly provides an insiders' look into black urban street life via crime and violence (Keyes 2004:4; Kitwana 1994:19).

Sociological scholarship on identity, culture, and violence in inner-city communities has largely overlooked rap music. Much of the existing literature assumes that the street code is a product of neighborhood processes and neglects additional sources such as popular culture, which may reflect, reinforce, or even advocate street-code norms. This study builds on existing literature through a content analysis of rap music that explores how the code is present not only in "the street," but also in rap music. This research, however, does not suggest that rap directly causes violence; rather, it examines the more subtle discursive processes through which rap helps to organize and construct violent social identity and account for violent behavior.

Theoretically, the study considers how structural conditions in inner-city communities have given rise to cultural adaptations—embodied in street code—that constitute an interpretive environment where violence

is accountable, if not normative. It focuses on the complex and reflexive relationship between the street code, rap music, and social identity. Empirically, the study examines how rappers' lyrics actively construct violent identities for themselves and for others. It explores the ways in which violence is justified and accounted for in terms that clearly resonate with the code of the street. I address these issues through a content analysis of 403 songs on rap albums from 1992 to 2000. As I will argue, the lyrics offer portrayals of violence that serve many functions, including establishing identity and reputation and exerting social control.

SOCIAL-STRUCTURAL CONDITIONS IN INNER-CITY COMMUNITIES: THE CONTEXT

Whereas studies of violent crime typically have been situated within an exclusively structural or subcultural theoretical framework, recent research argues that the causes of violence are both socio-structural and situational (Bruce, Roscigno, and McCall 1998; Fagan and Wilkinson 1998; Kubrin and Wadsworth 2003; Sampson and Wilson 1995). Growing recognition of the utility of an integrative approach has led researchers to consider the relationship between structural disadvantage, cultural and situational responses to such disadvantage, and the perpetuation of violence within African American communities.

Structurally, the combined effects of poverty, unemployment, family disruption and isolation from mainstream America define the neighborhood context for residents in many inner-city neighborhoods. These "concentration effects" contribute to social disorganization (Sampson and Wilson 1995) and violence (Krivo and Peterson 1996; Kubrin and Weitzer 2003). The social, political, and economic forces that have shaped these conditions include, among other things, globalization and deindustrialization (Rose 1994: 21–61; Wadsworth 2004; Wilson 1996), residential segregation (Keyes 2002:44–45; Massey and Denton 1993), punitive criminal justice policy (Tonry 1995), and a legacy of slavery and discrimination (Hawkins 1985). The concentrated disadvantage found in many urban African American communities is not paralleled in predominantly white neighborhoods.

An important element of such disadvantaged communities is the opportunity structure available for residents. The inner city affords limited avenues for adolescents to obtain the types of social status and social roles available to youth in other environments

(Rose 1994:27). Street-oriented peer groups dominate social roles, and few opportunities exist for broader participation in community life, such as after-school groups, volunteer organizations, or supervised athletics. Alternatives to conventional status attainment are thus limited to manifestations of physical power or domination, verbal agility, or displays of material wealth (Wilkinson 2001:235).

At the same time, illegitimate avenues for success abound. For many poor, young, black males, the opportunity for dealing drugs is literally just around the corner (Anderson 1999:114; Keyes 2002:184) and represents one of the most viable "job" options in the face of limited employment opportunities (Kitwana 2002:39). This is not to say that impoverished blacks bypass hard work as a prerequisite for success in life; young blacks, like most Americans who are given the opportunity to work, have demonstrated their willingness to do so (Newman 1999). But the continual demand for economic and social success, coupled with limited legitimate avenues and numerous illegitimate avenues by which to attain it, creates a unique situation unparalleled in white and middle-class black communities (George 1998:43).

The prevalence of drugs—and of crack cocaine in particular—generates more than increased illegitimate opportunities. Crack and the drug trade create neighborhood battles for the control over markets where violence is used as social control (George 1998:42; Keyes 2002:183). Elijah Anderson (1990) explains this phenomenon in his ethnography of Northton, a poor, urban, black community: "Dealers have certain corners and spaces 'sewed up,' marked off as their own territory, and may prevent other dealers from selling either at a particular corner or even in the general area. At times these corners are bought and sold, leading to turf disputes and violence to decide who owns them. A 'king of the hill' competition may ensue, awarding the corner to whoever can claim it" (p. 85). Contributing to the violence, the ready availability of guns in these communities increases the stakes, often turning what would have been an assault into a homicide (Fagan and Wilkinson 1998; Wilkinson 2001:232).

Tenuous police-community relations contribute to these problems (see especially Anderson 1990:190–206). Residents of disadvantaged black communities, arguably those most in need of police protection, tend to be wary of the police, in part because of concerns about racial profiling and the possibility of being wrongfully accused. These practices cause residents who might otherwise assist the police to avoid them, to not cooperate with investigations, to assume dishonesty on the part of officers, and to teach others that such reactions are prudent lessons of survival on the streets (Anderson 1990; Kennedy 1997:153; Kubrin and Weitzer 2003). Anderson (1990) notes, because the young black man is aware of many cases when an "innocent black person was wrongly accused and detained, he develops an 'attitude' toward the police. He becomes concerned when he notices 'the man' in the community . . . The youth knows . . . that he exists in a legally precarious state. Hence he is motivated to avoid the police and his public life becomes severely circumscribed" (p.196). For many poor and working-class blacks, police and brutality are synonymous (Rose 1994:106).

Scholars have documented the disparities between black and white communities. In many cities, racial differences in poverty, joblessness, and family disruption are so great that the worst urban contexts in which whites reside are considerably better than the average context of black communities (Sampson 1987:354). These inequalities are even greater considering that incarcerated blacks, typically the most economically and socially disadvantaged social bloc, are not included in census counts (Western 2002).

In addition to racial inequality, patterns of economic bifurcation within the African American community have become more pronounced: "At one end of this bifurcated class structure are poor and working class blacks in ghetto communities that experience social, economic, spatial, and demographic isolation. On the other end is a black middle- and lower-middle class buoyed by increased access to higher education and professional employment" (Watkins 2001:381). Although black middle-class residents may fare better than their lower-class counterparts. Mary Pattillo-McCoy (1999) finds that almost half of the black middle-class is concentrated in the lower-middle-class region, distinguished by its close proximity to the black working poor. Moreover, she finds that middle-class blacks do not perform as well as similarly situated whites on standardized tests, are more likely to be incarcerated for drug offenses, are less likely to marry and more likely to be single parents, and are less likely to be working. Thus, we should be cautious in celebrating the achievements of the "fragile black middle-class" (Kitwana 2002:42).

In sum, the extreme, concentrated disadvantage and isolation of black inner-city communities coupled with the quantity and potency of drugs and availability of guns have created a situation unparalleled in American history; such conditions represent "previously unseen challenges in African American life" (Kitwana 1994:45; 2002:xx). These are the social-structural community characteristics from which a "code of the street" has emerged.

THE CODE OF THE STREET AND NEIGHBORHOOD SUBCULTURE

In his ethnography of the moral life of the inner city, Anderson (1999) argues that a street code provides the principles governing much interpersonal public behavior. Given the bleak conditions, black youth in disadvantaged communities have created a local social order complete with its own code and rituals of authenticity (Anderson 1999; Henderson 1996; Keyes 2002:6; Kitwana 2002; Perkins 1996:20). This street code articulates powerful norms and characterizes public social relations among residents, particularly with respect to violence. Neighborhood structural conditions generate the subculture, so cultural differences reflect adaptations to structural inequality.

Social identity and respect are the most important features of the code. Respect—defined as being treated right or granted the deference one deserves (Anderson 1999:33)—often forms the core of a person's self-esteem. One way to acquire respect is by developing a reputation for being violent, by creating a self-image based on "juice" (Anderson 1999:72). On the streets, the image one projects is paramount, and at the top of the hierarchy is the "crazy," "wild," or "killer" social identity (Wilkinson 2001:246). A person's public bearing must send the message that he or she is capable of violence when necessary. In his study of inner-city Philadelphia communities, Anderson (1999:72) found that youth often created altercations with the sole purpose of building respect. Similarly, Deanna Wilkinson (2001) found that young men committed robberies in order to impress their peers and upgrade their social status. A third study found that youth from inner-city New York communities used violence for recognition (Fagan and Wilkinson 1998). In short, violence is thought to be the single most critical resource for achieving status among those who participate in street culture (Wilkinson 2001:243).

In this context, the gun becomes a symbol of power and a remedy for disputes. Since the 1970s, guns have been a central part of the changing character of youth violence (Fagan and Wilkinson 1998:106). For those who subscribe to the code, guns are the tactical choice for settling scores and asserting dominance in matters of honor, territory, and business (George 1998:42). The easy accessibility of guns in the inner city has raised the stakes of the street code even higher. Jeffrey Fagan and Deanna Wilkinson (1998) found that guns dominated social interactions; youth reported having one close by in case it would be needed during a conflict. Regarding one youth, Fagan and Wilkinson state, "It was understood that using a gun to harm his opponent was the best way to handle the situation both in terms of what was expected on the street and what an individual had to do to maintain a respected identity" (p. 139). For many youth, guns have become symbols of respect, identity, and power in addition to having strategic survival value.

Building a violent reputation not only commands respect but also serves to deter future assaults. For those invested in street culture, or for those who simply wish to survive (Keyes 2002:6, 166), a key objective of their demeanor is to discourage others from "testing" or "challenging" them. In some cases, manifest nerve—stealing another's possessions, mouthing off, pulling a trigger—builds a reputation that will prevent future challenges. However, when challenges arise or transgressions occur, violence is viewed as acceptable, appropriate, and even obligatory: "In the most socially isolated pockets of the inner city, this situation has given rise to a kind of people's law based on form of social exchange whose by-product is respect and whose caveat is vengeance or payback" (Anderson 1999:66). If a person is assaulted, for instance, it is essential in the eyes of his peers and others for him to seek revenge, otherwise he risks being victimized. Walking away from conflict is risky to one's health:

> To run away would likely leave one's self-esteem in tatters, while inviting further disrespect. Therefore, people often feel constrained to pay back—to seek revenge—after a successful assault. Their very identity, their self-respect, and their honor are tied up with the way they perform on the streets during and after such encounters. And it is this identification, including a credible reputation for payback, that is strongly believed to deter future assaults (Anderson 1999:76).

In instances of payback, violence is considered an appropriate reaction to crime, not a crime itself, and the offender operates on the assumption that the victim provoked his own injury (or death) through an act of wrongdoing. As Donald Black (1983) explained decades ago, much crime is moralistic and involves the pursuit of justice; it is a mode of conflict management, a form of punishment—in some cases, it may even be capital punishment (see also Polk 1994:113). Much inner-city violence involves residents who characterize their conduct as a perfectly legitimate exercise of social control, as vengeful "self-help" (Kubrin and Weitzer 2003). These residents are determined to show that justice is done, even if this means they will be defined as criminals; they do what they think is right and willingly suffer the consequences.

Violent social control is directly related to the availability (and effectiveness) of authoritative agents of dispute resolution such as the police—vengeful self-help emerges in the absence or weakness of third-party control (Black 1984:41; Horwitz 1990:128). In other words, crimes of self-help are more likely where the law is less accessible, such as, for example, in poor minority communities where residents have relatively less legal protection. When called, the police may not respond, which is one reason many residents feel they must be prepared to defend themselves and their loved ones (Anderson 1999:34). Indeed, a study of extremely disadvantaged communities in St. Louis found that problems confronting the residents were often resolved informally—without calling the police—and that neighborhood cultural codes supported this type of problem solving, even when the "solution" was a retaliatory killing (Kubrin and Weitzer 2003). That residents frequently bypass the police to resolve disputes on their own confirms the street code as a "people's law based on street justice"; the code begins where the influence of the police ends and the personal responsibility for one's safety picks up (Anderson 1999:27).

Finally, the code of the street encompasses other related dimensions of street life in inner-city communities. For example, the code highlights the appreciation for material wealth as another way to establish self-image and gain respect. Nice cars, expensive jewelry, and the latest clothing fashions not only reflect one's style, but also demonstrate a willingness to possess things that may require defending. Likewise, respect and recognition are gained through sexual promiscuity and conquest. For young men, sex is considered an important symbol of social status, which results in the objectification of women. The more women with whom a young man has sex, the more esteem he accrues. And given the harsh conditions in extremely disadvantaged communities, the street code recognizes a growing sense of nihilism in black youth culture, an outgrowth of living in an environment filled with violence and limited opportunities. Clearly these dimensions of the street code reinforce, and are reinforced by, respect and violence.

In sum, worsening conditions in inner-city communities over the last several decades have given rise, in large part, to the street code. These same conditions also define the context in which rap music has emerged. In studying rap, scholars maintain that "popular forms of music contain significant cultural traditions that cannot be severed from the socio-historical moment in which they take place" (Rose 1994:xiv; see also Keyes 2002; Watkins 2001). The production of rap, and gangsta rap in particular, corresponded with crucial shifts in the material worlds inhabited by young minority males. S. Craig Watkins (2001) notes, "The hypersegregated conditions of the postindustrial ghetto

became a fertile reservoir of cultural production" (p. 389). Rap music "anticipated the racial mood shifts and growing discontent of a generation of young black Americans who were either disillusioned by the racial hostilities brought on by participation in the societal mainstream or dislocated from the center of social and economic life altogether" (Watkins 2001:381). A question arises: what is the connection between inner-city life, the code of the street, rap music and social identity? This is the focus of the next section.

THE STREET CODE, RAP MUSIC, AND SOCIAL IDENTITY

A naturalistic approach to understanding the culture-music-identity nexus would treat the street code as an explanation of behavior that operates much like a set of subcultural directives (see Gubrium and Holstein 1997:19–37; Holstein and Jones 1992). The subculture shapes and constrains residents' behaviors, particularly with respect to violence. From this point of view, the code would be viewed as a source of motivations and sanctions that lead to violence (see Anderson 1999) and, as such, behavior would stem from rule compliance, or noncompliance, with the tenets of the code (see part I of Wieder 1988). From this perspective, the street code projects a compelling normative order, and rap lyrics would be viewed as reproductions of the code offered up to describe black urban street life. Put most simply, the street code could be viewed naturalistically as a source of inspiration for rap lyrics; the code inspired lyrics would then be understood to reflect—whether accurately or inaccurately—black urban youth culture. An analysis using this approach would treat rap lyrics as more or less verifiable reports of street life and violence in poor urban communities (see, for example, Allen 1996).

Alternatively, one could frame the street code as an interpretive resource used to constitute what is and what is not deviant (Gubrium and Holstein 1997:48; part II of Wieder 1988). Reality is organized and made sensible through language use: "It is a form of *social action* through which social actors assemble the intelligible characteristics of their own circumstances. Descriptions, accounts or reports, then are not merely *about* some social world as much as they are *constitutive* of that world" (Holstein and Jones 1992:305). Such an approach has been applied to studies of inmate accounts of "doing time" (Holstein and Jones 1992) and the informal code that permeates talk and conduct in a halfway house for convicted substance abusers (Wieder 1988).

In the latter work, Lawrence D. Wieder (1988) treats the convict code as a set of locally developed instructions for understanding resident conduct. In describing this approach, Jaber F. Gubrium and James A. Holstein (1997) explain, "It became clear to Wieder that residents were doing much more than merely reporting on the features of their lives when they 'told the code.' They were trying to accomplish things in the telling, 'doing things with words' to create the very social structures they were otherwise apparently just describing. They were, in practice, actively marking the border between deviance and nondeviance through talk and interaction" (p. 49). Wieder recognized that the code represents more than a normative structure available to members of a setting as well as to the researcher of their behavior: it is a set of interpretive guidelines that was variably conjured up by the residents themselves who used it to account for matters that required explanation. In other words, "The code was a living embodiment of social control, serving as a shared accountability structure for residents, action" (Gubrium and Holstein 1997:49–50).

Applying this perspective to the current study, I argue that both the street code and rap lyrics are constitutive elements of contemporary black urban culture. Here culture is akin to an interpretive tool kit (Swidler 1990) that is useful for understanding residents' experiences. As I will demonstrate, rap lyrics are discursive actions or artifacts that help construct an interpretive environment where violence is appropriate and acceptable. The lyrics—like the street code in Anderson's study—create the sense of a normative climate of violence. They provide sometimes graphically detailed instructions for how to interpret violence. From this point of view, a lyrical analysis is less concerned with how well rappers' accounts comport with objective reality and instead focuses on how such accounts are used by rappers to reflexively accomplish a sense of reality—for themselves and for others. In the process, rappers articulate "vocabularies of motive" (Mills 1940) and "grammars of motive" (Burke 1945) to explain and account for street reality. In line with these classic approaches to rhetorical analysis, the constitutive approach is concerned with how words and grammar are used to constitute rather than report historical reality and its causes. Thus, for the purpose of analysis, I suspend belief (or doubt) in the motivations and explanations rappers offer for events and action, and focus instead on account making as a persuasive project that constitutes situated realities.

This is not to suggest that the street code is insubstantial or without explanatory value. But neither the code nor culture more generally is deterministic. The code and rap music do not cause violence; violent conduct is far more complex than that. Because listeners interpret music in multiple ways, rap and its lyrics are appropriated and embedded into specific individual, familial, and community fields of reference. That rap music is a "localized form of cultural expression" is clearly evident in the work of Andy Bennett (1999b:77) and of Tricia Rose (1994), who explains "Los Angeles county, Oakland, Detroit, Chicago, Houston, Atlanta, Miami, Newark and Trenton, Roxbury, and Philadelphia developed local hip hop scenes that link various regional postindustrial urban experiences of alienation, unemployment, police harassment, social and economic isolation to their local and specific experience via hip hop's language, style, and attitude" (p. 60).

Lyrics have situational and situated meaning. Moreover, their reception may be oppositional. For example, Keith Negus and Patricia Roman Velazquez (2002:141) point out that listeners may disagree with or reject lyrics resulting in disaffiliation, ambivalence, and disengagement with (rap) music. Anticipated disaffiliation may even be part of the lyrics; design (as in instances of irony, sarcasm, or hyperbole). That media content has multiple meanings and that audiences actively construct this meaning implies no direct relationship between music and identity (or behavior). The street code and rap music lyrics do not compel one to act, but they do provide an accountability structure or interpretive resource that people can draw upon to understand violent identity and conduct.

That listeners of rap music are "actively involved in the construction of meaning" (Bennett 1999b:86) implies a complex and reflexive culture-music-identity relationship, as Simon Frith (1996), Negus and Velazquez (2002), and William F. Danaher and Vincent J. Roscigno (2004) all suggest. Instead of music lyrics reflecting preexisting identities, in this view, they help to organize and construct identity. Frith (1996) states, "The issue is not how a particular piece of music reflects the people, but how it produces them, how it creates and constructs an experience" (p. 109). Likewise, the development of cultural forms will be structured by the reciprocal and mutually influential dynamics of production and reception (Danaher and Roscigno 2004:52).

In short, rap lyrics instruct listeners in how to make sense of urban street violence and how to understand the identities of those who participate in (or avoid) it. They do so in ways that resemble what Anderson's (1999) informants told him about street violence. Both sets of instructions—the everyday telling of the code by residents and the rappers' telling of the code in music lyrics—provide potent and complementary sources of local culture. Through the telling of the code, both in the streets and in the music, residents and rappers actively construct identities and justify the use of violence. As I will show, the rap lyrics provide vivid "vocabularies of motive" (Mills 1940), which structure violent identities and justify violent conduct, providing a way for listeners to understand and appreciate violent conduct.

DATA, METHODS, AND ANALYSIS

To examine the street code in rap lyrics, I identified rap albums from 1992 to 2000 that had gone platinum (that is, had sold over 1,000,000 copies) during that period (N = 130) I examined rap albums generally, rather than only gangsta rap albums, because rap albums typically mix genres (Krims 2000:87), and many songs with street code elements would have been excluded from the analysis if only gangsta rap albums had been included. The criterion that an album had sold over 1,000,000 copies ensured that the music had reached a wide segment of the population.

The 1992 to 2000 period was chosen because gangsta rap emerged in the late 1980s/early 1990s (Kelley 1996:147; Keyes 2002:104; Kitwana 2002:xiv; Krims 2000:83; Smith 1997:346; Watkins 2001:389), and while still popular today, beginning around 1999, it became highly commercialized (Kitwana 1994:23; Krims 2000:71; Smith 1997:346; Watkins 2001:382). Therefore, the year 2000 represents a turning point in the rap music industry whereby production values more clearly addressed commercial competition, pushing cultural production and reproduction aside. I chose to examine this time frame to capture a period when the fiscal priorities of the music industry were not so clearly dominating cultural commentary.

The 130 albums had 1,922 songs. For the analysis I drew a simple random sample of 632 songs (roughly 1/3 of the sample) and coded each song in two stages. First, I listened to a song in its entirety while reading the printed lyrics in order to get an overview of the song. Second, I listened to the song again and coded each line to determine whether six street code elements were present (0 = no, 1 = yes): (1) respect, (2) willingness to fight or use violence, (3) material wealth, (4) violent retaliation, (5) objectification of women, and (6) nihilism. These elements were identified based upon a close examination of Anderson's (1999) work. They encompass the major points raised throughout his general discussion of the "code of the street." Although this article's focus is violence, I report the percentage of songs that discussed related themes

for comparison. I coded the data conservatively, identifying themes only where it was clear that the lyrics reflected the street code. In cases of uncertainty about the meaning of a word or phrase, I consulted *The Rap Dictionary*, a comprehensive online dictionary of rap and hip-hop terms. As most themes are intricately linked, in those instances where lyrics referred to more than one theme at a time, each scored a "1" to create overlapping categories. Finally, in the relatively few cases where lyrics criticized or made light of the street code, I scored those as "0" so as to include only statements that endorsed the code.

The findings are based on a sample size of 403 songs (64 percent of the total sample). During the course of coding, after song 350, I no longer encountered lyrics that described new aspects of the street code themes. I coded another 53 songs to ensure that I had reached saturation (Glaser and Strauss 1967:111). In all, 588 minutes of music were coded for the analyses.

To assess intercoder reliability, an independent researcher identified a random subset of the sample ($n = 64$, 16 percent of the final sample) and listened to the songs, read the lyrics, and coded the cases. Agreement percentages were computed, which reflect how often the researcher and agreed that the street code theme was present (or absent) in the lyrics. Although the percentages vary slightly by theme, overall they suggest fairly strong agreement: 70.3 percent for respect, 79.7 percent for willingness to fight or use violence, 75 percent for material wealth, 82.8 percent for retaliation, 73.4 percent for objectification of women, and 87.5 percent for nihilism.

The first analyses I present are quantitative and describe the occurrence of violence (and the other themes) in the sample. The second analyses are qualitative and determine how rappers portray violent identities—both their own and those of others—and account for the use of violence in everyday street lives. Using content analysis, I looked for instances of violence (and related issues) in the lyrics and illustrate the results using representative quotations. During coding, I looked for evidence of violence, respect for being violent, the role of guns and other weapons, violent personae, since subthemes did arise in the process of coding the lyrics (e.g., violent retaliation for snitching, projecting a mentally unstable violent persona), I carefully searched for additional meanings in the data and incorporated them into the findings. In this way, the findings not only address how violence is characterized in rap music, but they also contribute to the theoretical framework for understanding the street code.

THE "STREET CODE" IN RAP LYRICS

The street code is clearly a staple of rap music lyrics. I found each street code theme prominently represented in the lyrics, albeit to varying degrees. Respect was the most commonly referenced theme (68 percent of the songs), followed closely by violence (65 percent). Material wealth and violent retaliation were mentioned in 58 percent and 35 percent of the songs, respectively. Finally, nihilism was present in 25 percent, and only 22 percent had references to the objectification of women, despite the common assumption that misogyny pervades rap music.

The qualitative review of the data underscores the centrality of violence in rap music and suggests that violence has several components. The discussion below considers the two most prominent functions served by violent imagery in rap lyrics: (1) establishing social identity and reputation, and (2) exerting social control. The discussion below includes 45 direct quotations by 21 different rappers. These quotations do not exhaust the universe of violence examples, but are representative.

Constructing Violent Social Identity and Reputation

In extremely disadvantaged neighborhoods, residents learn the value of having a "name," a reputation for being (Anderson 1999:67). Accordingly, rappers often project images of toughness in their music, referring to themselves and others as assassins, hustlers, gangstas, madmen, mercenary soldiers, killas, thugs, and outlaws. Some rappers are even more colorful in their depictions: "untamed guerillas" (Hot Boys; "Clear Da Set"), "3rd world nigga" (Master P; "Making Moves"), "thuggish, ruggish niggas" (BTNH; "2 Glocks"), "hellraiser" (2Pac; "Hellrazor"), "trigger niggas" (Master P; "Till We Dead and Gone"), "the nigga with the big fat trigger" (Ice Cube; "Now I Gotta Wet' Cha"), "no limit soldier" (Silkk the Shocker: "I'm a Soldier"), "young head busta" (Hot Boys; "'Bout Whatever"), "wig splitas" (Juvenile; "Welcome 2 the Nolia"), "cap peelers" (Mystikal; "Mystikal Fever"), "grave filler" (Juvenile; "Back that Ass Up"), "gat buster" or "trigger man" (Jay-Z; "It's Hot"), "raw nigga" (Layzie Bone; "2 Glocks"), and "Sergeant Slaughter" (Killer Mike; "Snappin and Trappin").

To bolster this image of toughness, rappers describe how dangerous they and others are—or can be, if necessary. The Notorious B.I.G. raps, "Armed and dangerous, ain't too many can bang with us," while 2Pac boasts, "A little rough with a hardcore theme / Couldn't

rough something rougher in your dreams / Mad rugged so you know we're gonna rip / with that roughneck nigga named 2pacalypse (2Pac, "Strugglin'"). Cypress Hill references 187, the California penal code for murder, as a way to drive home their violent image: "1 for the trouble, 8 for the road / 7 to get ready when I'm lettin' off my load / I'm a natural- born cap-peela,' strapped [armed] illa / I'm the West coast settin' it on, no one's reala'" (Cypress Hill, "Stoned Raiders"). Master P describes the viciousness of his posse:

> We couldn't run from niggas cause we bout it bout it
>
> I'm from the set where my niggas get rowdy rowdy
>
> We gon' hang niggas
>
> We gon' bang niggas
>
> We gon' slang niggas
>
> Cause we trigger niggas. (Master P, "Till We Dead and Gone")

In projecting a tough image, rappers allude to violent reputations whether for "kickin' ass" or for "keepin' an extra clip" in their gun:

> "I'm an assassin known for kickin' ass
>
> Show me who them niggas are, and watch me start blastin'
>
> It's Mr. Magic, known for causin' havoc
>
> As long as I'm on your side, see there's no need for panic (C-Murder, "Watch Yo Enemies");
>
> "I was born and raised for this gangsta shit
>
> C- Murder be known for keeping' an extra clip
>
> My pops say look 'em in the eye before I kill 'em
>
> P crank the 'llac [Cadillac] up and let's go get'em" (C-Murder, "How Many").

Young inner-city males take reputation or "rep" seriously and exert effort into building it in order to gain respect (Fagan and Wilkinson 1998:148). Often rappers will instruct listeners on how to develop "rep" on the street: "Rep in New York is the cat burglar, the fat murderer / Slippin' the clip in the Mac [Mac 10 submachine pistol] / Hurtin' your pockets, droppin' your stock to zero profit / Holding heroes hostage and mansions for ransom like DeNiro mob flicks" (Big Punisher, "Fast Money"); "Sterling [B. G.'s friend] lived a soldier, died a soldier / Had respect for knockin' heads clean off the shoulder" (B. G., "So Much Death"); "Kickin' niggas down the steps just for rep" (Notorious B.I.G., "Ready to Die"). In these examples, rappers authorize the use of violence to establish identity. In other words, the lyrics "accomplish [identity] in the telling" (Gubrium and Holstein 1997:49).

At the top of the hierarchy is the "crazy" or "wild" social identity (Fagan and Wilkinson 1998:151). As a way to display a certain predisposition to violence, rappers often characterize themselves and others as "mentally unstable" and therefore extremely dangerous. Consider Snoop Dogg and DMX, both of whom had murder charges brought against them in the 1990s:

> Here's a little something about a nigga like me
>
> I never should have been let out the penitentiary
>
> Snoop Dogg would like to say
>
> That I'm a crazy motherfucker when I'm playing with my AK [AK-47 assault rifle] (Snoop Dogg, "DP Gangsta");
>
> Since I run with the devil, I'm one with the devil
>
> I stay doin' dirt so I'm gonna come with the shovel
>
> Hit you on a level of a madman whose mind's twisted
>
> Made niggas dreams caught the last train, mines missed it,
>
> Listed as a manic, depressin' with extreme paranoia,
>
> And dog, I got somethin' for ya'
>
> Have enough of shit, startin' off hard then only getting' rougher!
>
> Tougher, but then came the grease, so if you wanna say peace,
>
> Tame the beast! (DMX, "Fuckin' Wit' D")

An important element of the "crazy" persona is having a reputation for being quick tempered (Katz 1988:99). In the chorus of "Party Up," DMX warns others that even when he's at the club partying, the slightest thing may set him off: "y'all gon' make me lose my mind (up in here, up in here) / Y'all gon' make me go all out (up in here, up in here) / y'all gon' make me act a fool (up in here, up in here) / Y'all gon' make me lose my cool (up in here, up in here)" (chorus, DMX, "Party Up"). These lyrics show how the code is brought into play to account for matters that require explanation, in this case, for explaining a mood shift that may result in violence. DMX and others account for their violent behavior, which they render acceptable and appropriate given the circumstances. The lyrics supply a vocabulary of motive which, C. Wright Mills (1963) argues, offers "accepted justifications for present, future or past programs or acts" (p. 443).

Verbal assertions of one's violent tendencies are important in establishing identity, but physical assertions are necessary as well (Anderson 1999:68). So, while projecting the right image is everything, backing up the projection with violent behavior is expected. For this reason, some rappers project images of toughness by describing acts of violence that they have perpetrated on others. The Notorious B.I.G. explains how he point blank kills someone: "As I grab the glock, put it to your headpiece / One in the chamber, the safety is off release / Straight at your dome [head] homes, I wanna see cabbage / Biggie Smalls the savage, doin' your brain cells much damage" (Notorious B.I.G., "Ready to Die"). It is common for rappers to provide detail when describing violent situations. Some songs contain literally dozens of lines describing in rich detail incidents that precipitate violence, the persons involved, violent acts, weapons, ammunition, and the bloody aftermath. The descriptions often make explicit reference to elements of the street code: "Must handle beef, code of the street / Load up the heat, if these niggas think they could fuck around / Real niggas do real things / By all means, niggas knowin' how we get down" (Nas, "Shoot Em Up"). Here the rapper, Nas, accounts for his violent actions in ways analogous to what Wieder (1988) reported in his study of a halfway house. Wieder explains, "It [the code] was a device for accounting for why one should feel or act in the way that one did as an expectable, understandable, reasonable, and above all else acceptable way of acting or feeling" (p. 175). Nas's notion that one "must handle beef" not only accounts for his violent conduct; it also instructs listeners how to understand violent circumstances and violent responses, given the situation.

Firearms are often used to claim the identity of being among the toughest. In fact, guns—referred to by rappers as street sweepers, heaters, ovens, and pumps—have become *the* tactical choice for demonstrating toughness and for settling scores, as suggested by the Notorious B.I.G., "Fuck tae kwon do, I toto the fo'-fo' [.44 magnum]" ("One More Chance") and Dr. Dre, "Blunt in my left hand, drink in my right, strap [gun] by my waistline, cause niggas don't fight" ("Ackrite"). Both rappers acknowledge the important role of the gun in the ghetto and justify its use.

Further, rappers acknowledge an increase in gun use by showing how times have changed in the inner city (George 1998:42). Fagan and Wilkinson (1998:138) found that inner-city young males often characterized their neighborhood as a "war zone" and described the streets as dangerous and unpredictable, a sentiment echoed in many of the songs. For example, in "Things Done Changed" the Notorious B.I.G. reminisces about the past as he explains how conditions in the ghetto have become much more violent:

> Remember back in the days, when niggas had waves,
>
> Gazelle shades, and corn braids

Pitchin' pennies, honies had the high top jellies

Shootin' skelly, motherfuckers was all friendly

Loungin' at the barbeques, drinkin' brews

With the neighborhood crews, hangin' on the avenues

Turn your pagers to nineteen ninety three

Niggas is getting' smoked [killed] G. believe me
(Notorious B.I.G., "Things Done Changed").

The Notorious B.I.G. goes on to describe in detail how violence began to escalate as drugs, fighting, gambling, and general disorganization set in. Violent circumstances and experiences are frequently offered as emerging norms as rappers depict the "reality" of street life—for them and for others. When rappers portray life in the streets as dangerous and unpredictable, they implicitly authorize the use of violence to establish identity and supply a vocabulary of motives for describing and understanding violent conduct.

As a result of worsening conditions, guns have become an everyday accessory in the ghetto. One study found that most young males carry guns and describe them as central to their socialization (Fagan and Wilkinson 1998:140). For many, carrying a gun is as common as carrying a wallet or keys. Rapper 2Pac makes this point clear in the chorus of "High Speed." He is asked, "Whatcha gonna do when you get outta jail?" and answers matter-of-factly: "I'm gonna buy me a gun." The lesson to learn is summed up in the chorus of C-Murder's "Watch Your Motherfuckin' Enemies": "Stay strapped [carry a gun] cause the ghetto is so wicked now." C-Murder both rationalizes his decision to carry a gun and instructs the listener that in everyday life one must "stay strapped" to stay secure. The lyrics are implicit, interpretive instructions for understanding "life in the streets"—not just for rappers, but for others as well.

Collectively, rap lyrics show how toughness and a willingness to use violence are articulated as central features of masculine identity and reputation. The rappers implicitly and explicitly use the code of the street to construct identities and in so doing they resemble Anderson's (1999) respondents from inner-city communities in many important respects. As the above passages illustrate, rappers typically characterize life on the streets as violent and unpredictable and implicate this violence and their participation in it in their own identity work. The lyrics provide an implicit recipe for how to create a violent, but viable, street identity. The lyrics suggest that one learns the value of having a reputation for being tough in order to survive. The lyrics also enlist guns as signs of toughness; their possession is a significant identity marker. The lyrics tout "rep" as a means of gaining and sustaining respect

among peers and preventing future challenges. In sum, the lyrics provide both a formula and a justification for violent street identities.

Portraying Violence as Social Control

As the problems of the inner city become more acute and police-community relations grow increasingly tentative, residents claim they must assume primary responsibility in matters of conflict (Kubrin and Weitzer 2003). This often results in violence intended as punishment or other expression of disapproval. Most frequently violent social control is precipitated through disrespect. Rappers are virtually fixated on "respect"; they tell listeners that no one should tolerate disrespect and are clear about the consequences of such behavior, which can include death for the "perpetrator." Whether referenced only in passing or explained in more detail, the message is clear. There may be severe penalties for disrespect:

Y'all punk muthafuckas ain't got no nuts

I only be dealin' with real niggas

Them other niggas, they get they ass put in check

When they try to flex and disrespect me

And that's when I gotta get even with niggas, retaliation
(Krayzie Bone, "Thugz All Ova Da World");

Gotta push the issue

On the fools that dis you

Whether pump or pistol

When it's up in yo' gristle [face]

Hand yo' mama a tissue

If I decide to kiss [kill] you (Ice Cube, "Ask About Me").

In the latter passage, Ice Cube not only warns others about the repercussions of disrespecting him, but also makes explicit the rules of the game concerning disrespect: payback is a must. Cube's lyrics instruct listeners that on the streets when one is disrespected, one responds with violence. In this way, he constructs an interpretive environment where violence is accountable and acceptable, as both a means of constructing identity and of enforcing social control on the street.

Disrespect can come in a variety of flavors including disrespect by testing or challenging someone, disrespect through victimizing—usually robbing—someone, and disrespect by snitching. Each was serious enough to warrant violent self-help again in rap songs.

Responding to challenges. Rappers are often vague in what constitutes being "tested" or "challenged"—two words commonly encountered in the lyrics. What they make very clear, however, is the *reaction* to being "tested" or "challenged," summed up succinctly by the Notorious B.I.G., "Fifty-shot clip if a nigga wanna test," and Bone Thugs-N-Harmony, "A nigga wanna test, catch slugs, put 'em in the mud"; "187 is a lesson for them niggas that want to test, bring more than one cause me shotgun will be buckin' your chest."

One form of testing or challenging involves "fucking with" someone or with his or her family, friends, or "posse." To do so, according to the code, is to invite a virtual death sentence. In "It's On," Eazy-E bluntly states, "You try to fuck with E nigga run run run, cause if it's on motherfucker, then it's on G." DMK describes the implications of "Fuckin' Wit' D": "Fuckin' wit' me, y'all know somebody has / Told you about fuckin' wit' D, stuck in / A tree is what you will be, like a cat / And I'm the dog at the bottom, lookin' up" (DMK, "Fuckin' Wit' D"). In a song appropriately titled "Murder III," Mystikal tells the boyfriend, "I'm living for revenge": "I know what you did, I'm comin' to get'cha, you cannot live / Look, you sleep forever is the fuckin' price / Shit, a throat for a throat, a life for a life" (Mystikal, "Murderer III"). And consider the lyrics from a Juvenile song: "I ain't gon' let a nigga disrespect my clique / And I ain't gon' let a nigga come and take my shit / That'll make me look like a stone cold bitch / So ain't no way I ain't gon' grab my AK and let my shit spit" (Juvenile, "Guerilla"). Note Juvenile's reference to looking like a "stone cold bitch" if he does not to respond to "niggas disrespecting his clique." Here he strongly justifies the use of violent social control in order to not lose respect—a fundamental aspect of the code. As such, the lyrics serve as a vehicle by which Juvenile and other rappers explain and justify their actions. The message that one is not a pushover must be loud and clear. In this context, projecting the right image is everything, an image that must be substantiated with violent behavior (Fagan and Wilkinson 1998:136).

The code in the lyrics justifies a reciprocal exchange of punishments in cases where one's friends and family are victimized. This position is not difficult to justify. According to the street code, even verbal disrespect cannot go unpunished (Kubrin and Weitzer 2003). This seemingly mild form of disrespect is enough to provoke violent retaliation in numerous songs: "Talk slick, you get your neck slit quick / Cause real street niggas ain't havin that shit" (Notorious B.I.G., "Machine Gun Funk"). In another song, Ice Cube warns that you should "check yo self"—watch what you say and do—because otherwise the consequence will be "bad for your health"; "So come on and check yo self before you wreck yo self / Check yo self before you wreck yo

self / Yeah, come on and check yo self before you wreck yo self / Cause shotgun bullets are bad for your health" (Chorus, Ice Cube, "Check Yo Self").

Resisting Victimization. Inner-city communities pose high levels of risk for victimization. Yet an important part of the street code is not to allow others to "get over on you," to let them know that you are not to be messed with. So those who want to present themselves as streetwise signal to potential criminals (and anyone else) that they are not the ones to be targeted for victimization (Anderson 1999). Rap lyrics invoke such signals letting listeners know that being disrespected through robbery victimization is a costly transgression: "You play with my life when you play with my money / play around but this'll be the last time you think somethin's funny" (DMX, "One More Road to Cross"). Method Man insists that violent retaliation is an automatic response to robbery: "Niggas try to stick [rob] me, retaliation, no hesitation" ("Sub Crazy") And the Wu-Tang clan warns others that they can get "wild with the trigger" if need be: "Shame on a nigga who try to run game on a nigga / Wu buck wild with the trigger!/ Shame on a nigga who try to run game on a nigga / Wu buck-I fuck yo' ass up! What?" (Wu-Tang Clan, "Shame on a Nigga"). Rappers' lyrics actively define the border between what is acceptable and unacceptable behavior—in other words, what will or will not provoke violent retaliation, as well as what is an appropriate and warranted response. By invoking rules and elaborating their application to specific cases, these rappers describe and constitute their activities as rational, coherent, precedented, and orderly (Gubrium and Holstein 1997:45). The concluding message to the would-be *offender:* "If you ever jack [rob] this real nigga, you'd besta kill me or pay the price" (C-Murder, "Ghetto Ties").

Don't Snitch. Violence as social control is perhaps best personified in cases of snitching, where rappers are not at all reluctant to administer capital punishment: "My next door neighbor's having a convo with undercovers / put a surprise in the mailbox, hope she get it / Happy birthday bitch, you know you shouldn't a did it" (2Pac, "Only Fear of Death"). In many rappers' eyes, the worst case scenario is to "end up Fed": "And I don't know who the fuck you think you talkin' to / No more talkin'—put him in the dirt instead / You keep walkin'—lest you end up red / cause if I end up fed, Y'all end up dead" (DMX, "Party Up"). DMX concludes with, "Sun in to sun out, I'ma keep the gun out, Nigga runnin his mouth? I'ma blow his lung out." Entire songs may be devoted to warning others about the repercussions of snitching and testifying, as is Nas' song "Suspect" with the chorus: "To the suspect witness don't come outside / You might get your shit pushed back tonight" (Nas, "Suspect"). These excerpts provide a glimpse of why, after a violent incident, residents of extremely disadvantaged communities are often unwilling to cooperate with the police out of fear of retribution (Kubrin and Weitzer 2003). The lyrics virtually instruct observers to keep quiet and perpetrators to enforce silence. The code in the lyrics is strikingly similar to the one Anderson (1999) observed, whereby people "see but don't see" (p. 133). The neighborhood mantra is "Niggas do unto these snitches before it's done unto you" (2Pac, "Hell 4 a 'Hustler'") which clearly covers that snitching is unacceptable and offers guidelines for how one should respond when encountering a snitch. Again, the theme of justified violence is clear.

Retaliation. In cases of snitching or disrespect, violent retaliation is portrayed as punishment and is characterized as an acceptable and appropriate response as part of the street code. In many instances violent retaliation is claimed to be not only appropriate but also obligatory: "You fucked with me, now it's a must that I fuck with you" (Dr. Dre, "Fuck Wit' Dre Day"): "Otis from the thirteenth bit the dust / It's a must we strap up and retaliate in a rush" (B.I.G., "So Much Death"). In "Retaliation," B.I.G. describes acts of retaliation and expresses the sentiment that retaliation is expected, a given known to all, and therefore, clearly justified. It's simple: "You done took mine, I'ma take yours": "Ain't that cold? I heard a nigga downed my nigga / My partner just paged me and say they found my nigga / It's a bust back thang can't be no hoes / I got a hundred rounds plus for my Calico." And later in the song: "You sleep six feet I tear down the whole street / Bust ya head up leave ya deader yo blood redder / Nigga what, keep ya mouth shut retaliation is a must." Ms. Tee warns all in the chorus: "Niggas. . . . They comin' to get'cha / You betta watch ya back before they muthafuckin' split cha" (B.I.G., "Retaliation"). Retaliation, of course, builds "juice." According to the lyrics, it is also a way to deter future assaults, as Rappin 4-Tay explains to 2Pac: "Pac I feel ya, keep servin' it on the reala / For instance say a playa hatin' mark is out to kill ya / Would you be wrong, for buckin' a nigga to the pavement? / He gon' get me first, if I don't get him—fool start prayin'" (2Pac, "Only God Can Judge Me"). Again, we see how rappers justify the use of violence, this time as a deterrent.

Anderson (1999:33) suggests that everyone knows there are penalties for violating the street code. In their music, rappers use the implicit rules of the code as explanations for street behavior. By reference to aspects of the code, the lyrics mark what is acceptable and unacceptable behavior (e.g., don't challenge, victimize, snitch). The lyrics make sense of violence as an arguably accountable response to a wide variety of "offenses," while simultaneously identifying just what those "offenses" might be. The above passages show how the code is variably conjured up by rappers to instruct listeners on how to understand and account for their own and others' everyday actions. In this way, the code becomes a living embodiment of social control as it both serves to define offensive behaviors and accounts for the violence that might be forthcoming in response (Gubrium and Holstein 1997:49–50).

RAP MUSIC AND CULTURAL CODES

That violence constitutes a large part of rap music, particularly gangsta rap, is axiomatic. This study found that nearly 65 percent of the songs sampled make reference to some aspect of violence and many songs were graphic in their violent depictions. It is precisely for this reason that gangsta rap is controversial and unpopular while some use their street knowledge to construct first-person narratives that interpret how social and economic realities affect young black men in the context of deteriorating inner-city conditions. Other narratives may be more mythical than factual. Regardless of their source or authenticity, rap lyrics serve specific social functions in relation to understandings of street life and violence.

In cases of disrespect, the code—as evident in the lyrics—makes clear that payback is imminent. Rappers' lyrics delineate the rules and actively mark the border between acceptable and unacceptable behavior. Moreover, the lyrics teach listeners how to appropriately respond in the event that rules are violated; they authorize the use of violent retaliation in certain situations and thereby prescribe violent self-help as a method of social control. As the lyrics showed, the code requires constant application and articulation with concrete events and actions in order to make the events and actions meaningful and accountable.

In examining how rappers use violence to establish social identity and reputation and exert violent social control, the study has carefully considered the relationship between the street code, rap music, and identity and behavior. As argued earlier, one approach is to treat the code as an explanation of behavior that operates much like subcultural counter-directives. From this view, the street code is a compelling normative order and rap lyrics are reproductions of the code that describe black urban street life. Any examination, therefore would treat the lyrics as more or less accurate reports of street life and violence in poor urban communities.

The current analysis provides a different framing. Rather than encouraging residents to be deviant, here the code is seen as an interpretive resource—as a source of indigenous explanation whereby reality is organized and made sensible through language use—in this case, lyrics. As explained earlier, the code supplies an interpretive schema for seeing and describing violent identity and behavior, and the lyrics are treated as reality-producing activities. In terms of analysis, this has led us beyond the artists' own explanations (the simple telling of the street code) in order to determine what is accomplished by the use of the code as an explanation of behavior. In other words, the focus has shifted from what is said by rappers to how they say it and what is socially realized in the process. I have bracketed rappers' claims about the causes of behavior in order to examine what is accomplished by making the claims. This has meant suspending belief in whether or not rappers' claims are true (Burke 1945; Gubrium and Holstein 1997:51). My analysis is indifferent to whether the reality rappers portray in their lyrics is an "actual" or "literal" one. What is important is that rap artists *create* cultural understandings of urban street life that render violence, danger, and unpredictability normative.

Of course, this cultural understanding legitimizes certain aspects of the street code while ignoring other important and arguably more positive aspects of urban life. Anderson (1999) devotes a significant portion of his book to discussing "decent" families and daddies and reminds us "to be sure, hustlers, prostitutes, and drug dealers are in evidence, but they coexist with—and are indeed outnumbered by—working people in legitimate jobs who are trying to avoid trouble" (p. 24). But what we mostly hear in rap lyrics are rappers touting the virtues of violence with little of the more mundane, yet positive, elements that emanate from the black community. This is not to say that the lyrics are inaccurate. But as a cultural force, gangsta rap music offers a particular characterization of urban life. While this version of local culture may be at odds with other versions, it is the one that gets the most "air play," so to speak. In that sense, it widely promotes an accountability structure in which violence is legitimized and condoned.

This raises another important issue: the characterization of rap music and its messages in the context of mainstream culture. Although Theresa A. Martinez

(1997) and others (e.g., Negus 1999) recognize rap as a resistant, oppositional, countercultural form of expressive culture, they also argue that this culture "may be embedded within and even contribute to a dominant hegemonic framework" (Martinez 1997:272). I agree wholeheartedly. Rap music does not exist in a cultural vacuum. Rather, it expresses the cultural crossing, mixing, and engagement of black youth culture with the values, attitudes, and concerns of the white majority. Many of the violent (and patriarchical, materialistic, sexist, etc.) ways of acting that are glorified in gangsta rap are a reflection of the prevailing values created, sustained, and rendered accountable in the larger society. Toughness and a violent persona have been central to masculine identity in myriad American social contexts. And young men come to identify the connections between masculinity-power-aggression-violence as part of their own developing masculine identities (Messerschmidt 1986:59). In short, gangsta rap is just one manifestation of the culture of violence that saturates American society as a whole—in movies, video games, sports, pro-wrestling, and other venues. Therefore, it is important to recognize that the values that underpin some rap music are very much byproducts of broader American culture.

Indeed, in some cases rap music does not warrant the excessive criticism it receives. Recall that one finding from the analysis is that "objectification of women" or "misogyny" is not as pervasive in rap lyrics as originally thought. Likewise, it does not appear to be a significant part of the rappers' code—nowhere near as central as respect and violence. Of all the street code themes, "objectification of women" was least prominent in the lyrics. A greater percentage of the songs mentioned issues related to nihilism, a topic frequently overlooked in the literature and by critics. This is not to suggest that rap music and misogyny are not synonymous and acknowledge the variability in topics covered by rappers.

Findings from this study suggest that violence researchers might look beyond traditional data sources (e.g., census reports and crime statistics) for the empirical traces of "culture in action" (Swidler 1990) that render violence acceptable. As I have argued, rap music does not cause violence but extends the purview of the street code of violence and respect. Rappers' telling the street code in their music in conjunction with the everyday telling of the code by inner-city residents in community research (Anderson 1999; Fagan and Wilkinson 1998; Kubrin and Weitzer 2003) provide two potent sources of local culture—a culture of the streets in which violence is cast as a way of life.

REFERENCES

Abrams, Nathan. 2000. "Gansta Rap." P. 198 in *St. James Encyclopedia of Popular Culture*, edited by Tom Pendergast and Sara Pendergast. Farmington Hills, MI: Thomson-Gale.

Allen, Ernest, Jr. 1996. "Making the Strong Survive: The Contours and Contradictions of Message Rap." Pp. 159–91 in *Droppin Science: Critical Essays on Rap Music and Hip Hop Culture*, edited by William Ericperkins. Philadelphia: Temple University Press.

Anderson, Elijah. 1990. *Streetwise: Race, Class, and Change in an Urban Community*. Chicago: University of Chicago Press.

——. 1999. *Code of the Street*. New York: W. W. Norton and Company.

Bennett, Andy. 1999a. "Rappin" on the Tyne: White Hip-Hop Culture in Northeast England—an Ethnographic Study." *Sociological Review* 47:1–24.

——. 1999b. "Hip Hop am Main: The Localization of Rap Music and Hip Hop Culture." *Media, Culture society* 21:77–91.

Black, Donald. 1983. "Crime as Social Control." *American Sociological Review* 48:34–45.

Bruce, Marino A. Vincent J. Roscigno, and Patricia L. McCall. 1998. "Structure, Context, and Agency in the Reproduction of Black-on-Black Violence." *Theoretical Criminology* 2:29–55.

Burke, Kenneth. 1945. *A Grammar of Motives*. New York: Prentice Hall.

Danaher, William F. and Vincent J. Roscigno. 2004. "Cultural Production, Media, and Meaning: Hillbilly Music and the Southern Textile Mills." *Poetics* 32:51–71.

Fagan, Jeffrey and Deanna Wilkinson. 1998. "Guns, Youth Violence, and Social Identity in Inner-Cities." *Crime and Justice* 24:105–88.

Frith, Simon. 1996. "Music and Identity." Pp. 108–27 in *Questions of Cultural Identity*, edited by Stuart Hall and Paul du Gay. London: Sage.

George, Nelson. 1998. *Hip Hop America*. New York: Viking.

Glaser, Barney G. and Anselm L. Strauss. 1967. *The Discovery of Grounded Theory Strategies for Qualitative Research*. Chicago: Aldine Publishing Co.

Gubrium, Jaber F. and James A. Holstein. 1997. *The New Language of Qualitative Method*. Oxford: Oxford University Press.

Guevara, Nancy. 1996. "Women Writin' Rappin' Breaking," Pp. 49–62 in *Droppin Science Critical Essays on Rap Music and Hip Hop Culture*, edited by William Eric Perkins. Philadelphia: Temple University press.

Hawkins, Darnell F. 1985. "Black Homicide: The Adequacy of Existing Research for Devising Prevention Strategies." *Crime and Delinquency* 31:83–103.

Henderson, Errol A. 1996. "Black Nationalism and Rap Music." *Journal of Black Studies* 26:308–39.

Holstein, James A. and Richard S. Jones. 1992. "Short Time, Hard Time: Accounts of Short-Term Imprisonment." Perspectives on *Social Problems* 3:289–309.

Horwitz, Alan V, 1990. *The Logic of Social Control*. New York: Plenum Press.

Katz, Jack. 1988. *Seductions of Crime*. New York: Basic Books Inc.

Kelley, Robin D.G. 1996. "Kickin' Reality, Kickin' Ballistics: Gangsta Rap and Postindustrial Los Angeles." Pp. 117–58 in *Droppin' Science: Critical Essays on Rap Music and Hip Hop Culture*, edited by William Eric Perkins. Philadelphia: Temple University Press.

Kennedy, Randall. 1997. *Race, Crime and the Law*. New York: Vintage Books.

Keyes, Cheryl L. 2002. *Rap Music and Street Consciousness*. Chicago: University of Illinois Press.

Kitwana, Bakari. 1994. *The Rap on Gangsta Rap*. Chicago: Third World Press.

——. 2002. *The Hip Hop Generation: Young Blacks and the Crisis in African American Culture*. New York: Basic Books.

Krims, Adam, 2000, *Rap Music and the Poetics of Identity*. Cambridge: Cambridge University Press.

Krivo, Lauren J. and Ruth D. Peterson. 1996. "Extremely Disadvantaged Neighborhoods and urban Crime." *Social Forces* 75:619–50.

Kubrin, Charis E. and Tim Wadsworth. 2003. "Identifying the Structural Correlates of African-American Killings: What Can We Learn from Data Disaggregation?" *Homicide Studies* 7:3–35.

Kubrin, Charis E. and Ronald Weitzer. 2003. "Retaliatory Homicide: Concentrated Disadvantage and Neighborhood Culture." *Social Problems* 50:157–80.

Martinez, Theresa A. 1997. "Popular Culture as Oppositional Culture: Rap as Resistance." *Sociological Perspectives* 40:265–86.

Massey, Douglas S. and Nancy A. Denton. 1993. *American Apartheid: Segregation and the Making of the Underclass*. Cambridge, MA: Harvard University Press.

Messerschmidt, James W. 1986. *Capitalism, Patriarchy, and Crime: Toward a Socialist Feminist Criminology*. Totowa, NJ: Rowman & Littlefield.

Mills, C. Wright. 1940. "Situated Actions and Vocabularies of Motive." *American Sociological Review* 5:904–13.

——. 1963. *Power, Politics and People*. New York: Oxford University press.

Negus, Keith. 1999. *Music Genres and Corporate Cultures*. London: Routledge.

Negus, Keith and Patria Roman Velazquez. 2002. "Belonging and Detachment: Musical Experience and the Limits of Identity." *Poetics* 30:133–45.

Newman, Katherine S. 1999. *No Shame in My Game: The Working Poor in the Inner City*. New York: Vintage Books.

The Original Hip-Hop/Rap Lyrics Archive. 2002. Retrieved April 24, 2005 from http://www.ohhla.com/all.html.

Pattillo-McCoy, Mary. 1999. *Black Picket Fences: Privilege and Peril among the Black Middle Class*. Chicago: University of Chicago Press.

Perkins, William Eric. 1996. *Droppin' Science: Critical Essays on Rap Music and Hip Hop Culture.* Philadelphia: Temple University Press.

Polk, Kenneth. 1994. *Why Men Kill: Scenarios of Masculine Violence.* Cambridge: Cambridge University Press.

The Rap Dictionary, edited by Patrick Atoon March 21, 2005. Retrieved April 24, 2005 from http://www.rapdict.org/Main-page

Rose, Tricia. 1994. *Black Noise: Rap Music and Black culture in Contemporary America.* Hanover, NH: Wesleyan University Press.

Sampson, Robert J. 1987. "Urban Black Violence: The Effect of Male Joblessness and Family Disruption." *American Journal of Sociology* 93:348–82.

Sampson, Robert J. and William Julius Wilson. 1995. "Toward a Theory of Race, Crime and Urban Inequality." Pp. 37–54 in *Crime and Inequality,* edited by John Hagan and Ruth D. Peterson. Stanford, CA: Stanford University Press.

Smith, Christopher Holmes. 1997. "Method in the Madness: Exploring the Boundaries of Identity in Hip-Hop Performativity." *Social Identities* 3:345–74.

Swidler, Ann. 1990. "Culture in Action, "*American Sociological Review* 51:273–86.

Tonry, Michael. 1995. *Malign Neglect: Race. Crime and Punishment in America.* Oxford: Oxford University Press.

Wadsworth, Tim. 2004. "Industrial Composition, Labor Markets, and Crime." *Sociological Focus* 37:1–24.

Watkins, S. Craig. 2001. "A Nation of Millions: Hip Hop Culture and the Legacy of Black Nationalism." *The Communication Review* 4:373–98.

Western, Bruce. 2002. "The Impact of Incarceration on Wage Mobility and Inequality." *American Sociological Review* 67:526–46.

Wieder, Lawrence D. [1974] 1988. *Language and Social Reality.* Lanham, MD: University Press of America.

Wilkinson, Deanna. 2001. "Violent Events and Social Identity: Specifying the Relationship between Respect and Masculinity in Inner-City Youth Violence." *Sociological Studies of Children and Youth* 8:231–65.

Wilson, William J. 1996. *When Work Disappears: The World of the New Urban Poor.* New York. Vintage.

PART III

SEX CRIMES

Although I have not placed forcible rape in the prior category of violent crimes, where it clearly belongs, I have selected one article on sexual assault in this section together with two other studies of sexual abuse in order to illustrate a somewhat broader range of crimes that are also categorized as sexual in nature but not viewed as serious as actual sexual assault, but remain very harmful to victims in their consequences. These two crimes discussed in this section often do not gain media attention on a frequent basis, because they are not perceived as serious sexual illegalities and are usually not of great concern to the public or the criminal justice system. Nevertheless, the two crimes often result in long-term psychological pain to the recipients who experience this type of illegal, sexual offense.

Utilizing an anthropological method of storytelling, Roche, Neaigus, and Miller examined two forms of tales: street smarts and urban myths. These two forms illustrate the risks associated with sex work and drug use by inner-city prostitutes. Storytelling by these women served as a method used to communicate specific information concerning the risks and dangers associated with sex work as well as strategies for survival and decreasing the risk in their inner-city community.

Sexual intimacy between therapists and clients is explicitly recognized as one of the most serious violations of the professional-client relationship, subject to both regulatory and administrative penalties and, in several states, criminal sanctions. In this article, Pogrebin, Poole, and Martinez examine the written accounts submitted to a state's mental health grievance board by psychotherapists who have had complaints of sexual misconduct filed against them by former clients. The authors employed Scott and Lyman's classic formulation of accounts and Goffman's notion of the apology as conceptual guides in organizing the vocabularies of motive used by the group of therapists to explain their untoward, often illegal behavior.

In their analysis of 33 convicted rapists serving time in various correctional institutions in a southern state, Monahan and Marolla interviewed offenders who actually admitted to committing forced sexual acts on their victims. The authors, who have conducted well-known studies of incarcerated rapists in the past, explain how sexual assault offenders organize and carry out their offenses. They found that there are five phases that constitute the events involved in sexual assault, and the authors analyze each one in order to portray the organization of the sexual assaults.

7

STREET SMARTS AND URBAN MYTHS

Women, Sex Work, and the Role of Storytelling in Risk Reduction and Rationalization

BRENDA ROCHE, ALAN NEAIGUS, AND MAUREEN MILLER

This article utilizes a storytelling methodological technique which has a historical tradition found in inner-city communities, in order to examine storytelling patterns of a sample of drug-using women also engaged in sex work in New York City. Street smarts and urban myths are the two methods utilized for analyzing the risks that exist for these two dangerous activities.

INTRODUCTION

In this article, we consider sex work and risk experiences in the lives of women who use drugs in two low-income neighborhoods in New York City (NYC). The life narratives of these women are marked by the simultaneous presence of drug use, sex work, violence, and social isolation that augments the risks associated with illicit behaviors. What is striking are the ways in which women adapt to and navigate situations of risk and at times exert control in circumstances where their options are severely limited. The women establish the nature and boundaries of an array of risks that they face in their everyday lives, carving out choices and possibilities in a seemingly chaotic and unmanageable world. As a socially isolated group, they adapt to the environment around by constructing localized knowledge that can be conveyed through forms of storytelling (Worsley 1968).

Through their personal narratives of drug use and work, recurring patterns of storytelling offer the means for women to disseminate context-specific information about the dangers and risks associated with sex work and general survival strategies. Storytelling can function as a primary means of collecting and disseminating information within a community and can range in form and style from the biographical to the myth or legend (Lévi-Strauss 1979). Increasingly,

---

Source: Street Smarts and Urban Myths: Women, Sex Work, and the Role of Storytelling in Risk Reduction and Rationalization by authors Brenda Roche, Alan Neaigus, and Maureen Miller. Reproduced by permission of the American Anthropological Association from *Medical Anthropology Quarterly*, Volume 19, Issue 2 pp. 149–170.

researchers are examining the mechanisms of story-telling and "mythmaking" as tools in the transfer of information about risk and health behaviors (Dossa 2002; Rhodes and Cusick 2002; Singer et al. 2001). Storytelling has the potential to map out the cartography of "local and particularized notions of risk" (Feldman 2001:84) in everyday life, shedding light on the relationships that people have to the communities around them, for better or for worse (Dossa 2002; Epele 2002; Smith, Lucas, and Latkin 1999).

In this article, we consider two forms of storytelling: street smarts and urban myths. Street smarts refer to stories of behaviors (experienced or observed firsthand) that are used to illustrate skills at dealing with the array of risks associated with street-based drug use and sex work. Although we differentiate between forms of oral traditions from the biographical street-smart anecdotes to "friend-of-a-friend" accounts of urban myths—there is often considerable overlap and interaction between these oral traditions, making differentiation difficult and somewhat artificial. For the purposes of this article, however, there is value in teasing out and highlighting differences between these forms of storytelling. Particular attention is directed toward understanding how these differences may be harnessed to develop meaningful AIDS prevention messages or how stories may undermine prevention efforts.

Urban myths assume a distinctive storytelling pattern: depicting a situation (an event or behavior) that is made familiar by a loose notion of network proximity (friend-of-a-friend tales). The veracity and validity of the facts of the story are largely irrelevant. Instead, these accounts operate as tools of informal communication, conveying beliefs and norms in a culture or subculture (Tonklin 1992). Although people may dismiss popular stories that circulate in a community, they may also find themselves responding to the underlying message and adapting their behavior to conform to the moral of the story (Brunvand 1981; Whatley and Henken 2000). This theory is aptly illustrated in a familiar urban tale in which a woman narrowly escapes a killer lying in wait in the backseat of her car. That many women religiously and subconsciously check the back seat of their cars before getting in has been attributed to the impact of the urban tale (Whatley and Henken 2000). It is unimportant whether the story is based on a true event (though many urban tales contain an element of fact), rather the ways in which the stories evolve, persist, and are incorporated into the daily practices of individuals highlight the impact of urban myths (Best and Horiuchi 1985; Brunvand 1981).

Urban myths follow a specific pattern: they tend to circulate widely, undergo light modifications with each retelling, and, above all, are asserted to be true. These stories may be used in a range of ways, including the justification of certain behaviors or the reinforcement of existing social norms and boundaries. This range can be illustrated through popular urban myths that have circulated concerning HIV and AIDS.

In the late 1980s, an urban legend surfaced that described a casual sexual encounter with terrible consequences. A common version of this story tells of a young man celebrating his birthday in the arms of a prostitute, organized by his friends. When he wakes the next day, he finds, scrawled across the bathroom mirror in red lipstick, the phrase, "Welcome to the world of AIDS." In the 1990s, this story, dubbed "AIDS Mary," has mutated somewhat into two or three distinct variants. The next variant to be encountered—one still circulating in parts of the world today—dispensed with sexual contact and focused on random needle attacks, usually in nightclubs. The victim would feel a sharp pain and, when they investigated, would find a sticker on their clothing somewhere that reads, "Welcome to reality—you now have AIDS" (Wells 1999).

These types of stories have become so pervasive in recent years that the Centers for Disease Control and Prevention in Atlanta has responded with formal statements refuting the stories as false (Centers for Disease Control and Prevention 1999). However, these stories can function as more than simply scare tactics; they have the ability to impart valid information on risk behaviors and risk-reduction practices. They may enable individuals to rationalize engaging in risk behaviors rather than serving as cautionary tales.

Risk-rationalization stories have not gone unnoticed; however, they have been treated largely as folk beliefs. Distinguishing between the health beliefs of individuals and what may be an urban myth can, at times, be quite difficult. These ideas are separated here for analytical purpose, but they exist on a continuum. Folk beliefs, as they to risk, seem to reflect more coherent understandings of disease causation, health, and illness (Nemeroff 1995). For example, the beliefs that certain sexual behaviors, such as oral sex, carry no risks of disease transmission or that an individual can accurately gauge whether someone has a sexually transmitted infection (STI) by the way a person looks are common "social folklore" that circulate (Sanders 2004). These beliefs fail to embody the hallmarks of urban mythology, including the "real life" event tone of the narrative such as the friend-of-a-friend format (making it familiar at once and yet remote). Folk beliefs are instead tidbits of information that function as something akin to a diagnostic appraisal, conveying pseudo medical instructions.

Like folk beliefs, urban myths may be distinguished from other forms of oral communication that circulate. For example, individual stories similar to what Singer and colleagues (2001) term "war stories," in which individuals relate their rites of passage in the street drug scene, are common. Stories of this nature have been described as part of the folklore of drug use and sex work (Sanders 2004). What we have termed "street smarts" are a similar form of narrative in that these stories are driven by the real-life experiences of an individual or those of the immediate members of his or her social network. They hinge on what can be described as a compilation of lessons learned through experience and are bolstered by instinct and the observation of others in the social and environmental context. These stories are more than tales of hardship and endurance or war stories: they vividly express agency in dire circumstances, but they also openly highlight episodes of poor judgment and miscalculations of risk.

In this light, we see evidence of personal agency around risk taking, even if we question the judgment and action that are taken. Conventional wisdom and much of the research literature on women who use drugs suggest that powerlessness is pervasive in their lives (Phoenix 1999, 2000). From a structural standpoint, this is true. These women have few resources and severe poverty, homelessness, and the absence of opportunity mark their lives. Yet, these women manage to demonstrate power and decision making in critical ways. How they evaluate risks is one way in which they exercise choice, even if that choice opens them up to other situations of risk.

An extensive and rich body of ethnographic work has been conducted among women who use drugs and engage in sex work (Bourgeois and Dunlap 1993; Feldman et al. 1993; Goldstein, Oullet, and Fencrich 1992; Inciardi 1993; Maher 1997; Oullet et al. 1993; Ratner 1993; Sterk, Elifson, and German 2000) and on the concepts of risk and risk-reduction practices as defined, understood, and implemented by drug users (Connors 1992; Moore 1993). The current research builds on a long tradition of not only assessing risk and risk-reduction practices reported by the populations engaging in behaviors that place them at increased risk of negative outcomes, but a tradition that also examines the setting or context within which these behaviors occur (Zinberg 1984). Interpretations of actions that seem irrational from an outsider's perspective may then be viewed and understood within the system or context that surrounds the behavior. The narratives that fill this literature form a critical backdrop to anthropologists' ability to expand the research among street-based sex workers.

These works intersect in important ways. The ways in which women experience and react to risks are unique in relation to drug use and street-based sex work (Sanders 2004). The images that emerge of women drug users who engage in sex work are harsh. This is particularly true for women who use crack cocaine who have been cast as the "ultimate in shame and sexual degradation" (Furst, Johnson, and Dunlap 1999; Inciardi 1995; Ratner 1993). The image that has become most entrenched is of the "crack whore," who is ruled by her "crack pipe as pimp" (Bourgeois and Dunlap 1993; Inciardi 1993; Ratner 1993). This portrait is one in which all traces of agency evaporate and are replaced by a hypersexualized female addict in constant need of drugs (Fullilove, Lown, and Fullilove 1992; Oullet et al. 1993). The quintessential "crackhead" is portrayed as a woman driven to extremes at the expense of all because of addiction to crack. This image of the female crack whore has taken on mythical features and reawakens historical associations between sexuality and substance abuse (Erickson et al. 2000). Fueled by popular media accounts, this image is imbued with strong moral judgments that often operate in conjunction with harrowing images of "crack babies" (Hartman and Golub 1999; Logan 1999).

Stories of the crack whore appear repeatedly throughout the literature, sharing cardinal features despite variability in geography, time, and population. The stories of the crack whore serve as a "worst-case" scenario, against which norms or boundaries may be established and against which women evaluate their actions (Maher 1997). In this context, the story fulfills a function for women who use drugs and who also engage in sex work. The crack whore caricature exists as a symbol of the worst that can be experienced. Over and over in the ethnographic literature, women echo the disparaging description of the crack whore and distance themselves from that image. Some researchers have argued that this is a false separation, as the women are too humiliated to acknowledge themselves as participants in such extreme behaviors (Maher 1997). And yet, an aspect of these stories bears a resemblance to urban legend, in that these stories can act as social indicators, highlighting the boundaries of acceptable behaviors. It has been suggested that the power of these stories may extend beyond those directly affected and may successfully discourage the use of crack cocaine across a broader population (Furst, Johnson, and Dunlap 1999; Kolata 1990). It also might foster the belief that participation in this type of sex work could only be temporary and time limited.

A hierarchy of risks frame the lives of women drug users who do engage in street-based sex work. The risk of incarceration, for example, is a perpetual risk that women must work against. The threat of arrest is more pronounced in neighborhoods that are undergoing gentrification, as the police engage in arrest "sweeps" that mark an effort to confront and eradicate the street-based drugs and sex work trade (Feldman 2001). To reduce the risk of arrest, women may find themselves using drugs or engaging in sex work in more precarious settings, outside the scope of vision of law enforcement officers (Miller and Neaigus 2002). In these circumstances, the women have critically examined the everyday dangers they encounter and acted accordingly, albeit in a way that increases their risks for violence and unsafe sexual encounters.

STUDY BACKGROUND AND METHODOLOGY

In-depth, life history interviews were conducted with 28 women who used drugs from two low-income neighborhoods in NYC. All women were interviewed over a span of nine months, between March and November 2000. Women at least 18 years of age who used either injected or noninjected drugs (i.e., heroin, crack, or cocaine), and who were able to provide their own informed consent were eligible to participate. As part of the consent process, each woman was advised of the voluntary and anonymous nature of the study, the kind of questions that would be asked, the fact that the interview would be audiotaped, and the precautions that would be taken to protect the data. Data protection included a United States Federal Certificate of Confidentiality that enables researchers to legally withhold respondent identities and information from all persons not directly associated with the research. Women were provided with a copy of the informed consent and were advised that they could decline to answer questions that they felt were too sensitive or stop the interview at any time.

The women were recruited from out-of-treatment settings through a variety of methods, including street recruitment, snowball sampling, and referrals from community-based organizations and research institutes in the Lower East Side/East Village in Manhattan, a predominantly white and Latino neighborhood, and in Bedford-Stuyvesant in Brooklyn, the largest African American neighborhood in NYC (Booth, Watters, and Chitwood 1993; Heckathorn 1997; Kaplan, Korf, and Sterk 1987; Watters and Biernacki 1989). These neighborhoods are locations where drug markets and drug use have been established for many years. To achieve a sample with sufficient representation of categories of interest, women were recruited using purposive sampling, which provides minimum quotas in terms of age, type of drug used, and race and ethnicity.

The in-depth life history interviews followed a semi-structured interview guide. Although data collection was not standardized, efforts at consistency across interviews were maximized by the fact that one interviewer (MM) conducted all the interviews. Interviews lasted between 60 and 90 minutes, and all participants were given cash reimbursements for their time. Referrals to health care services, as well as to drug treatment services, were provided when requested. All interviews were tape-recorded and transcribed verbatim. Participant observation was also ongoing during the study and involved observing and talking with people in their own natural setting and reality (Agar 1980; Spradley 1979a, 1979b). Field notes were maintained of these ongoing observations and less formal conversations. Personal names are replaced with pseudonyms for all women.

Grounded theory, and inductive and field-based approach, provided in initial framework in which the qualitative data were examined in order to develop theoretical categories or typologies (Strauss 1990, 1998). Individual interviews and field notes were read and reread to allow complete familiarity with the data set in its entirety and to confirm narrative consistency within individual interviews. This review process also helped shape preliminary codes.

The process of coding also relied on the specific themes spelled out in the interview guide. These codes allowed for a directed and consistent coverage of the domains that were the focus of the actual interviews. Specifically, the data were coded for factors associated with sex work, safety, risk, and risk avoidance, as well as for sociodemographics, drug use and sex practices, and personal history. Codes were expanded, broken down, or merged to capture a greater sense of the patterns emerging in the data. From this exercise, we began to identify central themes in the narratives surrounding the concept of risk (both risk reduction and risk rationalization). The analysis then homed in on the central risks that women spoke about, including the avoidance and justification of risk from a variety of sources, such as arrest, violence, sex work relationships, drug use risk, and STIs, including HIV. Through these analytic exercises, narrative patterns emerged suggesting the use of storytelling strategies. This article explores the stories of survival strategies and techniques that formed a critical part of these narratives—the way in which they were shaped and articulated—as well as their purposes (actual and ideal) in the lives of these women. The story frameworks that emerge here do not operate in a rigid dichotomy. Instead, these women have used narratives in two ways. Although their current use depends on circumstance and context, these narratives may also open new opportunities for intervention.

Analyses were conducted using a computerized text based analytic tool, dtSearch (http://www.dtSearch .com), for qualitative analysis, and SAS 8.0 for data that were quantified using codes developed for this purpose (e.g., age).

Sociodemographics

Of the 28 women interviewed, nine (32 percent) were white, eight (29 percent) Latina, eight (29 percent) African American, and three (10 percent) of mixed race/ethnicity. Their mean age was 31 (s.d. 7; range 19–43). All women used heroin (79 percent), crack (39 percent) or cocaine (21 percent), and 18 (64 percent) had injected drugs. Nineteen (68 percent) had engaged in street-based sex work. Educational attainment was low in this sample: 13 (46 percent) women had either completed high school or acquired a general equivalency degree. Only one woman was currently working, as a means to receive her welfare payments. Just over one-third (36 percent) of the women had a history of formal economy employment.

RISK AND AVOIDING RISK

The narratives of the women contain an array of risks they face everyday that are related to drug use, sex work, and violence. These risks were articulated in a variety of ways. We have chosen to examine the risks most expressed in these women's narratives. These include risks involving arrests (for both drug use and sex work), risks due to violence, and risks related to sexual health.

Avoiding Arrest

Of central importance in the daily lives of these women is the successful avoidance of punitive measures related to drug use and to sex work. This priority was most clearly articulated in the street smart stories the women recounted, which focused on the delicate balance between the need for acquiring drugs and the resources required for survival versus the risk of arrest for either sex work or drug use and acquisition.

A key tactic the women used for avoiding arrest related to selling drugs is a simple and commonsense one: sell only to the people you know. A number of women were quick to note this as their first "line of defense." Realistically, however, such a strategy severely limits the sellers' share of an already circumscribed drug market. The women who were involved in the drug market tended to be low-level actors and did not have the luxury of dictating the parameters of their work. As such, they needed to devise protective strategies for successfully selling drugs. These strategies tended to hinge on knowledge of the women's experiences of street life and drug use. Alex, a 24-year-old white heroin sniffer/injector recounts a strategy she uses to assess if a customer is sincere or if the "customer" is an undercover police officer.

I ask, I ask questions that only a heroin addict could know.

[INTERVIEWER: Like what?]

Like . . . I would ask you, you know, what does it feel like when you throw up? You know, does it feel like drinking throwing up or does it feel different? And if you can't answer that question I'm not going to buy for you. You know, 'cause it feels very different. Actually, I enjoy throwing up. Every heroin addict that I ever met enjoys throwing up.

An important skill that was highlighted in the interviews is the ability to identify undercover cops. This skill is honed over time through observation and attention to detail. As police maneuvers shift, the ability of women to successfully spot an undercover cop suffers. They openly acknowledge times that they have been arrested for selling to undercover police and note that the police have been honing their skills to be less obvious—particularly the female officers.

Field note: Layla 31-year-old white injector says it is easy to spot the police, although admits they have got much more savvy. She says she can tell by the way they walk, talk, dress, and from her experience down at the tombs.[1] She says it is very easy to spot a bulletproof vest under people's clothes. And the worst are the ones that try to dress like them [the drug users]—they are totally obvious.

Alternately, women come up with arrangements for purchasing or selling drugs that remove them from a street-based arena. Contacting dealers through the use of pagers, for example, allows for the scheduling of

[1]"The tombs" refers to the central holding cells in downtown Manhattan for recently arrested individuals who are awaiting processing.

meetings in neighborhoods with a low police presence or devising a system of codes to ensure the smooth transfer of goods.

A key aspect of street smarts is being aware of the shifting patterns of law enforcement efforts directed at drug users. Although needle exchange programs are legal in New York State, this may not translate into the ability to carry drug paraphernalia without consequences. Phoenix (1999) notes this dichotomy between legal availability and the consequences of possession among her sample of street-based prostitutes in England, where possession of numerous condoms is perceived as evidence of sex work. The possession of syringes and associated works can likewise be taken as tangible proof of illegal activities. Princess, a 34-year-old black crack smoker who does not inject, describes acquiring a box of sterile needles and syringes due to the death of a friend.

> A friend of mine's died. He used to take the insulin. And I said, I'll keep the needles in case somebody that need it, because there's germs going around and people need clean needles. But then, again, I do not want to be walking down the street one day and the cops pull me over and get caught with all these needles. They'll think I'm selling them. And, then, you don't have no cleanin' facility to go with them. That's illegal. You know? And they think I'm using them. No, no, no. [LAUGHTER] So, I just gave them to somebody one day and said here, because I thought about it. It's bad enough I'm using drugs, and then selling them, and then get caught with needles on me? No. You know? Uh hm. So, I just hm. I am not going to go through all that. They'll call my mother in Washington just for selling needles.

A key concern for these women is arrest related to sex work. This has become a central issue in areas that have become the target of an aggressive police campaign to rid neighborhoods of drug users and street prostitution (Feldman 2001). The women deal with this by relying heavily on their knowledge and awareness of the changing atmosphere. Renee, a 25-year-old white heroin injector, passed out her phone number to potential "dates," thereby eliminating the need to be physically out on the "stroll" soliciting sex clients:

> Yeah. Well, what happened was, I used to work on the street like every day and then the cops were getting too bad so I gave people my number. Everybody I just gave my number to. And if they weren't worth it, you know, if it wasn't like $50 or better, then I'm not gonna really go out with them. You know, I don't want to, don't waste my time to come all the way down here cause I live uptown. You know, it's ridiculous to come down here for $30, $40.

So I'm not, I'm not trying to come down here for that. But, um, the good dates, you know, I take and, and it's just much easier, you know? When they call me or I'll call them, whatever, you know.

Anna, a 22-year-old white heroin injector, tried to blend in with the surroundings of an increasingly student dominated area.

> Like, I wouldn't stand right out on, like, they would stand right out in the street. I would sit on a stoop and act like I was reading a paper or something, so I looked like I was in the neighborhood or, you know, one of the college students at the dorm or something.

These strategies emerge in response to the ongoing evolution of the drug economy and the changing nature of street knowledge and strategies. They evolve over time and come largely from firsthand experience, or stories shared within social networks. As the landscape of NYC neighborhoods shifts and changes, the women adapt their street routines to reflect this. Interestingly, women were more concerned with avoiding arrest for prostitution than for drug-related charges. Renee articulated this quite clearly:

> I didn't like it anyway but the cops were everywhere. I didn't need to have that on my back with a prostitution charge, anyway, and I did get caught by a cop, which is prostitution. If you get caught just loitering, that's loitering or disorderly conduct. But if you are confronted by a cop that's prostitution and I said, I do not need that on my record. That's you know, not something you want to go in. You know drugs, you could maybe say to a, a job interview, oh yeah, oh I was a kid and I was a young girl and I saw stuff. Now I'm getting my life together. But prostitution, you know, what are you going to say, you know?

A drug-related charge could, in time, be glossed over as a careless act associated with a misspent youth—whereas a charge of prostitution carries more extreme connotations, implying a significant level of drug addiction.

The stories that circulate with reference to avoiding arrest emphasize street smarts. In this context, strategies are presented as markers of the women's credibility as "players" in the drug and sex trades and operate as a testimony to their survival skills.

Violence

The nature of street-based sex work brings with it risks related to a considerable degree of violence as well. In our sample, experiences ranged from physical assault (being punched, slapped, or hit) to rape and kidnapping. Women displayed a broad range of responses to the nature and degree of violence they experienced. For some, the extreme violence is viewed as somewhat inevitable—an occupational hazard, of sorts. This perspective seems to envelop the stereotype of "powerlessness" that is associated with this population (Ratner 1993). Yet, most striking were the accounts by women when they fought back. Such personal anecdotes are particularly noteworthy because of the additional physical threat to the women if their efforts are unsuccessful. Anna, a slight young woman, reported a great deal of violence as part of her street-based sex work experience.

Yeah, when I was working on the street. Some guy tried to strangle and suffocate me, and then another time. . . .

[INTERVIEWER: What did you do?]

I just like got this massive strength, because when you get scared, like, this strength, he was on, he threw me on a bed and was strangling me like this and pushing in, you know, the thing there and I somehow got my legs up like this underneath him and I just like kicked off, and he flew off me. And I grabbed the phone next to me, and I just started punching numbers and screaming into the phone. Well, it was at a hotel, as soon as you pick up the phone, it automatically goes to the front desk and they heard me because then, he threw me back, he threw the, ripped the phone out of the wall, threw me back down and had a pillow over me, over my face and all of a sudden, he just, I, because I couldn't hear anything, he got off me because somebody knocked on the door, and that's why he got off me. And then they started opening the door with a key, and then he, actually, no, he was still dressed. I was, I had on like a thong, my underwear, and he just like took off out the door.

Where women have responded to client violence *with* violence, the results are dramatic, but precarious. The vulnerability and potential hazards are clear. Their narratives capture the split-second nature of aggression by a client and their spontaneous reaction to it. Despite the efforts by women to present these episodes as indicative of street smarts, in reality, their responses come through as episodes of questionable judgment where reflex responses are used to deal with violence or the possibility of being "ripped off." At times, such reactions place the women at considerable, additional danger.

Then, another guy tried to put a gun to my head because he wanted the money back, and I was really stupid because I was like fuck you, no way! And I'm in the car and he has a gun to my head. It was kind of dumb.

[INTERVIEWER: So, what happened?]

I tried to jump out of the car, and he grabbed me by the back of my hair because my hair was longer, and then, well, first, well, he didn't have the gun yet. He said, he was, he said all right, give me that money back. And I was like no, I'm not giving it, and he was like, well, then you have to do it again. I was like no, I'm not, forget it. And so, I'm like oh, he's I don't even want to deal with this. So, we pulled up to the light and I opened the car door and went to jump out, but I wasn't fast enough and he grabbed me by the back of the hair and pulled me down onto his lap and then grabbed a gun beside him and put it to my head. And he's like which pocket did you put it in? Where is it? And I wouldn't tell him. And then, oh, I told him though, and then, finally I ended up telling him a pocket, but I told him the wrong pocket. I had a dollar in there, and he just took it out and didn't pay attention, and I jumped out of the car. So, I ended up having the money and he took the dollar. [Anna, aged 22]

The risk of violence associated with sex work is amplified by the poverty that has driven the women to street-based sex work in the first place. As the previous story demonstrates, the threat of being ripped off was considered to be as important, if not more, than the threat to her life. Yet, inevitably, the success of fighting back or escaping from an attacker will be incorporated into the repertoire of supposed street smarts, even if it is due to sheer luck.

In the stories the women recounted, the nature of violence is not only extreme, but beyond their control. This was particularly true of the stories we have categorized as akin to urban myths. As detailed by the women, these stories do not focus on the standard threat of rape or assault by a sex work client. Rather, the myth adopts a more extreme scenario: the customer/serial killer who is not just looking to avenge himself on any woman, but on the woman who works as a street-based prostitute. In essence, it is a continuation of the Jack the Ripper story (Walkowitz 1982).

Walkowitz (1982), in her historical exploration of Jack the Ripper, notes how the case almost immediately acquired mythical qualities. The idea of prostitutes being targeted by a serial killer is not an unreasonable one. This story has an established basis in reality—as evidenced by the notorious Joel Rifkin case of 1993[2] in NYC and, more recently, the gruesome discovery of the bodies of several women who were street-based sex workers in British Columbia (Krauss 2002).

In the narratives of street-based sex workers, the serial killer's presence is palpable: everyone knows "a friend of a friend" who has narrowly escaped a serial killer. The construct of the serial killer is one that has become part of the terminology of sex work related violence. Kitty, a 41-year-old, black heroin sniffer/injector tells of her brush with a possible serial killer:

> OK, this man had picked me up. As a matter of fact, the police had him, was looking for him anyway. The police was looking for him. I didn't know that. It was after all this stuff happened to me that I was able to put everything together. The police had us down there—picked us up, 'cause he was after the girls—to like go through a mug shot book and help them to find this guy because he was doing stuff to girls. He had gotten me and stabbed me in the back of my neck with an ice pick, and I think that might have gave me some kind of poisoning, blood poisoning or something, but I got really sick.

What is additionally intriguing in this specific case is the idea of "blood poisoning" as a result of her injury, which surfaces in her narrative linking the violence she encountered with subsequent illness. The dangers then linked with sex work are, perhaps, in her mind, more extensive: with potential repercussions for her health above and beyond physical violence.

The potential presence of a serial killer—however distant or rare—has the ability to prompt women to rethink and reevaluate their vulnerabilities related to street-based sex work. The value of the urban legend then is that ideally it *can* convey the horror of the worst-case scenario and can function as a mechanism prompting women to exercise greater caution and perhaps implement risk reduction strategies. Some women do devise and implement strategies as an attempt to offset their risks—such as refining their selection practices.

> I was always turning guys down like constantly. I'd be out there for hours and hours till I picked up someone because I'd only go to a certain, like places. I wouldn't go back home with them. I wouldn't just jump in a car. I'd make them park and get out of the car and talk to them and feel them out. [Anna, aged 22]

The women in our sample, however, spoke in generalities about the ways in which they could avoid violence related to street-based sex work. Few mentioned well-known risk reduction strategies used by those in the sex industry, such as working in pairs and having a colleague note specifics such as the make of a car and license plate number. In fact, the majority of the women in our sample worked the streets alone and in isolated areas. This may be indicative of an extreme degree of marginalization these women experience. Ultimately, it places them at an increased risk for violence.

Sexual Risk Reduction

Health risks associated with sex practices are an ongoing hazard associated with sex work. This group of women has a heightened awareness of the risks to sexual health they face. Most of them reported getting tested regularly for HIV and remained acutely aware of their status. In fact, ten (36 percent) women reported being HIV infected. And yet, with respect to reducing sexual risk for both the transmission and acquisition of sexually transmitted infections, their incorporation of this knowledge is less clear. Although many of the women spoke with confidence about the regular use of condoms, when asked, few could produce one on the spot. In a discussion about condom use, Mira, a 31-year-old Latina heroin injector, candidly admits to not using condoms:

INTERVIEWER: So you weren't using condoms for very often.

MIRA: Most of the time I wasn't because—a lot of clients out there don't like using them. And I would take the risks or the chances.

The risks were heightened for women who had used drugs beforehand, leaving some women unable to recall sexual events. For example, Helen, a 26-year-old mixed race/ethnicity heroin injector, found herself waking up alone in hotel rooms, naked and with no idea of how she got there or of what had transpired. These stark circumstances illustrate that sometimes the ability to reconcile the gap between sexual risk and street smart learned over time is simply not feasible for these women.

---

[2]Joel Rifkin was arrested in 1993 and confessed to killing 17 prostitutes in the NYC area.

In the ethnographic literature, there are stories about sexual risk practices that *seem* to embody the tone and feel of an urban legend. A popular anecdote relayed in the literature is that women engaging in street-based sex work are being offered more money to *not* use condoms (Dalla 2000; DeCarlo, Alexander, Hsu 1996). When this information first began to circulate in the HIV/AIDS prevention research literature, it was met with disbelief. Such a finding strikes at the heart of prevention efforts, as well as undermines the goals of researchers and sex workers alike.[3] Over time, this concept has been accepted as both factual and to some degree unavoidable. For example, Mira tells of the reactions of sex work clients when she tries to refuse to have sex without a condom: "They were automatically off 'cause I would say no, I'm not going to go with you without a condom and they would say, well, I'll give you an extra $20 or $30 or $40 and, oh, OK."

Respondents readily state that men offer more money to not use condoms. In a discussion about prices and sex acts, Kitty, a 41-year-old heroin injector, stated emphatically that unprotected sex yielded a higher price. However, when asked to detail prices of sex acts both with and without a condom, the prices she quoted were identical. The belief that men pay street-based sex workers more not to use a condom is one that has been widely accepted. If the notion that men pay more for sex without condoms is presented as standard practice, women may find themselves in a position where unprotected sex is justified as a means of rationalizing that they are getting paid more—regardless of whether an explicit negotiation has occurred. The widespread acceptance of the idea that not using a condom yields a higher price may, in effect, function like an urban myth, shaping women's behavior without the formal negotiations of price and condom use. But it is also possible that HIV infection may confound negotiations, as well, particularly in high background HIV prevalence communities. Although as HIV-infected woman may be concerned about spreading the virus to her sex partners, she may be less willing or able to negotiate condom use. HIV-infected women tread a precarious space, because public knowledge of their HIV-positive status could have a negative impact on business. Moreover, recent research in the central Brooklyn community where many of these interviews took place indicates that the mention of condom use by a potential sex partners is a tacit admission of HIV-positive status (Miller, Serner, and Wagner 2005), a factor that clearly decreases the willingness of all parties to negotiate condom use, particularly those who are HIV infected.

SEX WORK RELATIONSHIPS

Conventional wisdom in health research among sex worker populations is that women use condoms with men who are clients, but not with their regular non-paying sexual partners. In reality, these relationships are not always so clearly demarcated, especially for street-based sex workers. The "regular" sex work client is one with whom women often report taking risks. Over time, the regular client gains certain privileges, such as the possibility of vaginal sex without condoms, whereas other clients may only receive oral sex. Women are less likely to use condoms (or claim to have unusually high rates of "slippage" or "breakage") with these partners. Renee's account is typical of the process.

RENEE:	We had sex one time, he came over, and this is after I got bailed out of jail and like a few other times. And, um, it would break anyway so....
INTERVIEWER:	That's weird.
RENEE:	Yeah, I know. That was really weird, yeah. But they would, I mean, it wasn't it was my condoms and he wasn't doing anything, I mean, on purpose.

The regular client is treated differently than a one-time off-the-street pickup—straddling the world between client and boyfriend and reflects a process in which a steady partnership is shaped and cultivated over time. In this gray area, women may take greater sexual risks than in relationships with clients that are based strictly on a financial exchange for services. Even less clear and more complicated is the relationship with a "sugar daddy."

Sex work is often the catalyst for the development of sugar-daddy relationships. These are men who, over time, establish themselves are regular clients with a specialized arrangement. The sugar daddy enables a woman to transform herself from street-based prostitute to a

---

[3]Sex-worker collectives took exception to the images being promoted in the popular media of sex workers as "vectors" of disease and were especially vocal about practicing safer sex—something that was considered largely normative among sex workers.

"kept woman." However, our data challenge the societal assumption that it is the man who decides to become a regular client. Dannette, a 34-year-old woman of mixed race/ethnicity who smokes crack, has perfected the art of selecting men who become her sugar daddies. She cultivates relationships with several men over long periods of time. One man provides her with an ongoing opportunity to "get out of the city" for brief respites from the street, while another provides her with temporary housing, as well as drugs, though she claims he is unaware of this fact.

The idea of the sugar daddy has its roots in a number of cultural stories—perhaps best known as the myth of Pygmalion (Shaw 1946). This universal tale reemerges in slightly different forms in popular culture. Approximately nine months after her initial interview, Renee was recontacted, partly because of her interest in learning some of the results of the study.

Field note: Renee stopped using drugs and moved in with her older boyfriend who she met on the stroll. She is the "Pretty Woman" story. The reason that he had refused to let her into his apartment was that he was a pig. Renee agreed with this and as soon as she moved in with him, she threw out all his junk and cleaned up their home. She has been on methadone since she moved in with him and is in some kind of educational/training program. She has gained quite a bit of weight and is unhappy about that, but has decided to face things day by day.

Typically among our sample of women, however, the realities of the sugar-daddy relationship paled in comparison to the myth, with few actually leaving the streets for a better and more secure life. The sugar-daddy relationship, although failing to live up to the fantasy, does confer very tangible benefits to the women. Anna describes one of the several sugar daddies she met in the course of street-based sex work.

> Yeah. There's one guy that I ended up being friends with, this guy Jesse, that I met on the stroll. And he helps me out sometimes, like if I'm hungry or if I don't have any food. He doesn't like to give me money for drugs, but if I call and I say look, I'm really, really sick and I missed my methadone program already, then he'll reluctantly, but he'll give it to me usually if he has it.

In addition to providing a considerable amount of instrumental support directly to the women, sugar daddies were also reported to provide support and sometimes friendship to the women's families. Sugar daddies may also reduce the sex risk experienced by women, because their contributions may allow women to survive with fewer sex partners, and sugar daddies

are often older men who may have difficulty maintaining erections and prefer "safer" sexual experiences. Fay, a 41-year-old, black heroin sniffer, recalls one of her favorite sugar daddies.

> He used to give me $100 every week just to go. He'd have to take off all my clothes and let him look at my titties and play with my pussy. He's be so happy, like a boy in fags town. You know what I'm saying? Because his dick was this little. He couldn't get hard. It would be like a fucking finger in your mouth. . . . He was an older man. . . . He was nice, though. He was an ugly old man, and he was as crazy about my big ass. For $100, and you ain't got to do nothing. Just, you know, go on, play all you want to.

However, sexual behavior with the sugar daddy is more likely to be riskier, because once the relationship is transformed from sex-work client to regular client or sugar daddy, the couple is less likely to practice safe sex. Moreover, the women are often unfamiliar with a sugar daddy's history in terms of both sex and drug-use risk behaviors, which leaves them open to an array of sexually transmitted infections, including HIV. Even when women are aware of the infection status of their sugar daddies, they may agree to unprotected sex that they will regret in the future. Renee describes having unprotected sex with the HIV infected sugar daddy with whom she lives.

> I had unprotected sex yeah with him. . . . I don't know, I'm really, I'm nervous, I don't know where my head was. . . .

[INTERVIEWER: Were you high?]

> Yeah. I mean not high but just like this . . . just straight and yeah it might have been that. You know I wasn't nodding out that night, but I mean you know I thought I was really going to have a life with him and I didn't care at the point, I was just like, I really care for you.

The sugar-daddy scenario draws on both urban mythology and on an element of street smarts. The women tell stories about the merits of having a sugar daddy, of women who have successfully gotten out of "the life" through their sugar daddies, and how these women found the men who saved them. The women also use their knowledge as sex workers to carve out steady relationships with male clients. These relationships consistently hold great potential for instrumental support (both long and short term). In a sense, the women seek out these relationships to acquire some control of the chaos that is their daily lives. They may increase their risks in some ways, but they also manage to use these relationships to achieve temporary respite from the street and to decrease their sense of isolation.

Yet, the ability to simply rely on street smarts in this area remains limited. The women were able to assess some of the risks in the context of street dynamics using the reported lived experiences of others as a springboard for action. However, they often ignored their own lived experience and did not modify their behaviors to protect themselves as a result of their learned knowledge. Exposure to an array of risks came to be understood as part of the lifestyles in which they were currently (and, many believed, transiently) involved. As such, the existence of many kinds of risk was viewed as somewhat inevitable but temporary.

DISCUSSION

In this article, we have explored two narrative templates of storytelling in the lives of a sample of drug-using women who engage in street-based sex work: street smarts and urban myths. In the context of their daily lives, these women face risk related to drug use, sex work, and daily survival that include the risk of arrest, violence, and exposure to STIs. Through an examination of personal accounts of the day-to-day experiences of drug use and sex work, we have uncovered patterns of storytelling that have the potential to establish the boundaries and acceptability of risk behaviors. In part, the stories reflect an accumulation of knowledge through experience (street smarts). Information is also conveyed in the guise of worst-case scenario against which the women gauge their actions; these stories bear the hallmark of urban myths. Both forms of storytelling illustrate the complexity of agency in constrained life circumstances. The women do devise and implement strategies of resistance that help them survive in a complicated economy and continue to support their lifestyles, albeit intermittently.

In their narratives, women make clear links between what they see as risks and what they feel they can implement in terms of their preventive practices. The difficulty arises in evaluating which risk takes precedence.

In much of the literature on low-income sex worker populations, traditional thought suggests that women are powerless under the conditions of street-based sex work (Maher 1997; Phoenix 1999, 2000). For women who use drugs, the difficulties are amplified (Dalla 2002). Without doubt, critical structural forces impact negatively on the ability of women who use drugs and who engage in prostitution to exercise control over their lives.

Through an exploration of the stories that guide their behaviors, we uncovered some of the small ways in which women exhibit power and choice, though the reality is that sometimes the choices they exercise may still hold critical risks for them or their sex partners. The implementation of street smarts has the potential to enable women to maximize their economic opportunities while minimizing some of their risks. For example, the cultivation of regular sex-work clients or sugar-daddy relationships enables women to acquire some stability and minimize the variety of risks associated with multiple partners (e.g., violence, exposure to disease). At the same time, though, women are more likely to engage in riskier sexual practices with regular sex clients because of the more intimate and less transactional nature of their relationships. The centrality of men and sexual partnerships to the survival strategies of these women cannot be underestimated (Miller and Neaigus 2002). The purposeful selection of male partners is at once an act of choice, as well as of dependence, that challenges conventional notions of agency and victimhood.

The consistent patterns of certain stories told by a broad spectrum of women, such as that of the serial killer, suggest that women do, in fact, use storytelling to convey information concerning the dangers inherent in their work. A more unsettling story that was also widely reported concerns the explicit negotiation of condom use in the context of sex work.

Women in this study expressed serious concern that they would lose the opportunity to earn money if they ever raised the issue of condom use with their sex-work clients. As a result of this belief, many of the women acknowledged infrequent condom use in sex work and few were willing to discuss the dynamics of condom-use negotiation. Although this discussion does not seek to undermine the authority of accounts where women *do* report earning more money for sex without condoms, we wish to raise questions about the universality of this practice, as well as to the extent to which this concept has been promoted through storytelling rather than through real-life dynamics of street-based sex work.

Traditionally, the framework for understanding the lives of street-based sex workers situates women in the dichotomy of victim versus player in the drug economy (Maher 1997). Phoenix (1999, 2000) argues that to make sense of prostitution, we need to explore power and powerlessness as much more fluid concepts in the lives of women. In this article, we have sought to examine the ways in which women exercise choice in situations of limited opportunity.

Capitalizing on the oral traditions that constitute a strong component of life in inner-city communities, these women have at their disposal a combination of street-smart anecdotes and urban myths to help define the parameters of risk as well as to develop strategies for reducing the general array of risks they face in their daily lives. Unfortunately, it seems that few of the women capitalized on the greater instructive quality of the stories toward increased risk reduction and may even use storytelling to justify the risks they do take. In part, these gaps may reflect the extreme degree of marginalization the women experience due to the absence of a meaningful network of other sex workers (Cohen 1999; King 1988).

Despite the existence of a medium of information transfer, many of the women interviewed spoke in generalities about the ways in which they could actually protect themselves. Absent from the discussions are the "occupationally specific" strategies acknowledged in other studies of sex-worker populations (Maher 1996; Phoenix 1999, 2000), such as working as a team and noting any meaningful characteristics of the client. Few of the women worked the streets with any conscious form of "backup" to ensure some margin of safety. Traditional resources available to street-based sex workers, including pimps or a network of individuals loosely connected to the sex trade (e.g., bar and hotel owners), were notably missing in the environments in which these women sold sex. Predictably, some women found themselves in horrifying situations marked by extreme violence committed by clients.

It may be argued that women have no adequate way to protect themselves if they participate in street-based sex work. Yet, as Walkowitz (1982) notes, the mythology of the serial killer can function as a tool of "instructive resistance." More specifically, it can serve as a catalyst for the development of an informal support network of women sex workers and their regular clients who seek to minimize their risks of violence associated with sex work. The women in our study, however, implemented few meaningful practices to reduce their risk of violence. One reason why women might fail to embrace such risk-reduction strategies may relate of their distance from the identity of sex worker. The presumed temporary nature of their sex work may preclude women from forming a collective and supportive network based on the reduction of shared risks, because the formation of such a network is predicated on acknowledging that one participates in prostitution.

Stories have the ability to reveal the ways in which individuals are connected to the world around them (Dossa 2002). One of the most striking aspects of these stories is the sense of profound isolation in these women's lives. Popular representations of street-based sex work may evoke images of a well-connected social network, but these women have marginal contact with each other and even less contact in the larger communities in which they live. Instead, their social contacts were severely circumscribed, limited to clients, "boyfriends," and marginal relationships with social service agencies. An acute sense of isolation permeates the stories of these women, thinly disguised under the banner of "going it alone."

More optimistically, the stories and myths that circulate in the lives of women who use drugs and engage in street-based sex work can become an entryway for public health intervention efforts. A critical first message to be transmitted via the oral tradition is to teach street-based sex workers the "tricks of the trade," including working in pairs, observing key client characteristics, and publicizing "bad Johns" in locations frequented by the women such as at needle-exchange programs or other health and social welfare locations.

Anthropologists need to critically examine currently existing stories to identify those with accurate and achievable risk-reduction methods and those that may further justify risk taking (Moore 1993). With this information, it may be possible to harness the medium of the oral tradition and integrate public health-risk reduction messages into street smarts and urban myth, thereby equipping women with new tools to assert power in situations where they, and others, traditionally view women as powerless. Although authors have noted limitations on the implementation of risk reduction practices such as condom carrying for women involved in street based sex (Phoenix 1999, 2000), they do not place these practical methods in the framework of harm reduction. By applying this framework to achievable risk-reduction practices that may be disseminated through the narrative strategies that the women currently use (e.g., urban myths developed to share the benefits of working in teams—even for those working on a temporary basis), it may be possible to reduce the assumptions of risk, as well as the actual experience of risk among these very vulnerable women.

References

Agar, M. 1980. *The Professional Stranger: An Informal Introduction to Ethnography*. New York: Academic Press.

Best, J., and G. T. Horiuchi. 1985. The Razor Blade in the Apple: The Social Construction of Urban Legends. *Social Problems* 32(5):488–499.

Booth, R. E., J. K. Watters, and D. D. Chitwood. 1993. HIV Risk-Related Sex Behaviors among Injection Drug

Users, Crack Smokers, and Injection Drug Users Who Smoke Crack. *American Journal of Public Health* 83(8):144–148.

Bourgeois, P., and E. Dunlap. 1993. Exorcising Sex for Crack: An Ethnographic Perspective from Harlem. In *Crack Pipe as Pimp: An Eight-City Ethnographic Study of the Sex-for-Crack Phenomenon*. M. Ratner, ed. Pp. 97–132. New York: Lexington.

Brunvand, J. H. 1981. *The Vanishing Hitchhiker (American Urban Legends and Their Meanings)*. New York: W. W. Norton.

Centers for Disease Control and Prevention. 1999. *Needle Stick Hoaxes: Are These Stories True?* Atlanta: Centers for Disease Control and Prevention.

Cohen, C. J. 1999. *The Boundaries of Blackness: AIDS and the Breakdown of Black Politics*. Chicago: University of Chicago Press.

Connors, M. M. 1992. Risk Perception, Risk Taking and Risk Management among Intravenous Drug Users: Implications for AIDS Prevention. *Social Science and Medicine* 34:591–601.

Dalla, R. L. 2000. Exposing the "Pretty Women" Myth: A Qualitative Examination of the Lives of Female Streetwalking Prostitutes. *Journal of Sex Research* 37(4):344–353.

2002 Night Moves: A Qualitative Investigation of Street-Level Sex Work. *Psychology of Women Quarterly* 26:63–73.

DeCarlo, P., P. Alexander, and H. Hsu. 1996. What Are Sex Workers' HIV Prevention Needs? In HIV *Prevention: Looking Back, Looking Ahead*. San Francisco: Center for AIDS Prevention Studies, University of California at San Francisco. Online at http://www.caps.ucsf.edu/prosttext.html.

Dossa, P. 2002. Narrative Mediation of Convention and New "Mental Health" Paradigms: Reading the Stories of Immigrant Iranian Women. *Medical Anthropology Quarterly* 16(3):341–359.

Epele, M. E. 2002. Gender, Violence and HIV: Women's Survival in the Streets. *Culture, Medicine and Psychiatry* 26:33–54.

Erickson, P. G., J. Butters, P. McGillicuddy, and A. Hallgreen. 2000. Crack and Prostitution: Gender, Myths and Experiences. *Journal of Drug Issues* 30:767–788.

Feldman, A. 2001. Philocetes Revisited. White Public Space and the Political Geography of Public Safety. *Social Text* 19(3):57–89.

Feldman, H. W., F. Espada, S. Penn, and S. Byrd. 1993. Street Status and the Sex-for-Crack Scene in San Francisco. In *Crack Pipe as Pimp: An Eight-City Ethnographic Study of the Sex-for-Crack Phenomenon*. M. Ratner, ed. Pp. 133–158. New York: Lexington.

Fullilove, M. T., A. Lown, and R. E. Fullilove. 1992. Crack'hos and Skeezers: Traumatic Experiences of Women Crack Users. *Journal of Sex Research* 29(2):275–287.

Furst, R. T., B. D. Johnson, and E. Dunlap. 1999. The Stigmatized Image of the "Crack Head": A Sociocultural Exploration of a Barrier to Cocaine

Smoking among a Cohort of Youth in New York City. *Deviant Behavior: An Interdisciplinary Journal* 20:153–181.

Goldstein, P. J., L. J. Oullet, and M. Fencrich. 1992. From Bag Brides to Skeezer: A Historical Perspective on Sex-for-Drugs Behavior. *Journal of Psychoactive Drugs* 24(4):349–361.

Hartman, D. M., and A. Golub. 1999. The Social Construction of the Crack Epidemic in the Print Media. *Journal of Psychoactive Drugs* 31:423–431.

Heckathorn, D. D. 1997. Respondent-Driven Sampling: A New Approach to the Study of Hidden Populations. *Social Problems* 44(2):174–199.

Inciardi, J. A. 1993. Kingrats, Chicken Heads, Slow Necks, Freaks and Blood Suckers: A Glimpse at the Miami Sex-for-Crack Market. In *Crack Pipe as Pimp: An Eight-City Ethnographic Study of the Sex-for-Crack Phenomenon*. M. Ratner, ed. Pp. 37–68. New York: Lexington.

——. 1995 Crack, Crack House Sex, and HIV Risk. *Archives of Sexual Behavior* 24(3):249–269.

Kaplan, C. D., D. Korf, and C. Sterk. 1987. Temporal and Social Contexts of Heroin-Using Populations: An Illustration of the Snowballing Sampling Technique. *Journal of Nervous and Mental Disease* 175:566–573.

King, D. K. 1988. Multiple, Jeopardy, Multiple Consciousness: The Context of a Black Feminist Ideology. Signs: *Journal of Women in Culture and Society* 14(1):42–72.

Kolata, G. 1990. "Old, Weak and a Loser": Crack User's Image Falls. *New York Times*, July 23, A1, B1.

Krauss, C. D. 2002. Mounties Dig up Body Parts in Serial Killing Case. *New York Times*, November 23, A8.

Lévi-Strauss, C. 1979. *Myth and Meaning: Cracking the Code of Culture*. New York: Schoken.

Logan E. 1999. The Wrong Race, Committing Crime, Doing Drugs, and Maladjusted for Motherhood: The Nation's Fury over "Crack Babies." *Social Justice* 26:115–138.

Maher, L. 1996. Hidden in the Light: Occupational Norms among Crack-Using Street Level Sex Workers. *Journal of Drug Issues* 26(1):143–173.

1997 Sexed Work. *Gender, Race, and Resistance in a Brooklyn Drug Market*. New York: Oxford University Press.

Miller, M., and A. Neaigus. 2002. An Economy of Risk: Resource Acquisition Strategies of Inner City women Who Use Drugs. *International Journal of Drug Policy* 13(5):399–408.

Miller M., M. Serner, and M. Wagner. 2005. Sexual Diversity among Black Men Who Have Sex with Men in an Inner City Community. *Journal of Urban Health* 82(suppl. 1): i26–i34.

Moore, D. 1993. Social Controls, Harm Minimisation and Interactive Outreach: The Public Health Implications of an Ethnography of Drug Use. *Australian Journal of Public Health* 17(1):58–67.

Nemeroff, C. J. 1995. Magical Thinking about Illness Virulence: Conceptions of Germs from "Safe" Versus "Dangerous" Others. *Health Psychology* 14(2): 147–151.

Oullet, L. J., W. W. Wiebel, A. D. Jiminez, and W. A. Johnson. 1993. Crack Cocaine and the Transformation of Prostitution in Three Chicago Neighborhoods. In *Crack Pipe as Pimp: An Eight-City Ethnographic Study of the Sex-for-Crack Phenomenon*. M. Ratner, ed. Pp. 69–96. New York: Lexington.

Phoenix, J. 1999. Making Sense of Prostitution. London: Macmillan.

2000 Prostitute Identities: Men, Money and Violence. British *Journal of Criminology* 40(Winter):37–55.

Ratner, M. 1993. Sex, Drugs and Public Policy: Studying and Understanding the Sex-for-Crack Phenomenon. In *Crack Pipe as Pimp: An Eight-City Ethnographic Study of the Sex-for-Crack Phenomenon*. M. Ratner, ed. Pp. 1–36. New York: Lexington.

Rhodes, T., and L. Cusick. 2002. Accounting for Unprotected Sex: Stories of Agency and Acceptability. *Social Science and Medicine* 55:211–226.

Sanders, T. 2004. A Continuum of Risk? The Management of Heath, Physical and Emotional Risks by Female Sex Workers. *Sociology of Health and Illness* 26:557–574.

Shaw, G. B. 1946. *Pygmalion*. London: Penguin.

Singer, M., G. Scott, S. Wilson, D. Easton, and M. Weeks. 2001. War Stories: AIDS Prevention and the Street Narratives of Drug Users. *Qualitative Health Research* 11(5):589–611.

Smith, L. C., K. J. Lucas, and C. Latkin. 1999. Rumor and Gossip: Social Discourse on HIV and AIDS. *Anthropology and Medicine* 6:121–131.

Spradley, J. P. 1979a. *Participant Observation*. New York: Holt, Rinehart, and Winston.

———. 1979b *The Ethnographic Interview*. Albany: State University of New York Press.

Sterk, C. E., K. W. Elifson, and D. German. 2000. Female Crack Users and Their Sexual Relationships: The Role of Sex-for-Crack Exchanges. *Journal of Sex Research* 37(4):354–360.

Strauss, A. L. 1990. *Basics of Qualitative Research: Grounded Theory Procedures and Techniques*. Newbury Park, CA: Sage.

———. 1998. *Basics of Qualitative Research: Techniques and Procedures for Developing Grounded Theory*. Thousand Oaks, CA: Sage.

Tonklin, E. 1992. *Narrating Our Past: The Social Construction of Oral History*. Cambridge: Cambridge University Press.

Walkowitz, J. R. 1982. Jack the Ripper and the Myth of Male Violence. *Feminist Review* 8(3):543–574.

Watters, J. K., and P. Biernacki. 1989. Targeted Sampling: Options for the Study of Hidden Populations. *Social Problems* 36:416–430.

Wells, R. L. 1999. *The Needle and the Damage Done: Urban Legends Research Center*. http://www.ulrc.com.au.

Whatley, M. H., and E. R. Henken. 2000. *Did They Hear about the Girl Who? Contemporary Legends, Folklore and Human Sexuality*. New York: New York University Press.

Worsley, P. 1968. *The Trumpet Shall Sound: A Study Of "Cargo" Cults in Melanesia*. 2nd ed. New York: Schoken.

Zinberg, N. E. 1984. *Drug, Set, and Setting: The Basis for Controlled Intoxicant Use*. New Haven, CT: Yale University Press.

8

ACCOUNTS OF PROFESSIONAL MISDEEDS

The Sexual Exploitation of Clients by Psychotherapists

MARK R. POGREBIN, ERIC D. POOLE, AND AMOS MARTINEZ

Sexual intimacy between therapists and clients is explicitly recognized as one of the most serious violations of the professional-client relationship, subject to both regulatory and administrative penalties and, in several states, criminal sentences. This paper examines the written accounts submitted to the Colorado state mental health grievance board by psychotherapists who have had complaints of sexual misconduct filed against them by former clients. Neutralization theory is utilized to analyze the accounts these offending therapists provide for their deviant behavior.

Intimate sexual relationships between mental health therapists and their clients have been increasingly reported in recent years (Akamatsu 1987). In a survey of over 1400 psychiatrists, Gartell, Herman, Olarte, Feldstein, and Localio (1987) found that 65% reported having treated a patient who admitted to sexual involvement with a previous therapist. National self-report surveys indicate that approximately 10% of psychotherapists admit having had at least one sexual encounter with a client (Gartell, Herman, Olarte, Feldstein, and Localio 1986; Pope, Keith-Spiegel, and Tabachnick 1986). It is suggested that these surveys most likely underestimate the extent of actual sexual involvement with clients because some offending psychotherapists either fail to

respond to the survey or fail to report their sexual indiscretion (Gartell et al. 1987). Regardless of the true prevalence rates, many mental health professional associations explicitly condemn sexual relations between a therapist and client. Such relationships represent a breach of canons of professional ethics and are subject to disciplinary action by specific licensing or regulatory bodies.

PSYCHOLOGICAL IMPACT ON CLIENT

Individuals who seek treatment for emotional or mental health problems assume a dependency role in a professional-client relationship in which direction and

---

Source: Accounts of Professional Misdeeds: The Sexual Exploitation of Clients by Psychotherapists by Pogrebin, Mark R., and Eric D. Poole, Amos Martinez, *Deviant Behavior: An Interdisciplinary Journal, 13*: 229–252, 1992 http://www.informaworld.com. Reprinted with permission.

control are exerted by the therapist. The client's most intimate secrets, desires, and fears are revealed to the therapist. Therapeutic communication relies on the development of trust between client and therapist. In order to be successful, therapy requires the individual in treatment to abandon the psychic defenses that shield his or her genuine self from scrutiny (Pope and Bouhoutsos 1986). The lowering of these defenses in a therapeutic relationship increases the client's emotional vulnerability. Because the potential for manipulation or exploitation of the client is heightened in such relationships, Benetin and Wilder (1989) argue that the therapist must assume a higher degree of professional responsibility to ensure that personal trust is not abused.

As Finkelhor (1984) points out, the therapeutic relationship is fundamentally asymmetrical; thus, the controlling presumption is that a client's volition under conditions of therapeutic dependency must always be considered problematic. The client cannot be considered capable of freely consenting to enter into a sexual relationship with a therapist. The therapist's sexual exploitation of a client represents an obvious violation of trust, destroying any therapeutic relationship that has been established. The client often experiences intense feelings of betrayal and anguish at having been victimized by the very person who had been trusted to help (Pope and Bouhoutsos 1986). Sexual exploitation by a therapist can result in clients' suffering emotional instability, conflicts in interpersonal relationships, and disruptions in work performance (Benetin and Wilder 1989).

The Colorado State Grievance Board

Historically in Colorado, grievances against licensed mental health providers were handled by two separate licensing boards: the Board of Psychologist Examiners and the Board of Social Work Examiners. During the past 20 years, the state witnessed a proliferation of practitioners in the unregulated field of psychotherapy. Individuals trained in traditional professional fields of psychology, counseling, and social work may call themselves psychotherapists, but anyone else with (or without) training in any field may refer to their practice as psychotherapy. In short, psychotherapists are not subject to mandatory licensing requirements in Colorado. Largely through the lobbying efforts of licensed mental health practitioners, the state legislature was persuaded to address some of the problems associated with the operation of a decentralized grievance process that failed to regulate unlicensed practitioners of psychotherapy. The result was the passage of the Mental Health Occupations Act, creating on July 1, 1988 the State Grievance Board within the Colorado Department of Regulatory Agencies.

The State Grievance Board has the responsibility to process complaints and undertake disciplinary proceedings against the four categories of licensed therapists and against unlicensed psychotherapists. Upon the filing of a complaint, the eight-member board (comprising four licensed therapists and four public members) initiates the following action:

1. The named therapist receives written notice and is given 20 days to respond in writing;

2. When deemed appropriate by the board, the complainant may review the therapist's response and is given 10 days to submit further information or explanation; and

3. The board reviews the available information and renders a decision about the complaint.

If the board determines that disciplinary action against a licensed therapist is warranted, the board is increased by an augmenting panel of three members, each of whom is a licensed practitioner in the same field as the psychotherapist subject to sanctioning. The board can issue a letter of admonition, place restrictions on the license or the practice, require the therapist to submit to a mental or physical examination, or seek an injunction in a state district court to limit or to stop the practice of psychotherapy. When the complaint involves an unlicensed practitioner, injunctive action is the board's only disciplinary remedy.

The governing state statute further mandates that psychotherapists provide their clients with a disclosure statement concerning their credentials (e.g., degrees and licenses) and specific client rights and information (e.g., second opinion and legal confidentiality, as well as therapeutic methods and techniques and fee structure, if requested). In the Model Disclosure Statement developed by the State Grievance Board, the impropriety of sexual relations is specifically noted:

> In a professional relationship (such as ours [client and therapist]), sexual intimacy between a therapist and a client is never appropriate. If sexual intimacy occurs, it should be reported to the State Grievance Board.

During 1988 the state legislature also enacted a statute making sexual contact between therapist and client a criminal offense (Colorado Revised Statutes 18–3–405.5, Supplement 1988).

Since 1988, sexual intimacy between therapists and clients has been explicitly and formally recognized as one of the most serious violations of the professional-client relationship, subject to both regulatory or administrative and criminal penalties. Yet, between August 1, 1988 and June 30, 1990, 10% ($n = 33$) of the 324 complaints filed with the State Grievance Board involved allegations of sexual misconduct. Given the implications that these sexual improprieties raise for both the client as victim and the therapist as offender, we wish to examine the written accounts submitted to the board by psychotherapists who have had complaints of sexual misconduct filed against them.

THEORETICAL PERSPECTIVE

As Mills (1940, p. 904) observes, the "imputation and avowal of motives by actors are social phenomena to be explained. The differing reasons men give for their actions are not themselves without reasons." Mills draws a sharp distinction between cause and explanation or account. He focuses not on the reasons for the actions of individuals but on the reasons individuals give for their actions. Mills (1940, p. 906) views motive as "a complex of meaning, which appears to the actor himself or to the observer to be an adequate ground for his conduct." Yet, there may be another dimension: the individual's perception of how the motive will appear to others.

Mills argues that such motives express themselves in special vocabularies: first, they must satisfactorily answer questions concerning both social and lingual conduct; second, they must be accepted accounts for past, present, or future behavior. According to Scott and Lyman (1968), accounts are socially approved vocabularies that serve as explanatory mechanisms for deviance. These linguistic devices attempt to shape other's attribution about the actor's intent or motivation, turning it away from imputations that are harmful (e.g., personal devaluation, stigma, or imposition of negative sanctions).

It is no doubt true that, it many instances, being able to effectively present accounts will lessen the degree of one's moral responsibility. Moral responsibility is rarely a presentor-absent attribution. Just as there are degrees of deviation from expected conduct norm, there are probably types and degrees of accountability, as well as acceptability, to various audiences with respect to the accounts that individuals offer.

> "The variable is the accepted vocabulary of motives of each man's dominant group about whose opinion he cares" (Mills 1940, p. 906).

It is easy for most people to draw from a repertoire of accounts in explaining their untoward acts. This is not to suggest that their reasons are either sincere or insincere. Nor does it deny the validity of their claims; they may well have committed the disapproved behavior for the very reasons that are given. The important thing here is that they require an appropriate vocabulary of motive to guide their presentation of self. In the present study we seek to identify the meanings therapists imputed to the circumstances and events surrounding their sexual relations with clients. Of particular interest are the situated reasons or motives these individuals offer in accounting for their actions.

METHOD

To the 33 complaints of sexual misconduct filed from August 1988 through June 1990, 30 written responses from psychotherapists were submitted to the State Grievance Board.[1] Twenty-four therapists admitted to sexual involvement with clients; six denied the allegations. In the present study we examine the statements of the 24 therapists who provided accounts for their sexual relations with clients.[2] Twenty-one therapists are men; three are women.

The analytical method utilized in reviewing therapists' accounts was content analysis, which "translates frequency of occurrence of certain symbols into summary judgments and comparisons of content of the discourse" (Starosta 1984, p. 185). Content analytical techniques provide the means to document, classify, and interpret the communication of meaning, allowing for inferential judgments from objective identification of the characteristics of messages (Holsti 1969).

---

[1] Twenty of the 33 complaints involved unlicensed therapists. There were no discernible differences between the licensed and unlicensed therapists in type of account presented. Moreover, there was no association between type of account and disposition of the cases by the Grievance Board.

[2] The written statements submitted by therapists to the State Board have been obtained under provisions of Colorado's Public Records Act, which provides "any person the right of inspection of such records or any portion thereof" unless such inspection would violate any state statute or federal law or regulation or is expressly prohibited by judicial rules or court order. The first author serves as a public member on the Grievance Board. The third author is Program Administrator of the Mental Health Licensing Section in the Department of Regulatory Agencies and is directly responsible for the administration of the Grievance Board.

The 24 written responses ranged in length from 2 to 25 pages. Each response was assessed and classified according to the types of explanations invoked by therapists in accounting for their acknowledged sexual relations with clients. We employed Scott and Lyman's (1968) classic formulation of accounts (i.e., excuses and justifications) and Goffman's (1971) notion of the apology as conceptual guides in organizing the vocabularies of motive used by our group of therapists to explain their untoward behavior. Our efforts build upon the work of previous sociologists who have utilized the concept of accounts to analyze the vocabularies of motive of convicted rapists (Scully and Marolla 1984) and convicted murderers (Ray and Simons 1987) in prison interviews with researchers, as well as the vocabularies of criminal defendants in presentence interviews with probation officers (Spencer 1983) and of white-collar defendants in presentence investigation reports (Rothman and Gandossy 1982). We developed the following classification scheme consistent with the controlling themes identified in the written accounts:

1. Excuse: an account in which an individual admits that an act was wrong or inappropriate, while providing a socially approved vocabulary for mitigating or relieving personal responsibility.

   (a) Appeal of defeasibility: an excuse in which an individual seeks to absolve himself or herself of responsibility by claiming to have acted on the basis of either lack of information or misinformation.

   (b) Scapegoating: an excuse in which an individual attempts to shift responsibility by asserting that his or her behavior was a response to the actions or attitudes of others.

2. Justification: an account in which the individual acknowledges the wrongfulness of the type or category of an act but seeks to have the specific instance in question defined as an exception.

   (a) Sad tale: a highly selective portrayal of distressing biographical facts through which the individual explains his or her present act as the product of extenuating conditions.

   (b) Denial of injury: a justification in which the individual asserts that his or her act was permissible under the particular occasion since no one was harmed or the consequences were trivial (or even beneficial).

3. Apology: an account in which the individual acknowledges the wrongfulness of the act and accepts personal responsibility but seeks to portray his or her act as the product of a past self that has since been disavowed.

Excerpts from the therapists' written accounts, presented in our findings below, have been selected to illustrate the defining elements of each of the above types of accounts. Care has been taken to avoid disclosing any information that could be used to identify the source of the statements. All names are fictitious to ensure against any potential violation of anonymity.

FINDINGS

Accounts are "linguistic device[s] employed whenever an action is subjected to valuative inquiry" (Scott and Lyman 1968, p. 46). An important function of accounts is to mitigate blameworthiness by representing one's behavior in such a way as to reduce personal accountability. This involves offering accounts aimed at altering the prevailing conception of what the instant activity is, as well as one's role in the activity. Excuses, justification, and apologies all display a common goal: giving a "good account" of oneself.

Excuses

Appeal of Defeasibility

In an appeal of defeasibility, one accounts for one's behavior by denying any intention to cause the admitted harm or by claiming a failure to foresee the unfortunate consequences of one's act, or both. As Lyman and Scott (1989, pp. 136–37) explain:

> The appeal of defeasibility invokes a division in the relation between action and intent, suggesting that the latter was malfunctioning with respect to knowledge, voluntariness, or state of complete consciousness.

In the following account, the therapist claims ignorance of professional rules of conduct governing relations with clients:

> I did not know that seeing clients socially outside of therapy violated hospital policy.... [I]f I realized it was strictly forbidden, I would have acted differently.

The next case involves a female therapist who had engaged in a long-term sexual relationship with a female client. The therapist couches her account in terms of failing to be informed by her clinical supervisors that the relationship was improper:

> Both Drs. Smith and Jones had total access to and knowledge of how I terminated with her [the client]

and continued our evolving relationship. Neither of them in any way inferred that I had done anything unethical or illegal. I do not understand how I can be held accountable for my actions. There were no guidelines provided by the mental health center around this issue. Both Drs. Smith and Jones knew of and approved of my relationship with her.

Other appeals of defeasibility incorporate elements of defective insight and reasoning, or just poor judgment, in an effort to deny intent. An appropriate vocabulary of motive is necessarily involved in the presentation of such appeals. For example, Scully and Marolla (1984, pp. 540–41) report that convicted rapists attempted to

> . . . negotiate a non-rapist identity by painting an image of themselves as a "nice guy." Admitters projected the image of someone who had made a serious mistake but, in every other respect, was a decent person.

The deviant actor makes a bid to be seen as a person who has many of the same positive social attributes possessed by others. This individual presents the basic problem simply: "Everybody makes mistakes"; "It could happen to anyone"; or "We all do stupid things." Such fairly standard, socially approved phrases or ideas are used to sensitize others to their own mistakes, thereby reminding them of their own vulnerability and limiting their opportunity to draw lines between themselves and the individual deviant. The basic message is that the deviant act is not indicative of one's essential character (Goffman 1963). This message is supplemented by an effort to present information about the "untainted" aspects of self. In these presentational cues, deviant actors seek to bring about a softening of the moral breach in which they are involved and relieve themselves of culpability.

In the following example, a therapist admits that she simply misinterpreted her own feelings and did not consciously intend to become sexually involved with her client:

> It was after a short period of time that I first experienced any sexual feelings toward her. I did excuse the feelings I had as something which I never would act on. Unfortunately, I did not understand what was happening at the time.

Similarly, another therapist seeks to diminish culpability by attributing his sexual indiscretion to a misreading of his client's emotional needs:

I experienced her expressions of affection as caring gestures of our spiritual bond, not lust. And I had no reason to suspect otherwise from her, since I had been so clear about my aversion to romantic involvement. We had sexual intercourse only once after termination. I am not promiscuous, neither sexually abusive nor seductive.

Another variant of the appeal of defeasibility involves a claim that the inappropriate behavior was an unforeseen outcome of the therapeutic process itself. This denial of responsibility requires articulation of one's position in the professional argot of psychotherapy. Such professionals are able to provide rather complex and compelling accounts of themselves, attempting to convince an audience of peers of the "real" meaning or "correct" interpretation of their behavior. As Lofland (1969, p. 179) posits,

> . . . since they are likely to share in the universe of understandings and cultural ideology of expert imputors, they are more likely to be aware of what kinds of reasons or explanations such imputors will buy.

The therapist in the next account focuses on the unique problems arising in the professional-client relationship that contributed to the sexual misconduct:

> The two inappropriate interactions occurred when she was a practicing psychotherapist and I was seeing her as a client, supervisee, and socially. I believe that my unresolved counter-transference and her transference greatly contributed to the events.

In related accounts, therapists provide a professional assessment or opinion that the therapeutic techniques utilized in treating their clients got out of hand. This approach is shown in the following:

> The initial development of a change in the relationship cantered around my empathetic feelings that touched on unresolved feelings of loss in my own life. One aspect of the treatment centered around a lifetime of severe feelings of abandonment and rejection that the client felt from her family. This worked powerful feelings within me and I responded by overidentifying with the client, becoming emotionally vulnerable and feeling inappropriate responsibility to ease the client's pain.

Some of these professional accounts provide lengthy and detailed descriptions of various treatment techniques utilized because of the ineffectiveness of prior intervention attempts. These therapists stress the multifarious nature of the problems encountered in treatment that warranted the use of more complex and often more risky types of treatment. The following case shows the compromising position in which the therapist placed himself in attempting to foster the client's amenability to treatment:

> Because we were at an impasse in therapy I adjusted the treatment to overcome resistance. I employed several tactics, one of which was to share more of my personal life with her; another was to see her outside the usual office setting.

A slight variation of this defeasibility claim involves what Scott and Lyman (1968, p. 48) call the "gravity disclaimer," where the actor recognizes the potential risks involved in the pursuit of a particular course of action but suggests that their probability could not be predetermined.

> When she came in she was very down, to the point that she was staring at the floor. I felt she was not being reached in a cognitive way, so I tried to reach her using a sensory approach. I was trying to communicate to her: caring, love, acceptance, compassion and so on. Unfortunately, with the sensory approach there is a fine line not to be crossed, and I crossed it.

The appeal of defeasibility is a form of excuse that links knowledge and intent. Actors diminish blameworthiness by defining their acts as occurring without real awareness or intent; that is, they attempt to absolve themselves of responsibility by denying having knowingly intended to cause the untoward consequences. Had they known otherwise, they would have acted differently.

Scapegoating

Scapegoating involves an attempt to blame others for one's untoward behavior. Scapegoating is available as a form of excuse in the professional-client relationship because of the contextual opportunity for the therapist to shift personal responsibility to the client. The therapist contends that his or her actions were the product of the negative attributes or will of the client, (e.g., deceit, seduction, or manipulation). The therapist in the following example recognized the wrongfulness of his behavior but deflects responsibility by holding the client culpable for her actions:

> I am not denying that this sexual activity took place, not am I trying to excuse or justify it. It was wrong. However, the woman who complained about me is a psychologist. She was counseling me as well, on some vocational issues. So if anyone had cause for complaint under the regulations, it seems it would be me.

Another example of an account where the therapist attempts to "blame the victim" for the improper sexual activity reveals the focus on his diminished personal control of the relationship:

> That I became involved in a sexual relationship with her is true. While my actions were reprehensible, both morally and professionally, I did not mislead or seduce her or intend to take advantage of her. My fault, instead, was failing to adequately safeguard myself from her seductiveness, covert and overt.

Here we have a therapist recognizing the impropriety of his actions yet denying personal responsibility because of the client's overpowering charms. The message is that the therapist may be held accountable for an inadequate "self-defense" which left him vulnerable to the client's seductive nature, but that he should not be culpable for the deviant sexual behavior since it was really he who was taken in and thus "victimized." The therapist's account for his predicament presumes a "reasonable person" theory of behavior; that is, given the same set of circumstances, any reasonable person would be expected to succumb to this persuasive client.

Justifications

Sad Tale

The sad tale presents an array of dismal experiences or conditions that are regarded—both collectively and cumulatively—as an explanation and justification for the actor's present untoward behavior. The therapists who presented sad tales invariably focused on their own history of family problems and personal tribulations that brought them to their present state of sexual affairs with clients:

> Ironically, her termination from therapy came at one of the darkest periods of my life. My father had died that year. I had met him for the first time when I was in my twenties. He was an alcoholic. Over the years we had worked hard on our relationship. At the time of his dying, we were at peace with one another. Yet, I still had my grief. At the time I had entered into individual therapy to focus on issues pertaining to my father's alcoholism and co-dependency issues. I then asked my wife to join me for marriage counseling. We were having substantial problems surrounding my powerlessness in our relationship. Therapy failed to address the balance of power. I was in the worst depression I had ever experienced in my entire life when we began our sexual involvement.

Therapists who employ sad tales admit to having sexual relations with their clients, admit that their actions were improper, and admit that ordinarily what they did would be an instance of the general category of the prohibited behavior. They claim, however, that their behavior is a special case because the power of circumstance voids the defining deviant quality of their actions. This type of account is similar to Lofland's (1969, p. 88) "special justification," where the actor views his current act as representative of some category of deviance but does not believe it to be entirely blameworthy because of extenuating circumstances. One therapist outlines the particular contextual factors that help explain his misbehavior:

> The following situations are not represented as an excuse for my actions. There is no excuse for them. They are simply some of what I feel are circumstances that formed the context for what I believe is an incident that will never be repeated.
>
> (1) Life losses: My mother-in-law who lived with us died. My oldest son and, the next fall, my daughter had left home for college.
>
> (2) Overscheduling: I dealt with these losses and other concerns in my life by massive overscheduling.

Other therapists offer similar sad tales of tragic events that are seen to diminish their capacity, either physically or mentally, to cope with present circumstances. Two cases illustrate this accounting strategy:

> It the summer of 1988, my wife and I separated with her taking our children to live out-of-state. This was a difficult loss for me. A divorce followed. Soon after I had a bout with phlebitis which hospitalized me for ten days.
>
> My daughter, who lived far away with my former wife, was diagnosed with leukemia; and my mother had just died. Additional stress was caused by my ex-wife and present wife's embittered interactions.

Sad tales often incorporate a commitment to conventionality whereby one's typical behavior is depicted as conforming to generally approved rules or practices—the instant deviant act being the exception. The imputation is that "the exception proves the rule"; that is, one's normally conventional behavior is confirmed or proven by the rare untoward act. The transgression may thus be viewed as an exception to the deviant classification to which it would justifiably belong if the special circumstances surrounding the enactment of the behavior in question did not exist.

Given such circumstances, individuals depict themselves as more acted upon then acting. In the next case the therapist outlines the special circumstances that account for his behavior:

> I had "topped out" at my job, was being given additional responsibilities to deal with, had very little skilled staff to work with, and received virtually no support from my supervisor. I was unconsciously looking for a challenging case to renew my interest in my work, and she fit that role. My finally giving into her seduction was an impulsive act based n my own hopelessness and depression.

Sad tales depict individuals acting abnormally in abnormal situations. In short, their instant deviance is neither typical nor characteristic of the type of person they really are, that is, how they would act under normal conditions. They are victims of circumstance, for if it were not for these dismal life events, their sexual improprieties would never have occurred.

Denial of Injury

Denial of injury is premised on a moral assessment of consequences; that is, the individual claims that his or her actions should be judged as wrong on the basis of the harm resulting from those acts. Again, the actor acknowledges that in general the behavior in which he or she has engaged is inappropriate but asserts that in this particular instance no real harm was done. This type of account was prevalent among the therapists who had engaged in sexual relations with clients following the termination of therapy.

> A good therapy termination establishes person-to-person equality between participants. Blanket condemnations of post-therapy relationships also are founded on a belief that such relationships invariably cause harm to the former patient. I defy anyone to meet Gerry, interview her, and then maintain that any harm was done to her by me.

The issue of sexual involvement with former clients represents an unresolved ethical controversy among therapists. On the one hand, the American Psychiatric Association has no official policy which categorically bans sexual relations between a psychiatrist and a former patient; instead, there is a case-by-case analysis of such relationships conducted by an ethics committee to determine their propriety. On the other hand, some states have enacted statutes that expressly prohibit any sexual relations between psychotherapists and former clients during a specified posttherapy time period. The statutory period in Colorado is six months following the termination of therapy.

Despite this explicit restriction, some therapists in the present study still insist that their sexual relationships with former clients are neither in violation of professional standards of conduct nor in conflict with state law.

> Her psychotherapy with me was successfully concluded two months prior to her seeking a social relationship with me. She herself was unequivocal in her desire for a social relationship with me, which was entirely free from any therapeutic need or motivation. . . . I expressly clarified to her that in becoming socially involved I no longer could ever again function as her therapist. With the dual relationship problem laid aside, strictly speaking, such relationships are not unethical since no ethical rule to conduct has ever been formulated against them. . . . I hope that I have convincingly demonstrated that there is no generally accepted standard of psychological practice in . . . post-termination relationships, and so I cannot have violated the statute.

In denial of injury one seeks to neutralize the untoward behavior by redefining the activity in such a way as to reduce or negate its negative quality, such as injury, harm, or wrong. To some extent this involves structuring one's accounts to alter the dominant conceptions of what the activity is. Accounts thus sometimes go beyond the "linguistic forms" that Scott and Lyman have emphasized. Deviance reduction often involves manipulation of various symbols as basis for one's behavioral account. As seen in the preceding of injury, therapists sought to have their sexual relations with former clients redefined according to a professional code of conduct that is subject to individual interpretation. This ethical code may be seen as symbolically governing the therapist-client relationship, establishing the grounds on which the therapist may make autonomous moral judgments of his or her own behavior.

Apology

Scott and Lyman (1968, p. 59) assert that "every account is a manifestation of the underlying negotiation of identities." In a sense, it is probably more accurate to conceive of accounts as referring to desired outcomes rather than as negotiating techniques. They indicate a sought-after definition of the situation one in which the focus on the deviant act and the shame attached to the individual are lessened. For example, Goffman (1971) argues that the apology, as an account, combines an acknowledgement that one's prior actions

were morally reprehensible with a repudiation of both the behavior and the former self that engaged in such activity.

Two consequences of an accused wrongdoer's action are guilt and shame. If wrongful behavior is based on internal standards, the transgressor feels guilty; if the behavior is judged on external normative comparisons, the person experiences shame. Shame results from being viewed as one who has behaved in a discrediting manner. In the following three cases, each therapist expresses his remorse and laments his moral failure:

> I find myself in the shameful position that I never would have thought possible for me as I violated my own standards of personal and professional conduct.
> I feel very badly for what I have done, ashamed and unprofessional. I feel unworthy of working in the noble profession of counseling.

I entered into therapy and from the first session disclosed what I had done. I talked about my shame and the devastation I had created for my family and others.

Schlenker and Darby (1981) observe that the apology incorporates not only an expression of regret but also a claim of redemption. An apology permits a transgressor the opportunity to admit guilt while simultaneously seeking forgiveness in order that the offending behavior not be thought of as a representation of what the actor is really like. One therapist expresses concern for his actions and proposes a way to avoid such conduct in the future:

> I continue to feel worry and guilt about the damage that I caused. I have taken steps I felt necessary which has been to decide not to work with any client who could be very emotionally demanding, such as occurs with people who are borderline or dependent in their functioning.

This account seems to imply that one's remorse and affirmative effort to prevent future transgressions are sufficient remedies in themselves, preempting the need for others to impose additional sanctions. Self-abasement serves a dual purpose in the apology. First, it devalues the untoward behavior, thus reaffirming the moral superiority of conventional conduct. Second, it represents a form of punishment, reprimanding oneself consistent with the moral judgments of others. The message is that the actor shares the views of others, including their assessment of him or her, and both desires and deserves their acceptance. As Jones and Pittman (1982, pp. 255–56) contend,

To the extent that the threatened actor sustains his counteractive behavior or to the extent that the counteractive behavior involves effort and costly commitments, social confirmation will have the restorative power sought.

Several elements of self-management combine when an apology is offered. While confessing guilt and expressing shame, the individual directs anger at himself or herself-denouncing that act and the actor. The actor then attempts to insulate his or her identity from the stigma of the deviant act, reconfirming an allegiance to consensual values and standards of conduct. As Goffman (1971, p. 113) observes, the deviant

> . . . splits himself into two parts, the part that is guilty of an offense and the part that dissociates itself from the defect and affirms a belief in the offered rule.

In the following account, the therapist accepts responsibility for his behavior but attempts to make amends by demonstrating a desire to learn from his mistakes:

> I am firmly aware that my judgment at the time was both poor and impaired. I am also aware that my thinking was grandiose and immature. One cannot hold a position of public trust and violate community standards. I have incorporated that knowledge into my thoughts and acts.

The demonstration of shared understandings may also be seen as consistent with a desire to preserve self-respect; moreover, self-initiated or proactive response to one's own deviance may serve as a mechanism to lessen the actor's feelings of shame and embarrassment, to militate against negative affect, and to foster a more favorable image of self. Gottman (1971) calls this ritual attempt to repair a disturbed situation "remedial work." In the next account the therapist reveals his effort to repair his spoiled identity:

> I have been grieving for Betty and the pain I have caused her. I am deeply distressed by my actions and am doing everything within my power for personal and professional discipline and restoration. I have tried through reading, therapy, and talking with other men who had experienced similar situations to understand why I allowed this to happen.

Such impression-management strategies involving remedial work convey to others that the actor is "solicitous for the feelings of and sensibilities of others and . . . willing to acknowledge fault and accept or even execute judgment for the untoward act" (Lyman and Scott 1989, p. 143). Hewitt and Stokes (1975, p. 1) further note that actors "gear their words and deeds to the restoration and maintenance of situated and cherished identities." The vast majority of apologies were offered by therapists who sought restoration of self by immediately entering therapy themselves. In the following case, the therapist's realization of the emotional damage resulting from her homosexual affair with a client led to her self-commitment to a mental hospital:

> I truly had no prior awareness of my vulnerability to a homosexual relationship before she became a client. In fact, it was such an ego dystonic experience for me that I soon ended up in the hospital myself and had two years of psychotherapy.
>
> From this therapy, as well as some follow-up therapy, I have come to understand the needs which led to such behavior. I regret the negative impact it has on both of our lives.

Efforts to gain insight into their sexual transgressions appear critical to the therapists' transformation of self. By entering therapy, the individual becomes the object of the therapeutic process, whereby the "act" and the "actor" can be clinically separated. The very therapeutic context in which the initial deviance arose is now seen as the means by which the therapist can be redeemed through successful treatment. Through therapy individuals gain awareness of the causal processes involved in their deviant activity and are thus empowered to prevent such transgressions in the future. Introspective accounts convey a commitment both to understand and to change oneself. In this way, the therapist disavows his or her former discredited self and displays the new enlightened self.

DISCUSSION

The consequences of deviant activity are problematic, often depending on a "definition of the situation." When a particular definition of a specific situation emerges, even though its dominance may be only temporary, individuals must adjust their behavior and views to it. Alternative definitions of problematic situations routinely arise and are usually subject to negotiation. Thus, it is incumbent upon the accused therapist to have his or her situation defined in ways most favorable to maintaining or advancing his or her own interests. When "transformations of identity" are at stake, such efforts become especially consequential (Strauss 1962). The imputation of a deviant identity implies ramifications that can vitally affect the individual's personal and professional life. As noted earlier, the negotiation of accounts is a negotiation of identities. The account serves as an impression-management technique, or a "front," that minimizes the threat to identity (Goffman 1959). If the therapist can provide an acceptable account for his or her sexual impropriety—whether an excuse, justification, or apology—he or she increases the likelihood of restoring a cherished identity brought into question by the deviant behavior.

There is a close link between successfully conveying desired images to others and being able to incorporate them in one's own self-conceptions. When individuals offer accounts for their problematic actions, they are trying to ease their situation in two ways: by convincing others and by convincing themselves. An important function of accounts is to make one's transgressions not only intelligible to others but intelligible to oneself. Therapists sought to dispel the view that their deviation was a defining characteristic of who they really were; or, to put it another way, they attempted to negate the centrality or primacy of a deviant role imputation. The goal was to maintain or restore their own sense of personal and professional worth notwithstanding their sexual deviancy. In a way, laying claim to a favorable image in spite of aberrant behavior means voiding the apparent moral reality, that is, the deviance-laden definition of the situation that has been called to the attention of significant others (Grievance Board) by a victim-accuser (former client).

Goffman (1959, p. 251) maintains that individuals are not concerned with the issue of morality of their behavior as much as they are with the amoral issue of presenting a moral self:

> Our activity, then is largely concerned with moral matters, but as performers we do not have a moral concern with them. As performers we are merchants of morality.

The presentation of a moral self following deviance may be interpreted as an attempt by the individual to reaffirm his commitment to consensual values and goals in order to win the acceptance of others (Tedeschi and Riorden 1981). The demonstration of shared standards of conduct may also be seen as consistent with the wish to redeem oneself in the eyes of others and to preserve self-respect. The desire for self-validating approval becomes more important when circumstances threaten an individual's identity. In these instances an actor will often make self-presentations for purposes of

eliciting desired responses that will restore the perception of self by others that he or she desires. If discredited actors can offer a normal presentation of self in abnormal situation, they may be successful in having their instant deviant behavior perceived by others as atypical, thus neutralizing a deviant characterization.

Individuals seek a "common ground" in accounts of their deviant behavior, explaining their actions in conventional terms that are acceptable to a particular audience. These accounts should not be viewed as mere rationalizations. They may genuinely be believed in. While accounts do not themselves cause one's behavior, they do provide situationally specific answers about the act in question and manifest a certain style of looking at the world.

Finally, it should be noted that, as retrospective interpretations, accounts may have little to do with the motives that existed at the time the deviance occurred. In this case accounting for one's deviant behavior requires one to dissimulate, that is, to pretend to be what one is not or not to be what one is. As Goffman (1959) asserts, social behavior involves a great deal of deliberate deception in that impressions of selves must be constantly created and managed for various others. Thus, it is not logically necessary that one agree with others' moral judgments in order to employ accounts. Even where no guilt or shame is consciously felt, one may offer accounts in the hope of lessening what could be, nonetheless, accounts blur the distinctions between "appearance and reality, truth and falsity, triviality and importance, accident and essence, coincidence and cause" (Garfinkel 1956, p. 420). Accounts embody a mixture of fact and fantasy. As shown in the accounts provided by therapists, what is most problematic is determining the mixture best suited for a particular situational context.

References

Akamatsu, J. T. 1987. "Intimate Relationships with Former Clients: National Survey of Attitudes and Behavior Among Practitioners." *Professional Psychology: Research and Practice* 18:454–58.

Benetin, J., and M. Wilder. 1989. "Sexual Exploitation and Psychotherapy." *Women's Rights Law Reporter* 11:121–35.

Finkelhor, D. 1984. *Child Sexual Abuse: New Theory and Research.* New York: Free Press.

Garfinkel, H. 1956. "Conditions of Successful Degradation Ceremonies." *American Journal of Sociology* 61:420–24.

Gartell, N., J. Herman, S. Olarte, M. Feldstein, and R. Localio. 1986. "Psychiatrist-Patient Sexual Contact: Results of a National Survey. I: Prevalence." *American journal of Psychiatry* 143:1126–31.

——.1987. "Reporting Practices of Psychiatrists Who Knew of Sexual Misconduct by Colleagues." *American Journal of Orthopsychiatry* 57:287–95.

Goffman, E. 1959. *The Presentation of Self in Everyday Life.* Garden City, NY: Doubleday.

——.1963. *Stigma: Notes on the Management of Spoiled Identity.* Englewood Cliffs, NJ: Prentice-Hall.

——.1971. *Relations in Public: Microstudies of the Public Order.* New York: Basic Books.

Hewitt, J. P., and R. Stokes. 1975. "Disclaimers." *American Sociological Review* 40:1–11.

Holsti, O. R. 1969. *Content Analysis for the Social Sciences and Humanities.* Reading, MA: Addison-Wesley.

Jones, E. E., and T. S. Pittman. 1982. "Toward a Theory of Strategic Self-Presentation." Pp. 231–62 in *Psychological Perspectives on the Self,* edited by J. M. Suls. Hillsdale, NJ: Erlbaum.

Lofland, J. 1969. *Deviance and Identity.* Englewood Cliffs, NJ: Prentice-Hall.

Lyman, S. M., & M. B. Scott. 1989. *A Sociology of the Absurd* (2nd ed.). Dix Hills, NY: General Hall.

Mills, C. W. 1940. "Situated Actions and Vocabularies of Motive." *American Sociological Review* 5:904–13.

Pope, K. S., and J. Bouhoutsos. 1986. *Sexual Intimacy Between Therapists and Patients.* New You: Praeger.

Pope, K. S., P. Keith-Spiegel, and B. G. Tabachnick. 1986. "Sexual Attraction to Clients: The Human Therapist and the (Sometimes) Inhuman Training System." *American Psychologist* 41:147–58.

Ray, M. C., and R. L. Simons. 1987. "Convicted Murderers' Accounts of Their Crimes: A Study of Homicide in Small Communities." *Symbolic Interaction* 10:57–70.

Rothman, M. L., and R. P. Gandossy. 1982. "Sad Tales: The Accounts of White-Collar Defendants and the Decision to Sanction." *Pacific Sociological Review* 25: 449–73.

Schlenker, B. R., and B. W. Darby. 1981. "The Use of Apologies in Social Predicaments." *Social Psychology Quarterly* 44:271–78.

Scott, M. B., and S. M. Lyman. 1968. "Accounts." *American Sociological Review* 33:46–62.

Scully, D., and J. Marolla. 1984. "Convicted Rapists' Vocabulary of Motive: Excuses and Justifications." *Social Problems* 31:530–44.

Spencer, J. W. 1983. "Accounts, Attitudes, and Solutions: Probation Officer-Defendant Negotiations of Subjective Orientations." *Social Problems* 30:570–81.

Starosta, W. J. 1984. "Qualitative Content Analysis: A Burkean Perspective." Pp. 185–94 in *Methods for Intercultural Communication Research,* edited by W. Gudykunst and Y. Y. Kim. Beverly Hills, CA: Sage.

Strauss, A. 1962. "Transformations of Identity." Pp. 63–85 in *Human Behavior and Social Processes: An Interactional Approach,* edited by A. M. Rose. Boston: Houghton Mifflin.

Tedeschi, J. T., and C. Riorden. 1981. "Impression Management and Prosocial Behavior Following Transgression." Pp. 223–44 in *Impression Management Theory and Social Psychological Research,* edited by J. T. Tedeschi. New York: Academic Press.

9

CONSTRUCTING COERCION

The Organization of Sexual Assault

BRIAN A. MONAHAN, JOSEPH A. MAROLLA,
AND DAVID G. BROMLEY

This article is based on interviews with prisoners who committed forceful rape of women who they were not acquainted with prior to the assault. Five sequential stages of rape events are found to exist and this study explores the awareness of the offenders' interpretations of their own actions, as well as the types of interpretive meanings they provide and the different types of organization they utilize to commit the offense.

For many types of deviance, such as burglary, robbery, and homicide, there are numerous studies of how those activities are organized, and the analytic lens is focused on the organization of the activity by the perpetrator or the interaction of perpetrator and victim. By contrast, there are few comparable studies of rapists and rape situations. Of those studies that do analyze rapists and their activities, a substantial proportion consists of psychological or clinical case studies that seek to identify their personality characteristics and dynamics. Case studies often do contain descriptions of rape events, of course, but they typically foreground the personality configuration of the perpetrator and background situational characteristics. This research draws on a sample of convicted rapists to offer an interpretation of *how* rape events emerge and are organized from the perspective of the perpetrator. In this analysis, we reverse foreground and background, directing attention primarily to the situational characteristics as constructed and enacted by the perpetrator. We are analyzing here a specific type of rape and subset of rapists. These rapists are analogous to most "opportunistic" burglars and robbers in that offenders engage in minimal planning, enlist no confederates, and have little or no prior social connection to their victims (Conklin 1972; Lejeune 1977). The organization of the rapes in our sample should be distinguished from serial rapes (Burgess et al. 1988); those carried out in intimate relationships, such as marital rape (Finkelhor and Yllo 1985); and those committed in permissive subcultural contexts, such as fraternities (Sanday 1990) or prisons (Davis 1970). It is also important to emphasize that the sample consists of convicted, incarcerated rapists who have

---

Source: Constructing Coercion: The Organization of Sexual Assault by Monahan, Brian A., Joseph Morolla A., and Bromley, David G., *Journal of Contemporary Ethnography, 34* (3) June 2005, pp. 284–316. Reprinted with permission.

committed offenses that are organized coercively as opposed to the mixture of manipulation and coercion characteristic of some other types of sexual assault, such as date rape (Sanday 1996). We shall argue that rape events, like robberies and homicides, can be analyzed in terms of a sequence of analytically distinguishable phases. The overall development of the event through these phases involves a process that is both contingent and emergent. That is, each phase leads to and structures the following phase, but at the same time, the event sequence of action may be interrupted and redirected by the actions of perpetrator, victim, or third parties.

THEORY AND RESEARCH ON SEXUAL ASSAULT

We argue that rape events can be described in terms of a sequential series of phases that are analogous to those employed to describe homicide, robbery, and mugging. The five phases of the kind of rape events we describe include (1) preexisting life tensions, (2) transformation of motivation into action, (3) perpetrator-victim confrontation, (4) situation management, and (5) disengagement. The first phase, preexisting life tensions, provides context for understanding how the perceived problems in the lives of the offenders give rise to rape events, which the rapists then attempt to control and manage. The subsequent three phases describe the management and control process, and the final phase delineates how offenders attempt to exit the coercive relationship they have created.

Whereas previous conceptualizations of the stages of robberies, muggings, and homicides acknowledge the "unstable" and "fleeting" quality of the transactions involved, we emphasize this variability. We argue that within these five phases, perpetrators exhibit differential awareness of their own actions, apply divergent meanings to apparently similar actions, and engage in different degrees and types of organization. By presenting the rape event in terms of its developmental phases, we highlight the emergent order that the perpetrator seeks to create; by presenting the variability within the developmental phases, we highlight the contingent nature of the perpetrator's actions.

METHODS AND SAMPLE

The data on which this article is based were collected by Diana Scully and Joseph Marolla; findings from that study have been reported in a book and a series of articles (Marolla and Scully 1986; Scully and Marolla 1984, 1985; Scully 1990). The total sample consisted of 114 rapists incarcerated in seven Virginia prisons. Forty-six percent were white and 54 percent black; many were incarcerated for more than one crime, including 11 percent who had been convicted of first- or second-degree murder; their sentences ranged in length from ten years to seven life sentences plus 380 years.

Gaining access to a meaningful sample of rapists is inherently problematic. It is usually not feasible to become a participant observer in a high-security prison facility for an extended period as a means of identifying and interviewing specific categories of offenders. Identifying active, undetected rapists raises a host of ethical issues about protecting the identities of individuals potentially engaged in ongoing offenses. Former rapists who are identified through official records present problems of recall, given the long sentences they are likely to have served. The strategy of identifying convicted rapists within a prison population and conducting extended structured and semi-structured interviews is therefore a reasonable means of obtaining some insight into how sexual assault occurs (Athens 1974; Copes and Hochstetler 2003; Ferraro and Moe 2003). Clearly, this sample of rapists consists of those who resemble the type of rape that is most likely to be prosecuted and result in incarceration: incidents that (1) consisted of a violent attack by one or more strangers, (2) occurred in a public setting or private space through a break-in, (3) involved the use of force and/or weapons, and (4) resulted in physical injury.

The sample that constitutes the basis for this analysis draws on one of the key distinctions Scully and Marolla drew in their analysis between "admitters" and "deniers" (1985. 98). The former group (forty-seven respondents) acknowledged that they had forced sexual acts on their victims and defined the behavior as rape. Since these men admitted that they had committed rape and consented to the interview, they provided sufficient detail to reconstruct the sequence of events. The men in the latter group either denied all sexual contact or acquaintance with the victim (thirty-four respondents), typically claiming that they were not even at the scene, or admitted that they engaged in sexual acts with the victim but denied that their behavior constituted rape (thirty-three respondents), typically claiming that the sexual encounter had actually been consensual. Some of these men admitted they had engaged in sexual relations but stated that they were drunk or high at the time and could not remember what happened. Those men who denied rape either provided little detail on the sequence of events or offered limited descriptions that were simply designed to buttress their innocence claims. In addition to those who denied committing rape, cases involving admitters who declined to offer details on the rape event, multiple rapists (since the organization and dynamics of those rapes were influenced by the involvement of several perpetrators), and young child victims (who were incapable of resistance or negotiation) were not included in our analysis. Therefore, this article is based on interviews with the thirty-three admitters who acted alone and provided descriptions of the rape event in the course of the interview.

PREEXISTING LIFE TENSIONS

There is ample evidence by a number of measures that the lives of the incarcerated rapists in this sample were filled with problems and tensions. Based on survey data collected on these offenders, Scully (1990) reports that half had been abandoned by their fathers by the time they were eighteen years old, the same percentage stated that their childhoods had been characterized by instability, only 20 percent completed high school, and many had criminal records dating back to their teenage years. As adults, more than half were neither married nor cohabiting with a woman, 40 percent reported being unemployed, and 85 percent had criminal records (typically with multiple property-offense arrests).

The interviews with the thirty-three rapists in our sample support the larger sample demographic profiles. They expressed feelings of a lack of control that most often traced to their work and domestic lives in some combination. Twenty-eight of the respondents made statements that reflected these themes. For example, one rapist who reported that he was constantly "thinking about how fucked up my life was" traced his sense of futility to an unfulfilling marriage. He felt that he had been forced into marriage and as a result had forfeited an opportunity to attend college. Furthermore, he termed his marital expectations as unrealistic, a response to his own sexual inexperience and the fact that "my parents' marriage was not good, and [I] wanted this one to be perfect." These problems were exacerbated by his feeling that he had "too many responsibilities," that everyone was making decisions for him, and that he had "little control over [him]self." Another offender who raped his victim in her residence after following her there from a store described his mental state as one of extreme depression. He traced his depression to both his work and home life. He recalled, "Work pressures were overwhelming me, [I] wanted to be successful, but tension and pressure

were beyond my grasp." He also reported that he "was miserable at home" due to a poor relationship with his wife and children. Prior to the rape, he was "on a three-day leave from work" and in a terribly depressed state in which he "wanted to cry every minute" and "couldn't sleep for days." He stated that he regularly experienced periods during which he wouldn't sleep for days at a time and then would "crash for eighteen hours straight."

Twenty of the rapists reported having experienced these circumstances for an extended period of time, and another eight described equally troubling conditions that were of shorter duration. Whatever the duration, these men seemed to feel caught up in a situation that was hopeless. Their accounts suggest that they were consumed by the emotional threat posed by the onset of these feelings or the need to escape engulfment by them. A major focal concern for many offenders, then, was simply coping with daily life, and judging by the accounts they offered, their efforts had met with very mixed success.

These ongoing life tensions are more directly connected to the ensuing rapes by virtue of the fact that perpetrators were very likely to assert that their personal troubles became particularly acute in the period immediately prior to their commission of a sexual assault. One man who admitted having committed four rapes during the period of a year recalled experiencing tremendous depression for that entire year but also being more depressed and upset than usual on the nights when he committed rapes, often following conflict with a significant other. Another rapist discussed the intense sense of despair he experienced during the several days between the time he came home to find his wife in bed with another man and the point at which he raped his victim:

My parents have been married for many years, and I had high expectations about marriage. I put my wife on a pedestal. When I walked in on her, I felt like my life had been destroyed, it was just such a shock. I was bitter and angry about the fact that I hadn't done anything to my wife for cheating.

A particularly violent rapist traced his sexual violence to a misdiagnosis of venereal disease. His wife was diagnosed as having a venereal disease and accused him of contracting it through infidelities and then transmitting it to her. He reported that he became so enraged by his wife's lack of trust in him that he "wanted to break every bone in her body" and that he was "very angry, so [I] rode around and drank a lot."

The pervasive sense of futility that these offenders reported and the exacerbation of these feelings immediately prior to the rapes does not, of course, provide a direct connection to the sexual assaults that they were to later commit. However, there are several other factors that suggest why these men were good candidates to respond to the tensions they were experiencing by assaulting women—their gender attitudes, the prevalence of force as a means of control in their lives, and their acceptance of the use of force in sexual relationships (Scully 1990). While the rapists did not hold unusually conservative gender attitudes on occupational and domestic matters, they were more likely to subscribe to the "pedestal" idea, that women need male protection and should be more virtuous than men. This idea (note the explicit use of the term above by one of the rapists) oriented both their expectations of women and their conceptions of appropriate male behavior. It is instructive in this regard, for example, that about two-thirds of the rapists agreed that women caused their own rapes by their clothes and conduct. Second, these men were relatively supportive of and accustomed to force being exercised by males in families. In their reports about their child and adult family lives, about half of the offenders reported having grown up in families in which they witnessed violence against their mothers, and the same percentage admitted that as adults they had struck their partners at least once. Third, force was regarded as an appropriate means for men to control sexual relationships. In the attitude survey, more than three quarters of the men stated that a man should not give up when a woman says no to sex; 40 percent agreed that a man was justified in hitting his wife; and 45 percent said that some women like to be hit because it is a sign of caring by the male. Those men most accepting of violence were also most hostile toward women and accepting of rape stereotypes.

The rapists' accounts provide two other clues to the connection between tension in the rapists' lives and their subsequent sexual assaults. One is that seventeen of them attributed their problems to relationships with women, most frequently wives or girlfriends. As several of the preceding quotes from the rapists indicate, they frequently mentioned unfulfilling marriages, mistrust, and betrayal by their partner. Furthermore, whether the issues were domestic or occupational, the interviews with the rapists strongly suggest that they did not adopt other possible lines of action through which to address their problems directly. For example, there is little evidence that they confronted those against whom they harbored grievances (employers, coworkers, family members, or intimate partners), resolved differences with them, or searched for alternative relational partners. Unwilling or unable to confront the source of their problems, these men defined themselves as victimized and sought out alternative targets onto which to displace their aggression. As one rapist, who cited family problems as a primary source of his personal turmoil and went looking for a victim put it, "I knew I didn't want to be around my family because I knew I would hurt them if anything set me off." From their perspective, then, the assaults in which they subsequently became involved were perceived to be *defensive* in nature. The rapists generally depicted their assaults as a means of attempting to restore control in their lives. A perpetrator who described himself as out of control in every other part of his life stated that rape placed him in control, rape was "having my way." A second offender described himself as having been intimidated by women since boyhood. For him, rape constituted a way that he could feel there was someone of less worth than him. This theme was repeated by a third rapist, who also portrayed himself as bashful, timid, and intimidated by women. Rape was a means of reversing this relationship. As he put it, "In rape, I was totally in command, she [was] totally submissive."

The preexisting life tension phase summarizes what was usually an extended time period during which the individual who ultimately became a rapist experienced a variety of personally troubling events. These men were good candidates to become rapists, given their attitudes toward women and violence and their tendency to connect personal troubles to women. However, the mere presence of these factors did not make sexual assault inevitable. Perpetrators reported specific incidents that increased their sense of personal futility and anger and heightened their motivation to engage in sexual assault. However, these rapists did not confront what they deemed the source of their troubles but rather sought redress for their grievances by displacing their aggression onto surrogates.

TRANSFORMATION OF MOTIVATION INTO ACTION

The combination of personal tensions, violent proclivities, misogynous attitudes, and perceived victimization among this group of rapists created a predisposition toward a violent solution in which women were the targets. During this phase, the situation moved from one in which the perpetrator was emotionally agitated to one in which he determined what kind of action to undertake, selected a specific victim, and concluded that circumstances were safe enough to proceed. The interview data suggested three paths from motivation to action. Nine of the rapists indicated that they were determined to rape from the outset, nineteen reported that the transition from motivation to action had been mediated by the situation (giving assistance to a woman in four cases, participation in social encounters in three cases, and commission of another crime in seven cases) and was therefore indirect, and five stated that they had consciously suppressed their feelings only to find that those feelings had reemerged. There was similar variation in perpetrators' selection of victims. Most offenders chose victims simply because they were available, some others sought out surrogate attributes, and still others looked for what they deemed desirable physical characteristics. Finally, perpetrators varied in how much attention they paid to their personal security.

Several offenders reported that their turbulent emotions translated immediately into a decision to commit rape. An offender who admitted to raping five females during a period of one year reported that his "intent always was to rape" and that "when I left the house each time I wanted to rape and went out to find the right victim." He further added that "I had a 'Dracula attitude'—going out to get blood, to violate a female." Other perpetrators knew that they wanted to "act out" but were unsure of what they would do. A man whose girlfriend became pregnant stated that he had a fight with her mother immediately prior to the assault and that "[I was] predetermined to go out and get in trouble—to blow off aggression, but didn't know what I was going to do." Uncertainty sometimes persisted until the very moment when confrontation with the rape victim ensued, with rapists deciding to engage in sexual assault when they failed to achieve satisfaction over another grievance. In one incident, the offender reported that he was in the midst of severe financial hardship and went to the eventual victim's house to collect some money owed to him by the victim's husband. On being informed that the husband was not present and that the money the offender sought was unlikely to be forthcoming, the perpetrator became enraged, assaulting and then raping the victim. He asserted, "I did it to get even with her husband and her" and that he had decided he was going to "get it one way or another."

Another group of perpetrators reported that the rape event emerged within a context in which it was unexpected to the offender himself. These perpetrators typically were engaged either in mundane social encounters (such as providing assistance of some kind to the victim or participating in a social occasion) when something occurred in the situation that triggered their hostile feelings or in an illegal activity (such as burglary or robbery) that presented an opportunity for rape. In one case, a rapist offered assistance to a woman whose car had broken down. When he was unable to repair the car, he offered the victim a ride

home. He then decided he wanted to have sex with her. When she refused his advances, he raped her. Another incident involved a man helping a sixty-year-old female acquaintance move a table into her house. He reported that he suddenly began hitting her and then sexually assaulted her. He was unable to offer any explanation for his behavior except "I just did it." Rapes attending robbery and burglary were not uncommon. Several rapists reported burglarizing residences and then committing rape when they discovered a woman present in the house. The impulsive nature of many of these rapes is illustrated by a robber who was going to make payment to a bail bondsman to whom he owed money. He decided instead to rob the bail bondsman; spotting an attractive woman in the office while engaged in the robbery, he decided to rape her as well.

Perpetrators typically described victim suitability in terms of one of three characteristics: simple physical presence (fourteen), surrogate attributes (nine), or manifestation of characteristics the perpetrator deemed desirable (five). In some cases where the perpetrator had determined to proceed with a sexual assault, the mere presence of the victim in the vicinity was sufficient. One offender, who reported that he had been in a fight with a family member and went out to "blow off aggression," stated that he chose his victim simply because "she was just there, could have been anybody. I picked her because she was just there." It was not her personal characteristics; as he put it, "She was plain, healthy, and not too attractive." Another rapist echoed that same theme, stating, "It was someone I didn't know and it just happened. . . . She was in the wrong place at the wrong time. She was just the first person available." Finally, a perpetrator who had gone to a store late at night for cigarettes and who had thought about rape earlier in the evening selected a victim simply because she had driven down the street at the moment he was walking toward the store.

The search for surrogates to represent the actual object of the perpetrators' grievance sometimes led to the targeting of virtually any woman and at other times involved more specific characteristics. For example, a rapist who felt that his girlfriend had violated his "plans and trust in her" when she began having relations with other men upon moving away to college reported that he saw his victims and all females as representing this girlfriend. He admitted that during the rapes, "I was hating Sally [the girlfriend] and hating them [victims] because they probably messed men over." He went on to say that at the time he was "hating all females because they were deceitful" and that rape was his way of "getting revenge for what happened to me." Another rapist selected a victim because she resembled a woman who had previously, and he contended falsely, accused him of rape. It was more common for the perpetrator to seek out some kind of physical resemblance with the woman against whom the perpetrator felt a grievance, such as race, height, weight, or physique.

Finally, some perpetrators sought out females simply because they possessed physical characteristics the offenders found attractive. In such cases, the desired characteristics appear to have been those that the offender looked for in conventional and consensual relationships with females. Several offenders reported that the primary criteria employed when selecting a victim was that she met or exceeded what they described as their subjective standard for sexual attractiveness. One repeat offender indicated that "I choose attractive females, not just anybody." Another perpetrator described sizing up his victim as she left a store and was walking home. He thought about raping her only after seeing her and finding her attractive. He characterized her as "cute, 5' 3," a little chunky, blonde, no bra, and sexually appealing." Had she been older or less attractive, he reported, he would not have proceeded with the rape. For those offenders who did seek out surrogate or attractiveness characteristics, the search process involved rejecting potential victims that perpetrators simply seeking any woman would assault. An offender who committed five rapes during a one-year period reported that he would walk around and look into windows at various residences until he came upon a white woman in her forties (because he regarded mature women as more sexually experienced).

The other factor that determined how the rape event proceeded was the perpetrator's degree of concern for his personal security. A number of offenders who were in a rage or inebriated when they committed rape and selected the first available woman obviously took few precautions to protect themselves. For example, a perpetrator who initially intended to commit robbery abducted the victim at noon in front of a supermarket. A particularly candid offender who was discussing precautions stated, "Yes, I knew what I was doing, [I] just said the hell with the consequences." Not surprising, offenders who intended rape from the outset were much more likely to establish and verify the suitability of the circumstances first, and then wait for the necessary victim to emerge within that context. One repeat offender reported very specific techniques for raping, which he referred to as his "pattern." The "pattern was to check out the area, see if any dark spots, people around, dogs around before doing the rape." For him, victim characteristics were a secondary

concern. As he noted, when he entered his pattern, he "hadn't seen her yet and couldn't tell what she looked like when I picked her." Another offender chose his victims because they lived in an apartment complex that had minimal security and buildings that allowed him to identify victims easily. He recalled that "all of the victims had their blinds wide open, windows open, and it allowed me to see them." Furthermore, the victims were "always in bed, asleep in a ground-level unit." Indeed, he recalled, "I kept going back because it [the apartment complex] was an easy target" and "a child could do the same thing." One important implication, of course, is that many of these rapists intended to commit rapes on a number of other occasions but did not find the type of victim and/or situation they were seeking or observed a number of women before selecting a victim. There was therefore considerable indeterminacy in both the occurrence of particular rape events and selection of specific victims.

The phase in which perpetrators transformed their motivation into action was characterized by significant differences in how they were going to act out their intentions. While some perpetrators immediately initiated a rape and assaulted the first woman available, for others the decision to engage in rape was contingent on unfolding events and identifying victims with specific characteristics. Most of the offenders, then, were not fully cognizant of their own intentions at the beginning of the rape process: intervening events shaped the direction that their actions would take. The indeterminacy of the situation for a number of rapists was significant, as they were soon going to confront and then have to manage a victim to complete the rape. There was a similar indeterminacy in who would become a victim as some victims were chosen at random, others on the basis of surrogate characteristics, and still others for their physical attractiveness. The apparently uniform victim selection process actually thus was quite diverse, with perpetrators selecting victims as a product of anger, revenge, or attraction. Whichever choice the perpetrator made, of course, his intention was to use sexual coercion to redress the perceived violation of his identity. Finally, there was variance in the precautions offenders took to ensure their security. The combination of concern about the type of victim and the degree of security also produced temporal variability: some perpetrators invested considerable time in identifying a particular kind of victim and setting while others responded more viscerally. These differences were significant in the next phase as perpetrators who had more carefully selected victims and settings more readily gained control of the rape situation.

PERPETRATOR-VICTIM CONFRONTATION

Confrontation occurs once the perpetrator has identified a victim, concluded that an opportunity for action exists, and has directly encountered the victim. The perpetrator now becomes involved in interaction as opposed to purely personal reactions to troubling events in his life. Confronting the victim categorically changes the perpetrator's social situation because he is now committing assault, even if he terminates the encounter and does not carry out the rape. The situation is also dramatically altered for the victim, who finds her safety and well-being suddenly and unexpectedly threatened. Having crossed a significant normative boundary, the perpetrator's immediate problem becomes gaining control of the victim. As Katz (1988, 176) puts it, the offender seeks to "dramatize with unarguable clarity that the situation has been suddenly and irreversibly transformed." Perpetrators established control through the overt or implied use of force, and victims responded by capitulating, attempting to negotiate, or physically resisting. Victim resistance created a clear challenge to perpetrator control and was met with a rapid and often dramatic escalation of violence by the perpetrator.

The overt use of force involved assaulting the victim to the point where she was immobilized by some combination of injury and fear (Felson 1996). Techniques of overt force included brandishing a weapon in a threatening manner, beating the victim so as to cause injury beyond that involved in the rape itself, and using a weapon to injure the victim. For example, one offender reported, "I grabbed her and hit her a couple of times to get her to cooperate." Another offender abducted his victim at knifepoint and forced her into the car and then onto the floor. He held her down and slapped her across the face, leaving bruises on her forehead. In extreme cases, the perpetrator launched a savage assault on the victim. One rapist approached a woman sunbathing on a roof and told her he was going to have sex with her. When she tried to get him to take money and leave her alone, he grabbed her by the neck. During the rape, she resisted by punching him in the face. He then drew a knife and stabbed her at least fifty times before fleeing and leaving her there to die.

Perpetrators who relied on the implied use of force most often combined verbal persuasion with the display of a weapon or overwhelming physical superiority. These offenders typically contended that they did not physically harm their victims or use or brandish their weapon in a threatening manner. However, they also acknowledged that they made certain that the weapon was plainly visible. One offender who initially hoped to gain consensual sex began by fondling the victim who resisted his advances. He then "ignored her no's" and used his superior size to forcefully let her know he was going to have sex with her. He ordered her to put a blanket on the floor and then raped her. Another offender admitted that he showed his victim the weapon in his possession in a way that "suggested what would happen." A third rapist reported that he simply removed the fishing knife he was carrying from his belt and laid it on the ground, making sure that the victim saw it.

Overt and implied force strategies are not mutually exclusive, of course. In some cases, rapists employed combination or sequential strategies. A perpetrator who had given his victim a ride when she experienced automotive problems gained compliance with his demands through verbal threats of physical assault and through the disparity between his physical stature and hers. After gaining the desired capitulation, he reported that "I told her what to do, how to do it, and she did it." In another case, the offender gained entrance to the victim's residence by posing as a repairman and claimed that he hoped to obtain sex consensually. However, he stated that "I realized I was getting nowhere, so I grabbed her kitchen knife and put it to her throat. . . . I put the knife to her throat and told her to cooperate and she wouldn't be hurt."

From the victims' standpoint, the sudden, unexpected confrontation left them with little opportunity to formulate a resistance strategy. Some victims capitulated rapidly to the rapist's initial commands, but in a number of cases, the victim sought to exchange compliance for safety. Several perpetrators reported that their victims offered cooperation to avoid additional injury by saying "please don't hurt me. I'll do anything you want." By the perpetrators' accounts, at least, verbal or physical resistance by the victim usually occurred early in the confrontation phase, and rapes in which the perpetrator employed an implied force strategy obviously offered victims somewhat greater latitude for resistance. Victims who sought to negotiate with perpetrators usually made moral or self-interest appeals. Another offender who characterized his victim as "very unwilling" stated that she sought to convince him that sex should be consensual by asserting "no, you don't want it this way." Again, combination and sequential strategies were not uncommon. For example, one perpetrator reported that his victim kept trying to talk him out of carrying out the rape by referring to the implications of rape for his own family. He reported that "she [repeatedly] asked me to think about my sister and mother." When that appeal failed, the victim attempted to dissuade the offender by appealing to his self-interest, telling him that she was infected with a venereal disease.

Physical resistance was much more likely than verbal resistance to result in the perpetrator's escalating the level of violence to reassert control of the situation. A perpetrator who raped his victim in his apartment following a night of drinking in a bar reports that his victim attempted to prevent the rape by hitting him, sending him into a rage. He stated, "[I] got mad and hit her back with my fist as hard as I would hit a man." On encountering resistance, another rapist recalled, "[I] called her a bitch and then started to beat her. I hit her over the head with a vase and beat her with a vacuum cleaner." In some instances, physical resistance produced an outburst of uncontrolled rage. One perpetrator reported. "[I] punched her, choked her, loosened some teeth, bruises, and cuts over her eyes . . . beat her half to death, but someone came in and I left, or I might have killed her."

If the immediately prior phase in the rape process involved the transformation of motivation into action, this phase moved from action to interaction. Perpetrators for the first time had to engage the victim directly. Their actions were almost exclusively directed at gaining physical control of victims at this juncture. The major source of variability was whether force was overt or implied, but the message to victims was clear in either case. However, the situation now became more complex as perpetrators had to deal with both appeals from victims and their own anger, particularly when victims physically resisted their control. Ironically perhaps, at the very moment that rapists were focused on controlling the victim, offender self-control presented itself as an issue. This problem continued during the next phase, indicating the limited awareness perpetrators had of their own emotions and the extent to which the rape process was emergent for them as well as for their victims.

SITUATION MANAGEMENT

Once the victim's resistance had been overcome and dominance had been established, the rapist's problem became one of managing the coercive situation he had created. Managing the rape situation was considerably more complex than simply subduing the victim and compelling her to engage in sexual acts. The focus of activity for these rapists during the situation management phase was twofold: first, gaining control of their own emotions as well as the emotions and behavior of the victims, and second, developing a management strategy, domination or negotiation, through which to maintain control during the rape.

Achieving physical control of the victim did not end the process of maintaining control of the rape situation. Since these perpetrators typically initiated their assaults while in a state of emotional turmoil and engaged in very little prior planning, many appear to have been unprepared for their own reactions to the actions that they had initiated. Indeed, a recurrent theme in perpetrators' descriptions of the rape situation was the difficulty that they faced not only in controlling the victim but in maintaining self-control. One-third of the perpetrators openly acknowledged that they themselves were unnerved at the outset of the rape. It is not surprising that offenders were anxious because they knew unexpected events could occur. For example, an offender admitted to being extremely fearful upon entering his victims' residence because he "didn't know if a man would be there," while another acknowledged that "there was a time after I got into the house that 1 was fearful because I didn't know what to expect." One rapist reported just such an unanticipated event. After breaking into an apartment, the man first discovered a baby, which he moved to another room; a second woman then appeared and he raped her as well.

Even after dealing with predictable nervousness, a number of rapists struggled with self-control. As one offender put it, "[I was] not really in control, totally confused and frightened. I didn't take any clothes off. [I was] too scared" and "I kept questioning myself during the act." Another perpetrator reported feeling an intense inner conflict. As he put it, "Part [of me] wanted to stop and part [of me] wanted to go ahead" and then "I didn't really feel in control. . . . It was a fragile control. If anything had gone wrong, I would've run. . . . I felt a sense of control and dominance, although very loose control." This insecurity was echoed by another offender who stated, "If [she] had resisted aggressively, I probably would've taken off." Another said, "If she had screamed, I would have run." In some cases, this internal conflict produced a feeling that they were at war with themselves. As one perpetrator described those sensations, "I didn't feel in total control, it was like something was driving me to do it" and "it just seemed like things were happening and I couldn't control them." Several offenders described these feelings of lack of control in dissociative terms; one likened the rape to a dreamlike state and expressed frustration over the fact that he "couldn't get hold of it" while another stated that raping his victim was "like watching myself on TV do it."

Interestingly, a calming influence for these rapists was the capitulation of the victim. The fact that they had at least temporarily subdued the victim gave them confidence, frequently amid self-doubt. As one offender conveyed this feeling of empowerment, "Seeing her laying there helpless gave me confidence I could do it." Another perpetrator gained composure from the fact that the victim was calmer than he was. He commented that "I was nervous too and because she was relaxed, I was relaxed." However, a sense of control was rarely found so quickly but rather proved elusive to acquire and difficult to maintain throughout the duration of the rape event. The primary means through which perpetrators sustained control was by moving in the direction of situation management either by domination or negotiation.

The rapes were relatively evenly divided between those in which domination and negotiation were the primary means of control. Thirteen perpetrators relied primarily on domination, varying from coercive restraint to brutalization. These men simply overrode any doubt they had, recognizing that it could be their undoing. One offender indicated that the time for doubt had passed, making comments such as "Once I got into the rape, I didn't think about precautions, only before the rape"; "Once I entered the house and had female alone, I never hesitated or I would get caught"; and "I had made up my mind that this [rape] was what I was going to do." For those eleven cases that did not simply involve a brutal, physical assault on the victim, both the perpetrator and victim had an interest in "normalizing" the coercive situation so that it took on the appearance of consensual sex (initiating conversation, trying to please the victim sexually, establishing a rudimentary relationship), albeit for different reasons. Many perpetrators were experiencing a mixture of strong emotions—the turbulence that triggered their resort to rape in the first place, the anxiety associated with the initial confrontation, and the feelings of confusion and conflict about proceeding with the rape. Any behavior by the victim that perpetrators could take as evidence of victim desire served to diminish perpetrators' feelings of guilt and ambivalence. Perpetrators could believe at least to some extent that they were not forcing and victims were not resisting. From the victim's perspective, creating the appearance of a normal relationship might reduce the likelihood of injury and increase the probability the rapist would believe the victim would not later report the rape. The result was that both perpetrator and victim attempted to manage the other, and clearly rapists in some cases allowed themselves in the moment to believe that the relationship was not completely coercive.

In many instances, normalizing the situation merely involved nominal assurances that the victim would not be harmed if she cooperated. One offender stated, "I made an attempt to convey to her that I wouldn't hurt her," while a second tried to "explain to her that I was an everyday person and she needn't be afraid." Some perpetrators clearly allowed themselves to interpret victim compliance as implied consent, a conclusion that might well be attributable to their views on gender and sexuality. Several rapists stated this in remarkably similar ways, such as "[it] felt like she didn't seem to care because she didn't really resist" and "[I] felt like lack of fighting meant that she wanted it."

A number of perpetrators went well beyond simply making perfunctory assurances, however, by constructing a rudimentary personal relationship. In one incident, a perpetrator reported that upon grabbing the victim and dragging her into some bushes for concealment, he proceeded to talk to her before the rape about his family and other personal matters. Another perpetrator recalled that he and his victim were engaging in normal conversation during the rape event: "She didn't seem to care at the time. We carried on a normal conversation" about the victim's child and other issues. Still another rapist contended that conversation with his victim helped to reduce the tension and fear of the event and even served to create what he perceived to be a bond between the two. He stated that there "might have been a bit of feeling for her" and that they talked for awhile "about her divorce, her children." The inauthenticity of the relationship is revealed, however, in the perpetrator's acknowledgment that he lied about most matters pertaining to himself. While conversation was the most common mode of normalizing the encounter, seeking to please the victim sexually was another technique. A perpetrator reported that "I treated her as if it was normal, I tried to get her as high as me. . . . I was trying to please her. . . . We did it like normal sex, with foreplay."

At the same time, of course, victims were trying to manage the situation, and sometimes these efforts apparently were successful to some degree. In one case, the perpetrator said that the victim "made comments like I was the best she ever had, fantastic" and that he believed her at the time, although he later concluded she made such remarks out of fear. A rapist who had committed several rapes admitted that he would always ask his victims, "Does it feel good? Want more?" enabling himself to believe that the victims were enjoying the sexual acts. And "when they said 'good,' I believed it, even though I know it was crazy to do so."

As perpetrators entered the situation management phase, they had gained physical control of their victims, and now the problem became sustaining that control. Even after dealing with predictable initial nervousness, many of these rapists reported strong, unanticipated emotional reactions, such as inner conflict, lack of control, fright, and confusion. Perpetrators sought to stabilize and manage the volatile situation through either domination, simply suppressing these reactions by plunging ahead, or negotiation, trying to create a working agreement with the victim to normalize the situation. Both solutions created momentary order and control but also produced additional problems. Domination made it more difficult for perpetrators to preserve their initial perception of themselves as victims. Negotiating with the victim created a situation in which a number of these men deluded themselves into thinking the situation was partially voluntary, which of course meant that they were not so clearly perpetrators. Both domination and negotiation had important implications for the disengagement process. Rapists who opted to employ domination typically did not harbor illusions of a relationship with the victim that might deter her from reporting the incident to the police, and negotiation clouded the perpetrator's judgment about the veracity of any victim assurances to him.

Disengagement

Once the rape had been completed, perpetrators faced the problem of disengaging from the situation. Given that most of these rapes were precipitated by turbulent emotions and involved negligible planning, it is not surprising that the perpetrators had given little consideration to sealing actions that would protect them against future apprehension. Disengagement therefore most often assumed the appearance of a disorganized retreat; fifteen of the offenders reported lacking any real plan and simply fled the scene. By contrast, three perpetrators seemed unable to cope with the implications of what they had just done and simply waited with resignation for apprehension by the police. Where perpetrators did develop a disengagement plan to assure themselves the victim would not seek their arrest, their strategies assumed dramatically different forms: murder (three cases) or bargaining (seven cases). Whichever choice they made, these rapists faced the continuing prospect of arrest. The most common responses of the rapists was either to immediately resume their prior lives, both to normalize the situation for themselves and to arouse less suspicion, or to leave the community to avoid arrest.

The most common form of disengagement for these perpetrators was simply leaving the rape scene without doing much more than admonishing the victim not to move until they had departed or eliminating any evidence that would bring attention to themselves. As one rapist put it, his primary objective was simply "to get away and make sure I wasn't caught.... I knew I did something wrong." Another said he warned his victim not to scream before pulling the bed covers over her head and leaving. A third offender recalled that he "didn't say much, put [my] pants on and walked out the bedroom door." Finally, a man who committed a particularly brutal rape of a tenant in the apartment complex in which he was employed stated

> [I] looked at all the blood and ran down nineteen flights of stairs, went to the employee restroom, washed [the] blood off, put [the] jacket in bag, put [the] keys up and then left the building and took the bus home.

There were also cases in which the perpetrators did not regard their sexual assaults as a major reason for concern. For example, some believed victim assertions that they enjoyed the sex and would not report them to police while others regarded the burglaries they committed concurrently as the really serious crime for which they would be sought by police. These beliefs sometimes contributed to their minimal efforts to protect their identities.

By contrast, some rapists did not even leave the rape scene but simply waited for the police to arrive and apprehend them. In one instance, a man brutally assaulted and raped a woman in his home following an evening of drinking in a local bar. The victim managed to escape when the offender left the room to wash her blood from his hands. When the offender realized that the victim had escaped, he made no effort to conceal evidence or to leave the location. He recalled,

> After she left, I just sat there on the couch and felt drained. I was scared because I didn't know what I had done or what would happen.... I don't know why I didn't run, I had a car but just sat there until police came.

In another incident, a rapist who committed a particularly brutal and violent rape stated that he was scared and that his immediate concern at the time of exit was to wash the victim's blood off of his clothes and person. However, he took no further evasive action but simply "got plastered that night in my apartment and didn't think about leaving." The offender who raped and murdered multiple females during the period of one year claimed that he would experience a sense of disbelief about what he had done and then "go home, take a shower, try to eat, go to sleep, and escape into subconsciousness."

Those rapists who did try to engage in sealing actions had to somehow prevent the victim from alerting the police and identifying them. Confronted with this situation, a few perpetrators chose to murder their victims. One offender described how he tied his victim with rope and left her while he went back to his vehicle to wipe away fingerprints and remove evidence. Upon returning, he killed her and then disposed of her body in a nearby river. In this sample, murder was rarely chosen as a sealing action because rapists who contemplated homicide found that their own lack of planning or their own sensibilities deterred them from this course of action. Indicative of the relatively unplanned nature of these rapes, one rapist who was carrying a gun but no bullets reported that "if I'd had bullets, I would have shot and killed her." He went on to comment that murder would have been best for him because he would then have been able to hide the body and leave town. Yet other rapists came to the brink of murdering their victims only to encounter their own aversion to murder. One respondent described how he had "debated what he had gotten himself into and what I should do." Regarding killing his victim, he said, "Under the circumstances, it was normal to think about murder"; however, in the end he did not feel like he could "take a life" and he reported that he was proud of himself for not doing it.

Among those who engaged in sealing actions, it was more common for perpetrators to try to extricate from impending arrest by reducing the victim's motivation to report the rape to police. Perpetrators most often tried to apologize and seek forgiveness for their actions. One offender stated that he told his victim he was "sorry about what happened" and that he "offered her [money] to call the police" because he was upset with himself for inflicting physical injury upon her. Another reported that he dropped his victim off behind a tree and gave her cigarettes and beer and said he was sorry. The rapist who assaulted and raped his victim in response to his wife's infidelity recalled that "I apologized to her and started to cry." At least at that moment these offenders hoped that their apologies would suffice. As one offender stated, "I had illusions that I wouldn't [be arrested], that she wouldn't tell anyone because I didn't hurt her and I apologized for five minutes after it was over."

Most perpetrators who left the scene of the rape tended to return home or to the residence of a family member or significant other. Ten of the respondents reported that they were confident that their sealing actions were sufficient to protect them. These offenders were likely to immediately delve back into their routine by returning to daily work or recreational routines. An offender who committed several rapes said that after

exiting the rape event he "would go to work the next day like nothing had happened." Another offender reported feeling as though "I got what I wanted and had to get on with my business." He further insisted that the victim was of no concern to him and that he went directly from the rape event to pick up his girlfriend. However, none of the disengagement strategies employed by these rapists offered any real assurance that they would be able to evade identification and apprehension. Therefore, upon reflection, those offenders who were less confident that they took the measures necessary for adequate closure of the rape event chose further evasion. For example, one offender reported that he left the victim's house and went to work, and then started thinking about the rape and decided to leave town. He reported that he went into hiding for three months before deciding to surrender to authorities. Another perpetrator, who also left town, reported that he knew he was being pursued by the police and several months later was apprehended after he committed a minor traffic offense.

Accounts provided by perpetrators of the disengagement process offer compelling evidence that, as in the prior phases of the rape process, the majority of these men had neither a plan of action nor full control of their own emotions and actions. Despite the gravity of the situation, most of the rapists engaged in little organized effort to conceal their actions and identity: they either left the scene with but minimal effort to cover their escape or emotionally collapsed and fatalistically awaited apprehension. A number of perpetrators contemplated murder but then found they could not deal with the prospect of becoming murderers. Others emotionally broke down and apologized to their victims, a desperate strategy whether or not their emotions were authentic. Simply resuming normal life constituted another form of denial of their situation. A few perpetrators obviously continued to consider their vulnerability and days or weeks later decided to move to another community, a tactic that only delayed their arrest. By virtue of fully appreciating the implications of their actions only after the fact, this group of rapists virtually insured their ultimate apprehension.

DISCUSSION

In contrast to the extensive research literatures on homicide, robbery, and burglary, there is very little research on how perpetrators organize sexual assault. In this article, we have employed data from interviews with incarcerated rapists to develop an analogous developmental model for rape. At the most basic level, we have argued that rape events are socially patterned and not the idiosyncratic acts of mentally disordered individuals. We have described rape events as consisting of five analytically distinct phases: (1) preexisting life tensions, (2) transformation of motivation into action, (3) perpetrator-victim confrontation, (4) situation management, and (5) disengagement. This sequence of activity is comparable to those reported for both interpersonal and property offenses.

The perpetrators report lives pervaded with a sense of futility and emotional turmoil. They attribute their life problems mainly to domestic and occupational issues in which women are implicated directly or indirectly. In some cases, the perpetrators harbored grievances against particular women or women in general. In other cases, the rapists' personal backgrounds and attitudes (histories of force being exercised in their family lives, regarding force as an acceptable means of controlling sexual relationships, believing that women interpreted use of physical force as caring) rendered them likely candidates for coercively controlling women. In either event, the perpetrators reported that they engaged in sexual assault as a means of restoring a sense of control and self-respect in their own lives. However, in contrast to the homicidal violence described by Luckenbill and Katz, the rapists did not confront the immediate source of their grievance but rather displaced the violence on to a woman with whom they had little or no relationship. Once they transformed their motivations into action, the rapists focused on gaining control of the victim, managing the situation, and disengagement. One of the most intriguing findings concerning the perpetrators' orchestration of the rape event was that a number of offenders attempted to negotiate a quasi-voluntaristic relationship with the victim. Perpetrators were thus able to deny the full extent of the violence in which they were engaged, and victims apparently took advantage of the opportunity to minimize the violence that would be inflicted upon them. During the course of the rape event, their control of their own actions clearly was compromised by the emotional instability they continued to exhibit, which in part traced back to the perceived grievances that precipitated their actions, as well as the ingestion of drugs/alcohol.

It is important, however, not to allow the analytic template to reify rape event organization. The five developmental phases incorporate considerable variability in the perpetrators' alternative means of handling the issues that presented themselves. This variability manifested itself in issues such as victim selection, security concerns, means of gaining control of the victim and managing the situation, and disengagement strategies. More significant, one of the most striking findings was the emergent and contingent quality of rape events. While the various choices that

perpetrators made moved them along through the event phases, this was not an inevitable progression. For example, numerous perpetrators reported looking for specific types of victims or situations that might or might not have presented themselves, simply coming upon the victim or situation by chance, or being in one situation (a social event or a burglary) that the offender suddenly came to perceive as a potential rape opportunity. It is evident from the perpetrator accounts that, whether or not they had decided on rape from the outset, the events had an emergent quality for them. Most engaged in minimal planning and usually had little knowledge of the victim or the situational circumstances. In many cases, they did not know what they were going to do next and did not anticipate their own emotional reactions to the situation they were creating. Perpetrators clearly did not comprehend the full meaning of their actions until they were fully engaged in the situation or sometimes until after they had disengaged from the situation.

The cases reported on here have at least three implications for a more general understanding of rape. First, our data on the preexisting life tensions of offenders strongly reaffirm the connection between patriarchal orientations, in this case interpreted as a male right to sexual access, and sexual assault. Our data leave little doubt that the offenders' lives were in serious disarray on a number of dimensions. However, there were numerous possible alternative lines of action available that perpetrators could have pursued in addressing their personal troubles. These men attributed their problems to women, chose violence instead of other possible resolutions, engaged in sexual as opposed to other forms of violence, displaced their aggression onto women with whom they had no significant relationship, and tended to regard their assaults as appropriate responses to attacks on their identity. Clearly, the element of sexual dominance and control is exhibited in these cases.

Second, there is the issue of power versus sexual motivation in rape. The accounts provided by these rapists suggest both power and sexual motivations, and perhaps complex combinations of the two. Perpetrators most often described their initial motivations in terms of regaining a sense of personal control, asserting appropriate relationships, or simple revenge. These accounts suggest power motivations. However, some rapists specifically sought out women who were sexually attractive to them, some attempted to sexually arouse their victims or negotiate a pseudo-consensual relationship, and some asked victims whether they had been sexually satisfied. These behaviors suggest the presence of a sexual component in rape events. To put the matter another way, some men sought power through sexuality and others sought sexuality through power, but the two themes are linked in complex fashion. Further, we are not proposing a resolution of the power and sexual motivation issue because we are dealing with a very specific type of sexual assault, one that contrasts sharply with the organization of date rape or marital rape. We would be inclined to argue that the mixture of power and sexuality varies by type of rape and there is not a single motivational source.

Third, with respect to resistance/capitulation, and particularly recent discussions about women carrying weapons for self-defense, our data suggest that the implications of resistance to sexual coercion are difficult to predict. On one hand, a number of rapists reported becoming more violent when victims challenged their control. Since their actions were precipitated by feelings of absence of control in their lives and they were typically emotionally agitated at the time they initiated the assaults, there is a basis for arguing that resistance may increase violence. On the other hand, a number of the perpetrators reported seeking out victims who appeared vulnerable, and one of the most striking findings was the self-doubt and tenuous sense of control that these rapists reported, at least initially. Indeed, rapists commonly reported they were ambivalent about their actions. They were only marginally in control and then only because they perceived the victim to be calm or passive. Many rapists claimed that had they encountered resistance, they would have fled the scene. These observations suggest that at least in some cases, rapists who encountered immediate resistance in the form of screaming, fighting, or brandishing a weapon would have reduced the likelihood of a completed rape. Since the interviews were not constructed to address either of these issues, we cannot offer additional insight with confidence. It is also important to note that our respondents actually carried out sexual assaults. Other men who were deterred by early resistance would not appear in our sample. Data on attempted assaults would be critical to the resolution of the resistance/capitulation issue.

Finally, it is important to affirm that the present research findings represent only an initial statement on the social organization of sexual assault. We have reported on cases in which the perpetrators completed rapes but were apprehended and incarcerated and in which the rapists were the exclusive source of data. The utility of the analytic framework presented here should be tested with cases in which accounts from both perpetrator and victim are available. This analytic framework would also benefit from the incorporation of cases of undetected rapes; perpetrators in those cases might have employed tactics that were not utilized by the incarcerated rapists we studied. Correspondingly, it

would be valuable to include cases of unsuccessful rape attempts to gain additional perspective on tactics women used to avoid victimization. And, of course, ultimately it will be necessary to compare the types of cases we have analyzed with date, marital, prison, gang, fraternity, wartime, and other types of rape. A fuller theoretical statement on the social organization of sexual assault therefore awaits the interpretive context that will be created by such research.

REFERENCES

Athens, Lonnie H. 1974. The self and the violent criminal act. *Urban Life and Culture* 3:98–112.

Burgess, Ann, Robert Hazelwood, Frances Rokous, Carol Hartman, and Allen Burgess. 1988. Serial rapists and their victims: reenactment and repetition. *Annals of the New York Academy of Sciences* 528:277–95.

Conklin, John. 1972. *Robbery and the criminal justice system.* Philadelphia: Lippincott.

Copes, Heith, and Andy Hochstetler. 2003. Situational construction of masculinity among male street thieves. *Journal of Contemporary Ethnography* 32:279–304.

Davis, Alan. 1970. Sexual assaults in the Philadelphia prison system. In *The sexual scene,* edited by John Gagnon and William Simon, 107–24. Chicago: Aldine.

Felson, Richard. 1996. Big people hit little people: Sex differences in physical power and interpersonal violence. *Criminology* 34:433–52.

Ferraro, Kathleen, and Angela Moe. 2003. Mothering, crime, and incarceration. *Journal of Contemporary Ethnography* 32:9–40.

Finkelhor, David, and Kersti Yllo. 1985. *License to rape: Sexual abuse of wives.* New York: Holt, Rinchart, and Winston.

———. 1991. The motivation of the persistent robber. *Crime and Justice* 14:277–306.

Katz, Jack. 1988. *Seductions of crime.* New York: Basic Books.

Lejeune, Robert. 1977. The management of mugging. *Urban Life* 6:123–48.

Luckenbill, David. 1977. Criminal homicide as a situated transaction. *Social Problems* 25:176–86.

Marolla, Joseph, and Diana Scully. 1986. Attitudes toward women, violence, and rape: A comparison of convicted rapists and other felons. *Deviant Behavior* 7:337–55.

Sanday, Peggy. *Fraternity gang rape: Sex, brotherhood, and privilege on campus.* New York City: New York University Press, 1990.

Sanday, Peggy. *A woman scorned: Acquaintance rape on trial.* Garden City, NY: Doubleday, 1996.

Scully, Diana. 1990. *Understanding sexual violence.* Boston: Unwin Hyman.

Scully, Diana, and Joseph Marolla. 1984. Convicted rapists' vocabulary of motives: Excuses and justifications. *Social Problems* 31:530–44.

———. 1985. Riding the bull at Gilley's: Convicted rapists describe the rewards of rape. *Social Problems* 32:251–63.

PART IV

GANGS AND CRIME

The existence of gangs historically is not a new phenomenon, but it was not until the late 1980s and 1990s that youth street gangs began to grow in number and sustain themselves in urban America by their involvement in drug trafficking and sales, together with the publicized violence and use of weapons that fueled a national public outcry. For many urban youth from economically deprived neighborhoods, gang membership became a refuge from a violent and stressful home life, chaotic neighborhoods, other gang members, and a lack of social outlets. Gang membership provided a sense of belonging, another type of family that was accepting of marginalized and impoverished adolescents. Gangs do engage in various types of criminal behavior, as the articles in this section will illustrate. However, the gang offers a haven for the multiple problems that inner city youth face in their communities. Besides the monetary gains some gang members experience from membership, they also experience social ones in the way of peer acceptance and family-like unity.

Pete Simi, Lowell Smith, and Ann M. S. Reeser portray another type of gang that differs in many respects from Stretesky and Pogrebin's inner-city minority gangs. Here we explore a Southern California-based racist skinhead gang known as Public Enemy Number One. Although white-supremacist type gangs are not as well known to the public as ethnic and racial gangs are, due to media coverage of the violence and drug distribution, nevertheless the authors illustrate just who these gang members are and how their organization operates for profit-oriented criminal activities.

In their study of urban street gangs, Stretesky and Pogrebin explore how gangs promote violence and gun use. The socialization process that shapes a gang member's identity and sense of self is discussed within the context of gang membership. Imprisoned gang members were interviewed, who were convicted for committing a crime that involved the use of a firearm. Their retrospective stories about gang socialization and their willingness to put their lives on the line for their gang are indicative of the importance the gang plays in shaping their identity.

In their analysis of young woman gang members who become mothers while active in gang activities, Moloney, Hunt, Joe-Laidler and MacKenzie examine the experiences of 65 females who transition to motherhood while attempting to negotiate their identities as both gang members and mothers. Being a parent and gang member is a difficult task for many of these young women to reconcile. These two distinct role identities are analyzed and challenge the dominant stereotypical image of these young women as unfit parents. The researchers further reveal how becoming a mother and gang member influences their life trajectories.

10

FROM PUNK KIDS TO PUBLIC ENEMY NUMBER ONE

PETE SIMI, LOWELL SMITH, AND ANN M. S. REESER

This study examines the historical development of a racist skinhead gang located in Southern California. The gang, known as Public Enemy Number One, perceive themselves to be a racist skinhead gang without very much interest in any form of racist-political movement, which other skinhead gangs participate in. Their purpose is economic-oriented gain through illegal means by way of drug distribution, counterfeiting, and identity theft. A focus on the reconciliation of street gang activity and racist behavior is explored.

INTRODUCTION

On July 17, 2002, two members of Public Enemy Number One (PEN1), a racist skinhead gang based in Southern California, walked into the Orange County Jail in Santa Ana, CA, and posted bail for one of their "brothers" with a $500,000 counterfeit check. Law enforcement officials reported that this scam was a first in Orange County history (McDonald 2002). The escapee and the individuals who posted the counterfeit bail were later apprehended and the beneficiary of the jailbreak is now serving a life sentence for attempted murder (Anti-Defamation League [ADL] 2007). The attempted murder was related to PEN1's decision to "discipline" an associate who was suspected of giving information about the gang to local police in Orange County, CA. Three PEN1 members attacked the victim, repeatedly stabbing him in the chest, arms, and abdomen. The

victim survived the attack and although he initially refused to identify the perpetrators, he later said that he was shocked that one of the attackers had been a close friend and god-father to his child (McDonald 2002).

A string of brutally violent incidents committed by members of PEN1 have propelled them from relative obscurity into the spotlight. PEN1 has recently been the subject of numerous journalistic accounts depicting their volatile mix of white supremacy and criminal sophistication. Journalists have also focused on PEN1's rising membership and ruthless violence, yet the details of their emergence and development are less clear. Some journalists have mistakenly attributed their origins to the California prison system (Kemp 2005). Other reports have difficulty accurately characterizing PEN1's ability to balance a white supremacist ideology and profit-oriented criminal specialties. Drawing on participant observation, interviews, and secondary data analysis, we use a case study approach to examine PEN1, whose membership, which numbers between 300 and 500, makes it one of the single largest skinhead gangs in the United States. Although PEN1 shares the white supremacist philosophy that typically characterizes racist skinheads, their primary activities revolve around profit-oriented crime.

This article focuses on PEN1's organizational development. The first section examines the gang's initial formation while the second section discusses their transition from a relatively small youth clique that coalesced around style, music, and fraternal relations to a criminal enterprise with a presence on the streets as well as the prison yard. In both sections we emphasize the tensions that exist among members of PEN1 about how to balance their commitment to racial politics with their involvement in profit-oriented crime and the variation in attitudes among other racist skinheads about PEN1's criminal activity and drug use.

Conceptualizing Skinheads

We define a gang as an age-graded peer group that exhibits some permanence and establishes a sense of boundaries through gang-identified territory, style, and oppositional practices such as fighting or other criminal activity (Decker and Van Winkle 1996; Klein 1995; Short and Strodtbeck 1974). We argue that regardless of whether the street, youth, or criminal dimension is emphasized, skinhead groups meet each of these criteria commonly used to define gangs and thus fall within this conceptual rubric.

The tendency to view skinheads as distinct from other gangs is related to the dominant characterization that describes them as "neo-Nazi youth" primarily involved in bias-motivated political violence. For example, in one article the authors claim, "The majority of Skinheads across the country are racist, neo-Nazi whites who feel threatened by Jews, non-whites, and homosexuals . . ." (Landre et al. 1997, as quoted in Etter 1999:18), while another observer argues, "Skinhead crimes are usually violent and chosen for their political or racial impact rather than for profit motive . . ." (Etter 1999:19). Although these statements accurately describe a portion of racist skinheads, they ignore racist skinhead gangs who possess a white supremacist orientation and are also simultaneously organized around profit-oriented criminal activity. Unlike some white power revolutionary "cells" (e.g., the Silent Brotherhood, the Aryan Republican Army) that have engaged in profit-oriented criminal activity in order to

generate funds for a "racial revolution" (Flynn and Gerhardt 1995; Hamm 2002), there is currently no evidence that suggests PEN1 is using profits from their criminal activities to fund political endeavors. Rather than portraying skinheads as solely focused on political violence and activism, we propose that there is great diversity existing among racist skinheads and that PEN1 illustrates some of these differences. As the interview data obtained from PEN1 members clearly show, these skinheads see themselves as part of a white supremacist street gang. Their street gang orientation, however, has not prevented members of PEN1 from maintaining a white supremacist ideology. Instead, members strive to balance criminal operations that necessitate pragmatic decision making with a white supremacist political ideology that is rigidly idealistic.

The Emergence of Skinheads

Beginning in the rapidly deteriorating neighborhoods of London's East End (Moore 1994), skinheads were initially characterized as an attempt to "magically retrieve the sense of community that the parent working-class culture had lost" (Clarke 1976:99). Early British skinheads were directly tied to specific neighborhoods (much like many African-American and Hispanic gangs in the United States), class-conscious, and embraced traditional notions of masculinity. Although they did not explicitly associate themselves with Nazism, they were ardently nationalist in political orientation and fervently opposed to foreign immigration (Hebdige1979; Knight 1982). The first skinheads attended the poorest schools, lived in disorganized neighborhoods, and their employment prospects were primarily limited to low-wage jobs (Brake 1974: 188–190). Although skinheads defined themselves along themes of nationalism, ultra-masculinity, and working-class issues (e.g., lack of economic opportunity, poor housing, and neighborhood deterioration), they expressed political sentiments through stylistic imagery (Hebdige 1979). Toward this end, skinheads were described as creating a gross caricature of the working-class, "the look of the cartoonist lumpenworker" (Frith 1981:219).

By the mid-1970s, the number of skinheads had decreased but by the late 1970s, skinheads re-emerged and during this time some skinheads became associated with the extreme right's National Front (NF) and the British National Party (BNP) and spread beyond Britain emerging in several other European countries as well as North America (Knight 1982).

DATA AND METHODS

Tracing the history of PEN1 is difficult and required that we rely on a diverse array of data sources. Our analysis is grounded primarily on the 127 primary interviews we conducted with a variety of racist skinheads in Southern California and law enforcement officers between 1999 and 2006. We also interviewed "non-skinhead" racist leaders (e.g., Tom Metzger and Richard Butler) who were among the first to promote the importance of the skinheads to the larger white supremacist movement. We selected interview subjects through snowball and purposive sampling strategies, which enabled us to access a wide range of networks and groups among skinheads. The sample included 43 active or previously active skinheads in 17 different skinhead gangs; however, in this article we focus on data specific to the PEN1 gang. Of the 43 skinhead interviewees, 9 were members of PEN1 although we also asked skinheads affiliated with other gangs questions about PEN1. Most of our interviewees were male, which is not surprising as the skinhead subculture is a predominantly male one (Blee 2002). In terms of social class, no clear patterns existed among the skinheads we interviewed. This is also not surprising considering the cross-section of social classes represented in the larger skin-head subculture (Anderson 1987; Hamm 1993). We also conducted interviews with gang specialists in law enforcement who have experience investigating skinhead gangs.

We conducted archival research, including the analysis of watchdog organizations' official reports, newspaper accounts, and court documents. We analyzed secondary sources for evidence that would either corroborate or contradict insights about skinheads gleaned through primary interview data. Our multimethod approach allowed for triangulation across an array of data (Denzin 1978). Although the data is rich, it is not perfect. We encountered methodological difficulties, mainly related to skinheads' preference for secrecy and illegal activity. Clearly this obstacle prevented us from gathering certain types of data (e.g., gang rosters) and some skinheads were unwilling to participate.

THE EARLY DAYS: THE HISTORY OF PEN1

The origins of PEN1 lie at the margins of Southern California youth culture. By the mid-1980s, skinhead gangs were forming across the region. Many of these skinhead gangs in the Los Angeles area were directly influenced by the growing hardcore punk style (Blush 2001; Ruddick 1994; Simi 2006; Spitz and Mullen 2001; Wood 1999).

> By the 1980s a lot of the nonwhite gangs were really starting to push into Orange County and we wanted to put a stop to that shit, when my parents first moved to Santa Ana it was a nice white suburb and look at it now.... So yeah, we were like a defense mechanism against all these fuckin' gangs and we thought we [whites] should have a gang too so that we could protect ourselves and our neighborhoods ... (Lonnie, PEN1, September 3, 2001)

Despite such encouragement, PEN1 remained insular and primarily focused on local issues (e.g., conflict with local punk gangs and other street gangs, petty theft). PEN1 also developed antagonistic and conflictual relationships with other racist skinhead gangs as well as punk gangs like the LADS and the Suicidals. Trevor, an early member of PEN1, explains these conflicts between PEN1 and other skinheads:

> Yeah but back then we [PEN1] used to fuckin war [fight] with all kinds of people. I never understood when I would go out with those guys we would come across another set of skinheads and we would probably start fighting. Everybody was always battling each other. It's kind of good to see now that a lot of that shit got dropped. If anybody is fighting now it's a personal thing ... (Trevor, PEN1, May 14, 2001).

TRANSITIONAL PERIOD

In this section we describe how PEN1 transitioned from a small clique with a defensive orientation that was primarily involved in local turf conflicts with other gangs to a relatively large gang with an increasingly centralized leadership structure and involvement in sophisticated organized criminal activity. The story of PEN1's change in organizational emphasis is primarily connected to the experience of incarceration and their members' "openness" to drug use and street crime.

The Experience of Incarceration

By the late 1980s the moral panic surrounding racist skinheads in the United States was gaining momentum and law enforcement agencies were increasingly aware of the need to investigate and suppress skinhead activities in order to disband these gangs. Law enforcement efforts led to increasing numbers of skinheads arrested for a wide variety of offenses. Surveillance and arrests forced some skinheads to curtail their activities. The officers we interviewed described a growing awareness among Southern California police departments about skinhead gangs in the late 1980s. For example, one officer claimed:

> It took us a while to get a hold on things, but by 87, 88 and on we really cracked down on 'em. We weren't gonna let them get by with anything and when they staged an event, we were there and we busted people for anything we legally could. Didn't matter if it was violent or not, we picked people up on PVs [Parole/Probation Violations], suspended licenses didn't matter. If there were a bunch walking around down-town, we stopped 'em ... found out who they were running with that kind of stuff ... (Law Enforcement, January 29, 1999)

During the late-1980s some skinheads, like PEN1's leader, Popeye, were repeatedly arrested for various criminal offenses including drug charges, burglary, and strong-arm robbery (Simi 2003). PEN1's history of illegal activity resulted in an increasing number of members being incarcerated. Law enforcement interviews and analysis of court records reveal that many of PEN1's core members have relatively extensive criminal histories. Eventually the members of PEN1 who were incarcerated helped facilitate a hybridization of their organizational form and criminal activities, which is a finding that other researchers studying Latino and African-American gangs have also noted (Fleisher and Decker 2001; Fagan 1996; Hunt et al. 1993).

Once incarcerated, PEN1 members began forging new organizational ties with the Aryan Brotherhood (AB), the most powerful white prison gang in the United States. The AB's origins date back to a collective of white inmates in the California prison system known as the Blue Birds who were active in California's San Quentin State Prison in the 1960s (Fleisher and Decker 2001). The AB viewed whites as superior to blacks and displayed racial pride through symbolic gestures like tattoos of shamrocks, swastikas, and "Aryan battle warriors" (e.g., Thor). As the AB began gaining greater power, the California Department of Corrections (CDC) moved confirmed members to secure housing units (SHUs). Once the AB was segregated from the general population, they began to recognize the need for white inmates to serve as "middlemen" to continue running their criminal operations. As more skinhead gang members were being sent to prison, the AB leadership realized they were a good resource. Mutual interest in white supremacy increased the likelihood that the AB would consider skinheads as suitable partners. In a recent indictment, the Los Angeles County District Attorney explains the AB's search for assistants as a means "to maintain control over the Caucasian prison population, the Brotherhood needed to give authority and power to another group that had the accessibility and mobility to continue committing crimes in prison" (quoted in ADL 2001:1).

During the 1990s the AB expanded its inmate workforce by aligning with PEN1. As this alliance developed, PEN1's organizational strength increased and their membership continued to grow. The AB selected PEN1, in part, because the gang has traditionally maintained a small and relatively cohesive leadership and PEN1's street origins prevent them from being classified as a prison gang, thereby minimizing the level of confinement available to prison officials (Simi 2003).

The relationship that emerged between PEN1 and the AB is explained by the social contact that resulted from the incarceration of PEN1 members. Incarceration created opportunities for PEN1 to network with an older and more criminally sophisticated gang, which, in turn, helped them to evolve from unorganized petty crime to coordinated criminal activity. Incarceration also helped transform PEN1 into a "hybrid" gang with a presence in prison as well as the streets. In this respect, PEN1's connection to a long-standing prison gang reflects larger changes occurring among American gangs. In the past, street and prison gangs typically were unconnected but in recent decades this has begun to shift as rates of incarceration have skyrocketed helping produce a massive underground prison economy that generates millions of dollars in profits for those who are able to control these markets (Fagan 1996; Hagedorn 1998; Ralph et al. 1996; Spergel 1995).

Openness to Drug Use

Traditionally, skinheads have often held an anti-drug stance, not withstanding their notoriously large amounts of alcohol consumption (Hamm 1993). Although some skinhead gangs, especially the most politically oriented ones, have been vehement about their anti-drug stance, others, like PEN1, have been ambivalent about the use of methamphetamine and heroin. Some skinheads even claim that the use of methamphetamine is part of the larger Nazi tradition they belong to and are seeking to maintain. Our data reveal the symbolic connection to German Nazis through methamphetamine was rarely discussed among members of PEN1 and appears to have little direct relevance to participants. What seems far more important is "getting high" and finding illicit means to purchase even more drugs (e.g., theft, drug distribution, fraud). Of the nine PEN1 members we interviewed eight indicated current or past use of methamphetamine and four admitted past use of heroin. Law enforcement data suggests that methamphetamine use and/or distribution is relatively common among PEN1 members as evidenced, in part, by probation and parole searches that result in methamphetamine seizures.

Although PEN1's involvement in the distribution of methamphetamine was extended after developing ties with the AB, members used this drug before they became connected to the AB. The use and small-scale distribution of methamphetamine that characterized PEN1's early formation has gradually evolved into a more central role in the methamphetamine trade. This shift parallels some other gangs' increasing involvement in drug selling (Fagan 1996; Padilla 1992; Taylor 1990). PEN1's involvement in the meth trade has also helped them develop links to motorcycle gangs (e.g., the Vagos and Hells Angels) who are responsible for a significant proportion of the manufacturing of methamphetamine (Quinn 2001; Quinn and Koch 2003; Spergel 1995). PEN1, however, has not limited their criminal activity to drugs. In recent years, PEN1 has become increasingly involved in relatively sophisticated "white-collar" crimes such as identity theft, the creation of false documents, and even counterfeiting (ADL 2007). PEN1 commits home invasions, mail theft, and relies on girlfriends' employment (e.g., banks, mortgage companies, collection agencies) to gain access to financial information. Since 2004 members of PEN1 have been under investigation for their involvement in an alleged money laundering scam involving a bail bond company and a multi-million dollar money trail that stretches from Southern California to the Palestinian territories, Jordan, and Israel (Reza 2004). PEN1 has also conducted business (trading methamphetamine for guns) with minority gangs in Southern California. While PEN1 maintains a racist identity and a "whites only" membership policy, engaging in profit-oriented crime with minority gangs certainly seems to blur the line between what is acceptable and unacceptable behavior regarding their racist ideology.

Merging a Criminal and Skinhead Identity

In fact, the most difficult aspect of PEN1 to describe is their racial beliefs. PEN1 illustrates the capacity for certain gangs to simultaneously remain committed to both ideological principles associated with hardcore racism and profit-oriented criminal activity. PEN1 members embraced racism when they initially formed the gang, but they simply choose not to participate in political activism. Nonetheless, they often experienced an indirect effect of skinhead politicization, and although they did not meet with Metzger or other adult white supremacists, they still encountered the literature these organizations produced and distributed.

In 1999, PEN1 went through a series of discussions regarding whether they should move away from their white supremacist philosophy and open up their ranks to "nonwhites." Others wanted to move in the opposite direction and not only maintain their racist ideology, but embrace a more political stance and scale back their criminal operations. According to several of PEN1's core members, two factions co-exist within the organization; those who seek a greater political emphasis and would like to reform PEN1's criminality and those who want to continue with their profit-oriented criminal emphasis. This seeming contradiction is not completely unprecedented, as other white supremacist gangs in Southern California have also balanced a racist orientation with a willingness to maintain multiracial relations (Simi 2003).

PEN1's current ability to maintain criminal and social relationships with minorities while simultaneously maintaining relationships with traditional white supremacists is steeped in their origins as a white supremacist street gang as opposed to a political movement. During the late-1980s as some skinheads gravitated toward political activism and forged relationships with white supremacist groups like White Aryan Resistance and Ku Klux Klan, PEN1 intensified their commitment to delinquency and crime. PEN1 members began to strengthen their identity as "gangsters" and embraced a traditional criminal orientation (Katz 1988). Although PEN1 remained racist in a territorial and localized way, they did not organize their activities to promote broad social change based on racism. They shared racism and in some cases they talked politics with more political gangs, but there was a political line that they refused to cross and a political identity they refused to embrace. PEN1 created a narrative of difference with political skinheads resting on the notion that they were "nothing but a gang."

> Yeah we used to hang with WAR Skins and we'd talk to them about politics and stuff but we didn't want any part of all that leafleting and rallies and shit . . . we were a street gang and that's how we viewed ourselves . . . we banded together to protect each other and we did our fighting in the streets . . . we just never were interested in reading about all this political stuff . . . (Greg, PEN1, March 26, 2002)

We [PEN1] were a group of fucken white boys that formed together to protect each other, gang style. It wasn't nothing fucken political at all. Some of the members might have been more political . . . but generally we were only interested in being gangsters. (Travis, PEN1, February 21, 2003)

PEN1 embraced a gangster identity that included partying, fighting for fightings' sake, and protecting each other. Their activities were locally oriented and emphasized protecting their gang.

We mainly just hung out and someone would say, "So and so is playing at this fucking club. We should go." It was just like kind of go stir up some shit and unfortunately it seemed it started to evolve in a criminal element. (Shorty, PEN1, August 19, 2002)

Their peers who became political also referred to them as gangs: "It's a gang and they [PEN1] don't make any bones about that and they don't excuse that fact you know that they're a gang" (Seth, WAR Skin, June 12, 2001). Similarly, Shorty talked about PEN1's turn to criminal activities, which he described in the following way: "It's unfortunate. PEN1 has really never been a stand up political true skinhead-type clique. Kind of like a bunch of bros that hung out. We all looked out for each other" (Shorty, PEN1, August 19, 2002). They justified their lack of activism as a result of either laziness, the desire for fun, or simply wanting to be "brothers" who supported each other. PEN1 desired the immediate gratification street crime offered as opposed to political activism, which they saw as requiring significant commitment with little material incentive and less exciting than other forms of nonpolitical rebellion (see Katz 1988 regarding the seductions of crime).

To tell you the truth the politics was too much work and those guys weren't having nearly as much fun as we were, I mean we were a bunch of young fuck-ups . . . usually we just partied, we fought a lot and you know some other things but most of the time we were just crashed out . . . (Trevor, PEN1, July 21, 2002)

Fuck yeah we're a gang and we don't make no bones about it, we not trying to say we're something we're not. We kick ass when we need to and don't let any other gang fuck with us . . . that's just the way we've always been . . . (Vance, PEN1, September 2, 2001)

During the 1980s the Southern California skinhead scene's strongest emphasis involved race-based politics

(Simi 2003); however, in the 1990s, as gangs like PEN1 gained strength, an emphasis on profit-oriented crime became more prominent. Part of this shifting emphasis included a cross-over in membership as skinheads from WAR and other smaller political cliques joined PEN1. Yet, the increasing emphasis on economically oriented criminal activity has not been without its detractors among other skinheads in the scene. Not only have some factions within PEN1 emerged that discourage their criminal emphasis, some members of skinhead gangs outside of PEN1 claim that "real skinheads" do not commit non-political criminal activity. These skinheads will sometimes refer to criminally oriented skinheads as "scumbags" or "white trash" or offer statements such as: "blacks can't help it, it's part of their genes, but these guys know better and they do it anyway" (Jake, American Front, January 15, 2002). The criticism of criminally oriented skinheads is further illustrated by another skinhead who argues that drug use represents a racial characteristic not suited for members of the "white race":

Skinhead is not about using drugs. There is no justification for it. Look at the heroes of our race and movement; Adolph Hitler, Rudolf Hess, Bob Mathews, George Lincoln Rockwell, Ian Stuart. These men dedicated and gave their lives for our movement and race and none of them needed drugs to fight for our cause. Why would any self-respecting white man or woman disgrace themselves, our race, our movement, and the memory of these great men by soiling themselves with drugs? (Nathan, WAR Skin, July 28, 1999)

Another skinhead sees these trends as reflecting poorly on the entire skinhead scene:

Over the past year or two it's kind of been inundated with drug use and gang mentality. This unfortunately gives the Southern California skinhead movement a bad name around the world. There are a lot of good skinheads in Southern California . . . (Seth, WAR Skin, November 17, 2000)

Yet PEN1's organizational discipline and ruthless violence leads some political activists to consider them an asset to the racial movement. For example, although Tom Metzger (founder of White Aryan Resistance) preaches the necessity of maintaining racial purity and strict standards of conduct (e.g., no drugs), he sees the possibility of strategically using criminally oriented skinhead gangs to the advantage of the white supremacy movement. For example,

The NLR and the others, I think there is probably a bridge in some cases political and criminal. Mostly because we need money to operate. Like the left wing they use drugs to get money and of course some of the right wing have done that too. Some of these racist gangs have non-white Mexicans and stuff in there, that don't work with us, they can cause confusion and upset the system, that's fine. Making a strong link with a mixed up group. . . . I think the means justify the end; if it works, it's ok with me. If you feel your race is in that big of danger than there would be nothing you probably wouldn't do to save it. There are guys out there that are both racial and criminal I think probably they will become leaders some day because it's going to be, I mean the shits really going to get bad, it's going to get mean and it's going to take some people that are ruthless, I don't think I'm ruthless. I never had to be but there is a new breed coming on. Who knows, it's amazing how things start to evolve. (Tom Metzger, June 17, 1999)

And sometimes the same individual simultaneously holds contradictory views related to these differing subcultural emphases. For instance, Nathan, a skinhead who stated that "true skinheads" do not engage in drug-taking and other criminal activity, on another occasion, wagered that there might be room for different types of skinhead organizations and that in fact, these differences might be useful:

they [PEN1] got their way of doing things, I don't personally agree with all of it but a lot of those guys are good guys you know they back each other up and if one 'em goes down they all go down . . . sure there's scum out there that call themselves skinheads, but I do think it's possible for us to work together, maybe some of these guys will be good on the frontline [of the race war], we're gonna need as many as we can get . . . (WAR Skin, November 15, 2002)

Conclusion

Since the beginning PEN1 has maintained, in differing degrees, three organizational emphases: (1) social-stylistic, which includes an emphasis on fighting, camaraderie, and the punk music scene; (2) economic, which includes an emphasis on profit-oriented crime; and (3) political, which includes an emphasis on expressing support for and participating in white power activism. During the early days the social emphasis was most prominent but by the mid-1990s the economic orientation had become dominant.

Although the political emphasis has never been dominant, it has always been present in some fashion. This reflects the diversity that exists within many gangs despite the folk lore that tends to characterize them as monolithic groups.

The conflicts surrounding drugs and crime illustrate the deep cleavages within the racist skinhead scene. Yet, in the face of these seemingly insurmountable differences, racist skinheads find ways to bridge these divisions. Some of these efforts are "band-aids" to heal sore points among individual skinheads, whereas others are large-scale strategies designed to "squash" conflict and strengthen organizational alliances.

Although the popular conception of skinhead gangs associates them with bias-motivated violent attacks, skinhead violence and crime in general varies depending on organizational context. Skinhead gangs are not completely homogenous; there are co-existing emphases that move in different directions. Although PEN1 may operate for profit, they are also united around a white supremacist ideology. PEN1's economic emphasis is not automatic, but must be struggled for. Participants successful in pushing PEN1 in one direction may find that detractors are able to conjure support and resources needed to push the organization in another direction. PEN1's organizational emphases result from these struggles and should be viewed as accomplishments that necessitate nurturing and reinforcement.

In turn, PEN1 illustrates how race and racial conflict can be both a source of gang formation, providing a defense mechanism against "racial enemies," as well as a means for achieving unexpected alliances that help facilitate the development of new interests. PEN1 emerged as a social gang forming around shared interests in hardcore punk music and white racism; over time PEN1 developed into a criminal gang emphasizing drug use and distribution while still retaining a white supremacist orientation. These changes coincided with PEN1's greater willingness to interact with "racial enemies" for the sake of business. PEN1 may foreshadow a larger trend among skinhead gangs that parallels outlaw motorcycle gangs (OMGs) (Quinn and Koch 2003) in that these groups provide a context for individuals with high levels of criminal motivation to unite long enough to operate enterprises of relatively high criminal sophistication. PEN1's organizational development corresponds with Padilla's (1992) description of the "Diamonds," a Puerto Rican gang in Chicago, who evolved from a street-corner group with primary interests in partying and music to a fighting gang that was also involved in profit-oriented crime. The links between racist skinhead gangs like PEN1 and the AB and OMGs resemble the ties that other gangs (especially Asian ones) sometimes develop with adult organized crime groups (Chin 1995, 1990).

PEN1 illustrates there is significant diversity among racist skinheads. Some people characterize racist skinheads as primarily political and use terms like "neo-Nazi," which helps perpetuate perceptions of fascist "stormtroopers" working for the "white revolution." This ignores the existence of profit-oriented racist skinhead gangs, and the distinction between racism and adopting a neo-Nazi political program. The latter refers to the process of politicization, which for skinheads includes a racist identity, but also includes ties to and participation in criminal and non-criminal political activism. Currently, PEN1 maintains a racist identity, but is not politicized. If, however, subcultural development tells us anything, it tells us that this could change relatively quickly. This dynamic characteristic poses serious concerns for law enforcement who should be leery of pigeon-holing PEN1 as either a white supremacist group or a criminal street gang. PEN1 is both and although their combination of these is likely to continue privileging crime for the sake of profit, it would be a mistake to assume that PEN1 will not begin to venture into more politicized criminal activity such as further money laundering and other profit-oriented crime that may help fund terrorist groups and/or activities. Understanding these changes is an important piece of improving theories of gangs and suggests the importance of creating models that are able to account for their dynamic quality and how gangs change over time.

REFERENCES

Anderson, Erik. 1987. *Skinheads: From Britain to San Francisco Via Punk Rock.* M.A. thesis, Washington State University, WA.

Anti-Defamation League (ADL). 1995. *Annual Report.* New York: Anti-Defamation League.

———. 2001. *Racist Groups in U.S. Prisons.* New York: Anti-Defamation League.

———. 2002. *Dangerous Convictions: An Introduction to Extremist Activities in Prison.* New York: Gorowitz Institute.

———. 2007. *Public Enemy Number 1 (PEN1): California's Growing Racist Gang.* New York: ADL.

Blee, Kathleen M. 2002. *Inside Organized Racism: Women in the Hate Movement.* Berkeley: University of California Press.

Blush, Steven. 2001. *American Hardcore: A Tribal History.* Los Angeles, CA: Feral House.

Brake, Michael. 1974. "The Skinheads: An English Working Class Subculture." *Youth and Society* 6:179–199.

———. 1985. *Comparative Youth Culture: The Sociology of Youth Cultures and Youth Subcultures in America, Britain, and Canada.* London: Routledge.

Chin, Ko-lin. 1990. *Chinese Subculture and Criminality: Non-traditional Crime Groups in America.* Westport, CT: Greenwood.

———. 1995. *Chinatown Gangs.* New York: Oxford University Press.

Clarke, John. 1976. "The Skinheads and the Magical Recovery of Community." Pp. 99–102. In *Resistance Through Rituals,* edited by Stuart Hall and Tony Jefferson. London: Hutchinson.

Decker, Scott and Barrik Van Winkle. 1996. *Life in the Gang: Family, Friends and Violence.* Cambridge, UK: Cambridge University Press.

Denzin, Norman K. 1978. *The Research Act: A Theoretical Introduction to Sociological Methods.* New York: McGraw-Hill Book Company.

Etter, Greg. 1999. "Skinheads: Manifestations of the Warrior Culture of the New Urban Tribes." *Journal of Gang Research* 6:9–21.

Fagan, Jeffrey. 1989. "The Social Organization of Drug Use and Drug Dealing Among Urban Gangs." *Criminology* 27:633–670.

———. 1996. "Gangs, Drugs, and Neighborhood Change." Pp. 39–74. In *Gangs in America,* edited by Ronald Huff. Thousand Oaks, CA: Sage Publications.

Fleisher, Mark S. and Scott H. Decker. 2001. "An Overview of the Challenge of Prison Gangs." Pp. 157–168. In *Understanding Contemporary Gangs in America: An Interdisciplinary Approach,* edited by R. D. Petersen. Upper Saddle River, NJ: Prentice Hall.

Flynn, Kevin and Gary Gerhardt. 1995. *The Silent Brotherhood.* New York: Signet.

Frith, Simon. 1981. *Youth, Leisure, and the Politics of Rock 'N' Roll.* New York: Pantheon Books.

Hagedorn, John. 1988. *People and Folks: Gangs, Crime, and the Underclass in a Rustbelt City.* Lakeview Press: Chicago, IL.

———. 1998. "Gang Violence in the Postindustrial Era." *Crime and Justice* 24:365–419.

Hamm, Mark S. 1993. *American Skinheads: The Criminology and Control of Hate Crime.* Westport, CT: Praeger Publishers.

———. 2002. *In Bad Company: America's Terrorist Underground.* Boston, MA: Northeastern University Press.

Hebdige, Dick. 1979. *Subculture, the Meaning of Style.* London: Methuen.

Hunt, Geoffrey, Stephanie Riegel, Tomas Morales, and Dan Waldorf. 1993. "Changes in Prison Culture: Prison Gangs and the Case of the Pepsi Generation." Pp. 175–184. In *In Their Own Words: Criminals on Crime,* edited by P. Cromwell. Los Angeles, CA: Roxbury Publishing Company.

Katz, Jack. 1988. *Seductions of Crime.* New York: Basic Books.

Kemp, Ross. 2005. "Gangs in America: Orange County." London: Suncoast Broadcasting Company.

Klein, Malcolm. 1995. *The American Street Gang: Its Nature, Prevalence, and Control.* New York: Oxford University Press.

Knight, Nick. 1982. *Skinhead.* London: Omnibus Press.

McDonald, John. August 20, 2002. "Counterfeit Checks Used to Spring Skinhead," p. 3. In *The Orange County Register.*

Moore, David. 1994. *Lads in Action: Social Process in an Urban Youth Subculture.* Brookfield, VT: Ashgate Publishing Company.

——. 1991. *Going Down to the Barrio: Homeboys and Homegirls in Change.* Philadelphia, PA: Temple University Press.

Padilla, Felix. 1992. *The Gang as an American Enterprise.* New Brunswick, NJ: Rutgers University Press.

Quinn, James. 2001. "Angels, Outlaws, and Pagans: The Evolution of Organized Crime Among the Big Four 1% Motorcycle Clubs." *Deviant Behavior: An Interdisciplinary Journal* 22:379–399.

Quinn, James F. and Shane Koch. 2003. "The Nature of Criminality Within One-Percent Motorcycle Clubs." *Deviant Behavior: An Interdisciplinary Journal* 24:281–305.

Ralph, Paige, Robert Hunter, James W. Marquart, Steven J. Cuvelier, and Dorothy Merianos. 1996. "Exploring the Differences Between Gang and Nongang Prisoners." Pp. 123–136. In *Gangs in America,* edited by Ronald Huff. Thousand Oaks, CA: Sage Publications.

Reza, H. G. "Bail Agency Tied to Racist Gangs, Officials Believe." *Los Angeles Times,* October 11, 2004.

Ruddick, Susan M. 1994. *Young and Homeless in Hollywood: Mapping Social Identities.* London: Routledge.

Short, James and Fred Strodtbeck. 1965/1974. *Group Process and Gang Delinquency.* 2nd ed. Chicago, IL: University of Chicago Press.

Simi, Pete. 2006. "Hate Groups or Street Gangs? The Emergence of Racist Skinheads." Pp. 145–159. In *Studying Youth Gangs,* edited by James Short Jr. and Lorine Hughes. Walnut Creek, CA: AltaMira Press.

——. 2003. "Rage in the City of Angels: The Historical Development of the Skinhead Subculture in Los Angeles." Ph.D. dissertation, Department of Sociology, University of Nevada-Las Vegas.

Spergel, Irving. 1995. *The Youth Gang Problem: A Community Approach.* Oxford: Oxford University Press.

Spitz, Marc and Brendan Mullen. 2001. *We Got the Neutron Bomb: The Untold Story of LA Punk.* New York: Three Rivers Press.

Taylor, Carl. 1990. *Dangerous Society.* East Lansing: Michigan State University Press.

Wood, Robert. 1999. "The Indigenous, Nonracist Origins of the American Skinhead Subculture." *Youth and Society* 31(2): 131–151.

11

GANG-RELATED GUN VIOLENCE

Socialization, Identity, and Self

PAUL B. STRETESKY AND MARK R. POGREBIN

The purpose of this research is to examine socialization as the mechanism between street gang membership and violence. Gangs are important agents of socialization that help shape a gang member's sense of self and identity. Guns are important tools of impression management that helped to protect and project a rough reputation. The way gang socialization leads to gun-related violence has implications for policies aimed on reducing gang related violence.

This study considers how gangs promote violence and gun use. We argue that socialization is important because it helps to shape a gang member's identity and sense of self. Moreover, guns often help gang members project their violent identities. As Kubrin (2005, 363) argues, "The gun becomes a symbol of power and a remedy for disputes." We examine the issue of gang socialization, self, and identity formation using data derived from face-to-face qualitative interviews with a sample of gang members who have been incarcerated in Colorado prisons for gun-related violent crimes. Our findings, although unique, emphasize what previous studies have found—that most gangs are organized by norms that support the use of violence to settle disputes, achieve group goals, recruit members, and defend identity.

Prior to our analysis of gang members, we briefly review the literature on the relationship between gangs, crime, guns, and violence. In that review, we emphasize

the importance of socialization and the impact of gangs on identity and self. We explain how guns help gang members shape and convey their identity. Finally, in our discussion we relate our findings to the relative efficacy of different intervention strategies that are focused on reducing gang violence.

GANGS AND VIOLENCE

Research suggests that gang members are more likely than non-gang members to engage in crime—especially violent crime (Gordon et al. 2004). According to Thornberry et al. (1993, 75), the relationship between gang affiliation and violence "is remarkably robust, being reported in virtually all American studies of gang behavior regardless of when, where, or how the data were collected." Whereas the relationship between gangs and violence is pervasive, "little is known about

Source: Gang-Related Gun Violence: Socialization, Identity, and Self by Stretesky, P. B., & Pogrebin, M. R., *Journal of Contemporary Ethnography,* *36* (1). Feb. 2007. pp. 85–114. Reprinted with permission of Sage Publications, Inc.

the causal mechanisms that bring it about" (Thornberry et al. 1993, 76). Do gangs attract individuals who are predisposed to violence or do they create violent individuals? The debate in the literature about these explanations of gang violence is rather extensive.

Thornberry et al. (1993) point out that there are three perspectives that inform the debate concerning the relationship between gangs and violence. First, the selection perspective argues that gang members are individuals who are delinquent and violent prior to joining the gang. Thus, gang members are individuals who are likely to engage in violent and deviant behavior even if they are not gang members (Gerrard 1964; Yablonsky 1962). From this perspective, what makes gang members more criminal than non-gang members is that criminal individuals have self-selected or been recruited into gangs. The second perspective is known as the social facilitation perspective. This perspective argues that gang members are no different from non-gang members until they enter the gang. Therefore, the gang serves a normative function. In short, the gang is the source of delinquent behavior because new gang members are socialized into the norms and values of gang life, which provides the necessary social setting for crime and violence to flourish. The enhancement perspective is the third explanation for the relationship between gang and crime (Thornberry et al. 1993). The enhancement perspective proposes that new gang members are recruited from a pool of individuals who show propensity to engage in crime and violence, but their level of violence intensifies once they enter the gang because the gang provides a structure that encourages crime and violence (see also Decker and Van Winkle 1996).

According to McCorkle and Miethe (2002, 111) the second and third explanations for gang-related crime are the most popular explanations in the literature because both perspectives rely on the assumption that social disorganization increases socialization into the gang subculture, which produces crime. Recent criminological research suggests that the enhancement perspective is the most likely explanation for the association between gang involvement and criminal behavior. For instance, Gordon et al. (2004) discovered that individuals who join gangs are, in general, more delinquent than their peers *before* they join the gang. However, Gordon et al. also found that violent behavior among individuals who join a gang significantly increases *after* they become gang members. Although Gordon et al.'s work provides some answers concerning the potential causal mechanisms of gang violence, it still leaves open the question about why gang members increase their violent behavior after they join a gang. It is for that reason that we focus our research on the concept of socialization as a mechanism that leads to gang-related gun violence.

GANG SOCIALIZATION

Research on gang socialization—the process of learning the appropriate values and norms of the gang culture to which one belongs—suggests that group processes are highly important (Miller and Branson 2000; Sirpal 1997; Vigil 1988). In addition, Moore (1991) believes that many city gangs have become quasi-institutionalized. In these cities, gangs have played a major role in ordering individuals' lives at the same time that other important social institutions such as schools and families play less of a normative role (see also Bjerregaard and Lizotte 1995; Blumstein 1995; Bowker and Klein 1983; Vigil 1988). Vigil (1988, 63) has found that gangs help to socialize "members to internalize and adhere to alternative norms and modes of behavior and play a significant role in helping . . . youth acquire a sense of importance, self-esteem, and identity." One way to attain status is to develop a reputation for being violent (Anderson 1999). This reputation for violence, however, is likely to develop (at least to some degree) after an individual joins a gang.

The reasons individuals join gangs are diverse (Decker and Van Winkle 1996). According to Decker and Van Winkle (1996), the most important instrumental reason for joining a gang is protection. In addition to instrumental concerns, a large portion of all gang members indicate that their gang fulfills a variety of more typical adolescent needs—especially companionship and support, which tend to be more expressive in nature. That is, the gang is a primary group. The idea that the gang is a primary group into which individuals are socialized is not new. For instance, long ago Thrasher (1927, 230) pointed out,

> [The gang] offers the underprivileged boy probably his best opportunity to acquire status and hence it plays an essential part in the development of his personality. In striving to realize the role he hopes to take he may assume a tough pose, commit feats of daring or vandalism, or become a criminal.

Thus, gang violence may often be viewed as expressive in nature. The value of masculinity as a form of expression plays an important role in gang socialization (Miller and Decker 2001). Oliver (1994) argues that gang violence is often a method of expressing one's masculinity when opportunities to pursue conventional roles are denied. Acts of manhood, note Decker and Van Winkle (1996, 186), are "important values of [a member's] world and their psyches—to be upheld even at the cost of their own or others' lives." Katz (1988) also believes violence plays an important and acceptable role in the subculture of people living in socially isolated environments and economically deprived areas because violence provides a means for a member to demonstrate his toughness, and displays of violent retaliation establish socialization within the gang.

According to Short and Strodtbeck (1965; see also Howell 1998), a good portion of all gang violence can be attributed to threats to one's status within the gang. Gang membership, then, helps to create within-group identity that defines how group members perceive people outside their formal organizational structure. By way of altercasting (i.e., the use of tactics to create identities and roles for others), gangs cast nonmembers into situated roles and identities that are to the gang's advantage (Weinstein and Deutschberger 1963). Altercasting, then, is an aggressive tactic that gangs often use to justify their perception of other gangs as potentially threatening rivals, and it is used to rationalize the use of physical violence against other gangs. If the objective of a gang is to be perceived by the community, rival gangs, law enforcement officials, and others in a particular way, then their collective group and individual identities will be situated in these defining situations. Even though there is a good deal of research examining the important relationship between violence and status within the gang as it relates to socialization, little is known about the specific ways that status impacts gang violence.

Socialization into the gang is bound up in issues of identity and self. Identity, according to Stone (1962), is the perceived social location of the person. Image, status, and a host of other factors that affect identity are mostly created by group perceptions of who we are and how we define ourselves. "People see themselves from the standpoints of their group and appropriate action in relation to those groups becomes a source of pride" (Shibutani 1961, 436). Berger (1963, 92) notes that "identities are socially bestowed, socially maintained, and socially transformed."

Moore (1978, 60) has suggested that "the gang represents a means to what is an expressive, rather than an instrumental, goal: the acting out of a male role of competence and of 'being in command' of things." The findings of Decker and Van Winkle (1996) and Moore suggest that although instrumental reasons for joining a gang are important, once a member joins a gang they largely see the gang as an important primary group that is central to their lives and heavily influences their identity and personality. Because this is a primary group, the approval of gang peers is highly important. It is this expressive reason for remaining in a gang that may help to explain gang crime and violence, especially as it relates to socialization. Hughes and Short (2005) provide insight into the area of identity and gang violence. Specifically, they find that when a gang member's identity is challenged, violence is often a result—especially if the challenger is a stranger. If a gang member does not comply with gang role expectations when they are challenged, the result may be a loss of respect. It is important to project a violent reputation to command respect and deter future assaults. Walking away from conflict is risky to one's health (Anderson 1999). Gang members must by necessity make efforts to show a continued commitment to role expectations to the group (Lindesmith and Strauss 1968). From this perspective, it appears that character traits that are a consequence of being socialized into street gangs may result in youthful acts of violence through transformations in identity (Vigil 1996).

Initiation rights are one important aspect of identity formation (Hewitt 1988; Vigil 1996). Initiation rights that new gang members are obligated to go through demonstrate commitment to the gang and attest to an individual's desire to gain official membership in the organization. Hewitt (1988) argues that these types of acts help create a "situated self" where a person's self can be defined and shaped by particular situations. Thus, notions of identity formation are highly consistent with notions of gang violence as a function of social facilitation and enhancement perspectives in that they explain why gang members may increase their levels of crime and violence once they join the gang. Moreover, research suggests that the more significant the relationship to a gang is, the more committed an individual is to a gang identity (Callero 1985; Stryker and Serpe 1982). In short, gangs provide a reference group for expected role behavior and shape a member's identity and sense of self (Callero 1985). The greater the commitment a person has to a gang identity, the more frequently that person will perform in ways that enact that identity, ways that include acts of violence (Stryker and Serpe 1982).

Guns also play an important role in many gangs and are often reported to be owned for instrumental reasons (Decker and Van Winkle 1996). Gang members who perceive a threat from rival gangs are believed to carry guns to protect themselves and their neighborhoods (Decker and Van Winkle 1996; Horowitz 1983; Lizotte et al. 1994; Wright and Rossi 1986). Gang membership "strongly and significantly increases the likelihood of carrying a gun" (Thornberry et al. 2003, 131).

However, the reason that gang members carry guns is still unclear. It is likely that in addition to instrumental reasons for carrying a gun, gang members carry guns for expressive reasons (Sheley and Wright 1995). That is, guns provide gang members with a sense of power, which may be extremely important in identity formation. Guns help gang members project a tough image. Thornberry et al. (2003, 125) report that gang members who carry guns may feel "emboldened to initiate criminal acts that they may otherwise avoid."

Sociologists have long recognized that symbols are important indicators of identity. This is especially true of gangs (Decker and Van Winkle 1996; Vigil 2003). Gang members often display symbols of gang membership, and this is part of being socialized into the role of a gang member:

> Wearing gang clothes, flashing gang signs, and affecting other outward signs of gang behavior are also ways to become encapsulated in the role of gang member, especially through the perceptions of others, who, when they see the external symbols of membership respond as if the person was a member (Decker and Van Winkle 1996, 75).

Bjerregaard and Lizotte (1995, 42) argue that it is plausible that "juveniles are socialized into the gun culture by virtue of their gang membership and activity."

Although there is some indication that gang members are more likely to own guns than non-gang members prior to joining a gang, gang membership also clearly appears to increase the prevalence of gun ownership. Bjerregaard and Lizotte (1995) believe that future research needs to focus on why gang membership encourages gun ownership. In this vein, Sanders's (1994) research on drive-by shootings provides some insight into why gang membership may encourage gun ownership. Drawing on Goffman's (1961) notion of realized resources, Sanders argues that gangs are organizations that provide the necessary context for drive-bys. Sanders is clear when he states that guns and cars are the least important resource in producing drive-bys. However, it is also true that guns are necessary for drive-bys to occur and as such are an important part of gang culture to the extent that drive-bys help gang members "build an identity as having heart" (Sanders 1994, 204). Thus, notions of character and identity provide a way to look at drive-by shootings as a product of the gang structure, where guns are important instruments in building identity. Given the importance of guns to a gang member's identity, it is interesting to note that little research exists that examines the relationship between guns and gangs in terms of identity formation.

METHODS

The interviews in tin's study of twenty-two gang members were taken from a larger qualitative study of seventy-five Colorado prison inmates who used a firearm in the commission of their most recent offense. Inmates were asked general questions about their families, schools, peer groups, neighborhoods, prior contact with the criminal justice system, and experiences with firearms. They were also asked a series of questions surrounding the circumstances that lead up to the crime for which they were currently incarcerated. It was from this vantage point that we began to see the importance of gang socialization, self, and identity as important aspects of violence and gun use.

Inmates we interviewed were located in eleven different correctional facilities scattered throughout Colorado and were randomly selected by means of a simple random sample from a list of all inmates incarcerated for a violent crime in which a firearm was involved. The overall sample was composed of 39.1% whites, 40.6% African Americans, 15.6% Hispanics, and 4.7% Asians and Middle Easterners. Eight percent of our subjects were female. The demographics of the inmates in our study correspond closely to the demographics of inmates incarcerated in Colorado prisons (see Colorado Department of Corrections 2005).

We used official inmate case files located at the Colorado Department of Corrections to verify that the twenty-two self-identified gang members were likely to have actually been gang members prior to their incarceration. That validity check substantiated what our subjects said—they did indeed appear to be gang members. Case files were also used to gain information about offenders' past criminal records to determine the validity of each inmate's responses with respect to previous offending patterns as well as characteristics associated with their most current offense.

During the interview process, we made every effort to ensure that inmates understood that our conversations were both voluntary and confidential. We told each inmate that only we would be able to identify their answers and that any information they provided to us would be used only for research-related purposes. Moreover, we informed inmates that if they were uncomfortable with any of the topics of discussion, they could simply tell us that they felt uncomfortable and we would proceed to other topics of interest. Finally, we emphasized that we did not want any details that might compromise an inmate's pending legal case. It is important to point out that we did discover—through our conversations with inmates—that those subjects who refused to be interviewed were mainly concerned about legal repercussions associated with our interviews. Still, we have good reason to believe that the inmates we did interview were surprisingly open and honest about their past behavior. Again, we are confident in the validity of our data because inmates often gave answers that closely matched available information recorded in their official inmate files. Finally, we should point out that a few inmates who felt uncomfortable with a particular line of questioning asked the interviewer to momentarily turn off the tape recorder so that their responses were not recorded. These brief, unrecorded conversations were often focused on a particular aspect of an inmate's crime and are largely inconsequential to the current research.

The appendix lists the characteristics of the inmates in our gang sub-sample. The median age of the twenty-two gang members in our sample was 25 years old, though their age at the commission of the crime was considerably younger. Thirteen of the inmates were black, five were white, one was Asian, and three were Hispanic. Six of the inmates we interviewed were convicted of murder or nonnegligent manslaughter, four were convicted of attempted murder, two were convicted of robbery, eight were convicted of assault, and two were convicted of kidnapping. At the time of the interviews, our subjects had been incarcerated for an average of 4.7 years. All but one of the inmates in our sample of gang members were male, and all subjects used a handgun in the commission of their most recent violent crime.

In order to arrange times to interview inmates, we sent a letter to the case worker of each inmate we selected into our sample. The purpose of these letters was to (1) identify the inmates selected for inclusion in our study, (2) explain the nature of the study, and (3) indicate that inmate participation in the study was voluntary. Correctional case workers were asked to provide inmates with information about the study, tell them that their participation was voluntary, and inform them of the dates that the researchers would be at the prison to conduct interviews. We also informed subjects that as an incentive to participate in the interview, we would put five dollars into their inmate account.

Prison officials were notified of our visits prior to our arrival, and they helped us locate the inmates in our sample and arrange for a place for the interviews to be conducted. All interviews were conducted in the prison in private conference rooms, vacant staff offices, and empty visitation rooms. Each interview was tape-recorded with the subjects consent and lasted between 60 and 120 minutes. A semistructured format was used that relied on sequential probes to pursue leads provided

by the inmates. This technique allowed subjects to identify and elaborate important domains they perceived to characterize their life histories. Generally, these included their gang experience, engagement in violent encounters throughout their life, and their involvement with a firearm in those situations.

The interview tapes were transcribed for qualitative data analysis, which involves scanning and identifying general statements about relationships among categories of observations. We looked for explanations concerning gang members' perceptions about how they learned to become gang members and their perceptions of the importance of guns in that process. Thus, we used an inductive-methods approach where the inmates' responses directed our empirical generalizations and conclusions. As Schatzman and Strauss (1973, 110) note, "The most fundamental operation in the analysis of qualitative data is that of discovering significant classes of things, persons, and events and the properties which characterize them." Our face-to-face interviews allowed our subjects to elaborate on important domains they perceived to characterize their criminal life history as it related to their perceptions of gang involvement.

It is important to point out that although we would have preferred to conduct and establish a long-term relationship with our subjects and observe their behavior as they went about their daily lives, such an approach is, unfortunately, highly unrealistic in the case of the most violent gang members. This is important as there are some researchers who believe that ethnography excludes qualitative research approaches where the researcher has not spent a long period of time observing study participants in the field in order to become sufficiently knowledgeable of the setting being studied (Glaser and Strauss 1967). We, however, agree with Lofland and Lofland (1995, 18) that the distinction between participant observation and intensive interviewing is "overdrawn and any invidious comparisons are [typically] unwarranted." Moreover, Hobs and May (1993) suggest that in-depth interviews are the best way to gather data that could never be obtained just by observing the activities of people. Given the fact that intensive interviews are often part of participant observation, we argue that they are sufficient to draw conclusions regarding gang socialization and the creation of a gang identity among the gang members in our sample—those who find themselves incarcerated for violent crimes.

One potential methodological issue that could be interpreted as cause for concern has to do with the generalizability of our sample. The gang members we talked with were probably more highly integrated into their gang than the typical gang member. We believe this because our subjects were incarcerated for gang-related violence, which we interpreted as a sign of high commitment to their group. Thus, we should expect that our subjects' gang experiences are quite different from gang members in general who have not displayed similar levels of violence. Such selection bias might be problematic if the purpose of the study is to generalize our findings to all gang members. The purpose of this research, however, is more modest in nature. We are interested in the experiences of violent gang members in our sample precisely because they are likely to be the most committed to the gang and because that commitment is likely to be translated into gang-related gun violence. As studies of gang violence indicate, a large percentage of gang violence is committed by a small percentage of gang members (Piehl, Kennedy, and Braga 2000, 100). The gang members in our study, then, are likely to have the most to offer in terms of their gang and gun experiences, and their stories are likely to be the most useful in thinking about policy-related issues surrounding gang- and gun-related violence.

FINDINGS

We divide our findings into four sections. First, we focus on our subjects' socialization into the gang and the impact that socialization has on their self and identity. Second, we explore the importance of gang commitment as reinforcing a gang member's self and identity. Third, we focus on masculinity as a central value among gang members. During our discussions of masculinity, gang members often referred to notions of respect and reputation. Reputation is a way that gang members can project their image of masculinity to others. Respect was often referenced when their masculine identity was challenged. Finally, we focus on the importance of guns as instruments central to the lives of our gang members in the sense that they help project and protect masculine identities.

Gang Socialization, Self, and Identity

Goffman (1959) argues that as individuals we are often "taken in by our own act" and therefore begin to feel like the person we are portraying. Baumeister and Tice (1984) describe this process as one where initial behaviors are internalized so that they become part of a person's self-perception. Once initial behaviors are internalized, the individual continues to behave in ways consistent with his or her self-perception. Related to the current study, the socialization process of becoming a

gang member required a change in the subject's self-perception. That is, who did our gang members become as compared with who they once were? Social interaction is highly important in the process of socialization because it helps create one's identity and sense of self, as Holstein and Gubrium (2003, 119 [emphasis added]) point out:

> As personal us they seem, our selves and identities are extremely social. They are hallmarks of our inner lives, *yet they take shape in relation to others. We establish who and what we are through social interaction.* In some respects, selves and identities are two sides of the same coin. Selves are the subjects we take ourselves to be; identities are the shared labels we give to these selves. We come to know ourselves in terms of the categories that are socially available to us.

Most inmates we interviewed appeared to indicate that their socialization into the gang began at a relatively young age:

> At about fifteen, I started getting affiliated with the Crips. I knew all these guys, grew up with them and they were there. . . . I mean, it was like an influence at that age. I met this dude named Benzo from Los Angeles at that time. He was a Crip and he showed me a big wad of money. He said. "Hey man, you want some of this?" "Like yeh! Goddamn straight. You know I want some of that." He showed me how to sell crack, and so at fifteen, I went from being scared of the police and respecting them to hustling and selling crack. Now I'm affiliated with the Crips: I mean it was just unbelievable.

Another inmate tells of his orientation in becoming a member of a gang. He points out the glamour he associated with membership at a very impressionable age:

> I started gang banging when I was ten. I got into a gang when I was thirteen. I started just hanging around them, just basically idolizing them. I was basically looking for a role model for my generation and ethnic background; the main focus for us is the popularity that they got. That's who the kids looked up to. They had status, better clothes, better lifestyle.

One of our black study participants residing with his father in a predominantly white, suburban community felt estranged from the minority friends he had in his former neighborhood. He discussed his need to be among his former peers and voluntarily moved back to his old neighborhood.

A lot of the people that lived where my father was staying were predominantly white. I mean, not to say I didn't get along with white kids but, you know, it was just two different backgrounds and things of that nature.

His racial and socioeconomic identification in the white community, where he resided with his father, offered little opportunity for him to fit in. When he returned to the city, he became involved with a gang quite rapidly.

I started getting charged with assaults. Gang rivalry, you know, fighting, just being in a gang.

Because he was better educated and did not use street vernacular as his peers did, our participant claims he had to continually prove his racial proclivity to his peers.

Other kids would call me "white wash" because I spoke proper English. Basically, I wanted to be somebody, so I started hanging around with gang bangers. I was planning on being the best gang member I can be or the best kind of criminal I can be or something like that.

Consistent with Goffman's (1959) observations, once our subjects became active gang members, their transformation of identity was complete. That is, consistent with the notion of social facilitation and enhancement perspectives (Thornberry et al. 1993), the self-perceptions and identity of the subjects in our study appear to have changed from what they were prior to joining the gang. Shibutani (1961, 523) explains such changes by claiming that violent behavior appeared to play an important role in this transformation of identity and self. Most gang members noted that they engaged in violent behavior more frequently once they joined the gang.

A person's self-perception is caused by a psychological reorientation in which an individual visualizes his world and who he thinks he is in a different light. He retains many of his idiosyncrasies, but develops a new set of values and different criteria of judgment.

At an early age, it was encouraged that I showed my loyalty and do a drive-by . . . anybody they (gangster disciples) deemed to be a rival of the gang. I was going on fourteen. At first, I was scared to and then they sent me out with one person and I seen him do it. I saw him shoot the guy. . . . So, in the middle of a gang tight I get pulled aside and get handed a pistol and he said. "It's your turn to prove yourself." So I turned around and shot and hit one of the guys (rival

gang members). After that, it just got more easier. I did more and more. I had no concern for anybody.

A further illustration of situated identity and transformation of self is related by another inmate, who expresses the person he became through the use of violence and gun possession. Retrospectively, he indicates disbelief in what he had become.

As a gang banger, you have no remorse, so basically, they're natural-born killers. They are killers from the start. When I first shot my gun for the first time at somebody, I felt bad. It was like, I can't believe I did this. But I looked at my friend and he didn't care at all. Most gang bangers can't have a conscience. You can't have remorse. You can't have any values. Otherwise, you are gonna end up retiring as a gang banger at a young age.

The situations one finds themselves in, in this case collective gang violence, together with becoming a person who is willing to use violence to maintain membership in the gang, is indicative of a transformed identity. Strauss (1962) claims that when a person's identity is transformed, they are seen by others as being different than they were before. The individual's prior identity is retrospectively reevaluated in comparison with the present definition of a gang member. Such a transformation was pail of the processional change in identity that our prisoners/gang members experienced.

Commitment to the Gang

"As a creature of ideas, man's main concern is to maintain a tentative hold on these idealized conceptions of himself, to legitimate his role identities" (McCall and Simmons 1966, 71). Commitment to the gang also serves individual needs for its members. We found that gang identification and loyalty to the group was a high priority for our subjects. This loyalty to the gang was extreme. Our subjects reported that they were willing to risk being killed and were committed to taking the life of a rival gang member if the situation called for such action. That is, gang membership helped our subjects nourish their identity and at the same time provided group maintenance (Kanter 1972). As Kanter (1972) points out, the group is an extension of the individual and the individual is an extension of the group. This notion of sacrifice for the group by proving one's gang identification is expressed by an inmate who perceives his loyalty in the following terms:

What I might do for my friends [gang peers] you might not do. You've got people out their taking bullets for their friends and killing people. But I'm sure not one of you would be willing to go to that extreme. These are just the thinking patterns we had growing up where I did.

Another inmate tells us about his high degree of identity for his gang:

> If you're not a gang member, you're not on my level ... most of my life revolves around gangs and gang violence. I don't know anything else but gang violence. I was born into it, so it's my life.

The notion of the gang as the most important primary group in a member's life was consistently expressed by our study subjects. Our subjects often stated that they were willing to kill or be killed for the gang in order to sustain their self-perception as a loyal gang member. This extreme degree of group affiliation is similar to that of armed services activities during wartime. The platoon, or in this case, the local gang, is worth dying for. In this sense, the notion of the gang as a protector was an important part of gang life. All members were expected to be committed enough to aid their peers should the need arise. The following gang member points to the important role his gang played for him in providing physical safety as well as an assurance of understanding.

> That's how it is in the hood, selling dope, gang bangin. Everybody wants a piece of you. All the rival gang members, all the cops, everybody. The only ones on your side are the gang members you hang with.

For this particular member, his gang peers are the only people he perceives will aid him from threatening others. The world appears full of conflicting situations, and although his gang affiliation is largely responsible for all the groups that are out to harm him in some way, he nevertheless believes his fellow gang members are the only persons on whom he can depend.

Violence against rival gangs was a general subject that the majority of the inmates interviewed discussed freely. However, only a few of our study participants focused on this subject compared with the less violence-prone gang-affiliated inmates. The violent gang members perceived other gangs as ongoing enemies who constantly presented a threat to their safety. As our literature review suggests, there is some debate about whether gang members would be violent without belonging to a gang, or if formal membership in the group provided them with the opportunity to act out this way. However, we find clarity in the inmate accounts that a gang member's identity provided the context necessary to resort to violence when confronted with conflicting events, as the following inmate notes:

> I have hate toward the Crips' gang members and have always had hate toward them cuz of what they did to my homeboys. . . . I never look back. I do my thing. I always carry a gun no matter what. I am a gang member, man! There are a lot of gang members out to get me for what I done. I shot over forty people at least. That's what I do.

This perception of being a person who is comfortable with violence and the perception of himself as an enforcer type characterizes the above inmate's role within his gang. Turner (1978) suggests that roles consistent with an individual's self-concept are played more frequently and with a higher degree of participation than roles that are not in keeping with that individual's self-concept. Our study subject in this situation fits Turner's explanation of role identity nicely. His hatred for rival gangs and his willingness to retaliate most likely led to his incarceration for attempted murder.

Masculinity, Reputation, and Respect

For those gang members we interviewed, socialization into the gang and commitment to the gang appear to be central to the notion of masculinity. That is, all gang members we interviewed spoke of the importance of masculinity and how it was projected (though the creation of a reputation) and protected (through demands for respect). The notion of masculinity was constantly invoked in relation to self and identity. In short, masculinity is used to communicate to others what the gang represents, and it is used to send an important signal to others who may wish to challenge a gang's collective identity. A gang member's masculine reputation precedes him or her, so to speak. On an individual level, similar attributes apply as well.

> Whatever an individual does and however he appears, he knowingly and unknowingly makes information available concerning the attributes that might be imputed to him and hence the categories in which he might be placed. . . . The physical milieu itself conveys implications concerning the identity of those who are in it. (Goffman 1961, 102)

According to Sherif and Wilson (1953), people's ego attitudes define and regulate their behavior toward various other groups and are formed in concert to the values and norms of that person's reference group. They formulate an important part of their self-identity and their sense of group identification. For our gang member study population, the attributes that the gang valued consisted of factors that projected a street image that was necessary to sustain. It was a survival strategy.

Masculinity. "Every man [in a gang] is treated as a man until proven different. We see you as a man before anything." This comment by a gang member infers that masculinity is a highly valued attribute in his gang. The idea of manhood and its personal meanings for each interviewed prisoner was a subject consistently repeated by all participants. It usually was brought up in the context of physical violence, often describing situations where one had to face danger as a result of another's threatening behavior or testing of one's willingness to use physical force when insulted by someone outside of the group.

> Even if you weren't in one [gang], you got people that are going to push the issue. We decide what we want to do: I ain't no punk. I ain't no busta. But it comes down to pride. It's foolish pride, but a man is going to be a man. And a boy knows he's going to come into his manhood by standing his ground.

Establishing a reputation coincides with becoming a man, entering the realm of violence, being a stand-up guy who is willing to prove his courage as a true gang member. This strong association between a willingness to perpetrate violence on a considered rival, or anyone for that matter, was a theme that defined a member's manhood. After eight years in the gang, the following participant was owed money for selling someone dope. After a few weeks of being put off by the debtor, he had to take some action to appease his gang peers who were pressuring him to retaliate.

> I joined the gang when I was eleven years old. So now that I'm in the gang for eight years, people are asking. "What are you going to do? You got to make a name for yourself." So we went over there [victim's residence] and they were all standing outside and I just shot him. Everybody was happy for me, like "Yea, you shot him, you're cool," and this and that.

A sense of bravado, when displayed, played a utilitarian role in conflicting situations where a gang member attempts to get others to comply with his demands by instilling fear instead of actually utilizing violent means. Having some prior knowledge of the threatening gang member's reputation is helpful in preventing a

physical encounter, which is always risky for both parties involved. Again, the importance of firearms in this situation is critical.

> The intimidation factor with a gun is amazing. Everybody knows what a gun can do. If you have a certain type of personality, that only increases their fear of you. When it came to certain individuals who I felt were a threat. I would lift my shirt up so they would know I had one on me.

In this case, the showing of his firearm served the purpose of avoiding any altercation that could have led to injury or even worse. Carrying a gun and displaying it proved to be an intimidating, preventative factor for this gang member. The opposite behavior is noted in the following example of extreme bravado, where aggressive behavior is desired and a clear distinction (based on bravery) between drive-by shootings and face-to-face shootings is clear.

> If someone is getting shot in a drive-by and someone else gets hit, it is an accident. You know, I never do drive-bys. I walk up to them and shoot. I ain't trying to get anyone else shot to take care of business.

A final example of masculinity and bravado, as perceived by this particular study participant, illustrates his commitment to being a stand-up guy, a person who will face the consequences of gang activity. The situation he discussed had to do with his current incarceration. Here he explains how he adhered to the gang value of not being a snitch, and refused to provide information about rival gang members' involvement in two homicides to the police, which could have helped in his prosecution for murder.

> I know what I did [gang war murder], you know what I mean? I'm not gonna take the easy way out [snitch on rival gangs for two homicides], I know what I did. I'm facing my responsibility.

An interesting note in this scenario has to do with the above inmate's continued loyalty to the values of his gang when he was outside of prison. His information on the rival gang's homicides most likely could have had the criminal charges against him reduced and subsequently he would have received a lesser prison sentence. We are taking into consideration that the inmate's cultural code is similar if not the same as the gang code, and our study participant was simply adhering to the same value system.

The image of toughness fits well under masculinity and bravado as an attribute positively perceived by gang members we interviewed. Its importance lies in projecting an image via reputation that conveys a definition of who the collective group is and what physical force they are willing to use when necessary. A clear explanation of this attribute is related by the following subject.

> Everybody wants to fight for the power, for the next man to fear him. It's all about actually killing the mother fuckers and how many mother fuckers you can kill. Drive-by shootings is old school.

The implication here is that having a collective reputation for being powerful motivates this prisoner. He notes that the tough image of shooting someone you are after instead of hiding behind the random shooting characterized by drive-bys projects an image of toughness and power.

There are others who prefer to define their toughness in terms of physical fighting without the use of any weapons—though it was often noted that it was too difficult to maintain a tough reputation under such conditions. For instance, the predicament the following gang member found himself in is one where rival gangs use guns and other lethal instruments, and as a result of this, his reputation as an effective street fighter proved to be of little value. In short, his toughness and fighting skills were obsolete in life-threatening encounters.

> Like my case, I'm a fighter, I don't like using guns. The only reason I bought a gun was because every time I got out of the car to fight. I'd have my ribs broken, the back of my head almost crushed with a baseball bat. I was tired of getting jumped. I couldn't get a fair fight. Nobody wanted to fight me because I had a bad reputation. Then I decided, why even fight? Everybody else was pulling guns. It's either get out of the car and get killed or kill them.

The fact that this prisoner had good fighting skills ironically forced him to carry a gun. The rules of gang fighting found him outnumbered and unarmed, placing him in a very vulnerable position to defend himself. The proliferation of firearms among urban street gangs is well documented by Blumstein (1995) and others. Lethal weapons, mainly firearms, have drastically changed the defining characteristics of gang warfare in the late 1980s and 1990s, when most of our study subjects were active gang members in the community.

Reputation. On a collective group level, developing and maintaining the gang's reputation of being a dangerous group to deal with, especially from other groups or

individuals who posed a threat to their drug operations, was important. The following inmate points out the necessity of communicating the gang's willingness to use violent retaliation against rivals. Guns often played an important role in the development and maintenance of reputation, though they were rarely utilized in conflicting situations:

> We had guns to fend off jackers, but we never had to use them, 'cause people knew we were straps. People knew our clique; they are not going to be stupid. We've gotten into a few arguments, but it never came to a gun battle. Even when we were gang bangin', we didn't use guns, we only fought off the Bloods.

Aside from a collective reputation, the group serves the identifying needs of its individual members (Kanter 1972). Our study participants related their need to draw upon the reputation of the gang to help them develop their own reputation, which gave them a sense of fulfillment. People want to present others with cues that will enhance desired typifications of who they are. They desire to present who they are in ways that will cause those they interact with to adhere to their situated claims (Hewitt and Stokes 1975). The following participant discusses the way gang affiliation enhanced his reputation as a dangerous individual, a person not to be tested by others.

> There are people that know me; even ones that are contemplating robbing me know of me from the gang experience. They know if you try and rob me [of drugs and money], more than likely you gonna get killed. I was gonna protect what was mine. I'll die trying.

Another study subject perceives gang membership differently. He attained a reputation through gang activity, and guns clearly played an important role in that process.

> Fear and desire to have a reputation on the streets made me do it. When I got into the streets, I saw the glamour of it. I wanted a reputation there. What better way to get a reputation than to pick up a pistol? I've shot several people.

> Although each prisoner/gang member interviewed expressed a desire to be known in the community for some particular attribute, there were some gang members who simply wanted to be known, sort of achieving celebrity status. You basically want people to know your name. It's kind of like politicians, like that, you wanna be known. In my generation you want

somebody to say, "I know him; he used to hang around with us."

Respect. One constantly associates the subject of disrespect in gang vernacular with retaliatory violence. Interactions with rivals stemming from an affront to one's self-image often became the excuse to use a gun to redeem one's reputational identity. Strauss (1969) argues that anger and withdrawal occur when a person is confronted with a possible loss of face. For our subjects, this anger was apparent when rivals challenged their self-identity (i.e., when our subjects were disrespected).

According to the gang members we talked to, disrespect, or rejection of self-professed identity claims by others, often was the cause of violence. Violence is even more likely to be the result of disrespect when no retaliatory action may lead to a loss of face. The following inmate relates his view on this subject in general terms.

> Violence starts to escalate once you start to disrespect me. Once you start to second guess my manhood, I'll fuck you up. You start coming at me with threats, then I feel offended. Once I feel offended. I react violently. That's how I was taught to react.

The interface of their manhood being threatened seems to be directly associated with Strauss's (1962) concept of identity denial by an accusing other. This threat to one's masculinity by not recognizing another's status claims is apparently an extremely serious breach of gang etiquette.

> When someone disrespects me, they are putting my manhood in jeopardy. They are saying my words are shit, or putting my family in danger.... Most of the time, I do it [use violence] to make people feel the pain or hurt that I feel. I don't know no other way to do it, as far as expressing myself any other way.

Hickman and Kuhn (1956) point out that the self anchors people in every situation they are involved in. Unlike other objects, they claim that the self is present in all interactions and serves as the basis from which we all make judgments and plans of reaction toward others that are part of a given situation. When being confronted by gang rivals who have been perceived as insulting an opposing gang member, the definition of street norms calls for an exaggerated response. That is, the disrespectful words must be countered with serious physical force to justify the disrespected individual's maintenance of self (or manhood). A prime example of feeling disrespected is discussed in terms of territory

and the unwritten rules of the street by one gang member who told us of an encounter with a rival gang who disrespected him to the point that he felt he was left with no other alternative choice of action but to shoot them.

> So, as we were fighting, they started saying that this was their neighborhood and started throwing their gang signs. To me, to let somebody do that to me is disrespect. So I told them where I was from.

A little while later the gang members in question showed up in our study subject's neighborhood and shot at him as he was walking with his two small children to a convenience store to get ice cream. He continues to recite the tale:

> I was just so mad and angry for somebody to disrespect me like that and shoot. We got a rule on the street. There is rules. You don't shoot at anybody if there is kids. That's one of the main rules of the street. They broke the rules. To me that was telling me that they didn't have no respect for me or my kids. So, that's how I lost it and shot them. I was so disrespected that I didn't know how to handle it.

The notion of disrespect is analogous to an attack on the self. Because many of the inmates in our sample reported that masculinity is an important attribute of the self, they believed any disrespect was a direct threat to their masculinity. For those brought up in impoverished high-crime communities, as these study population participants were, there are limited alternatives to such conflicting situations (Anderson 1999). Retaliation to redeem one's self-identity in terms of his internalized concept of manhood precludes a violent reaction to all actions of insult. To gang members caught in those confrontational encounters, there is a very limited course of action, that of perpetrating violence toward those who would threaten their self-concept of who they believe they are.

Gangs and Guns

The perceived necessity by gang participants to carry handguns became a reality for our study group. They collectively expressed the danger of their life on the street, whether it was selling narcotics, committing a robbery, being a provocateur against rivals, or being the recipient of violent retaliation on the part of perceived enemies. They viewed their world fraught with potential danger, thus the need for the possession of guns. It is necessary, then, to take the person's definition of the situation into account in explaining their unlawful conduct (Hewitt 1988). Often, the interviewed prisoners emphasized the importance of the gun as an attribute that communicated their masculinity in some situations but was protection in others. Quite often, both definitions of the situation existed simultaneously.

Our analysis of the interview data dichotomized those gun-using encounters as expressions of either power or protection, based on each participant's perceived definition of the situation.

Carrying a firearm elicits various feelings of power:

When I have a gun, I feel like I'm on top of it, like I'm Superman or something. You got to let them know.

Another participant explains that the larger the gun, the more powerful he felt:

I was fifteen at that point in time and I had a fascination with guns. It was like the more powerful impact the gun had, the more fascinated I got and the more I wanted it.

The actual use of a firearm is described in a situation that most lethally expressed the power of guns in an attempt to injure those belonging to rival gangs. In this situation, our subject points out that they were not trying to injure or kill anyone for personal reasons but rather to display a sense of willingness to commit a lethal act for purposes of dominance.

When I was younger, we used to do drive-bys. It didn't matter who you were. We didn't go after a specific person. We went after a specific group. Whoever is standing at a particular house or wherever you may be, and you're grouped up and have the wrong color on, just because you were in a rival gang. You didn't have to do anything to us to come get you, it was a spontaneous reaction.

When not being involved in collective gang violence, individual members find themselves being involved in gun-use situations as instigators when confronting rivals on one's own.

My cousin told me if you pull it you better use it. So you gotta boost yourself. When the time came I was just shooting.

Our findings showed that in the vast majority of gang member-related shootings, most of these violent gun-using situations involved individuals as opposed to large numbers of gangs confronting each other with firearms. Yet, we were told that in gang representation, either on an individual basis or in a small group,

whether it be in a protective or retaliatory mode, gang members needed to display a power position to those confronting them to maintain their reputations, and guns were important in that respect.

The issues surrounding gun possession often have to do with interpersonal conflict as opposed to collective gang situations. The fear of being physically harmed within their residential environment, coupled with the relative ease in which a person can attain a firearm, has resulted in a proliferation of weapons in the community. Growing up in such high-crime neighborhoods and then joining a gang can shape a minority teen's perceptions of his or her social world,

There's a lot of brutality, there is a lot of murder around us. There is a lot of violence, period. There are enemies and all. A lot of pressure, you know. If you're not going to do this, then they're going to do it to you. I'd rather get caught with a gun than without.

The perceived fear for potential harm caused this female gang member to carry a gun with her outside her home. When she expresses the violence that is prevalent in her environment, she is also telling us how random threats can often occur and sees the necessity to harm rivals before they ham her.

Individually or collectively, rival gang members constantly pose a physical threat according to the next inmate. He also discusses the need for protection and how drug sales caused him to be a target for those who would try and rob him.

I carried a gun because I knew what I was doing, especially since I was in a gang. Other gangs are gonna try and come after us. So I used it [gun] against those gangs and to make sure that my investments in the drugs was protected. I don't want nobody to take money from me.

Last, one study subject relates the need to carry a gun all the time to protect his jewelry, which he openly displays as a symbol of his monetary success through the use of illegal means.

I basically carried a gun for protection. Just like you have a best friend. You and your best friend go everywhere. I got over ten thousand dollars of jewelry on me. People see all this jewelry and may try and beat me up. There may be two or three and just myself.

For our prisoner/gang member study population, the descriptive attributes they related all played an important role in shaping their individual gang identity. The roles they learned to play through their processional development into bona fide gang participants were accomplished by group socialization. Their acting upon those perceived valued attributes resulted in their transformed identity. Once the socializing process is complete, the novice gang member has to sustain his reputation and status personally as well as collectively with the formal group.

> An individual who implicitly or explicitly signifies that he has certain social characteristics ought in fact to be what he claims he is. In consequence, when an individual projects a definition of the situation and thereby makes an implicit or explicit claim to be a person of a particular kind, he automatically exerts a moral demand upon others, obliging them to value and treat him in the manner that persons of his kind have a right to expect. (Goffman 1959, 1–5)

For Goffman, the claims (attributes) our sample of gang members desired to convey to others of just who they perceived themselves to be directly affected their sense of self.

DISCUSSION AND CONCLUSION

Gangs not only fulfill specific needs for individuals that other groups in disadvantaged neighborhoods may fail to provide, but as our interviews suggest, they are also important primary groups into which individuals become socialized. It is not surprising, then, that self-concept and identity are closely tied to gang membership. Guns are also important in this regard. We propose that for the gang members in our sample, gang-related gun violence can be understood in terms of self and identity that are created through the process of socialization and are heavily rooted in notions of masculinity. Thus, our analysis provides insight into the way gang socialization can produce violence—especially gun-related violence.

We find that related to the issue of gun violence, the possession and use of guns among gang members is relatively important because, in addition to protecting gang members, guns are tools that aid in identity formation and impression management. As many of our subject narratives suggest, guns were often connected in some way to masculine attributes. Gang members reported to us that they could often use guns to project their reputation or reclaim respect. We believe that the consequences of our findings regarding gang violence and guns are important for public policy for three reasons.

First, because our sample only consisted of those gang members who committed the most severe forms of violence (i.e., they were incarcerated for relatively long periods of time for their gun-related violence), there may be some interest in targeting individuals like the ones in our sample early in their criminal careers to "diminish the pool of chronic gang offenders" (Piehl, Kennedy, and Braga 2000, 100). We believe this may be one potential method for reducing gang-related violence because the gang members in our sample often had extensive violent histories. Moreover, in studies of gang violence, researchers have generally found that a small number of offenders commit most of the crime. For instance, Kennedy, Piehl and Braga (1996) found that less than one percent of Boston's youth were responsible for nearly sixty percent of the city's homicides. Thus, identifying the rather small pool of chronic gang members may be a useful approach to reducing gang violence because they are the ones engaged in most of the violence. This approach, however, is somewhat problematic because identifying chronic offenders is both difficult and controversial (Walker 1998). Moreover, Spergel and Curry (1990), who studied the effectiveness of various gang-related intervention strategies, argue that law enforcement efforts seem to be one of the least effective methods for reducing gang-related problems.

Second, our research suggests that policies aimed at reducing gang violence should take gang socialization into account. Simply reducing gun availability through law enforcement crackdowns on violent gang members is probably not sufficient (see Piehl, Kennedy, Braga 2000). In addition, our interviews suggest that guns are probably far more important to the daily lives and identities of gang members than most policy makers might imagine, precisely because they help project a reputation and create respect. Thus, it might be pointed out that if gang culture could be changed through the resocialization of gang members, gun-related gang violence might significantly decrease. Indeed, studies of gun initiatives such as the Boston Gun Project suggest that gang violence is reduced when gang culture is changed. As Piehl, Kennedy, and Braga (2000, 100) point out, one reason homicides in Boston decreased as a result of the Boston Gun Project was because that initiative focused on "establishing and/or reinforcing nonviolent norms by increasing peer support for eschewing violence, by improving young people's handling of potentially violent situations."

Overall, however, the strategy of focusing on gang socialization, however, falls most closely in line with social intervention perspectives that have not proved to be highly successful in various situations (Shelden, Tracy, and Brown 2001). In short, altering the values of gang members to make gang-related violence less likely may not be the most promising approach to reducing gang violence. As Klein (1995, 147) recently noted,

"Gangs are byproducts of their communities: They cannot long be controlled by attacks on symptoms alone; the community structure and capacity must also be targeted." Whether gang violence can be reduced by the resocialization of gang members appears to remain open to debate, but it is clearly one avenue of intervention that requires further attention in the research.

Third, it is not clear from our research whether simply eliminating or reducing access to guns can reduce gun-related gang violence. For example, studies like the Youth Firearms Violence Initiative conducted by the U.S. Department of Justice's Office of Community Oriented Policing Services does suggest that gun violence can be reduced by focusing, at least in part, on reducing access to guns (Dunworth 2000). However, that study also indicates that once these projects focusing on access to guns end, gang violence increases to previous levels. Moreover, our interviews suggest that there is little reason to believe that gang members would be any less likely to look to gangs as a source of status and protection and may use other weapons—though arguably less lethal than guns—to aid in transformations of identity and preserve a sense of self. Thus, although reduction strategies may prevent gang-related violence in the short-term, there is little evidence that this intervention strategy will have long-term effects because it does not adequately deal with gang culture and processes of gang socialization.

Overall, our findings suggest that gang socialization produces gang-related gun violence through changes to identity and self. Although the problems of gang-related violence appear to play out at the micro-level, the solutions to these problems do not appear to be overwhelmingly situated at this level. Instead, we believe that intervention efforts must reside at the macrolevel and impact socialization processes at the microlevel. We agree with Short (1997, 181) that "absent change in macro level forces associated with [gang violence], vulnerable individuals will continue to be produced" (see also Shelden, Tracy, and Brown 2001). Thus, it may be more fruitful to focus on intervention efforts aimed at improving the economic and social environments that create gangs.

Appendix

Characteristics of Inmates in Sample

ID	Age	Sex	Race/Ethnicity	Education (Years)	Offense	Sentence (Years)	Years Served	No. Previous Felonies
1	28	M	Hispanic	11	Attempted first degree murder	16	7	0
2	21	M	Black	7	Second degree kidnapping	16	3	1
3	20	M	Black	11	Attempted first degree murder	21	J	3
4	21	M	Hispanic	11	Second degree assault	3	2	2
5	21	M	Black	12	First degree murder	Life		
6	48	M	White	12	Second degree assault	14	6	7
7	33	M	Black	12	Attempted first degree murder	16	9	2
8	22	M	Black	9	Second degree assault	25	5	4
9	38	M	Black	12	Manslaughter	22	9	1
10	28	M	White	12	Second degree murder	30	8	
11	25	M	Black	11	First degree murder	Life	4	2
12	23	M	Black	12	First degree assault	14	2	
13	24	M	White	10	Aggravated robbery	20	5	2

ID	Age	Sex	Race/Ethnicity	Education (Years)	Offense	Sentence (Years)	Years Served	No. Previous Felonies
14	32	M	Black	12	First degree murder	40	16	0
15	29	M	Hispanic	12	Second degree assault	5	4	1
16	25	M	Black	12	First degree assault	3	1	1
17	32	M	Black	10	Attempted first degree murder	20	3	
18	20	M	Asian	9	Second degree kidnapping	40	3	0
19	26	F	Black	11	Aggravated robbery	8	4	0
20	43	M	White	12	First degree assault	9	0	2
21	33	M	Black	12	Second degree murder	35	5	0
22	23	M	White	11	First degree assault	45	5	1

REFERENCES

Anderson, Elijah. 1999. *Code of the street: Decency, violence, and the moral life of the inner city.* New York: W.W. Norton.

Baumeister, Roy, and Dianne Tice. 1984. Role of self-presentation and choice in cognitive dissonance under forced compliance. *Journal of Personality and Social Psychology* 46:5–13.

Berger, Peter. 1963. *Invitation to sociology: A humanistic perspective.* Garden City, NY: Doubleday.

Bjerregaard, Beth, and Alan Lizotte. 1995. Gun ownership and gang membership. *Journal of Criminal Law and Criminology* 86:37–58.

Blumstein, Alfred. 1995. Violence by young people: Why the deadly nexus? *National Institute of Justice Journal* 229:2–9.

Bowker, Lee, and Malcolm Klein. 1983. The etiology of female juvenile delinquency and gang membership: A test of psychological and social structural explanations. *Adolescence* 18:739–51.

Callero, Peter. 1985. Role identity salience. *Social Psychology Quarterly* 48:203–15.

Colorado Department of Corrections. 2005. *Statistical report, fiscal year 2004.* Colorado Springs: Office of Planning and Analysis.

Decker, Scott, and Barrik Van Winkle. 1996. *Life in the gang: Family, friends, and violence.* New York: Cambridge University Press.

Dunworth, Terence. 2000. *National evaluation of youth firearms violence initiative, research in brief.* Washington, DC: U.S. Department of Justice, Office of Justice Programs, National Institute of Justice.

Gerrard, Nathan. 1964. The core member of the gang. *British Journal of Criminology* 4:361–71.

Glaser, Barney, and Anselm Strauss. 1967. *The discovery of grounded theory: Strategies for qualitative research.* New York: Doubleday.

Goffman, Erving. 1959. *The presentation of sell in everyday life.* Garden City, NY: Doubleday.

——. 1961. *Encounters: Two studies in the sociology of interaction.* Indianapolis, IN: Bobbs-Merrill.

Gordon, Rachel, Benjamin Lahey, Kriko Kawai, Rolf Loeber, Magda Stouthamer-Loeber, and David Harrington. 2004. Antisocial behavior and youth gang membership: Selection and socialization. *Criminology* 42:55–88.

Hewitt, John. 1988. *Self and society.* Boston: Allyn and Bacon.

Hewitt, John, and Randall Stokes. 1975. Disclaimers. *American Sociological Review* 40:1–11.

Hickman, C. Addison, and Manford Kuhn. 1956. *Individuals, groups, and economic behavior.* New York: Dryden.

Hobs, Dick, and Tim May. 1993. Forward. In *Interpreting the field accounts of ethnography,* eds., Dick Hobbs and Tim May (vii–xviii). New York: Oxford University Press.

Holstein, James, and Jaber Gubrium. 2003. *Inner lives and social worlds.* New York: Oxford University Press.

Horowitz, Ruth. 1983. *Honor and the American dream.* New Brunswick, NJ: Rutgers University Press.

Howell, James. 1998. Youth gangs: An overview. *Juvenile Justice Bulletin* August 1998. Washington, DC: U.S. Department of Justice, Office of Juvenile Justice and Delinquency Prevention.

Hughes, Lorine, and James Short. 2005. Disputes involving youth street gang members: Micro-social contexts. *Criminology* 43:43–76.

Kanter, Rosabeth. 1972. *Commitment and community: Communes und Utopias in sociological perspective.* Cambridge, MA: Harvard University Press.

Katz, Jack. 1988. *Seductions of crime: Moral and sensual attractions in doing evil.* New York: Basic Books.

Kennedy, David, Ann Morrison Piehl, and Anthony Braga. 1996. *Youth gun violence in Boston: Gun markets, serious youth offenders, and a use reduction strategy.* Research in Brief. Washington, DC: U.S. Department of Justice, Office of Justice Programs, National Institute of Justice.

Klein, Malcolm. 1995. *The American street gang.* New York: Oxford University Press.

Kubrin, Charis. 2005. Gangstas, thugs, and hustlas: Identity and the code of the street in rap music. *Social Problems* 52:360–78.

Lindesmith, Alfred, and Anslem Strauss. 1968. *Social psychology.* New York: Holt. Rinchart and Winston.

Lizotte, Alan, James Tesoriero, Terence Thornberry, and Marvin Krohn. 1994. Patterns of adolescent firearms ownership and use. *Justice Quarterly* 11:51–74.

Lofland, John, and Lyn H. Lofland. 1995. *Analyzing social settings: A guide to qualitative observation and analysis.* Belmont. CA: Wadsworth.

McCall, George, and Jerry Simmons. 1966. *Identities and interactions: An examination of human associations in everyday life.* New York: Free Press.

McCorkle, Richard, and Terance Miethe. 2002. *Panic: The social construction of the street gang problem.* Upper Saddle River. NJ: Prentice Hall.

Miller, Jody, and Rod Branson. 2000. Gender dynamics in youth gangs: A comparison of males' and females' accounts. *Justice Quarterly* 17:419–48.

Miller, Jody, and Scott Decker. 2001. Young women and gang violence: Gender, street offender, and violent victimization in gangs. *Justice Quarterly* 18:115–40.

Moore, Joan. 1978. *Homeboys: Gangs, drugs, and prison in the barrios of Los Angeles.* Philadelphia: Temple University Press.

———. 1991. *Going down to the barrio: Homeboys and homegirls in change.* Philadelphia: Temple University Press.

Oliver, William. 1994. *The violent world of black men.* New York: Lexington.

Piehl, Anne Morrison, David Kennedy, and Anthony Braga. 2000. Problem solving and youth violence: An evaluation of the Boston gun project. *American Law and Economics Review* 2:58–106.

Sanders, William. 1994. *Gang-bungs and drive-bys: Grounded culture and juvenile gang violence.* New York: Walter de Gruyter.

Schatzman, Leonard, and Anselm Strauss. 1973. *Field research strategies for a natural sociology.* Englewood Cliffs. NJ: Prentice Hall.

Shelden, Randall, Sharon Tracy, and William Brown. 2001. *Youth gangs in American society.* Belmont, CA: Wadsworth.

Sheley, Joseph, and James Wright. 1995. *In the line of fire: Youth, guns and violence in America.* New York: Aldine de Gruyter.

Sherif, Muzafer, and Milboume Wilson. 1953. *Group relations at the crossroads.* New York: Harper.

Shibutani, Tomatsu. 1961. *Society and personality: An interactionist approach to social psychology,* Englewood Cliffs, NJ: Prentice Hall.

Short, James. 1997. *Poverty, ethnicity, and violent crime.* Boulder, CO: Westview Press.

Short, James, and Fred Strodtbeck. 1965. *Group processes and gang delinquency.* Chicago: University of Chicago Press.

Sirpal, Suman K. 1997. Causes of gang participation and strategies for prevention in gang members' own words. *Journal of Gang Research* 4:13–22.

Spergel, Irving, and G. David Curry. 1990. Strategic perceived agency effectiveness in dealing with the youth gang problem. In *Gangs in America,* ed. C. Ronald Huff (288–309). Newbury Park, CA: Sage.

Stone, Gregory. 1962. Appearance and self. In *Human behavior and social processes,* ed. Arnold Rose (86–118). Boston: Houghton Mifflin.

Strauss, Anselm. 1962. Transformations of identity. In *Human behavior und social processes: An interactional approach,* ed. Arnold Rose (63–85). Boston: Houghton Mifflin.

———. 1969. *Mirrors and mash: The search for identity* New York: Macmillan.

Stryker, Sheldon, and Richard Serpe. 1982. Commitment, identity salience and role behavior. In *Personality, roles and social behavior,* eds. William Ikes and Eric Knowles (199–218). New York: Springer-Verlag.

Thornberry, Terence, Marvin Krohn, Alan Lizotte, and Debra Chard-Wierschem. 1993. The role of juvenile gangs in facilitating delinquent behavior. *Journal of Research in Crime and Delinquency* 30:75–85.

Thornberry, Terence, Marvin Krohn, Alan Lizotte, Carolyn Smith, and Kimberly Tobin. 2003. *Gangs and delinquency in developmental perspective.* Cambridge. England: Cambridge University Press.

Thrasher, Frederick. 1927. *The gang.* Chicago: University of Chicago Press.

Turner, Ralph. 1978. The role and the person. *American Journal of Sociology* 84:1–23.

Vigil, James. 1988. *Barrio gangs.* Austin: University of Texas Press.

———. 1996. Street baptism: Chicago gang initiation. *Human Organization.* 55:149–53.

———. 2003. Urban violence and street gangs. *Annual Review of Anthropology* 32:225–42.

Walker, Samuel. 1998. *Sense and no sense about crime and drugs.* Belmont. CA: Wadsworth.

Weinstein, Eugene, and Paul Deutschberger. 1963. Some dimensions of altercasting. *Sociometry* 26:454–66.

Wright, James, and Peter Rossi. 1986. *Armed and considered dangerous: A survey of felons and their firearms.* New York: Aldine de Gruyter.

Yablonsky, Lewis. 1962. *The violent gang.* New York: Macmillan.

12

Young Mother (in the) Hood

Gang Girls' Negotiation of New Identities

Molly Moloney, Geoffrey P. Hunt, Karen Joe-Laidler, and Kathleen MacKenzie

This research study's focus is on female gang members who become mothers. The project examines their thoughts about their new role as a parent. The way these gang member mothers transition their new identities and their negotiation of femininities in their attempt to reconcile these two statuses is analyzed. The loss of autonomy they experience as mothers from the more autonomous status of gang member is now changed and the effects of their diminished gang girl role are discussed.

Introduction

Despite declines in teen births internationally, young motherhood has been the subject of much heated media attention and policy debate in locales from the USA to the UK to Australia and New Zealand (McDermott and Graham 2005, Angwin and Kamp 2007). Policy discussions, drawing from scientific discourse, center on diet problems associated with early motherhood, including poor perinatal outcomes, child neglect or abuse, unstable employment, marital instability, and poor educational outcomes for both mother and child (Wilson and Huntington 2006). Young motherhood is presented as threatening the very foundation of society, undermining beliefs and values associated, with childhood, innocence, marriage, and family (Roseneil and Mann 1996, Furstenburg 2003). Given

the opposition between childhood and adulthood, combining childhood and motherhood provokes a deep sense of unease: "...it is adults who bear and beget children; a child cannot beget or bear a child. Yet that is precisely what a pregnant teenager is about to do" (Murcott 1980, p. 7). Although traditional objections connected to moral prescriptions and ideologies of feminine sexual purity have not disappeared, they have been joined by other arguments. For example, policymakers find it difficult to accept the moral affront young mothers present in today's neo-liberal state where welfare dependency and social exclusion are being replaced by new educational and employment opportunities meant to spur economic growth and allow individuals to construct a reflexive and autonomous self (Harris 2004; Wilson and Huntington 2006). These young mothers are deemed as having rejected these opportunities, and hence, are defined as an 'at risk' group and 'a risk' to social stability (Mitchell and Green 2002, McDermott and Graham 2005). In this article, however, we wish to move beyond this one-sided, negative view of young motherhood.

This article is concerned with one particular group of young mothers: gang-involved girls. We hope to demonstrate, drawing from qualitative interviews, the ways these young women negotiate and attempt to reconcile their identities as young mothers and gang girls. The lifestyle of girl gang members, including violence, drug and alcohol use, drug sales, and other criminal activities, has been noted by some gang researchers as an environment that may be harmful for raising a healthy child and conducive for the generational transmission of delinquency (Fleisher 1998). Motherhood and gang membership join together moral concerns about under-age sexual activities, childhood parenting and welfare dependency, as well as law-and-order worries about delinquency. Given the recent attention not only with girl gang members but also young motherhood in general, it is somewhat surprising that the issue of motherhood and gang membership has not generated more research (see Campbell 1991, Moore 1991, Dietrich 1998, Moore and Hagedorn 1999, Miller 2001, Vigil 2008 for key exceptions). In contrast to popular stereotypes of gang girls as either irredeemably violent or sexually promiscuous (Joe and Chesney-Lind 1995, Nurge 2003), an understanding of their experiences of pregnancy and motherhood may challenge these dominant images. An analysis of these young mothers will reveal the extent to which becoming mothers shapes their life trajectories, as well as provide an opportunity to understand how these young women negotiate between two conflicting identities: gang member and mother.

From Teen Mothers to Young Mothers

In spite of ongoing public concerns with teen pregnancy, recent research has questioned earlier studies purporting problematic outcomes of young mothers (Furstenburg et al. 1987, Luker 1996, Furstenburg 2003, SmithBattle 2009). Increasingly studies challenge commonly held assumptions that perinatal and post-natal outcomes are worse for teenagers than for older women. Also, although studies consistently show that early motherhood is related to dropping out of school, the path to leaving school is more complex than previously understood. Pregnancy may follow, rather than lead to leaving school early (Furstenberg et al.

1987, Social Exclusion Unit 1999, Dawson 2006). Moreover, motherhood can be a driving force for re-engaging in education (Hosie and Selman 2006, Angwin and Kamp 2007). Many early studies were plagued by issues of selection and failed to control for confounding factors; poor maternal or child outcomes associated with teenage births may be the result of underlying causes or contributors to teenage pregnancy rather than the teenage births themselves.

Recent research indicates that the key factor in determining the outcome of teenage pregnancy and motherhood is not age but poverty (Konner and Shostak 1986, Luker 1996, Geronimus 2003). Poverty, and related risk-factors, may explain unfavorable outcomes associated with teenage motherhood (Furstenberg 2003, Holmlund 2005, Hotz et al. 2005). Moreover, poverty combined with social and institutional stigmatization can negatively affect the transition to early motherhood (Kirkman et al. 2001, Yardley 2008). In considering the role of poverty and stigma, feminist researchers challenge implicit middle-class assumptions about the appropriate age for childbearing and the importance of delaying parenthood (Murcott 1980, Phoenix 1991, Jacobs 1994, McRobbie 2000, Edin and Kefalas 2005). While historically late-adolescence was perceived as physiologically an ideal time for young women to give birth, and motherhood in later years (over age 30) was identified as a period of increasing risk, this 'age appropriateness' has been redefined in the opposite direction (Wilson and Huntington 2006). Today, delayed parenthood is promoted in public policy as consistent with the expansion of opportunities for women to attain higher education and a career outside the home, and the rise of a new 'democratized family,' (McDermott and Graham 2005) within the 'new competitive meritocracy' (McRobbie 2007). As such, today's young mothers are marked as not having taken advantage of those opportunities, and instead have made 'bad choices' rather than being in 'bad circumstances' (Rolfe 2008). And as a result, teen (as distinct from young) mothers are highly stigmatized individually and collectively.

In response to this backlash, feminist scholars have emphasized the importance of understanding not only the cultural, economic and social factors that encourage early motherhood in marginalized communities but also the ways in which these youth negotiate new identities as women and as mothers within these structural constraints. Studies show that young mothers are fully aware of their stigmatization as being irresponsible, immoral, and lacking respectability (Kaplan 1997, Hanna 2001, Yardley 2008). Moreover, young mothers face the challenge of coming to terms with no longer having the freedom of adolescence, giving up youthful pleasures of partying, isolation from friends, financial insecurities, and feelings of unattractiveness (Kirkman et al. 2001, Baker 2009). In essence, this is a period of transition in femininity—from girlhood to motherhood, but is complicated by the stigma attached to their age.

Yet young mothers are highly resilient, negotiating poverty and stigma through social support from family and others. They report positive experiences with motherhood, finding it provides personal satisfaction, an impetus to pursue school or work, or a healing of family relationships (Rolfe 2008, Arai 2009, Gregson 2009). Despite the challenges of securing childcare and scheduling class time, young women find not only self-satisfaction, but also a way to build self-confidence for entering the job market (Dawson 2006). But more than this, for many young mothers, the transition to motherhood marks the transition to adult femininity with 'good mothering' as a key to this new identity and defined by the belief in their strengths such as competence as a mother and the advantage of youthful age (McDermott and Graham 2005, Baker 2009). Young mothers are engaged in 'consoling plots' (Prettyman 2005) or competitive parenting (Higginson 1998), an interactional process in which they reject the 'teen mother' as 'unfit mother' identity by 'investing in the good mother identity' (McDermott and Graham 2005, p. 71). This includes 'othering' the 'welfare mom' and projecting a self-sufficient and autonomous image (i.e., mature, responsible, financially independent) (Higginson 1998, Rolfe 2008). As McDermott and Graham (2005) have observed, this projected autonomous self is consistent with, although by a route counter to the middle-class prescription, the neo-liberal agenda of new twenty-first century woman (Harris 2004). Young mothers who are or have been involved in gangs, though, may face additional obstacles to challenging the 'teen mother' and 'unfit mother' stigma and to securing this autonomous identity, due to their gang involvement.

YOUNG MOTHERS IN THE HOOD

Early gang studies traditionally downplayed and minimized the roles that young women play in street gangs as well as the social processes and consequences of their involvement in gangs. Female gang members were portrayed in stereotypical ways from personal property to sexual chattel to maladjusted tomboys (Joe and Chesney-Lind 1995). Female gang participation has generated much public concern and media attention in recent years, in part because they are becoming more visible, and in part because they are presumed to be rebelling against traditional notions of femininity. In recent decades, there has been a significant expansion of scholarship focusing on young women in gangs (Quicker 1983, Fishman 1988, Harris 1988, Campbell 1991, Moore 1991, Joe-Laidler and Hunt 1997, 2001, Fleisher 1998, Venkatesh 1998, Chesney-Lind and Hagedorn 1999, Miller 2001, 2009, Miranda 2003, Nurge 2003, Hunt et al. 2005, Valdez 2007). Gang researchers have particularly focused on how these young women interpret their participation in delinquency and violence (Joe-Laidler and Hunt 1997, Campbell 1999, Chesney-Lind and Hagedorn 1999). This focus on delinquency, violence, and other public/street features of gang girls' lives, although important, has been questioned by some feminist writers. They argue that a focus on the traditionally masculine space of the street misses key elements of the social world of girls, which are often in more private or domestic locations (McRobbie and Garber 1976, Griffin 1993, see also Hunt et al. 2000, Wingood et al. 2002). Understanding their experiences in the private sphere may be just as essential to understanding their gang involvement as the more visible street activities. Having a child is one development that may lead a gang girl to alter her involvement in gang life. Furthermore, an analysis of how these young women view their relationships to their boyfriends and their families once they become pregnant and have children may illuminate their changing notions of femininity. Although in becoming gang members these young women may resist normative femininity (Joe-Laidler and Hunt 2001), by having children they may be obliged to accept some elements of traditional femininity.

Many key predisposing factors likely to encourage pregnancy are quite common among young women in gangs. Involvement with men significantly older (six or more years) is associated with both young mothers (Office of Population Affairs 2000) and with young women in gangs (Dietrich 1998). Experiences with childhood sexual abuse or assault may be related to adolescent pregnancy, with some estimating 50–75% of teenage mothers have histories of such abuse (Stevens-Simon and McAnarney 1996, see also Mason et al. 1998). Family abuse, physical and sexual, has been identified as a feature common among female gang members (Joe and Chesney-Lind 1995, Miller 2001, Fleisher and Krienert 2004, Gosselin 2005, Valdez 2007). Neighborhood influences are also linked to early pregnancy, particularly in communities where adolescent childbearing is increasingly common or socially acceptable (Schlegel 1995, Anderson 1999).

This may be especially true in impoverished neighborhoods where the 'lack of opportunities for personal advancement may lead to a lack of motivation to avoid pregnancy,' and where 'adolescent childbearing is considered normative' (Stevens-Simon and McAnarney 1996, p. 318). Similar social and cultural factors encouraging early pregnancy have been identified by gang researchers in studies of female gang members (Moore 1991, Dietrich 1998, Miller 2001).

However, these predisposing factors may not be the only elements in determining either the likelihood of female gang members becoming mothers or the ways they care for their children. We also need to consider the perspectives of these young women themselves. Although their choices are shaped by structural constraints at home and on the streets, these young women attempt to establish an identity of being a gang member within often conflicting cultural forms of femininity. Girls' participation in gangs offers an avenue for challenging and testing normative gender roles or what Connell (1987) calls 'emphasized femininity.'

Miller (2001) argues that young women in gangs participate in masculine gender norms, attempting to display toughness and fit in as 'one of the guys.' This street reputation and status translate as power for girls who operate within the patriarchal power structure of the gangs, the streets, and community. At the same time, many girl gang members embrace some forms of 'culturally appropriate' femininity (Messerschmidt 1997, p. 83). Ethnographic studies on female gangs find that gang girls concentrate on 'feminine activities' such as appearance and conversation. Many also find themselves in typically gendered lower- and working-class jobs like cleaning services, babysitting, and clerical work (Campbell 1991, Joe and Chesney-Lind 1995). Gang girls also achieve their identity of emphasized femininity by engaging in such gender-specific activities as cooking and preparing food within the gang (Messerschmidt 1997). Messerschmidt contends that female gang violence and displays of toughness are 'resources' for establishing a particular notion of femininity, that of the 'bad girl.' Others emphasize how these adolescent girls respond to two conflicting cultural forms of femininity. For example, Dietrich (1998) observes that Latina adolescents 'are confronted by a conflict between their gender and their gang membership' (p. 151). In adopting a masculine code of conduct or 'macho' homegirl image, they reject a more traditional Latino cultural norm of 'femeninidad.' '[T]he homegirls are a symbol of improper femininity' (Dietrich 1998, p. 151).

Given this already existing conflict between multiple, sometimes opposing, forms of femininity, how do gang girls negotiate femininity once they become pregnant and become mothers? This paper focuses on how these young women attempt to resolve their notions of being 'bad girls' with being pregnant and a mother while at the same time maintaining respect within the gang. Our objective is to uncover the process by which they negotiate early motherhood, how they handle the reactions and controls placed upon them by family members, and how they reconcile these potentially conflicting identities of gang girl and mother.

RESEARCH METHODS

The data for this paper are drawn from an ongoing comparative qualitative study of ethnic youth gangs in the San Francisco Bay area. We conducted face-to-face interviews with 350 self-identified female gang members, who were located using a snowball-sampling approach (Biernacki and Waldorf 1981). Approximately one-fifth (exactly 65) of these gang members were mothers. The analysis in this article is based on these interviews.

The mixed-methods interviews included a pre-coded quantitative schedule and semi-structured, open-ended questions about substance use, violence, and criminal activities as well as kinship and support networks. The interviews were conducted by field-workers who were matched to the groups they were sampling, either by their knowledge of the neighborhoods, their ethnic background, or their own experiences with gangs. The interviews took place in a variety of settings including residences, parks, church youth centers, and coffee shops. We gave a $50 honorarium in recognition of their participation and time.

We utilized self-nomination as the most reliable way of assessing gang membership (Esbensen et al. 2001, p. 124). We took several steps to address validity and reliability issues. Given the interviewers' familiarity with the scene and some of the respondents, respondents were less likely to exaggerate or minimize their experiences. During the interview, questions were rephrased at different times to detect inconsistencies. Interviewers were required to assess the respondent's veracity at the end of the interview, and found them to be truthful.

Audio recordings of the interviews were transcribed verbatim. The transcripts were then read and coded using qualitative textual-analysis software (NVIVO), using categories to capture different aspects of the respondents' narratives (e.g. gender relations, substance use, family relations, children).

Sample

The sample for this analysis is based on interviews with 65 mothers from the larger sample of 350 gang-involved young women. They came from a variety of low-income neighborhoods in the San Francisco Bay area. The majority of the women had just one child, with 14% having two or more. Five of the mothers were pregnant at the interview.

Almost half of the sample were Latinas (32 in all), 32% were African-American, 6% Pacific Islanders and 12% had classified themselves as being of mixed ethnicity. Twenty-three percent were immigrants, 12 having been born in Mexico or Central America, one in the Philippines, one in Samoa, and one in Germany. This is a diverse sample and clearly ethnicity may have a major influence on both experiences within the gang as well as kinship networks and experiences with motherhood. However, in the various narratives we discuss below, we find a remarkable commonality among young women from very different cultural backgrounds. Despite being raised with very different cultural and familial traditions, and participating in different ethnic-gangs, many of the young women faced similar challenges in reconciling gang and mother identities. In addition, our sample size (n = 65) is not large enough to comfortably be able to make generalizations about key differences in the gang/mother experience based on race or ethnicity. Hence, in this article, contrasts between gang members of different races and ethnicities will not be a primary focus.

At the time they were interviewed the mothers ranged in age from 15 to 31 years old. The median age was 21 with slightly over 47% of them under 18 when they had their first child, and nearly half were 16 or less. Six of the respondents were 13 years old when they had their first child and two were 12. Nearly two-fifths (38.5%) of the mothers had neither finished high school nor were they pursuing any other form of education. Over 40% of the mothers had either full- or part-time jobs, the remaining women relied on a number of different sources of income, including public assistance (9%) and family members or male partners (8%).

The respondents were members of a variety of types of gangs, from large, multigenerational gangs, with many sub-groups on types of gangs, from large, multigenerational gangs with many sub-groups on different blocks or regions, to smaller, more transitory gangs and cliques, and are similar to those described in the Eurogang project—which exhibit flexibility, a street orientation and crime involvement (including drug use and sales and violence) (Klein and Maxson 2006, p. 415). There was also diversity in the gender structure of the gangs represented, including all-female gangs as well as gangs with male and female members. The young women we interviewed typically had engaged in multiple risk behaviors, especially early on in their gang affiliation, including street fighting, drug sales, substance abuse, assaults, robbery, boosting (shoplifting), and other criminal behaviors, As we will see, however, for many of the young women involvement in these behaviors began to modify, decrease, or even cease upon pregnancy or the birth of their child.

GANG GIRLS AND MOTHERHOOD

While there are many reasons for joining a gang, many respondents identified the familial bond with the group as one of the most important as it offers acceptance and protection within a group they come to see as a surrogate family. In attaching themselves to the gang, they often found themselves in relationships with men who are significantly older and more experienced. The girls often feel under pressure to become sexually attached and in some cases encouraged and even pressured to have children. In opposition to the stereotypes of gang girls as being either too sexually available (sluts) or not sexually available enough (tomboys) (Joe and Chesney-Lind 1995), and in spite of their becoming pregnant, our respondents' accounts of their relationships with their boyfriends and the fathers of their children suggest a more nuanced picture. The majority of respondents had had little sexual experience prior to discovering that they were pregnant. About one-fifth of our sample became pregnant by their first sexual relationships.

For instance, Aesha (African-American, 20) described how at the age of 14 she was pursued by an 18-year-old man who lived in the same neighborhood. They got involved sexually and 'ain't never really went anywhere but in his room.' She ran away from home, moved in with the boyfriend and his mother, and 'then [I] popped up pregnant.' During the pregnancy, her boyfriend went to jail and, while incarcerated, denied he was the father. Prior to the start of this relationship she had no previous boyfriends because 'I wasn't wanting to pop.'

Yet their first relationships were not solely with older men. Approximately one-half of those who had children as a result of their first relationship were with young men of a comparable age. For example, Sonya, (African-American/Latina, 17), described how her boyfriend, who although the same age, 'was a little bit more advanced . . . I was like a little good girl . . . I didn't do anything at all that you weren't supposed to.' Because of their different sexual experiences, they decided to break up. But, at age 15, it was different because 'I was already into the gang. And then I was kickin' it around there more.' Soon after, she got pregnant, at the age of 16. He told her, 'You ain't gonna get an abortion . . . and you ain't gonna give him up for adoption. So, we're gonna take care of it.'

Respectability

According to Sonya, the father's willingness to look after the child was due to his strong belief that the child was his: 'I only had sex with him. That was it. Nobody else. And he knew that . . . He knew I wasn't sluttin' around with no dudes.' Sonya emphasized her respectability; she was not a 'slut,' and was not that enthusiastic about sex:

> I'm the type of girl who has had sex. I'm not into sex . . . I have sex with him because he wants to. I'm even embarrassed . . . I'm not that kind of girl . . . he's my man and because I got feelings for him.

This young mother, like others in this study, took pains to assert and establish her 'respectability.' Although teen motherhood may cast young women as embodying deviant femininity, as violating norms for sexual propriety, many respondents present their sexual experiences and resulting pregnancies in a more traditional light, appealing to their disinterest in sex, their commitment, or desire to become a mother.

Paradoxically the concern for respectability may also be a factor in explaining erratic birth control use. Sonya went on to explain:

> I was taking birth control. I got pregnant maybe four months after I started taking birth control because I would take it sporadically. Like, during the day, I would take it one day at three o'clock, the next day at four, the next day at nine . . . And so I got pregnant even on birth control.

While contraceptives offer protection, their use also signifies that she is sexually active and can raise doubts about her respectability or 'spontaneity' (Kaplan 1997, p. 42, see also Luker 1996, Dietrich 1998). This points to the extent to which she must attempt to negotiate competing cultural forces. Young women in gangs wished to be 'bad girls' but they were also concerned about their reputations. If they insist on using birth control they may stray into the male sphere of power and control and become identified not as sexually knowledgeable

but much more damagingly as sexually promiscuous. To be characterized as such may lead to the loss of reputation as a 'decent' girl and being labeled as a 'ho.' Consequently, femininity is constructed within these boundaries. Regardless of whether she knows about contraceptives she may be unwilling to enforce their use and thus risks pregnancy. Issues of respectability weigh heavily on some of the girls. Esmeralda (Latina/African-American, 15) expressed relief at attending a high school for teenage mothers: 'So another girl can't say, "She's a ho cuz she has a baby,"' something she says she hears 'all the time.'

Good Mothers

Becoming pregnant requires a gang girl to accommodate to a new identity of mother while at the same time negotiating what this will mean for her as a gang member. Becoming a mother does not mean that she necessarily gives up her identity as a 'bad girl,' but it does require her to find a compromise between being a good gang member and a good mother if she wishes to maintain respectability (Hunt et al. 2005). Similar to other work on young motherhood (Higginson 1998, Yardley 2008) gang girls invest in the good mother identity by distancing themselves from other young mothers, and are particularly critical of other gang girls who continued to 'hang out' on the block and even took their children out with them:

'There are so many other girls that I know with kids and they're still out there banging with their kids two, three in the morning. So many things have happened to babies because their moms are stupid, taking them out to parties, parks, while they're drunk, drinking in front of them, smoking in front of them. That's something I wouldn't do' (Giggles, Latina, 16).

Similarly, when asked how her life might differ from other young women, Frosty (Latina/African-American, 17) commented, 'Some girls don't even take care of their babies . . . going to the street all the time and nothing about babies, you know.' By highlighting the actions of 'bad mothers,' these young women shore up their claim to good motherhood.

Yet their attempts to construct themselves as good mothers do not always go without challenges. One source of conflict is often between the new mother and her own mother or grandmother, who in many cases provides a great deal of financial and/or childcare support for the babies. Becoming a mother means that the girls, who often joined the gang as a way of seeking greater independence beyond the private domestic sphere, now find themselves in a situation where they need assistance from others. The most common domestic arrangement was the young mother lived with her children and members of her family of origin (57%), often with her mother (41%), grandmother (6.5%), or both her parents (12%). The young women's families frequently provide financial support as well as childcare, which is crucial for the young mothers who are attempting to graduate from high school or get jobs. Many of the young mothers express gratitude for the help and support they have received from their families. It was common for them to comment that becoming a mother brought them closer to their own mothers, whereas relations had often been strained when they were more involved with the gang or the streets.

However, this family support presents its own dilemmas. Given the troubled family history of many gang girls (Joe and Chesney-Lind 1995, Hunt *et al.* 2000), these adolescents are often drawn to gang life as an alternative family and as a way of removing themselves from family controls and the consequences of family problems, including alcohol- and drug-related violence and physical and sexual abuse. Consequently, to return to the family and become reliant on family members may produce a new set of problems. As McRobbie noted, 'It is not hard to see the more negative dimensions of the "advantages" of a supportive family . . . dependency on the parents puts the young mothers in a powerless position' (2000, p. 167).

Whereas before they faced controls and criticism for not being good girls, they were now criticized for not being good mothers. Were they looking after their children properly and spending enough time with them? Were they spending too much time still 'hanging out' and 'partying'? As Esmeralda recounted, her mother:

Tell[s] me how to raise my son, or if I wanna go out: 'No, you're not bringin the baby with you, it's too cold outside,' She doesn't trust me with him so she takes him from me. And if I leave him, usually she'll say she'll call the police cuz I'm abandoning him or whatever. It's too much.

Criticisms of their mothering skills came not only from mothers but also grandmothers: 'I don't get along with my grandma 'cuz she makes me feel like a bad mother. She's like, "I know Teon better than you. Why are you making Teon suffer?"' (Gorda, Latina, 17). These new criticisms were difficult to accept, especially given their relationships with their mothers, whom many of the girls believed had failed to be 'good' parents (Hunt et al. 2000).

Still many young women report that while they feared telling their mothers about their pregnancy and the announcement initially led to heated tension, ultimately motherhood enabled many young women to become closer to their families, particularly their mothers. Motherhood led them to mature and allowed them to spend time with their families. Deici (Latina, 20) comments: 'Oh yeah, now I get along with my mom really good. And cause, I think because me getting pregnant, it was like a way for me to mature. Now I'm seeing things different.'

Off of the Streets, Into the Home

Before becoming mothers, the gang girls had been able to leave home and 'hang out' if things got too difficult, or even run away. They now found themselves tied to the home because of their children. For many young women, one of the most significant transitions to motherhood involves the realization of a loss of adolescent freedom. They report a decline in the amount of time spent on the streets with their friends and gang members, and increase in the amount of time spent within the home. Graciela (Latina, 19) comments 'Before I used to go out a lot with my friends . . . I don't go out no more, and I just stay home with the baby.' Ebony (African-American, 17) concurs:

I don't have time to have friends now . . . I want to like take care of my son, and just go home and be with my son . . . Sometimes I do feel like goin out, but that's kinda like once every six months.

Some describe separation from their friends, because their friends continue to socialize primarily through 'partying,' smoking weed, and other activities they choose not to partake in when they have their children with them. Star (Latina, 21) expresses feeling isolated from even her friends with children: 'I don't really talk ta my friends anymore . . . Most of 'em got kids and everything now . . . It's just different cuz we can't go outside.'

This can be seen as a retreat from the male-dominated sphere of the street (in which they nevertheless had often carved places for themselves), to the domestic sphere of the home (where they often feel out of place, especially initially), and hence a physical move from an oppositional femininity within a masculine sphere to inhabiting a seemingly more conventionally feminine sphere. This move inside removed them from some of the real dangers of violence and victimization they faced on the streets. It also, however, sometimes meant they grew apart from the social networks and support with then-fellow gang girls. And, as so many of them are in their mothers' homes, it meant difficulties finding a place to assert their independence.

Not surprisingly, some yearned for a place of their own:

> I would like to get my own place because everybody's always telling me like how to raise my baby . . . Like every time she cried, my grandma'll be like 'Oh, what's wrong with her? Did you feed her? Did you change her?' And I already changed her. And I already fed her. (Lucia, Latina, 17)

However, few of the women had the necessary financial resources to set up home independently. Attempts to be self-sufficient are often undermined as they find themselves totally ill-equipped, not only because of their youth and inexperience but also because of their lack of financial resources. Only 12% of the respondents lived on their own with their children, and those that did so were typically the older members of the sample. This increasing distance from peers marks the loss of adolescent autonomy and the negotiation of a new sense of adult autonomy, one which is based on demonstrating to others (and the self) one's mothering skills. These 'good mothering' skills entail not only being a good care giver but also financial provider.

The Fathers of the Children

To rely on the fathers of their children was not feasible in most cases. Some young men were unwilling to help, and of those who desired to help, many lacked the resources to do so. From the available data, only 31% of the respondents said that they had any relationship with their children's fathers. An additional 6% said that a relationship did exist, but that the fathers were currently in jail. Twelve of the 65 respondents lived with their child's father, sometimes as a couple alone, but often with his or her family. Although for many of the aspects studied we did not see clear racial/ethnic differences among our sample, we do see a suggestive association between ethnicity and cohabitation. The only two African-American respondents who were living with the father of their child were both biracial (African-American/ Latina). On the other hand, an additional 10 other Latina respondents were living with the fathers of their children, including the only two respondents who were married. This finding matches other research that has found cultural variation in the meaning of cohabitation with unmarried African-American mothers significantly less likely to cohabit with their child's father than Latinas or non-Hispanic whites (Manning and Landale 1996, Smock 2000).

The most common reason for the father's absence was his violence. Indeed, nine young women specifically recounted stories of the fathers behaving violently toward them after the pregnancy was announced. A second important reason for the father's absence was that they had proved to be unwilling to provide childcare either emotionally or financially.

Rocio (Latina, 19) complained that although her boyfriend 'had always wanted a baby,' when she had the child, he was unwilling to help in childcare activities. 'If I ask him like to change the diaper, he's like 'Oh, I don't wanna change a diaper, she's a girl' and I'm like, 'Don't use that excuse . . . He only wants to do the fun things.' Given this unwillingness to help look after the child, she now rarely sees him, a situation that she regrets:

> I wish I had like a real family to bring her up in. I know I hated it when my dad wasn't around. And look at my child's dad. He's out doin' who knows what. I can't even imagine spending one day without my baby, how is he about to spend two months?

As in many of the other cases, this young woman faced a situation where initially her boyfriend had been keen on looking after his child, but gradually lost interest in caring for his daughter and drifted away. Esmeralda similarly recounts: 'He came by a couple of times. And that was it. He doesn't show up no more . . . He don't care no more . . . so it's just me and the baby.'

A Gang Member and a Mother?

In some instances, gang girls were able to turn to their fellow members for support. Four women belonged to one all-female Latina gang. As they became mothers, the group took on a new focus.

> After you have a baby, you can only be friends with other people who have babies because all the single ones think, 'Oh, she probably can't go out. She got the baby.' . . . I mean, it's like once you have a baby, you only stick to people that have babies mostly. A lot of my friends have babies . . . We'll be there at my house or someone else's house with all our kids. We'll be like, 'the Baby-Sitters Club.' (Rocio)

This group continued to get together after they became mothers. Previously they tended to gather on the streets and were actively involved in risky behaviors, including substance use and fighting. Now their interaction occurs in the private sphere, getting together for occasions like baby showers and birthday parties. Moving beyond the public gaze of the street, the group has become a distinctive context to support one another emotionally, to exchange information, advice, childcare, and even items like baby clothes. This social outlet serves to reduce social isolation and disconnection from others of their age. This type of 'baby club,' in which the young women support one another and their babies, is not uncommon among street girls (Hagan and MacCarthy 1997, Anderson 1999). However, as found in previous research (Lauderback et al. 1992, Joe-Laidler and Hunt 2001), these are exceptions in the world of gangs and may occur primarily in female-only gangs, as opposed to the more common mixed-gender, often male-dominated gang formations.

While in this baby-club example, the women found support for their mother identity from their gang group, in most other cases, they describe conflict between their ability to remain good members of their gang and their responsibilities as a mother. Some young mothers described a newfound wariness of the dangers of gang-related violence, now that they had children to worry about. Some expressed a desire to curtail hanging out and partying due to their commitment to be a responsible parent and role model. Others expressed concerns about not 'being there' for the gang or not being able to blow off steam with the gang, though they'd like to, due to having to be at home. Nearly one-half of all respondents were either no longer or less involved in the gang. Over one-half of them specifically mentioned their children as the primary reason for this change.

Many young women believed that becoming a mother was a positive development, which allowed them to reassess their role in the gang. Graciela described her transformation:

It kind of made me grow up faster than I should have because now it's like I think about my baby first before I think about myself . . . Before, I don't care about nothing and, you know, I'm goin to do what I want to do. And then when I had my baby, I thought of him first and I changed my way of thinking.

Some of their modified behaviors occurred because they were unwilling to expose their children to everyday gang life, especially in the use of drugs and alcohol.

Well, I stopped talking to them really because, my friends go out a lot. . . . and I don't want to take my baby out with me and hang around my friends, and drink and hang out on the corner or whatever . . . I don't want my baby there. (Graciela)

In these cases, motherhood enabled an important shift in the girls' outlook, priorities, and time spent in gang-related risk activities. Their new mother identity, and the desire to be the 'good mother,' increasingly supplanted their gang identity.

Upon becoming a mother, keeping themselves and their children safe by avoiding the streets, reduces the risks associated with gang violence and leads most mothers to cease some if not all of the common gang risk behaviors, including shoplifting, fights, and drug sales. The most pervasive activity that many young moms continued is the use of marijuana. A third of the mothers admitted to still smoking marijuana which demonstrates the increasing trend toward normalization of marijuana use (MacKenzie et al. 2005). Many mothers who carry on using marijuana generally do so in private and not in the presence of their children. The ongoing use of more serious and more addictive drugs, such as crack cocaine and methamphetamine, is sporadic and minimal among most of the mothers.

Some young women (18%) decided they would still hang out and party with the gang but remained committed to being responsible. For them, the key to balancing the tension between adult responsibilities and adolescent freedoms was to define acceptable boundaries of motherhood. Deliberately exposing their children to 'harmful activities' such as using drugs was deemed unacceptable, and too much like those mothers they distanced themselves from. Yet leaving their children in the care of trusted others while hanging out meant they were still acting as responsible mother.

I smoke weed like every once in a while. I don't like doin' it 'cuz I'm always with my baby . . . My mom sometimes she goes 'Okay, you can get away for like three hours.' I'll go around my neighborhood with my friend . . . we'll go smoke, and I'll go back home when I'm better . . . I breastfeed her, so that's one of the reasons I don't like smoking weed. Or we go outside. (Smiley, Latina, 17)

These respondents describe a somewhat compartmentalized identity—sometimes highlighting their motherhood, taking care of their children, other times highlighting their gang membership, hanging out with their homegirls, while their mother or grandmother watched the baby or only engaging in gang behaviors when they were not with the child. Frosty describes:

As long as I don't have my baby with me, I'm down [will join in a fight]. If I got my baby with me, I'm a punk [won't join in a fight]. Cuz I'm not gonna do nothing violent with my kid with me.

Yet motherhood did not automatically lead them all to sever the ties to the gang. Twenty-nine percent of young mothers gave little or no indication that they had lessened their involvement or modified their behaviors. One mother, for example, brought her infant son to the interview, wearing shoes and sports gear that she pointed out as being associated with her gang. Drug sales were a continuing activity for this third of the mothers in the sample, who are willing to take a risk to subsidize or supplement their incomes. Many of the mothers who engage in sales rationalize their activity as a critical income-producing option in a competitive market, and a risk that a good mother is willing to take to provide for her children.

For those who continued gang involvement, it was not uncommon for them to find themselves with their children in potentially violent situations.

> I don't wanna get jumped [attacked] because of the baby . . . Like for a month, I had to go to [a rival gang's street] . . . I was confronted . . . I was like 'I'm with my baby, what the fuck are you coming up ta me? Come up ta me when I'm by myself. I don't care what you do ta me, but with my baby, no.' (Silvia, Latina, 16)

And even for those who choose to leave the gang to take care of their children, this poses a number of challenges. Some were challenged by members of rival gangs who are unaware that they are no longer in the gang. Others describe resentment from their fellow gang members for having left. However, many do report that leaving the gang for motherhood is an acceptable exit route from gang life, one that does not, for instance, require being 'jumped out' [beaten up to leave]. Still, constructing a motherhood identity around a gang identity proves challenging.

CONCLUSION

This analysis suggests that gang girls who become mothers share much in common with young mothers, more generally, in other locales around the world (McDermott and Graham 2005, Rolfe 2008, Yardley 2008). The initial discovery of pregnancy is often met with disbelief and yields mixed reactions from family and the father. After the initial period, the father's presence and support often remains tenuous with his own struggles with young adulthood (e.g. finances, employment, freedom, and male peer interactions). This can be a source of anxiety as she comes to terms with the realization of her loss of adolescent freedom and of the sacrifices of responsible adulthood. These findings run counter to the popular characterizations of the 'teen mother' as the irresponsible dependent and the gang girl as 'bad girl.' These young women clearly understood and rose to the challenge of moving from girlhood to womanhood.

Similar to other studies (Baker 2009), we also found respectability to be a key dimension in young mothers' attempts to negotiate adult femininity. In our earlier work on gang girls, we argued that respect is highly gendered and that it must be understood beyond the masculine power of the street (Joe-Laidler and Hunt 2001, et al. 2003). For gang girls, adolescent femininity is connected with the pursuit of respect (ability) and enacted through demonstrations of personal autonomy and sexual reputation. Maintaining respect alters for many of these gang-involved girls when they become mothers. Whereas previously respectability was negotiated in their role as gang girl where much time was invested in demonstrating to others one's autonomy and sexual reputation on the street, once pregnant, their gang identity often conflicts with maintaining respect as a good mother. Caring for children while still being a gang member places these young women in a precarious, contradictory position. They also face challenges in reconciling respectability with their visibility as teenagers who are pregnant or young mothers. Whether still heavily involved in the gang, or having left the gang entirely, for most of the young women in this study, the meaning and negotiation of respect (ability) shifts as they move into motherhood. The pursuit of autonomy is no longer tied to wanting to be on the street and out of family controls and conflict but linked to the desire to feel independent (e.g. financially, emotionally) from others including the child's father and her own family members.

We were struck by how their new motherhood responsibilities—and specifically their return to family homelife and the necessity to rely on the support of parents and other relatives—did not allow many of these young women to fully express or experience feelings of adulthood or independence. Whereas prior to becoming mothers, they countered family criticisms and controls by being involved in the gang, once they have children, their older relatives may question their ability to raise her child or to be good mothers. Other studies have observed young mothers' resistance to what they perceive as 'adversarial advice' from family and relatives (Higginson 1998). Because young mothers are newly reliant on family support, they may find themselves even more restricted than previously. Moreover, their ability to negotiate some private space to define their own identity can become more curtailed as they seek to care for their children.

Overall, most respondents attempted to care for their children in difficult circumstances with often insufficient support. For many of the young mothers the task was especially difficult and tiring: 'It was like kinda hard because you don't get much sleep, and they're always waking up and they're always hungry' (Rocio). Given these difficult circumstances it is not surprising that some of them, although loving and caring for their children, wished motherhood came at a later stage in their lives. 'I don't regret my daughter because I love her but I wasn't ready, you know' (Giggles). Nevertheless, most young mothers expressed resiliency, and in spite of severe problems with families and boyfriends, few gave the impression of being downtrodden. In fact, they articulated a sense of agency and willingness to be a responsible, good mother.

Our study cannot and is not meant to generalize the experience of gang girls and young motherhood, and reflects a small group of young women in a particular locale. Young women in gangs are more likely to have histories of substance abuse, of drug sales, of criminal involvement, and of participation in fights and violence (Wingood et al. 2002, Miller 2009). The challenges faced by these young women if they attempt to finish their education or enter the workforce to support their children may be even greater than those faced by non-gang-involved young mothers, due to their criminal records and the stigma of gang membership as well as pressures from fellow gang members. Despite this, we found many similarities in gang girls experiences with young women reported elsewhere who had no affiliation with gangs. In spite of the structural inequalities and the stigma of 'teen motherhood,' gang and non-gang girls are resilient in navigating from adolescence into adulthood. At the core of this journey is a realization of the new meanings and responsibilities of adult femininity. As others have observed, this is articulated in their discourse as 'good mothers,' independence, and self-growth; attributes associated with middle-class neo-liberalism. Yet as these young mothers try to balance the desires and demands of motherhood and the gang, they are still constrained by the possibilities of the neo-liberal state which although on the surface promise greater freedom for young women, in fact, place further controls on their everyday life.

References

Anderson, E., 1999. *Code of the street: decency, violence, and the moral life of the inner city.* New York: W.W. Norton & Company.

Angwin, J. and Kamp, A., 2007. Policy hysteria in action: teenage parents at secondary school in Australia. In: J. Mcleod and A. Allard, eds. *Learning from the margins: young women, social exclusion and education.* London: Routledge, 95–107.

Arai, L., 2009. What a difference a decade makes: rethinking teenage pregnancy as a problem. *Social policy and society,* 8, 171–183.

Baker, J., 2009. Young mothers in late modernity: sacrifice, respectability and the transformative neo-liberal subject. *Journal of youth studies,* 12, 275–288.

Biernacki, P. and Waldorf, D., 1981. Snowball sampling: problems and techniques of chain referral sampling. *Sociological methods & research,* 10, 141–163.

Campbell, A., 1991. *The girls in the gang.* 2nd ed. Cambridge, MA: Basil Blackwell.

Campbell, A., 1999. Female gang members' social representations of aggression. In: M. Chesney-Lind and J. M. Hagedorn, eds. *Female gangs in America.* Chicago, IL: Lake View Press, 248–255.

Chesney-Lind, M. and Hagedorn, J. M., eds. 1999. *Female gangs in America. Chicago,* IL: Lake View Press.

Connell, R., 1987. *Gender and power.* Stanford, CA: Stanford University Press.

Dawson, N., 2006. In a class of their own? The education of pregnant schoolgirls and schoolgirl mothers. In: H. S. Holgate, R. Evans, and F. K. O. Yuen, eds. *Teenage pregnancy and parenthood: global perspectives, issues and interventions.* London: Routledge, 63–76.

Dietrich, L. C., 1998. *Chicana adolescents: bitches, 'ho's, and schoolgirls.* Westport, CT: Praeger.

Edin, K. and Kefalas, M., 2005. *Promises I can keep: why poor women put motherhood before marriage.* Berkeley, CA: University of California Press.

Esbensen, F. -A., et al., 2001. Youth gangs and definitional issues: when is a gang a gang, and why does it matter? *Crime & delinquency,* 47, 105–130.

Fishman, L., 1988. The vice queens: an ethnographic study of female gang behavior. Paper *presented at the American Society of Criminology.* University of Vermont, Burlington.

Fleisher, M. S., 1998. *Dead end kids: gang girls and the boys they know.* Madison, WI: The University of Wisconsin Press.

Fleisher, M. S. and Krienert, J. L., 2004. Life-course events, social networks, and the emergence of violence among female gang members. *Journal of community psychology,* 32, 607–622.

Furstenberg, E. E., Jr., 2003. Teenage childbearing as a public issue and private concern. *Annual review of sociology,* 29, 23–39.

Furstenberg, F. F., Jr., Brooks-Gunn, J., and Morgan, S. P., 1987. *Adolescent mothers in later life.* Cambridge, UK: Cambridge University Press.

Geronimus, A. T., 2003. Damned if you do: culture, identity, privilege, and teenage childbearing in the United States. *Social science & medicine,* 57, 881–893.

Gosselin, D. K., 2005. *Heavy hands: an introduction to the crimes of family violence.* Upper Saddle River, NJ: Pearson/Prentice Hall.

Gregson, J., 2009. *The culture of teenage mothers.* Albany, NY: State University of New York Press.

Griffin, C., 1993. *Representations of youth: the study of youth and adolescence in Britain and America.* Cambridge, UK: Polity Press.

Hagan, J. and MacCarthy, B., 1997. Mean *streets: youth crime and homelessness.* Cambridge, UK: Cambridge University Press.

Hanna, B., 2001. Negotiating motherhood: the struggles of teenage mothers. *Journal of advanced nursing,* 34, 456–464.

Harris, A., 2004. *Future girl: young women in the twenty-first century.* New York: Routledge.

Harris, M., 1988. *Cholas: Latino girls and gangs.* New York: AMS Press.

Higginson, J. G., 1998. Competitive parenting: the culture of teen mothers. *Journal of marriage and family,* 60, 135–149.

Holmlund, H., 2005. Estimating long-term consequences of teenage childbearing: an examination of the siblings approach. *The journal of human resources,* XL, 716–743.

Hosie, A. and Sehnan, P., 2006. Teenage pregnancy and social exclusion: an exploration of disengagement and re-engagement from the education system. In: H. S. Holgate, R. Evans, and F. K. O. Yuen, eds. *Teenage pregnancy and parenthood: global perspectives, issues and interventions.* London: Routledge, 77–94.

Hotz, V. J., Mcelroy, S. W., and Sanders, S. G., 2005. Teenage childbearing and its life cycle consequences: exploiting a natural experiment. *The journal of human resources,* 40, 683–715.

Hunt, G., Joe-Laidler, K., and Mackenzie, K., 2005. Moving into motherhood: gang girls and controlled risk. *Youth & society,* 36, 333–373.

Hunt, G., Mackenzie, K., and Joe-Laidler, K., 2000. I'm calling my mom: the meaning of family and kinship among homegirls. *Justice quarterly,* 17, 1–31.

Jacobs, J. L., 1994. Gender, race, class and the trend toward early motherhood: a feminist analysis of teen mothers in a contemporary society. *Journal of contemporary ethnography,* 22, 442–462.

Joe, K. A. and Chesney-Lind, M., 1995. Just every mother's angel: an analysis of gender and ethnic variations in youth gang membership. *Gender & society,* 9/408–431.

Joe-Laidler, K. and Hunt, G., 1997. Violence and social organization in female gangs. *Social justice,* 24, 148–169.

Joe-Laidler, K. and Hunt, G., 2001. Accomplishing femininity among girls in the gang. *British journal of criminology,* 41 (4), 656–678.

Kaplan, E. B., 1997. *Not our kind of girl: unraveling the myths of black teenage motherhood.* Berkeley, CA: University of California Press.

Kirkman, M., et al., 2001. 'I know I'm doing a good job': canonical and autobiographical narratives of teenage mothers. *Culture, health & sexuality: an international journal for research, intervention and care,* 3, 279–294.

Klein, M. W. and Maxson, C. L., 2006. *Street gang patterns and policies.* Oxford, UK: Oxford University Press.

Konner, M. and Shostak, M., 1986. Adolescent pregnancy and childbearing: an anthropological perspective. *In:* J. B. Lancaster and B. Hamburg, eds. *School-age pregnancy and parenthood: biosocial dimensions.* New York: Aldine De Gruyter, 325–345.

Lauderback, D., Hansen, J., and Waldorf, D., 1992. Sisters are doin' it for themselves: a black female gang in San Francisco. *Gang journal,* 1, 57–72.

Luker, K., 1996. *Dubious conceptions: the politics of teenage pregnancy.* Cambridge, MA: Harvard University Press.

MacKenzie, K., Hunt, G., and Joe-Laidler, K., 2005. Youth gangs and drugs: the case of marijuana. *Journal of ethnicity in substance abuse,* 4, 99–134.

Manning, W. D. and Landale, N. S., 1996. Racial and ethnic differences in the role of cohabitation in premarital childbearing. *Journal of marriage and family,* 58, 63–77.

Mason, W. A., Zimmerman, L., and Evans, W., 1998. Sexual and physical abuse among incarcerated youth: implications for sexual behavior, contraceptive use, and teenage pregnancy. *Child abuse and neglect,* 22, 987–995.

McDermott, E. and Graham, H., 2005. Resilient young mothering: social inequalities, late modernity and the "problem" of "teenage" motherhood. *Journal of youth studies,* 8, 59–79.

McRobbie, A., 2000. *Feminism and youth culture.* 2nd ed. New York: Routledge.

McRobbie, A., 2007. Top girls?—Young women and the post-feminist sexual contract. *Cultural studies,* 21, 718–737.

McRobbie, A. and Garber, J., 1976. Girls and subcultures: an exploration. *In:* S. Hall and T. Jefferson, eds. *Resistance through rituals: youth subcultures in post-war* Britain. London: Hutchinson University Library, 209–222.

Messerschmidt, J. W., 1997. *Crime as structured action: gender, race, class, and crime in the making.* Thousand Oaks, CA: Sage.

Miller, J., 2001. *One of the guys: girls, gangs, and gender.* Oxford, UK: Oxford University Press.

Miller, J., 2009. Young women and street gangs. *In:* M. A. Zahn, ed. *The delinquent girl.* Philadelphia, PA: Temple University Press, 207–224.

Miranda, M. K., 2003. *Homegirls in the public sphere.* Austin, TX: University of Texas Press.

Mitchell, W. and Green, E., 2002. I don't know what I'd do without our mam: motherhood, identity and support networks. *The sociological review,* 50, 1–21.

Moloney, M., et al., 2009. The path and promise of fatherhood for gang members. *The British journal of criminology,* 49, 305–325.

Moore, J. W., 1991. *Going down to the barrio: homeboys and homegirls in change.* Philadelphia, PA: Temple University Press.

Moore, J. W. and Hagedorn, J. M., 1999. What happens to girls in the gang? *In:* M. Chesney-Lind and J. M. Hagedorn, eds. *Female gangs in America.* Chicago, IL: Lake View Press, 177–186.

Murcott, A., 1980. The social construction of teenage pregnancy: a problem in the ideologies of childhood and reproduction. *Sociology of health and illness,* 2, 1–23.

Nurge, O., 2003. Liberating yet limiting: the paradox of female gang membership. *In:* L. Kontos, D. Brotherton, and L. Barrios, eds. *Gangs and society: alternative perspectives.* New York: Columbia University Press, 161–182.

Office of Population Affairs, 2000. *Trends in adolescent pregnancy and childbearing* [online]. US Department of Health and Human Services. Bethesda, MD: Office of Population Affairs. Available from: http:/Meb.arcbiveorgMeb/20000615040037/http://hhs.gov/progorg/opa/pregtrnd.html [Accessed 10 March 2010].

Phoenix, A., 1991. *Young mothers?* Cambridge, UK: Polity Press.

Prettyman, S. S., 2005. "We ain't no dogs": teenage mothers (re)define themselves. In P. J. Bettis and N. G. Adams, eds. *Geographies of girlhood: identities in-between.* Mahwah, NJ: Lawrence Erlbaum, 156–174.

Quicker, J. C., 1983. *Homegirls: characterizing Chicana gangs.* Los Angeles, CA: International University Press.

Rolfe, A., 2008. "You've got to grow up when you've got a kid": marginalized young women's accounts of motherhood. *Journal of community & applied social psychology,* 18, 299–314.

Roseneil, S. and Mann, K., 1996. Unpalatable choices and inadequate families: lone mothers and the underclass debate. In E.B. Silva, ed. *Good enough mothering? Feminist perspectives on lone mothering.* London: Routledge, 191–210.

Schalet, A., Hunt, G., and Joe-Laidler, K., 2003. Respectability and antonomy the articulation and meaning of sexuality among the girls in the gang. *Journal of contemporary ethnography,* 32 (1), 108–143.

Schlegel, A., 1995. A cross-cultural approach to adolescence. *Ethos,* 23, 15–32.

SmithBattle, L., 2009. Refraining the risks and losses of teen mothering. MCN. *The American journal of maternal/child nursing,* 34, 122–128.

Smock, P., 2000. Cohabitation in the United States: an appraisal or research themes, findings, and implications. *Annual review of sociology,* 26, 1–20.

Social Exclusion Unit, 1999. *Teenage pregnancy.* London: Her Majesty's Stationery Office (HMSO).

Stevens-Simon, C. and McAnarney, E. R., 1996. Adolescent pregnancy. *In:* R. J. Diclemente, W. B. Hansen, and L. E. Ponton, eds. *Handbook of adolescent health risk behavior.* New York: Plenum Press, 313–332.

Valdez, A., 2007. *Mexican American girls and gang violence: beyond risk.* New York: Palgrave Macmillan.

Venkatesh, S. A., 1998. Gender and outlaw capitalism: a historical account of the Black Sisters United "girl gang." *Signs,* 23, 683–709.

Vigil, J. D., 2007. *The projects: gang and non-gang families in East Los Angeles.* Austin, TX: University of Texas Press.

Wilson, H. and Huntington, A., 2006. Deviant (m)others: the construction of teenage motherhood in contemporary discourse. *Journal of social policy,* 35, 59–76.

Wingood, G. M., et al., 2002. Gang involvement and the health of African American female adolescents. *Pediatrics,* 110, 57–62.

Yardley, E., 2008. Teenage mothers' experiences of stigma. *Journal of youth studies,* 11, 671–684.

PART V

WHITE-COLLAR OCCUPATIONAL CRIME

Although there are a wide variety of white-collar criminal offenses such as price fixing, insider stock trading, and bribery—which mainly occur at the corporate level—there are also numerous other types of white-collar crimes that prey on citizens by the use of fraud. Those particular offenses include a wide variety of ways in which criminals obtain property or money under false pretenses. Fraudulent activity usually is in the form of confidence games or swindles and involves deception and misrepresentation that tend to manipulate the victims. Gaining the trust of the potential victim is a very important part of a fraudulent scheme when committed on innocent victims.

The readings in this area of criminal behavior deal with persons whose illegal acts involve fraud and identity theft, which are categorized as white-collar crimes. However, the realization that I have selected three readings that only represent a small component of white-collar crime needs to be noted. But, the subjects they discuss are probably familiar to most students reading this book and thus were chosen for inclusion.

Most people have been contacted by telemarketers by phone at one time or another. Shover, Coffey, and Sanders interviewed 47 telemarketing offenders convicted of violations of federal law. These offenders are very much like other criminals who wish to gain economically from their unlawful activities in order to experience a lifestyle that they wish to maintain. The authors point out that the number of people victimized by fraud is considerable in number and far exceeds those citizens victimized by street crime felonies. Telemarketing fraud steals approximately $40 billion dollars a year from the public in this country alone. The rapid increase in this white-collar offense has been largely a result of the ease in which victims are contacted.

Identity theft's rapid growth in recent years poses a threat to an unsuspecting public. The criminal activity occurs when citizens' personal information is stolen for purposes of economic gain by another. The identifying information includes: names, telephone numbers, address(es), financial information such as bank or stock accounts, and the most important item—an individual's social security number. With the advancement of technology, computers have provided identity thieves with the necessary venues in which to carry out this offense.

Heith Copes and Lynne M. Vieraitis examined the crime of identity theft by interviewing 59 offenders who were serving time in various federal prisons for committing this criminal activity. Their study attempts to determine if identity theft should actually be categorized as a type of white-collar crime because the backgrounds of offenders are of such a diverse nature. To provide an answer to this definitional question, they focused their study on their sample offenders' backgrounds and the techniques the offenders utilized to gain the victims' identifying information, as well as the methods for using this information for purposes of financial gain.

The subject of illegal digital pirating is explored by Thomas J. Holt and Heith Copes. They were interested in the impact of the process of online learning as it affects individual behavior by examining online media piracy. The increased growth of media files and the advances in technology have resulted in the creation of a subculture on a world-wide basis; this subculture is one of media piracy. The authors discuss how individuals become familiar with the motives and techniques of media piracy by online interactions involved in this illegal practice. Risk factors, motivations, methods to lessen risk of being caught, and overall justifications for committing digital offenses are discussed.

13

Dialing for Dollars

Opportunities, Justifications, and Telemarketing Fraud

Neal Shover, Glenn S. Coffey, and Clinton R. Sanders

Based on interviews of 47 federally incarcerated telemarketers, this study describes and analyzes the backgrounds and criminal pursuits of people involved in this type of fraudulent criminal behavior. The income produced from telemarketing fraud was quite lucrative, which enabled these offenders to enjoy a comfortable economic lifestyle. Their manipulative abilities—which required very few credentials— provided their access to participate in this form of white-collar crime.

The dawning of the twenty-first century has ushered in fundamental changes in the structure and dynamics of economic relationships and communications technology. Most important, widespread use of telecommunications and electronic financial transactions presage a depersonalized, cashless economy. Electronic financial transfers among banks and businesses, automatic teller machines, and home banking increasingly are used across the globe.

Not only has the nature of business transactions been altered fundamentally by transformations of economic relationships, but capacity for credible oversight Blum (1972:14) observed:

> It is well not to overlook how "normal" it is to be a confidence man or swindler. In our society,

salesmanship is valued, commerce is based on the ability of people to persuade others whom they do not know that their products are worthy. The promise of gain is central to our—and to most—societies . . . It is also not extraordinary to lie, nor to misrepresent and to deceive in ordinary business. Viewed in this light, what the confidence man does is simply an extreme expression of normal business dealings.

Contemporary fraud is nonconfrontational, violates trust, and can be carried out over long distance. In organizational complexity and reach, it ranges from itinerant vinyl siding scamsters to international banking crimes that can destabilize national economies. The number of Americans victimized by fraud is large and substantially exceeds the number of those victimized

Source: Dialing for Dollars: Opportunities, Justifications, and Telemarketing Fraud, by Neal Shover, Glen S. Coffey, and Clinton R. Sanders. *Qualitative Sociology, 27* (1), Spring 2004. Used with kind permission from Springer Science+Business Media B.V.

by serious street crime (Rebovich and Layne 2000; Titus 2001). A 1991 survey of U.S. households, for example, found that compared to crimes of burglary, robbery, assault, and theft, fraud "appears to be very common" (Titus, Heinzelmann and Boyle 1995, p. 65).

The state and the array of largesse it makes available to citizens and organizations are frequent targets of fraud offenders, ones they need not leave home or office to exploit. Federally funded health care programs, for example, have given physicians and hospitals access to new pools of tax revenue for which oversight is so weak that it has been called a "license to steal" (Sparrow 1996). The growth of health insurance fraud, therefore, can be seen as "emblematic of the emerging forms of . . . crime that reflect the changing economy of the late twentieth century" (Tillman 1998, p. 197).

The rapid growth and correlative criminal exploitation of telemarketing parallel these larger trends in commercial deviance. In 2000, legitimate telemarketing sales accounted for $611.7 billion in revenue in the United States, an increase of 167 percent over comparable sales for 1995. Total annual sales from telephone marketing are expected to reach $939.5 billion by the year 2005 (Direct Marketing Association 2001). The reasons for the growth of telemarketing are understood easily in the context of the "general acceleration of everyday life, characterized by increasingly complicated personal and domestic timetables" (Taylor 1999, p. 45). The daily schedule no longer permits either the pace or the style of shopping that were commonplace a few decades ago, and the need to coordinate personal schedules and to economize on time now drives many household activities. In the search for convenience, telemarketing sales have gained in popularity.

Telemarketing's increasingly important role in the legitimate economy means criminal deviants have been quick to exploit the opportunities it presents. Although it was nearly unheard of until recent decades, few citizens today are unfamiliar with telemarketing fraud, a form of economic exploitation that is estimated to take $40 billion a year from its gullible victims (Doocy et al. 2001, p. 9). There are countless variations on the basic scheme, but typically a consumer receives a phone call from a high-pressure salesperson who solicits funds or sells products based on false assertions or enticing claims. Callers offer an enormous variety of products and services and often they use names that sound similar to those of bona fide charities or reputable organizations (U.S. Congress, Senate 1993). Goods or services either are not delivered at all, or they are substantially inferior to what was promised.

METHOD

Most of the data used for this discussion were gathered in semi-structured interviews with 47 telemarketing offenders convicted of federal crimes. We began the process of identifying respondents by examining major metropolitan newspapers for the years 1996 through 2000 and an assortment of approximately 75 web sites that contain information about telemarketing fraud and names of convicted offenders. This search yielded the names of 308 persons who were convicted of telemarketing fraud during this period.

Under terms of an agreement with the Federal Bureau of Prisons, the names were submitted to personnel in their Office of Research and Evaluation, who reported to investigators the institutional locations of those currently incarcerated. The institutional warden or the warden's designate subsequently presented to the inmates a written description of the research and its objectives and inquired if she or he was agreeable to meeting with an investigator when he visited the institution. Investigators then traveled to a number of institutions to meet with those who responded affirmatively in order to describe and explain research objectives and to interview those who elected to participate in the study. Twenty-five respondents were incarcerated in 12 federal prisons when they were interviewed.

To ensure that the interviews included respondents with diverse telemarketing experience, 22 offenders under federal probation supervision in Las Vegas and 7 other cities also were interviewed. This was done because we reasoned that probationers' involvement in telemarketing fraud probably was neither as lengthy nor as serious as was that of those who had been incarcerated. On average, the 47 interviewees were employed in criminal telemarketing for 8.25 years. Their ages when interviewed ranged from 26 to 69, with a mean of 42.4 years. Their ranks included 38 white males, 3 African American males, and 6 white females. Nearly all had been married at least once, and most had children. While the precise relationship of those interviewed to fraudulent telemarketers in general is difficult to determine, our interview data does capture persistent fraud offenders, deviant actors who are worthy of analytic attention and official concern.

All interviews followed an interview guide, which was revised as data collection progressed and analytic insights were developed. The interviews explored a range of topics, including respondents' background and criminal history, their employment history, and the circumstances of their entry and continued participation in telemarketing fraud. We also inquired about the interviewees' perceptions of the benefits and risks of fraudulent telemarketing. Interviews were tape recorded and later transcribed for analysis using *NVivo*, a software package for text-based data (Richards 1999).

In addition to interviews, we used three additional sources of information on fraudulent telemarketing. We were granted access to presentence investigation reports for 37 of the 47 interviewees. Examination of these reports served not only as an independent check on the quality of information elicited during the interviews but also gave a more complete picture of the interviewees' backgrounds, lives, and circumstances. We also interviewed 4 acquaintances who formerly worked as telemarketers for short periods of time, 5 legitimate telemarketers, 2 of whom once held office in telemarketing trade associations, 4 assistant U.S. attorneys with extensive experience prosecuting telemarketing offenders, and 4 U.S. probation officers who have supervised a large number of convicted telemarketers. Last, we examined 10 depositions of victims of telemarketing fraud made by law enforcement personnel and 3 voluminous criminal trial transcripts containing detailed descriptions of criminal telemarketing organizations and operations.

The Work

Like its legitimate forms, criminal telemarketing is a productive form of collective action that requires the coordinated efforts of two or more individuals. To work in it, therefore, is to work in an organizational setting (Francis 1988; Schulte 1995; Stevenson 2000). The size of these organizations can vary substantially; some consist of only two or three persons, but most are considerably larger (e.g., *Atlanta Journal-Constitution* 2000). Many, therefore, take on the characteristics and dynamics of formal organizations; they are hierarchical, with a division of labor, graduated pay, and advancement opportunities. Typically, they are established by individuals with previous experience in fraudulent sales.

The permanence and geographic mobility of criminal telemarketing organizations vary as well. Some remain in one locale for a year or more, while others may set up and operate for only a few days before moving on. These "rip and tear" operations, some of which use long-distance cards with mobile, cloned, or pay telephones, count on the fact that up to six months may pass before law enforcement agencies become aware of and target them. "Boiler rooms" (operations featuring extensive telephone banks and large numbers of

employees) have become less common in the U.S. in recent years, largely because of the law enforcement interest they attract. Increasingly, however, criminal telemarketers are locating boiler rooms in countries with weak laws and oversight, and operating across international borders (e.g., Australian Broadcasting Corporation 2001).

New recruits to criminal telemarketing generally start as sales agents, the industry's rank and file employees. They work on commission. Sales agents call potential customers, make the initial pitch, and weed out the cautious and the steadfastly disinterested. They do not call individuals randomly but work instead from "lead lists" (also known as "mooch lists"). Lead lists are purchased from any of dozens of businesses that compile and sell information on consumer behavior and expressed preferences. Individuals whose names appear on lead lists typically are distinguished by their disposable income and by previously demonstrated interest in promotions of one kind or another. Lead lists and names are purchased also from other criminal telemarketers after they have successfully exploited the listed individuals.

Sales agents work from written scripts that lay out both successful sales approaches and responses to whatever reception they meet with from those they reach by phone. Promising contacts are turned over to "closers," who are more experienced and better-paid sales agents. "Reloaders" are the most effective closers. Much like account executives in legitimate businesses, they maintain contact with individuals who have previously sent money to the company (i.e., "purchased" from it) in hopes of persuading them to send more. Employment mobility by criminal telemarketers is common; individuals move from one firm to another, with some eventually taking managerial positions (Doocy et al. 2001). At the time of their arrests, 22 interviewees were owners, 8 were managers, and 17 were closers, reloaders, or sales agents.

The products and services offered by criminal telemarketers run the gamut. Examples of commonly employed schemes include prizes and sweepstakes deals, magazine sales, credit card sales, work-at-home schemes, advance fee loan offers, credit card loss protection programs, buyers' clubs, and travel/vacation offers. Those we interviewed included some who identified and located owners of vacant property, led them to believe that buyers for the property could be found easily, and then charged high fees to advertise it. One respondent sold inexpensive gemstones with fraudulent certificates of grossly inflated value and authenticity. The stones were sealed in display cases such that purchasers would have difficulty getting them appraised, particularly since they were told that if they broke the seal, the value of the stones would decrease and the certificate would become invalid. Other telemarketers sold "private stocks" that by definition are not listed or traded on a stock exchange. Nevertheless, they were able to entice investors with smooth talk and a promising prospectus. Dependent upon their salespersons for market reports, those who invested soon discovered that the value of their nonexistent stocks nose-dived, and they lost their investments. Some interviewees solicited money for nonexistent charities or for legitimate organizations they did not represent. A high proportion of the companies represented by the interviewees promised that those who purchased products from them were odds-on winners of a prize soon to be awarded once other matters were settled. Typically this required the customers to pay fees of one kind or another up front.

To the unsuspecting, the day-to-day activities of a fraudulent telemarketing operation may be indistinguishable from those of a legitimate business. Therein lies a major reason for its deviant potential and its appeal; fraudulent telemarketing lends itself easily to respectable constructions of organizational and individual activities. Both its illicit nature and individual culpability can be managed behind an organizational front and shared rhetorical scripts. The telemarketers we interviewed typically employed the rhetoric of legitimate business when describing their operations and activities. Their narratives were filled with references to "customers," "purchases," "account executives," "premiums," and such. When they talked, however, of "customers" who "bought" from their establishments, they were referring to men and women who sent them money and whom they hoped could be induced to make additional "purchases" despite receiving little of value in return for earlier ones.

THE WORKERS

In stark contrast to those of street criminals, the telemarketers we interviewed typically described the financial circumstances in their parental homes as secure if not comfortable and their parents as conventional and hard working. They were raised by parents who prided themselves on how well they provided materially and whose conversations and admonitions stressed the importance of financial matters and "taking care of business." Their fathers were the principal source of family income, but one-half of the mothers were employed outside the home as well. The occupations reported for the fathers ranged from machinist to

owner of a chain of retail stores, but a striking 68 percent ($n = 32$) were business owners or held managerial positions. Consequently, a substantial proportion of the men and women interviewed for this research were exposed to entrepreneurial perspectives and understandings while young. Business ownership, financial independence, and wealth were goals for many of them. One told the interviewer:

> You're always pursuing more money, most of us are. We're raised that way, we are in this country. And that's the way I was raised. But I also wanted to do my own thing. I wanted to be in business for myself, I wanted the freedom that came with that.

Another said: "I had certain goals when I was a teenager, you know. And I had a picture of a Mercedes convertible on my bedroom mirror for years." Another interviewee told us: "You know, I do have a major addiction, and I don't think I'll ever lose it. And I don't think there's any classes [treatment] for it. And it's money, it's Ben Franklin."

Whatever one's social background, legitimate pathways to success are not always identified easily or pursued diligently by the young. This was true of most of the men and women interviewed for this research; they dawdled or became distracted while pursuing marketable skills. Their educational careers, for example, were unexceptional; 8 dropped out of high school, although most graduated. Twenty-one attended college, but on average they invested only 2 years in the quest for a degree. Five claimed holding a baccalaureate degree. As they reached early adulthood, their directionless and lackluster performance only heightened the felt need to identify and settle upon a means of livelihood that would "pay off." They had little interest in occupations that required confining routines, hard or sustained physical labor, or subordination to others. As one interviewee said:

> You know, I've never been a firm believer [that] you got to work for a company for 30 years and get a retirement . . . I'm all about going out [and] making that million and doing it, doing it very easily. And there's a lot of ways to do it.

In short, they found themselves in economically precarious and frustrating circumstances. Despite their ambitions, most either had stalled or were making little progress on conventional paths. They were mindful of the possibility of growing economic marginality if they did not find and settle upon a satisfactory means of livelihood. One interviewee described his entry into telemarketing fraud as prompted by his relative lack of economic success:

> I got into telemarketing, how it all came about is, I was working for a car wash, right up the road here. And I'd been there eight months, you know. And I wasn't really making, I mean, I made pretty decent money, what I thought was decent, you know. And . . . I see all these people coming through driving these brand-new cars and all this, you know. Younger people, you know, a little bit older than me, but still . . . it would be nice to do that someday, you know. And most of them were in [telemarketing].

His remarks were echoed by another respondent:

> Yeah, I'm not complaining, but, you know, when you see someone next to you and it's coming that easy for them, you always want to work twice as hard. To get everything twice as fast, to stay one step ahead of him. And I think everybody, in life, has an opportunity to go a different route. But a lot of people, they're scared. You don't know. But when I saw that opportunity to go a different route that would get there twice as fast as somebody else, I took it.

Along with their frustrated legitimate aspirations, the frequency with which interviewed telemarketers had been in trouble with the law suggests a measure of moral marginality as well. This may have increased their receptiveness to deviant solutions. Thirteen respondents had previous criminal convictions, 7 for minor offenses (e.g., petty theft and possession of marijuana) and 6 for felonies. Of these, the previous convictions of 3 interviewees were for telemarketing offenses. It is clear that some of these men and women were not one-time or accidental violators. Taken together, our findings and reports by others suggest strongly that significant numbers of relatively affluent offenders appear to have recurrent trouble with the law and, like street criminals, they are persistent users of alcohol and other drugs (Doocy et al. 2001; Weisburd, Chayet and Waring 2001; Benson and Moore 1992). It suggests further that when these men and women were presented with attractive opportunities to engage in deviant economic exploitation they did not have to overcome strong internalized beliefs about obeisance to the law.

The initial exposure to telemarketing for the men and women interviewed for this study was fortuitous and fateful. While still in high school or, more commonly, while in college, they either responded to attractive ads in the newspaper or were recruited by friends or acquaintances who boasted about the amount of money they were making.

> [A former acquaintance] . . . looked me up, found me and said, "You gotta come out here . . . We're gonna make a ton of money." I went out for three weeks—left my wife back home. And I got on the phones, and I was making a thousand dollars a week. I'm like, "Oh, my God, Jenni, pack the stuff, we're going to Arizona" . . . He was like, "Man . . . you're a pro at this shit." And I just, I don't know what it was. I was number one . . . I don't know, I loved it.

For this respondent, as for others, criminal telemarketing was a godsend; it appeared at a time when they needed to show that, beyond becoming merely self-supporting adults, they could be economic successes. Another telemarketer said that it was "a salvation to me as a means of income. And being able to actually accomplish something without an education." His comments were echoed by a man who told the investigator that telemarketing "gave me a career, [and] to me it was my salvation." Despite their class origins, the interviewees were poorly prepared to maintain the standard of living provided by their parents, and thus they were predisposed to adopt deviant pathways to success.

THE REWARDS

The primary attraction of criminal telemarketing was the income it offered. Overwhelmingly, the men and women interviewed said they got into and persisted at it for "the money." Some reported that telemarketing was their reason for having dropped out of college:

> Telemarketing was just something I picked up as a part-time job, when I was sixteen . . . When I was in college, my second year in college, [fellow students] were talking about finishing their four years of college and making $28,000 or $30,000 a year. And I was making $ 1,000 a week part time, you know . . . And I just couldn't see doing it. I mean, I wound up, after the end of my second year of college, I never went back. I was making too much money. It just seemed so easy.

Only one person reported earning less than $1,000 weekly. Most of those interviewed said their annual earnings were in the range of $100,000 to $250,000 and 5 claimed that their annual earnings exceeded $1 million. The fact that they could make considerable amounts of money quickly and do so without undue restrictions and responsibilities increased the attractiveness of telemarketing. The telemarketers found appealing both the flexible hours and the fact that the work required neither extensive training nor advanced education. Few employers imposed rigid rules or strictures. Generally, there were neither dress codes nor uniforms; the work could be done in shorts and a T-shirt (Doocy et al. 2001). Twenty- to 30-hour work weeks were common and the need for close oversight by owners or managers decreased substantially once operations were up and running.

The high income returned by criminal telemarketing made it possible for practitioners to enjoy self-indulgent lifestyles featuring conspicuous consumption and display. The younger segment of the workforce generally lived "life as party," enjoying "'good times' with minimal concern for obligations and commitments external to the immediate social setting" (Shover 1996, p. 93). Use of cocaine and other illicit drugs was common in the venues and among those who pursued this lifestyle. Asked how he spent the money he made, one telemarketer responded:

> Houses, girls, just going out to nightclubs. And a lot of blow [cocaine], lots and lots of blow, enormous amounts. And other than that, you know, I look back, I get sick when I think about how much we spent, where the hell I put it all. I'm making all this money [but] I don't have a whole hell of a lot to show for it, you know. That lifestyle didn't allow you to save.

Similarly, another said:

> The hours were good. You'd work, sometimes, from about 9 to 2, 9 to 3, sometimes from 12 to 4. Basically, we set our own hours. It was freedom. The money was fantastic . . . You got the best of the girls. For me, it wasn't really about the job, it was a way of life . . . I had an alcohol problem at a young age, and to be able to support the alcohol and drug habit with the kind of money that we were making seems to go hand in hand. And then you've got the fast lifestyle . . . up all night, sleep all day, you know. So, everything kinda coincided with that fast lifestyle, that addictive lifestyle.

Heavy gambling was also commonplace. One respondent said that he "would go out to the casinos and blow two, three, four, five thousand dollars a night. That was nothing—to go spend five grand, you know, every weekend. And wake up broke!"

For those criminal telemarketers who eventually married and took on more conventional and more time-consuming responsibilities, their lifestyle changed in degree if not in kind. An increasingly larger portion of their lives now centered around home and family and conspicuous display:

> I played some golf. [In the summer] water skiing, fishing. I'm real heavy into bass fishing, me and my dad and my brothers. Hunting. Doing things with my wife and kids I spent a lot of time with them. Evenings, maybe just walking the golf course, or whatever. Watching the sunset.

Their interest in the faster aspects of life as party remained, but it had to compete with family responsibilities and with the pursuits thought appropriate for successful citizens. Those who succeeded to this degree were much less likely to frequent the strip clubs and gambling joints they patronized when they were younger. However, the rewards and attractions criminal telemarketing held for them went beyond the income it returned and the pleasures of life as party. In addition to material and lifestyle rewards, the deviant occupation offered workers an opportunity to experience a strong sense of personal mastery and construct self-definitions in which the ability to control and manipulate others was central. The most striking characteristic shared by nearly all of the interviewees was the belief that they were outstanding salespersons. They were supremely confident of their ability to sell over the telephone by overcoming whatever resistance they encountered, and doing so successfully gave them a sense of competitively earned distinction and power:

> The ability to impose one's will upon another person—and to achieve a measurable financial reward for doing so—is highlighted in many of the reports of illegal telemarketing practices. Enforcement officials told us that sellers often have mirrors in the cubicles in which they work. They are told to look into the mirror and see the face of a hotshot salesperson. Sometimes there will be a motto on the wall, such as: "Each No gets me closer to the Yes I want." Boiler room owners and managers . . . may put large bills on a bulletin board and say that the next sale or the highest total for the day will qualify for this extra reward. Often the salespeople have to stand up when they consummate a transaction, so that the boss can note them and they can take pleasure in the achievement (Doocy et al. 2001, p. 17)

Successful sales were intoxicating. As one telemarketer described it:

> You could be selling a $10,000 ticket, you could be selling a $49.95 ticket. And it's the same principle, it's the same rules. It's the same game I like to win. I like to win in all the games I play, you know. And the money is a reason to be there, and a reason to have that job. But winning is what I want to do. I want to beat everybody else in the office. I want to beat that person I am talking to on the phone.

His remarks were echoed by another respondent:

> [I] sold the first person I ever talked to on the phone. And it was just like that first shot of heroin, you know. I'm not a heroin addict ... I've only done heroin a couple of times. But it was amazing. It was like, "I can't believe I just did this!" It was incredible. It was never about the money after that ... Yeah, it was about the money initially, but when 1 realized that I could do this every day, it was no longer about the money. It was about the competition, you know. I wanted to be the best salesman, and I want to make the most money that day. And then it became just the sale. It wasn't the money. I didn't even add the figures in my head anymore. It was just whether or not I can turn this person around, you know, walk him down that mutual path of agreement, you know. That was exciting to me. It was power, you know, I can make people do what I wanted them to do And they would do it.

Another interviewee expressed his experience of this "sneaky thrill" (Katz 1988) intrinsic to the activity of fraudulent telemarketing most simply when he said that the work "gives you power. It gives you power."

Reared in social circumstances where they were commonly exposed to conventional values that stressed success was achieved through diligence and effort, fraudulent telemarketers were confronted with a situation in which their personal and social identities were potentially degraded. As with many categories of those who live at the margins of conventionality or outside of the law, fraudulent telemarketers adopted perspectives that guarded against self-blame and moral rejection. In order to retain feelings of self-worth and continue to hold some measure of allegiance to conventional moral codes, they employed various "techniques of neutralization" (Sykes and Matza 1957). Given the relative privilege of their backgrounds, the "excuse" (Scott and Lyman 1968) that their rule-breaking was necessitated by a structurally determined lack of opportunity was not readily available. Central to the "vocabulary of motive" (Mills 1940) fraudulent telemarketers used to legitimate their deviant occupational activities and defend their personal identities was the "justification" (Lyman and Scott 1970) that their customers deserved to be victimized. They routinely expressed the belief that "the mooch is going to send his money to someone, so it might as well be me" (Sanger 1999, p. 9). Telemarketers felt neither concern nor sympathy for their victims. "Customers" were thought to be so greedy, ignorant, or incapable that it was only a matter of time before they would throw away their money on something unobtainable. One interviewee expressed the typical view of customers when he said:

> If these people can't read, so be it. Screw them, you know. It [doesn't say] *everybody's* gonna get the diamond and sapphire tennis bracelet. They're dumb enough not to read, dumb enough to send me the money, I really don't care, you know. I'm doing what I have to do to stay out of jail. They're doing what they have to do to fix their fix. They're promo junkies, and we're gonna find them and get them, and we're gonna keep getting them. And they're gonna keep buying, and, you know what I used to say, "They're gonna blow their money in Vegas, they're gonna spend it *somewhere*. I want to be the one to get it."

While this "denial of the victim" (Sykes and Matza 1957) rationale was the justification most commonly presented by interviewees, they also employed a definitional tactic Goode (2002, p. 32) refers to as "normalization." Fraudulent telemarketers often expressed the view that they were involved in sales transactions that were, in fact, not appreciably different from those typically encountered in legitimate commercial settings. Telemarketers did not see themselves as exploiting innocent and undeserving victims. Instead, they were simply engaging in what they defined as routine sales transactions.

As one interviewee observed:

> Yeah, I still do to this day think it's more of a moral line than a legal line because 1 think [the feds] just had a hard-on to get us as an industry, not as a company. I really think [our operation] is as legal as what Ed McMahon is doing, if not more ... Yeah, I'm charging exorbitant amounts for vitamins. I'm sending them out. But there's no law against that ... I used to say, "Hey, I went and I bought a shirt over at whatever. You know this shirt costs a dollar to make for the manufacturer, but I'd pay 50 [dollars] at the store. So, am I getting screwed here? Oh yeah, technically I guess I am, but I'm paying a markup. How is it illegal for me to do the same thing? That's free enterprise.

DISCUSSION

Since its original formulation (Merton 1938), strain theory has arguably been the most influential etiological perspective in the sociology of deviance and the focus of considerable criticism. Many of these critiques have focused on the failure of the strain perspective to offer a general explanation for deviance or to adequately account for forms of rule violation (e.g., suicide, homosexuality, assault, mental disorder, recreational drug use) that are not reasonably seen as the consequence of an actor's innovative attempts to achieve conventional economic goals through the use of illegitimate means (see the various discussions in Clinard 1964). Strain theory has also been accused of being inadequate as an explanation of rule violations by affluent members of the society who enjoy positions of privilege and have ready access to legitimate means of goal achievement (Taylor, Walton and Young 1973; Void and Bernard 1986).

Recent reformulations of strain theory (e.g., Passas 1990; Messner and Rosenfeld 2000, 2001) have emphasized the domination of economic institutions over, and interpenetration of, other social institutions. Contemporary advocates of strain theory also point to the decline of "sentiments of mutual obligation" that undergird "collective solidarity" (Messner and Rosenfeld 2001, p. 156) as a key factor promoting exploitative interactions by all social actors regardless of their class backgrounds and economic resources.

The contemporary cultural emphasis on monetary success, individual achievement, competition, and the exercise of power over others through duplicity (Barron 1974) provides the foundation for our understanding of the movement of fraudulent telemarketers into their deviant occupation and the ongoing appeal it has for them. As we have seen, fraudulent telemarketers stressed the economic rewards of their work, valued the power they exercised over their victims, and enhanced their personal identities by emphasizing the persuasive skills that allowed them to effectively exploit the targets of their fraudulent activities.

Social structure and one's position in it, like all elements of social life, are not objectively given. Opportunities, advantages, and alternatives are, instead, subjectively problematic. The means one chooses in pursuing conventional (and unconventional) goals depend on what he or she defines as reasonable and, in the case of the fraudulent telemarketers presented here, most easily available. The telemarketers we interviewed grew to adulthood in comfortable material circumstances and they aspired to and lived the American Dream. They were committed to the goal of material success which was to be achieved by all individually and competitively (Messner and Rosenfeld 2000, p. 5). Although their class backgrounds ostensibly offered ready access to conventional means of achievement, their perceptions of viable alternatives were limited by their desire to avoid the disadvantages, effort, and encumbrances of legitimate occupational pursuits.

Once involved in fraud the telemarketers found it to be both an effective means of achieving their instrumental goals and an occupational activity that offered the intrinsic "sneaky thrills" (Katz 1988) that came from exercising control over their victims. Seduced into the deviant activity primarily by their desire for easy economic gain, fraudulent telemarketers soon

discovered that employing their persuasive skills to exploit gullible victims provided feelings of power and control. The deviant work was "a kind of game … that produce(d) a clear winner and loser" (ibid., p. 67). Success in this power game had the added advantage of enhancing the telemarketers' positive definitions of self as they came to see themselves as skilled players in the game of fraud. In short, the rewards they derived from their deviant activities went well beyond the limited economic goals emphasized in most analyses of deviance premised on conventional strain theory.

In addition to moving beyond a narrow focus on the pursuit of economic rewards and the presumption that opportunities for achievement are an objective consequence of one's structural position, our discussion emphasizes the definitional perspectives that are readily available in both the larger culture and the more narrow and practically focused occupational culture in which fraudulent telemarketers operate. By casting the victims of their economic exploitation as deserving their fate because of their greed or gullibility and defining their occupational activities as merely a variant of "normal" business practices, telemarketers could retain both their positive self-definitions and their general commitment to what they still, at some level, regarded as the dominant moral order.

Conclusion

With few exceptions, all who aspire to the American Dream are encouraged to pursue material success and upward mobility, and all are evaluated on the basis of individual achievement. An important corollary of this universal entitlement to succeed is that the hazards of failure are also universal (Messner and Rosenfeld 2000). Fellow citizens thus become rivals in the struggle to achieve social rewards and, ultimately, to validate personal worth. Given such a value orientation, pressure to achieve can be intense, and the belief that "it's not how you play the game; it's whether you win or lose" (ibid., p. 63) can gain broad acceptance. Individual competition to succeed can cause some to creatively reconstruct or totally disregard normative restraints on behavior when they threaten to interfere with the realization of personal goals.

Like commonplace criminal deviants, fraudulent telemarketers engage in illegal economic activities in order to maintain a style of living they experience as satisfying. Unlike those involved in more mundane property crimes, however, their deviant decisions and illegal operations blend imperceptibly into legitimate ones. Prompted by perceptions of blocked opportunity and desiring the culturally prescribed rewards of economic success, they choose a deviant career that offers significant economic gain while exacting few of the conventional costs of hard work and sustained effort (Agnew 2000). Despite their apparent embrace of some of the trappings of conventionality, they are best described as "marginal middle-class persons" (Doocy et al. 2001).

Deviant economic exploitation of the kind discussed here is likely to increase as the current economic contraction proceeds and legitimate opportunities for those with middle-class backgrounds and aspirations become more scarce. The growing importance of the Internet as a vehicle for economic transactions will provide further impetus to fraudulent exchanges as deviant entrepreneurs exploit the Web to expand the scope of victimization (see Ulick 2003). It is reasonable to expect that fraudulent telemarketing and its new technological variations will be important features of the landscape of deviant economic exploitation well into the future.

REFERENCES

Agnew, R. (2000). Sources of criminality: Strain and subcultural theories. In J. F. Sheley (Ed.), *Criminology: A contemporary handbook, 3rd edition* (pp. 349–371). Belmont, CA: Wadsworth.

Atlanta Journal-Constitution (2000). Alleged scam on elderly by telemarketers is revealed. September 6, B3.

Australian Broadcasting Corporation (2001). Beyond the boiler room. September 24. www.abc.net.au/4corners/.

Barron, M. (1974). The criminogenic society: Social values and deviance. In A. Blumberg (Ed.), *Current perspectives on criminal behavior* (pp. 68–86). New York: Knopf.

Benson, M. L., & Moore, E. (1992). Are white-collar and common criminals the same? *Journal of Research in Crime and Delinquency,* 29, 251–272.

Blum, R. (1972). *Deceivers and deceived.* Springfield, IL: Charles C. Thomas.

Clinard, M. (Ed.) (1964). *Anomie and deviant behavior: A discussion and critique.* New York: Free Press.

Direct Marketing Association (2001). www.the-dma.org.

Doocy, J., Shichor, D., Sechrest, D., & Geis, G. (2001). Telemarketing fraud: Who are the tricksters and what makes them trick? *Securities Journal,* 14, 7–26.

Francis, D. (1988). *Contrepreneurs.* New York: Macmillan.

Goode, E. (2002). *Deviance in everyday life.* Prospect Heights, IL: Waveland.

Katz, J. (1988). *Seductions of crime: Moral and sensual attractions in doing evil.* New York: Basic Books.

Lyman, S. M., & Scott, M. B. (1970). *A sociology of the absurd.* New York: Appleton-Century-Crofts.

Maurer, D. W. (1940). *The big con.* New York: Bobbs-Merrill.

Merton, R. K. (1938). Social structure and anomie. *American Sociological Review,* 3, 672–682.

Messner, S. F., & Rosenfeld, R. (2000). *Crime and the American dream, 3rd edition.* Belmont, CA: Wadsworth.

Messner, S. F., & Rosenfeld, R. (2001). An institutional-anomie theory of crime. In R. Paternoster & B. Bachman (Eds.), *Explaining criminals and crime* (pp. 151–160). Los Angeles: Roxbury.

Mills, C. W. (1940). Situated actions and vocabularies of motive. *American Sociological Review,* 5, 904–913.

Passas, N. (1990). Anomie and corporate deviance. *Contemporary Crisis,* 14, 157–178.

Rebovich, D., & Layne, J. (2000). *The national public survey on white collar crime.* Washington, DC: National White Collar Crime Center.

Richards, L. (1999). *Using NVivo in qualitative research.* Newbury Park, CA: Sage.

Sanger, D. (1999). Confessions of a phone-scam artist. *Saturday Night,* 114, 86–98.

Schulte, F. (1995). *Fleeced! Telemarketing rip-offs and how to avoid them.* New York: Prometheus.

Scott, M. B., & Lyman, S. M. (1968). Accounts. *American Sociological Review,* 33, 46–62.

Shover, N. (1996). *Great pretenders: Pursuits and careers of persistent thieves.* Boulder, CO: Westview.

Sparrow, M. K. (1996). *License to steal: Why fraud plagues America's health care system.* Boulder, CO: Westview.

Stevenson, R. J. (2000). *The boiler room and other telephone sales scams.* Urbana: University of Illinois Press.

Sykes, G., & Matza, D. (1957). Techniques of neutralization: A theory of delinquency. *American Sociological Review,* 22, 667–670.

Taylor, I. (1999). *Crime in context: A critical criminology of market societies.* Boulder, CO: Westview.

Taylor, I., Walton, P., & Young, J. (1973). *The new criminology.* New York: Harper and Row.

Tillman, R. (1998). *Broken promises: Fraud by small business health insurers.* Boston: Northeastern University Press.

Titus, R. (2001). Personal fraud and its victims. In N. Shover & J. P. Wright (Eds.), *Crimes of privilege: Readings in white-collar crime* (pp. 57–67). New York: Oxford University Press.

Titus, R. M., Heinzelmann, F., & Boyle, J. M. (1995). Victimization of persons by fraud. *Crime and Delinquency,* 41, 54–72.

Ulick, J. (2003). The dark side of the Internet. *Newsweek,* March 17, E5.

U.S. Congress, Senate (1993). *Telemarketing fraud and S. 568, The Telemarketing and Consumer Fraud and Abuse Protection Act.* Hearing before the Subcommittee on Consumers of the Committee on Commerce, Science, and Transportation, 103rd Congress, 1st session. Washington, DC: U.S. Government Printing Office.

Void, G., & Bernard, T. (1986). *Theoretical criminology, 3rd edition.* New York: Oxford University Press.

Weisburd, D., Chayet, E. F., & Waring, E. (2001). *White-collar crime and criminal careers.* Cambridge: Cambridge University Press.

14

UNDERSTANDING IDENTITY THEFT

Offenders' Accounts of Their Lives and Crimes

HEITH COPES AND LYNNE M. VIERAITIS

This study offers the perspective of 59 federally incarcerated identity thieves. The research that describes the characteristics of this type of offender and the techniques they use to gain the personal information of victims necessary to commit their criminal activity. Identity thieves are a diverse group that are demographically comprised of all groups of age, race, gender, socioeconomic class, and criminal background. The methods these thieves use to attain peoples' identity information poses questionable concerns as to whether this particular criminal offense falls under the category of white-collar crime.

The definition of white-collar crime has engendered much confusion and debate among criminologists since it was introduced nearly seven decades ago and agreement over conceptual boundaries has yet to be achieved. Perspectives on how best to conceptualize white-collar crime tend to fall into one of two camps, what Shover and Cullen (2008) refer to as the populist and patrician paradigms. The populist paradigm is perhaps best exemplified by the work of Sutherland who saw the respectable status of the perpetrators as the defining characteristic of white-collar crime. Those who take this perspective conceive of white-collar crime as involving the "illegal and harmful actions of elites and respectable members of society carried out ... in the context of legitimate organizational or occupational activity" (Friedrichs, 2004, p. 5). When seen through this lens, white-collar crime evokes images of powerful elites who use their position to fraudulently obtain money and evade prosecution and elicits a critical, reform oriented stance to research.

The patrician perspective of white-collar crime "takes a narrower, more technical, and less reform-oriented view of white-collar crime" (Shover & Cullen, 2008, p. 156). Those who define white-collar crime from this perspective place emphasis on the characteristics of the crime rather than the characteristics of the

Source: Understanding Identity Theft: Offenders' Accounts of their Lives and Crimes by Copes, Heith and Lynne M. Vieraitis, *Criminal Justice Review*, *34* (3), September 2009, pp. 329–349. Published by Sage Publications on behalf of Georgia State University Research Foundation. Reprinted with permission.

criminal. The work carried out at the Yale Studies of White Collar Crime typifies this perspective (Weisburd, Wheeler, Waring, & Bode, 1991). By reviewing the pre-sentence investigation reports of federal offenders, Weisburd et al. (1991) painted a portrait of white-collar offenders as mundane and ordinary. This camp points out that the notion of white-collar crime being com-mitted only by elites is an exaggeration and, therefore, emphasis should be placed on "collaring the crime, not the criminal" (Shapiro, 1990). As Shapiro (1990) notes, researchers should be "exploring the modus operandi of their misdeeds and the ways in which they establish and exploit trust" (p. 363). Edelhertz (1970) suggests that white-collar crime is "an illegal act or series of illegal acts committed by nonphysical means and by concealment or guile, to obtain money or property, to avoid the payment or loss of money or property or to obtain business or personal advantage" (p. 3). Edelhertz (1970) makes clear the belief that "the char-acter of white-collar crime must be found in its modus operandi and its objectives rather than in the nature of the offenders" (p. 4).

Regardless of whether one emphasizes the status of the offender (populist) or the nature of the crime (patrician), Friedrichs (2004, p. 4) notes that most criminologists who study white-collar crime agree that it occurs in a legitimate occupational context and is motivated by the goal of economic gain or occupa-tional success. This issue was also raised by Newman (1958) who argued that "the chief criterion for a crime to be 'white-collar' is that it occurs as a part of, or a deviation from, the violator's occupational role" (p. 737). Typologies of white-collar crime also illuminate the difficulties in defining white-collar crime and classify-ing actors and/or actions as white-collar. Numerous typologies have emerged since Sutherland's (1949) *White Collar Crime* with some classifying types of white-collar crime based on the context in which the activity occurs, the status or position of the offender, the pri-mary victims, the primary form of harm, or the legal classification of the offense (Friedrichs, 2004).

According to Braithwaite (1985), the most influential partition has been Clinard and Quinncy's (1973) separa-tion of white-collar crime into occupational and corpo-rate crime. In doing so, the term *corporate crime* preserves the original definition of white-collar crime as delineated by Sutherland, but recognizes that lower level white-collar and even blue-collar workers commit crimes in the con-text of their occupations. Others have added forms of governmental crime, hybrid forms of white-collar crime (e.g., state-corporate crime, crimes of globalization, and finance crime), and "residual" forms such as technocrime and avocational crime (Friedrichs, 2004).

When labeling acts as *white-collar* researchers typi-cally use definitions from one of the two camps. But some crimes are hard to classify in either of these broad categories, which makes it difficult to determine the best conceptual lens with which to understand these crimes. Friedrichs (2004, p. 187) argues that identity theft is a classic example of a hybrid form of white-collar crime based on the observation that a victim's identifying information is often taken by an employee and passed along to others. Thus, the employee and his/her actions may be classified as white-collar criminal and white-collar crime, respec-tively, but how does one classify the use of the identify-ing information that likely follows? Many perceive identity theft to be so sophisticated that it is commit-ted predominantly by computer specialists, organized criminal networks, or sophisticated "hackers" who access such databases. Others see it as a crime so mun-dane that it has become the crime of choice for those who have succumbed to the effects of methamphet-amine addiction (Gayer, 2003). Thus, current discus-sions of identity theft focus either on drug addicted, unsophisticated mail thieves, and dumpster divers or more commonly on high-tech hackers aid phishers. Such varied portrayals of the crime raise the question, is identity theft a white-collar crime? Our goals for this study are to contextualize previous research based on victimization surveys and law enforcement case files and to determine if identity theft should be treated as a white-collar offense using either of the two broad definitions. To do this we rely on the accounts of 59 federally convicted identity thieves to examine their personal backgrounds and the techniques they use to acquire identifying information and convert it into cash or goods.

IDENTITY THEFT IN CONTEXT

Although it is difficult to gauge the extent of identity theft, it is possible to determine a general pattern of the crime by comparing the various attempts by public and private agencies to measure it. Numerous sources support the claim that identity theft rose considerably over the past decade. According to reports from the Federal Trade Commission (FTC), identity theft has been the most prevalent form of fraud committed in the United States for the past 7 years, comprising 36% of fraud complaints filed in the year 2006 (FTC, 2007). According to the Gartner Survey and the Privacy and American Business (Privacy and American Business [P&AB], 2003) survey, the incidence of identity theft almost doubled from 2001 to 2002. The Social Security

Administration's fraud hotline received approximately 65,000 reports of Social Security number misuse in 2001, more than a five-fold increase from the 11,000 reported in 1998 (U.S. General Accounting Office, 2002). Data from the FTC (2004) suggest that identity theft rose from 86,212 in 2000 to 214,905 in 2003, nearly a 250% increase. Recent data from the FTC indicate that identity theft reports have been relatively stable the past 3 years.

In 2007, the FTC released a report on estimates of the incidence and costs of identity theft. According to the report, approximately eight million people experienced identity theft in 2005 and total losses were nearly $16 billion (Synovate, 2007). According to the National Crime Victimization Survey (NCVS), in 2005, 6.4 million households, representing 5.5% of the households in the United States discovered that at least one member of the household had been the victim of identity theft during the previous 6 months. The estimated financial loss reported by victimized households was about $3.2 billion (Bureau of Justice Statistics [BJS], 2006). Regardless of how identity theft is measured, reports indicate that it is a growing and costly crime.

IDENTITY THEFT OFFENDERS

Despite the creation of identity theft task forces throughout the country, clearance rates for identity theft are low. Available evidence suggests that offenders are seldom detected and rarely apprehended (Allison, Schuck, & Lersch, 2005; Gayer, 2003; Owens, 2004).The paucity of research on identity theft coupled with the low clearance rate makes it difficult to have a clear description of those who engage in this offense. To date only two studies have provided data on identity thieves, both rely on law enforcement files (e.g., closed cases or police reports). To gain an understanding of the type of individual who commits identity theft Gordon, Rebovich, Choo, and Gordon (2007), examined closed U.S. Secret Service cases with an identity theft component from 2000 to 2006. They found that most offenders (42.5%) were between the ages of 25 and 34 years when the case was opened. And another one-third fell within the 35 to 49 years age group. Using data from a large metropolitan police department in Florida, Allison et al. (2005) found that offenders ranged in age from 28 to 49 years with a mean age of 32 years.

Both studies found similar patterns regarding race. Gordon et al. (2007) found that the majority of the offenders were Black (54%), with Whites and Hispanics accounting for 38% and 5% of offenders, respectively.

Allison et al. (2005) found that the distribution of offenders was 69% Black, 27% White, and less than 1% were Hispanic or Asian. The two studies differed in terms of the gender of offenders. Gordon et al. (2007) found that nearly two-thirds of the offenders were male, whereas Allison et al. (2005) found that 63% of offenders were female.

TECHNIQUES OF IDENTITY THEFT

To be successful at identity theft would-be offenders must secure identifying information and convert it into goods or cash. Identity thieves have developed a number of techniques and strategies to do this. Researchers and law enforcement agencies have collected information, primarily from victimization surveys, on the techniques identity thieves commonly employ.

The first step in the successful commission of identity theft is to obtain personal information on the victim, which is relatively easy for offenders to do. Offenders obtain this information from wallets, purses, homes, cars, offices, and business or institutions that maintain customer, employee, patient, or student records (Newman, 2004). Social security numbers, which provide instant access to a person's personal information, are widely used for identification and account numbers by insurance companies, universities, cable television companies, military identification, and banks. The thief may steal a wallet or purse, work at a job that affords him/her access to credit records, may purchase the information from someone who does (e.g., employees who have access to credit reporting databases commonly available in auto dealerships, realtor's offices, banks, and other businesses that approve loans), or may find victims' information by stealing mail, sorting through the trash, or by searching the Internet (Davis & Stevenson, 2004; Lease & Burke, 2000; LoPucki, 2001; Newman, 2004).

Based on victim surveys, most offenders commit identity theft by obtaining a person's credit card information, which they use to forge a credit card in the victim's name and use it to make purchases (P&AB, 2003). According to the P&AB survey, 34% of victims reported that their information was obtained this way. In addition, 12% reported that someone stole or obtained a paper or computer record with their personal information on it. Eleven percent said someone stole their wallet or purse: 10% said someone opened charge accounts in stores in their name; 7% said someone opened bank account in their name or forged checks; 7% said someone got to their mail or mailbox; 5% said they lost their wallet or purse; 4% said someone went to a public record; and 3% said someone created false IDs to get government benefits or payments (P&AB, 2003).

Data from the FTC suggest that of those who knew how their information was obtained (43%), 16% said their information was stolen by someone they personally knew; 7% during a purchase or financial transaction; 5% reported their information was obtained from a stolen wallet or purse; 5% cited theft from a company that maintained their information; and 2% from the mail (Synovate, 2007). Other techniques have been identified such as organized rings in which a person is planted as an employee in a mortgage lender's office, doctor's office, or human resources department to more easily access information. Similarly, these groups will bribe insiders such as employees of banks, car dealerships, government, and hospitals to get the identifying information. Others have obtained credit card numbers by soliciting information using bogus e-mails (phishing) or simply by watching someone type in a calling card number or credit card number (Davis & Stevenson, 2004).

According to the FTC, the most common type of identity theft was credit card fraud followed by "other" identity theft, phone or utilities fraud, bank fraud (fraud involving checking and savings accounts and electronic fund transfers), employment-related fraud, government documents or benefits fraud, and loan fraud (FTC, 2007). Although not directly comparable due to differences in methodology, units of analysis, and definition of identity theft, data from the NCVS indicate that of the 6.4 million households reporting that at least one member of the household had been the victim of identity theft, the most common type was unauthorized use of existing credit cards (BJS, 2007).

METHODS

The present study is based on data collected from interviews with 59 inmates incarcerated in U.S. federal prisons for identity theft or identity theft-related crimes. The interviews were conducted from March 2006 to February 2007. A purposive sampling strategy was employed to locate suitable participants, which involved an examination of newspapers and legal documents from across the United States. Lexis-Nexis News, an electronic database that organizes newspapers from around the United States by region and state, was used as the source for the newspapers. The Lexis-Nexis Legal Research database, containing decisions from all federal courts, and the Westlaw database, were also searched using the term *18 U.S.C. § 1028*, which is

the U.S. federal statute for identity theft. Finally, the websites of U.S. Attorneys in all 93 U.S. districts were searched for press releases and indictments regarding individuals charged with identity theft.

The online Federal Bureau of Prisons Inmate Locator (www.bop.gov) was then used to determine whether the offenders identified during the earlier searches were housed in federal facilities at the time of the study. In total, this process yielded the names of 297 identity thieves. To sample participants, visits were made to the 14 correctional facilities that housed the largest number of inmates in each of the six regions defined by the Federal Bureau of Prisons (Western, North Central, South Central, North Eastern, Mid-Atlantic, and South Eastern). A total of 65 individuals who were incarcerated for identity theft, primarily aggravated identity theft, were interviewed. However, six interviews were excluded from the analysis because the offenders denied taking part in or having knowledge of the identity theft (if they had a codefendant) or because they committed fraud without stealing the victims' identities. The final sample consisted of 59 people who had engaged in identity theft.

Some argue that interviews with active, free-ranging offenders have numerous advantages over those with incarcerated offenders (Jacobs & Wright, 2006). Purportedly, findings based on inmate interviews may be biased because the participants are "unsuccessful," fearful of further legal sanctions, and likely to reconstruct their offenses in an overly rational manner. However, many of these claims against captive populations are overstated (Copes & Hochstetler, in press). In fact, a recent study examining target selection of burglars found a "striking similarity" between studies using free-ranging and prison-based samples (Nee & Taylor 2000, p. 45). Little is gained by denying that the interview setting colors narratives or that conversations with social scientists are not different than what might be said elsewhere. Yet offenders appear to report similar patterns of behavior regardless of how they were originally contacted or where they were interviewed.

Semistructured interviews were used to explore offenders' life circumstances at the times of their crimes, their reasons for becoming involved in and continuing with identity theft, and the techniques they used to secure information to commit fraud and convert it into cash or goods. This style of interview allows the participants to discuss their crimes in their own words and with detail. Moreover, it allows the researcher to gain in-depth knowledge about the subject matter, in this case, the backgrounds and modus operandi of identity thieves.

The interviews took place in private rooms in the correctional facilities, such as offices, visiting rooms, and attorney-client rooms. For the majority of the interviews the authors interviewed as a pair, with one acting as lead and the other taking notes and ensuring that important questions were not left out. The one constant in the interview settings was that interviewers were alone with participants during the interview. Although correctional officers were nearby, they were unable to listen in on the conversations. This was important because participants may be hesitant to speak freely with the worry of staff overhearing the details of their lives and crimes. When possible interviews were audio recorded and then transcribed verbatim. However, some wardens denied us permission to bring recording devices into their facilities and some offenders agreed to the interview only if it was not recorded. All but nine interviews were recorded. Detailed notes were taken during the interviews that were not recorded. The transcribed interviews and detailed notes taken from nonrecorded interviews were analyzed with QSR NVivo 7 (Richards, 1999). To ensure interrater reliability, the two authors read independently each transcript to identify common themes. The authors then convened to determine the overarching themes they had identified.

BACKGROUND CHARACTERISTICS OF IDENTITY THIEVES

The common perception of identity thieves is that they are more akin to middle-class fraudsters than they are to street level property offenders. That is, they hail disproportionately from the middle-classes, they are college educated, and they have stable family lives. To determine if identity thieves resemble other fraudsters various demographic characteristics, including age, race, gender, employment status, and educational achievement were collected. In addition, offenders were asked about their socioeconomic status, family status, and criminal history. Overall, it was found that identity theft was a democratic crime. Its participants came from all walks of life and had diverse criminal histories. In fact, they were just as likely to resemble persistent street thieves as they were middle-class fraudsters.

Gender, Race/Ethnicity, and Age

Table 1 shows the gender, race, and age distributions of the sample. The final sample of 59 inmates included 23 men and 36 women, which was consistent with the findings of Allison et al. (2005).

However, the discrepancy in gender in our sample is likely due to our sampling strategy and the higher response rate from female inmates rather than the actual proportion of identity theft offenders. For example, the gender makeup of the full list of located identity thieves was more similar to that found by Gordon et al. (2007): 63% male and 37% female. The racial makeup of the sample was 44% White, 53% Black, and 3% other. The makeup for the full list of located inmates was 50% White, 46% Black, and 4% other. This is a higher percentage of White offenders than found by either Gordon et al. (2007) or Allison et al. (2005). Offenders in the sample ranged in age from 23 to 60 years with a mean age of 38 years. The majority of offenders were aged 25 to 34 (34%) or 35 to 44 (32%). Only 7% were aged 18 to 24 years and 5% were older than 55 years. The age distribution matches closely with the larger sampling pool and that found by Gordon et al. (2007) and Allison et al. (2005).

Table 1 Gender, Race, and Age of Identity Thieves[a]

	Sampling Pool		Final Sample	
	N	Percentage	N	Percentage
Gender				
Male	187	63.0	23	39.0
Female	110	27.0	36	61.0
Race				
White	148	50.8	26	44.1
Black	137	46.1	31	52.5
Other	12	4.0	2	3.4
Age (Years)				
18–24	15	5.1	4	7.0
25–34	91	30.6	20	33.9
35–44	113	37.8	19	32.2
45–54	61	20.6	13	22.0
>55	17	5.9	3	5.1

[a]Information collected from Bureau of Prisons Inmate Locator.

Employment History

Most offenders had been employed at some point during their lifetimes (see Table 2). The diversity of jobs included day laborers, store clerks, nurses, and attorneys. At the time of their crimes 52.5% were employed and a total of 35.5% of the sample reported that their employment facilitated the identity thefts. The majority of those who used their jobs to carry out their crimes committed mortgage fraud. Others worked at businesses that had access to credit cards and/or social security numbers (e.g., department stores that granted credit or government agencies). These people used their position to obtain information and either used it themselves or sold it to others who then committed fraud. For instance, one offender worked as a junior recruiter for the National Guard and used his position to obtain identifying information. In his words:

> The military has [a form], which has all of your history on it. Social Security numbers, dates of birth. Last known addresses that kind of stuff. And we use that to solicit people to come into the National Guard. . . . After I had gotten out [of the National Guard] I still had the information. . . . I had talked to some other people about how to get credit cards and stuff like that. Then I started, you know.

Table 2   Employment Histories

	N	Percentage
Employed during lifetime		
Yes	47	79.7
No	3	5.1
Unknown	9	15.3
Employed during ID theft		
Yes	31	52.5
No	21	35.6
Unknown	7	11.9
Employment facilitated ID theft		35.6
Yes	21	35.6
No	32	54.2
Unknown	6	10.2

Not all used their positions to steal information, some used their employment to facilitate identity theft. For example, several worked at local Department of Motor Vehicles offices and used their position to help others obtain fraudulent identification. Most of them claimed that they sought employment at these places legitimately and then were approached by others to commit the fraud. Few said that they sought employment for the purposes of gaining easy access to sensitive information or to facilitate the thefts. Although the majority of thieves we spoke with did not commit identity theft through the course of their occupations, a significant number of offenders indicated that their past employment experience gave them insiders' knowledge that enabled them to carry out their crimes. This included knowledge of real estate transactions and how banks, credit agencies, and department stores operated and extended credit.

Criminal History

A total of 37 (63%) of the offenders reported that they had been arrested for crimes other than those for which they were currently incarcerated (see Table 3). Of those who had prior arrests most were for financial fraud or identity theft ($n = 26$) but drug use/sales ($n = 11$) and property crimes ($n = 13$) were also relatively common, which is consistent with Gordon et al.'s (2007) findings. A total of 26 had also been convicted of a crime. Again, most of these convictions were for financial fraud or identity theft ($n = 15$).

Researchers are unclear as to the degree that offenders specialize in particular crimes. Here again our sample showed diversity. Prior arrest patterns indicate that a large portion of them had engaged in various types of crime, including drug, property, and violent crimes. Yet the majority of them claimed that they only committed identity thefts or comparable frauds (e.g., check fraud). Although several offenders described having committed other crimes in the past, they stopped these other criminal endeavors because they could make more money through identity theft. For example, one offender said, "[selling drugs is] not the answer. That's not where the money is" and another, who switched from burglaries to identity theft, argued that, "[identity theft] is easier and you get the money, you know. You get a lot of money."

Inmates were also questioned about their prior drug use (see Table 4). A total of 34 (58%) had tried drugs in their lifetime, mostly marijuana, cocaine in various forms, and methamphetamine. Only 22 reported having been addicted to their drug of choice. Of those offenders who said that they were using drugs

| Table 3 | Criminal Histories |

	N	Percentage
Prior arrest		
Yes	37	62.7
No	19	32.2
Unknown	3	5.1
Prior arrests by crime types[a]		
Property crime	13	35.1
Violent crime	4	10.8
Drug possession/sales	11	29.7
Fraud	19	51.4
ID theft	7	18.9
Other	3	8.1
Unknown	2	5.4
Prior convictions		
Yes	26	44.1
No	25	42.4
Unknown	8	13.6
Prior convictions by crime types[a]		
Property crime	5	19.2
Violent crime	2	7.7
Drug possession/sales	2	7.7
Fraud	13	50.0
ID theft	2	7.7
Other	1	3.8
Unknown	8	30.8

[a]For some categories percentages do not add up to 100% because some offenders reported more than one answer.

| Table 4 | Drug Histories |

	N	Percentage
Drug use ever		
Yes	34	57.6
No	22	37.3
Unknown	3	5.1
Drug addiction		
Yes	22	37.3
No	31	52.5
Unknown	6	10.2
Drug use during ID theft		
Yes	25	42.4
No	31	52.5
Unknown	3	5.1
Type of drug used during theft[a]		
Cocaine (powder and crack)	10	40.0
Heroin	3	12.0
Marijuana	6	24.0
Prescription	1	4.0
Methamphetamine	7	28.0
Unknown	8	32.0
Drug use contributed to ID theft		
Yes	14	23.7
No	41	69.5
Unknown	4	6.8

[a]For some categories percentages do not add up to 100% because some offenders reported more than one answer.

while committing identity theft, only 14 reported that the drug use contributed to their identity thefts. Despite current claims about the link between methamphetamines and identity theft, only five of those with whom we spoke said that methamphetamine use directly contributed to their crimes. One respondent claimed, "I started smoking meth, then I stopped working, and then I started doing this for money." This finding is supported by Gordon et al. (2007).

Family Background, Marital Status, and Educational Attainment

To gain an understanding of their life experiences offenders were asked to describe their past and current family situation (see Table 5). To assess social class a subjective measure was used by asking offenders to self-identify with a class based on their parents' occupations and lifestyles. When asked to describe their family's status growing up most offenders classified their family background as either working-class (47.5%) or middle/upper-middle class (42.4%). Whereas a few of the parents of those who self-defined as working class made a living through crime, the majority said that their parents worked at jobs such as manual laborers. A typical response to what their families were like was, "Growing up, my mom was actually in prison. She was here actually for ten years and then my dad, like I said I don't know about him." Another replied:

> I had a rough background. Since I've been incarcerated, I've been able to reflect on everything that led me up to where I was a couple of years ago. Let's see. I'm a middle child of 5 girls and I'm from Chicago. My mother was a single parent. She was physically abused by my father. They were divorced when I was 4, but I remember the fights, you know? My mother was remarried. Her second husband had sexually molested me and that was like one time. I was 12 years old, but that never was able to be dealt with and I think I had a lot of anger starting at 11 years old that I held in. So my anger wanted to get back but I didn't know how.

Not all came from such humble beginnings. As over half claimed to hail from middle-class or upper-middle-class families. The parents of those who self-defined as middle-class held jobs such as doctors, nurses, engineers, or other white-collar positions. When asked to describe their childhood one respondent said, "Typical middle-class. Both parents, actually my mother didn't work until the children were grown and out of the house (I have two younger sisters). My father's always been in law enforcement he's also military, he's a colonel in the army." Another described, "[My] parents went to work and we went to school.... We had computers. Pretty much didn't want for anything."

Of those for which information was available, 39% came from broken homes, which is reflected in some of the above quotes. Most offenders were currently or had been married in their lifetimes: 25% of offenders were married, 30.5% were separated/divorced, 32.2% had never been married, and 5.1% were widowed. Divorces

Table 5 Family Background, Marital Status, and Educational Attainment

	N	Percentage
Socioeconomic class		
Under/working class	28	47.5
Middle/upper-middle class	25	42.4
Unknown	6	10.2
Family background		
Broken	23	39.0
Intact	17	28.8
Unknown	19	32.2
Marital status		
Never married	19	32.2
Divorced/separated/widowed	21	35.6
Married	15	25.4
Unknown	4	6.8
Children		
Yes	44	74.6
No	11	18.6
Unknown	4	6.8
Educational attainment		
No high school diploma	9	15.3
High school diploma	10	16.9
Some college	19	32.2
College degree	12	20.3
Unknown	9	15.3

or separations were factors, among many, that instigated identity theft for 10 people. One female offender's remarks exemplify this process:

> I had gotten divorced. I was a single mom, and I was struggling. I was working, but I've worked for a number of years as an independent contractor doing medical transcription, and I lost some of my accounts. I was struggling with depression and dealing with a lot of

things. I had met some ladies and we started talking and . . . we began to socialize and they said, "We do identity theft and we think you would do really good going into a bank and taking some money out. We can split that with you and you can have some money.'" I said okay and that's how I started.

Only one individual said that her thefts led to her divorce. Approximately 75% of offenders had children. With respect to educational achievement, the majority of offenders had had at least some college.

Based on the background characteristics of the identity thieves in our sample, it would be difficult to classify them as white-collar offenders. They came from a variety of socioeconomic classes, occupations, and varied in their employment histories. Weisburd et al.'s (1991) study also reported a diversity of classes represented in their sample of *white-collar* offenders with the majority hailing from the middle class. Thus, if one were to adhere to the populist perspective regarding the definition of white-collar crime, the majority of identity thieves in our sample would not be considered white-collar criminals, nor would their crimes be considered white-collar. The majority of offenders were not of high economic, social, or occupational status nor did most of them commit their thefts through the course of their occupation. In fact, most of the offenders who were employed at the time of their crimes did not use their positions to gain identifying information and commit identity theft.

METHODS AND TECHNIQUES OF IDENTITY THEFT

Identity thieves use a variety of methods to acquire victims' personal information and convert that information into cash and/or goods. Data from victimization surveys and interviews with law enforcement officials have been used to describe the techniques identity thieves commonly employ to commit their crimes (Lease & Burke, 2000; Newman, 2004). In what follows we contextualize previous research on the topic by providing a description of the techniques participants used to commit identity theft.

Acquiring Information

When asked where the information came from nearly all were able to answer. However, some individuals worked in a group where other group members obtained the information. They claimed that they merely played their role in the crimes and chose not to

ask too many questions. Those who did know where information came from did not specialize in a single method of procuring identifying information. Instead, they preferred to use a variety of strategies. Although some offenders acquired identities from their place of employment, mainly mortgage companies, the most common method of obtaining a victim's information was to buy it. Offenders in our sample bought identities from employees of various businesses and state agencies who had access to personal information such as name, address, date of birth, and social security number. Information was purchased from employees of banks, credit agencies, a state law enforcement agency, mortgage companies, state Department of Motor Vehicles, hospitals, doctors' offices, a university, car dealerships, and furniture stores. One individual bought information from an employee of a state department of law enforcement. He described how he was able to do so:

> I just happen to meet this lady that was a drug user. She smoked crack and worked for [law enforcement agency], so that told me that she could be bought. She was very discreet with it, but I knew that she had a weakness. Her weakness wasn't necessarily the crack, the weakness was the money from my part. I couldn't supply her with crack, but I could definitely give her the money to buy crack. So I would make her offers that she could not refuse as far as, "Look, I need you to go into the file for me, pull up some clean names for me."

He was not alone in the ability to locate employees willing to sell private information. According to one female identity thief, "It's so easy to get information and everybody has a price." Another, said. "People are easily bought these days. You can get IDs anywhere. You can get IDs from a driver's license place if you find somebody corrupt working in there." When describing how she obtained information from a bank employee, one participant said:

> [The bank employee] was willing to make some money too, so she had the good information. She would have the information that would allow me to have a copy of the signature card, passwords, work address, everything, everything that's legit.

Offenders who purchased information did so from persons they knew or who they were acquainted with "on the streets." As one male offender explained, "[People on the streets] knew what I was buying. I mean any city, there's always somebody buying some information." The majority of the people who were providing this information were drug users and/or petty street hustlers. The identity thieves bought information from other offenders who obtained it from burglaries, thefts from motor vehicles, prostitution, and pick-pocketing. For the most part, the participants did not know or care where their sellers obtained their information. As long as the information was good they asked no questions. When asked where the information came from one offender explained, "I didn't ask . . . they just said. 'Hey I got this and I got that.' And I said, 'Okay well here's a little bit of dope.' There you go."

Other individuals obtained information by using the mailbox method or searching trash cans. These offenders typically stole mail from small businesses such as insurance companies or from residential mailboxes in front of homes or apartments. Apartment complexes or other areas with rows of boxes in close proximity were popular targets. When asked where they got information, a female identity thief answered:

> I would go into an apartment complex that would have the square boxes. There would be like 60 in one, because there's like a little community in there. You just pop it open and there's just all kinds of slots there. You just start taking it all out as fast as you can, real late at night, in the early morning like when people are just about ready to go to work.

Others simply drove through residential areas and pulled mail out. These offenders took steps to appear legitimate. One middle-class offender explained how he did this, "I usually had a flyer I was putting in the mailbox and I was dressed like I was getting a flyer out for these businesses so no I was never confronted." This strategy was similar to that used by residential burglars looking for a suitable home to break into (Wright & Decker, 1994). Mailboxes and trashcans for businesses that send out mail with personal information (account numbers, social security numbers, and date of birth) such as insurance companies were also popular targets. One offender, who paid people to get information for him, said, "I had a dude running into the banks and stealing the trashcans out the bank." Some would even steal from store cash registers to obtain credit and check information. Another offender would:

> Go to a department store register and pull out the under-box and pull out whatever they had for their credit receipts and stuff like that. They'd write social security number and date of birth on them. And pull that kind of stuff out.

Although most of the offenders interviewed did not know their victims, of those who did, half said that the victim willingly gave them the information in exchange for a cut of the profits. In these cases, the "victim" gave the offender information to commit the identity theft and then reported that their identity had been stolen. According to one, 'What I did was I had got this guy's personal information, he actually willingly gave it to me." The other half used family members' information without their knowledge. One identity thief used a good friend and roommate's identity because of his high credit score. He explained:

> [He] moved into my home out of his apartment to save him money. And from there I just kept track of his credit. I kept track of what he was spending and his credit limits. From there whenever I needed to use his credit [I did]. . . . He just didn't know about it.

Another, who worked for a mortgage company, used her infant son's identity to buy property. In her words, "I bought another property in a false alias, I used my son's social security number and my maiden name and bought a property." Historically, deceased victims have been thought to be the targets of choice for identity thieves (Newman & McNally, 2005). Only two individuals used this type of information and one was a family member. Pontell, Brown, and Tosouni (2008) also found that only a limited number of people stole deceased people's identities.

Other methods of acquiring victims' information included various thefts (house and car burglary, purse-snatching). One individual claimed to have stolen mailbags from an unattended mail truck. Others conned or manipulated people to get their information. One individual set up a fake employment site to get information from job applicants. In his words:

> I put an ad in the newspaper, company in a new area, seeking employees. . . . I would write a synopsis up on the computer as to what the job was offering, the benefits. In the paper I always put excellent benefits and dental after ninety days, and I would take that and attach it to an employment application and put it in a folder. . . . Each person that filled out an application, I had a digital camera, I would take a picture of and I actually fashioned the application for the information that I needed. You know height, weight, color of eyes, date of birth, Social Security number. . . . Then I would take the applications and screen the ones that were close to my makeup and shred the rest. I would take folders and I built the identities in case I needed one quick. So I would have

the information, birth certificate, and Social Security card, everything you needed.

Another used the birth announcements in newspapers to get the names of new parents and, posing as an insurance representative, called the parents to get information for "billing purposes." Interestingly, the offender made the phone calls from the waiting room of the hospitals where the infants were born so that the name of the hospital would appear on the victims' caller ID if they had it. Another offender used rogue internet sites to run background checks and order credit reports on potential victims.

Converting Information

After they obtain a victim's information the offender then has the task of converting that information into cash or goods. Offenders used a variety of methods to profit from the stolen identities including applying for credit cards in the victims' names (including major credit cards and department store credit cards), opening new bank accounts and depositing counterfeit checks, withdrawing money from existing bank accounts, applying for loans, and applying for public assistance programs. Identity thieves often used more than one technique when cashing in on their crimes.

The most common strategy for converting stolen identities into cash was applying for credit cards. Offenders used the information to order new credit cards. In a few cases the information was used to get the credit card agency to issue a duplicate card on an existing account. They used credit cards to buy merchandise for their own personal use, to resell the merchandise to friends and/or acquaintances, or to return the merchandise for cash. A typical response was, "you buying things so that you could then sell it for cash or just items for yourself." Offenders also used the checks that are routinely sent to credit card holders to deposit in the victim's account and then withdraw cash or to open new accounts. Offenders also applied for store credit cards such as department stores and home improvement stores. According to one offender who used this technique:

> [I would] go to different department stores or most often it was Lowes or Home Depot, go in, fill out an application with all the information, and then receive instant credit in the amount from say $1,500 to $7,500. Every store is different. Every individual is different. And then at that time, I would purchase as much as that balance that I could at one time. So if it was $2,500, I would buy S2,500 worth of merchandise.

She went on to explain that sometimes she took orders from customers before making the fraudulent purchases or just sold them later. Gift cards were popular purchases. One participant explained, "I was buying like gift cards and things like that.... Gift cards were like money on the streets. People were buying them off me like hotcakes."

Another common strategy to profit from identity theft was to produce counterfeit checks. Offenders either made fraudulent checks on their own or knew someone who would produce these checks for them. Sometimes identity thieves would use the stolen identities to either open a new bank account as a way to deposit fraudulent checks or to withdraw money from an existing account. One offender described how her and her team would work this scam:

> They had fake checks deposited into the account. And because we were in Washington, I was required to go to Oregon because for [this bank], Washington, Idaho, Oregon, California are not on the same computer system. Every day you can make three transactions on an account without a flag coming up. So they would deposit monies into the account and for a two day period, he would drive me to Oregon and we would go to different bank branches and I would go in and I would withdraw money from the account and you could do three a day and so I would take $1,500 from each, so that'd be $4,500.... We would do 2 days at a bank, so we'd go to 6 different branches. Sometimes there would be a third day if there was still a balance on the account.

Another identity thief, who also worked in a group, described their process thus:

> There were some people in my cases that had fake ID and stuff like that. We use other people's names and stuff to go in [the bank] and cash checks. First they get your account, then they get your name and stuff. Make some ID and send a person in there to cash checks on your account.

Another offender, who acted as a ringleader, described how he would get a "writer" to cash checks from stolen identities:

> Say that the person already got an existing account. I would teach the [co-defendant] how to do the signature. I would let him do it couple of times, like send him in there and let him practice on it. Then once I feel like he got it down pat, I send them in there and let them cash checks in that person's name.... If the person got an account at any kind of bank, you ain't really got to go in

there and cash a check, you can go through the drive through. So, I send the [co-defendant] through the drive through with a rented car and just cash the check. But if the person doesn't have an account, what I'm going to do. I'll just take three grand and I'm going to go open up a checking account somewhere. And I just hit the branches around that area.... I might get ten pieces in one day, with that three grand in there.

Identity thieves also applied for and received loans with the stolen identities. The majority of those who applied for loans engaged in some type of mortgage fraud. These types of scams often involved using a victim's information to purchase homes for themselves. In one case, the offenders were buying houses and then renting them for a profit. Others applied for various auto loans, home equity loans, or personal loans.

When cashing checks in other people's names, applying for loans, or extracting money from the victim's bank account it was necessary to have fraudulent identification to pose as these individuals. Most commonly, offenders used the information to acquire or produce additional identity related documents such as driver's licenses or state identification cards. Some offenders created the cards themselves with software and materials (e.g., paper and ink, purchased at office supply stores or given to them by an employee of a state Department of Motor Vehicles [DMV]). One participant described her process for making fraudulent identification:

> We studied IDs. Then I went to the stamp shop, the paint shop, got the logos right and I know the [Bank] was one of the hardest banks for us to get money out, but when I found out about the logos, when I passed it through the black light, it became real easy.... I went to the stamp shop and bought a stamp and sat there for hours and hours with the colors and I made like seven different IDs before it come through under the black light.

Another claimed to have access to software that allowed them to produce realistic looking driver's licenses:

> My friend, he made me the IDs and he was good at it and of course we have DMV program from people working at DMV and they get you the program. So we have DMV program. We even have real DMV holograms, backing, and the paper.

Several offenders claimed to get driver's licenses directly from the Department of Motor Vehicles either through fraud or by paying off employees. One prolific identity thief described how he obtained a driver's license from a small town DMV:

> I was at a DMV and the lady said "something's not right." I said. "Yeah I don't understand why it's not coming up on your computer that I have a license." She goes, "Well, I think you did. I believe you did." And she gave me one anyway, because it was a transfer from another state.

Others used their contacts at their local DMVs to purchase driver's licenses. In these cases they would bring stolen information on the victim and present it to the compromised employee. Then the employee would process the information as if it were legitimate, resulting in a driver's license with the offender's photo but the victim's information.

CONCLUSION

The goals of the research presented here were to contextualize previous research on identity theft and to highlight the complexities in labeling the crime as white-collar. Our interviews with 59 offenders incarcerated in federal prisons revealed information about their backgrounds and the methods they employed to acquire information and convert it into cash and/or goods. Results show that identity thieves were a diverse group. The majority of them were between the ages of 25 and 44 years, have had at least some college, and were employed in a wide range of legitimate occupations. Although White offenders made up the largest proportion of offenders, Blacks were overrepresented in relation to their distribution in the population. In addition, offenders employed a variety of methods to both acquire information and convert it to cash. When seeking out identifying information, identity thieves were more likely to buy it from others. Those they purchased information from either obtained this information from their place of employment or through other crimes like burglaries. For those who obtained information on their own they typically did so by simple methods such as dumpster diving or stealing from mailboxes. Few in the sample used sophisticated computer technologies like phishing to obtain identities. When converting this information into cash the most common strategies were to apply for credit cards, apply for loans, or to counterfeit and/or forge checks.

Depending on which perspective one adheres to, identity theft may or may not be classified as a white-collar crime committed by white-collar offenders. Although the characteristics of our sample would seem to support the patrician view of white-collar crime that emphasizes the act rather than the populist view that emphasizes the actor, we find it difficult to categorize all identity theft as a white-collar crime. If one defines identity theft by the act itself, regardless of whether it occurs in an occupational context, then it would be included as a white-collar crime under the patrician perspective. Edelhertz (1970) suggests that white-collar crime is "an illegal act or series of illegal acts committed by nonphysical means and by conceal-ment or guile, to obtain money or property, to avoid the payment or loss of money or property or to obtain business or personal advantage" (p. 3). Thus, if we ignore the offender's occupational position or social status we might conclude that identity theft is a white-collar crime.

If we take a more middle of the road position regarding the definition of white-collar crime, then some identity thieves can be classified as white-collar offenders, whereas others might best be classified as property offenders. If, as Friedrichs (2004) suggests, most criminologists support the basic assumption that white-collar crime must occur in the context of a legitimate occupation, identity theft is sometimes but not always white-collar crime. The majority of the offenders in our sample did not meet this requirement as many were either unemployed or, if employed, did not acquire information through their place of employ-ment. We should reiterate however that many of them noted that they were able to engage in identity theft because of their knowledge gained from previous employment experiences. According to our findings, identity thieves include property offenders (e.g., those who acquire information from other street offenders or from employees of certain businesses) and white-collar offenders (e.g., employees who acquire information from their place of work).

Identity theft is often portrayed as a sophisticated crime committed by well-organized groups through the use of computers and as such it is often portrayed as white-collar crime. Considering that the research on identity theft is rather limited and there are limita-tions to our own study (as discussed below) it is likely impossible to conclude that identity theft is a white-collar or even primarily a white-collar crime. But we should be careful not to overlook the fact that identity theft is committed by people from a wide range of classes and backgrounds. Based on the employment status of our sample of offenders, and the methods they used to acquire and convert identifying informa-tion, we do not advocate classifying it as a white-collar crime. It is best categorized as an economic crime committed by a wide range of people from diverse backgrounds through a variety of legitimate (e.g., mortgage broker) and illegitimate (e.g., burglar) occupations.

It should be noted that this project was designed to be a starting point for understanding identity theft from the offenders' perspectives. As such, the study does have limitations that should be addressed in future research on the topic. The primary limitation of the study is that it relied exclusively on interviews with federally convicted thieves. Although appropriate for an exploratory study, this type of sample does have its shortcomings. Generally, any sample based on con-victed offenders may actually tell us more about enforcement patterns and priorities than about the actual distribution of crime (Jesilow, Pontell, & Geis, 1993). Those convicted at the federal level may not be characteristic of the typical identity thief. Federally convicted thieves may be responsible for unusually high monetary losses or have clear evidence against them making prosecution easier. However, the self-reported financial gains of those interviewed are com-parable to reports from other researchers (BJS, 2006; FTC, 2004; Gordon et al., 2007).

Our findings also suggest directions for future research. Expansion of the sample to include those convicted at the state level and those who are still active is warranted and desirable. Those charged and convicted at the federal level may not necessarily reflect the larger population of identity thieves for those reasons listed above. Expanding the sample accordingly would certainly increase our understand-ing of the problem. To address the problems associated with relying on data from federally convicted offend-ers, both state and federal prosecutors should be sur-veyed to assess the types of cases they handle. Questions may include those designed to ascertain the differences between the types of cases prosecutors accept for prosecution and those they decline and the types of cases that start at the state level and are picked up by federal prosecutors for processing. In addition, collecting data using a self-report questionnaire may provide relevant information about those who commit this crime. Doing so would allow for a considerably larger sample and would allow for quantifiable data, both of which were outside the reach of the current project. The information gleaned from the current research and from others could be used to develop an appropriate questionnaire.

Despite public perceptions of identity theft being a high-tech, computer driven crime, it is rather mun-dane and requires few technical skills. Identity thieves do not need to know how to hack into large, secure databases. They can simply dig through garbage or pay insiders for information. No particular group has a monopoly on the skills needed to be a capable identity thief. This should not be taken to dismiss or diminish the impact of large-scale, sophisticated identity theft organizations that do exploit modem information systems. These types of breaches do occur and exact considerably large costs to victims, but they are a rarity in comparison to the typical identity theft incident.

References

Allison, S., Schuck, A., & Lersch, K. M. (2005). Exploring the crime of identity theft: Prevalence, clearance rates, and victim/offender characteristics. *Journal of Criminal Justice, 33*, 19–29.

Braithwaitc, J. (1985). White collar crime. *Annual Review of Sociology. 11,* 1–25.

Bureau of Justice Statistics. (2006). *Identity theft. 2004.* Washington. DC: Government Printing Office.

Bureau of Justice Statistics. (2007). *Identity theft. 2005.* Washington, DC: Government Printing Office.

Clinard, M., & Quinncy, R. (1973). *Criminal behavior systems: A typology* (2nd ed.) New York: Holt, Rinechart, & Winston.

Davis, K., & Stevenson, A. (2004). They've got your numbers. *Kiplinger's Personal Finance,* 58, 72–77.

Edelhertz, H. (1970). *The nature, impact, and prosecution of white-collar crime.* Washington, DC: U.S. Department of Justice, National Institute of Law Enforcement and Criminal Justice.

Federal Trade Commission. (2004). *National and state trends in fraud and identity theft January-December* 2003. Retrieved December 29, 2007, from http://www.ftc.gov/

Federal Trade Commission. (2007). *National and slate trends in fraud and identity theft January-December* 2006. Retrieved December 29, 2007, from http://www.ftc.gov/

Friedrichs, D. O. (2004). *Trusted criminals* (2nd ed.). Belmont, CA: Wadsworth.

Gayer, J. (2003). *Policing privacy: Law enforcement's response to identity theft.* Los Angeles: CALPIRG.

Gordon, G. R., Rebovieh, D., Choo, K. S., & Gordon, J. B. (2007). *Identity fraud trends and patterns: Building a data-based foundation for proactive enforcement.* Utica, NY: Center for Identity Management and Information Protection.

Jacobs. B., & Wright, R. (2006). Street justice: *Retaliation in the criminal underworld.* New York: Cambridge University Press.

Jesilow. P., Pontell, H., & Gcis, G. (1993). *Prescription for profit: How doctors defraud Medicaid.* Berkley, CA: University of California Press.

Lease, M. L., & Burke, T. W. (2000). Identity theft a fast-growing crime. *FBI Law Enforcement Bulletin.* 69, 8–13.

LoPucki, L. M. (2001). Human identification theory and the identity theft problem. *Texas Law Review, 80,* 89–135.

Nee, C., & Taylor, M. (2000). Examining burglars target selection: Interview, experiment or ethnomethodology? *Psychology, Crime & Law,* 6, 45–59.

Newman. D. J. (1958). White-collar crime. *Law and Contemporary Problems,* 23, 735–753.

Newman, G. R. (2004). *Identity theft. Problem-oriented guides for police* (Problem-Specific Guide Series, Guide No. 25). Washington. DC: U.S. Department of Justice, Office of Community Oriented Policing Services.

Newman, G. R., & McNally, M. (2005). *Identity theft literature review.* Washington, DC: U.S. Department of Justice, National Institute of Justice.

Owens, M. (2004). *Policing privacy: Michigan law enforcement officers on the challenges of tracking identity theft.* Ann Arbor: Public Interest Research Group in Michigan.

Pontell, H. N., Brown, G. C. & Tosouni, A. (2008). Stolen identities: A victim survey. In M. McNally & G. Newman (Eds.). *Perspectives on identity theft* (pp. 57–86). New York: Criminal Justice Press.

Privacy and American Business. (2003). *Identity theft: New survey and trend report.* Retrieved December 29. 2007 from http://www.bbbonlinc.org/idtheft/lDTheftSrvyAug03.pdf

Richards. L. (1999). *Using NVIVO in qualitative research.* London: Sage.

Shapiro, S. (1990). Collaring the crime, not the criminal: Reconsidering the concept of white-collar crime. *American Sociological Review,* 55, 346–365.

Shover, N., & Cullen, F. T. (2008). Studying and teaching white-collar crime: Populist and Patrician perspectives. *Journal of Criminal Justice Education,* 19, 155–174.

Sutherland, E. (1949). *White-collar crime.* New York: Dryden.

Synovate. (2007). *Federal Trade Commission—2006 identity theft survey report.* Retrieved December 29, 2007, from www.ftc.gov/os/2007/1 l/SynovateFinalRcportIDTheft2006.pdf

U.S. General Accounting Office. (2002). *Identity theft: Prevalence and cost appear to be growing.* Report to Congressional Requesters GAO-02-363. Washington, DC.

Weisburd. D., Wheeler, S., Waring, E., & Bode, N. (1991). *Crimes of the middle classes: While collar offenders in the federal courts.* New Haven, CT: Yale University Press.

Wright, R., & Decker, S. (1994). *Burglars on the job.* Boston, MA: Northeastern University Press.

15

TRANSFERRING SUBCULTURAL KNOWLEDGE ON-LINE

Practices and Beliefs of Persistent Digital Pirates

THOMAS J. HOLT AND HEITH COPES

The nature and impact of the on-line learning process as it affected the behavior of individuals is examined by studying the deviant behavior of those people who participate in on-line piracy. Criminal subcultures form around this illegal behavior and through their interactions with other on-line pirates, they learn the norms and values that encompass this illegal activity.

The majority of delinquent behavior is by necessity a social enterprise. Delinquents rarely work alone and even when they do, they often require tutelage and a social network to be successful (e.g., McCarthy 1996; Morselli et al. 2006; Warr 2002). In fact, interacting with others who have similar problems can lead people to develop solutions to collectively experienced social problems by creating an alternative frame of reference or delinquent subculture (Cohen 1955). This frame of reference, which is both social psychological and cultural, provides individuals with specific techniques for committing crime and ways to make sense of their actions. Interactions with likeminded others engender the transmission of shared understandings of actions (e.g., beliefs, goals, and values that approve of

and justify involvement in deviance), the skills to be successful, and codes of conduct for interacting with others (Akers 1998; Sutherland 1937, 1947). Sutherland suggests that the key intervening factor between deviant associations and delinquency is the acquisition of techniques and other symbolic elements that are favorable toward the violation of law. Through continued interactions people learn and articulate a discourse that structures the generation, activation, and diffusion of these ideas, objects, and practices.

Elaborating on this idea with his theory of "differential identification," Glaser (1956) focused on the subjective role-taking process that occurs in both social interaction and private thought. Thus, "a person pursues criminal behavior to the extent that he identifies himself with real or imaginary persons from whose perspective his criminal behavior seems acceptable" (1956:440). The more an individual identifies with a particular group the more likely he or she is to accept the definitions promoted and incorporate them into his or her belief and knowledge systems.

To that end, passive interaction through media or non-verbal interactions via computer-mediated communications can be important locales for passing on and learning subcultural knowledge (DiMarco and DiMarco 2003; Holt 2007; Taylor et al. 2006; Williams and Copes 2005). Interactions in virtual environments through computer-mediated communications have become an important aspect of everyday life for a growing number of people across the world. The Internet and computer-mediated communication methods, such as newsgroups and Web forums, allow individuals to exchange information almost instantaneously and without regard to geographic boundaries and limitations (DiMarco and DiMarco 2003). The ubiquity of computers and easy access to the Internet allows peers to communicate on-line across great distances, facilitating the global transmission of subcultural knowledge without the need for physical contact with one another (Holt 2007; Taylor et al. 2006).

It must be noted that Internet and computer technologies provide more than just a means to connect individuals. These technologies also encourage offenders to change their values, norms and behaviors as they adapt to scientific and technological innovations (Quinn and Forsyth 2005). This new aspect of social life has important implications for how deviant and criminal knowledge is passed on. Despite this, we know little about how technology, specifically participation in on-line groups, influences the learning process of offending and the transmission of subcultural norms (for an exception, see Mann and Sutton 1998).

To that end, this study explores the nature and impact of the on-line learning process on individual behavior by examining one of the most common and easily recognized forms of on-line deviance: media piracy. The tremendous growth of digital media files and technologies designed to play them has stimulated the creation of a global subculture of chronic media pirates (Cooper and Harrison 2001). The members of this subculture focus on the rapid distribution of diverse media content to a wide audience and achieve status and respect through the dissemination and maintenance of large volumes of media (Cooper and Harrison 2001). Thus, we examine how individuals learn the motives and techniques of digital piracy through on-line interactions with others. Specifically,

we describe the initiation process of digital piracy, perceptions of risk and strategies to minimize risk, motivations, and justifications for illegal downloading.

DIGITAL PIRACY SUBCULTURES

Before exploring the learning process of digital piracy, it is important to understand how interaction and identification among digital pirates facilitates the dissemination of techniques and meanings of illegal downloading. One of the few studies on piracy subcultures found that its members share commonalities with computer hackers (Cooper and Harrison 2001; see also Furnell 2002). Pirates in the late 1990s and early 2000s often used Internet Relay Chats (IRC) or other communications channels to exchange files quickly. A small population of individuals within this subculture also break copyright protections, operate communications channels, and host file-sharing services to provide access to pirated materials. In fact, the persistent piracy subculture places significant value on high speed Internet connectivity and the ability to host significant amounts of data (see Hinduja 2001). This is due to the main goal of persistent pirates, to rapidly disseminate electronic media in large quantities to people around the globe (Cooper and Harrison 2001).

We address the process of criminal learning through technology by analyzing the accounts of persistent digital pirates. Using a series of semi-structured interviews with persistent pirates and ethnographic observation of an on-line forum devoted to piracy, we explore the expression of subcultural norms pirates articulate when discussing how they became involved in piracy as well as their accounts or justifications for their involvement in piracy. In addition, we explore the formal and informal risks pirates associate with their actions, and the strategies employed to minimize these risks. The findings can expand our knowledge of the practices of technology-focused criminals and how they use technology to transmit subcultural knowledge and beliefs.

DATA AND METHODS

The current study is based on data collected from semi-structured interviews with 34 individuals who actively, engaged in the illegal downloading and from ethnographic observations of an on-line forum. Our goal was to understand the justifications, practices, risks, and rewards that high frequency, persistent pirates associate with their downloading and how these aspects of their crimes were shaped or learned through participation in on-line communities. To be eligible for inclusion in the interview section of the study pirates had to have downloaded digital information at least once in the two weeks prior to the interview and had to average five files a week for the previous six months.

Interviewees were identified through the use of a field-worker at a university in the southern United States and by solicitations made via e-mail, Internet forums, and instant messaging programs. In fall of 2007 we began face-to-face interviews with nine participants recruited by the fieldworker using prior contacts and snowball sampling. These pirates had been downloading music, movies, television shows, and software for a number of years and were members of pirating communities. Face-to-face interviews were conducted in private locations and audio-recorded. The interviews lasted between 45 minutes and two hours.

We sought to expand the sample outside of the local area because downloading is not confined to specific geographic regions. In addition to face-to-face interviews, 25 respondents from two on-line forums and two IRC channels devoted to piracy and referrals from the original sample were interviewed using instant messaging programs (Gross 2004). We began with an Internet site that acted as an index for torrent file and is the source of many illegally uploaded and distributed copyrighted data. Its forums have active participants from throughout the world who discuss piracy in most, if not all, of its forms. The fieldworker became a member of the forums for both websites and made posts calling for help on the project. Several of the participants were hesitant to participate in the interviews until the fieldworker provided proof that she was not law enforcement and proved her authenticity as a member of the piracy subculture. This was done through answering questions on the forum and, perhaps most importantly, by showing her adeptness at open-source programs. The use of electronic interview methods allowed us to expand the sample without regards to geographic limitations. In fact, the pirates interviewed in this way lived in Australia, Europe, and North America.

Regardless of the type of interview conducted, the protocol probed individual experiences with piracy, the technology they used to download media, and any connections to larger piracy communities. We began the interviews by asking participants about their educational and occupational backgrounds, living situations,

and other aspects of their lives. Pirates were also asked about when and how they began actively pirating copyrighted data, what programs they used, and their thoughts about their downloading activity. In addition, we asked questions about how their behavior and beliefs had changed over time, why and how they currently pirated, the risks and rewards of illegal uploading and downloading, and how they managed the risks associated with piracy.

The interview sample consisted of male pirates from Australia, Canada, Holland, the United Kingdom and the United States. Participants were between the ages of 14 and 32, with the average age of 20 years old. The majority were white, unemployed students with no technical computer training. All but five were male. None of the participants had faced any convictions of piracy or had been incarcerated, although many experienced informal victimization caused by downloading viruses. The majority of participants pirated a combination of music, movies, television shows and software through popular peer-to-peer (P2P) file-sharing and torrenting programs, although several discussed key-code cracking, video streaming, and other methods of accessing copyrighted materials.

In order to gain more insight into the subculture of piracy we also performed ethnographic observations on one of the on-line forums where we located the additional participants. We chose this forum because it was affiliated with one of the largest and most popular torrent websites devoted to on-line piracy. The forum had over 65,000 members, with nearly 6,000 of them classified as active. Participants interact with one another by posting on "threads" within the forum. Threads are textual conversations that are organized chronologically on the forum's Web page and constitute its "conversational life" (Denzin 1999:114).

The data were collected through passive ethnographic observations without focused interaction with participants to produce a content analysis of forum threads (Bainbridge 2000). During our analysis of these early posts, we noticed that on-line pirates discussed the same focal concerns that emerged during the interviews with pirates. Additional forum threads were identified that pertained to piracy techniques, beliefs about theft, experiences with guilt, and other topics that were similar to those raised by the interviewees. In total, over a dozen threads with more than 300 posts were analyzed, and the data sets were triangulated, allowing the distinct contexts of the data to be connected while situating each in its specific social setting. To protect the privacy and on-line identity of those who posted on-line we have assigned them an alias when quoting them. The data that follow come from both the interviews and the forums. Unless otherwise noted the quotes come from the interviews with pirates.

INITIATION AND PERSISTENCE IN ILLEGAL DOWNLOADING

All of those we interviewed defined themselves as active pirates, although many indicated that they were not significantly involved in a piracy subculture. They said this despite being active members of invitation only piracy forums and private tracker groups (websites devoted to downloading files). This suggests that the membership in virtual piracy subcultures is fluid and without rigid boundaries. People can log onto the forum, browse, or interact without investing fully. Access to the group is not limited to those with technical knowledge. In fact, unlike in previous research on piracy, few of those we interviewed had a technical background in computer science (Cooper and Harrison 2001; Hinduja 2001, 2003; Simms et al. 1996). This may be a result of significant changes in the penetration of computer technology and the Internet, as well as increased awareness of piracy in the general public (Furnell 2002; Taylor et al. 2006). Computer piracy was a much more underground behavior in the late 1980s and early 1990s, which changed as many individuals began to use the Internet in the mid 1990s. During this time computer technology became increasingly user-friendly and file-sharing programs were easily accessible (Furnell 2002; Taylor et al. 2006).

In fact, most of the individuals interviewed became involved in piracy in the late 1990s with the development of easy to use file-sharing software such as Napster and Kazaa. The creation of programs with an easy to navigate graphical user interface enabled young people to easily and quickly identify free music and other media. Mass Weasel demonstrated this point, stating, "When I was, oh, seven, my cousins found this amazing music software. Oh, how wonderful it was. You could get music just like that, no strings attached! This wonderful music software? Napster." The concurrent emergence and ubiquity of inexpensive CD-burning technologies also increased some individuals' desire to engage in piracy (see Hinduja 2001). The ability to easily create CDs that could be played anywhere from pirated materials made piracy a more attractive practice. This was exemplified by Fighting Tears who stated that he started pirating "when Napster came out" and "downloaded individual songs . . . then burned mix

CDs and jammed out." Scott also wrote that he began to use Napster after "my friend showed me I would never have to pay for a CD."

Most all of the interviewees described using Bittorrent or another type of torrent program as their primary means of piracy currently. Torrents are a method of file sharing that provide a greater level of safety for the user (torrents minimize the likelihood of detection) and provide a faster level of download speed. The process of torrent file sharing was succinctly described by Mass Weasel:

> Bittorrent works by, when you run a torrent, sniffing out other torrenters who are currently "seeding" files on their computer. It takes random bits of it [the pirated file] from random seeders [users], making it difficult to trace since not even the program knows exactly where the data is coming from. Of course, if there's only a couple of seeders, the safety lowers, and if there's none, the damn thing is useless.

The perceived safety, elegant programming, and fast download speeds associated with torrents have made them extremely popular among pirates.

It is clear from the pirates that their skills and knowledge about pirating evolved through continued practice and, perhaps more importantly, through interactions with others. Their lack of technical computer skills suggests that they did not learn these techniques from legitimate study of computer technology as their skill with illegal downloading was not generalized to other computer applications. Instead, it was focused interactions about the topic of downloading that facilitated their persistence with the activity.

RISKS OF PIRACY AND RISK REDUCTION STRATEGIES

One of the technical skills that pirates learned through on-line interactions was how to recognize and avoid the risks associated with their piracy. Most of the pirates interviewed thought "there is hardly any risk of being caught in today's climate" (Section8) (see also Al-Rafee and Cronan 2006; Chiou et al. 2005; Higgins and Makin 2004). This notion was so prevalent that Celebmacil suggested he had "a better chance of getting hit by a car or lightning" than being prosecuted for piracy. In fact, pirates thought they were very safe while pirating regardless of the methods they employed to reduce their likelihood of detection. Rev. Ben Dover succinctly described this point, stating that "it's like jaywalking—everybody does it and no one cares."

Despite the relative lack of concern from legal threats, pirates recognized that the formal sanctions for piracy have increased to include suspicion of services, fines, and jail sentences. Pirates argued that the individuals who receive these sanctions are unfairly singled out by law enforcement or had it coming due to their poor downloading choices. M3thic demonstrated the former stating:

I don't think people get caught, I think the government/ companies pick people to make an example out of them. . . . I think they take someone who they know cannot pay for it or is a regular person and try to make an example of them to scare people.

When people are formally caught and prosecuted the pirates frequently blamed the event on the inexperience of the downloader. For example, when discussing the guilty party of one of the few successful prosecutions for illegal downloading a forum member from the United States commented that the defendant was "just fucking stupid and uneducated, not knowing much about the subject of file-sharing." In addition, several interviewees suggested that the risk of detection increased significantly due to excessive downloading. FightingTears wrote that "people get caught up in the thrill of downloading and then download waaaay too much." When describing the types of people who were caught for downloading, Celebmacil said, "It's people with tens of thousands of files on their computers . . . they run the software non-stop over a broadband connection, and eventually trip investigative software flags. Or, in short, they're dumb."

Several pirates suggested that they took formal threats seriously and used certain technological practices to reduce their risk of detection. For example, Polite Boy used encryption software to hide his home IP address while pirating. Celebmacil used a different tactic to introduce doubt that he pirated materials from his home Internet connection. He described using:

an unsecured wireless modem network, so that theoretically, anyone within range could use it to download files. While "reasonable doubt" is not a standard for civil cases, it would certainly introduce the potential that someone other than me was using the IP.

Similarly, Mass Weasel stated that, "I don't pirate at home. . . . I have what could be called a mobile piracy station, in the form of a flash drive and a mental list of contacts, websites, and whatever."

The most significant risks that pirates claimed to face were from informal threats, particularly viruses and malicious software that could infect and damage

their system (Bachman 2007; Wolfe et al. 2008). Malicious software writers often post their programs in locations where individuals are likely to inadvertently access and execute their malware (Furnell 2002; Szor 2005; Taylor et al. 2006). Piracy sites are a key place to house malware, as pirates download and run all manner of files. This fact has led many pirates to abandon once popular downloading programs for ones they see as safer. Bee claimed that his computer became infected because of the software he used, stating, "I was using crappy programs—Kazaa. Kazaa gave you adware and spyware." Similarly, Abe Lincoln and Orchid suggested that "Limewire is a virus whore."

In light of this risk, pirates took multiple steps to reduce the likelihood of infection. In describing their strategies for avoiding harmful or bad files the pirates articulated the importance of experience. The pirates across the data sets articulated that they developed the ability to spot files that are infected with malicious software before downloading them. This ability to recognize and distinguish the quality of files helped differentiate the experience level of pirates. Konink elaborated on this point, stating:

I've seen enough to know who good resources are and when someone is posting something fake, plus you can actually see what types of files are in the torrent before you download. There are minimal things newbs [inexperienced pirates] wouldn't recognize, but when you see it enough you just kind of know. For example, torrent users can post comments about the content or quality of the file, and note if it is infected.

The ability to determine the quality of a file was developed through repeated downloads and the use of cues provided by other pirates. As reflected in the above quote, one approach to reducing the risk of downloading junk torrents or files was to read the comments on the site or to look at the number of seeders, which is a practice they claimed inexperienced pirates neglect to do. Those who have inadvertently downloaded malicious files will often leave warnings. Others who may be unaware that they downloaded bad files will leave comments asking for passwords or special video players to view the files. These types of comments become red flags to those in the know. In a forum thread devoted to detecting bad torrents SubDra stated, "I hate getting calls from people, 'Why won't my torrent work?' 'Errr, did you read the comments before you downloaded it?' 'No. Okay. Looks like it's a fake.' Grrr." This idea was demonstrated by Polite Boy, "If you read what people say you can usually tell if it's legit or not." Similarly, the number of seeders is a good indication of the content of a file. In fact, this information may be more important than the number of comments. Posting in the same forum from above, Hüsker explained the importance of comments:

> A good way is just to look at the seeders, I always do that. If a torrent has 10,000+ seeds and the next in the list only has 700+ seeds then it is 100% a fraud, even if the 10,000+ have zero comments and the 700+ have 100+ comments.

Thus, the poster is suggesting that too many individuals attempting to share a file relative to the other files available is an indication of something unusual, and by extension, risky.

The participants also noted that one could examine the size of a file and compare it against other resources to potentially determine if it is infected. Materials that were either too small or too large could be a potential risk. Abe Lincoln avoided "weird filenames and weird file sizes" claiming that "if it looks weird, it probably is." Others suggested that looking for obscure or unusual materials helped to reduce their risk of detection. Celebmacil suggested that his taste in music:

> mitigates my odds of being found, and what charges could be prosecuted.... I'm pretty certain there are certain artists, file types, and price points that are far more common to be transferred and that any investigative firms use their own software to track patterns and users within those file searches. Personally, my files (in my opinion) are pretty fringe, so I'd say I run a pretty fixed value.

All of these methods provide a modicum of protection from formal and informal risks, although it is important to note that the practices of pirates are dynamic and may change with the introduction of new technologies. As a consequence, pirates alter their methods to minimize their likelihood of detection. This was exemplified by Mass Weasel who wrote, "As law enforcement technology increases, so does the technology to fool it." The fact that the pirates across the data sets shared their security techniques with others on-line demonstrates the value of forums and on-line interaction as an effective means to transmit subcultural knowledge. As the forum user StillRolling explained, "A sharing community is supposed to be a caring one, and not an 'I got what I want now screw you' one."

Benefits of Digital Piracy

In addition to learning risk avoidance strategies, pirates also learned the beliefs and excuses of their actions through on-line interactions. It is not uncommon, however, for those who engage in stigmatized behavior to make clear boundaries between themselves and unacceptable others (Copes et al. 2008). The pirates with whom we spoke were no exception, as they utilized a larger philosophical issue commonly found in the technology focused hacker subculture to make distinctions between themselves and others. In particular, pirates articulated the belief that information should be free to all and that once a product or piece of information has been placed on the Internet it should be made available for anyone to use (Furnell 2002; Holt 2007; Jordan and Taylor 1998; Levy 1984). In the words of Kibbe:

> My view point on items found on the Internet is that I believe that it is open source. If a product is produced and put on the Internet then it should be available for all to use. If not, then do we not create a segregated population? Those who cannot afford it cannot use it or hear it or see it? Is that fair?

Similar comments were made by forum members in a thread about why they download instead of buying media, such as Brownie who wrote:

> I am denied access to information and other tools that could be at my disposal, because we live in an economic system that is ruled by the greed of other people. Not that I'm an anarchist or communist or hippie or anything, I think it works quite well. That's why I pirate. It's a bit of a moral imperative actually, I think.

Thus, the idea of sharing files and making information freely accessible had important consequences for how some pirates defined themselves and others.

One of the main distinctions about respectability they made focused on profiting from pirating—a practice all of the participants denied doing. In fact, profiting from piracy was strongly and uniformly condemned. Pirates like Lemur saw "a moral difference between downloading for personal use and for profit." This idea was perhaps best reflected by Polite Boy when responding to a question about whether he sold pirated material, "No! Only lowlife shit do that." The adherence to a non-profit mindset allowed pirates to portray themselves as non-criminals and, thus, morally acceptable. Those who made money were not, however, acceptable participants in the piracy subculture.

The pirates in this study also operated within a hierarchy based on their downloading and file-sharing activities (Cooper and Harrison 2001). It was evident that file-*sharing* played a critical role in maintaining the piracy subculture. Without cooperation and assistance, downloading media would be extremely difficult. Thus, those who maintained an even ratio of files downloaded and shared, or seeded, were given status in the group. Those who simply downloaded materials without sharing files were condemned and referred to as leeches and, in some communities, formally banned. Bluebeard explained the perception and reaction to leeches, stating, "A public tracker won't punish them . . . but they're definitely looked down on. Whereas private trackers will ban people if they don't have a high enough ratio—forcing people to seed." All of those who spoke with us claimed that they tried to maintain an even ratio of seeds to downloads. Some even bragged about the high number of seeds they maintained even when not downloading.

In light of these perceptions of respectability, pirates articulated specific reasons for their downloading that was consistent with the larger beliefs of the piracy subculture. All of the pirates interviewed claimed that they simply wanted to listen to or watch the media they downloaded (see Cooper and Harrison 2001; Ingram and Hinduja 2008). Pirates have a variety of options when seeking entertainment media, including purchasing it from retailers. While the pirates acknowledged that this was an option, they claimed that downloading was better because they could obtain media for free, access media conveniently, and preview it before they purchased it.

While profiting from piracy was condemned, the pirates acknowledged that downloading materials allowed them to save significant amounts of money when obtaining desired content (see also Chiou et al. 2005; Ingram and Hinduja 2008). When asked why he downloaded material illegally, Bluebeard answered succinctly, "I couldn't afford to buy the albums." Mass Weasel explained that piracy was necessary because, "I can't afford to spend money on entertainment. So I have to take it. I pirate out of necessity. If I could afford to, I'd just buy everything I've pirated over the years."

Saving money was not the only benefit of downloading media. When asked why they download, pirates also claimed that they did so because of convenience (see also Ingram and Hinduja 2008). Many interviewees stated that they preferred to stay home and interact with friends on-line. Thus, pirating allowed them to access the desired media without having to leave their homes. Lemur stated, "It's more convenient than the store, in addition to being faster, because if I'm given a name of an artist I can get it immediately instead of hoping to remember it." Similarly, Konink said:

> Convenience was a big factor. . . . Instead of having to run to the store (and pay there) I could just download the film, album, etc. right here. It is very convenient to do it in the privacy of my home.

When discussing the convenience of downloading, pirates also argued that it was an important way to identify sources and materials that they could not find in local retail stores. When referring to this, Slimmy McGee said that "sometimes there are songs you want that weren't on any CDs—they were random songs. You can't really find CDs for that. They weren't mainstream." Polite Boy echoed this sentiment, stating, "I've found tons of music from piracy. A ton of my music is stuff I've never seen at Best Buy." Lemur explained his motives by arguing that "there's no way that my reasonably small town's store would have music like Captain Beefheart or Strawberry Alarm Clock." For some, the emphasis placed on finding, possessing, and sharing these hard-to-find materials was a means to gain respect in piracy subculture as they became a valuable source of material for others.

ACCOUNTING FOR DIGITAL PIRACY

Although the previously mentioned benefits of illegal downloading are important, pirates must be able to make sense of their actions and maintain a positive self-image when engaging in piracy. These excuses and justifications become an aspect of piracy culture that contributes to persistent offending. The interviewees acknowledged that they wanted the media they obtained, but would not engage in any form of crime to get it. All agreed that stealing physical copies of music or movies on compact discs or DVDs was beyond their capacity as they perceived it to be morally wrong. The fact that they were merely copying the media and that no one was harmed because of their actions allowed them to easily justify their actions. This idea is consistent with the contention that when offenders contemplate committing criminal acts they find ways to neutralize the guilt associated with their actions (Maruna and Copes 2005; Sykes and Matza 1957). To do this, offenders used linguistic devices that blunt the moral force of the law and neutralize the guilt of criminal participation. While there are a number of ways that offenders justify or excuse their crimes, digital pirates relied primarily on: denial of injury, denial of victim, condemnation of the condemners, and denial of responsibility (Hinduja 2007; Ingram and Hinduja 2008; Morris and Higgins 2009).

The most common neutralization technique pirates used to justify their activities was to deny that they caused any real or significant injury. Many pirates said they were merely borrowing the media and if it was good, they would eventually purchase it. In this sense piracy was not only benign but actually helped artists and record companies. Section8 said, "I will buy Dexter when season 2 comes out on DVD because I love that show and wish to support it. But without downloading it I would never have watched it." In an ongoing discussion about why they pirate, Dwight a forum member from the United Kingdom, replied, "I actually purchase the movies/games that I download and like. Similarly, Bluebeard said:

> Well, people say that piracy is costing companies billions. . . . I think that these multi-million dollar record companies and movie studios and fortune 500 companies aren't losing any extra business if I download their stuff. In fact if I download something and like it I'm more likely to buy it, whereas if I couldn't download and preview it I wouldn't get it all, so they're actually gaining business.

Other pirates claimed that their illegal downloading actually gave recognition and fame for artists, especially independent musicians and filmmakers. Celebmacil stated, "Many of the artists I am interested in are not commonly known, and encourage file sharing of their music to spread their listener base." According to FightingTears, "I like a lot of indie music and those are bands that are pretty much stoked that you are listening to their music. You paying for it usually isn't an issue." They point out that many independent artists encourage downloading and sometimes even thank pirates in the credits. As such, the creators suffered no loss of revenue from piracy. While the validity of these claims may be suspect, pirates eased their conscience by pointing to the minimal harm they caused and by emphasizing how they helped artists.

Another way that pirates denied they actually caused harm was by claiming that they would not have bought the media anyway. They pointed out that they downloaded the material only because of its availability. It was common for pirates to browse content without specific material in mind. When they came across interesting media they downloaded it. As a result of this type of search strategy, Section8 argued, "Data on the Internet may never have been bought in the first place. So there is no loss in revenue as data has no price-tag." Celebmacil echoed this sentiment, stating, "Much of the software that I [pirated] (full Adobe suite for example), while expensive, would not have been something I personally would have considered getting."

Sometimes digital pirates admitted that their actions may possibly have harmed those they stole from, but they neutralized moral indignation by denying victim status to recording artists, record and movie producers, and software developers. Pirates excused their crimes by saying that artists should expect piracy because media is too expensive and often is of low

quality. Pirates defined their own actions as a form of rightful retaliation or punishment for artists being self-indulgent and producing low quality material. According to Abe Lincoln, "Metallica got stupid and kicked off people sharing their music from Napster. I was one of them. I no longer support Metallica. They can fuck themselves, which is what they think of me so it is alright." Similar comments were found in the forum data, as noted by an Italian member who wrote:

> CDs are becoming increasingly expensive loosing quality and contents. You want over 20 Euros for a CD with 12 songs in it? Are you kidding me? Even if I would, often in a CD there is a good track, used as "trailer," while the remaining tracks are poor.

Pirates claimed that artists get paid far too much and that they have no right to complain since downloading is not what harms their income, but rather it is the artists' expensive habits. Konink summed it up by saying, "I mainly download movies and I see everyday how someone in Hollywood is complaining about how piracy could bring them down when in actuality the $300 [U.S.] dinner they just had was unnecessary or the limo rides (drive yourself?)." Pirates also argued that record companies charge too much for their products. Rebekah made a similar point, "[Downloading] was cheaper than buying CDs or buying entire albums for just a few songs. I didn't feel that buying them was a good investment since albums did not get full CD play." The nigh costs of albums coupled with the perception that most songs on albums were of low quality allowed pirates to sidestep responsibility by laying the blame on the artists. Thus, according to the pirates, if artists want to slow illegal downloading then they should produce better albums at a more affordable cost for the consumer.

When justifying their illegal behavior, pirates often pointed to negative, bullying, and perhaps corrupt behaviors of those actively trying to stop them. Pirates condemned their condemners through claims that the practices of the RIAA (Recording Industries Association of America) foster an attitude of resistance. The consensus among the pirates was that the RIAA "goes overboard in their prosecution of individuals" (Randally) and has "treated this generation of downloaders as thieves and evil" (Section8). This perceived unfair treatment by those in charge of preventing piracy created a sense of pride and accomplishment when downloading. As MY explained, "There is also some slight smug satisfaction that some corporate big-wig has his panties in a bunch because I was running a downloader. A forum member from England justified his actions:

I am a completely honest person with exception to ignoring copyright laws. I cannot even lie as my conscience doesn't support it. . . . In regards to copyright [laws] I simply feel I am reclaiming some of what has been extorted out of me since I was a kid as far as the entertainment industries are concerned and so feel justified to that end.

Such comments demonstrate a deep-seated distrust of corporations and the media industry as a whole. The acceptance of these larger beliefs enabled pirates to easily reject the claim that corporation are victims of illegal downloading.

The least common neutralization technique used by pirates was the denial of responsibility. When this technique was used, it was primarily used when pirates were young and unaware of the illegal nature of their activities. For example, a few downloaders heard about Limewire or other programs from their friends or family, but were not told that what they were doing was illegal. When explaining why they started downloading, Mass Weasel and Elisa both made a nearly identical statement, "I had no idea I was even pirating, I had no idea." These denials were only effective when the pirates were young and naive. Each of these pirates acknowledged that their interactions on Internet forums led to changes in their understanding of the illegal nature of their activities.

Conclusions

Edwin Sutherland (1947) argued that the key intervening factor between deviant associations and crime is the acquisition of techniques, attitudes, motives, and drives that favor the violation of law. Criminal subcultures form around deviant behaviors as a consequence of persistent interactions with like-minded others that facilitate the transmission of norms, values, and beliefs. Though researchers have regularly explored the value of social interactions in the real world to facilitate social learning of deviant behavior, fewer have considered how learning occurs through virtual interactions (see Holt 2007). This study sought to explore how the beliefs and practices of digital piracy are spread through virtual interactions to better understand the ways that technology facilitates criminal learning.

Our findings suggest that pirates share a belief promoted in hacker subculture that information should be shared (Cooper and Harrison 2001; Holt 2007; Jordan and Taylor 1998; Levy 1984). This belief structured pirate identities and relationships with others within this subculture. It allowed them to distance themselves from those they defined as unacceptable pirates, such as profiteers and leeches. Through interactions on-line, pirates articulated the norms and values of digital piracy and the means of gaining status within this group. These interactions fostered a consensus in how persistent pirates made sense of and justified their illegal downloading. Namely, they argued that their actions caused no real harm to the artists themselves, victims should not be given victim status, and that they were validated in their actions because of poor practices by recording companies.

Exploring pirates' beliefs and attitudes also demonstrated that formal sanctions from law enforcement played a very small role in their decision-making process. Those interviewed were aware that legal sanctions could result from piracy, although they thought they were unlikely to be detected because of their careful downloading practices.

The findings also reflect the idea that deviant behavior adapts to accommodate new technology (Quinn and Forsyth 2005). This is particularly important in light of the increasingly rapid lifecycle or technology and innovations in Web-based applications that can spawn new forms of offending that did not otherwise exist (Taylor et al. 2006). Digital piracy is an excellent example of crime resulting from technological change as it is one of several crimes that stem directly from technological innovations (see Holt 2007; Quinn and Forsyth 2005; Taylor et al. 2006). The pirates interviewed for this study indicated that they were not necessarily skilled computer users, although their methods of piracy changed as a direct consequence of innovations in technology.

This study showed a clear growth in sophistication among digital pirates with regard to the type of programs they used, frequency of downloading, and the strategies used to reduce formal and informal risks. Participation in on-line forums and interactions with others enabled pirates to improve their skills and gain status among one another. In addition, they learned the acceptable ways to neutralize responsibility for their crimes and justify piracy through sophisticated, yet morally acceptable, terms. Thus, the ability to interact on-line was instrumental in this learning process.

In addition, our findings point to a key issue in the study of on-line subcultures. The pirates interviewed articulated common ways of engaging in piracy and similar excuses and beliefs about their actions, although most did not identify themselves solely as pirates. Rather, the interviewees acknowledged that they engaged in piracy and even interacted regularly with others who could be seen as pirates, but maintained closer ties with conventional society. They drifted between groups as it suited their needs, which may explain the widespread prevalence of neutralizations (Sykes and Matza 1957).

Interactions through on-line forums coupled with adjustments to evolving technologies have implications for the ways that we understand the structure of digital communities. Subcultures based on face-to-face interactions require a relatively high level of commitment as it is much harder for participants to locate, interact and learn from members. There is an ease of interaction in digital communities where people can simply log on, read posts, take what they want from the group, and move on with minimal commitments. Thus, the spread of deviant behaviors through on-line communities can occur without full enculturation into a deviant subculture.

As more deviant groups develop on-line communities, it is possible that involvement in deviant behavior may spread to larger populations of non-deviants. For example, in their discussion of Internet newsgroups devoted to cable theft, Mann and Sutton (1998:221) stated that they "might play an increasing, if somewhat unwitting, role in the recruitment and education of property offenders." Although the use of on-line communications has made it easier for sociologists and criminologists to study deviant groups, the relationship between deviants and non-deviants in this environment may require the creation of new theoretical frameworks to understand the formation and spread of subcultural knowledge. Further research is needed with all manner of deviance to improve our understanding of the influence of technology on the nature of crime and deviance in the twenty-first century.

References

Akers, Ronald L. 1998. *Social Learning and Social Structure: A General Theory of Crime and Deviance.* Boston: Northeastern University Press.

Al-Rafee, Sulaiman and Timothy P. Cronan. 2006. "Digital Piracy: Factors that Influence Attitude Toward Behavior." *Journal of Business Ethics* 63:237–259.

Bachman, Michael. 2007. "Lesson Spurned? Reactions of Online Music Pirates to Legal Prosecutions by the RIAA." *International Journal of Cyber Criminology* 1:213–227.

Bainbridge, William S. 2000. "Religious Ethnography on the World Wide Web." Pp. 55–80. In *Religion and the Social Order: Religion on the Internet,* edited by J. K. Hadden and D. E. Cowan.

Chiou, Jyh-Shen, Chien-yi Huang, and Hsin-hui Lee. 2005. "The Antecedents of Music Piracy: Attitudes and Intentions." *Journal of Business Ethics* 57:161–174.

Cohen, Albert. 1955. *Delinquent Boys: The Culture of the Gang.* Glencoe, IL: The Free Press.

Cooper, Jon and Daniel M. Harrison. 2001. "The Social Organization of Audio Piracy on the Internet." *Media, Culture, and Society* 23:71–89.

Copes, Heith, Andy Hochstetler, and Patrick Williams. 2008. "We Weren't Like No Regular Dope Fiends: Negotiating Hustler and Crackhead Identities." *Social Problems* 55:254–270.

Denzin, Norman K. 1999. "Cybertalk and the Method of Instances." Pp. 107–25. In *Doing Internet Research: Critical Issues and Methods for Examining the Net,* edited by S. Jones. Thousand Oaks, CA: Sage.

DiMarco, Andrew D. and Heather DiMarco. 2003. "Investigating Cyber-society: A Consideration of the Ethical and Practical Issues Surrounding Online Research in Chat Rooms." Pp. 164–79. In *Dot.cons: Crime, Deviance, and Identity on the Internet,* edited by Y. Jewkes. Portland, OR: Willan Publishing.

Furnell, Steven. 2002. Cybercrime: *Vandalizing the Information Society.* Boston, MA: Addison-Wesley.

Glaser, David. 1956. "Criminality Theories and Behavioral Images." *American Journal of Sociology* 61:433–444.

Gross, Elisheva F. 2004. "Adolescent Internet Use: What We Expect, What Teens Report." *Journal of Applied Developmental Psychology* 25:633–649.

Higgins, George E. 2005. "Can Low Self-Control Help with the Understanding of the Software Piracy Problem?" *Deviant Behavior* 26:1–24.

Higgins, George E., Brian D. Fell, and Abby L. Wilson. 2006. "Digital Piracy: Assessing the Contributions of an Integrated Self-Control Theory and Social Learning Theory Using Structural Equation Modeling." *Criminal Justice Studies* 19:3–22.

Higgins, George E. and David A. Makin. 2004. "Self-Control, Deviant Peers, and Software Piracy." *Psychological Reports* 95:921–931.

Higgins, George E., Scott E. Wolfe, and Catherine D. Marcum. 2008. "Digital Piracy: An Examination of Three Measurements of Self-Control." *Deviant Behavior* 29:440–460.

Hinduja, Sameer. 2001. "Correlates of Internet Software Piracy." *Journal of Contemporary Criminal Justice* 17:369–382.

———. 2003. "Trends and Patterns among Software Pirates." *Ethics and Information Technology* 5:49–61.

———. 2007. "Neutralization Theory and Online Software Piracy: An Empirical Analysis." *Ethics and Information Technology* 9:187–204.

Holt, Thomas J. 2007. "Subcultural Evolution? Examining the Influence of On- and Off-Line Experiences on Deviant Subcultures." *Deviant Behavior* 28:171–198.

———. 2010. "Exploring Strategies for Qualitative Criminological and Criminal Justice Inquiry Using On-line Data." *Journal of Criminal Justice Education* 21, 466–487.

Ingram, Jason and Sameer Hinduja. 2008. "Neutralizing Music Piracy: An Empirical Examination." *Deviant Behavior* 29:334–366.

Jordan, Tim and Paul Taylor. 1998. "A Sociology of Hackers." *The Sociological Review* 46:757–780.

Levy, Steven. 1984. *Hackers: Heroes of the Computer Revolution.* New York: Dell.

Mann, David and Mike Sutton. 1998. "Netcrime: More Changes in the Organisation of Thieving." *British Journal of Criminology* 38:201–229.

Maruna, Shadd and Heith Copes. 2005. "What Have We Learned from Fifty Years of Neutralization Research?" *Crime and Justice: A Review of Research* 32:221–320.

McCarthy, Bill. 1996. "The Attitudes and Actions of Others: Tutelage and Sutherland's Theory of Differential Association." *British Journal of Criminology* 36:135–147.

Morris, Robert G. and George E. Higgins. 2009. "Neutralizing Potential and Self-Reported Digital Piracy: A Multitheoretical Exploration among College Undergraduates." *Criminal Justice Review* 34:173–195.

Morselli, Carlo, Pierre Tremblay, and Bill McCarthy. 2006. "Mentors and Criminal Achievement." *Criminology* 44:17–43.

Quinn, James F. and Craig J. Forsyth. 2005. "Describing Sexual Behavior in the Era of the Internet: A Typology for Empirical Research." *Deviant Behavior* 26:191–207.

Simms, Ronald R., Hsing K Cheng, and Hildy Teegen. 1996. "Toward a Profile of Student Software Pirates." *Journal of Business Ethics* 15:839–849.

Sutherland, Edwin. 1937. *The Professional Thief.* Chicago: University of Chicago Press.

———. 1947. *Principles of Criminology.* Philadelphia: Lippincott.

Sykes, Gresham and David Matza. 1957. "Techniques of Neutralization: A Theory of Delinquency." *American Sociological Review* 22:664–670.

Szor, Peter. 2005. *The Art of Computer Virus Research and Defense.* Upper Saddle River, NJ: Addison Wesley.

Taylor, Robert W., Tory J. Caeti, D. Kall Loper, Eric J. Fritsch, and John Liederbach. 2006. *Digital Crime and Digital Terrorism.* Upper Saddle River, NJ: Pearson Prentice Hall.

Warr, Mark. 2002. *Companions in Crime: The Social Aspects of Criminal Conduct.* New York: Cambridge University Press.

Williams, Patrick and Heith Copes. 2005. "How Edge Are You? Constructing Authentic Identities and Subcultural Boundaries in a Straightedge Internet Forum." *Symbolic Interaction* 28:67–89.

Wolfe, Scott, George Higgins, and Catherine Marcum. 2008. "Deterrence and Digital Piracy: A Preliminary Examination of the Role of Viruses." *Social Science Computer Review* 26:1–17.

PART VI

Drugs and Crime

Having experienced a recent "law and order" campaign in this country with the 1980's and 1990's "war on drugs," federal and state convictions for drug offenses have increased more than 100% as compared with drug-related convictions prior to the 1980s. Many states have enacted mandated sentences for the possession of narcotics, which has resulted in our nation's prisons, both federal and state systems, experiencing drastic increases in prisoner population growth in recent years. This has led to prison overcrowding and placed financial burdens on state governments for the costs of maintaining and constructing new prison facilities. Much of this correctional population growth is a direct result of punitive policies formulated by state and federal legislation to get tough on narcotic violators.

The disproportionate drug arrest rate for cocaine use between blacks and whites is a consequence of laws against possession and use of crack cocaine, a narcotic used mainly by African Americans. Penalties against crack were more stringent than those judicial sentences handed out to white offenders for powder cocaine violations. These legal disparities in the laws for drug offenses, as the example of cocaine illustrates, are indicative of just how disparate the laws are for the differing sanctions between black and white drug users. The selected studies in this part of the book offer a penetrating look into the world of narcotic addict lifestyles as well as the risks and hazards they face from life on the street and detection from law enforcement agencies.

In the first article, Robert Jenkot collected data from 31 imprisoned women in two different state prison systems who were methamphetamine users, dealers and manufacturers, *and* were serving sentences for narcotics-related crimes at the time he interviewed them. The study explored the hierarchies of the methamphetamine producing groups. The hierarchies have multiple layers with users at the lowest level and cooks at the top. Because the study subjects were women involved at various levels of that hierarchy, Jenkot analyzed how gender relations are effected by producing groups in the hierarchical arrangement of methamphetamine-producers.

Hustler and crackhead identities within the street culture in open-air drug markets are examined by Heith Copes, Andy Hochstetler and J. Patrick Williams. They investigate how the street economy of crack cocaine participants attempt to create a "hustler" identity in order to prevent being labeled a crackhead which connotes a low status street identity, characterized by addiction and street hustling failure. By studying how their identity perception as hustlers allowed them to shape their hustler identity in positive terms, and their desire to distance themselves from the negative identity of the low status crack user was highlighted. In short, the image of street hustler permitted them to self-identify as respectable people in the social order of drug-street culture.

Aline Gubrium utilizes an anthropological method in deconstructing the negative stereotype of the black-woman crack-user as the monstrous person others perceive them to be. Gubrium uses personal stories of one black-female crack-cocaine user to document the various ways culture is portrayed through the use of one woman's stories. The author demonstrates through discourse how this recovering crack-addicted woman constructs herself as a recovering addict and simultaneously a spiritually strong woman as well. Through her narrative, she is able to contrast her recovery attempts with stereotypes as a monstrous female crack-addict.

16

"Cooks Are Like Gods"

Hierarchies in Methamphetamine-Producing Groups

Robert Jenkot

This particular study is of female involvement with the use, sales, and production of methamphetamine. The research reveals the relationships between the women involved and the drugs within this drug culture, and is particularly concerned with the types of hierarchies that exist within these methamphetamine-producing groups.

In 1965 members of the Hell's Angels Motorcycle Club found that they could produce the synthetic drug methamphetamine; their efforts provide the first documented clandestine methamphetamine production (Lavigne 1996a,b). The "discovery" of clandestine methamphetamine production roughly coincided with legislation to control its illicit use (Young et al. 1977). Since the 1970s, we have seen an increase in the domestic clandestine production of methamphetamine and a proportionate rise in known methamphetamine use through the 1990s (DEA 2000). Little is known about the social relations within the groups that produce methamphetamine. Even less is known about women's social position within these groups.

The present study, part of a larger study of women involved with methamphetamine use, sales, and production, seeks to inform our understanding of the social relations within these groups. This study in particular uncovers the types of hierarchies present within methamphetamine-producing groups. Understanding the types of hierarchies that exist within these groups

can shed light on how members of a methamphetamine-producing group function over time as new members arrive, members leave, or new groups are formed. Further, because the sample is exclusively female, some findings will also illuminate how gendered relations are affected by the hierarchies present in methamphetamine-producing groups.

LITERATURE REVIEW

Studies of domestic methamphetamine use, sales, and production have uncovered four unique characteristics when international smuggling is omitted. First, methamphetamine production is dominated by white Anglo-Americans (Pennell et al. 1999; Riley 2000). Second, white women's use of methamphetamine is often on par with men's use patterns (Riley 2000). Third, much of the methamphetamine supply is due to domestic production (DEA 2000). Fourth, small, tight-knit groups of economically marginalized people

Source: "Cooks Are Like Gods": Hierarchies in Methamphetamine-Producing Groups. Jenkot, Robert, *Deviant Behavior, 29* (8) 667–689. Reproduced by permission of Taylor & Francis Group, LLC., http://www.taylorandfrancisgroup.com.

perform much of the domestic production of meth-amphetamine (Lavigne 1996a,b).

Beyond the generalizations noted, determining who is producing methamphetamine is not as clear as who uses the drug. The ADAM (Arrestee Drug Abuse Monitoring) project, as well as associated federally funded projects, have little if any mention of who is involved with methamphetamine production (Meth et al. 2001; Pennell et al. 1999; Riley 1999a,b, 2000). Research on women involved with methamphetamine production is limited to non-academic reports (Kurtis 1997). Although the gendered relationships that exist within these groups has not been explored, it is clear that women are taking part in the production process. The production of illicit drugs goes beyond the expected behavior of women who take part in deviant activities. In effect, women have limitations on their behavior in both licit and illicit groups (Denton and O'Malley 1999). However, there is a distinct lack of research detailing women's involvement with the pro-duction of drugs. It is here that I believe that this research can begin to fill that gap in the literature.

Comparing methamphetamine production to the manufacture of other drugs is troublesome. Although cocaine is a drug with similar psychopharmacological effects, it is usually produced in clandestine laborato-ries in South America. Crack cocaine is easily produced locally and by a single individual (Bourgois 1996). The result is that hierarchies have not been explored within crack cocaine manufacturing; the literature on crack cocaine focuses on the sale of the drug and the subse-quent hierarchies that exist within the distribution networks (see Schatzberg and Kelly 1997).

Another drug that is readily "manufactured" domestically is marijuana. Much research exists on the topic but is often relegated to social relations outside of the producing group or apart from the producer. For example, Hafley and Tewksbury (1995, 1996) consider the social relationships between the marijuana grow-ers and the communities in which they exist. Weisheit (1990, 1991) approaches the idea of hierarchies in marijuana cultivation, but his research subjects reflect more on their personal accomplishments and rewards from the behavior. In short, he finds that growers self-rank themselves based on the quality and/or potency of the marijuana they cultivate (Weisheit 1991). Also, Weisheit's research shows that much marijuana culti-vation is performed by individuals and not groups (1990, 1991).

The differences between methamphetamine pro-duction compared to crack cocaine and marijuana include: only the production of methamphetamine can result in fire and explosions, the chemicals necessary for methamphetamine production are controlled, and the production of methamphetamine takes greater specialized knowledge than either of the other drug's production. The production of methamphetamine is a multi-stage process where specialized knowledge, risky tasks, and time-consuming processes are necessary. In fact, the production of methamphetamine can easily necessitate a division of labor. Unlike the domestic pro-duction of crack cocaine and marijuana, methamphet-amine production could—and does—benefit from group involvement.

Adding gender into the phenomena of metham-phetamine production supports much recent research that illustrates women's involvement in criminal behavior. Until the 1980s, women were often depicted as secondary to males with regard to their criminality. Female offenders have historically been considered status offenders and non-violent (e.g., runaways) or took part in very gender-specific crimes (e.g., prostitu-tion) (Schur 1984). Recently we have seen women tak-ing greater part in crimes of all sorts. There are rising numbers of women being arrested and convicted for drug and drug-related offenses as well as violent offenses. Women's prison facilities are getting more crowded. Also we have seen the emergence of "girl gangs" that are involved in violence and drugs. But what are the effects within single- and/or mixed-sex groups taking part in criminal behavior?

Warr (2002) provides a concise means of under-standing the interaction between social learning and peer pressure. Using three key issues, solidarity within the peer group can be established and maintained. These three issues are loyalty, status, and fear of ridi-cule (Warr 2002). Although maintaining loyalty to fel-low group members is clear, Warr provides mechanisms for the establishment of statuses. The more experi-enced, loyal, and skilled the group member is at either leadership or deviant techniques, the higher the status of that group member. Aiding the division of group members within a hierarchy is the use of ridicule to maintain group cohesion and norms. Using Warr's concepts we can see that within criminal groups hier-archies can be established and maintained.

Through interviews with women who have been charged with drug-related offenses, a recurring theme of status within their peer group was evident. This study seeks to uncover what statuses are present in methamphetamine-producing groups. Further, how do group members maintain these statuses? By iden-tifying what statuses exist within the groups, we can better understand the mechanisms that provide for new members to enter the group and mobility within the group.

Methods

This project was approved by the Human Subjects Committee at Southern Illinois University. The data for this study was obtained through in-depth surveys with 31 women incarcerated in county jails in Missouri and Arkansas. Using current lists provided by each facility, every female inmate charged with drug-related offenses (i.e., possession, intent to deliver, maintaining a drug premises) was contacted personally and requested to take part in the study. Two women refused to take part in the study. Each participant selected a pseudonym to allow for confidentiality. Each interview lasted at least one hour, to a maximum of three hours. Most of the interviews were recorded on audio-tape; several participants did not want to be recorded. During every interview copious notes were maintained as well.

Realizing the presence as a large white male can be intimidating to incarcerated women, the researcher relied on the idea of assuming the role of an "acceptable incompetent" (Lofland and Lofland 1984; Lofland et al. 2006). In this way the researcher was able to minimize the potentially intimidating persona, and rely on the participants to "teach" what they knew and relate their experiences. Using this method also showed deference to their knowledge and experience.

The location of the interviews were multi-purpose rooms located either in the cell-pods themselves, attached to the cell-pods, or in the visitor section of the facilities. The rooms consisted of molded plastic furniture within cinder block walls painted gray. Each room had a window in the door for security reasons, although no correctional staff ever looked in.

Demographics of the Sample

The average age of the sample was 36 years old, with a range of 18 to 48 years old. One woman was 18 years old. Seven women were between 21 and 29 years old, 12 women were between 30 and 39 years old, and 11 women were between 40 and 49 years old. The sample consisted of 28 white women, 1 African-American woman, and 2 Hispanic women. The majority of the sample, 19 women, were single at the time of their interview; 4 women were married, 4 women were separated, and 4 women were divorced. Of the 31 women involved in this study, 18 stated that they had "cooked" methamphetamine; the same 18 reported that they had sold or traded methamphetamine for money or other items of value. All 31 women reported that they had used methamphetamine at least one time.

Every woman interviewed was employed prior to incarceration; however, their employment status varied considerably. Fifteen women had regular legitimate occupations (e.g., restaurant managers, retail clerks, and fast food cooks), 11 women were employed in seasonal or family-operated businesses (e.g., drywall installers, roofing companies, and house painters), and the remaining 5 women drifted between low-level minimum wage jobs and/or maintained illegitimate occupations (e.g., methamphetamine production, prostitution).

With regard to educational attainment, 26 women had a high school diploma or a GED and the remaining 5 women possessed an Associate's degree, Bachelor's degree, or some form of post-secondary education (e.g., Med-Tech training, Paramedic training).

The combination of educational attainment and occupation can be considered hallmarks of class standing. The women in this sample can be considered largely lower- to working-class individuals. Many, if not most, had illegitimate income in addition to income derived from their occupations (e.g., illicit drug sales and/or prostitution). The result is that many reported indicators of wealth (e.g., multiple new automobiles, high grade stereo equipment, and cash on hand), yet none of the participants reported assets that are normally associated with the wealthy (e.g., real estate, stocks).

The demographic data provided can be used to illustrate that a typical participant in this study would be a single white woman in her mid-thirties employed in either a service sector job or manual labor position. She would also hold a high school diploma and live comfortably, but financially would have little to no net worth. She would also be a regular methamphetamine user who occasionally sells the drug, and is capable of producing the drug.

Findings

The hierarchy within methamphetamine-producing groups focuses on maintaining a supply of the drug. From the participant's comments, every action is connected with the production process or used to rank the people present. Of the 18 participants who had experience as a cook, they all related that a similar hierarchy was present in their group. The responses from these women varied in detail. Annie relates the hierarchy present in her group in great detail from highest status to lowest: Cook, Gas Man/Juicer, Shopper, Dope Ho, and lastly the "simple user." Because Annie's experiences with a methamphetamine-producing group were related in the greatest detail, her comments comprise the bulk of the narrative regarding statuses within these groups.

The Methamphetamine Cook

Annie (a 32-year-old white woman) is 5'2" tall, blonde, currently separated from her second husband, and she has 3 children. She appears to be in good health and claims that the jail food has "bulked" her up. Annie has a long sentence yet appears in good humor. Her good humor was evidenced by the pseudonym she chose. She said that Annie was short for anhydrous ammonia, a key ingredient to the production of methamphetamine. She has earned a college degree and worked as a Registered Nurse and has had paramedic training. Her second husband began sexually molesting her oldest child from her first marriage; she subsequently separated from him. She stated that the stress of the abuse of her child combined with being alone caused her to gain weight. Her weight ballooned to 285 pounds. Annie stated that her existing stress was compounded by her own self-image as being "fat." It is at this point that she contacted an old friend from high school. The old friend and Annie used to use drugs together during high school. It was this old friend who first offered Annie methamphetamine as a means to control her weight and feel better. She initially began to use methamphetamine to escape from her feelings of powerlessness regarding her second husband's sexual abuse of her oldest daughter. As she said, "I had to just [long pause] get my mind off that shit; meth'll do that for ya for sure." A bounty hunter captured Annie; she had multiple outstanding warrants for drugs. Upon her arrival at the jail, she was in possession of both methamphetamine and marijuana.

All 18 women stated that the cook holds the highest position of privilege and prestige within the group. Annie explains:

If you are a cook you are all set. I mean, like, you could have anything you wanted. You want other drugs? You got 'em. You want a stereo? You got it. It might be hot, but you got it. Everyone in every group I saw was like tuned-in to the cook. [What do you mean, "tuned-in"?] Well, like the cook is the top dog. Without the cook you'd have to go buy meth on your own—or schmooze [persuade] it outa somebody else.

Reinforcing her experience with methamphetamine-producing groups, Annie clarifies the position of cooks:

Anyway, at the top of the group was the cook. There might be like two or three cooks in a group—like mine, we had, wait, let's see, 5 people who could cook decent dope. Cooks are like gods. I mean everyone does whatever they can to keep the cook happy. Food, stereos, supplies, sex, whatever they want they got.

Annie's recollection of methamphetamine cooks as "top dog" constructs the position of methamphetamine cook as a goal for non-cooks. Attaining this position includes a constant supply of methamphetamine, deference from others, and the ability to have anything you want. This power can be considered economic in nature, with methamphetamine being the currency.

Group members had to learn that the cook was the most valued member of the group. Although learning this may appear to be simple, learning who holds the greatest power within the group aids in the neophyte understanding the entire structure of the group. As Annie's comments continue, we see how members of the group relegate value and status to its members relative to their behavior within the group.

The Gas Man/Juicer

Annie also provides another position in the hierarchy of methamphetamine-producing groups:

Above the Shoppers were the Gas Men or Juicers. [What is a Juicer or Gas Man?] These are the guys—usually guys—that would go get the anhydrous ammonia. It was a real ordeal trying to get anhydrous, if ya fucked up you'd blow up or get burned by the anhydrous. A couple of weeks back I was driving on 55 [Interstate 55] and I saw this car burning on the side of the road and you could smell the, well, it smells special, that smell of anhydrous. They fucked up.

Second only to the cook, whose behavior is very risky and highly valued by the group, being a Gas Man is much more risky. A Shopper (discussed later) can succeed in her or his role by legitimately buying the necessary items while a Gas Man cannot. Gas Men run the risk of arrest but also run the risk of injury and death.

The increased risk Gas Men face is due to the need for anhydrous ammonia. Anhydrous ammonia (a key precursor chemical in the production of some forms of methamphetamine) is a "dry" form of household ammonia that is in a gaseous state and when it comes into contact with air, it chemically tries to bond with the water molecules present in the air (Falkenthal 1997; Hargreaves 2000). If it comes into contact with human skin, it leaches out the water in the skin, resulting in a chemical burn (Falkenthal 1997; Hargreaves 2000). If inhaled, the anhydrous ammonia will leach out the water in the mouth, sinuses, throat, and lungs, resulting in internal chemical burns (Falkenthal 1997; Hargreaves 2000). Additionally, anhydrous ammonia is explosive (Falkenthal 1997; Hargreaves 2000). With this in mind, Gas Men are at substantially higher risk than any other group member who does not handle the substance. The higher risk accords them more status and privilege within the group.

Whereas 17 women noted the status of Gas Man or Juicer from their experiences, 1 woman was involved with a group that did not use anhydrous ammonia. Elizabeth detailed her assistance in the production process: "They needed red phosphorus to cook with, so I would get it for 'em." Elizabeth (a 45-year-old white woman) is 5'7" tall, blonde, divorced, and she has 2 children. She stated that she was bi-polar and had only received one of her two daily injections to control her condition. As a result she was pacing in the small interview/visitor's room. Although she was very pleasant and talkative, she was apparently agitated, or on edge. She had a high school diploma and worked (until recently) at her husband's restaurant. Elizabeth claimed that her husband was the son of the local mafia boss. As her marriage began to dissolve, largely due to her husband's use of crack cocaine, she stated that her husband had hired a "hit-man" to kill her and that her husband had tried to kill her with a kitchen knife as well. She began using methamphetamine when friends offered it to her husband, as she said, "When in Rome." She was arrested after a traffic stop resulted in the police finding methamphetamine in her purse. She is unable to pay her bond because none of her friends will accept a collect call from jail, and she is too afraid of her husband to call him. As a result, she is just waiting for her case to come to court.

Regardless of the method of producing methamphetamine used, the person who supplied the integral ingredient held a higher status. Again, status in the group is connected with the risk taken by the group member. With regard to the hierarchy Annie detailed, Elizabeth would hold a status about equal with a Shopper and below a Gas Man. Elizabeth explains:

Interviewer: Did you buy it [red phosphorus], or what?

Elizabeth: Well, I used to think that you bought like a can of it but all you gotta do is scrape off the striker part of book of matches. [You mean the match heads? The top end that you light with?] Oh no! On the actual book, the little strip that you use to light the match. That is where the red phosphorus is. All you gotta do is scrape it away. Takes forever, but you gotta do it just so. I mean if you dig too deep you get paper, but you want all the red phosphorus. So ya

gotta do it just so and I was good at it. So I'd lend a hand doing it. I'd sit there for hours scraping away with a knife. We'd have piles of matchbooks but no way to light them! [laughs] [So, you'd watch them cook and just scrape away huh?] Yeah, separating those pills takes a while. So we'd bullshit as I would scrape and then by the time they were ready for the red phosphorus I'd be about done. Course if I wasn't done they'd have to wait for me. Shit I remember once I showed up and there was this asshole scraping matchbooks, I was kinda pissed cuz he was like taking my job ya know. Then Joe [a pseudonym] told him to stop and for me to take over.

Elizabeth's status was reaffirmed when the "temp scraper" was pushed aside by the cook so that she could resume her "job." In order for Elizabeth to perform her task within the production process, she had to learn the techniques specific to the task. How did she come to know that the red phosphorus was contained in the striker of the matchbook and not the match head? She learned this from an existing "scraper."

The Shopper

There are other levels of power and status within these groups, as Annie explains:

Now above the users and Dope Ho's were the people that would actually help out. First ya got the Shoppers. [What did the Shoppers do?] They would go get anything. I mean anything. They'd get the supplies to cook with: pills, buckets, lithium, tubing, whatever. Shit, I remember this one cook's car broke down and she asked for a Thunderbird. So this Shopper I know goes out and steals one—bingo! The cook is happy again. The best Shoppers were the ones who would really put their ass on the line. The ones that used like real money to buy pills were still good and all, but the ones that would hold up a store and take all their pills—now that was great. You still had your cash, and the pills. So I guess there is levels within the levels of power there.

The establishment of a specialized role in the methamphetamine-producing group to obtain the goods requested by the cook reaffirms the formal social structure within the group. In their quest to obtain the requested goods any means were acceptable, even theft. In fact, Annie states that the more risk the Shopper takes, the greater she or he is valued. What is important to note is that Shoppers are integral to the production process within the group.

Brandy (a 42-year-old white woman) is 5'5" tall with dark brown hair; her skin appears to be blotchy, red, and irritated. She is single and has a 19-year-old son. She considers herself to be a functioning addict. She will use a class of drugs (e.g., stimulants or depressants) for a time, then switch to another class of drugs. Much of her drug use parallels what she can obtain via theft and fraud. She has an off-putting personality and is not very talkative. When she responds to a question it is usually a one-word response. Further probing gains little additional information. She is currently in jail for cooking methamphetamine in her house.

Brandy could produce methamphetamine on her own, but often chose to be an assistant. As she stated, "I would shop a lot, you know go get the pills. Truck stops are great for that, plus you get to go on a nice drive!" Additionally, she would, " …just lend a hand here or there."

Each of the 18 women spoke of their group having at least 1 Shopper; some groups had up to 4 Shoppers. As they described the behaviors of these group members, they echoed Annie's comments. If members of the group wanted anything, especially the cook, the shopper was the person slated to obtain it.

The Dope Ho

Although "simple users" may be at the bottom of the methamphetamine group hierarchy, another status, Dope Ho, is only slightly above them. Most of the participants knew Dope Ho's (15 of the 18 participants); the remaining 3 had heard of men and women trading sex for drugs but had never personally experienced the phenomena. Annie explains the in-group social position of Dope Ho's:

Along with users are Dope Ho's. Now Dope Ho's are not a problem really. They are around just to trade a blow or a lay for some meth. They are ALWAYS there. Like I said, they are not a problem like the users but they really don't do anything to help out. Dope Ho's are like baggage, they are there taking up space. Now some guy cooking meth would like to have 'em. [Why would guy cooks like them?] OH! Well, the Dope Ho's take care of the cook, with sex. They are not there for everyone to fuck, just the cook. So, like guys are right, they always wanna get laid so the Dope Ho's handle that. You know, there might be a few Dope Ho's at a time. It's funny, it's like the cook has a choice who he's gonna bang, "No, not her, not her, yeah I'll bang her today!" That sort of thing.

Positions similar to that of a Dope Ho are not unique among drug-using groups. We know about people trading sex for crack cocaine, even for a hit of that drug (Ratner 1993; Maher 1997). However, with regard to crack cocaine, many of these women are prostitutes who trade sex with "Johns for the drug that they hold (Maher 1997; Ratner 1993). As Annie reports, Dope Ho's are accepted members of the group unlike the "simple users." Dope Ho's function to keep the cook happy (sexually), which aids in the production process. The fascinating thing about the presence of Dope Ho's is how this (usually) heterosexual relationship interacts with other heterosexual relationships.

Interviewer: What about a wife or girlfriend? Wouldn't they get mad? Or were the wives and girlfriends of these guys the Dope Ho's?

Annie: Nah, they were nobody's girlfriend or wife, just Ho's. Nobody really cared about them either, they were just always there. They were cool and all, just kinda looked down at, I mean, shit, you know, they were tradin' a blowjob for a buzz—not a bag of Dope, just a buzz. Kinda sad now that I think of it.

Interviewer: Were there guys as Dope Ho's too?

Annie: Yeah, I saw a few and heard of more. But, you know how girls are, they can get laid anytime they want and they don't have to give meth away to get laid! Guys will jump on anything, anytime—"sex? I'll do it!"—so why have the burden of carrying someone else's habit just to get laid. Still, some chicks would have some around but it was not like normal to see Guy-Ho's.

Annie's comments regarding the relationship between Dope Ho's and men are important. As Annie said, "nobody really cared about them," indicating that Dope Ho's hold a certain status within the group. They occupy a low status position in which they are marginalized to such a degree that wives and girlfriends apparently do not consider them threats to their monogamous relationship with the male cooks.

To hear Annie talk about Dope Ho's, her inflection is important; these people are looked down on. However, the status of Dope Ho can be considered slightly higher than that of the "pain in the ass" user.

The User of Methamphetamine

Every women involved in this project agreed that the position that lacks any prestige is that of the simple user. Annie provides a very clear image of the user:

> At the bottom were the users. These were the people that just wanted to buy meth, if ya think of the most strung out, tweeked freaks, that is the user. They are not really in the group. I mean, we all know them, but they are more of a pain in the ass. They always show up at the worst times. They show up when the batch [of methamphetamine] ain't done yet. They show up when you wanna sleep. They show up, well just like a pain in the ass, there is no good time.

The presence of users in a group creates the issue of risk and trust as being at odds with each other. Members of the group know the users or else they would not be allowed to socialize with the group. However, these people also pose a risk if they are undercover police officers or user-informers. Users are a burden to the group.

Users Versus Simple Users

It is important to differentiate between the types of methamphetamine users: users and "simple users." All of the participants in this study had used methamphetamine at some point in their lives. Most of the methamphetamine cooks (16 of the 18 cooks) were also current methamphetamine users. However, those women who took part, in whatever way, in the production process held a status above the "simple user." The "simple user" only uses the drug. The methamphetamine user is part of the group; the "simple user" is a "pain in the ass," meaning not part of the group.

As Annie (and others) relate, there is a distinct hierarchy within methamphetamine-using groups. Status within these groups is related to the activity regarding the methamphetamine production process. The greater the involvement and/or risk with the production process, the higher the status. Other participants in this study provided information on the process of upward mobility in the group as well as some variations of the statuses in these groups.

In-Group Mobility and Status Variations

There is a process involved in the production of methamphetamine. This process includes multiple people performing specific tasks. The performance of these tasks relates to the performance of social roles in the group. Brandy stated that she was able to cook, purchase the pills used as the base for the drug, and help out where needed. Other tasks that need to be completed in order for the methamphetamine production to be successful include: obtaining key precursor chemicals (P2P, red phosphorus, or anhydrous ammonia), obtaining the other items and compounds used in the production process (containers, lithium, hydrochloric acid, and hot plates), and the actual production of methamphetamine. These associations form a peer group for Brandy where she would, " . . . shop a lot." Her performance at this task was positive for the group and she was not stopped from doing it. Because she was able to cook methamphetamine as well, she was able— and allowed—to perform other functions.

The key point to understand is that these groups grow and splinter into networks that maintain some degree of association with each other. In these groups, gender differences fade as the actor rises in status within the group. Once the status of cook has been achieved, the drive for quality drugs equalizes the gender disparity evident at lower levels of these methamphetamine production groups.

Annie knew how to cook and did so frequently. However, she would also take part in schemes to obtain anhydrous ammonia, illustrating her mobility within her group. She has earned the highest status, but was able to choose to work at a lower status. For example, Annie stated:

> Me and another girl would get all dolled up and go to farmers' houses. We'd knock on the door, wiggle, wink, giggle and shit. Then just ask if we could have some anhydrous. That always worked. [So would you be treated as a Juicer when you did that?] Fuck no! [laughs] Shit once you can cook you are golden, you know. I was just helpin' out. Now the guy we was with, he was the Juicer. [What about the woman you went with?] Well, actually she was a Dope Ho. But she was cool.

Status can be earned by working with other members of the group and learning by their example. However, a formal learning process also takes place within methamphetamine-using groups. Cammy (a 42-year-old white woman) is 5'3" tall with brown hair and lives in a suburban area. She is fairly thin, but not as thin as some of the women in this study. Cammy appeared to be depressed and sad about her current situation. She was willing to take part in the interview, yet would often reply with one-word answers and little more when prodded. She did not want to say if she had any children, but she was separated from her husband. Her arrest occurred at a methamphetamine lab raided by the police. She possessed marijuana. Cammy illustrates how she learned to cook within the structure of the methamphetamine-producing group when she states:

> I was livin' with this cook right. We was jus' like in the same house, not fuckin' or nothin.' OK, so I know how to cook but not real good. I asks this guy, don't wanna say his name, if he can teach my boyfriend to cook right. So he's like, "cool," right. OK, so he's showin' my man how to cook and I am learnin' too right. OK, so like now we both are cooks and we get our own thing goin' and we cook like crazy! It was cool.

Cammy, due to her status with her house-mate and as a cook, was able to bring her non-cooking boyfriend up in status. Once she and her boyfriend were both cooks, their position within their group was solidified; however, shortly afterward they left this group to form their own group. In their new group they were able to complete all of the functions necessary to produce methamphetamine. Cammy's experiences provide us with a way that methamphetamine groups spread. As the unique knowledge is disseminated so too do the groups that hold this knowledge spread. It should be clear that these groups will be connected in a network of multiple cells of methamphetamine production.

The goal for these groups is the production of methamphetamine, not its sale. The various members of the group operate within a hierarchy where a neophyte can be upwardly mobile within the group, roles are defined, and power and prestige are linked to the status one holds. Interestingly, because the goal is paramount, in these groups they are more willing to dispose of social constructs valid in the dominant culture in order to further their goal. As a result, women who move up in the hierarchy of the production process are not stigmatized for the roles they play. Instead, women appear to become, or perceive themselves to be, the equals of their male counterparts.

GENDER AND STATUS IN METHAMPHETAMINE-PRODUCING GROUPS

Producing methamphetamine is rather easy even though it involves a number of processes and chemicals that can be hard to obtain. Annie and Brandy illustrated that their ability to change the role they played within the group is tied to their ability to cook methamphetamine themselves. This reflects the status that a methamphetamine cook holds within her group. Brandy can decide to cook one day and go for a drive the next day to obtain other material for the production of methamphetamine. Annie would cook methamphetamine, or choose to assist in obtaining anhydrous ammonia. Holding the status of a cook can be equated with the freedom to play the role of their own choosing, not to be relegated to a subordinate role defined by others within her group.

In every case, the women reported that they were able to complete the entire production process themselves. Their choice to simply "assist" was personal: every woman interviewed stated that she never felt that she was pressured to stand aside. Bea (a 41-year-old Hispanic woman), a homemaker in a suburban community who has a GED, is 5'3" tall with long blonde hair and she is apparently healthy. Although some people appear to be younger than their actual age, Bea is the opposite; she appears to be much older than she actually is. Bea is married; her husband was also in the jail for unrelated charges. She has no children, but would have liked to have had some. Bea has been a methamphetamine user since the 1970s. She was very willing to discuss every aspect of her involvement with methamphetamine. At times her explanations sounded almost canned, as if she had been telling people about her experiences for years. Bea was arrested for possession of methamphetamine during the course of a traffic stop.

As Bea stated, "Shit, all we wanted was meth. You cook, I cook, who cares so long as it's good! I been cooking for what now [long pause] 20 years? Yeah, been about 20 years of cookin.' I am cool with the guys that cook, and they are cool with me."

Bea's statement identifies that the goal of these groups was methamphetamine, not money, nor material goods, nor quibbling over traditional gender expectations. However, as Bea stated, the higher the quality of the methamphetamine, the more desirable it is. This is an important point as it relates to gendered relationships within the hierarchy of methamphetamine-producing groups. This perceived equality intimates that methamphetamine cooks hold a status that transcends constructed gender statuses evident among female users. The master status for female methamphetamine cooks appears to change from "female" to "methamphetamine cook" due to the group's focus on the production of the drug.

The finding that female cooks can hold power over other group members is contrary to traditional gender expectations. Considering this finding we must recall that the goal of the group is acquiring more methamphetamine. The group members are not trying to replicate the dominant cultural view of women, nor are they overtly trying to maintain male dominance in the methamphetamine subculture; all they want is more methamphetamine. Realizing that the group's goal is task-oriented, it makes sense that the group members would not care who produces—so long as the drug is being produced and a supply of methamphetamine is maintained.

These findings support Warr's (2002) research on peer pressure. The presence of a hierarchy (statuses) aids in the maintenance of loyalty and solidarity among group members. Marginal, unneeded, or unwanted persons are derided for their behavior (the "pain in the ass user"). Importantly, Warr's work is centered on the theoretical premise of social learning and Sutherland's differential association; aspects of such learning can be seen in the methamphetamine-producing group.

Although gendered behavior appears to fade away at the upper levels of methamphetamine-producing groups, female cooks are still willing to use gendered expectations to achieve their ends. For example, Annie relates two other events that occurred with some regularity:

> Well, if you cook in the woods, like way out, we always had a guy and a girl cookin.' That way if ya hear someone walkin' up ya just start rollin' in the leaves kissin.' Shit we got by a bunch of Park Rangers that way. They smell the cook right, they find us makin' out and they freakin' apologize—can ya believe that! We get all huffy right, then we just leave . . . never got busted that way, never.

This recollection is one strategy to disguise their illegal activity. Often methamphetamine production takes place on public lands; the cook[s] will remain nearby, but not necessarily at the production site (Falkenthal 1997; Hargreaves 2000). During his investigation, the Park Ranger comes upon a couple kissing and apologizes for interrupting a behavior that has been constructed as "normal." Interestingly, Annie and her friend showed that they understood the social construction of gender. They used expected gender roles to hide the fact that they were actually producing methamphetamine. The reaction by the Park Ranger reinforced their idea that their use of constructed gender roles was accurate. However, there are other means employed to disguise illegal activities that take place in public places. Annie continues:

> Another thing we'd do, and it is kinda funny too, while the guys would be gettin' anhydrous I'd hang by the car with the hood up like somethin's wrong. If anybody stop, I just say that my boyfriend would be back soon with a wrecker. Plus that way I was a lookout too. Any cop roll up, I just ask for help and I'll be damned if the car don't start! [laughs] I drive off and then circle back in a bit and pick up the boys [laughs]. Funny huh?

In the second instance, Annie used the traditional gendered idea of a "damsel in distress." Relying on widely held constructions of gender Annie had been able to avoid arrest. Throughout these two recollections, Annie and her group knowingly used gendered behavior to dispel any thoughts that deviant activity was taking place.

CONCLUSION

The roles that the women in this study play within their methamphetamine-producing groups are varied. The findings show that some statuses are more highly valued by the group, whereas others are not. The value placed on certain statuses indicates the presence of a hierarchy.

It should also be noted that illicit drug sales was not incorporated in the hierarchy of a methamphetamine-producing group Annie (or any other participant) detailed. At no time did Annie or any other participant provide a rank or status for a dealer of methamphetamine or any other drug. However, it is telling that members of these groups did trade and sell methamphetamine yet do not fit the ideal type of drug dealers.

The statuses that these women hold in their methamphetamine-producing groups range from "simple user" to cook. Introduction into the group would begin at the user level. The low status of the neophyte must be negotiated to obtain higher status. The neophyte would not simply obtain high status (e.g., a Juicer) until she or he had shed the label of "pain in the ass" user. Group members in the upper echelon could easily take part in behavior that was "below" them without losing status. The rationale for this mobility is that the goal of the group was preeminent: the production of more methamphetamine.

The consensus among the participants is that the status associated with being a methamphetamine cook carries with it power and prestige within the group. It is expected that group members would seek to achieve this status. The data does not provide any intimation regarding persons holding a status that is disagreeable to them (for example, a Shopper who disliked holding that position). We can assume that the ready supply of methamphetamine would ameliorate any discontent as the group members could use the drug free of charge.

Central to understanding methamphetamine-producing groups is the realization that they are organized to produce the drug they use. By producing their own supply of methamphetamine, they eliminate the need for a dealer (middle-man), save money, decrease their risk of arrest, and are assured of the quality of the drug they will use. To facilitate that goal, these groups have developed a hierarchy to achieve their aim.

Understanding the statuses and relationships within methamphetamine-producing groups illustrates the difficulties encountered by women as they leave jail or prison. Successful reintegration can be hampered by the loss of power and status they once enjoyed in methamphetamine-producing networks. This loss is exacerbated by the unwelcome realization that they are viewed as just another drug user. Although that label is accurate in societal terms, the women are reduced to what they once despised—"pain in the ass users." Thus, imprisonment results in a crisis of self-identity as well as the loss of power and status in a former social network.

Providing drug treatment, diversionary programs, or other social services to these women should include an acknowledgment of the statuses that these women have held. Beyond a general idea of reintegration, these women will face their crisis of self-identity in any conforming group they would join. Having once been the "top dog," finding themselves as anything less is another hurdle for the recovering drug user to overcome.

References

Bourgois, Philippe. 1996. *In Search of Respect: Selling Crack in El Barrio* Cambridge, MA: Cambridge University Press.

DEA. 2000. *United States Drug Enforcement Administration Internet Site.* Available at (www.usdoj.gov/dea).

Denton, Barbara and Pat O'Malley. 1999. "Gender, Trust, and Business: Women Drug Dealers in the Illicit Economy." *The British Journal of Criminology* 39:513–530.

Falkenthal, Greg. 1997. "Clan Labs: A Modern Problem." *Fire Engineering* 150(9):41.

Hafley, Sandra R. and Richard Tewksbury. 1996. "Reefer Madness in Bluegrass Country: Community Structure and Roles in the Rural Kentucky Marijuana Industry." *Journal of Crime and Justice* 19(1):75–94.

———. 1995. "The Rural Kentucky Marijuana Industry: Organization and Community Involvement." *Deviant Behavior* 16(3):201–221.

Hargreaves, Guy. 2000. "Clandestine Drug Labs." *FBI Law Enforcement Bulletin* 69(4):1–7.

Kurtis, Bill. 1997. *Investigative Reports: Meth's Deadly High.* [Video]The Arts and Entertainment Television Networks.

Lavigne, Yves. 1996a. Hell's Angels: *"Three Can Keep a Secret If Two Are Dead."* Secaucus, NJ: Carol Publishing Group.

———. 1996b. *Hell's Angels: Into the Abyss.* New York: HarperCollins.

Lofland, John, Davis Snow, Leon Anderson, and Lyn H. Lofland. *Analyzing Social Settings: A Guide to Qualitative Observation and Analysis,* 4th ed. Belmont, CA: Wadsworth.

Lofland, John and Lyn Lofland. 1984. *Guide to Qualitative Observation and Analysis,* 2nd ed. Belmont, CA: Wadsworth.

Maher, Lisa. 1997. *Sexed Work: Gender, Race, and Resistance in a Brooklyn Drug Market.* New York: Oxford.

Meth, Marcia, Rebecca Chalmers, and Gail Bassin. 2001. *Pulse Check: Trends in Drug Abuse Mid-Year* 2001. Washington, DC: Office of National Drug Control Policy.

Pennell, Susan, Joe Ellett, Cynthia Rienick, and Jackie Grimes. 1999. *Meth Matters: Report on Methamphetamine Users in Five Western Cities.* Washington, DC: U.S. Government Printing Office.

Ratner, Mitchell S. 1993. "Sex, Drugs, and Public Policy: Studying and Understanding the Sex-for-Crack Phenomenon." Pp. 1–36. *In Crack Pipe for Pimp: An Ethnographic Investigation of Sex-for-Crack Exchanges,* edited by M. S. Ratner. New York: Lexington.

Riley, Jack. 2000. 1999 *Annual Report on Drug Use Among Adult and Juvenile Arrestees.* Washington, DC: U.S. Government Printing Office.

———. 1999a. 1998 *Annual Report on Drug Use Among Adult and Juvenile Arrestees.* Washington, DC: U.S. Government Printing Office.

———. 1999b. *Research Report:* 1998 *Annual Report on Methamphetamine Use Among Arrestees.* Washington, DC: National Institute of Justice.

Schatzberg, Rufus and Robert J. Kelley. 1997. *African-American Organized Crime: A Social History.* Piscataway, NJ: Rutgers University Press.

Schur, Edwin M. 1984. *Labeling Women Deviant: Gender, Stigma, and Social Control.* New York: McGraw Hill.

Warr, Mark. 2002. *Companions in Crime: The Social Aspects of Criminal Conduct.* New York: Cambridge University Press.

Weisheit, Ralph A. 1991. "The Intangible Rewards From Crime: The Case of Marijuana Cultivation." *Crime and Delinquency* 37(4):506–527.

———. 1990. "Domestic Marijuana Growers: Mainstreaming Deviance." *Deviant Behavior* 11(2):107–129.

Young, Lawrence A., Linda G. Young, Marjorie M. Klein, Donald M. Klein, and Dorianne Beyer. 1977. *Recreational Drugs.* New York: Berkley Books.

17

"We Weren't Like No Regular Dope Fiends"

Negotiating Hustler and Crackhead Identities

HEITH COPES, ANDY HOCHSTETLER, AND J. PATRICK WILLIAMS

By utilization of social identity, this research describes and analyzes two distinct street identities in open-air drug markets. Hustler and crackhead identities are explored within the economy of crack cocaine. Hustlers contrast their social behavior styles to avoid the negative connotation of crackhead, which has lower status than that of hustler in the street culture of drug dealing in inner-city neighborhoods.

In the 1980s, when crack cocaine began transforming poor, urban neighborhoods into even more socially distressed and impoverished areas than they were previously, it became clear to social analysts that the devastation wrought upon those in close proximity to crack addicts would be serious and lasting. Crack proliferation had effects beyond damage to souls and families, however. Its presence changed many distressed inner-city streets into busy open-air drug markets filled with violence and other forms of victimization (Williams 1992). The social settings of residents in places that would eventually be termed "crack alleys" were affected as citizens were divided, if imprecisely at times, into those who traded in crack and those who did not.

Law abiding citizens living near America's crack corners took great pains to separate themselves socially from the conditions outside their doors, necessarily changing their attitudes toward and interactions with those who had fallen either into addiction or to the enticements of the drug economy. Those up close also saw adjustments under their language and interactions as enduring drug markets transformed relationships between dealers and customers, creating new social types (Anderson 1999). An emergent social identity—the "crackhead"—became almost universally recognized and derided. Not only were crackheads failures at achieving the "American Dream," they also failed to project an image of "cool transcendence" that is admired by those embedded in street life (Katz 1988).

The label crackhead is commonly used in casual speech as a metaphor and illustration of personal failure and lack of responsibility. The crackhead serves as go-to material among a seemingly endless series of

---

Source: "We Weren't Like No Regular Dope Fiends": Negotiating Hustler and Crackhead Identities by Copes, Heith Andy Hochstetler, and J. Patrick Williams, *Social Problems,* 55(2), pp. 254–270. Reprinted with permission from University of California Press.

dark humored comics who make their living by portraying tragic characters in poor neighborhoods and making light of unpleasant, stereotypical interactions that might arise in dealing with them. The identity resonates with a wide audience because the physical effects of severe crack cocaine addiction are so apparent that they can be seen by the most casual observer, and because the spatial concentration of crack addiction allows for convenient allusion to the impoverished conditions and supposed moral failure in the inner city.

The devastating effects of local crack economies changed the behaviors and language of those in street life as well as their shared understandings of what the streets mean. Street identities and street language have adjusted to make sense of and arrange ordinary dealings in the illicit drug market. We contend that the resulting divisions between crack addicts and others engaged in street life entrench identity hierarchies by orienting offenders toward sub-culturally constructed criteria associated with the tough, capable hustler and away from those associated with the weak, incapable crackhead. Indeed, some of the most significant symbolic values prevalent in street life today are found in the meaningful distinction between hustlers and crackheads.

Hustler and crackhead identities are actively created through interactions among persons proximate to and distant from places where the categories are used in interaction. Each identity is imprecise and fluid and can have local variety. Yet, there is a more or less consistent ideal-typical form at the level of everyday use. These identities offer convenience when defining recurring interactional moments on the street and in making sense of the street scene. They encapsulate notions of what and who is valued and reflect what offenders are trying to be in the eyes of their peers. While mutuality functions to establish feasible identities, there is always subjectivity and some creativity in judging and using boundaries appropriately. Thus, to understand the social identity of the hustler it is necessary to examine how street offenders talk about themselves in terms of that identity category, as well how they construct relevant outgroups—in this case, crackheads.

In this study we employ a conception of social identity (Hewitt 2003; Jenkins 2004) to describe and examine two street identities in open-air drug markets. Drawing on interviews with 28 men who were convicted of committing violent street crimes, we explore how they identified themselves using distinct, contrasting social categories. Our analysis shows how contemporary street offenders construct meaningful identities that distance themselves from those exhibiting distasteful symptoms of crack cocaine addiction,

which they see as a striking and noticeable form of street failure. We study how their identity work allows them to make sense of the social world they know best and to portray themselves in culturally relevant and positive terms. On the streets, the boundaries that hustlers use to separate the demonized crack customer from themselves are significant. These identity boundaries shape how self-defined hustlers behave, their beliefs about how others should view and treat them, and the extent to which they self-identify as respectable and noteworthy characters.

CLASSIFICATIONS AND SOCIAL IDENTITIES

The process hustlers use to identify themselves vis-á-vis crackheads is not an arcane subcultural ability. Rather, classification is a basic social process that shapes the minute details of people's everyday lives (Zerubavel 1997). To make sense of their physical and social surroundings, human beings classify everything they encounter. People attach meaning to physical objects as well as gestures and words. In so doing, they shape their own and others' beliefs about and behaviors toward them (Blumer 1969). Dichotomies such as "attractive" versus "unattractive," "powerful" versus "weak," and "valuable" versus "worthless" employ socially-constructed boundaries that may become culturally standardized and utilized routinely in interaction. Such distinctions can provide a great deal of information as culturally shared shorthand that individuals use to orient to situations.

Identities are social constructs that classify persons. While some social scientists reduce identity to psychologically-based personality traits or sociologically-based categories substantiated by racial, ethnic, class, or gender-based groups, others conceptualize identity as a robust, malleable, and intricate phenomenon (e.g., Hogg and Ridgeway 2003; Hogg, Terry, and White 1995; Stets and Burke 2000). The former obscures the fact that identity is enacted and purposeful. In accord with conceptualizations that portray identities as negotiated and situational, we shift the focus from the internal structure, functions, and cultural makeup of identity categories to the *processes* through which such categories become meaningful to people in their everyday lives. One of the most fundamental is found in the use of culturally bounded contrasts and comparisons to establish the scope of identities and to make claims to membership.

Social identity is a multivalent process through which individuals identify themselves in terms of similarity to some people and difference to others. Social identification occurs when people identify both themselves and others as members of social categories (Hewitt 2003; Jenkins 2004). These can be almost ubiquitous categories such as white or male or subculturally-specific categories such as "righteous dope fiend" or "sick addict" (Sutter 1966). To be someone, such as a hustler for instance, "is to identify with others who are perceived as like oneself and whose real or imagined presence evokes positive feelings" (Hewitt 2003:107). When identifying with a desired social category, people regularly describe their own actions in terms of positively-defined behaviors associated with its members. Those who see themselves as hustlers describe admirable characteristics of hustlers and relate stories of their own behaviors in the hope of convincing their audience that they are authentic. Jack Katz (1988) makes sense of the lure and form of much crime according to the dictates of offenders desire to maintain "respectable" street identities. Moreover, he points out that many of the rewards and enticements of crime can be understood only by peering through the lens of these identities at potentially criminal situations.

To understand the social identity of the hustler it is necessary to examine how they talk about themselves in terms of identity categorization, as well as how they construct relevant out-groups. To the uncritical or uncaring eye, there may be little visible difference between hustlers and crackheads. One reason is that crackheads and hustlers inhabit the same physical environment, separated (by some combination of agency and structure) from legitimate means of achieving mainstream social prestige. Most participants in urban drug economies, and particularly in the crack trade, have fewer opportunities for the development of meaningful selves than mainstream Americans (Gubrium and Holstein 2000). Despite what is shared, the distinction is extremely salient in contemporary urban street life and is arguably more significant in offenders thinking, self-concept, and daily interactions than the divide between law-abiding citizens and themselves. The methods through which individuals immersed in street life construct a positive self-concept while engaging the drug economy is one type of "growing concern," which characterizes "relatively stable, routinized, ongoing patterns of action and interaction . . . that explicitly structure or reconfigure . . . identity" (Gubrium and Holstein 2000:102).

A growing concern for those embedded in street life is the ability to stay close to the drug economy without succumbing to its debilitating effects. Slipping into uncontrollable addiction is antithetical to the hustler identity, and it can have many debilitating and dangerous costs; yet, that slippage is oftentimes unavoidable. Edward Preble and John Casey (1969) found that heroin users in New York used the drug to make their lives busy and meaningful heroin use and its accompanying activities provided gratification that came from successfully accomplishing the challenges of being an addict and acquiring drugs. It also distracted from ensuing and occurring damage. "Righteous dope fiends" admire those who can acquire and use hard drugs in stylistically appropriate ways, whereas they mock ordinary poor people and those who lack such wherewithal. The fact that heavy drug use can devastate only serves to reinforce the sense that those who can "take care of business" and successfully manage a habit are admirable (Johnson et al. 1985; Preble and Casey 1969). Those who are capable of more than eking out an existence through crime and drug use garner special attention and accolades from their peers (see also Boeri 2004; Lewy and Preble 1973; Stephens 1991), and young hustlers learn that the ability to avoid the dismal fate of the crackhead, one form of the sick addict, is a mark of character and distinction that serves as essential proof of their social identity. In short, when constructing identities it is important for self-proclaimed hustlers to set themselves apart from those who have succumbed to drugs.

Discerning these growing concerns through offenders' talk means not simply taking at face value their claims of being hustlers rather than crackheads, but instead studying the identity-boundaries they construct through narrative. Such a focus leads to an understanding of the meanings that extend beyond the shorthand and labels and recognizes that the "critical focus of investigation [ought to be] the . . . *boundary* that defines the group, not the cultural stuff that it encloses" (Barth 1969:15, emphasis in original). This shift is pragmatic in the sense that it avoids reifying the cultural "stuff" (including identities) of population categories. It also encourages attention to the active construction of identity categories, and turns attention away from claims-makers constructions of identities as essential or natural. Hustler and crackhead are not objective identity categories; they are dialectically paired status symbols that are constantly being (re)negotiated.

For decades, investigators of street life and its dictates have recognized the prominence and power of the hustler identity and have described many of its behavioral and attitudinal components (Shover 1996). Less attention has been given directly to how identities valued by offenders are sustained interpersonally. Typically, interviews with offenders address neither meanings attributed to identities in depth nor precisely what hustlers have on their minds pertaining to relevant identities. In what follows, we describe how we struck upon the significance of the hustler/crackhead distinction while interviewing street offenders. We proceed to describe the distinction as street offenders presented it and show how interactions are used to reinforce these distinctions. We conclude by arguing that the salience of these identities and narratives highlights their significance for forming what contemporary offenders believe and how they conduct themselves. Such identity narratives therefore should not be neglected by any who would understand street crime, criminal decision-making, or related behaviors that otherwise might seem senseless.

DATA AND METHODS

The current study is based on the accounts of 28 violent male street offenders gathered in semistructured interviews. At the time of the interview, these individuals were serving sentences for various offenses in two Louisiana medium security prisons. Like most prisons in Louisiana, the populations are overrepresented by those who are young and black; our sample reflects this population. To locate participants within these prisons we used a purposive sampling strategy. Clerks in the prisons collected the names of individuals convicted of carjacking, the initial type of crime that the study was about, and we solicited these individuals. Due to a low number of convicted carjackers in the prison we also asked correctional officers if they knew inmates who had forcibly stolen vehicles. We interviewed those individuals who admitted to forcible auto theft even if they were convicted for other offenses. Thus, our sample consisted of individuals who had engaged in carjacking regardless of whether they were convicted of it or not.

Respondents ranged in age from 21 to 40 (mean age = 25). Five participants were white and 23 were black. Most had long criminal records that reflected years of persistent offending. Crimes in offenders' adult records revealed offenses ranging in severity from low-level drug distribution to robbery and attempted murder. The vast majority of them reported being involved in drug use and/or drug distribution around the time they were last arrested. The bulk of the respondents were heavily engaged in and surrounded by the drug economy and street life in poor neighborhoods in mid-sized to large cities in Louisiana.

When we began interviewing offenders for this project our intent was not to explore the phenomenon of managing social identities, but rather to explore the social world of those who engage in violent street crime and, more specifically, how participation in street culture

constrained the criminal decision-making process. Thus, in each interview we asked study participants about their educational backgrounds, families, occupations, criminal histories, drug use, and current lifestyles. The interviews were loosely structured to allow participants to elaborate on issues they thought relevant. These types of interviews are advantageous when investigators choose not to identify significant themes before research begins. Loosely structured interviews are often necessary when researchers suspect that their subjects thinking and categorical schemes may be foreign or when discovery hinges on understanding how participants interpret and narrate their lives and actions. As interviews progressed, it became clear that fostering a view of themselves as hustlers rather than crackheads was significant to participants. Upon recognizing this trend we adjusted the interview guide accordingly to collect more identity-related data. At first, this was done informally simply because of the way the conversations were going and as the interviewer carried information across interviews.

Among other questions, we asked if they self-identified as addicts or heavy drug users. Sometimes this question led to specific probes about whether the participants considered themselves to be junkies, addicts, or crackheads depending on context in the interview. Another question asking offenders how they interacted with drug customers elicited additional data. As these questions became more focused, we were intrigued by the emergence of the symbolic importance of the crackhead and hustler identities and the maintenance of the boundaries between them. We subsequently asked offenders how those in their neighborhoods treated crackheads generally and how they personally treated such people.

The interviews took place in private rooms in the facilities administrative wing. Only the study participants and the interviewer were in the room during the interview. While correctional officers were nearby, they were unable to listen in on the conversations. The interviews varied in length from 30 to 90 minutes. We transcribed all interviews verbatim and analyzed them with QSR NVivo 7 (Richards 1999). To ensure interrater reliability, the first two authors read independently each transcript to identify common themes. This was done midway through the research and again when interviews were completed. By the midpoint of the study, it was clear that the coding scheme should include offender concepts of self and others, and that the crackhead distinction would be an important subcomponent of the latter. At that point, an intentional decision was made to elicit more information on offenders' self-conceptions and specific identities. Of course, this allowed for greater elaboration by offenders when more questions on these topics were asked in the latter half of the study, but the coding scheme developed at the midpoint remained throughout the duration of the study. We should note that there were other self-concepts that were salient to offenders. For example, it was important for many to make distinctions between themselves and more violent offenders, whom they characterized as monstrous brutes or erratic madmen. The passages of interviews where offenders talk about themselves or others or spoke directly to the meanings of identities form the bulk of the talk included in what follows.

When interviewing inmates it is important to ensure that they are neither coerced into participating nor exposed to any undue harm by relaying information about crimes for which they have not been convicted. The potential exists that they may feel coerced into participating from either excessive prodding from staff or from the mistaken belief that they will accrue legal benefits (e.g., parole considerations). As Richard Wright and Scott Decker (1997) point out: "No matter how much inmates are assured otherwise, many will continue to believe what they say to researchers will get back to the authorities and influence their chances for early release" (p. 4). To address the possibility of coercion and harm we assured them of confidentiality and that we could not help their position in the prison or their case for release in any way. We warned offenders not to reveal information so specific that it could help a prosecutor, which alleviated many fears about our motives as interviewers. In addition, we guaranteed that we would take all possible measures to keep their responses private. If prison staff did come into the room, which happened only a few times, we stopped asking questions until they exited. Additionally, before entering the prison we had promises from prison administrators that they would not ask for any information elicited during the interviews. As a way to assess whether they were coerced, we asked the offenders why they agreed to be interviewed. The reasons they gave—a chance to talk to new people, to help out, and to do something consistent with being on the right track—suggested that they were neither coerced nor reluctant to discuss their current and past lives (Copes and Hochstetler 2006).

One could argue that the accounts given by these self-proclaimed hustlers were designed to present positive images solely for us and that these presentations may differ from those given on the streets (Presser 2004). At times, common sense led us to be skeptical of some details in their accounts and we expect the reader may be as well. Some degree of

dishonesty is expected and assumed (Jacobs and Wright 2006). Like others, we think that distorted facts and stories impart meaning, however. Exaggerations and fictions may reveal as much about people as "facts," especially when they are discussing their self-conceptions in relation to others. We believe, however, that offenders' talk gives us insight into more than just the situational construction of a personal "hustler" identity within the context of the interview. Their talk also represents some of the processes through which they construct meaningful social identities on the street. In what follows we describe the process through which individuals who self-identified as capable hustlers established boundaries between themselves and a social type that they perceived to epitomize those who are weak and unworthy of respect.

SEMANTIC BOUNDARIES OF THE HUSTLER IDENTITY

To understand offenders' self-identifications as hustlers we examined talk about who they refused to be. While they were not conventional hardworking citizens, this needed little consideration or attention as it was so far-fetched. After even short conversations or interactions with these men, few would mistake them for the ostensibly square and boring but legally employed citizens in their communities. Consequently, they made little effort to articulate this apparent division. The strongest and most adamant contrast they made was with crackheads.

Many offenders we interviewed reported using, though most denied being controlled by the substance. Despite their persistent use of crack, they insisted they could maintain their "style." Others, they claimed, were not capable of handling their addictions. Those who failed to manage their drug use (i.e., crackheads) became an important symbol and antihero. Assignment to that category could be stylistically avoided despite heavy drug use. Almost all offenders rejected their membership in the crackhead category and those few who admitted that they shared much in common with crackheads described how the stereotypical identity resulted in an inadequate understanding of their position in the context of the local drug market. Some purported hustlers interviewed here found it humorous that someone might see them as a crackhead, but understood the confusion over appropriate labels among those with little or no direct knowledge of street life and were more than willing to correct it. Yet if someone from the street inferred that they were crackheads the response would not be so jovial. As

Jarret stated, "That's an insult. You insulted my character. I'm gonna deal with you, you know."[1]

Hustlers took special care to establish boundaries between themselves and crackheads in their neighborhoods, especially during face-to-face interactions. Their narratives represent, therefore, the maintenance of social distance from those they defined as crackheads to audiences on the street, including peers, potential drug customers, and the crackheads themselves. The offenders we interviewed constructed their hustler identities along five semantic boundaries: being clean, having things, being cool, being criminally able, and having heart.

Being Clean

Hustlers viewed themselves as being cleaner than crackheads, both morally and hygienically. This perspective was linked to the credit given to unusual cleanliness in dress and appearance among those who wish to "create a look of cool transcendence" (Wright and Decker 1997:40; see also Katz 1988). Cleanliness has long been a noteworthy feature of criminal underworlds and of street life in general, most likely deriving from the importance of demonstrating that one has it together despite, or because of, criminal activity (Katz 1988). Indeed, clean is a word that offenders were fond of using in describing their style of dress and ostentatious displays. Shawn, a self-defined hustler, emphasized what he spent his money on: "I love to dress clean, you know. Clothes!" By contrast, crackheads were viewed as incapable of cleanliness—unkempt and dirty in every sense of the word. When asked to describe the defining characteristics of someone who had succumbed to drugs, Charles offered the following: "That's somebody who is strung out and looks bad. Don't keep they self up. Don't do nothing with they self." Whereas respectable street hustlers represented themselves with the latest fashions, they perceived crackheads as either oblivious to these fashion trends or as simply incapable of following them.

Crackheads disgust conventional citizens and hustlers alike and contact with them taints. Several offenders recalled that crackheads were so physically filthy as to be almost untouchables in the street criminals social hierarchy. The fact that the drug had taken them was too obvious. As Chantey explained: "It's like they living zombies or something." Jarrett echoed this sentiment: "Somebody come up to you with their lips all white and shaking. Let me suck your . . . Let me get this hit. Yeah, that's at the bottom." Shawn explained that the rules

among his friends, for whom few other boundaries were inflexible, were fairly clear even when crackheads were otherwise attractive as sexual partners:

> You don't want to mess with them [sexually]. Like very few of the guys that I hang with will knock them down a cut. No. Uh-uh, that is a no no! I mean cluckers [crack addicts] do some wild things for their crack and you might catch a bad disease messing with them.

Three offenders mentioned that, to them, crack itself was dirty and crack use was not as respectable and clean a habit as heroin, but most made no such distinction. Generally, in the street offenders view the crackhead's taint is not acquired directly from heavy drug-use or choice of drug, but through some stylistic reflections of heavy use or a particular set of apparent symptoms of severe addiction. Other distinctions interviewees made were rooted in the ability to secure a place to sleep, shower, and perform other hygienic behaviors, as well as the symbols of elevated street tastes.

Having Things

Fashion, consumption, and material display are often markers of identity membership. The "ostentatious enjoyment and display of luxury items" is vital to understanding street life and perhaps even the motivation to steal (Shover and Honaker 1992:283; see also Shover 1996; Wright and Decker 1994, 1997). In many of the hustlers' portrayals, one could not be a crackhead and have things, or more precisely one could not be a crackhead and successfully accumulate material goods. It seems that while doctors and lawyers on their way down feasibly can be crackheads, "successful" street criminals cannot. It is the ability to demonstrate appropriate tastes and to acquire and provide material goods at any given moment that separated hustlers from crackheads. Philip's self-description exemplified this idea:

> I never considered myself a junkie until I come to jail I never was staring at walls and stuff like that I always sold drugs so I always had money. I was never broke . . . I got money. I got nice clothes. I got a roof over my head. I go do this and that when I want.

Whatever the current street terminology—flossing, stunting, flashing, or shining—all of these professed hustlers claimed to enjoy the expensive styles and tastes

---

of the successful street criminal. These tastes were exhibited in the right style of car, clothing, weapons, phones, jewelry, and other fashionable accoutrements associated with street life. Charles described why he and his partners were not true crackheads despite their drug-use:

> We weren't like no regular dope fiends though. You catch us with like five hundred dollars worth of clothes riding around in stolen luxury vehicles, man. [We had] beaucoup money . . . You gotta be presentable. You gotta come with some valued gifts . . . If you going after all this money to get this dope, believe one thing, you done got the money to keep yourself up too.

For Charles it was the availability of resources and material goods that separated him from other drug addicts. Being a good provider is part of what it means to be a man and a hustler and through proper hustling, Charles and others like him avoided the crackhead label because they were sufficient providers for themselves and those around them (Copes and Hochstetler 2003; Kersten 1996).

When street offenders like Charles and Philip spoke of "having things," generally they referred to having the resources necessary to put on appropriate displays of criminal success, although they also needed a place to live, transportation, and other things that almost everyone wants. Material displays showed others that they were *not* facing tough times and were *not* becoming desperate. The hustler might have empty pockets, but he was sure that he could still provide adequately for his needs.

Another resource was the social connections that benefitted them in criminal pursuits. Most respondents liked to think of themselves in the center of a criminal network where there was some camaraderie or mutual respect based on one's character. Some interviewees reported social relationships that provided resources and respectful deference. Most had an abstract understanding that nothing was dependable in the hustling life. Nevertheless, a modicum of street success and display of success meant that other hustlers included them in crimes and shared with them. Also, drug customers, friends, family, or lovers would contribute to their needs and tastes, supporting their lifestyles and their leisure interests.

> I wasn't stealing from my mom . . . I didn't have to do none of that. I had money. I had friends. I had a girlfriend. She works two jobs and got a nice Mustang; a brand new car. I got a place to stay; a house. So, I bring her to work and she gives me money to go get my dope.

> Save her a bag or two. I use her car and her cell phone all day to run drugs . . . So I didn't most of the time have to pay for my own dope. She was paying for my own habit. I just save all of my money. [Philip]

Interviewees tended to believe that crackheads, unlike hustlers, are incapable of maintaining possessions for a reasonable amount of time. Hustlers, like Thomas, believed and furthered the stereotype that "[crackheads] sell everything; sell everything in they house." When asked if he feared retaliation from a crackhead that he robbed, John responded, "If he ever had a gun, he done sold it by now," reflecting the extent to which crack addicts could not maintain possessions. Determining whether it was their addiction or some underlying flaw that forced crackheads to sell or trade away belongings was not important. The perception that crackheads possessed significantly less than hustlers and were viewed as beyond the position where they could turn things around was reason enough to categorize them accordingly. For hustlers, material well-being could be acquired and enhanced despite occasional crises, slips, or setbacks if they only managed to make the right situational moves and fortune shone. The crackheads trajectory was predictably and steadily downward. Temporary poverty was something the hustler might have to endure, but complete material failure was a problem to which only a crackhead was susceptible.

Being Cool

Hustlers appreciated a cool, detached persona, probably because they associated this with the ability to roll with punches, stay calm, and be ruthlessly cold when required. According to Katz (1988): "To be cool is to view the immediate social situation as ontologically inferior, nontranscendent, and too mundane to compel one's attention" (p. 97). This image is far from the erratic, paranoid, fast, and sketchy mannerisms of the ideal-typical crackhead. On the streets, crackhead mannerisms imply all of the wrong things about them. Although a great many of the valued mannerisms associated with respectable street styles might be viewed as those of the slightly numbed or sedated, no one emulates the disjointed walk or awkward mannerisms of the stereotypical crack addict except in jest. Shawn's description of a "clucker" certainly negated any sense of coolness:

> A clucker is one who do drugs. The reason that we call them cluckers is when they don't have the crack they be clucking. They be like how a chicken will do because

they nervous so we call them cluckers, or chews because they be chewing on their lips.

As shown in this pitiless description, it is nearly impossible to be seen as cool when one is in such a nervous affective state or when being compared with the least flattering features of barnyard poultry.

Another element of being cool that emerged was remaining calm in the face of imminent danger. Katz (1988) argues that putting oneself in perceivably uncontrollable and chaotic situations and coming out unharmed is one of the sensual attractions that lure people into committing robbery. Confronting adversity with unflinching resolve and handling the potential for chaos without being flustered is admired. According to our interviewees, the dope corner gave the hustler plentiful opportunities to show their mettle, but crackheads seldom displayed any sense of will of character. According to Jason: "See the ones that was on drugs, the drugs do something to them. They be spooked. They be scared." Those we spoke with made a point to emphasize that they could handle themselves with fearlessness and bravado no matter what situations they encountered. Unlike crackheads, they were seldom spooked and if they were, it would be unperceivable.

Being Criminally Able

None of our interviewees talked about their moneymaking endeavors in the rational and calculable ways that approximate the deliberations and cost/benefit analyses that accompany corporate careers. Many did acknowledge, however, that they had a specialist's knowledge—a larceny sense—of how to navigate the drug and crime underworld and make something of the lifestyle that accompanied it (Nee and Meenaghan 2006; Sutherland 1937; Wright, Logie, and Decker 1995). The most derisive condemnations of crackheads centered on the theme that they had lost so much mental capacity and control of themselves that they could barely survive (let alone prosper) on the streets. When they were not begging others for drugs and money or searching the ground desperately for possibly dropped drugs, they relegated themselves to petty thefts and demeaning hustles. As Jarrett explained:

See people like us, we go big. Crackheads will go do what they gotta do like steal lawnmowers and shit like that. Might do that shit every day. I might go pull off an act everyday too ... Whatever we do it's gonna be worth something, you dig?

On the streets and in prison, the status and prestige given to people based on the types of crimes they commit remains remarkably unchanged. There is little doubt that those seeking status and respect are aware of these distinctions or that they think that crimes of hardmen and hustlers can reflect positively on their character and repute. Michael recounted his rise from being a generally respected but ordinary sneak thief into a recognized neighborhood heavy:

[Carjackings] helped my reputation. People knew— "you're jacking now." [They] say, "You went from stealing cars to jacking, ah man!" All it takes is one person who tell a friend, who tell a friend you doing such and such. "Yeah, that Michael runnin around"; and everybody want to be with you 'cause they know what you do on the street. They know how you done made out ... You get more respect like that. Really, one time I was nothing man, but I done got my reputation.

When addicts did not act like respectable hustlers, others assumed their inability was due to character flaws, signifying them as unworthy of respect as well as being easy marks. Crack addicts carried out crimes and hustles that had low payoff and that were seen to be subservient. This portrayal of crackheads often emerged during discussion of "rock rentals"—the practice of renting out one's vehicle in exchange for a small amount of crack—and the foolishness of the addicts engaging in these transactions (Copes, Forsyth, and Brunson 2007).

They should know one thing. I am going to take their shit [car] and sell it. But, they be stupid enough to give it to me. You wanted that to happen, you know what I am saying. I ain't the one tweeking on rocks. You want something, I want something ... See they gotta watch out for people like me. [Michael]

Interview participants recognized that crack addicts engaged in rock rentals in an attempt to avoid some of the stigmatizing behavior associated with being a crackhead. However, purported hustlers did not accept this interpretation. Instead, they saw it as a desperate attempt by an addict and as proof of crackhead's inability to succeed.

If crackheads were judged harshly for their ineptitude, they are even more resolutely condemned for passively accepting their status in the street due to fear of confrontation. Open air drug dealing, for them, is out of the question for all the obvious reasons. Likewise, their habit of committing crimes so petty that they could not possibly provide meaningful thrill or bragging rights reinforced our interviewees' beliefs that crackheads are not to be taken seriously. In this idealized distinction, real hustlers did what they wanted, but crackheads accepted their dismal fate, demeaned themselves, and scavenged scraps. The state of crack addicts and their inability to provide for themselves was perhaps best described by Brennon:

> A crackhead … ain't got a ride. They ain't got a house to live in. [They] ain't got no food to eat. You know I always had all that. A crackhead goes and suck dick for rock—now you know I ain't about all that … I'd rob, that was my thing … Why you go and try to hustle a person at a gas station for a dollar or fifty cent to get a rock?

And while the men we spoke with did recognize that they were prone to victimization, they did not think it likely that their victimizers would be "crackheads" but rather other hustlers. On this matter and others, we were surprised at how firm the division was between crackheads and hustlers, and there is no way of knowing if offenders simply forget about exceptions to the rules and those who fall somewhere in the middle range on the boundaries. The point is not to describe a realistic division, only the boundaries constructed in interviews. Surely, pride means that no self-professed hustler can admit being robbed by a crackhead easily. Such an event is rendered highly implausible due to the limited but great freedom to assign labels in the streets and the unrestricted freedom in the interview. As Jason, who did worry over robbery, remarked about crackheads: "1 didn't fear none of them."

Having Heart

As hustlers saw it, crackheads not only lacked the ability to commit noteworthy crimes, they also lacked the heart required to show courage when confronted. Hustlers knew that they inhabited a dangerous world but were confident that they would do relatively well in protecting themselves from victimization and demeaning nuisances (this went beyond criminal capability for acquisitive and respectable offenses). Self-identifying hustlers were confident that they would not be degraded by street-corner peers or rivals more than once. When asked why he did not concern himself with possibly being scammed by a crackhead, Thomas replied: "Reputation of what we could do to him." For Thomas, and others like him, vigilantly protecting one's reputation kept many would-be scammers, con men, and robbers at bay (Jacobs, Topalli, and Wright 2000).

Interviewees reluctantly admitted that when it came to protecting themselves from danger, their options were constrained by background and previous choices, but they pointed out that crackheads had no options at all. Failure in both the legitimate and criminal world left the crackhead vulnerable in every sense of the word. Crackheads were thought to lack the courage, physical capacity, and social connections necessary to intimidate others and protect themselves in the streets. They either could not or were unwilling to take up for themselves, and any meaningful alliances to help them do so were beyond their grasp. Even if they consumed crack, the individuals we spoke with made it clear they were different from "real" crackheads because they (as hustlers) were capable and in some instances eager to violently stand up for themselves. Derrick explained why he could always take from a crackhead: "They know the type of person that I am. They know that if they come mess with me its gonna be trouble." Jason, an experienced carjacker, best explained the difference between crackhead behavior and his own:

> See the ones that was on drugs you basically can do anything to them. They ain't about no trouble. The drugs done took their heart and courage and just make them feel like they ain't even nothin, so they don't even try to fight or nothin.

Thomas echoed this sentiment, but added that unwillingness to defend oneself also meant that no one else would or should come to their aid because the "weak get what they deserve":

> They don't want no trouble. He's a clucker, man. You can beat the piss out of a clucker any time you feel like it. Hate them, you understand me? I wouldn't give a can of shit … I'd piss on a clucker right now.

Crackheads were thought to lack the mental fortitude to enact revenge, which meant they were unworthy of the aid of others. Indeed, it was too late to turn this state of affairs around. Once marked as this sort of street failure, significant challenges to those higher in status would surely be met with severe retaliation. Short of disappearing from the street scene or committing murder, there were few alternatives to continued degradation for crackheads, as no hustler could tolerate an affront from them that went beyond playful street banter.

The above references to prototypical hustler and crackhead behaviors highlight the boundaries that would-be hustlers constructed. Such boundary constructions consisted on the one hand of hustlers emphasizing the negative characteristics of crackheads, while on the other hand extolling their own accomplishments and importance as hustlers. Interviewees used these idealized descriptions as a form of symbolic mobilization to more neatly distinguish and distance themselves from the maligned category. For example, Gerald explained that he could not be a crackhead in his own neighborhood because he would not be treated as one. "I'm still a homeboy, I'm just a user." In his view, the slight respect garnered by being a homeboy made assigning him to the category crackhead difficult even though he admitted sharing more attributes with the crackhead class than did most of our other respondents. Membership in the crackhead category was rejected using semantic strategies not unlike those described by Derek Edwards (1997). The potential member compares himself to a prototypical member on a list of category attributes and reasons out an explanation of varying complexity, for how he is not one of "them" (see also Widdicombe 1998).

Disrespectful Interaction

The distance interviewee's narratives emphasized between themselves and crackheads was not only maintained through verbal constructions but also enacted symbolically in face-to-face interactions. One way social boundaries could be maintained was by simply avoiding any but the most detached and short-lived interaction with those they defined as crackheads. To ensure that others did not inaccurately view them as crackheads, many of those with whom we spoke limited friendly exchanges and conversation with crackheads beyond what was necessary. Interactions and transactions were kept short, depersonalized, and business oriented. The point was illustrated by a diversity of comments about keeping social distance from the crackhead and maintaining the status division in dealer/customer relationship. Describing his interactions with addicts to whom he sold crack, Jason said, "Well, I never had no relationship with them, you know, except for dealings with the dope." Michael echoed this sentiment: "[Crackheads] are out in the hood so you know who they are. I knew them, but they weren't friends. They just people I conversate with, if you know what I'm saying."

The social world of the open-air drug market requires and contains plentiful customers. Those addicted to crack must interact with drug dealers and others who may look down on them. Many crack addicts live in very confined social and geographic worlds and proximate to other street offenders, but manage their everyday interactions with little conflict.

However, due to hustlers' desires to maintain an obdurate boundary between themselves and crackheads, interactions had the potential to be degrading dramatizations of boundaries.

Crackheads fulfilled simple, and sometimes important, functions to hustlers on the street by providing cheap labor for routine, demeaning, or unchallenging tasks and services. Because the derided addict would do most anything, tasks described were wide-ranging. Typically, they required no assumption on the part of the contractor that the crackhead was reliable or criminally capable, simply that they were willing. In describing the nature of his prolonged interactions with those he considered crackheads, Shawn pointed out that crackheads provided services because of who he and his friend were (i.e., "real" hustlers).

> We might hide in their house, lay low for a couple of days. We ain't got to come out. Send them to run errands. You get whatever you need, bam! You can chill right there, especially if you are like all of us. I mean we jack cars and run to Houston and drop them off and we get a clucker that will come up and bring us back for two twenty dollar rocks. He'll come up there and break the speed limit coming up for that, you know.

Others denied "clowning" or using crackheads but relayed thoughts as to why others treated crack addicts so poorly:

> They use [crackheads] to go get sound systems, or to wash their cars. You know what I'm saying, you want to be a big bailer standing out there with a bunch of jewelry on and watch them boys wash your car, wash and wax their car. Makes them look good; like they the big man around there. [Brennon]

Some hustlers frequently established boundaries through deliberate interactions that were one-sided, exploitative, and demeaning to others. We interpret these interactions as mechanisms that put crackheads in their "rightful" place in the street hierarchy—the bottom. These stories suggest that demonstrating power was important for establishing the hustler's status at the top of the street culture hierarchy and that this could be done easily, almost without risk, against those at the bottom. Philip described one such interaction: "[We] made one chick one time give a Rottweiler head . . . Man we used to call her Rottweiler from then on too." Shawn related an interaction he witnessed:

> [They] made a couple of them [crackheads] stick their hand up in an ant pile—them red ants. They'd stir 'em

up and stick their hand up in there and hold it down for so many minutes . . . They be seated there man and them ants be tearing them up.

Chantey reported a situation where he exhibited little compassion for the drug user:

We was up in the projects and everything . . . They got a rock head to climb a building, you know what I'm saying. Tell him if he jump off the building they'll give him ten rocks—his stupid ass jumped off of it and broke both ankles.

Despite the humiliation and physical pain caused to the drug users, Philip, Shawn and Chantey relayed these stories not out of concern for the crackheads but to prove that hustlers like themselves would not be subject to such degradation because of their street sense and command over those of lower social status.

Even offenders who saw such degradation as senseless clowning, or as behavior engaged in by insecure men still striving to gain their place in the street culture hierarchy, reported on similar interactions in ways that made clear the message that their social world required and emphasized certain attributes. Pragmatically, it is in these dramatizations that the axiom "some have what it takes and some do not" is obtained. Brennon recalled an instance of playing with a crackhead:

He was like out on the front where they sell all the dope and I was out there too. He come passing by and all them boys was laughin at him. I say, "Watch this. Watch what I do to this dude." And I grabbed a tire out of my trunk and he come right there and I told him, I said, "look I'll give you twenty dollar stone if you let me hit you hard as I can across your ass." I say, "Bend over and touch your ankles." He bend over and I hit him hard as I could with that tire. He did a whole flip. When he stood up, he wanted his rock. [I did it] just to make them boys laugh, to show them how much a crackhead he really is.

His account began by explaining that both men were hanging out on a crack corner where drugs are sold. Brennon then illustrated how he was sufficiently respected by the street corner dealers to afford security and safety, in contrast to the crackhead. In addition, he shows that he is sufficiently well positioned to dispose of a twenty-dollar piece of cocaine on a lark. Brennan concludes by noting that the message he intended to send was confirmed successfully in interaction. From the hustlers perspective, such interactions provide distraction from the business and long hours that many offenders spend sitting or standing on bleak street corners. They also function to exaggerate the hustler's status by setting up crackheads as a polar opposite and of being devoid of value and status. The following example suggests how common such practices were.

I'll give him some crumb if he will do something stupid. [I said] "Go to the back of that truck and take that man on. He got a refrigerator back there. Bet you won't take that refrigerator back there." [He asked] "What you gonna give?" [And I said] "I'll give you a twenty." He go back there to take the man's refrigerator and then I tell the man, "Somebody trying to steal your refrigerator." The refrigerator man come out and beat him up. Be out there trippin out laughing. Because they will do anything. Go down and trip off them all day. [John]

To some degree, to be seen as anything other than posturing, hustler identities must be successfully enacted, and in the social world herein, empty posturing as a hustler is dangerous. When there is a supposed hierarchical arrangement where some are valued and others devalued, individuals can use enactments that draw on divisions to establish their place, and to sustain boundaries they perceive as beneficial. Exploitive interactions solidify the boundaries between the "legitimate" hustlers and the "weak" crackheads.

CONCLUSIONS

Through interaction, individuals actively construct boundaries and identities that separate them from others who they view as having lower status. Just as social elites differentiate themselves from members of the underclass despite being members of the same society, so too do hustlers differentiate themselves from others on the streets. In general terms, the study of social identity provides insight into the pragmatic links among structural conditions and individuals' behaviors. Identities are not merely situational constructs. Rather, through their embeddedness in everyday interaction they accrete into culturally identifiable categories that become useful as markers of pride or disgrace. Identities such as the hustler and the crackhead are arbitrary (rather than essential) constructs that emerge from a finite range of going concerns that frame interactions. Those who engage in illegitimate drug economies on the street construct types to show status in the business and surrounding social structure.

The way one's self is imagined, portrayed, and accepted by others, and the value she or he and others assign these conveyances, are important aspects for the study of social behavior. In his work on behavior in public places, Erving Goffman (1963) notes that individuals "give off" information about themselves simply by being present in a situation. On the street, those engaged in the drug economy give off a certain amount of information about themselves through their relation to that economy. Interviewees expressed some understanding that the label crackhead might be a tempting way for outsiders to sum up their lives as few seemed particularly shocked at mention of it in the context of interviews. Further, they were behind bars during the interview and were well aware of the stigmatized identities likely placed upon them by outsiders. While not particularly interested in denying or neutralizing their criminal exploits (Topalli 2005, 2006), including their use of illegal drugs such as crack cocaine, the men were active in constructing a clear boundary between themselves and the average drug users with whom they shared the street. The self-described hustlers in our research succeeded, at least in their own minds, in establishing an identity whose status is at the top of the crack economy rather than at the bottom. To the extent their reported behaviors are accurate, that identity must carry significant weight on the street as well.

Given that they are regularly in the company of stigmatized members of the "street society," hustlers must remain constantly vigilant to avoid or minimize having low-status labels such as crackhead attached to them. This is true not only because they wish to maintain a positive self-concept, but because their financial future is at stake. Studying how street offenders construct a sense of self is therefore sociologically important inasmuch as these identities are directly linked to the interaction order (Goffman 1983) and to the obligations and expectations attached to social identities. For offenders proximate to, or involved in, the crack economy but who do not use crack, constructing a hustler identity is a convenient explanation for their abstinence. It comes with the reward of being confident in their place at the top of this underworld. Drawing on the power of societal condemnations of the crackhead in combination with the attributes defined as street success, hustling can be a comfortable identity in the face of adversity and the disapproval of polite society. Sustaining the identity also provides a coherent strategy for imagined success and perhaps helps avoid the temptation to imbibe in self-destructive habits (Furst et al. 1999; Jacobs 1999; Williams 1992). It also expresses free will and natural ability. For those who use drugs including crack, the ability to be identified as a hustler due to other attributes aids in managing the stigma associated with their drug use and criminal activities.

Giving off a successfully cultivated hustler identity makes it less likely that those in street life will need to deal with some of the ordinary shakedowns or half-hearted attempts to get them to balk in confrontation or in potential thefts. Our respondents did not believe that their violent reputations would universally protect them, at least not by reducing their overall chances of being accosted by others. They knew well the dangers of their lifestyles, and that continued participation in crime would likely result in their victimization. A "heavy" reputation does mean, however, that those who have sufficient knowledge and ability to judge such things will not take them lightly or take from them without possibly incurring high costs. All those contemplating such a move will, in the hustlers mind, give due respect by considering the odds of retaliation (Jacobs and Wright 2006). Fostering the hustler identity affords a layer of protection from victimization that crackheads do not possess.

This insight sheds substantive light on the symbolic interactional construction of street-level power relations and inequalities. The men we interviewed constructed an image of the crackhead not only to frame their own sense of self, but more generally to frame the social reality of street life. This social reality is constituted by an ongoing "conversation of gestures" (Mead 1934:179) by which hustlers and crackheads come to define themselves, each other, and their social environment. Understanding how hustlers identify themselves and others thus sheds light on the dialectic ties between social relations and the criminal decision-making process, including target selection.

Assigning people to identity categories provides convenient justifications for choosing victims. Those who are surrounded by and participate in street crime have an increased likelihood of victimization. In attempting to explain this phenomenon some have pointed out that hustlers are ideal candidates for victimization because they are likely to have desirable goods (i.e., cash, drugs, or valued accessories) and they are unlikely to involve police (Jacobs 2000; Wright and Decker 1997). Our study suggests that there may be additional reasons why hustlers choose to rob or victimize other offenders. Part of what it means to be a hustler is the ability to take advantage of others. Confronting those with reputations as hustlers can send a message that respect is deserved. Hustlers seemed to believe that crackheads could not manage such a crime or deal with the repercussions.

Sociologists have long known that offenders justify their crimes by defining certain types of people as acceptable victims (Maruna and Copes 2005; Sykes and

Matza 1957). It is remarkably easier to victimize someone when she or he is thought to deserve such treatment. Typically, this deserving status is assigned to those who have personally wronged the offender, but this is not always the case. The crackhead label conveniently places those defined as such into a deserving category for all those reasons previously described. Thus, when preying on crackheads, hustlers can more easily justify how and why they choose their marks. They can victimize without ordinary reservations about taking from the helpless and also can circumvent the subcultural dictates that crime should be done only for financial reasons and when insulted. In this sense, our analysis offers substantive support for other microsociological work on the reproduction of inequality through explicit and implicit processes of boundary maintenance and "othering" (Schwalbe et al. 2000).

In a review of a book about offender self-narratives and endorsement of deeper analysis of offenders assigned meanings, David Gadd (2003) asks of a quoted offender's account: "What depictions of him (a wimp, not a man, a pushover, a failure, or maybe a psycho, 'trash', an 'idiot'?) were ruminating round in his head when he was lying in bed thinking" (p. 321). Gadd implies that offenders choose from a range of alternative selves. Some of these are more stable categories than others. While our analysis only scratches the surface of self and meaning, we show that consciously, culturally, and intuitively persistent street offenders incorporated crackhead into their categorical arrangements for self-definition. This hardens them to the plight of a certain type of addict and affirms the view that acts of violence, ruthlessness, and conspicuous pride in criminal accomplishments are the makings of good criminals. Interactions with and interpretations of crack addicts helped convince offenders that being bad, if done properly, is a worthwhile goal and that hustler identities should be adhered to except in exceptional circumstances (Topalli 2005). In all ranks, unforgiving and harsh condemnations of moral failure alongside the rigid categorizations that typically accompany them can harden the heart and result in destructive and oppressive behaviors.

REFERENCES

Anderson, Elijah. 1999. *Code of the Street.* New York: W. W. Norton and Company.

Barth, F. 1969. *Ethnic Groups and Boundaries.* Bergen, Norway: Universitets Forlaget.

Blumer, Herbert. 1969. *Symbolic Interactionism.* Berkeley: University of California Press.

Boeri, Miriam W. 2004. "Hell, I'm An Addict, But I Ain't No Junkie': An Ethnographic Analysis of Aging Heroin Users." *Human Organization* 63:236–45.

Copes, Heith and Andy Hochstetler. 2003. "Situational Constructions of Masculinity among Male Street Thieves." *Journal of Contemporary Ethnography* 32:279–304.

———. 2006. "Why I'll Talk: Offenders' Motives for Participating in Qualitative Research." Pp. 19–28. In *In Their Own Words: Criminals on Crime,* 4th edition, edited by Paul Cromwell. Los Angeles, CA: Roxbury.

Copes, Heith, Craig Forsyth, and Rod Brunson. 2007. "Rock Rentals: The Social Organization and Interpersonal Dynamics of Crack-for-Cars Transactions in Louisiana, USA." *British Journal of Criminology* 47:885–99.

Edwards, Derek. 1997. *Discourse and Cognition.* Beverly Hills, CA: Sage.

Furst, R. Terry, Bruce D. Johnson, Eloise Dunlap, and Richard Curtis. 1999. "The Stigmatized Image of the 'Crack Head': A Sociocultural Exploration of a Barrier to Cocaine Smoking among a Cohort of Youth in *New York City." Deviant Behavior* 20:153–81.

Gadd, David. 2003. "Making Criminology Good: A Response to Shadd Maruna." *The Howard Journal* 42:316–22.

Goffman, Erving. 1963. *Behavior in Public Places.* New York: The Free Press.

———. 1983. "The Interaction Order." *American Journal of Sociology* 48(1):1–17.

Gubrium, Jaber and James Holstein. 2000. "The Self in a World of Going Concerns." *Symbolic Interaction* 23:95–115.

Hewitt, John P 2003. *Self and Society: A Symbolic Interactionist Social Psychology.* Boston: Allyn and Bacon.

Hogg, Michael A. and Cecilia L. Ridgeway. 2003. "Social Identity: Sociological and Social Psychological Perspectives." *Social Psychology Quarterly* 66:97–100.

Hogg, Michael A., Deborah J. Terry, and Katherine M. White. 1995. "A Tale of Two Theories: A Critical Comparison of Identity Theory with Social Identity Theory." *Social Psychology Quarterly* 58:255–69.

Jacobs, Bruce 1999. *Dealing Crack: The Social World of Streetcorner Selling.* Boston, MA: Northeastern University Press.

———. 2000. *Robbing Drug Dealers: Violence Beyond the Law.* New York: Aldine de Gruyter.

Jacobs, Bruce and Richard Wright. 2006. *Street Justice: Retaliation in the Criminal Underworld.* New York: Cambridge University Press.

Jacobs, Bruce, Volkan Topalli, and Richard Wright. 2000. "Managing Retaliation: Drug Robbery and Informal Sanction Threats." *Criminology* 38:171–97.

Jenkins, Richard. 2004. *Social Identity.* 2nd ed. London, UK: Routledge.

Johnson, Bruce, Paul Goldstein, Edward Preble, James Schmeidler, Douglas S. Lipton, Barry Spunt, and Thomas Miller. 1985. *Taking Care of Business: The Economics of Crime by Heroin Abusers.* Lexington, MA: Lexington Books.

Katz, Jack. 1988. *Seductions of Crime: Moral and Sensual Attractions in Doing Evil.* New York: Basic Books.

Kersten, Joachim. 1996. "Culture, Masculinities, and Violence against Women." *British Journal of Criminology* 36:381–95.

Lewy, Marc G. and Edward Preble. 1973. "Tragic Magic: Word Usage among New York City Heroin Addicts." *Psychiatric Quarterly* 42:228–45.

Maruna, Shadd and Heith Copes. 2005. "What Have We Learned from Five Decades of Neutralization Research?" *Crime and Justice: An Annual Review of Research* 32:221–320.

Mead, George H. 1934. *Mind, Self, and Society.* Chicago: University of Chicago Press.

Nee, Claire and Amy Meenaghan. 2006. "Expert Decision Making in Burglars." *British Journal of Criminology* 46 935–49.

Preble, Edward and John Casey. 1969. "Taking Care of Business: The Heroin Users Life on the Streets." *International Journal of Addictions* 4:1–24.

Presser, Lois 2004. "Violent Offenders. Moral Selves: Constructing Identities and Accounts in the Research Interview." *Social Problems* 51:82–101.

Richards, Lyn 1999. *Using NVivo in Qualitative Research.* London, UK: Sage.

Shover, Neal. 1996. *Great Pretenders: Pursuits and Careers of Persistent Thieves.* Boulder, CO: Westview.

Shover, Neal and David Honaker. 1992. "The Socially Bounded Decision Making of Persistent Property Offenders." *Howard Journal of Criminal Justice* 31:276–93.

Schwalbe, Michael, Sandra Godwin, Daphne Holden, Douglas Schrock, Shealy Thompson, and Michele Wolkomir. 2000. "Generic Processes in the Reproduction of Inequality: An Interactionist Analysis." *Social Forces* 79:419–52.

Stephens, Richard C. 1991. *The Street Addicts Role. A Theory of Heroin Addiction.* New York: SUNY Press.

Stets, Jan E. and Peter J. Burke. 2000. "Identity Theory and Social Identity Theory." *Social Psychology Quarterly* 63:224–37.

Sutherland, Edwin. 1937. *The Professional Thief.* Chicago: University of Chicago Press.

Sutter, Alan G. 1966. "The World of the Righteous Dope Fiend." *Issues in Criminology* 2:177–222.

Sykes, Gresham and David Matza. 1957. "Techniques of Neutralization: A Theory of Delinquency." *American Sociological Review* 22:664–70.

Topalli, Volkan. 2005. "When Being Good is Bad: An Expansion of Neutralization Theory." *Criminology* 43:797–836.

——. 2006. "The Seductive Nature of Autotelic Crime: How Neutralization Theory Serves as a Boundary Condition for Understanding Hardcore Offending." *Sociological Inquiry* 76:475–501.

Widdicombe, Sue. 1998. "But You Don't Class Yourself: The Interactional Management of Category Membership and Non-Membership." Pp. 52–70. In *Identities in Talk,* edited by C. Antaki and S. Widdicombe. Thousand Oaks, CA: Sage.

Williams, Terry. 1992. *Crackhouse: Notes from the End of the Line.* New York: Penguin Books.

Wright, Richard, Robert Logie, and Scott Decker. 1995. "Criminal Expertise and Offender Decision Making: An Experimental Study of the Target Selection Process in Residential Burglary." *Journal of Research in Crime and Delinquency* 32:39–53.

Wright, Richard and Scott Decker. 1994. *Burglars on the Job Street Life and Residential Break-Ins.* Boston: Northeastern University Press.

——. 1997. *Armed Robbers in Action.* Boston: Northeastern University Press.

Zerubavel, Eviatar. 1997. *Social Mindscapes: An Invitation to Cognitive Sociology.* Cambridge, MA: Harvard University Press.

18

Writing Against the Image of the Monstrous Crack Mother

Aline Gubrium

This article examines how the cultural stereotype of "monstrous crack mother" relates the experiences in the personal story of one African-American woman's involvement in the use of crack cocaine over a long period of time. The use of storytelling portrays the various ways culture is represented through one woman's account of her drug-related world and contrasts this drug world with her participation in a twelve-step rehabilitation program. The part her spirituality plays presents another side to the negative stereotype that exists for women who have been involved in the use of crack cocaine.

In *Managing Monsters: Six Myths of our Time*, Marina Warner (1994, 250) describes mothers who are represented as monsters in cinema. The film *Jurassic Park*, for example, portrays female characters, including dinosaurs, as out of control and/or domineering in the name of motherhood. The mother-as-monster image also is evident in media portrayals of women who use crack cocaine; African American users living in inner-city neighborhoods especially are depicted as grossly irresponsible mothers (Baker and Carson 1999; Lilt and McNeil 1994; Lubiano 1992; Roberts 1997). They are presented as lazy, overly reproductive, welfare-dependent women, who care more about their own material needs (crack) than their

children—perpetuating the associated view of a bio-underclass of "ruined" children or crack babies (Lilt and McNeil 1994; Roberts 1997; Willz 1996).

The mother on crack is seen as wholly unfit to properly care for children; she is not even aware of their needs (Lubiano 1992; Seccombe, James, and Walthers 1998). Racialized, this is deployed into a stigmatizing meta-narrative on Black mothering that comes in mythic proportions (Klee 1998). Wahneema Lubiano (1992) refers to this as a "cover story" that confers a hegemonic influence on maternal identity. Cover stories are used by the influential to obscure complexities hidden beneath and within. They are applied to others by those with the power to convey

---

Source: Writing Against the Image of the Monstrous Crack Mother by Gubrium, Aline, *Journal of Contemporary Ethnography, 37*(5), pp. 511–527. Reprinted with permission.

images, which, in their routine communication, telegraph the ostensibly obvious character of those portrayed: "Such narratives are so naturalized, so pushed by the momentum of their ubiquity that they seem to be the reality" (329).

This article examines how the cultural stereotype of the monstrous crack mother is "unsettled" by focusing on the narrative representation of experience in the personal story of an African American woman who has been a long-time user of crack cocaine. As Lila Abu-Lughod (1991) argues in her essay "Writing Against Culture," it is important to document the complexity of culture from below in storytelling, rather than in relation to a uniform cover story. By considering the various ways culture is represented in personal stories, in working through one woman's account, I highlight the flexibility of her usage as a way of demonstrating how narrative can differentially frame experience to contend with cultural stereotypes. My analysis first considers her use of the Twelve-Step recovery framework to present her experience and then her contrasting account of the spirituality that belies monstrosity.

Focusing on Muncell

Muncell is the pseudonym of an African American woman born in Port Charles, a small town located in North Central Florida. Muncell was 43 years old when I interviewed her. She had used crack for roughly 15 years over the course of two of her three pregnancies. She had been in one long-term relationship, but never married. At the time of the interview, she had a 23-year-old son and two daughters, 10 and 13 years of age. Her son resided out of state and her daughters lived intermittently with her or with their grandmother in a small town 15 miles away.

Muncell was interviewed as part of a larger study (Gubrium 2005) in which I conducted semi-structured interviews with 20 participants. Participants were rural African American women, between the ages of 18 and 65, living in or near Port Charles. The purpose of the larger study was to document the cultural contours of the gender socialization narratives of rural African American women. I was especially interested in how the women constructed their growing up experiences in relation to commonplace troubles such as narcotics addiction and domestic violence. Several community members had agreed to be interviewed after assisting in another research project on health-related dimensions of African American women's use of crack cocaine in the rural south (Brown 2003; Brown and Trujillo 2003).

Of the 20 women participating in my larger study, seven spoke of past or current addictions to crack cocaine. For this article, I chose to focus on the narrative of only one of the seven women, because her interview reflects the broadest range of narrative representation related to the monstrous mother stereotype. More than in the accounts of the other six women. Muncell applies aspects of two narrative resources—Twelve-Step recovery language and elements of African American spirituality—to narratively contend with the image of the monstrous crack mother.

Muncell was not selected on grounds of conventional representation; her story most extensively elaborates on the elements found to a lesser degree in the other women's stories. Several of the other women interviewed cast themselves more narrowly, while a few did come close to Muncell in the elaboration in their self-constructions. Muncell's account bears witness to the narrative possibilities that can grow from contending with a stereotype, the narrative and self-identifying imperatives she and women like her deal with on a daily basis.

As Muncell's narrative will show, Twelve-Step language serves to construct women on crack, among others, as individuals with a disease, an addiction, and as ultimately redeemable, but never fully cured, so long as they "work" the steps in the process toward recovery. Of particular concern here is Narcotics Anonymous (NA) discourse (NA 1986, 1992). This discourse highlights the strength that emanates from giving oneself over to a "Higher Power" in the service of recovery. In this facet of her account, she constructs herself in much the same way that Leslie Irvine's (1999) participants did in her book *Codependent Forevermore: The Invention of Self in a Twelve Step Group.*

Another narrative resource running through Muncell's interview relates to African American spirituality. Recent scholarship in the area of African American women's recovery from substance abuse has highlighted a different narrative resource, one that does not necessarily implicate institutional recovery, such as in a Twelve-Step program. Several studies have pointed to the integral connection between African American women's personal spiritual relationship with God, in particular spiritual and religious practices, including daily prayer and intimate conversations with God, and church attendance as effective in coping with and recovering from substance abuse (Brome et al. 2000; Brown 2006; Curtis-Boles and Jenkins-Monroe 2000; Green, Fullilove, and Fullilove 1998; Klein, Elifson, and Sterk 2006). For example, Emma J. Brown (2006) flags the importance of spirituality and religion in the everyday lives of rural African American women addicted to crack and examines the way that individual spirituality and personal religious practices affect recovery from addiction. By intentionally juxtaposing a Twelve-Step theme with a contrasting theme of spirituality—foregrounding spiritual strength as much as the shame of addiction—this analysis of Muncell's interview serves to write against cultural uniformity.

RECOUNTING ADDICTION AND RECOVERY

> God grant me the serenity to accept the things I cannot change, the courage to change the things I can, and the wisdom to know the difference. (NA 1986)

The narrative linkages of this "serenity" epigraph drawn from NA resonated significantly in Muncell's recollection of her addiction and recovery. In this context, she drew heavily from Twelve-Step discourse to redeem herself, but this did require an admission of failure and a continuing identity of a recovering addict. This plan of her account followed NA's narrative map (Pollner and Stein 1996), which is a pathway with three milestones: before drug use, during drug use, and after drug use (see Rafalovich 1999).

Before Drug Use

Muncell began the interview describing her family of origin, which consisted of nine surviving siblings and her mother. The family was "closeknit." All family members lived instate, six of her siblings nearby. Her mother for a time was a resident of a rehabilitation facility, hoping to save a leg threatened by gangrene resulting from diabetic complications.

In the Twelve-Step framework of her account, Muncell's description of her childhood was central to her conception of herself as an addict. The glowing description stood in marked contrast to the kinds of problems that she implied contributed to drug use as a form of self-medication. While her biological father died while she was quite young and she mentions being teased at school for being shy and her use of wigs to cover her sparse hair, these were not construed as precursors to her addiction. Rather, Muncell described her addiction as something innate to her personality— as an organic slate that was just waiting to emerge. Speaking in Twelve-Step terms, Muncell speaks of herself as one of two kinds of addict, whose body is naturally "allergic" to drugs and who, on smoking crack, loses control of herself (see Rafalovich 1999).

A charmed upbringing was no defense against a propensity to addiction. She explains:

> I had a drug problem, and the drugs got worse and worse! I couldn't hold a job. Some people could work and smoke crack and I don't see how they could do it. But I was one that couldn't smoke crack. I couldn't just get me one hit and then I'm through. I would call and tell them [at work] that I couldn't make it, or make certain kind of lies, you know. It's a mind thing. It's that kind of thing.

Muncell spoke of her initial crack use as occurring in the mid-1980s, when her boyfriend brought a piece of crack back from a big city south of Port Charles, encouraging her to "try it." Once she tried crack, she found that it was not easy to give up. While her boyfriend was able to quit using after five years, she could not shake her habit for ten years after that, despite her boyfriend's pleas—she being the type who was naturally "allergic" to drugs. Muncell does not blame her boyfriend for her addiction, even though he introduced her to the drug. Rather, as she "works a step," she takes full responsibility for her addiction in admitting that she and her body were to blame. At this point of her story, what led up to her addiction was not as morally consequential for her identity as what happened from that point onward.

During Drug Use

Elaborating this framework, Muncell soon begins to represent her growing monstrosity in Twelve-Step terms. She contrasts her identity now, as a capable mother, with the way she used to be, when she was "swallowed up by addiction" (see Rafalovich 1999).

> I got girls coming up and they seein' me like this, and my son, you know, he was like, you know, always sayin' things. Like, I was a crackhead. When he would get mad with me. You know, that hurt. I'm different now because I don't. I don't smoke crack no more. And it make me, you know, I can do things with my kids. I can hold a job now. I can keep a car. You know. I can pay my bills without messin' my money up. And I can keep money in my pocketbook. And um . . . uh, that's different (laughs). Because when I was smoking crack I couldn't keep anything. You know. I would crack (my body) up, punt it out, sell it out. You know. I was doin' it all . . . I was just doin' anything to, to make my money to get . . . get my high.

Muncell relates that her son, her oldest child, had a difficult childhood as a result of her addiction. One outcome was that he grew up an "angry young man" witnessing the effects of his mother's drug use throughout much of his youth and altogether dismissed her as a mothering figure up until recently, when she was able to apologize for her past indiscretions and make amends as a recovering addict.

Vividly detailing the depths of her drug-induced depravity in "hitting bottom," or in Muncell's terms "rock bottom," she explained that her attention focused exclusively on acquiring crack, her children often relegated to the sidelines of what became a drugging lifestyle.

> The drugs got worse and worse! So I couldn't hold a job. I started hanging out. Cause, like I say, if I'm going to work, here comes somebody with piece [of crack] there. I started staying out . . . and I had to slap my own face and like, now I'm up and, you know, I've been up a whole week. I hadn't really had any *sleep*! Nothing too much to eat. And I would rent my, I would get new cars and vans. Nice vehicles. And I would rent 'em out to, when I got no money. I would rent 'em out to the dope boys. You know, and that was bad! That was bad! And then people come. I done prayed and read my Bible. People come knocking on my back door (knocks on the table), late at night, you know. And my kids had got used to it because, I was in my own home with my girls and . . . and I would leave 'em! I was stoned on crack, honey. I would get me my chair right up there by the back window and I would crawl out that window and go! And I would go and stay and, and my oldest daughter, she was just a little something but she end up towing the younger one next door to my mom's . . . late, late at night. Knocking on the door. So then my mom was like, she couldn't really rest when I was home because she didn't know . . . when I was gonna jump and leave the kids in the house as I did. Some other times I end up hauling them in the back seat of my car. And they would cry and they'd wanna go home and I would still be tryin' to get a piece together of crack. You know? I mean, I went down . . . (makes a hissing sound) . . . I mean. I, I know I did. Cause I went *way* down! Like this carpet here, like you stepping on it. I mean, it was just . . . I know I hit rock bottom because I *lost* a lot. I lost everything. The things I would do. Like I say, I lost everything and looked like I was losing *everybody*. You know, losing out on my family and . . . friends . . . I didn't have a lot of them.

The account speaks of the lows to which Muncell sank. Describing her maternal relations with her daughters, Muncell noted that they often came second to procuring crack. She points to the responsibility that her older daughter had to take on while still quite young to protect her even younger sister from neglect, and does not even include her son in the picture—perhaps because he had already had enough with her drugging lifestyle and was living with a friend at the time. Integral to the during-drug-use phase of a Twelve-Step narrative is when the recovering addict tells her "rock bottom" story—of being in the throes of addiction and what this was like for the addict and those around her (Brown & Trujillo 2003). Muncell describes herself as an out-of-control mother who abandoned her children to satisfy a craving, casting herself in the stereotypical role of crack mother who prioritizes drug use above everything. In this phase of the typical Twelve-Step narrative, crack has taken over and produced the monstrous drug user, in Muncell's case the monstrous crack mother. She elaborates on the lengths she would go to obtain crack, endangering her children to acquire it, and harming herself and others in the process. She details the monstrosity of being "willing to do almost anything to get crack." In the world of crack use, one's primary concern is "the score." Portraying herself as a "real mess," this is clearly a self to loathe.

True to the Twelve-Step story, Muncell describes the horrors and tragedies that resulted from her addiction. She describes herself as "doing things she never thought she would do," such as selling food stamps and her body to buy crack. She lost things that were valuable to her, including her job, her children, her home, and her self-respect. The monstrous mother is now the complete crackhead her son assailed: "I was no different from [other crack users] when I was out there in the world, you know, I did it all!"

Stripped of the special circumstances of her addiction, she is reduced to being one of many who typify individuals with a raging problem, monstrously portrayed in the dominant image.

Muncell "bottoms out" in two ways, and thus begins to tame the endless stigmatic descent. In one way, she bottoms out through institutional influence, in which she is finally forced to attend a 60-day treatment facility for addicts, having been threatened with having her children taken away if she does not. Muncell relates:

> I was made to go to rehab. And I went to rehab for sixty. I *had* to go to a sixty-one day program. I had to go. Or they was gonna take the kids. So I went, and did me sixty-one days. Cause I was messing up the food stamps, you know. I was selling food stamps and . . . everything else. Couldn't maintain . . . a job. I could get them . . . but I couldn't keep 'em, because of the crack.

In the process she evokes the image of the monstrous crack mother who is concerned more about acquiring crack than she is about the well being of her own children. Referring to the poor Black mother's nightmare of being investigated for her worthiness as a mother by "the man," she reiterates how in the end she was given a choice by child welfare services of entering a drug rehabilitation program or losing her children.

However, perhaps more important to Muncell than being forced to attend a rehab program is her betrayal of the faith that her family constantly held out for her to quit using crack. Though her family was always supportive, even during her drug binges, after ten years her addiction was so bad that they could no longer offer support: "So my mom and them really, they didn't want to [call child welfare], but they really got tired of me and I was driving them *crazy*! Cause you know, when you on, on a drug like that, and you got a family that really care for you and love you. It bothered them also, it just got to be where they can't rest, they can't, you know, it really bothered them." In this way, she links the institutional and the interpersonal, with Muncell's family instigating "the call" that led to her forced participation in a drug rehab program.

Completing the rehabilitation program, Muncell said that she managed to stay sober for six months. However, on her birthday that year, she and her boyfriend decided to use crack, reasoning that she should have been able to control her addiction after going through the program. Reflecting back on this experience, Muncell appropriates a Twelve-Step narrative framework to differentiate between passively "going through" rehabilitation and actively "working" the steps of the program on the path to recovery. From a Twelve-Step perspective, she was not taking the creed to heart if she was able to rationalize her drug use. Indeed, as a now recovering addict, she admits that she was not the type of person who could use crack in moderate quantities. Describing herself as someone who "binges until [she] passes out," she constructs herself as one who will never really fully recover from her addiction, again confirming Twelve-Step reasoning.

Falling off the wagon after her participation in the rehabilitation program, Muncell explains that she "got back out there for seven years again" and "fell apart." She takes up Twelve-Step language in contrasting a drug-using world "out there" with a sober, safer world "inside," reproducing the parallel "us" (addicts) and "them" (the sober community) found in NA texts (see Rafalovich 1999). At this point, this time at "rock bottom," she describes an epiphany of sorts—the moment when a virtual looking-glass self spoke directly to her, telescoping her monstrous maternal identity (Cooley 1964/1902). She looked into a mirror and saw her addicted self reflected back.

[I was talking] to myself in the mirror. I'm saying, "This is not me! Why can't I stop?" My question was "Why?! Why do this?" I hurt my mom. I'm giving her all this pressure with the kids and me on top of that, but she's still holding on, trying to help. So (sighs), every day and night. I look [in the mirror] and I talk and cry. And I want to drive my vehicle into another vehicle when I done went out there and messed up my money, and I can't get no more crack. I'm ready to die. And I'm like, "Lord, if I got to live like this, why don't you just take me away? Please take me out of this world, so I won't have to live like this!"

It is at this point that Muncell finally asks God to "grant her serenity," to either help her to overcome her addiction or to let her die.

An integral component of a Twelve-Step program is the narrative of recovery, such that storytelling and/or relating one's past experiences are crucial to the practice of recovery itself. Thus, Muncell was actively practicing recovery by focusing so much on her "crack story" during her interview. In this relatively public discussion of her past behavior and emphasis on the way that she "once was." Muncell relates that she was able to quit using crack "cold turkey" three years preceding our interview, perhaps ironically, on Mother's Day.

After Drug Use

Muncell turns to her recovery, which in a Twelve-Step discourse one is said to never fully achieve (Rafalovich 1999). She speaks of God as being in the driver's seat on her road to recovery, which figures into the Twelve-Step logic of turning one's life over to a Higher Being to reclaim one's life. The crux of a Twelve-Step program rests on the assumption that the only way an addict is going to maintain sobriety is by forming a strong relationship with a higher power (NA 1986).

The shame of addiction is given over to a growing serenity. Muncell speaks of herself at this point as being God's servant, working the Twelve Steps by "serving the Lord" through prayer and good deeds. As if to construct a small part for herself in a more positive cosmic drama, Muncell refers to her former addiction and her current recovery as a "plan" that God had for her. She is to serve as a role model for other crack addicts, and to talk to them about their own problems as a way to begin the process toward recovery: "I like to help 'em [others addicted to crack]. You know, I talk to 'em. But . . . I can't do it for 'em. They have to do it for themselves, um hmm. But if they start talking to me about they problems, you know. I'm here to, you know, talk to 'em." While she encourages other addicts to speak with her about their problems, she also takes up a Twelve-Step perspective in relating that the only way to achieve sobriety is for the addict to walk the road to recovery herself.

The Spiritual Strength That Challenges Monstrosity

Muncell did not speak directly of African American spirituality in her interview. But her repeated references to her relationship with God, daily prayer, and the strength and salvation she has gained through her connection with God unsettles a stereotype based on a recovery narrative. While in one framework Muncell may be seen as avidly taking up Twelve-Step discourse to construct her addiction, another framework gains inspiration from the significance of spirituality and religion in the everyday lives of African American women (Abrums 2000; Gubrium 2005; Black 1999; Callahan 2006; Eugene 1995; Mattis 2000, 2002; McRae, Thompson, and Cooper 1999; Newlin, Knafl, and Melkus 2002; Wilson and Miles 2001). In this framework, Muncell's story illuminates the importance of a distinctly cultural spirituality in dealing with life's trials and tribulations. The narrative imperative of the monstrous mother image again recedes, but this time in relation to her cultural heritage, not in relation to the amelioration narrative of Twelve-Step recovery shared by many Americans. Black or White. Here, her story unsettles Twelve-Step recovery as "the way back" from being a monstrous mother, putting in its place a different cultural theme on the indigenous spiritual strength that challenges monstrosity.

In the Framework of Personal Spirituality

Like many of the other women interviewed for my larger project on gender socialization, Muncell spoke of growing up in the church: "Well, we often went to church. When we was young, sometimes we were ... *made* to go. And up to the day, I go, but I don't go like I should go. But I still give God the praise. And ... um ... I do have sisters, they be there every time the churches are open (laughs)." Discussing her church background, Muncell made a clear distinction between church attendance and one's spirituality. In her interview she referred to being forced to attend church.

In this framework, Muncell exhorted the importance of her own spirituality and God's personal involvement to help her and her family to get by. Rather than describing herself as an addict strengthened through fellowship with other addicts, as might be

realized in the Twelve Steps, Muncell instead spoke of the painful conversations that she had with God in trying to overcome her addiction, even while she borrows from Twelve-Step language.

> You know, I just did different things when I hit rock bottom. I would go out to the grave yard and I would lay out there and I would scream to the Lord ... you know, I'd scream so loud, you know, because I really got tired. And I was like ... you know, I asked the Lord to deliver me and *help* me ... and ... I'm praying and asking, this man up here, because all the time, he know. God knows ya,' cause he made us.

Muncell's exhortations to God were made in solitude, away from an institutional structure that may have told her to work the steps to achieve sobriety. Indeed, Muncell narratively counterposes her stay at the 61-day rehab facility, and the eventual failure that this program was for her on the one hand, with her success with her individual ministrations to God and the realization that no one was going to quit using crack for her, on the other. Through God's help she needed to make this decision for herself.

> I realized [that I needed to quit] on a Sunday (Mother's Day). And it's that Monday that I finally quit. So I stopped that Monday. And um ... like I say, a lot of people prayed for me. But you gotta really want to do something yourself. You gotta wanna stop doing things yourself. So I did. So I really, really got, um ... sincere about, you know, stopping. You know. God was first. And so, I started praying and reading my Bible ... all kind of little good things, different things that were really working and helping me. And um ... then I, like I said, I started working with a little bit and got me a job and I started, you know, getting myself together. And ... ever since that day, up to now, you know, like I say, I've been clean.

Muncell spoke of the debt of gratitude that she owed God in helping her to overcome her addiction, while also speaking of the strength that she gained through her spiritual convictions. While she is fortified through her connections with God as described in a Twelve-Step discourse, in more distinctly Afrocentric terms she falls back on the faith that was ostensibly always there within reach to help her become the person she once was: "It's a great feeling, you know, I feel like I'm me again. You know, cause when I was out there smoking crack it was like ... it wasn't me. I was a *whole* totally different person. Really, I was a mess!"

Muncell spoke of her "true" self as a caring woman who took pains to protect her family from her addiction and who has worked as a certified nursing assistant over the course of her adult life, caring for others—a description that comes close to applying the myth of the strong Black woman so commonly found in portrayals of Black womanhood (cf. Beauboeuf-Lafontant 2003, 2005; Cole and Guy-Sheflall 2003; Mullings 2002, 2006). Working the narrative borders of what it means to be a strong Black woman, Muncell refers to her career as a certified nursing assistant employed in a nursing home in University Town, located 40 miles from Port Charles. The job is not presented as something she would eventually lose, but as a remnant of her former self. During her interview she described her calling to the nursing profession as a desire to care for other people: "I just like working with people that need my help. I really do. And I wanted, I have always wanted to do that." Despite her inability to hold onto a job while addicted to crack, Muncell emphasized that she always had a job or was always actively in search of another one. This contrasts with the view that crack addicts are lazy individuals "soaking off the system."

Muncell also contrasted her adherence to the myth of the strong Black woman with her own selfish pursuits, in which she prioritized acquiring and using crack over the well-being of her children and her relationship with God. In this context, while she may have been "strong on the outside," on the inside her spirituality was weak, her own selfishness emanating from a spiritual naiveté. She was not mindful of God and guarding that precious gift that God had made to her.

She evoked this spiritual naiveté while tracing her drug use through two of her three pregnancies. Muncell was not using crack when she was 20 years old and first pregnant with her son, but related that she had begun using crack by the time she gave birth to her first daughter ten years later. She continued to use crack through the birth of her second daughter, three years after that. She nonetheless marveled at the successful birth of big and healthy babies, events that ostensibly worked against the odds and certainly against the alleged birthing outcomes of crack addiction.

> I had [my son] in '81. And I started using drugs in, I wanna say '86, yeah. And I was pregnant, ten years after I had my son. I got pregnant. So I was using drugs. I used drugs the whole time while I was carrying my [first daughter]. So, and um, I even went to the hospital high. I was getting high while I was in labor, you know. And then, she came out okay and beautiful, and beautiful today. *Thank God* we don't, we didn't, you know, she didn't have HIV or nothing. And three years later I was still smoking crack and I used it with my next baby! And she was bigger than him and bigger [than her]! She done beat both of 'em! But healthy and well,

everything's okay. Smart in school, A/B honor roll student. And I used drugs with both of the girls the whole time.

In the framework of what Muncell now relates to be the work of God in protecting her family from the potentially deleterious effects of using crack while pregnant, "back then" was viewed as somewhat of a surprise. What might have been spun into yet another tale of a monstrous mother contributing to the production of bio-underclass of crack babies (and possibly ameliorated through a Twelve-Step experience) is subverted by Muncell through a spiritual metaphor. She marvels at the unexpected biological success of her daughters because of God's grace on them.

Cognizant of the narrative details swirling beneath the cover story of ruined crack babies, Muncell contrasts images of listless, underweight babies plagued by breathing and heart problems on one hand, with the births of her two large and healthy daughters on the other. Her babies flourished in comparison, the birth of a smaller infant son born before she had even begun to use crack. She had successful daughters, who soon were to become strong Black young women in their own right despite the odds. And of equal importance, this was because of God's protection, transcending what might have been a tragic story.

In this narrative framework, Muncell has been able to look the monster of addiction in the face and through God's help wrestle with her demons to become a better woman and caring mother. Virtually echoing bell hooks' (1981, 1984) call to Black women to develop their own feminist theories because nobody else is going to do this for them, Muncell has fashioned what is now a self-reliance story informed by spiritually wizened sensibilities. If Muncell describes herself as having exposed her children to danger in her quest for crack cocaine, she now undermines the individual failure theme of Twelve-Step discourse by recollecting that God has always been there to help protect her children. What may be overlooked in a Twelve-Step framework is that women who use crack cocaine do not exist in a cultural vacuum. The importance of Twelve-Step language supports the alleged bad mothering of all addicted women, because it is drawn through a lens that ignores the particularities of culture, in this case the importance of spirituality in the African American community.

CONCLUSION

It would be inappropriate to ask whether the Twelve Steps or Afrocentric spirituality best describes Muncell's recovery experience. Instead, this article has treated them as narrative resources, asking how their frameworks can be used to unsettle cultural stereotypes. Muncell's identity work does not unfold in relation to a uniform understanding of women of her experience, but rather she takes on board from the variety of ways of framing herself that her particular social circumstances make available to her (see Butler 1990; Holstein and Gubrium 2000; Schrag 1997). As symbolic interactionists, third-wave feminists, and some postmodern scholars advocate, a turn to the work that is done in articulating identity directs our attention to multiplicity rather than homogeneity, to the use of cultural particulars rather than to its reproduction (Chase 2001; Loseke 2001; Snow and Anderson 1987). Equally important are the resources available for doing identity work, which the case material presented here shows is not uniformly available to everyone in society.

Muncell applied both Twelve-Step and Afrocentric spirituality discourses to contend with the image of the monstrous crack mother that challenged who and what she had become as a woman. Being African American, she and other Black women have an indigenous narrative resource in Afrocentric spirituality that is unavailable to other groups, a spirituality that valorizes the potential for good mothering underneath it all. In that sense, she and others like her can contend with the identity implications of monstrous crack motherhood in a way specific to themselves, even while they do and can share other narrative resources such as Twelve-Step discourse with other groups.

I note two implications of recognizing such differences. First, differences in narrative resources offer groups distinctive ways of assembling their identities and, relatedly, constructing their cultures. What bad, monstrous, or even good mothering for that matter means, depends on the resources available to assign them meaning. The resources that one group, such as African American women, have as part of their cultural heritage, is not available to other groups. Other groups, in turn, may have indigenous resources unavailable to African American women. In that regard, it would be disingenuous, if also empirically inappropriate, to treat them all as members of the same social category, such as all being crack mothers, or even monstrous mothers, whose recovery is understandable through a common language of recovery.

A second implication relates to social, especially health, policy. Social researchers and policy makers need a more robust way of capturing a target population's experiences with problems such as mothering on crack cocaine and their stereotypes. They need to look to the potential for contending with problems, not just what is typically done or said, which is the reason Muncell's interview, in particular, was selected for analysis. Putting into place the concept of narrative resources, which Muncell's interview evoked more than the others, turns us to the ways culture can be made meaningful. Monstrous motherhood is a tremendous experiential burden for women. We would do well to document the narrative tools that women variously have available for dealing with this before striving headlong to formulate uniform interventions based on homogenized statuses such as crack users, mothers, or even African American crack mothers.

Muncell's story is useful precisely because she is narratively an outlier. Her story can serve to inform us as social researchers, women with addictions and policy makers, of the varied ways one *could* tell one's story and, in turn, the varied ways one *could* understand one's troubles and their stigmatizing consequences for identity. It is the outliers of social distributions that inform us of what, for better or worse, we could do to unsettle culture and destigmatize experience.

REFERENCES

Abrums, Mary. 2000. "Jesus will fix it after awhile": meanings and health. *Social Science & Medicine* 50:89–105.

Abu-Lughod, Lila. 1991. Writing against culture. In *Recapturing anthropology: Working in the present,* ed. R. G. Fox. Santa Fe: School of American Research Press.

Baker, Phyllis L., and Amy Carson. 1999. "I take care of my kids": mothering practices of substance-abusing women. *Gender and Society* 13 (3): 347–63.

Beauboeuf-Lafontant, Tamara. 2003. Strong and large Black women? Exploring relationships between deviant womanhood and weight. *Gender & Society* 17 (1): 111–21.

——. 2005. Keeping up appearances, getting fed up: the embodiment of strength among African American women. *Meridians: Feminism, Race, Transnationalism* 5 (2): 104–23.

Black, Helen K. 1999. Life as gift: spiritual narratives of elderly African American women living in poverty. *Journal of Aging Studies* 13 (4): 441–55.

Brome, Deborah Ridley, Michelle Deaneen Owens, Karen Allen, and Tinaz Vevaina. 2000. An examination of spirituality among African American women in recovery from substance abuse. *Journal of Black Psychology* 26 (4): 470–86.

Brown, Emma J. 2003. Double whammy: accessing, recruiting and retaining the hidden of the hidden. *Journal of Ethnicity in Substance Abuse* 2(1): 43–51.

——. 2006. The integral place of religion in the lives of rural African American women who use cocaine. *Journal of Religion and Health* 45 (1): 19–39.

Brown, Emma J., and Teresa Henchan Trujillo. 2003. "Bottoming out?" among rural African American women who use cocaine. *Rural Health Research* 19 (4): 441–49.

Butler, Judith. 1990. *Gender trouble: Feminism and the subversion of identity.* New York: Routledge.

Callahan, Allen Dwight. 2006. *The talking book: African Americans and the Bible.* New Haven: Yale University Press.

Chase, Susan. 2001. Universities as discursive environments for sexual identity construction. In *Institutional selves,* ed. Jaber F. Gubrium and James A. Holstein, 142–157. New York: Oxford University Press.

Cole, Johnnetta Betsch, and Beverly Guy-Sheftall. 2003. *Gender talk: the struggle for women's equality in African American communities.* New York: Ballantine.

Cooley, Charles Horton. 1964/1902. *Human nature and the social order.* New York: Scribner.

Curtis-Boles, Harriet, and Valata Jenkins-Monroe. 2000. Substance abuse in African American women. *Journal of Black Psychology* 26 (4): 450–69.

Eugene, Toinette M. 1995. There is a balm in Gilead: Black women and the Black church as agents of a therapeutic community. *Women & Therapy* 16 (2–3): 55–71.

Green, Lesley L., Mindy Thompson Fullilove, and Robert E. Fullilove. 1998. Stories of spiritual awakening: the nature of spirituality in recovery. *Journal of Substance Abuse Treatment* 15 (4): 325–31.

Gubrium, Aline. 2005. Growing up stories: narratives of rural African American women. PhD diss. University of Florida, Gainesville.

Holstein, James A., and Jaber F. Gubrium. 2000. *The self we live by: narrative identity in a postmodern world.* New York: Oxford University Press.

Hooks, Bell. 1981. *Ain't I a woman: Black women and feminism.* Boston: South End Press.

——. 1984. *Feminist theory: from margin to center.* Boston: South End.

Irvine, Leslie. 1999. *Codependent forevermore: the invention of self in a twelve step group.* Chicago: University of Chicago Press.

Klee, Hilary. 1998. Drug-using parents: analyzing the stereotypes. *International Journal of Drug Policy* 9:437–48.

Klein, Hugh, Kirk W. Elifson, and Claire E. Sterk. 2006. The relationship between religiosity and drug use among "at risk" women. *Journal of Religion and Health* 45 (J): 40–56.

Lilt, Jacquelyn, and Maureen McNeil. 1994. "Crack babies" and the politics of reproduction and nurturance. In *Troubling children: studies of children and social problems,* ed. J. Best. New York: de Gruyter.

Loseke, Donilene. 2001. Lived realities and formula stories of "battered women." In *Institutional selves,* ed. Jaber R Gubrium and James A. Holstein, 107–126. New York: Oxford University Press.

Lubiano, Wahneema. 1992. Black ladies, welfare queens, and state minstrels: ideological war by narrative means. In *Racing justice, en-gendering power: essays on Anita Hill, Clarence Thomas, and the construction of social reality,* ed. T. Morrison. New York: Pantheon.

Mattis, Jacqueline S. 2000. African American women's definitions of spirituality and religiosity. *Journal of Black Psychology* 26(1): 101–22.

——. 2002. Religion and spirituality in the meaning-making and coping experiences of African American women: a qualitative analysis. *Psychology of Women Quarterly* 26:309–21.

McRae, Mars B., Delores A. Thompson, and Sharon Cooper. 1999. Black churches as therapeutic groups. *Journal of Multicultural Counseling and Development* 27 (4): 207–20.

Mullings, Leith. 2002. The Sojourner syndrome: race, class, and gender in health and illness. *Voices* 6 (1): 32–36.

——. 2006. Resistance and resilience: The Sojourner syndrome and the social context of reproduction in central Harlem. In *Gender, race, class & health: intersectional approaches,* ed. A. J. Schulz and L. Mullings. San Francisco: Jossey-Bass.

Narcotics Anonymous. 1986. *NA white booklet.* Narcotics Anonymous World Services, Inc.

——. 1992. *Another look.* Narcotics Anonymous World Services, Inc.

Newlin, Kelley, Kathleen Knafl, and Gail D'Eramo Melkus. 2002. African American spirituality: a concept analysis. *Advances in Nursing Science* 25 (2): 57–70.

Pollner, M., and J. Stein. 1996. Narrative mapping of social worlds: the voice of experience in Alcoholics Anonymous. *Symbolic Interaction* 19 (3): 203–23.

Rafalovich, Adam. 1999. Keep coming back! Narcotics Anonymous narrative and recovering-addict identity. *Contemporary Drug Problems* 26 (Spring): 131–157.

Roberts, Dorothy. 1997. Making reproduction a crime. In *Killing the Black body: Race, reproduction, and the meaning of liberty,* ed. D. Roberts. New York: Vintage.

Schrag, Calvin O. 1997. *The Self after postmodernity.* New Haven: Yale University Press.

Seccombe, Karen, Delores James, and Kimberly Battle Walters. 1998. "They think you ain't much of nothing": the social construction of the welfare mother. *Journal of Marriage and the Family* 60 (4): 849–865.

Snow, David, and Leon Anderson. 1987. Identity work among the homeless: the verbal construction and avowal of personal identities. *American Journal of Sociology* 92: 1336–71.

Warner, Marina. 1994. *Managing monsters: Six myths of our time, the Reith lectures.* London: Vintage.

Wilson, Sonja M., and Margaret S. Miles. 2001. Spirituality in African American mothers coping with a seriously ill infant. *Journal of the Society of Pediatric Nurses* 6 (3) (electronic): 1–6.

Willz, Teresa. 1996. Kicking crack. *Essence:* 1–6.

PART VII

GENDER AND CRIME

Until the 1970s, interest in women's involvement in crime was thought to be not very serious in nature. Due to gender roles, women offenders were most often involved in prostitution, child abuse, shoplifting, and the like. However, in the era of the 1970s through the 1990s, women's involvement in more serious crimes was thought to have increased. But according to official crime data, women are still arrested for the same minor crimes that they have committed historically. Although women's crime rates for more serious crimes are somewhat higher than in the past, their poverty rate, victimization, and economic dependency is more likely an explanation for their increased offense rate.

In order to provide some insight into women's involvement in what is considered more masculine criminal behavior, the selections in this part of the anthology analyze female crimes that are atypical of the majority of offenses that women usually commit.

Candace Kruttschnitt and Kristin Carbone-Lopez's study of women who commit violent crime attempted to uncover just how these women construct their participation in the use of violence against another person. In short, what were their motivations to commit such a serious criminal act? Their analysis consisted of narratives provided through key interviews with 205 women incarcerated at a large metropolitan jail. The authors attempted to understand the various types of motivating factors the sample group provided. They analyzed the life events of their jail sample group of women 36 months prior to their incarceration to find their involvement in violent criminal events, both as victims and perpetrators. They found 66 female jail inmates being involved in 106 violent incidents within 36 months prior to their incarceration, and that there was a wide range of violent events that occurred. The authors concluded that women's acts of violence cannot be stereotyped on the basis of gender alone.

In her analysis of elite prostitutes, Ann M. Lucas collected data from call-girls and escorts through an interview process that explored prostitutes' perceptions of the world of sex work. Lucas utilizes prostitution as work, as a model in which to study the attitudes and experiences from an elite prostitute's viewpoint within the context of an illegal activity. These women view themselves as providing a service and perceive competency and integrity as important characteristics of their trade. Factors that contribute to the meaning of work for elite prostitutes include their career orientations, customer relations, their consumer market, and their views of prostitution in general.

The last article on gender discusses the relationship between being a mother, criminal activity, and being imprisoned. Here, Kathleen J. Ferraro and Angela M. Moe focus on the relationships between violent victimization and incarceration of economically marginalized women who committed crimes for monetary benefit to avoid homelessness or hunger. Those women who had children experienced the socioeconomic results of unequal division of labor as well as opportunities to not accept their marginalized status in society.

19

MOVING BEYOND THE STEREOTYPES

Women's Subjective Accounts of Their Violent Crime

CANDACE KRUTTSCHNITT AND KRISTIN CARBONE-LOPEZ

This research focuses on a wide range of violent behavior committed by women who are incarcerated in county jail. The analysis looks at female violence in both private and public domains and particularly concentrates on the role of situational aspects in relation to drugs, alcohol, and weapons as well. Race contributes to violent encounters and also to the types of explanations the interviewed women provide for their involvement.

S cholars, the courts, and especially the media have shown increasing interest in women's involvement in violent crime. However, their interest in this topic has been perhaps more prurient than analytic. Focusing in particular on women who kill, the question has been, how do we explain this aberration in the "kinder and gentler" sex? The answers appear to have changed relatively little over time and include biological defects, hormonal influences or, more recently, psychological syndromes that emerge from a history of severe victimization (Downs, 1996; Rasche, 1990). What all of these approaches have in common is that they deny women's agency or the possibility that women are involved in violent acts as active, rational human subjects (Morrissey, 2003).

There is, however, a growing body of literature that is beginning to question these common "anti-agentic"

views of women's violent offending. Some have pointed to the need society has for abnormalizing women's violence, arguing that to view violence by women as normative endangers traditional scripts about women's appropriate place in society and gendered social boundaries (Gilbert, 2002; Jones, 1980; Stanko, 2001). Others challenge feminists' general unwillingness to acknowledge that women's acts of violence aren't always a product of personal or social oppression (Daly, 1994: 131; Morrissey, 2003). But, to date, relatively few scholars have actually examined how women depict and characterize their involvement in violent crimes and even fewer have moved out of the realm of what might be considered the somewhat atypical act of violence— homicide (for example, Baskin and Sommers, 1998; Maher, 1997; Maher and Curtis, 1998; Matravers, 2006; Miller, 1998, 2001)

Source: Moving Beyond the Stereotypes: Women's Subjective Accounts of Their Violent Crime by Kruttschnitt, Candace and Kristin Carbone-Lopez, *Criminology*, 44(2), 2006. Reprinted with permission from the American Society of Criminology.

We aim to contribute to this scholarship by analyzing narratives of 106 incidents in which sixty-six women used violence toward another person, whether an intimate partner or someone else. We want to determine how they construct their involvement in these violent incidents. Do they describe them, consistent with the dominant depictions of women's violent offending found in popular culture and scholarly discourse, as a response to their victimization or do they convey other motivations that may arise from broader social disparities—motivations described in the criminological literature as disrespect and self-help (Black, 1983, 1993; Wolfgang, 1958: 191)? Although narrative analysis is certainly not new, it remains provocative and important precisely because it has "transformative" potential, serving to rewrite common assumptions and social scripts (Ewick and Silbey, 1995; more generally see, for example, Abu-Lughod, 1993; Rollins, 1995).

AGENCY AND INTERSECTIONALITY

The problem with an approach that pits the aggressive and inherently evil female offender against the victimized or incapacitated offender is that it ignores the complexity of gender identities and fails to see women as active subjects and responsible human beings (see Downs, 1996; Miller, 2001; Morrissey, 2003; Motz, 2001). Recent ethnographic work on female offenders, though not ignoring gender distinctions in crime, suggests that women's involvement in violence, like men's, has multiple motives and meanings in different contexts.

In one of the earlier attempts to deconstruct women's involvement in violent crime, Baskin and Sommers (1998) conducted life history interviews with 170 black and Hispanic women in three "hyperghettoized" neighborhoods in New York City. The framework for this research encompasses a more traditional "generalizability" approach to the study of women and crime (see Daly and Chesney-Lind, 1988), examining the relevance of social learning, control, and disorganization theories for understanding the nature and timing of women's participation in violent crime. Nevertheless, their findings challenge "generic and gender-based generalizations" about violent female offending (Baskin and Sommers, 1998: 146). Women's motivations for offending and their choice of victims were often rational (to recover stolen money or to avenge a disrespectful act, for example) but not devoid of gendered considerations as they were careful to target those who looked weak or vulnerable. The authors' life history perspectives also provide important insights into how the timing of initiation into offending shapes

opportunities for either gender-congruent or more wide-ranging criminal lifestyles.

Perhaps the most central study in this field is Lisa Maher's (1997) ethnography of forty-five racially diverse women living and working in the drug markets of the Bushwick neighborhood in Brooklyn, New York. Focusing on the problem of the overdetermined female offender, she shows how women navigate their way through the highly gendered informal economy that governs drug sales and consumption. Given women's limited access to making money in the drug market, they turn not only to selling their bodies but also robbing their clients. But, she argues, the violence perpetrated by these women was largely reactive, a response to their living conditions and the collapsing economy rather than evidence of a new breed of violent female offenders. Maher's study is also notable for the attention it draws to intersectionality, or the ways in which the confluence of race and gender shape interaction and outcomes. Race was critical in determining women's life chances, influencing when they worked, how often they worked, and how much they earned (Maher, 1997: 202–3). And, though all women operating in the drug market were at a relative disadvantage compared to men, as is true in the legal market economy, white women fared better than minorities.

Miller's (2001) ethnography of primarily black gang (N = 48) and nongang (N = 46) girls in St. Louis and Columbus furthers this line of work by illustrating the importance of particular structural contexts in determining how gender is played out. Here we learn that though the motives for gang involvement are not necessarily gendered, the types and levels of their involvement in gang activities are. Further, Miller's analyses of these girls' subjective views of their positions and activities in the gang reveal a surprising level of complexity: though they readily acknowledge that the gangs reify existing gender relations, they are able to see themselves as operating outside of this traditional framework.

Finally, in a somewhat different vein, yet also challenging the dominant narratives of women and violence, Gartner and McCarthy (2006) examined police records of 103 neo-naticides and infanticides committed over the course of the twentieth century in Seattle and Buffalo. They also reviewed coroners' records to examine the characteristics of cases involving newborn and infant deaths that went officially unrecorded. Probing the veracity of the stock portrayals of women who kill their children as "mad, bad, or victims," they do find that the female perpetrators were often constrained by poverty, social isolation, and other personal problems. However, they also discover evidence suggesting that many of these women were rational and resourceful when disposing of their children.

These studies each suggest that we are only beginning to uncover the subjectivities of women offenders. They also suggest that though gender plays a role in the nature of women's involvement in crime, it is not the entire story. As these works highlight, where and under what conditions a crime occurs—in disadvantaged neighborhoods, in drug markets, and in gangs—has as much to do with the patterns and motives of criminal activity as gender, at least in terms of street level violence. Yet, as Gartner and McCarthy's (2006) study suggests, much of women's violence is private. Controversy continues over whether women's involvement in domestic violence is primarily reactive or proactive (Johnson, 1995), but less attention has been given to the ways in which structural position and context influence how women construct and understand their involvement in domestic violence. Richie's (1996) unique exploration of the life histories of incarcerated black and white women remains an important exception. Although essentializing the victimization experiences of these offenders, the findings draw attention to the way in which race conditions the formation of gender identity and the implications this has for intimate relationships, especially when they involve violence (Richie, 1996:157–58).

In the following analysis, we aim to build on this body of research challenging dominant conceptions of women's involvement in violent crime. Our work, however, differs in at least two important respects from previous research in this area. First, we focus neither on celebrated acts of homicide that are largely decontextualized nor gang or drug activity that, by its very nature, may be overcontextualized. Rather we consider violence in a wide range of contexts—including not just the illegal economy but also in recreational, home, and even carceral settings. Broadly conceived, and consistent with the extant research, we analyze how women's violence is played out in private and public domains. Second, in examining these two domains, we draw attention to the way particular aspects of situations (drugs and alcohol, weapons), and the race of those involved, shape violent encounters and women's characterization of them.

DATA AND METHODS

The women whose narratives we analyze were part of a racially diverse sample of 205 women drawn from the female population incarcerated in the Hennepin County Adult Detention Facility (Minneapolis,

Minnesota). This is a short-term jail (postsentence) that provides separate housing for both male and female offenders. The women who were selected for interviews, based on the proximity of their release dates, were invited to participate in a project designed to gain a greater understanding of women's experiences with violence as offenders, victims, and "avoiders" of violence. A life events calendar, programmed on laptop computers, was used to assess women's involvement in these encounters over the 36 months before their incarceration. We collected data on a maximum of eight recent violent and eight avoided violent incidents involving both partners and nonpartners. The interviews were conducted by the authors and two graduate students. Depending on the number of violent incidents in which a woman was involved, each interview took between 2 and 8 hours to complete. The narrative sample (N = 66) is distinguished from the larger sample (N = 205) on the basis of reports of perpetrating violent acts, regardless of whether the women involved in these acts also were the victims of violence in the same or different encounters. Forty-six reported that they perpetrated at least one act of violence and twenty reported between two and five acts of violence. Some women are, therefore, overrepresented in these data. However, it is important to remember that our interest centers not on the particular female offender but rather on whether the existing portrayals of women's violence do justice to the range of circumstances and reasons for women's violent encounters.

Generally, the women who provided narratives of their violent encounters are quite comparable to the total interview sample. Only two exceptions appear. First, American Indian women are slightly overrepresented in the narrative sample. Given our focus on the question of intersectionality, however, we feel that this broader representation of American Indian women provides a unique opportunity to explore the experiences of this vastly understudied population. The second exception appears in the data on criminal history. Here we find that the women reporting involvement in acts of violence have had significantly more arrests over their lifetimes, and were arrested for the first time at an earlier age, than women offenders with no self-reported acts of violence. However, in terms of age, education, and, notably, experience with childhood abuse (physical and sexual), we find no significant differences between our subsample of violent female offenders and the larger sample of interviewed offenders.

The narratives women gave us of their violent encounters undoubtedly reflected how they wanted to be viewed in these situations, and we make no claim that we can really know what happened in these incidents. What we can know, however, is how these women depicted and framed their actions and the actions of those around them. As such, this discourse is an important indication of their subjectivity and identity (Butler, 1993: 225; Silverman, 1983).

Working inductively, we each coded the narratives separately according to what we thought was the primary motivation for the encounters. We cross-classified our individual results and we found substantial reliability in our categorization of these events. We added three sets of variables to our coding of each narrative: whether an incident involved a partner or nonpartner (relative, friend, acquaintance, or stranger); the situational context of the incident (for example, alcohol or drugs involved; weapons used, did it occur in a public or private domain); and demographics (the race of the offender, and the race and sex of the opponent). We present first the categories we found that characterize the common motivations underlying these acts of violence. We then turn to see whether particular categories of violence are more likely to be associated with incidents involving a partner as opposed to a nonpartner. We chose this method of analysis because much of the research on women's involvement in violent crime, as both victims and offenders, centers on its private nature (Kruttschnitt, McLaughlin, and Petrie, 2004). Finally, we consider the situational and demographic characteristics of these incidents to determine whether there are certain common correlates or relationships that are defining features of specific types of violent encounters.

CHARACTERIZING WOMEN'S VIOLENT ENCOUNTERS

Most of the women we interviewed were poor; many had drug habits, and some were street prostitutes. As a result, violent encounters were hardly unusual events for them.

Although occasionally violence seemed to have multiple meanings and motives (16 of 106 incidents), we were able to identify what seemed to be the main reason for their involvement in each violent encounter in the majority of cases. We begin by describing the five main motives for violence as these women recounted them to us: jealousy, disrespect, self-defense, self-help, and victim precipitation.

The most common reason for a violent encounter among these women was perceived disrespect or humiliation (20 percent of the cases). Here we are referring to the notion that the offender feels challenged by a comment or gesture that threatens her sense of self or dignity. Such reactions are commonly noted as a motive for men's involvement in homicides (see, for example, Katz, 1988: 20–21; Polk, 1994: 58–92; Wolfgang, 1958: 191) but rarely are they considered as a rationale for women's involvement in violence (compare Mullins, Wright, and Jacobs, 2004). Consider, for example, how the following black woman reacted to the allegation that she was shoplifting.

> Me and my girlfriend were walking in [a large chain grocery] and looking for some medication for my three-year-old but they didn't have it and we walked out and this man said we were stealing batteries so I let the guy check me and my purse and everything 'cause I wasn't taking no damn batteries and as we were leaving he grabbed me hard and pulled me back. I almost fell and we started fighting. He wasn't even security; he was like a stock guy and I was like, "We weren't even near the battery aisle" and we were at court and this guy didn't even know where the battery aisle was. And he grabbed me back and I fell on the ground against this metal bar and so I maced him and since I sprayed mace I was the bad one and the cops arrested me and not him at all. My girlfriend jumped on him too 'cause he was jumpin' on me and that made her jump on him, hitting him with my purse you know, 'cause he is on me for no reason. [The grocery store] called the cops and they actually called me names and said I was resisting arrest and this other guy come out the back room choking me before the cops came and I was choking and couldn't breathe and trying to yell at my friend and the cops took my friend to the car and then slowly walkin' to me and this guy is still choking me and then they say I was resisting arrest. I couldn't even breathe and how could I resist arrest? I was so mad at the police 'cause they called me black bitch and everything and it's just sick; the whole situation is wrong, just wrong and here I am in jail for protecting myself from someone assaulting me for no reason.

Despite the initial humiliation of being accused of shoplifting, she nevertheless complies with a search of her purse, believing that by so doing she will be vindicated. Although the stolen goods were not found on her, the store clerk attempts to physically restrain the woman and her reaction turns violent. Her characterization of her acts of violence are framed by both the injustice of his attempts to physically restrain her and her understanding that this was someone who had no authority to act in this fashion, someone perhaps who had no greater social status than her own. Notably, as she describes it, compliance with the store clerk's attempts to physically restrain her was not an option.

The second most common motivation we found for women's violence was jealousy (19 percent of the cases). Usually, this involved discovering a partner's infidelity and, typically, confronting him about his indiscretions. However, sometimes it also involved the "other woman." What is particularly interesting about these cases is the unapologetic descriptions women provide of the violence they direct toward the alleged culprits. One black woman, who initially tried to cut her boyfriend, only regrets that she didn't go after the "other woman" before attempting to assault him.

> We were at a friend's house and we were arguing about drugs and I was talking to this one girl and he knew who she was and I didn't think he knew anyone there. So, I got upset and jealous and we was arguing and he said "shut up about it" and I went to the kitchen sink and picked up a knife and threw it at him and he left out of the house and that was it. I went after the girl then and she ran to the head of the house and stay in the room with him and then I left. I didn't hit him with the knife, but I was really tryin' but just missed. I should have just gone after the girl in the first place 'cause I was pissed at her.

Not all women, of course, impart such agentic accounts of their attempts to rectify instances of perceived infidelity. One American Indian woman, for example, provides what might be considered a more typical depiction of female aggression by framing her violence on one side by her drinking and on the other by his more serious acts of retaliation.

> We were sitting there drinking and he had cheated on me with this one girl. I slapped him upside his head and punched him a few times. He went and grabbed a whip that I had bought from Sex World. He started whipping me with it. His brother had came down to stop it. He told his brother to mind his own business. He was whipping me so hard with the whip that the leather came off and it was just a metal rod. I have permanent bruises on my thigh and butt cheek.

As this last case demonstrates, jealousy not only ignites aggression but it can also provoke self-defense—perhaps the most popular explanation for women's involvement in violence. We found that though self-defense was a relatively frequent motivation for violence (18 percent of the cases), it occurred slightly less often than both disrespect and jealousy. Self-defense can be readily identified by the fact that

women's violent actions emerge only in reaction to someone initiating an attack against them. Their violence in these encounters remains reactive and contained, unlike mutual violence, where it is difficult to determine who initiated the violence and who is the victim. The following description of a prostitute's exchange with a stranger who wanted her services after she had completed her work shift, exemplifies self-defense or the perceived use of violence as a reasonable response to the situation.

> I was in no money-making mood. I had already given Leo over a hundred dollars. I was in no mood to have a date. I kept walking straight and this car kept following me. And he must have parked his vehicle and came to me and instinct told me it was the driver of the truck. I had a small knife I never carried, you know, but for some reason that one day Leo gave it to me even though I didn't want it. So this guy comes walking and I put my hands in my pocket. He started talking to me and I was just ignoring him, you know, and as he was saying something to me, he kicked me and my knife went flying out. He just totally attacked the shit out of me, for no reason, and we were in the street. My head hit the curb and smashed my cheek bone like you know. When I hit everything got blurry. I thought I was gonna die, everything went white and shit. I was laying there and my body was heavy and couldn't move and then out of the blue I just kicked him in the balls. . . . I kicked him and that is what saved me.

A fourth motivation we uncovered for women's violence was self-help (12 percent of the cases). Originally described by Black as conduct that "is intended as a punishment or other expression of disapproval" (1983: 35), this broad definition could encompass what we have referred to as disrespect and jealousy. We use the term more narrowly to refer to efforts to obtain restitution or compensation that a woman believes is owed her. Prostitutes frequently resorted to "self-help" to obtain what they believed they were owed.

> We (a "John" and I) were on Clinton and 31st and he had felt all on me and try to drop me off without paying and said that he changed his mind so I reached over him and took his keys and he grabbed my hand and tried to stop me. I hit him over the head and I said "you want your keys back, you will give me all that is in your wallet or you won't have a car to drive when I throw your fuckin' keys on the roof." He gave me all his money and I gave him his keys back.

This woman describes herself as deserving of compensation and willingly uses force to obtain it, regardless of the potential costs to her individual safety. Further, her threats to dispose of his keys, which she could easily have done, are merely that—threats designed to enforce the contract she believes this client entered into with her. Not all cases of self-help, however, involved prostitution. Sometimes they involved exacting revenge for damaged property, uncompensated rewards for engaging in dope deals, and unpaid loans.

Finally, we also saw, albeit to a lesser extent, instances of victim precipitation (7 percent of the cases). Drawing on the work of von Hentig (1948/1979), Wolfgang (1958) popularized this concept in his study of homicides in Philadelphia. Wolfgang noted that in many homicides, the victim was the first one in the altercation to have used physical force against his slayer. Although it is commonly assumed that this term is only appropriate for violent encounters involving males, Wolfgang (1958: 253) noted a number of slayings in which the husband initiated the violence that ultimately resulted in his own death. Consistent with this theme, we found that in some cases women didn't initiate the violent encounters they were involved in, but once they were started their level of violence clearly exceeded that of their victims.

> He told me we were going to this party, it was nighttime. It was his ex-girlfriend's party. She was like "why did you bring this bitch?" We left. We were in the truck on the expressway. I was like "why did you bring me to this party?" He reached over and punched me in the mouth. Something made me react and put my hand in my pocket and I grabbed a box-cutter. I started slicing him up. We were by [the] hospital. We got off the expressway. He was bleeding so bad. I felt sorry for him.

What is particularly interesting about this case, and similar cases of victim precipitation, is that she eschews being hit (clearly a legitimate and the dominant rationale for reacting aggressively) and only refers to "something" that made her respond so violently. This suggests that the physical blow she sustained may have been less salient to her than the insult she encountered at the party from an obvious sexual rival.

Beyond these five major categories, we also found four incidents of mutual violence. These cases always involved a partner and were largely consistent with what is now referred to as "common couple violence" (Johnson, 1995; Johnson and Ferraro, 2000; Johnson and Leone, 2005). Here women attributed the violence to "arguing" that turned into a fight, suggesting few attributions of responsibility—to either themselves or their partners—for the violence.

Illicit gain was a similarly infrequent occurrence (four cases) among these women. Women involved in this type of violence described their actions, "putting a gun to his head and taking his money" in the course of "selling some weed," in unapologetic and very matter-of-fact terms. Like the women who engaged in self-help, their violence is depicted as part of a business transaction; however, unlike self-help cases, these women are not acting to right some perceived wrong. Their motive for violence is money or drugs and their transactions leave little room for their own victimization.

Taken together, these incidents suggest that women's involvement in violent offending is wide-ranging. Their actions, encompassing jealousy, self help and disrespect, reflect not only common themes identified in the prior literature on women and girls living in dangerous and disadvantaged neighborhoods (Baskin and Sommers, 1998; Maher, 1997; Miller and White, 2003) but also behaviors found in studies of homicide and domestic violence, such as victim precipitation and self-defense. But do these contexts, one public and the other private, script women's violent encounters? To answer this question, we turn now to explore what types of violence are more likely to emerge with romantic partners and expartners, as opposed to those that involve nonpartners. By using this frame for our analysis, we are able to examine the validity of the dominant theoretical framework that has dichotomized women's violence into the public and private spheres—a framework that contributes to the anti-agentic views of women offenders.

CONTEXTUALIZING WOMEN'S VIOLENT ENCOUNTERS

In each of the categories of violence we coded, we were able to determine what proportion of the incidents involved a partner or a nonpartner. Not surprisingly, the three types of violent encounters most likely to involve partners or former partners were jealousy, victim precipitation, and mutual violence. In the jealousy cases, even when the victim was an acquaintance or a stranger, the reason for the violence usually centered on an argument involving a boyfriend or an ex-partner.

A close examination of the situations and women involved in these incidents suggests that little of the dominant discourse around women's involvement in domestic violence supported.

The use of alcohol and drugs played an important role in half of the mutual violence cases but in less than a third of the jealousy and victim precipitation cases (compare Straus and Gelles, 1992: 203–24). The role of alcohol and drugs in domestic violence, though commonly noted, is not well understood (see, for example, Gelles and Cavanaugh, 2005). What insights these women provide into the impact of substance use on their violent encounters with partners provide support for the "time out" perspective, or the notion that their normal interaction is suspended during periods of intoxication. Consider, for example, how this woman characterizes her aggression with a former partner. She does not cast herself or her partner as the primary offender, but rather their drug habit.

> We [respondent and ex-boyfriend] were both tired and up for more than a week on drugs—doing crack. We got done fighting about who is spending the most money on dope and we were drinking. And, I smacked him in the head or somethin' or hit him on the shoulder and all of a sudden we were just fighting. We just got tired of just boxing each other. When we go at it, we are just ridiculous. I can barely remember the fight, we were both torn up. We were both a mess. We fight all of the time. We were both tired of trying to get dope and took it out on each other.

Another notable feature of these domestic encounters, which were disproportionately likely to occur in private residences, is the role of bystanders or witnesses to the violence. Whereas bystanders in violent incidents are often equivocal in terms of whether they act to escalate or de-escalate the violence (Sacco and Kennedy, 2002: 49), in these cases they often seemed to further provoke the violence. In large part, this is due to the fact that the bystander was often the other woman or someone closely aligned to one of the parties involved in the dispute. Consider the following case that was motivated by both jealousy and self-help.

> I had moved out, stressed over being the only one working. My daughter stayed with her, she had a new partner who moved in. My jealousy overtook me a little bit. I called her and told her that I was coming over to see my daughter and her kids. She told me no, another time. So I took it upon myself to go over to the house, not knowing her partner was there. Her partner was telling me to leave, that I wasn't going to see the kids. Eventually I left but came back in one to two hours. Upon my return she was home and my daughter was on the porch playing. She called my name out and everyone else came out to the porch. We were arguing, but my ex-partner told me that I could only visit her on the

> porch. Her kids wanted to come out to see me. Her new partner didn't think it was a good idea. So I was getting angry, like "fuck this." She came out with her loudness, and we are arguing. Her nephews come out. My ex-partner is telling me to leave. Her new partner came up in my face, she shoved me toward the window, I shoved her back. We got into a fist-fighting altercation. My partner got between us, I don't know if she was trying to break it up, but I took it as she was trying to help me. The kids are crying; people's shirts are getting ripped off. Finally her nephew came and clocked me one. I wasn't completely out. He threw or carried me off the porch.... The neighbor called the police.

This woman invokes her competing notions of identity—ex-partner and mother—to explain her violence, but she is also careful to note that she was not alone in this predicament. Bystanders were clearly taking sides (with "shirts getting ripped off") and, as she acknowledges, the encounter only ended after the police arrived on the scene, called by a neighbor. Notably, she did not use a weapon (as they were not typically found in cases of partner violence), nor did she enlist the help of others when she returned to see her children.

More generally, we found that in cases of partner violence, unlike studies of street-life retaliation, women did not seek out males to even the score with a cheating partner (Mullins, Wright, and Jacobs, 2004: 930–31). Instead, they directed their anger against either the men they thought were cheating on them or the women that were threatening their relationships. Because these cases were disproportionately likely to involve black men, these violent responses to instances of infidelity may also have been influenced by a well-founded perception that there is a limited supply of young black males. As Pattillo and her colleagues (2004) have shown, due to the massive growth in incarceration over the past two decades, prison time is now a modal experience for young, undereducated black males. This fact may also be readily apparent to other women accessing the same limited pool of eligible males, because the majority of the jealousy and mutual violence cases involving partners were interracial, and such cases often involved white women and American Indian women with black males.

The types of violent encounters most likely to involve nonpartners are disrespect, self-help, and self-defense. In these more public encounters, we found that alcohol or drug use on the part of the offender or the victim was slightly more common than in incidents involving partner violence. Again, however, the use of weapons was rare (only 25 percent of the cases).

Perhaps what distinguishes these three types of encounters is the fact that they are stratified by the race of the offender, suggesting that women in different social locations perceive and respond violently to different types of affronts.

In the case of disrespect, the dominant portrayal of violence relayed to us, American Indian women were substantially overrepresented (40 percent) relative to their representation in the narrative sample (29 percent). The notion of respect has gained significant attention in explanations of young Hispanic and black male violence. Their social and economic disenfranchisement is alleged to create particularly fragile masculine identities, thereby heightening the need to rebuff verbal humiliations (see, for example, Bourgois, 1995; Messerschmidt, 1993). This approach is consistent with the notion that "doing crime" also explains "doing gender," or that criminality is an expression of masculinity. Our findings, however, suggest that violent responses to disrespect may have relatively little to do with gender and more to do with social locations (see also Miller, 2002). By this we mean that, regardless of gender, it may be that individuals who feel culturally and socially ostracized are especially likely to react violently to personal affronts from others, particularly those who they perceive as having no higher social status than their own. The American Indian women in this study, who are extremely marginalized in the economic and social hierarchy, were especially vulnerable to verbal slights, and not just from strangers. Usually, their encounters involved friends or acquaintances, as noted in the following narrative.

> She [friend from childhood] used to hang with me and my friend when we were kids and now she's way out on drugs and we don't hang with her that often anymore, but me and my home-girls changed a little bit and got out of drugs and she didn't. So, one day she called and she was drunk saying "you ain't no better than me" and started saying stuff about my kids like I don't even take care of my kids. And I said, "I'm gonna kick your ass when I see you next" and I just hang up the phone and it was probably a week later and I saw her even though she didn't see me 'cause I was in the back of the van when my other girlfriend pulled up to her on the street and I was like "pull over, pull over" and I jumped out of the back of the van and hit her in the mouth sayin' "why'd you say that about my kids?"

As this woman's confrontational tone suggests, questions about her identity as a mother were raised by a black woman who she perceived was no longer her peer. Because her identity had been refigured—to one

that no longer involves drugs—but has not been acknowledged by her friend ("you ain't no better than me"), it ignites a violent reaction.

Slights from white men in public also seemed to be particularly threatening to American Indian women, even when they involved the relatively uncommon instances with a partner. Consider the following dispute that took place in a bar.

> He was drunk. He was sitting at a table with a bunch of people. I came in to cop some dope and my connect wasn't there. I told him I was meeting someone but [Tom] was not there. That's when he called me a dope whore. All the people kind of stopped. I said, "That's bullshit; we both know that, but I bet you don't say that again." He got about half of it out his mouth and I cracked him. Then he asked the waitress (a friend of mine) if she had seen that; she said she didn't see anything.

In contrast to these cases, self-help seems to cut across race but is more likely to involve a male victim than a female victim. Although prostitution provides the template for this type of violence, we found that more generally these cases involved women—black, white, and American Indian—looking for ways to obtain what they perceived were their just desserts. This might involve money or drugs, or even avoiding unwanted sexual advances.

> I just remember I was cleaning my house and my brother-in-law come in and I told him to leave me alone and when he's drinking he's always messin' with the women, grabbing body parts and touching and stuff but he was messin' with me and I kept tellin' him to leave me alone, and I just swung around and hit him with the broom cause I was cleanin' in the kitchen, and I hit him in the knees and legs and he left after that. He was just being so physical you know, and I don't need that. He was tryin' to touch my breasts and butt and all of that and we have had our run-ins before, so I knew he was just in one of those states where he is drunk and tryin' to get up on me.

This black woman's understanding of the world did not include having to put up with a drunk relative's advances. As a result, she has no apologies for her aggression. A white woman also relayed how her implicit view of what was excessively deviant (spending too much money on drugs) led her to assault her male companion.

> We was kind of seeing each other, staying in a motel room. We finished smoking all the crack we had. And I

still had some money left but I wanted to save it for the rent. I was tired and had been up for days. He wanted to go buy some more drugs. I was like no, when I give you money to buy drugs you buy bullshit. It escalated to screaming and stuff. Finally, I just snapped and stood up and threw the lamp at him. I threw something else but I don't know what and it hit him in the face.

As these cases demonstrate, women's attempts at self-help generally involved friends and acquaintances which may explain why these incidents were slightly more likely to be intraracial than interracial. When a stranger was targeted in these cases, it usually involved a prostitute attempting to ensure that she was paid for her services.

Although self-defense cases are most commonly associated with domestic violence, we found that these women used self-defense in a variety of contexts. Only slightly more than one-third of the incidents (37 percent) involved a woman defending herself against her partner's or ex-partner's violence. The remaining cases spanned instances of street violence, including prostitution, as well as domestic encounters with relatives and roommates. In these cases, women were always careful to note that their use of violence arose only because they were trying to protect themselves, almost equally as often against a male as a female.

> It was over drugs and I wouldn't spend time with him or get back with him because I'm with the boyfriend I have now and he took it upon himself to grab me by the throat and I kicked him in his private parts and I fought back. He didn't hurt me physically aside from holding me back, but I was able to get in kicks and punches and stuff. He had a good hold on my throat for a while and I was fighting but he wasn't fighting back very much. He just pulled my hair though I guess. It was right in the middle of the street too in front of all kinds of people too. It was so stupid. He said I was the first white woman who fought back; guess I showed him. A lot of it had to do with me not supporting his habit as well 'cause I wouldn't give him the drugs I had anymore either like I used to. Other people kind of got involved and my friends told him to get lost.

What is particularly notable about this case is the attention this woman draws to her willingness, being a "white woman," to fight back against a black former boyfriend in a public arena. Although such interracial encounters were more common in self-defense cases involving partners than nonpartners, when a stranger of a different race assaulted women, they were quick to

point this out, perhaps believing that this factor added justification for their acts of self-defense.

Finally, women situated themselves relatively equally between public and private domains when they described their involvement in acts of illicit gain. Their violence to obtain money or drugs, or both, sometimes involved targeting known victims and sometimes total strangers. Although we are cautious about drawing any definitive conclusions from these relatively unusual cases (N = 4), they do suggest, consistent with the other motivations, that weapons are likely to be invoked primarily when women are targeting male victims.

CONCLUSION

Our aim in this study was to examine and challenge the dominant narratives of women's involvement in violent crime. The popular press (particularly the print media) has characterized women's involvement in violence as a result of either an inherently evil or pathological nature or earlier victimization. Scholarly research has further contributed to these depictions by dichotomizing women's violence into determinative public and private spheres. By contrast, and consistent with the growing body of work that questions anti-agentic views of women offenders, we used women's narratives of their violent encounters in the hope of illustrating their general understanding of the world and how these understandings either reproduce or deflect the dominant discourse on gender and violence.

Women unveiled their experiences in a wide range of violent encounters; some aspects of these experiences clearly support common depictions of women's violent offending. For example, in terms of the situational dimensions of these encounters, we saw that partner violence (often motivated by jealousy, victim precipitation, and mutual violence) involves primarily males and it occurred for the most part in private arenas with few bystanders. More generally, we also found that weapon use is an infrequent aspect of women's violent incidents, and that violence that emerges from disrespect is largely an intragender phenomenon (Baskin and Sommers, 1998; Maher, 1997; Miller, 1998).

Yet, our findings depart from existing research in their ability both to depict a broader array of motivations for women's violence and to speak to the issue of whether and how they are gendered. Ethnographies of female offenders that have moved beyond the dominant discourse on this topic alternate between gendered (for example, Baskin and Sommers, 1998) and economic and related social status, motivations for violent crime (Maher, 1997; Gartner and McCarthy, 2005).

Our findings suggest that both perspectives are probably correct but not always readily transparent. Specifically, our analyses of these narratives revealed both explicit and implicit explanations for women's violence. Consistent with the notion that violence is motivated by gendered considerations, the explicit explanations women gave contained more hegemonic, or taken for granted, assumptions about their place in the world (Comaroff and Comaroff, 1991; Messing and Heeren, 2004). Here we are referring not just to the fact that women drew on the common notions of jealousy and mutual violence to explain their behavior but also on their identities as partners or mothers, or both, to justify their acts (see Messing and Heeren, 2004). Their stories often directed attention to their perceived threats to their status as a good mother or a faithful partner. Occasionally, they also drew attention to their status as violent victims, primarily, but not exclusively, in their tales of self-defense.

When we considered how race, in addition to gender, shaped these encounters, a second, more implicit set of motivations emerged. For example, we found that partner violence was more likely to occur between interracial than intraracial couples, and particularly interracial couples with a black male partner. Explicitly, many of these cases involved threats to a woman's status as a partner; implicitly, they direct attention to a politicized consideration—the scarcity of young black males in the community. Race also conditioned women's responses to their violent encounters with non-partners. For example, recall the pride a white woman took in publicly fending off the blows of a black ex-boyfriend. Or, consider the black woman who found accusations of shoplifting from a white stock clerk intolerable. In each of these cases, the implicit motivation may be related to perceived status differences that adhere to different races and women's attempts to subvert social reality. In choosing to attack those who drew attention to this status differential, or in some cases fight back, these women offer a valuable reflection on the execution of politics in their lives.

Although our attention to intersectionality is an important contribution to the research on female offending, there is no question that this study is only the first step. We have analyzed a relatively atypical group of women who are not necessarily representative of all female offenders. However, to obtain detailed information about violent incidents and their situational correlates, we need to study a population with higher than average exposure to violent encounters. Excepting the ethnographies we have highlighted, most of our information about women's involvement in violence comes from victimization surveys or interviews with women in shelters. Although provocative, these findings provide a somewhat skewed picture of women's violent encounters. By targeting women who are at high risk for violence but not selected based on their victimization or violent offending, we have been able to capture a greater range of violent encounters—though certainly not the full extent of them (see Roberts et al., 2005)—than previous research.

Summarily, we believe that this research contributes to the growing body of scholarship that is challenging the common views of women's involvement in public and private violence and the socially constructed images of anti-agentic women. Women's violence occurs, and expresses itself, in a wide range of circumstances. Its triggers are not limited to victimization and bad domestic relationships but also include the desire for money, respect, and reparation. In this sense, expressions of male and female offending share many similarities and, as we have seen, are often determined by the same sorts of personal and political concerns. Perhaps, then, our greatest challenge lies in reconciling the seemingly contradictory notion of the centrality of gender to crime and the acknowledgement that gender is interwoven with other social statuses—social class and race—that may be at least as important as, if not more important than, gender in facilitating crime. It may be that the answer to this challenge will require a significant scholarly investment in research on identity formation and the relative roles of culturally determined gender scripts and economic status and prospects in identity work. Hints of this have appeared in some of the most compelling research to date on the questions of whether there are gendered pathways into and out of crime (Giordano, Cernkovich, and Rudolph, 2002; Heimer and DeCoster, 1999). Although these suggestions are provisional, we believe they are worth considering. After all, we all have much to gain by challenging our common sense assumptions about gender and crime and unpacking the intersections of disadvantage that make violence a rational act for women, as well as men.

REFERENCES

Abu-Lughod, Lila. 1993. *Writing Women's Worlds*. Berkeley: University of California Press.
Baskin, Deborah R., and Ira B. Sommers. 1998. *Casualties of Community Disorder: Women's Careers in Violent Crime*. Boulder, CO: Westview.
Black, Donald. 1983. Crime as social control. *American Sociological Review* 48:34–45.
Black, Donald. 1993. *The Social Structure of Right and Wrong*. San Diego: Academic Press.

Bourgois, Philippe. 1995. *In Search of Respect: Selling Crack in El Barrio.* New York: Cambridge University Press.

Butler, Judith P. 1993. *Bodies That Matter.* New York: Routledge.

Comaroff, Jean, and John Comaroff. 1991. *Of Revelation and Revolution.* Chicago: University of Chicago Press.

Daly, Kathleen. 1994. *Gender, Crime and Punishment.* New Haven, CT: Yale University Press.

Daly, Kathleen. 1998. Women's pathways to felony court: Feminist theories of lawbreaking and problems of representation. In *Criminology at the Crossroads,* eds. Kathleen Daly and Lisa Maher. New York: Oxford University Press.

Daly, Kathleen, and Meda Chesney-Lind. 1988. Feminism and criminology. *Justice Quarterly* 5:497–538.

Downs, Donald Alexander. 1996. *More Than Victims: Battered Women, the Syndrome Society, and the Law.* Chicago: University of Chicago Press.

Ewick, Patricia, and Susan Silbey. 1995. Subversive stories and hegemonic tales: Toward a sociology of narrative. *Law and Society Review* 29:197–226.

Gartner, Rosemary, and Bill McCarthy. 2006. Maternal infanticide and the dark figure of homicide: Beyond the mad, the bad, and the victim. In *Gender and Crime: Patterns in Victimization and Offending,* eds. Karen Heimer and Candace Kruttschnitt. New York: New York University Press.

Gelles, Richard J., and Mary M. Cavanaugh. 2005. Association is not causation: Alcohol and other drugs do not cause violence. In *Current Controversies on Family Violence,* eds. Donileen R. Loseke, Richard Gelles, and Mary M. Cavanaugh. Thousand Oaks, CA: Sage Publications.

Gilbert, Paula Ruth. 2002. Discourses of female violence and societal gender stereotypes. *Violence Against Women* 8:1271–1300.

Giordano, Peggy C., Stephen A. Cernkovich, and Jennifer L. Rudolph. 2002. Gender, crime, and desistance: Toward a theory of Cognitive Transformation. *American Journal of Sociology* 107:990–1064.

Heimer, Karen, and Stacy De Coster. 1999. The gendering of violent delinquency. *Criminology* 37:277–317.

Johnson, Michael P. 1995. Patriarchal terrorism and common couple violence: Two forms of violence against women. *Journal of Marriage and the Family* 57:283–94.

Johnson, Michael P., and Kathleen J. Ferraro. 2000. Research on domestic violence in the 1990s: Making distinctions. *Journal of Marriage and the Family* 62:948–63.

Johnson, Michael P., and Janel M. Leone. 2005. The differential effects of intimate terrorism and situational couple violence. *Journal of Family Issues* 26:322–49.

Jones, Ann. 1980. *Women Who Kill.* New York: Fawcett Columbine.

Katz, Jack. 1988. *Seductions of Crime: Moral and Sensual Attractions of Doing Evil.* New York: Basic Books.

Kruttschnitt, Candace, and Rosemary Gartner. 2005. Marking Time in the Golden State: *Women's Imprisonment in California.* New York: Cambridge University Press.

Kruttschnitt, Candace, Brenda L. McLaughlin, and Carol V. Petrie, eds. 2004. *Advancing the Federal Research Agenda on Violence Against Women.* Washington, DC: National Academy Press.

Maher, Lisa. 1997. *Sexed Work, Gender, Race and Resistance in a Brooklyn Drug Market.* Oxford: Clarendon Press.

Maher, Lisa, and Richard Curtis. 1998. Women on the edge of crime: Crack cocaine and the changing contexts of street-level sex work in New York City. In *Criminology at the Crossroads,* eds. Kathleen Daly and Lisa Maher. New York: Oxford University Press.

Matravers, Amanda. 2006. *Women Sex Offenders.* Cullumpton, Devon, UK: Willan Publishing.

Messerschmidt, James W. 1993. *Masculinities and Crime: Critique and Reconceptualization of Theory.* Lanham, MD: Rowman and Littlefield.

Messerschmidt, James W. 2002. On gang girls, gender and a structured action theory: A reply to Miller. *Theoretical Criminology* 6:461–75.

Messing, Jill Theresa, and John W. Heeren. 2004. Another side of multiple murder: Women killers in the domestic context. *Homicide Studies* 8:123–58.

Miller, Eleanor. 1986. *Street Women.* Philadelphia, PA: Temple University Press.

Miller, Jody. 1998. Up it up: Gender and the accomplishment of street robbery. *Criminology* 36:37–66.

Miller, Jody. 2001. *One of the Guys: Girls, Gangs, and Gender.* New York: Oxford University Press.

Miller, Jody. 2002. The strength and limits of 'doing gender' for understanding street crime. *Theoretical Criminology* 6:433–60.

Miller, Jody, and Christopher W. Mullins. 2006. The status of feminist theories in criminology. In *Taking Stock: The Status of Criminological Theory,* eds. Francis T. Cullen, John Wright, and Kristie Blevins. *Advances in Criminological Theory,* vol. 15, series eds. Freda Adler and William Laufer. Piscataway, NJ: Transaction Publishers.

Miller, Jody, and Norman A. White. 2003. Gender and adolescent relationship violence: A contextual examination. *Criminology* 41:1207–48.

Morrissey, Belinda. 2003. *When Women Kill: Questions of Agency and Subjectivity.* New York: Routledge.

Motz, Anna. 2001. *The Psychology of Female Violence: Crimes Against the Body.* Wolverhampton, East Sussex, UK: Brunner-Routlege.

Mullins, Christopher W., Richard Wright, and Bruce A. Jacobs. 2004. Gender, streetlife and criminal retaliations. *Criminology* 42:911–40.

Pattillo, Mary, David Weiman, and Bruce Western, eds. 2004. *Imprisoning America: The Social Effects of Mass Incarceration.* New York: Russell Sage Foundation.

Polk, Kenneth. 1994. *When Men Kill: Scenarios of Masculine Violence*. Cambridge: Cambridge University Press.

Rasche, Christine E. 1990. Early models for contemporary thought on domestic violence and women who kill their mates: A review of the literature from 1895 to 1970. *Women and Criminal Justice* 1:31–53.

Richie, Beth E. 1996. *Compelled to Crime: The Gender Entrapment of Battered Black Women*. New York: Routledge.

Roberts, Jennifer, Edward P. Mulvey, Julie Horney, John Lewis, and Michael L. Arter. 2005. A test of two methods of recall for violent events. *Journal of Quantitative Criminology* 21:175–94.

Rollins, Judith. 1995. *All Is Never Said: The Narrative of Odette Harper Hines*. Philadelphia, PA: Temple University Press.

Sacco, Vincent F., and Leslie W. Kennedy. 2002. *The Criminal Event: Perspectives in Space and Time*. Belmont, CA: Wadsworth.

Silverman, Kaja. 1983. *The Subject of Semiotics*. New York: Oxford University Press.

Stanko, Elizabeth A. 2001. Women, danger and criminology. In *Women, Crime and Criminal Justice,* eds. Claire M. Renzetti and Lynne Goodstein. Los Angeles, CA: Roxbury.

Straus, Murray A., and Richard J. Gelles. 1992. *Physical Violence in American Families: Risk Factors and Adaptations to Violence in 8,145 Families*. New Brunswick, NJ: Transaction.

von Hentig, Hans. 1948/1979. *The Criminal and His Victim*. New York: Schocken Books.

Wolfgang, Marvin E. 1958. *Patterns of Criminal Homicide*. Philadelphia: University of Pennsylvania Press.

20

THE WORK OF SEX WORK

Elite Prostitutes' Vocational Orientations and Experiences

ANN M. LUCAS

This article examines women's views of prostitution as paid work. Emphasis is placed on differences in motivation, experience, and working style among these women. Exploring their career orientations, perceptions of the market for their services, and their customer relationships together with the factors that led to their decision to engage in prostitution offers a "Crime as work" perspective that defines much of the accounts provided for participation in the elite sex trade.

INTRODUCTION, METHODS, AND LITERATURE REVIEW

Polsky (1967) argued that sociological and criminological scholarship would be greatly advanced if, in examining illegal commerce, it devoted as much time to analyzing the vocational aspects of such activity as it did analyzing illegality or deviance. While the state of scholarship has changed in the ensuing four decades, in some ways Polsky's argument remains timely. For example, although scholarly accounts of prostitution examine a variety of issues, including policy options, prostitution's effects on its practitioners and society, and the motivations of prostitutes and clients, relatively few examine prostitutes' views of their work as work. Yet prostitution is more than a set of signs and symbols about gender, sexuality, or power, more than a deviant identity, and more than a social problem; it is a practice,

a repeated event. Although its settings and participants vary, it is (re)enacted hour after hour and day after day. Because prostitution simultaneously involves deviance, criminality, and sexual labor, it is a rich site in which to explore the meaning of work, and offers an intriguing counterpoint to legitimate employment.

Prostitutes are found in a variety of circumstances. While some prostitutes are juvenile runaways fleeing sexual abuse, and some are drug-dependent adults, as stereotypes depict, others turn to prostitution to support themselves or to augment insufficient incomes; their ranks include housewives, nurses, teachers, college and graduate students, secretaries, single mothers, and women on welfare (Leigh 1998; Wardlaw 1998; West 1998). Their fees range from as little as five dollars for ten minutes (Goldsmith 1993) to five hundred dollars an hour or more. In general, prostitutes choose their work for the same reasons other people choose other work. The primary incentive leading individuals to engage in prostitution appears to be economic (Alexander 1998; Scambler 1997), but prostitutes also are influenced by common non-economic considerations: flexibility and freedom, enjoyment or variety, and available options (Alexander 1998; Canadian Organization for the Rights of Prostitutes [CORP] 1987; Carter 1998; French and Lee 1988; Niles 1998; Rhode 1989; Scambler 1997). And despite the stigma, isolation, and risks that often accompany prostitution, in at least two surveys large majorities of prostitutes reported overall job satisfaction (Rhode 1989).

Nearly all women arrested for prostitution in the United States are street prostitutes, even though street prostitutes likely comprise just 10–20% of all prostitutes (Alexander 1998; Cooper 1989; Hampton 1988; Rhode 1989). Women of color are also over-represented among those arrested and given jail sentences (Alexander 1998; Rhode 1989; West 1998). Not surprisingly, then, stratification within prostitution mirrors stratification in the larger society, and this fact in turn suggests that prostitutes' work experiences may vary widely from one stratum to another.

The material in this article is based on open-ended interviews I conducted with 30 American female prostitutes from mid-1996 through mid-1997, along with follow-up conversations in the ensuing years, concluding in 2002. Interviews were conducted in person or by telephone and tape-recorded. Interviewees were identified through chain referral, also called snowball sampling. At the time of the interview, most lived on the west or east coasts of the United States, with a few living in the south. All of these interviews involved prostitutes who worked off the streets, in the middle- to upper-levels of the profession.

A few scholars have examined aspects of prostitution as work. Bryan (1965) examined how new call girls learned their trade through a type of apprenticeship. Romenesko and Miller (1989) detailed the life histories of female street hustlers, including their reasons for engaging in prostitution and their experiences with legitimate work. Ford (1998) compared prostitutes to hospital workers to explore prostitution as service work. Albert (2001) studied women working in a legal Nevada brothel, including their attitudes toward work and their reasons for choosing it. Lastly, Brennan (2002) studied prostitutes in sex tourist destinations seeking to meet men who would sponsor their migration to another country. However, because there is a relative paucity of scholarship of this kind in regard to illegal work, generally, and illegal prostitution, in particular, neither has received the same level of sustained attention as has legitimate employment, resulting in insufficient attention to

different orientations toward illegal commerce and different styles of working. In regard to indoor prostitutes, this article attempts to offer a more extended consideration of differences in motivation, experience, and working style among this group, with the goal of improving our knowledge of variation in lived experience among those engaging in illegal commerce.

PROSTITUTION COMPARED TO OTHER WORK

Many prostitutes argue that their work is no worse, and may be better, than other work women perform. For example, because they are paid for sexual services, sexual harassment is generally not an unwanted part of the economic bargains they make with clients (Carole 1998b). Several of my informants reported that they experienced sexual harassment in "straight" jobs, which they felt they had to accept or ignore.

> Actually, I've been selling myself a long time. I had to be nice to people, working service jobs, be pretty. And when I was working as a dishwasher I had to put up with all kinds of advances from my bosses, pinches, sexual suggestions.
> When I was . . . doing data entry . . . the fellow who delivered the mail would come by and torment me every day: "You want it, girl, blah, blah, blah . . ." [I thought,] "This sucks." And I was really frightened; I was such a stupid little boob, and we didn't have a word for sexual harassment then, that I had no idea what to do about it. But I think I just quit my job; I was really anxious to get out of there. And that was at the glorious fucking university, too.
> When I worked in bars, or waitressing, you'd get these comments [from customers, like], "Hey, baby, if you took off your bra you'd make better tips," and I was like, "Shut up, I'm a bartender." And finally I thought, "Why don't I go somewhere else where I can take off my damn top and I will make better tips?" You're gonna have to deal with sexism anywhere you go. As a woman you're gonna have to put up with all this bullshit—you might as well be compensated for it. But . . . I think I get more respect for doing this [prostitution] from my clients than I did for other jobs.

In addition, several women reported that working as prostitutes taught them how to resist harassment more effectively than they had in the past. For example, the woman who was harassed as a university worker argued that today she would respond differently:

> I don't know if it's just because I'm older, but honestly, I think that my ability to handle all kinds of interpersonal stuff is really enhanced, because I do it all the time [in

prostitution] . . . I've had many years of being able to see myself as the head of a very successful business [as an independent call girl] and it's very hard for me to imagine that I would just sit there while the mail boy tormented me.

Another made a similar claim about prostitution enhancing her ability to set boundaries.

I [was] harassed by bosses when I worked in offices or worked in the restaurant. I don't get harassed now; my clients don't harass me. Sure, sometimes I might get some idiot that calls me; I'll just hang up the phone. I was on the bus one day and a young man came from the back of the bus and petted my hair and said, "Oh, I like your hair," and my arm just . . . shot up automatically and . . . knocked his arm [away]. I said, "You keep your hands off of me." And he went, "Whoa!" and he backed up and . . . ran off the bus, and all the men on the bus were nice, they're saying, "Well, have, have, have a good afternoon, ma'am." [laughs] I take whatever measures are necessary to maintain my boundaries. You have to do that with men generally, whether you're with them in a professional capacity or not. A lot of them are just like naughty boys, and they're going to try to get away with whatever they can get away with. And once they see that you're not going let them get away with what you don't want them to do, then they'll stop it.

Still another made the same observation in a more general way:

Women are going to be treated as sex objects [by men]. . . . I think that non-working women could learn much from working women [i.e., prostitutes] . . . I've learned so much from [prostitutes] who have worked longer than I have about valuing yourself and doing what you think is right and so I don't think it threatens women's rights . . . I don't think it threatens women's power, I think that it really empowers a lot of women.

Because the "sexual contract," to use Carole Pateman's (1988) term, is explicit in prostitution, sexual harassment need not be an unspoken part of the bargain. Indeed, some of what would be harassment in another setting may be entirely appropriate in sex work (Sundahl 1998). As women, prostitutes still experience some sexual harassment in their daily lives; however, in the context of work, harassment is much less frequent, because nothing sexual needs to be brought in clandestinely. Moreover, sex work may enable its practitioners to resist sexual harassment, in that it can make clear when a woman is appropriately treated as a sexual being, and when her sexuality should be irrelevant to any interaction. A prostitutes' rights activist forthrightly argues that "for some women to get paid for what all women are expected to do for free is a source of power for all women to refuse any free sex" (Lopez-Jones 1998:273).

In addition, the terms of the bargain are not simply dictated to the prostitute; many prostitutes emphatically assert that they decide what they will do for money. In setting the terms of the transaction—deciding how to express their sexuality and what their time and talents are worth—prostitutes may find another means of empowerment (Alexander 1998; CORP 1988; French and Lee 1988; Metal 1998). As one of my informants stated,

[Working as a prostitute] taught me a lot about dealing with people, and I was always very shy, I was a very shy child. . . . [Setting the terms in prostitution] was really nice. I had gone from an abusive boyfriend, who raped me, to a succession of men that I slept with that I didn't really care about. So [prostitution] was the first time I had any kind of power in a relationship. It was great! It changed my life in that respect, because I learned that I could have power in a relationship.

In regard to clients, another said,

I think that they think, a lot of times, that they've rented me for an hour so I should have to do anything that they want to. I think, maybe, it takes them by surprise that I walk in and take charge of the situation, and I'm like, "OK, let's do this," and they can make suggestions but if I don't want to do something I'm not gonna do it.

In other words, just as in the case of sexual harassment, prostitution can offer benefits—in the form of development of interpersonal skills—that extend beyond the work setting. This possibility appears to be especially available to women who work independently, because they manage all aspects of the business themselves. They find, screen, schedule, and negotiate with clients, collect fees, find and maintain workplaces, manage transportation and other logistics, decide which services to provide, and the like. However, to some extent these kinds of benefits are available to workers in more structured settings such as escort agencies or illicit brothels, since a large portion of their work involves private, negotiated, one-to-one contact with clients.

In addition to these benefits, prostitutes emphasize the income potential, autonomy, and flexibility of prostitution. In this regard, many of my informants argued that prostitution again compares very favorably with other work they have performed.

> I never once felt any of [my prostitution clients] was disgusting. I think that's an important thing.... Let's talk about real degradation and humiliation ... and yes, I have had both experiences. [Working] at the dry cleaners, and granted this was when I was ... 15, but still, I can't imagine anything more horrible than having to put my hands in these gross polyester pants with little bits of gross Kleenex and old Certs crudded up in the bottom of them. It was so disgusting. And to pull out a penny or a nickel and they would say, "Oh, you can keep that!" So disgusting. And to never see a soul or the daylight and just sit back there with piles of filthy, disgusting clothes and chemicals and take five minutes to eat your lunch with the stuff all still on your hands, because you can't really wash it off. And the environment was one little old lady who worked at the front, and then every once in a while I would get to work the cash register, which I never knew how to work, and have to deal with people [saying], "Look at this horrible thing! You did it all wrong! It was fine when I brought it in!" Just unhappy, mean people coming and going all day being totally dissatisfied, no matter what you did. And bringing in filthy, gross, gross things. [Later, working as a consultant] ... the thing that was unpleasant—I didn't have to do anything that was disgusting, ... we'll just move on to degradation and humiliation—was just having some client follow me all the way from downstairs to upstairs screaming that I don't know what I'm doing, and she's a social worker and she knows everything about how you should run a business, and trying to calm that one down while another one is complaining that I broke the rules ... and now they're going to sue. It's just, so completely unappreciated, nobody supporting me, the entire [staff] was just as glad to see me, outside consultant, go down in flames, "Fuck you, lady." ... I was a female outsider working within a male power structure.... My feelings about that [job] are that it was absolutely the most horrible work I've ever had, and the money was good enough that I stayed for a while, but nobody could possibly put up with that over time. I can't believe people get up in the morning and go through that ... it was intolerable.
>
> I haven't had a job in ten years except working for myself doing other things, and I went and got a job last year for two days as a waitress. I said, "Oh my God, this is so hard, it's hideous!" ... You go through all this trouble and you have $80.00 at the end of eight hours. It just was a real eye opener.... [W]hen I see ... those talk shows [where the topic is sex work], somebody in the audience will stand up and say, "I put myself through college and I worked three jobs and I worked at Dunkin'

> Donuts and I did this and that, and I didn't have to do what you do." I just think to myself, "You're an idiot. You could have worked one night and been home studying, taking care of your kids or whatever."

Having engaged in many kinds of work, these women expressed a clear preference for prostitution. Despite its risks or deficiencies, prostitution enabled them to avoid some of the disadvantages of more traditional work, particularly those associated with regimented or hostile workplaces, or poorly paid service work that involves demanding, unsatisfied customers. Continuing on this theme, two other subjects stated,

> The thing I get a lot is, "How did a smart girl like you get into the business?" and I tell them it's because I'm too smart to work for corporate America.... I hear my friends talk about their jobs and they hate them. They hate the work they do, they work for people who won't listen to their ideas and they have them doing these asinine things, and I can't work like that. It would make me nuts.
>
> [Another's answer to a client question about why she isn't working on Wall Street:] Well, I'd rather be rich and happy than rich and unhappy, that's why.

These women's belief, correct or not, that they have the mettle to succeed in corporate America shows that they view sex work not as a last-ditch alternative to destitution, but as a preferred choice. Like the bookmakers studied by Coontz (2001), my subjects entered their vocation voluntarily and valued the independence, autonomy, and control it offered (see also Polsky 1967).

Over and over again, my interviewees emphasized wages and freedom as the primary attractions of prostitution. Indeed, whether or not their primary reasons for engaging in prostitution were financial, many women emphasized the ready demand for their services, which enabled them to pay bills or raise cash quickly:

> [Sometimes my husband] and I have financial problems and I just miss the ease [of prostitution], because money is something that when you need it you can just reach out and grab it. It's like picking fruit off trees—when you need it, you get it. [For example,] I needed $300 to pay my electric bill, and I could just see someone—and it's not like the way work is set up in this country [comparing to paycheck regime].
>
> Definitely sometimes I see [prostitution] as just paying the rent. Sometimes it's not even ... business, I see it as just money.... It's really distinct, it's like scooping out something, not even business-like.

For these women, one key benefit of their work is that it is a cash business with a fairly consistent demand; their references to "picking fruit," "grab[bing]," and "scooping out" money vividly demonstrate this fact. To a certain extent, they can tailor their working hours to their financial needs, working more when they have debts, and working less when they need time off.

Of course, the fact that prostitution is both illegal and, for most clients, a discretionary expense rather than an essential service, means there are also times of financial insecurity, such as when police arrests of clients receive prominent coverage on the evening news, or alarmist reports about sexually transmitted diseases are published in local newspapers. Events unrelated to prostitution also affect business; as one of my informants explained,

> [T]here's fluctuation with the work, so sometimes I might see three people in one day, and sometimes I might have a work week which is very, very slow. . . . [L]ike when they had the stock-market crash, the phone didn't ring for two days. [Then]I get very nervous, because I do have a lot of financial pressures, I've got my mother out of a nursing home and she's in my house [elsewhere], and I'm having to pay for a caregiver. And the house payments are very expensive, and my insurance on my house is nine hundred dollars a month there. So I'm trying to develop other [income], so that I don't have to be feeling so on the edge, and having this financial insecurity. . . . This eventuality, then, importantly qualifies the claim that prostitution is like picking fruit. Much of the time it may be, but there are other times, some foreseeable (Christmas) and some not (September 11, 2001), when there will be few or no fruit to harvest, even if the prostitute has done everything right.

Indeed, asked what a bad work day is like, nearly all of my informants said a typical bad day was a day when no one called, when those who called seemed like bad risks, or when some other circumstance prevented them from working.

> A really bad work day is, nobody's calling, [you're] stressed trying to pick from people that you kind of don't want to have over because you don't know them, they might be—they're probably not cops but it's not clear, because they either won't give their work number or they won't do something [else that is part of her screening process]—and trying to [decide] to see them or not to see them, since it's already pledged as a work day and not [a day off]. . . . Just sitting around and waiting is really one of the higher-level bad days, I think.

> The worst day . . . [is] when the building supervisor decides they have to put a screw into something stupid in your [apartment]. It's like, I really don't need to have the water faucets fixed . . . but you can't get rid of them and you don't know when they're going to come, so all day long [clients] call and say "Can I come over now? Can I come over now?" and you're like, "No, no, no, I'm waiting for someone to come in and put a screw into my water faucet," and just watching everything good pass you by. I think that's an awful day. It's a totally wasted day. Sitting by yourself having nothing better to do and watching your work day disappear. I don't know if there's any analogy . . . Lots of [other] people lose a work day, but they don't lose a month's income in a flash because of a screw that nobody needed to put in anyway, but you can't tell them why they can't.

As these statements demonstrate, coupled with its illegality the independence and autonomy that can be found in prostitution also may result in insecurity. When demand is high and the legal climate calm, prostitution can offer a good income, free time, and interesting clients. But when demand is slow or other exigencies interfere with the ability to work, a prostitute may be vulnerable to financial strains or feel it necessary to see clients she might otherwise reject.

These are similar to the pressures faced by many self-employed people, but for the prostitute these pressures are magnified by the illegality of her work. To avoid raising suspicions or putting her "cover" story in question, for example, she may feel unable to tell the building superintendent to reschedule repairs. Because she may have no recourse if a client mistreats her or refuses to pay, seeing a questionable client is a risky and difficult decision. Advertising more widely or working with other prostitutes may increase her risk of arrest. Finally, although some surges and slumps in demand are predictable, many are not, and those who work alone may have no way of knowing whether everyone in the business is suffering, or whether her ad has become stale, her rates undercut, or some similar factor she could address is the cause.

WORKING STYLES: PROSTITUTION AS A MEANS TO AN END

Among my subjects I found three basic attitudes toward work and money: One group worked as little as possible, just enough to support themselves at whatever standard of living they preferred (from minimal and ascetic to fairly lavish); another group worked more diligently, usually due to specific financial and personal commitments; and the third group were particularly savvy businesswomen who approached the work as a profession or trade and thought strategically about ways to increase business, to invest, and to insure their futures. The demarcations are not exact, and some women exhibited overlapping orientations. However, the overall variation in responses supported this tripartite categorization.

Those who worked to support a specific lifestyle stressed their ability to be independent, to have control over their work and non-work lives, to be able to afford some indulgences, and to vary how much they worked each month. Exemplifying this attitude toward work, one interviewee once explained that working as an escort means that she has "rarely set an alarm clock, and . . . never had cheap champagne" (DePaulo 1997:38). As one subject elaborated,

> One kind of really great work day is just to do a personal best, financially . . . [S]ome days all of your favorite people will come over exactly spaced out throughout your day and each one will give you a tip or a present, and tell you how you've made their life totally better. And at the end of the day you'll have scads of money and have been appreciated till you're going to turn blue. And the other best kind of work day is the day when you do exactly what you wanted in the pursuit of love, health, and happiness: Plug in the phone for five minutes, work for two hours, and have enough money to pay for the rest of the month.

Another put similar thoughts this way:

> I don't have to be rich, but I'd like to be comfortable, be worth maybe . . . $100,000 or so, that's not a lot, maybe $200,000, maybe more. I'm not really willing to work that hard. I could probably be rich if I wanted to be, but I'm not willing to work that hard to make that much of a fortune. I'll settle for a small fortune. Yeah, I like beautiful things, but I don't have to have everything beautiful, just some nice things that inspire me. They could all burn up in a fire! 1 like to enjoy my life, I like my leisure time, I like to have time to goof off or play on my computer or watch television or play with my [pet]. I don't want to be a slave to my business. Maybe for short periods of time, if I have to be, to get things done. Sometimes you have to. But, no, [not in general].

Still another maintained a more modest standard of living but took this same approach to her work. She once worked full-time in prostitution, and now works in another part of the sex industry, engaging in prostitution occasionally:

> I know I'll do [prostitution] for as long and whenever I need money. I'm practical in that way . . . I just use it in a way to have enough money to do nothing, basically, so I can work a little bit and sit on my butt the rest of the time. . . . I live very humbly and I'm happy with what I have. . . . [Full-time prostitution was a] good way to earn money to do other things, it wasn't total drudgery, [but] . . . it wasn't like this was my life's work. . . . I hate working, I'm just basically lazy. I liked the money, and the freedom. I didn't get a big ego boost out of it. . . . I guess the money was the main motivator, and the hours. . . . We were pretty lazy . . . we really didn't work that hard. We'd met our minimum and had a little bit left over to have fun, and basically didn't work the rest of the week. . . .

Even if they are not saving for the future, women like these are mindful that prostitution enables them to achieve a certain standard of living otherwise unavailable to them without a significant alteration in lifestyle. The women in this group generally treat prostitution as their primary, and often only, source of income, so there are certainly times when they work very hard in order to maximize their earnings. Nonetheless, they are more likely than the women in the other groups to adjust the frequency with which they see clients and the energy they devote to obtaining them, depending on what other goals they have. That is, should a woman in this group desire a shopping spree at Neiman Marcus or a new sports car, she may work extremely hard. When she wants time to garden, paint, or see friends, she may devote only minimal hours to prostitution.

A second group was more clearly instrumental about their work in prostitution, seeing it not so much as a career but as a good means to fulfill or facilitate other obligations. This group's work orientation might seem to be simply a variation of the first, in that for both groups prostitution functions as an efficient mechanism to support a certain lifestyle. However, they are better understood as distinct groups because the first takes a more casual attitude toward work, depending on how it fits in with what else they want to do. The second group, in contrast, may indeed set alarm clocks and forego expensive luxuries because of obligations such as fixed expenses for which a delinquent payment might be disastrous. One interviewee, for example, has chosen to work in prostitution until she finds an equal but more stable source of income:

> I think that my main problem now is that my overhead is so high, because of my house and my responsibilities [support of dependents]. If it wasn't for that I . . . wouldn't also have to demand that, oh, I have to have

this much money.... [When I was in my twenties] I lived like a yogi, I lived very simply.... I'm into ... low consumption. I don't have a lot of desires, like, oh, I want to fly around the world, I have to go to Chanel; that's not me. My car is ten years old. And I was happy to get new tires, you know. So I feel like it's a challenge just to meet my obligations right now.

Prostitution's lucrativeness enables some prostitutes to pursue other projects that are unpaid but meaningful to them. Thus, some women use prostitution instrumentally not just to meet pre-existing financial obligations, but to do so and still have time, energy, and funds for other projects, as the following subject explained:

I worked at a nonprofit organization one summer in college and the vice president was someone who said, "Don't tell your parents, I'm a masseuse." And I was like, "I don't know what that is and I don't know why I shouldn't tell them," but in retrospect [I understand what she was saying]—if you want to work full-time at some of the unpaid, important work, then [prostitution] is probably a really good job to have. And I didn't realize it at the time [I began working as a call girl], but I had already met people who were in the business so, upon reflection, when I finally figured out what it was they were talking about I [thought] "Oh, that's a really good role model."

A retired prostitute had similar comments:

Well, for me, [what I like about prostitution is] the freedom that you can buy by working an incredibly small number of hours to do things that are important [to you], which [things] changed over time—whether it was art work, or political work, or some other sort of thing. I think I got to capitalize on a lot of opportunities that a person who wasn't basically independently wealthy, almost, would never have gotten to do. And a lot of people who know me actually still think that I have a trust fund—somehow they're having a harder time believing that I worked for the money than that I just inherited it, because I pop up in weird places doing weird stuff like producing plays, or suddenly taking a ... job that's unpaid—that's not the luxury that most people have.

Although not all of my interviewees were so self-consciously aware of this benefit as a luxury available to very few Americans—nor would all have valued it if pointed out to them—it was nonetheless considered a significant asset by more than a few. Such women best

fit in the second group in that they are more disciplined about prostitution as a job, saving money to support political activism or forays into the arts and creating the impression they have trust funds. The women in the first group, in contrast, live more hand-to-mouth, even if they do so in comfort.

A third attitude toward work belonged to those I have termed "savvy businesswomen." For these women, like the previous group, prostitution serves instrumental purposes. However, the difference in this last group is that they have thought carefully and at length about prostitution as a business or career, and have taken steps to try to maximize its long-term benefit to them. The following subject epitomizes this orientation:

[T]he business side of things, I've been learning more about as I've been getting older. There was a madam who once said, "If you stay in the business over time, you're forced to become more entrepreneurial," and that's true.... I like going out and trying to network.... I've joined the Chamber of Commerce [recently, as an escort]—now that's a challenge, trying to work with these conservative, established business types. I'm going to get rejected [by some], but there's others that will probably be intrigued, and who knows what'll happen. I've always had some guts, and that's paid off. I think those are just tools, learning how to run a business—that's just a [way to] manifest one's vision.... For me [prostitution] is [a career]. I like it, for different reasons. I think it's an easy business—the demand is very strong—and if you're good, you can learn how to distinguish yourself from your competition and ... how to make this business something good, in the sense that you can retain your integrity and your sense of who you are.... I think it's important to have a strong positive vision why you do this work. Because if you don't, and I see this all the time, you're in danger of internalizing society's stigma, and then that can be destructive to oneself, and also to the clients. And I think you have to care about what you're doing and the quality of the service that you're providing, and you have to see it as a business. That's what it is.... [How does work differ in different cities?] I think a lot of it has to do with how you position yourself in the market; that determines what market you're going to attract. I've been trying to find ways to attract more of a professional and business clientele, that's what I prefer.... I think the larger cities have more stratified economies, and they're more diverse. For example,——'s main industry is tourism, so I've been trying to focus more on the business and pleasure travelers. Yeah, there's more diversity. If you live in a small town, then you don't have that.

Prostitutes in this third group, then, take the time to think about their markets, how to establish a niche, how to network, and how to maintain a sufficient client base, taking advantage of new tools like the Internet and reflecting on past experience to plan for the future.

In sum, as with workers in other professions, prostitutes exhibit a range of approaches to their work and a range of understandings about what paid work offers them. Work can buy free time, pay for living expenses, fund investments or other opportunities, ensure future financial security, or any combination thereof. The diversity of these responses, from within only one segment of prostitution, moreover, challenges stereotypes that "all prostitutes" are lazy, seek easy money, fail to plan for the future, have no business sense, and crave wealth and luxury.

PROVISION OF SERVICES: SEXUAL AND NON-SEXUAL SERVICES

Whatever their attitudes toward money, most prostitutes view prostitution as work. However, many argue that sex is not the only service they provide, or even the most important one. According to several women, for many men, sex is the pretext for the visit, and the real need is emotional. They reported that it was not unusual for men to pay for an hour of their time and yet ask for sex only in the last few minutes of the session. The following accounts are representative of this perspective.

> [For] a lot of the guys I see, more than anything they want some companionship. They just want somebody to sit and talk to them and make them feel like they're interesting and that they're good people. The sex is— they want sex but it's kind of like icing on the cake, is the impression that I get.

> [Why do you think clients come to see you?] I honestly think they are too busy, they are lonely . . . and nobody listens to them. And that the sex part is the annoying little thing that they have to use as an excuse, and most of them say, like, "Well, three minutes left, let's get it over with." And some people will spend five hours just to tell me about their accomplishments, and get a hug. It's not all of them, but it happens often enough that I think it describes a really big bunch [of men], that [sex] is not the reason that they even came over, but they needed it as an excuse so that they can feel more masculine—which is therapeutic—at the same time as having an opportunity to do a bunch of really feminine things, like hugging and touching and talking and

being really listened to, and having somebody think about them. Or sometimes they don't want to think about themselves at all, but [want] to just plain old connect with another person. Sometimes they just want to . . . have another human being [who's] there with them and not doing anything else. So I think they come because they're lonely.

> You get these relationships going, and they're not real relationships, but there's a connection. People misunderstand that and think it's just a sexual service, but it's not. It's men looking for an intimate emotional connection, too, that they aren't getting [elsewhere] and maybe they don't know how to get. Oh God, you hear that story so many times, "My wife doesn't understand me." I don't know if they have sex with their wives or not, but there's something that they're not getting anywhere else that they know that they can get [from me], and I think those are the ones who call, because they want someone to talk to—that's why it takes an hour. No man takes an hour [for sex]. No man. If he takes twenty minutes he's doing pretty good. But there's time to talk, to get to know each other, to have a glass of wine. . . . Many of these people need to express things to someone, and sometimes there's no one in their life that they can talk to, even just about superficial stuff. [When I was working I had] my little entourage because I was real pretty, but also I always liked to listen to people and I always had this maternal energy. I think of it as nurturing sometimes; maybe sometimes men can only express their need to be nurtured in the context of sex. They've already paid to show that they're manly enough. Some of my regular "dates" were very romantic, very sweet. We would laugh and laugh, and then it would be like, "Time's almost up, we'd better get down to it."

> [When you see a client, how does his experience differ from yours?] A lot of [clients] see it as specifically a stress-reduction technique that works into their time schedule. And it's not sexual, but it happens to include [sex], but it's just like, "I need to relax, I've had such an awful day." . . . I think that most of them don't consciously register that they're just looking for the company, I think that's my interpretation, but I think that . . . anybody who was going to look at this from a management consulting standpoint would have to say that the need here, expressed or not, is not for sex. [What would clients say they're looking for?] Off the tops of their heads, I think they would say that they didn't come looking for sex, they came looking for a "relaxing sex mini-vacation." You actually can't separate them out. That if they thought it was sex that wasn't a mini-vacation or wasn't relaxing they wouldn't do it. And a treat . . . beyond mini-vacation that it's like a lollipop for

them. It can be a reward. . . . None of them come over saying, "I need sex," or almost never. But "I need a treat," almost always. A relaxing treat or a treat.

These arguments were made by women who span the spectrum of approaches to business. That is, not only the savvy businesswomen but also women who exhibited no particular interest in techniques of entrepreneurial success made these observations. These women's references to an hour of their services as a vacation or a treat, and their perception of sex as the "excuse" or the "icing on the cake" suggest that, from the women's perspective, the services they provide are more than purely physical. Although sex seems to be completely absent from very few prostitution encounters, it seems undeniable that for some women it is a small part of the services they offer (see also Carter 1998; CORP 1988; French and Lee 1988; Lever and Dolnick 2000). Moreover, this claim can be true even if clients would describe their needs and desires entirely differently.

Of course, not all prostitutes understand their work this way; many believe that sex is a primary reason clients seek them out. But even many of these prostitutes also do not describe their services as exclusively physical:

> I get to know all kinds of interesting people, and I get to play with them. I like to touch other people, I like to make them feel good, I like to see them smile, I like to pull out my toys and have them look at me like, "Ooh, what's she going to do with me now?" All this is just sort of fun. So that's what I really like about it.

> The good [clients] were, for the most part, in their late 40s, early 50s, they would come and they'd talk and establish a rapport like human beings, and then when you came right down to the "down and dirty" it was so sweet. They were appreciative and loving. It was nice. It was gentle. . . . And they leave strutting, they're like cock of the walk—they just had themselves a woman.

> I think that the men in general, they're going to be more desirous [due to strong sex drives and not having sex often enough]. That's why they're coming to me. Because they're not getting satisfied in whatever life they have; often they're very busy businessmen. They enjoy sex, they want to get away and just relax for an hour, do something for themselves. They see this as a way of pampering themselves. And I think they enjoy the fact that . . . I make sure that I enjoy the situation, and I set certain limits, if something's uncomfortable for me, and they can count on me to do that. So I'm sure that makes them feel much more comfortable, because then they

don't have to feel the added guilt of "Well, I'm imposing . . . on somebody, or invading somebody's body space when they don't want me there." And I think that can make me more successful.

Even women who see sex as the defining, integral characteristic of their work, then, may intuit client needs that are intertwined with sexual desire, and/or may recognize sexual services as fulfilling certain non-sexual functions. They recognize that in doing their jobs well—sexually, interpersonally and emotionally—they not only satisfy a client's sexual need but also can make him feel happy, more confident, relaxed, and less alone. This may increase the likelihood of a repeat visit, and also enables the prostitute to feel positive about her work.

Prostitutes who view the sexual side of their work as often incidental may, of course, attempt to select for clients who have the same understanding. In addition, it is likely that prostitutes who work on the streets and have shorter sessions than call girls and escorts experience less emotional connection with clients. For example, it is unlikely that British actor Hugh Grant was in the back seat of a car with Los Angeles street prostitute Divine Brown because he wanted someone to listen to him. Rather, one might guess that this encounter was motivated on his part by a combination of desire, excitement, risk, and taboo. However, my interviewees almost universally agreed that there is a certain proportion of clients who patronize call girls and escorts to satisfy some emotional need. Some prostitutes may look for such clients, others may screen out such clients, but almost all of them recognize this as a client type.

RELATIONSHIPS WITH CLIENTS

Given these perspectives on the work, it is not surprising that prostitutes describe a variety of relationships with clients, from purely business exchanges to more personal bonds.

> I had a nice gentleman . . . who paid for my company for the weekend, and we stayed at a lovely bed-and-breakfast. . . . [H]e was just a very nice man, a delightful man. Treated me well. . . . [A]fterwards I sent him a pretty card, and . . . I had a photo of myself, and I signed it, to give him something, a keepsake. . . . These men are single, they want a woman to be with them. I don't know if they'll ever do it again. It's like a one-time thing; it's expensive for them. They're middle-class men and that's an expensive investment for them, but they're curious; it's an experience.

Some [clients] I still keep in touch with for different [reasons]—my lawyers, accountants, computer consultants—that's how my networking works. Most of [my clients] were really my friends, but they're not friends in the same way that my friends in my regular address book are. They're like business associates who I would call . . . if my car needed fixing, but I wouldn't call them because I was lonely. [But] I would be delighted to cross paths with them. [They're] definitely not on the despising range, at all.

This work has given me the opportunity to . . . have connections with men that are helping me, and that will be helping me in my [other] businesses. I mean, from the telephone man to advertising, to helping get people to rent my house in [location] with a travel agent. So it's sort of an unfair advantage. It's going to be helping me.

Well, the [clients] who know me really well really do know my whole life story, or they know parts of it, and I pretty much know theirs. . . . [But knowing them like this] is all within [the] business context. It really reminds me of the way that people would know each other around the water cooler. We do know intimate stuff about each other, but we don't have an intimate relationship. For the most part. . . . [However], there's my wonderful old physicist friend who I think kind of mixes me up with a daughter, or some kind of niece or relation of some sort, and we just sit around and talk about [our] dogs. And he's my favorite, and I definitely see him in some sort of almost family role, I'm just delighted by him. . . . And then there's the great gob of the [ones who are strangers] that I don't know well and didn't see again.

They all really like me, and especially ones who are regulars—you have a relationship with them. You have a lot of affection and love and appreciation for each other; it's in certain strict boundaries. And I think that gives them a sense of safety or security, knowing that I'm not a mistress, I'm not going to be infringing on their lives. . . . [But] there's a kind of poignancy, especially if you are close to someone. . . . I was very close to [one client]. He really wanted me . . . to be a mistress and just move in and all with him, but he was too much into drugs, and I would never do that. He was into drugs, so I had to draw the line. And he ended up dying. So there was a kind of sadness. Because if I go to the funeral, none of the friends know me, none of the family, [and] I can't really say how I knew him. But you still have a lot of grief, and you still may know the person very deeply. You might know the person in ways no one else knows that person.

Like the call girls in Bryan's (1965) sample, virtually all of my informants defied the stereotype of prostitutes as exploitative, man-hating con artists; whether friendly or strictly professional, these women largely appreciated and respected their clients—especially the long-term clients—as the lifeblood of their enterprises. Here we see another parallel with Coontz's (2001) bookies. Both prostitutes and bookmakers engage in "victimless" crimes; their clients are willing participants in law-breaking. As such, many prostitutes and bookmakers strive for honesty and integrity in dealing with clients, to maximize income and career longevity.

My subjects' statements demonstrate a range of connections and experiences with clients, from impersonal (if not anonymous) single encounters, to warm but fleeting engagements, to repeated dealings and networking on a business level, to close and lasting friendships—much like service providers and professionals have with clients in the legitimate business world. In their relationships with clients, where these women largely make their own decisions about when and how often they will work, who they will see, and what they will offer, they have the ability to structure the relationship to suit their needs or interests much more so than do people whose workplace autonomy is more limited. Their relationships with clients are more characteristic of service providers and clients than sales people with their customers, although of course the distinction is not absolute. As such, prostitution appears to involve the provision of a sexual service more than the sale of a commodity, challenging the image of prostitutes as "selling themselves," selling their bodies or selling sex per se (Lucas forthcoming).

Choosing Prostitution

Whatever their work experiences, many prostitutes absolutely insist that their work is chosen. Indeed, the prominent prostitutes' rights activist Dolores (French and Lee 1988:178) argues that prostitution must be an option for women if women are to achieve self-determination: "As long as women [are] not allowed to voluntarily use our bodies to make a living, we [will] always, on some level, be denied the right to choose our own destinies. Everyone's body is a commodity. . . . A ballet dancer, a construction worker. All the rest is misplaced puritanism."

In this vein, some argue that for women with little job experience, few employment opportunities, or sudden, extraordinary expenses, prostitution is a rational choice. One prostitute emphasizes prostitution as work that is economically empowering for women, especially those from lower educational and income backgrounds; other than marriage, prostitution (and other sex work) offers women virtually the only opportunity "to hopscotch a few economic classes" (Cagan 1993; see also Skipper and McCaghy 1970). In the first of the following interview excerpts, my informant reports being "pushed" into prostitution by a lack of alternatives. However, as she describes her work history, it becomes clear she had the skills and experience for other jobs, but they did not pay sufficient wages. The second and third interviewees more explicitly see prostitution as the most agreeable and lucrative choice among available options, given economic realities.

> I was basically a student at the time I met my [ex-] husband, a music student, and so I was basically taken care of by my husband for, maybe, ten years. And this was one of the reasons that I was pushed into this type of thing [prostitution], because I had no job experience. I was basically destitute when my husband had financial problems and . . . cut me off completely, financially. I had taken care of my husband's mother; I was a caretaker, she [had] Alzheimer's. And I was also active in the community. . . . I was involved with different kinds of . . . political activism. . . . And so I was very busy . . . but it was never paid work. I think when I was younger I just worked [in] a fast-food place, and I worked in an ice-cream place, and I worked taking care of this elderly woman. . . . I did mostly volunteer work, unpaid work. I was the coordinator of a national . . . ecological activist group. It was also unpaid. So I think if I wasn't in this, I would be going into some kind of non-profit sector. And I'm also basically self-educated. I went to college maybe two years, and then I went to study business, and I never succeeded very well in that—business undergraduate—so I never completed my degree. And I . . . tried to go back to school for a while, and I think younger women are able to do that, but because I have my family that I'm supporting right now, I don't have the extra money or time.

> Especially with no [college] education, when you're 18 years old [like I was], there really is not much else out there that you can do that you can earn a living wage at. When you consider what people making minimum wage bring home for a week, how do they afford to live? . . . There are not that many other avenues. . . . [discusses glass ceiling, workplace discrimination, and low wages in female-stereotyped occupations]

> Basically I had gotten really, really broke and I needed money quick, so I started working at a strip club and I didn't like that very much. It wasn't a good environment for me, they were very strict and they were taking too much of my money. I just didn't like it. So I went to a lingerie shop [as a model] and I worked there for two months and I made better money but it still wasn't enough to get myself out of debt. And I thought to myself, "You know, I have slept with so many people just because I didn't want to hurt their feelings or whatever. Why can't I do it for money?" And I'd always been curious about it. So I called a bunch of escort services and the first night I worked I made $480 and I hadn't had sex with a single person and I thought, "OK, I like this job!"

Other women say they chose prostitution for significant non-economic reasons. As noted earlier, prostitution enables some women to engage in unpaid projects. Others state that they chose prostitution in part because they rejected mainstream social values and gender norms.

> [*How did you get into prostitution?*] I just saw a need for some sort of match-making service, or something like that, and the more I looked into it the more I thought, "that's not what people need, that's not really the need." The other thing is that I was 19, and it was 1980, and there was nothing radical to do. The sixties were over, the seventies seemed a little passé, and we were in the early Reagan era, and there wasn't anything to do. But I was bloody well not going to be a part of that culture, and there weren't that many ways to not be, and I feel like doing something that was obviously beyond the law and annoyed society would have been a good enough reason all by itself. And to discover that it also made sense to me in a human way, that I was working with people who seemed to have, not just a need for something they'd spend money on, but a real human need for companionship or whatever. I thought, "Well, this is even more radical and more fabulous than I thought. This totally fits for me and I'm doing something that I really, sincerely, find is good for me and good for the world, and bad for the current order." What could be more satisfying?

> A lot of my clients will tell me, "Wow, you're really nice and I didn't expect this," or "I've never had this experience." A lot of clients are really just in awe of the whole situation, that somebody could just say "Fuck the social stigma . . . I'm gonna do this [i.e., be a prostitute] because I want to do it," and just go out and do it. And . . . the stereotype of women in our culture is [that] we're weak and we can't do this and we can't do that, so I think it's kind of shocking that we are doing it.

What is interesting about these comments is not only the extent to which they reveal rational, goal-oriented decision-making, although that is important. What also is significant is that prostitution's stigma and illegality, in this context, magnified its attractions (even as they also magnified its risks). Women like these embrace prostitution's outlaw status, in this regard, because it enables them to make an overt political statement, or to support themselves in a way that comports with their beliefs, challenges the status quo, and rejects gender-based constraints.

CONCLUSION

Letkemann (1973:9) notes that "a purely economic model of man does not adequately explain variations in work behavior and job satisfaction" either in legitimate or unlawful work. The same can be said of prostitution: a model of prostitution as simply deviance (or exploitation) does not adequately explain variations in attitudes and experience. By looking at prostitution as work, this article has tried to begin overcoming that deficit. My subjects' statements reveal myriad aspects of prostitution as work from the elite practitioner's point of view. In some ways indoor prostitution is very similar to other work, especially service sector work and self-employment. It has the problem of uneven demand and the periods of financial insecurity common in many service occupations, as well as the flexibility and autonomy offered by some forms of self-employment. It has room for specialization, rewards professionalism, and can offer job satisfaction. But its benefits are importantly qualified by its legal status, because the criminalization of prostitution in the United States inevitably makes the work more insecure, dangerous, isolating, and socially disreputable (Lucas 2005). Yet despite this fact, the women quoted here are not ashamed of being sex workers. As Scambler (1997:109) argues, prostitutes often "have their own sub-cultural, or counter-cultural, notions of honour/dishonour.... Dishonour for many sex workers is not associated with sex work per se, but with a lack of competence and integrity in the conduct of work."

Moreover, perhaps because these women provide sexual services for a living, they have thought about sex in different ways than many non-sex workers do. During our interviews, their comments revealed that they recognize safe sex as a prudent and necessary business practice, for example; they can see sexual desires and needs as legitimate and integral to well-being; and being familiar with clients who vary tremendously in sexual aptitudes, attitudes, and experience, they often observe the potential benefit of their services to people other than the client himself. Of course, not all prostitutes make these claims about their work. Moreover, it is important to recall that my interviewees had the financial, social, and emotional wherewithal to structure their work largely in ways that suited them and provided them the time for such reflection and the ability to maintain healthy self-images. Nonetheless, the fact that even a portion of prostitutes have these perspectives is instructive about prostitution's significance for its practitioners and society. Despite its illegality and stigma, my informants found a range of positive meanings in their work. Their insights suggest that absent criminality and stigma, prostitution might be a very different institution than the one it is today, and perhaps even an institution that society could value as a service or helping profession (Lucas 2005).

REFERENCES

Albert, Alexa. 2001. *Brothel: Mustang Ranch and Its Women.* New York: Random House.

Alexander, Priscilla. 1998. "Prostitution: A Difficult Issue for Feminists." Pp. 184–230. In *Sex Work: Writings by Women in the Sex Industry,* 2nd ed., edited by Frédérique Delacoste and Priscilla Alexander. San Francisco: Cleis Press.

Brennan, Denise. 2002. "Selling Sex for Visas: Sex Tourism as a Stepping-Stone to International Migration." Pp. 154–68. In *Global Woman: Nannies, Maids, and Sex Workers in the New Economy,* edited by Barbara Ehrenreich and Arlie Russell Hochschild. New York: Metropolitan Books.

Bryan, James H. 1965. "Apprenticeships in Prostitution." *Social Problems* 12:287–97.

Cagan, Sasha. 1993, April. "Sex Under the Table." *The Fine Print* 2:5.

Canadian Organization for the Rights of Prostitutes. 1988. "Realistic Feminists: An Interview with Valerie Scott, Peggy Miller, and Ryan Hotchkiss of the Canadian Organization for the Rights of Prostitutes." Pp. 204–7. In *Good Girls/Bad Girls: Feminists and Sex Trade Workers Face to Face,* edited by Laurie Bell. Toronto: The Seal Press.

Carole. 1998a. "Interview with Barbara." Pp. 166–74. In *Sex Work: Writings by Women in the Sex Industry,* 2nd ed., edited by Frédérique Delacoste and Priscilla Alexander. San Francisco: Cleis Press.

Carole. 1998b. "Interview with Debra." Pp. 91–95. In *Sex Work: Writings by Women in the Sex Industry,* 2nd ed., edited by Frédérique Delacoste and Priscilla Alexander. San Francisco: Cleis Press.

Carter, Sunny. 1998. "A Most Useful Tool." Pp. 159–65. In *Sex Work: Writings by Women in the Sex Industry,* 2nd ed., edited by Frédérique Delacoste and Priscilla Alexander. San Francisco: Cleis Press.

——. 2000. "Power and Control in the Commercial Sex Trade." Pp. 181–201. In *Sex for Sale: Prostitution, Pornography, and the Sex Industry,* edited by Ronald Weitzer. New York: Routledge.

Coontz, Phyllis. 2001. "Managing the Action: Sport Book-Makers as Entrepreneurs." *Deviant Behavior,* 22(3):239–266.

Cooper, Belinda. 1989. "Prostitution: A Feminist Analysis." *Women's Rights Law Reporter* 11:98–119.

DePaulo, Lisa. 1997, July. "The Prostitutes' Convention." *Marie Claire,* pp. 34–39.

Ford, Kimberly-Anne. 1998. "Evaluating Prostitution as a Human Service Occupation." Pp. 420–34. In *Prostitution: On Whores, Hustlers, and Johns,* edited by James E. Elias, Vern L. Bullough, Veronica Elias, and Gwen Brewer. New York: Prometheus Books.

French, Dolores and Linda Lee. 1988. *Working: My Life as a Prostitute.* New York: E.P. Dutton.

Goldsmith, Barbara. 1993, April 26. "Women on the Edge." *The New Yorker,* pp. 64–81.

Hampton, Lynn. 1988. "Hookers with AIDS—The Search." Pp. 157–64. In *AIDS: The Women,* edited by Ines Rieder and Patricia Ruppelt. San Francisco: Cleis Press.

Leigh, Carol. 1998. "The Continuing Saga of Scarlot Harlot IV." Pp. 88–90. In *Sex Work: Writings by Women in the Sex Industry,* 2nd ed., edited by Frédérique Delacoste and Priscilla Alexander. San Francisco: Cleis Press.

Letkemann, Peter. 1973. *Crime as Work.* Englewood Cliffs, NJ: Prentice Hall.

Lever, Janet and Deanne Dolnick. 2000. "Clients and Call Girls: Seeking Sex and Intimacy." Pp. 85–100. In *Sex for Sale: Prostitution, Pornography, and the sex Industry,* edited by Ronald Weitzer. New York: Routledge.

Lopez-Jones, Nina. 1998. "Workers: Introducing the English Collective of Prostitutes." Pp. 271–78. In *Sex Work: Writings by Women in the Sex Industry,* 2nd ed., edited by Frédérique Delacoste and Priscilla Alexander. San Francisco: Cleis Press.

Lucas, A. 2005. "Paying a Premium: Prostitutes Under a Regime of Criminalization." Unpublished manuscript.

——. 2005. "The Currency of Sex: Prostitution, Law and Com-modification." Pp. 248–270. In *Rethinking Commodification: Cases and Readings in Law and Culture,* edited by Martha M. Ertman and Joan C. Williams. New York: NYU Press.

Metal, Phyllis Luman. 1998. "One for Ripley's." Pp. 119–21. In *Sex Work: Writings by Women in the Sex Industry,* 2nd ed., edited by Frédérique Delacoste and Priscilla Alexander. San Francisco: Cleis Press.

Niles, Donna Marie. 1998. "Confessions of a Priestesstute." Pp. 148–49. In *Sex Work: Writings by Women in the Sex Industry,* 2nd ed., edited by Frédérique Delacoste and Priscilla Alexander. San Francisco: Cleis Press.

Pateman, Carole. 1988. *The Sexual Contract.* Stanford, CA: Stanford University Press.

Polsky, Ned. 1967. *Hustlers, Beats, and Others.* Chicago: Aldine Publishing.

Rhode, Deborah L. 1989. *Justice and Gender: Sex Discrimination and the Law.* Cambridge., MA: Harvard University Press.

Romenesko, Kim and Eleanor M. Miller. 1989. "The Second Step in Double Jeopardy: Appropriating the Labor of Female Street Hustlers." *Crime and Delinquency* 35:109–35.

Scambler, Graham. 1997. "Conspicuous and Inconspicuous Sex Work: The Neglect of the Ordinary and Mundane." Pp. 105–20. In *Rethinking Prostitution: Purchasing Sex in the 1990s,* edited by Graham Scambler and Annette Scambler. London: Routledge.

Skipper, James K., Jr. and Charles H. McCaghy. 1970. "Stripteasers: The Anatomy and Career Contingencies of a Deviant Occupation." *Social Problems* 17:391–405.

Sundahl, Debi. 1998. "Stripper." Pp. 175–80. In *Sex Work: Writings by Women in the Sex Industry,* 2nd ed., edited by Frédérique Delacoste and Priscilla Alexander. San Francisco: Cleis Press.

Wardlaw, Cecelia. 1998. "Dream Turned Nightmare." Pp. 108–12. In *Sex Work: Writings by Women in the Sex Industry,* 2nd ed., edited by Frédérique Delacoste and Priscilla Alexander. San Francisco: Cleis Press.

West, Rachel. 1998. "U.S. PROStitutes Collective." Pp. 279–89. In *Sex Work: Writings by Women in the Sex Industry,* 2nd ed., edited by Frédérique Delacoste and Priscilla Alexander. San Francisco: Cleis Press.

21

MOTHERING, CRIME, AND INCARCERATION

KATHLEEN J. FERRARO AND ANGELA M. MOE

This article examines the relationships between women's perceptions of parenting, crime, and incarceration. The women's responsibilities of child care—together with the economic realities of being poor combined with being victims of domestic violence—resulted in most of the incarcerated women to commit crimes for economic gain. Some of the study sample of women suffered psychological problems due to the loss of custody of their children and became involved in drug- and alcohol-related crimes. Incarcerated women with children, being an absent parent, represents the gendered inequality of harm between mothers and fathers in the responsibilities for child care.

This article focuses on women's experiences with mothering, crime, and incarceration. Each of these socially constructed categories reflects and reinforces gendered expectations for women's performance, as well as race and class hierarchies. Some research has suggested that the legal system tends to de-emphasize, excuse, justify, and downplay women's crimes, even those that are targeted at or incidentally harm their children (Allen 1987; Daly 1994). According to such reports, women are portrayed within the legal system in ways that are consistent with paternalistic hegemonic standards of passivity and weakness and, as such, are unable to be held fully accountable for their criminal activities. Such research, supportive of the chivalry thesis in criminology (see Pollak 1950), contrasts with other studies that find that women are processed through the criminal justice system in misogynist ways, demonized and vilified for countering hegemonic womanhood and motherhood vis-á-vis their criminal offenses (Chesney-Lind 1997; Gilbert 1999; Nagel and Hagan 1983; Young 1986). The women most likely to benefit from hegemonic notions of womanhood and motherhood within the criminal justice system are those that fit the ideal image within society at large, namely white, middle to upper class, heterosexual women (Belknap 2001). Much current research suggests that the disproportionate rate of incarceration of women of color is a reflection of racist perceptions, policing, and sentencing policies (Belknap 2001; Gilbert 1999; Richie 2001).

While women are capable of and certainly do commit many forms of crime, including interpersonal

Source: Mothering, Crime, and Incarceration by Ferraro, Kathleen J. and Angela M. Moe, *Journal of Contemporary Ethnography, 32*(1), February 2003, 9–40. Reprinted with permission.

violent crimes that in some cases harm their children, they also commit their crimes from gendered, as well as raced and classed, positions that are politically, economically, and historically rooted (Allen 1987; Humphries 1999). Despite instances in which the contexts of women's crimes resemble those of men's (see as examples Miller 1998; Sommers, Baskin, and Fagan 2000), overall, women are more likely to commit minor property offenses than serious or violent offenses as compared to men and are less likely to recidivate than men (Smart 1995). The crimes for which they are most often arrested and incarcerated are suggestive of their gendered and raced social positioning (Richie 2001; Ross 1998). Such crimes include nonviolent and minor property crimes such as prostitution, larceny, shoplifting, check or credit card fraud, forgery/counterfeiting, and drug possession (Immarigeon and Chesney-Lind 1992; Bloom, Chesney-Lind, and Owen 1994; Chesney-Lind 1997; Chesney-Lind, Harris, and deGroot 1998; Greenfield and Snell 1999; Watterson 1996). The growth in the number of incarcerated women between 1990 and 2000 is composed largely of drug offenders (Harrison and Beck 2002).

Despite the relative infrequency and nonviolent nature of female offending, the numbers of women under control of the "correctional" system in the United States have been growing over the past twenty years at a faster pace than the numbers of men (Chesney-Lind 1997; Greenfield and Snell 1999; U.S. General Accounting Office 1999). Between 1990 and 2000, the rate of female incarceration increased by 108 percent (Beck and Harrison 2001). Yet the proportion of women composing the total correctional population remains small. Only about 6.7 percent of the total prison population and about 11 percent of the local jail population are women (Greenfield and Snell 1999; Stephan 2001). The research, facilities, and programs for criminal offenders in the United States focus primarily on adult male offenders. Knowledge of incarcerated women's experiences and responsiveness of prisons and jails to women's circumstances have both been retarded by neglect of the gendered dimensions of incarceration.

The vast majority of prisons and jails have not developed the most rudimentary resources for women inmates (Morash 1998; U.S. General Accounting Office 1999). Women are assessed and classified using instruments designed for males, and programming is designed without consideration of the differing needs of women. Although at least 70 percent of women in jail have minor children, few jails have programs that foster parenting skills or contact between mothers and children, and there are virtually no programs designed

to assist children with problems related to the incarceration of their mothers (Greenfield and Snell 1999).

METHOD AND SAMPLE CHARACTERISTICS

Our study was formulated to examine the relationships between women's experiences of violent victimization and incarceration. We developed a semistructured interview schedule designed to elicit topical life-history narratives. Such an approach has become a preferred means of data collection among those working with incarcerated and otherwise marginalized populations whose experiences are not easily predetermined or quantifiable (see as examples Arnold 1990; Gilfus 1992; Richie 1996). This methodology allowed us to center our analysis on the specific vantage points of the jailed women and to honor their location for developing understanding of mothering and incarceration (Elliott 1994; Hartsock 1987; Narayan 1988; Smith 1987). Assuming that members of marginalized groups can offer meaningful accounts of the ways in which the world is organized according to the oppressions they experience, we felt it appropriate to center our data collection and analysis on the direct accounts provided by the women about their life experiences (Sandoval 2000). In analyzing these accounts, we do not assume that they represent the objective truth of women's mothering any more than probation and court records represent such truth. Incarcerated women may have a unique stake in constructing accounts of mothering that emphasize their conformity to social expectations to counterbalance the stigma attached to criminalization (see Orbuch 1997). While strategies of self-presentation are always a concern in conducting interviews, we did not find that women portrayed their mothering in a particularly positive light. Rather, women were very emotional, often crying and on one occasion ending the interview, and expressed remorse and guilt over the impact of their crimes on their children.

The women ranged in age from twenty-one years to fifty years, with an average of thirty-four years. Fifteen (50 percent) women identified as white, seven (23 percent) as Black, three (10 percent) as Latina, three (10 percent) as American Indian, and two (6 percent) as biracial. This distribution was comparable to the proportions of women in each racial/ethnic group in the jail at the time of our interviews in which 53 percent were white, 24 percent Latina. 13 percent Black, and 9 percent American Indian. Few of the women had stable or sustainable employment prior to their incarceration and generally identified themselves as lower to working middle class. Twenty-seven (90 percent) of the women had children, with an average of three children each. Two of these women were also pregnant at the time of their interviews.

IMPACT OF THE ROLE OF MOTHERING ON CRIMINAL OFFENDING

Arizona, like most states in the United States, provides a very low level of financial and social support for mothering. Overall, 16.5 percent of Arizona women live in poverty, with the proportion rising to 22.3 percent in rural counties bordering Mexico and 53.3 percent on American Indian reservations (Caiazza 2000). Throughout the slate, approximately one-third of Latina and African American women and one-half of American Indian women live in poverty. Poverty data by race and family composition are not available, but overall, 41.5 percent of single women with children live in poverty, which is comparable to the national rate of 41 percent (Caiazza 2000). Nearly 25 percent of Arizona women do not have health insurance (compared with a national rate of 18.5 percent), and the average annual cash benefit provided to single mothers through Temporary Assistance for Needy Families in Arizona, $3,345, is considerably lower than the U.S. average of $4,297. Child support is awarded in about 30 percent of mother-headed households, but only 43.6 percent of orders for collection result in actual collections. Single mothers, especially those with less than a high school education and women of color, face harsh economic constraints and a lack of low-cost housing, child care, and medical services.

Some of the mothers interviewed correlated this economic situation directly with their participation in criminal activity. Women with children in their custody conceptualized crime as an alternative to hunger and homelessness. Women without dependent children did not discuss the relationship between economic survival and economic crimes and most often referenced drugs and alcohol as the basis for their offenses. Several women linked their financial difficulties, and the crimes they committed to obtain money, to efforts to escape from or cope with violent men while providing for their children. These women articulated the structural barriers to successful mothering and viewed nonviolent crime as a rational, responsible action taken to meet their children's needs. This interpretation of the reasonableness of crimes contrasted with individualistic and self-blaming views expressed by most women incarcerated for drug and prostitution crimes committed to support addictions. In this way, the role of mothering served as catalyst and a rationale

for crime that was not available to women without children in their custody.

Racial differences were apparent in the accounts of women, as African American women were more fully cognizant of the ways in which race, gender, and poverty were intertwined through institutionalized patterns of exclusion. All the African American women in our sample had been battered, and they were the most realistic about economic exclusions and their sole responsibility for meeting the economic needs of their children. American Indian women also discussed their experiences with racism but linked them more to addictions than to poverty. Latina women most often described their offending in terms of individual deficiencies and/or victimizations rather than structural economic constraints.

Alicia, a twenty-one-year-old biracial (African American/white) woman with two children, ages three and five, reported that she had been on her own since she was seventeen, having left the abusive father of her children. She completed a training program as a nursing assistant and had been working as well as selling crack. She was in jail for possession of crack, powder cocaine, and paraphernalia. The "paraphernalia" was the cigarette case she used to transport the drugs for sale. Although she thought that selling was wrong "because crack destroys people's lives," she felt her actions were "right at the time" because they allowed her to support her children:

> I don't regret it because without the extra income, my kids wouldn't be fed every day. Even though I do have a good job when I work and stuff like that, it's hard raising two kids by yourself. . . . You get used to having money every day and you don't have to worry about the electric being off or the rent being paid. Your cheek is like your hard earned money: you're not going to spend it ridiculously like, "Oh, let's go buy a hundred-dollar pair of shoes with it." You know what I'm saying? You budget it because it's the only thing you look forward to for paying your bills. . . . But with that other money [paycheck] it goes so fast. As soon as you get it, the kids need new clothes or spend twenty dollars at the Circle K for candy. . . . We may not have chosen the right paths to go along in life, but I'm not a dummy. . . . They get mad at you if you can't get a job in two weeks. Who in the hell is going to employ you? I'm not going to McDonald's. McDonald's is not going to pay my rent. That's what they want you to do, lower your self-esteem to where you will take anything. I'm sorry, I have never worked for a five dollar an hour job, not since I was a teenager. I'm not going to now. I have two kids to support. Where am I going to live with them? In a shelter, making five dollars

an hour. I'm not going to subject my kids to something like that. I'd rather just do my prison time if I have to do it and get rid of all of this.

Although she was one of the youngest women in the sample, Alicia rejected total, individual responsibility for her crime. Her explanation for selling crack reflects some of the aspects of individual worth in the African American community described by Gilbert (1999, 239): self-help, competence, confidence, and consciousness. She understood that the options available to her as a single mother were limited and that she was "a grain of sand" in the underground economy that would grind on with or without her participation. Her "good job" as a nursing assistant was sporadic and unreliable and paid about ten dollars an hour. She made a decision to sell crack to support her family and preferred going to jail to working at a minimum wage, dead-end job and living in a shelter with her children. She had a boyfriend who was also in jail, but she had no expectation that he would support her or her children.

Angel also committed crimes to support her seven children. A forty-one-year-old African American woman who grew up in an extremely abusive and violent environment. Angel disclosed that her father was a pimp and that she grew up in a house full of people who "used drugs twenty-four/seven." She moved out and lived on her own at age seventeen and put herself through two and a half years of college. She had been working at a well-paying sales job when her violent husband tracked her down and began to harass her. She quit her job and moved her family to Phoenix but was unable to find a job that would pay her bills. She began writing bad checks as a way of making ends meet. When asked if she was receiving any benefits while she was writing checks, she responded:

Sometimes yes, as the check writing went off and on for a period, for a number of years, so yes. Sometimes I was getting benefits; sometimes I wasn't. I would have to supplement my income writing the checks, buying the groceries, stealing money from the bank to pay for rent or to pay for a car repair. You know, it was always something. [Question: How much is your restitution?] Six thousand dollars, which isn't that bad, because most of it I was buying was just stuff for the kids: groceries, and clothing for the children, toys for the kids, just basic stuff, and my rent. There were a couple of times I went to the bank and wrote checks for cash and made it out for one thousand dollars cash that was for covering things, bills, stuff like that. There's a lot of girls in here that have restitution much greater than mine.

Restitution was one of the burdens women faced as they left jail, which added to their already precarious economic situations. The other significant burden was the terms of probation. Eight women (27 percent) had been incarcerated because of minor probation violations, such as failing to inform a probation officer of one's whereabouts or missing an appointment because of work, sickness, or lack of transportation. Complying with probation requirements, or drug court requirements, places tremendous demands on the resources of single mothers, which are already strained. Alicia explained the difficulties of parenting and following the guidelines of intensive probation services (IPS):

This is my probation's terms. Three to four times a week, counseling, but you have to pay for it. One girl said she was paying like sixty dollars a week just for three counseling sessions. Every time it was twenty bucks, bang. . . . They expect us to have a full-time job, which is fine, counseling four times a week, on top of community service two hours a day, so that's ten hours a week, so where is the time for your kids? And they know some people have kids, but they don't care. You mess up any step of the law and they're violating you and putting you in prison. That's a lot of things to look forward to. That's a lot of stuff. And if you don't go to counseling when they say to go, you're violated even if you drop clean every day. If you mess up in any of those areas. Say the traffic is bad, or say my daughter is asthmatic. She goes into an asthma attack in the middle of the night. I have to make sure I page my IPS worker and make sure he calls me back in time before I go to the doctor. My daughter could be suffocating in this time while he's taking his time calling me back and they don't care. You leave without them knowing, you're violated. They don't care if you're dying or your kids are dying. Good thing my daughter hasn't been in the hospital. She has a heart murmur. Anything can happen to her, and I don't feel like that's right for them to violate if I am at the hospital with my child. Even if I get there right away and I page them, they say. "Well, too bad. You're prison bound." That's what IPS stands for: in prison soon. A lot of people say that.

One other African American woman's original crime, welfare fraud, was obviously related to providing for her three children. She was not incarcerated for welfare fraud, however, but for violating the probation she received for that original offense by smoking marijuana. Her "dirty" urine analysis prompted the judge to revoke her probation and give her a felony conviction plus 120 days in jail. She felt this was unfair, created additional problems for her children, and limited her opportunities for employment. Patrice explained that at the time she "signed the welfare check," her baby's father was in prison, and she had no source of funds:

> I wanted my baby a baby bed and wanted her this and I wanted her that, and he wasn't there. I didn't know where he was. Just one day he disappeared and I didn't know where he was. When I went for my sentencing, I thought he was going to let me go because I paid for all of my restitution for the welfare check and everything. My lawyer's like, "We think she should be released." And the judge goes. "No. I'm going to give her about 121 days." I said. "Why?" He goes, "Cause you shouldn't have smoked that joint."

Patrice had recently obtained work release status and was trying to find a job. She wanted to get her three children back from her sister and move into a house but was worried about finances. Her story reflects the spiraling effects of getting caught up in the criminal justice system while trying to make ends meet:

> Is there anything preventing me from getting a job? Yes, the felony that he gave me because of a little joint. I don't think he was very fair at all. I think that a felony is for somebody who did something really actually bad or something like that. I ain't sayin' what I did wasn't a crime. I know it was a crime. I just can't imagine why he would give me a felony because I broke probation and smoked a joint. I write down "felony" on my applications and everybody goes, "Oh no, we can't hire you." . . . A lot of us are in here for probation violations. The judge didn't care that we had kids or care that we lost our house or anything.

Lonna, a thirty-one-year-old biracial (Latina/white) woman with three children, was also in jail for violating probation after arrest for welfare fraud. She blamed her abusive husband for taking her money and creating an economic situation in which she felt compelled to commit welfare fraud:

> I don't want to make it sound like it was all his fault, but it is. I've been married since 1986. There came a time, about 1995, when there was sometimes no water in the house, no electric, no food. So while I was working I collected welfare. Not only that, sometimes he would take my money anyway no matter if he was working or not. It didn't matter. Sometimes he'd just take my money anyway, so I would go and get extra checks.

Lonna was sentenced to probation and was able to maintain a good job. After she was switched to a new probation officer, however, she had trouble maintaining contact, was arrested, and was jailed for four months.

While these women's initial crimes were motivated by a desire to provide for their children, it was minor violations of probation terms that caused the greatest problems for them. Women attempted to manage the demands of motherhood, interlaced with traditional prescriptions for femininity, while providing income and dealing with prior and ongoing victimization. Scripted notions of successful mothering and of femininity made compliance with elaborate probation terms difficult as the women's lives were filled with expectations of caring for others while under the gaze of the state.

Jail as a Retreat

For many women, life was so arduous and precarious that incarceration was actually perceived as an improvement. This was particularly true for women who had lived in extreme battering situations, who felt protected from their abusers while in jail (although some women continued to be terrorized through prison and jail networks and threats to their children). Jail and prison are also dangerous for women, as abuse by correctional staff, neglect of health, and overuse of medications are common (see Human Rights Watch Women's Rights Project 1996; Amnesty International 1999, 2001; Moe and Ferraro 2002). The women in PCAD described many problems with the care and level of safety they experienced, but some also commented on the jail as a break from the demands of mothering, street life, and male violence. Angel, for example, was passionate about literature and was using her time to read and write. She said she had read more than fifty books since she had been in jail and was writing a novel called *My Sister's Wedding* in longhand. She also had plans for another book designed to help women find jobs after getting out of prison. She planned to write at least three books if she received the longest prison term possible. With six young children at home and her oldest son in prison, she viewed her time in jail as a "vacation":

> Yeah, this has really been like a vacation for me in a way, 'cause I get a chance to, when I was at home with the kids, I never got a chance to sit down and read books. It's impossible to find the time to write when you have to work and you have to get the kids off to school or you have to do all of the things. I want to try to take this time and use it the best that I can to prepare myself for a career as a writer. If I'm paid to write and that's all I

have to do, well then I can do that at home when my kids are at school. I don't have to get up and go to work.

Angel had a positive outlook on life. "You have to try to find the goodness in all the bad things that happen to us in life, and there's plenty if you look." She placed all six of her little girls with her mother in Florida when she was arrested. Although she was in a good relationship with a man at the time of her arrest, "he wasn't able to handle all six of the girls 'cause they're all girls." She discussed working with this man as photographers in a restaurant, but she had no expectation that he would share in parenting activities. The children's biological fathers were abusive or had abandoned them, and thus Angel took full responsibility for their care and delayed her personal goals. This was true for all women, none of whom had male partners on whom they could rely for child care.

Other women viewed the minimal health and nutrition services as a respite from street life. Boo was pregnant with her fourth child, and she felt the care she received in jail was positive. She had been incarcerated so many times that she knew the guards like family:

> To me this is my home away from home 'cuz I don't have nobody on the outside. So it's kind of hard for me but then at the same time I like it in here 'cuz I get that special attention that I crave. . . . I know all of the COs [correctional officers] here. They're like my uncles and aunts in my way, you know what I'm saying. They're real good people to me. I like them. . . . I get taken care of in here very well. They give us three pregnancy bags a day which contain two cartons of milk, two orange juices, and two fruits, and you get three pills three times a day during breakfast, lunch, and dinner, so you have your little snack bag.

Although most women complained about the food and health care available in the jail, for Boo, who lived on the streets, the jail provided a relatively healthy environment for her pregnancy.

Other women viewed their incarceration as a way to get away from an abusive husband. Lonna, quoted earlier, who was jailed for violating her probation for welfare fraud, explained that her jail time allowed her to break from her husband and that she would not return home. Her children were having problems while she was in jail, but she felt a divorce would benefit them eventually:

> They don't have a mom or a dad. My mother-in-law asked my son, "Why are you acting this way?" He says, "Why do I have to come home? I don't have a family." I hear in the background my older daughter says, "It's true. My mom's in jail and my dad's out partying." Damn. Anyway, I think

it's a good thing that I came to jail. . . . I'm not going back home. I'm getting a divorce when I leave here. I'm just going to take the kids and leave. That's my plan when I leave here. . . . It's a good thing I'm here I guess. Not for the kids but it will be better in the long run.

Lonna had tried for fifteen years to make her marriage work, keep her family together, and have their bills paid. She assumed all the responsibility for her three children while her husband used her paycheck to buy drugs and liquor. She was attending classes in jail, which she believed were helping her to break free of that relationship and to help her children.

Similar to the women in Bosworth's (1999) study of women prisoners in England, femininity established the burdens and constraints women at PCAD faced as well as provided a grounds for resistance. The socially structured mandate for maternal responsibility for children's well-being and the failure of fathers and other men to provide support for parenting create a situation in which low-income women must struggle for money while providing care and denying their own dreams and interests. The state's intervention creates additional burdens through incarceration and terms of probation that further complicate the already overwhelming demands on mothers. Jobs and wages are lost due to violent husbands, women are arrested for crimes of economic survival, and criminal records make it more difficult to find good jobs. At the same time, the care of children provided a grounds on which women could focus on future goals and improvements: a career in writing, a healthy pregnancy, and divorcing an abusive husband. While some women could embrace the role of mothering as an opportunity for personal growth and social acceptance, for others, that opportunity had already been lost through state intervention in custody.

ADDICTIONS AND CHILD PROTECTIVE SERVICES

The majority (80 percent) of women interviewed were addicted to illegal drugs or alcohol. Crack cocaine was the most common drug, followed by heroin and crystal methamphetamine. Both crack and crystal were cheap and easily available in southern Arizona. A small "rock" of crack could be purchased for five dollars on the street. Heroin from Mexico was also quite easy to obtain. Thirteen women (43 percent) indicated that they were addicted to crack, with several of these women also using heroin, powder cocaine, or alcohol. Three women were alcoholics, and two women used crystal methamphetamine. Three of the six women who were not addicted to any substance were in jail because of their sale of crack or crystal. As Chesney-Lind (1997) and others have noted, the war on drugs clearly translates into a war on women.

Many women had lost custody of their children because of their addictions. Twelve women had children removed by CPS because of their alcohol or drug use. Ten had their parental rights severed and could not see their children until they turned eighteen, and two were still actively trying to have their children returned. The other twelve women with addictions had placed their children with relatives prior to incarceration. Several women indicated that the final severance decision was what pushed them into resumption of drug or alcohol use or into more serious addiction.

Theresa, a thirty-nine-year-old white woman with four children younger than sixteen and a twenty-two-year-old son, had much difficulty during her interview because of her extreme sadness and pain over the loss of her children. She showed no expression and spoke in a monotone. She was not pressed to elaborate on answers as it was obviously hard for her to remember and talk about her life. She was in jail because of a second driving under the influence charge that occurred when she resumed drinking after being sober for three and a half years. Her parental rights were severed because she reunited, briefly, with her abusive husband:

> I quit for three years, three and a half years, since 1995, and then when they said severance and adoption, I slightly fell off the wagon. [Question: You actually quit for three years and they still?] Yeah, they just brought up so many different things. They said we caused problems for the kids because of our arguments and our fighting and this and that. They bring up so many different things. [Question: Don't they have a plan, though, that you follow? And if you follow the plan then you get your kids back?] Yeah. I followed the plan. But then I got back with their dad, and he messed up and so then CPS said because it was my choice to get back with him that it ruined both of our chances of getting the kids back. And I told them, "I don't see how." That's when I lost it. The hardest I've ever drank in my life was last year. They were doing random drug testing and I was dropping clean. And I was doing all of their parenting classes and all their going to their psychiatrists plus going to my own psychiatrist plus doing my groups and doing AAs [Alcoholics Anonymous] and still, it didn't matter.

According to Theresa, her husband had received a two-and-a-half-year prison sentence for "trying to kill us." As she explained, "He beat me up severely so where one eye, this whole side of my face was just black and blue and swollen shut for like a whole month, and he cut me, stabbed me, three times." Although her husband was out of the situation because of his incarceration, CPS severed Theresa's rights and placed her children up for adoption. As Theresa phrased it, "Until they're eighteen they've been sentenced to adoption." Her plans focused on the day of their reunification: "What are my plans? To stay sober. I want to finish my education, get on with my life. Hopefully it will go a little faster so I can see my kids when they're eighteen."

Theresa's case illustrates the importance of children to women's recovery from alcohol and drugs and the despair that emerges when rights are severed. Her case also reflects the ways in which CPS agencies fail to respond appropriately to domestic violence by removing children from women who are abused. The district court ruling in *Nicholson v. Scoppetta* found that New York City's Administration for Children's Services had demonstrated "benign indifference, bureaucratic inefficiency and outmoded institutional biases" in removing children from the custody of women who had been beaten by their abusers (Friedlin 2002).

Marie's situation was similar, only she turned to crack and powder cocaine, heroin, and methadone when her children were removed. Marie, a twenty-seven-year-old white women with two young children (three and five years old), had also lost her children due to her husband's conduct. They were removed after he had gotten high on drugs and pushed them in a stroller onto a busy highway. Marie was home sick when the incident occurred. Because her family was living in a motel room at the time, the environment was considered unfit and CPS removed the children. Marie started using drugs after this but stopped, filed for divorce, rented an apartment, and followed all of the demands of CPS when she thought she had a chance of reunification:

> Everything was goin' good. Got an apartment of my own to get my kids back up on the north side of town where it's really expensive so they could live in a good place. The psychological evaluator was there and he suspected that I was doing this just to fool CPS, but he never voiced his suspicions to me. He voiced them to my CPS worker and he just changed it. The night before we went to court, he changed the whole plan from givin' them back to me to severance and adoption. I called up the psychological evaluator and asked, "How come you didn't ask me about this?" He said, "I told them there wasn't any furniture." I said, "Well, that's because I had just moved in. I have lots of furniture now." "Oh. well. I didn't think about that." And then he said, "Well, you don't have no food in your

house." I said, "That's because I live by myself and I work in a restaurant and I eat there all the time. I don't need food." "Well, yeah, I guess I didn't think about that." And I said, "Well, why didn't you ask me before you told my CPS worker?" It was too late then because they were changin' things. They told me again that they were going to take my kids away, so I started doin' drugs again. And then, prostitution came in.

Marie had been sentenced to six months in jail for prostitution, plus a $1,000 fine and two years on supervised probation. Although her children were in an adoptive home and CPS was moving to sever her rights, she believed she still had a chance of getting them back, and that was her motivation for staying clean:

> I know I'll get them back. They have no reason to keep them from me. I know I'll get them back. Plus, I pray. I know I will have them. [Question: Do you see any barriers to getting your kids back? Staying out of the drugs?] No. I think getting them back is a real strong drive for me to stay out of drugs. It gives me something to concentrate on. I know if I touch those drugs, the kids are gone. I'll never even have a fighting chance. So, I know I can't. The only barriers I see is just the last court date. I didn't go because I was high. I knew they were takin' them and I couldn't bear to hear a severance and adoption as they planned, so I just didn't go. That didn't help. I just hope it ain't the same judge.

Gillian, a thirty-six-year-old white woman, also began using crack after CPS severed her rights to her daughter. Her only child was removed from the home after reporting to her grandmother that her father had sexually molested her. Gillian and her daughter moved in with Gillian's mother after her husband assaulted and threatened to kill her. Her daughter was nine at the time and intellectually gifted, while Gillian had a learning disability and had not graduated from high school. Although she was following all the guidelines set by CPS, her rights were severed and she felt as if she had lost everything:

> She [her daughter] had been sexually molested when she was younger than that. I didn't know it. I had been going through the courts doing everything they asked me to, and they lied to me. [Question: Child protective services?] Yeah. CPS lied to me. [Question: What did they lie to you about?] Saying that if I did everything they told me to I would get her back. They lied to her too saying that she was going to be moving back in with me. They lied to both of us. We went to court. I didn't have a GED [general equivalency diploma]. I

have dyslexia. I have a learning disability. They said her intelligence would be wasted if they gave her back to me because I couldn't afford her education and I couldn't teach her how to read as she got older. I have dyslexia and I see words backward sometimes if I'm not careful. They used her IQ. It was 121 at the age of seven. She could not read. They figured her being with me would be a waste of time because I couldn't give her the education she needed. I didn't know that education was more important than love. I guess it is in their eyes. . . . I was like, "They've been lying to me all this time." Finally we went to court and they tried to say I had a drug and alcohol problem. I didn't even do drugs back then. I smoked pot, but since I've been in Tucson, I haven't smoked no weed. I did drink. They said I had a drug problem, and I don't even know where they got that. I wasn't even doing drugs. I did start drugs after I lost her. About two to three months later, I did it. I was like, "Hell, they said I did it." I didn't have nothing to lose then. I had already lost her, so that's when I started doing drugs.

Certainly, there is a possibility that women misunderstood or misrepresented the severance process that resulted in the loss of their children. The important point that can be drawn from these narratives, however, is that women's use of drugs or alcohol was often related in their own minds to the loss of their children. With "nothing to lose," and easy access to crack and alcohol, these women were drawn into usage that eventually resulted in their incarceration.

For some addicted women, use of crack cocaine preceded state intervention; however, they felt it was impossible to stop using. The threat of losing their children, or even damaging their children, could not overcome their dependence on crack. All the women indicated their sincere desire to stop using crack and their belief that crack had "taken everything." Many were awaiting limited bed space in residential treatment centers. All were attending Narcotics Anonymous and AA groups, and most felt that God was helping them get off drugs by sending them to jail. Women addicted to crack indicated that it was not possible for them to stop using while they lived in the neighborhoods where crack was easily available and all their acquaintances were using.

Two women had used crack while they were pregnant and felt enormous grief and guilt about endangering their babies. Peaches, a thirty-two-year-old African American woman, gave birth to a stillborn baby because of her use of crack. In jail for prostitution, she described a horrendous history of childhood sexual abuse. Peaches was the youngest of thirteen children, and her mother forced her to have sex with all of her siblings, as well as herself and her boyfriend. Her father took her away from this situation when she was six, but he also sexually abused her. She had a seventeen-year-old daughter and fourteen-, thirteen-, twelve-, and nine-year-old sons and had lost custody of all of them. Of all of the traumas she had experienced, however, she described the death of her baby as the worst:

> I have six kids. I have four boys, and I have a daughter, and then I have a little boy who passed away. [Question: Oh. I'm sorry. When did that happen?] In 1990. He was a crack baby. He was stillborn. I carried him for the whole nine months. I felt his last kick. That was the hardest thing I had to go through in my life. I don't think all the molestation and everything that I've been through has been worse than having a stillborn. I carried that baby for nine months. I don't think none of that that I've been through can top that day. I think that's the biggest problem that I'm having. I can't forgive myself for that. That's my biggest problem. [Question: You think the drugs did it?] Oh yes. There's no doubt in my mind that the drugs did it. I was doin' drugs as I was in labor. [Question: Did the doctors actually say that it was because of the drugs?] No, they didn't exactly say it was because of the drugs, but deep down inside, I know that was what it was. They wanted to go before a judge and get court orders to do autopsies. At that time, they had just passed a law that if a woman has a baby that's dead or something's wrong with the baby . . . like, my baby was dead so they could have charged me for murder on that child because I had been smokin' drugs. I didn't want that to happen so I did not give them permission to do an autopsy on my baby. The judge wouldn't give them permission because at the time that I was going for prenatal care, they were tellin' me that the baby was fine.

Peaches could not forgive herself and had little hope of ever seeing her children again. She had decided, however, that she was at the end of the line with crack and had to give it up or die:

> When I leave, I'm leaving here with nothing. No probation. When I do go to rehab, it's because I want to. . . . Matter of fact, I think it is the only option for me because there's only two lives. If we choose drugs, that's death. That's the way I feel. If you choose to not do drugs, that's life. I don't want to die doin' drugs. I don't want to die and have to be put in a cardboard box and buried in a cemetery because nobody claims me. That's the only option for me.

Tina's baby did not die, and she had not yet lost custody of her two children who were living with her parents. A twenty-seven-year-old Latina, Tina had been taken directly to jail after giving birth. She was arrested for violating probation, which she had received for drug trafficking and racketeering. During her interview, she lifted her T-shirt to show forty to fifty small, round burn scars on her stomach that had been caused by hiding her hot crack pipe in the waistband of her maternity pants. Tina had also been molested as a child, raped at age twelve, and stabbed and beaten by a group of girls who attacked her for her jewelry. At the time of the interview, her baby was a month old and Tina had been in jail for three weeks and four days. She had stopped using crack for six months during her pregnancy and was living far from town with a friend. There was no public transportation available, and she did not have a car, so her probation officer issued a violation for missed appointments. Tina knew she was facing IPS anyway, so she decided to attend a party with her friend and succumbed to the offer of crack. She cried heavily as she explained:

> I did it; and I was laughing; and remember hitting it and then feeling her move inside of me, like right after I hit the crack: and I still didn't stop; and then the fourth time I hit it, my plug broke and then my water broke. They wanted to go get more drugs and I was there by myself, and I called my dad and I told him. I was scared, you know? What if she died? They could at least treat her for the cocaine. They didn't violate me for probation for it or anything. I figured I couldn't stop; I mean. I stopped because I was away from it. But I couldn't stop when I was around it. So that's why I needed the help. And after seeing her go through the IV, you know, they were testing her, making sure. . . . It threw her complete blood count off. It was real bad; it was real off. But she's healthy now, but to see her hooked up to all them things and bruised up from them. She's just a little baby. It's awful, just seeing her. . . . She's a little angel from God. For me to just imagine one hit . . . what it does to me. Imagine what it did to her little brain. . . . Looking at her little eyes, her little smiles, thinking every little thing, "Is that because I did crack?" You know? "Is that because I had smoked when she had first developed?" I was scared, 'cuz I didn't know I was pregnant. But every little thing that I saw, I was just paranoid. Excuse me [crying hard], I'm like, just like for me to hurt her, just horrible. . . . CPS got involved: I mean, I don't blame them, the hospital called them, and you know, they treated me like a monster, and I felt like a monster; I *knew* I was a monster. But the remorse I feel, the

hurt. . . . My dad gets mad when I tell him I love my kids and I'm gonna change. He says, "Don't tell me you love them; every time you tell me, that makes me sick after what you did."

Tina and Peaches expressed a desire to stop using crack and bore tremendous sadness and guilt about the harm caused to their babies and their families. They shared the hegemonic public view of crack mothers as evil baby killers who deserve nothing but contempt, and they felt self-contempt as "monsters." They desperately wanted help and had long histories of abuse in addition to their addictions. The intensive assistance required to help them recover from their addictions and return to a mothering role was not available to them. Instead, the only motivation for recovery, their children, had been taken away, and they have nothing to look forward to except guilt and regret. These data suggest that decisions about child custody play a central role in women's resistance to the psychological anesthesia offered by drugs and alcohol. Balancing the need to protect children and promote women's health and well-being requires programs that are attuned to both mothers and children and flexible in their ability to provide support to both.

Mothering and Identity From Inside

The majority of women in jail had identities that reflected some of the social approbation that their incarceration signified. Like Tina and Patrice, cited earlier, the linkage of their drug usage with harm to their children contributed to self-images as "monsters," and they were unable to forgive themselves. Women who had prostituted for drugs or lost custody because of drugs also had negative judgments about those aspects of their identities. Other women resisted stigmatization by contextualizing their offenses within the realities of economic marginalization and violent victimization. As Alicia pointed out. "We're not all bad people."

In struggling to develop positive identities, mothering was critical in sustaining perceptions of value and goodness. In the abstract, motherhood is a highly valued status, and women viewed the facts of their motherhood as a potential source of social acceptance. At a deeper level, however, many women indicated that their links to their children were central to their selfhood. Children were extensions of their own identities, separate yet constitutive of women's subjectivity. In one case in which it was physically possible, a woman

returned to one of us with pictures of her children after her own interview ended. Other women indicated regret that they did not have photographs available to show us and spoke of how beautiful and cute their children were.

India, a thirty-one-year-old American Indian woman with six children, illustrated the importance of children to women's identities most graphically. She had tattoos for each child's name on various parts of her body. A heart with flowers around a blank space on her right breast was reserved for her youngest child whose name she had not yet had tattooed. She had lost her children to CPS at one point but regained custody after following their requirements. Her children were with their father's sister, and she planned to reunite with them after completing her sentence.

Even women whose rights had been terminated and who were prohibited from interacting with their children believed that they would be reunited one day. Julianna had lost custody of her four children but believed that some day they would be together again:

I believe in my heart of hearts, once you birth a child, they can take your child from you for so long, but that child will come back. Listen to a lot of these talk shows on how families are starting to reunite. Just look at the awesome power of God to bring families back together that haven't been together for fourteen, twenty, thirty years. I have a dream that one day my two children that is within the state, I will see them. We will reunite and be together. With my other children in Nebraska. I have no doubt that I will see them. They'll be family. God will show me the way for us to reunite and be together again. That's my strong belief.

The likelihood of Julianna reuniting her family was small, but focusing on this dream gave her the hope and strength to go on living. Like many jailed women, she believed that God was guiding her life and would ultimately return her children to her. She described what she believed to be direct communication with God:

That's when He spoke to me, sternly this time. "I'm gonna pick you up, and I will turn your life around, and I will make you want success and great things. Most of all, I will make you a great woman of God and you will be a great woman. I'm gonna bring you back to your children again." That, right there, is enough for me to hold on, to walk through the storm and the rain, and move on with my life.

Linda, who lost custody of three children because of her crack and heroin addictions, also believed that God would return her children to her:

> I ask God to give me my life back, give me my children back. And so now, this is a start. I'm okay with where I'm at because I know when I leave here it won't be long before I can reunite with my children. Not right away, but eventually it's goin' to come together. I know God is gonna give them back to me. I know I'm goin' to see them real soon. Without them. I'm nothin.' I just thank God.

Even women whose children had died carried their memories and the grief over their loss as a central aspect of their identities. Buckwheat's son had been killed in a drive-by shooting five years before we met her. She said that she went into a "blackout" for eight days and was finally awakened by the boy's father. He told her. "You didn't do nothin.' I had to go up to you and put the mirror to your face to see if you were alive." She described how a recent Valentine's Day visit at the jail had confirmed her son's eternal life and continued relationship to her:

> This past Valentine's, they had these Christian women come out here for a Valentine's thing in here. They gave out these little heart-shaped doilies and they had a little prayer on them, and they said to all of us, "These are special gifts that we're goin' to give you and hopefully the right one is goin' to reach you." Well, it surprised me about the one that they gave me because it said. "I gave my son to the Lord and for. . . ." I can't think of all of it but that he would live forever. I said. "Oh my God." And He told me to let it go. To let him go.

The continued importance of children to women's identities, despite severance or even death, was clear in all the women's narratives. This connection helped women to survive and look forward to the future with hope. It also made incarceration and separation from children more painful and worrisome due to the impact on children and the difficulties of mothering from inside the detention facility.

Conclusion

Mothering in an environment of scarce resources places women in a web of demands and constraints that may lead to incarceration. Selling drugs or cashing bad checks to meet bills and turning to drugs and alcohol as a way of coping with the psychological pain of childhood sexual abuse or the ongoing pain of domestic violence

are the primary pathways that lead women to jail (Daly 1994; Henriques and Manatu 2001; Katz 2000). Incarceration then creates greater burdens for maintaining positive relationships with children and for managing the demands of probation once released. Women interviewed at the PCAD had survived horrendous abuse and poverty yet maintained hope for a positive future and eventual reunion with their children.

Mothering simultaneously reproduces the unequal sexual division of labor and provides possibilities for resistance to marginalization and despair. The assumption that women will be primary caretakers and will provide resources and love for children when men do not demands that women obtain money and dispense care without much assistance. The possibility that women will become involved in crime as a result of trying to meet these demands is exacerbated by race and class hierarchies that restrict access to incomes adequate to support children.

The chaotic and demanding community contexts that lead women to view jail as a "vacation" suggest that there are complex problems facing low-income mothers that cannot be resolved either through programs for the children of incarcerated mothers or through revisions in sentencing policies. Reversing the trend of incarceration of minor drug and property offenders would ameliorate some of the harsh circumstances for both mothers and children created by incarceration. However, the violence, poverty, drug abuse, and mental health problems that women face outside of jail can only be addressed through systematic attention to the sources of these problems for women. Recent social policy trends exacerbate the obstacles facing many women. Exclusion of convicted drug offenders from social welfare programs, zero-tolerance housing policies that evict battered women from public housing, punitive and restrictive Temporary Assistant to Needy Families guidelines, and programs that encourage women to marry as a solution to poverty make it more difficult for low-income single mothers to survive in the United States than at any time since the Great Depression. The narratives of jailed women reflect this difficulty and the failure of social policies to remedy the cumulative effects of violent victimization, poverty, racism, drug addictions, and mental health problems on women's abilities to mother their children.

While mothering complicates women's abilities to negotiate marginalized existence, it also provides a resource for hope and positive identity. The dominant ideology of motherhood is reflected in women's accounts of their inadequacies and failures but also in their insistence on fighting against addictions, male violence, and poverty. Although the desire to be a "good mother," and the dimensions of that construct, may be a vector of the social control of women, it is simultaneously a grounds from which women challenge structural and individual sources of oppression.

References

Allen, Hilary. 1987. Rendering them harmless: The professional portrayal of women charged with serious violent crimes. In *Gender, crime and justice,* edited by Pat Carlen and Anne Worrall. 81–94. Philadelphia: Open University Press.

Amnesty International. 1999. "*Not pan of my sentence*": Violations of the human rights of women in custody. Available from http://web.amnesty.org.

———. 2001. *New reports of children and women abused in correctional institutions. Findings from Amnesty International research trip.* Available from http://webaninesty.org.

Arnold, Regina. 1990. Processes of victimization and criminalization of black women. Social Justice 17:153–66.

Beck, Allen J., and Paige M. Harrison. 2001. *Prisoners in 2000.* Washington, DC: U.S. Department of Justice.

Belknap, Joanne. 2001. *The invisible woman: Gender, crime, and justice.* 2nd ed. Belmont. CA: Wadsworth.

Bloom, Barbara, Meda Chesney-Lind, and Barbara Owen. 1994. *Women in California prisons: Hidden victims of the war on drugs.* San Francisco: Center on Juvenile and Criminal Justice.

Bosworth, Mary. 1999. *Engendering resistance: Agency and power in women's prisons.* Aldershot, UK: Ashgate.

Caiazza, Amy B. et al. 2000. *The status of women in the states: Women's economic status in the United States.* Washington, DC: Institute for Women's Policy Research.

Chesney-Lind, Meda. 1997. *The female offender: Girls, women, and crime.* Thousand Oaks. CA: Sage.

Chesney-Lind, Meda, Mary Kay Harris, and Gabrielle deGroot. 1998. Female offenders. *Corrections Today* 60 (7): 66–144.

Daly, Kathleen. 1994. *Gender, crime and punishment.* New Haven. CT: Yale University Press.

Elliott, Terri. 1994. Making strange what had appeared familiar. *Monist* 77:424–33.

Friedlin, Jennifer. 2002. Judge exposes agency harm to battered mothers, kids. *Women's ENews.* April 28.

Gilbert, Evelyn. 1999. Crime, sex, and justice: African American women in U.S. prisons. In *Harsh punishment: International experiences of women's imprisonment.* edited by Sandy Cook and Suzanne Davies, 230–49. Boston: Northeastern University Press.

Gilfus, Mary E. 1992. From victims to survivors to offenders: Women's routes of entry and immersion into street crime. *Women and Criminal Justice* 4:63–90.

Greenfield, Lawrence A., and Tracy L. Snell. 1999. *Bureau of Justice Statistics special report: Women offenders* (NCJ 175688V). Washington. DC: U.S. Department of Justice.

Harrison, Paige M., and Allen J. Beck. 2002. *Bureau of Justice Statistics bulletin: Prisoners in 2001* (NCJ 195189). Washington, DC: U.S. Department of Justice.

Hartsock, Nancy. 1987. The feminist standpoint: Developing a ground for a specifically feminist historical materialism. In *Feminism and methodology,* edited by Sandra Harding. 157–76. Milton Keynes. UK: Open University Press.

Henriques, Zelma W., and Rupert N. Manatu. 2001. Living on the outside: African American women before, during, and after imprisonment. *The Prison Journal* 81 (1) 6–19.

———. 2000. *Black feminist thought: Knowledge, consciousness, and the politics of empowerment.* New York: Routledge.

Human Rights Watch Women's Rights Project. 1996. *All too familiar: Sexual abuse of women in U.S. state prisons.* New York: Human Rights Watch.

Humphries, Drew. 1999. *Crack mothers.* Columbus: Ohio State University Press.

Immarigeon, Russ, and Meda Chesney-Lind. 1992. *Women's prisons: Overcrowded and overused.* San Francisco: National Council on Crime and Delinquency.

Katz, Rebecca S. 2000. Explaining girls' and women's crime and desistance in the context of their victimization experiences: A developmental lest of revised strain. *Violence Against Women* 6 (6): 633–60.

Miller, Jody. 1998. Up it up: Gender and the accomplishment of street robbery. *Criminology* 36:37–65.

Moe, Angela M., and Kathleen J. Ferraro. 2002. Malign neglect or benign respect: Women's health care in a carceral setting. Paper presented at the annual meetings of the Academy of Criminal Justice Sciences. March 5–9, Anaheim, CA.

Morash, Merry. 1998. *Women offenders: Programming needs and promising approaches.* Washington, DC: U.S. Department of Justice.

Nagel, Irene H., and John Hagan. 1983. Gender and crime: Offense patterns and criminal court sanctions. In *Crime and justice,* vol. 4, edited by Michael Tonry and Norval Morris. 91–144. Chicago: University of Chicago Press.

Narayan, Uma. 1988. Working together across difference: Some considerations on emotions and political practice. *Hypatia* 3 (2):31–47.

Orbuch, Terri L. 1997. People's accounts count: The sociology of accounts. *Annual Review of Sociology* 23:455–78.

Pollak, Otto. 1950. *The criminality of women.* Westport. CT: Greenwood.

Richie, Beth E. 1996. *Compelled to crime: The gender entrapment of battered black women.* New York: Routledge.

———. 2001. Challenges incarcerated women face as they return to their communities: Findings from life history interviews. *Crime & Delinquency* 47:368–89.

Ross, Luana. 1998. *Inventing the savage.* Austin: University of Texas Press.

Sandoval, Chela. 2000. *Methodology of the oppressed.* Minneapolis: University of Minnesota Press.

Smart, Carol. 1995. Criminological theory: Its ideology and implications concerning women. In *Law, crime and sexuality: Essays in feminism,* edited by Carol Smart. 16–31. London: Sage.

Smith, Dorothy. 1987. *The everyday world as problematic: A feminist sociology.* Toronto, Canada: University of Toronto Press.

Sommers, Ira B., Deborah Baskin, and Jeffrey Fagan. 2000. *Workin' hard for the money: The social and economic lives of women drug sellers.* Huntington, NY: Nova Science Publishers.

Stephan, J. J. 2001. *Census of jails 1999.* Washington, DC: U.S. Department of Justice.

U.S. General Accounting Office. 1999. *Women in prison: Issues and challenges confronting U.S. correctional systems.* Washington, DC: U.S. General Accounting Office.

Watterson, Kathryn. 1996. *Women in prison: Inside the concrete womb.* Rev. ed. Boston: Northeastern University Press.

Young, Vernetta D. 1986. Gender expectation and their impact on black female offenders and victims. *Justice Quarterly* 3:305–27.

PART VIII

Support Systems and Crime

This new section of the book was added to illustrate the importance that supportive relationships play with offenders either currently serving time in an adult correctional facility or out in the community on parole. These relationships are important in order to prevent re-offending. In short, support systems, whether family members, religious groups, close friends, employers, or a host of other significant persons or groups in the life of ex-prisoners have been recognized as important entities of positive support for offenders. All such support systems seem to be necessary factors in helping a stigmatized criminal know that there are those who care about their future and will help them when called upon.

You may ask yourself, "Why are we reading research that involves offender support type groups when the very next section focuses on offender desistence?" The answer lies in the differences between these two subjects. Distance and support issues do overlap to some extent; however, support systems discuss those persons who interact with the offender (i.e., families) while desistence mainly pertains to the offender's life and experiences once back in the community.

One of the most difficult adjustments for both released prisoners as well as their families is the challenge of and integration back into the family structure. Damian J. Martinez and Johanna Christian examine the ex-prisoner's families and the degree of supportive relationships they provide. They analyze how family members and former prisoners renegotiate their past and present relationships. They recognize the problems that exist based largely on previous history between the two but go further by providing an in-depth picture of the dynamics of the relationship, which find various degrees of support or lack thereof.

In his book, *Doing Time on the Outside,* anthropologist Donald Braman devotes the entire study to families of young African American men who are incarcerated and come from the lowest socioeconomic area of Washington, D.C. The chapter I selected to reproduce for this section on family support offers the experiences of one couple, Londa and Derek, and their relationship as it presently exists with Derek's use of drugs and a long prison sentence as a direct result of his addiction. Braman so insightfully portrays Londa's trials and tribulations throughout their marriage best characterized as one of a husband and father of three children *and* incarceration. This leaves Londa to face the hardship, pain, and regret experienced by so many impoverished families whose loved ones are serving lengthy criminal sentences in our nation's prisons. Braman's extremely insightful portrayal of Londa and Derek's family struggles offers all of us in the academic criminology/criminal justice world a most sensitive and honest view of the realities of family support for loved ones who are, in a very real way, serving time while on the outside.

22

THE FAMILIAL RELATIONSHIPS OF FORMER PRISONERS

Examining the Link Between Residence and Informal Support Mechanisms

DAMIAN J. MARTINEZ AND JOHNNA CHRISTIAN

Ex-prisoners face great challenges when they return to the community. One of the most important challenges is their reintegration into family relationships. Family support is a vital factor for former prisoners to avoid being returned to prison. This study examines how former prison inmates and their families exchange support within the context of residing at the family residence, and residence in a halfway house. The study also considers the ways in which support effects the relationship between both parties.

Imprisonment has many consequences for prisoners and for their families alike. One significant obstacle that former prisoners encounter on release is their reintegration into relationships with their families. Existing research findings also demonstrate that the absence of an individual because of incarceration causes emotional suffering to the prisoner's family (Carlson and Cervera 1991; Hairston 2001, 2003) and negatively affects the socioeconomic stability of his or her community (Clear, Rose, and Ryder 2001). Studies of the reentry of former prisoners, however, have focused largely on the socioeconomic impacts of incarceration, effective parole strategies, and circumstances related to employment (Festen and Fischer 2002; Liker 1982; Petersilia 2003). Detailed exploration of former prisoner and family relationships is largely absent from the literature.

Such research is, however, important. If prisoners receive family support during incarceration then the likelihood of recidivism and future criminality is reduced (Hairston 1998). A case also has been made that reconstruction of former prisoners' narrative identities can do much to ensure that they avoid engaging in new criminal activity, thereby decreasing recidivism

---

Source: The Familial Relationships of Former Prisoners: Examining the Link Between Residence and Informal Support Mechanisms, by Martinez, Damian J., and Johnna Christian, *Journal of Contemporary Ethnography, 38*(2), April 2009, pp. 201–224. Reprinted with permission.

(Martina 2001). Although some evidence indicates that, on release, former prisoners most often return to their families of origin (Fishman 1986; Nelson, Deess, and Allen 1999; La Vigne, Visher, and Castro 2004; Nurse 2002; O'Brien 2001), not much is known about what actually happens in adult family relationships—particularly regarding the various forms and levels of support exchanges—on their return.

At least 95 percent (592,000) of state-incarcerated prisoners eventually are released, and in Illinois more than 670,000 adults are under state parole supervision (Hughes and Wilson 2003). On release, most of these former prisoners return to their families and must renegotiate their relationships and relearn how to interact with their families. The family has functioned without the former prisoner, and when the former prisoner makes the transition from incarceration to (typically) community supervision (i.e., parole) to home, his or her return can be problematic. Both the former prisoner and the family must begin to negotiate the challenge of giving and receiving support.

For the most part, the literature has assumed support is offered to former prisoners by their family, but not that former prisoners are able or willing to provide support to their family members in return. Moreover, the literature has not considered whether residential context influences the mutual exchange of support, and the unique manifestation of support in different settings. This article addresses these gaps through an analysis of in-depth interviews, suggesting former prisoners and their family members engage in reciprocal exchanges of informal social support. Residence in either the family home or a halfway house is an important factor in the type of support exchanged between family members and former prisoners. The family members in our study made assessments of the former prisoner's needs based on where he lived. When family members perceived they could compensate for resources the former prisoner might lack, they offered support accordingly. We examine these issues by reviewing existing knowledge about such exchange processes, explaining the study's methodology, describing the analysis of informal social support processes, and discussing the findings.

The Need for Research about Reciprocal Relationships

In particular, the studies demonstrate that former prisoners' perceptions of received support are particularly important to their mental health. The existing research, however, does not examine specifically how former prisoners and family members renegotiate their relationships and whether residential context is an important factor in the exchange. The recognition and negotiation of the former prisoners' and family members' responsibilities underlie some of the problems associated with the prisoners' return home. Support—in its many forms—is not a one-way street. While previous studies have viewed support as fixed and unidirectional and also have implicitly viewed the former prisoner's (and current prisoner's) role as fixed, recipient and receiver do not exist in isolation. The dynamics of a family relationship involve interactions with various types and levels of support (or lack of support). In some cases, support is not immediately recognized as such. In short, the former prisoner has been seen as the sole recipient of support.

Also, from studies to date, more is known about the opinions of former prisoners than is known about the family structure when the former prisoner returns home. If family members are not queried about their relationships with former prisoners, researchers cannot obtain an accurate picture of the situation. Much research on former prisoner-family member relationships has been limited because it has not discussed the various types of support (i.e., emotional, instrumental, informational, companionship, and validation), even though attention to these variants is essential to understanding support as a whole (Cohen, Gottlieb, and Underwood 2000; Gottlieb 2000; Reis and Collins 2000; Wills and Shinar 2000).

Method

We conducted in-depth, face-to-face interviews with formerly incarcerated men and their family members. Participants were identified through the first author's attendance at meetings of the Illinois Going Home Program. Potential participants (1) had to be male; (2) must not have been convicted of a sex-related crime; (3) must have returned to the North Lawndale, Chicago, community; (4) must have been within sixty to ninety days of release from prison; and (5) subsequently must have been transferred to the North Lawndale adult transition center. The individuals were contacted after they had been released from the adult transition center, had been placed on parole, and had completed the Illinois Going Home Program.

The individuals interviewed consisted of six dyads: six former prisoners and six corresponding family members. Because most of the individuals (94 percent) who returned to North Lawndale were African American

(La Vigne and Mamalian 2003), the sample consisted primarily of African Americans (ten), and reflected the community's racial makeup, except for one dyad of Mexican origin. In terms of residence, three former prisoners resided with a family member: one with an aunt, one with a sister, and one with a brother. The other three former prisoners resided in a recovery home.

Data Collection

While ideally the study would have used ethnographic methods that included observation of interactions in the home and other settings, this was not feasible given the scope of the project. To gain the insights that ethnographic methods could produce, we needed a method that approximated, as closely as possible, ethnographic field methods. Therefore, we followed Spradley's (1979) guidelines for ethnographic interviewing, particularly using ethnographic, descriptive, and structural questions. We used an interview method that allowed us to get the kind of rich detail that field methods provide, what Geertz (1973) calls "thick description." To capture former prisoner-family member relationships in this way. the general question that guided the interview was: "For the next part of our discussion, I would like to ask you about your family. Please describe for me, in general, what your relationships with your family are like now." Additional questions were asked to gain understanding of former prisoners' and their family members' experiences and the exchange of support. These included questions about family contact and support, the former prisoners' roles and responsibilities within their families, the family members' views of the former prisoners' roles, and their exchanges of various types of support.

The interviews were conducted in a church in the North Lawndale community and at the University of Chicago, initially by two interviewers (a research assistant and the first-listed author). Each former prisoner and family member was interviewed once for approximately one to two hours, and the interviews were scheduled and conducted privately (as much as possible) and separately: they were tape-recorded and then transcribed verbatim. Each participant was paid $50 for the interview.

Analytic Strategy

Because the study centered on how former prisoners and family members made sense of and renegotiated their relationships once the former prisoner returned home, our analysis emphasized the concept of *social support*. We used a coding scheme of the five types of support as outlined in Wills and Shinar (2000, 88):

[E]motional support, the availability of one or more persons who can listen sympathetically when an individual is having problems and can provide indications of caring and acceptance. *Instrumental support* involves practical help when necessary, such as assisting with transportation, helping with household chores and child care, and providing tangible aid such as bringing tools or lending money. *Informational support* is defined as providing knowledge that is useful for solving problems, such as providing information about community resources and services or providing advice and guidance about alternative courses of action. *Companionship support* involves the availability of persons with whom one can participate in social and leisure activities such as trips and parties, cultural activities (e.g., going to movies or museums), or recreational activities.

A fifth type of support can be termed validation, which is based on the notion that social relationships can provide feedback and information about the appropriateness of one's behavior (Wills and Shinar 2000). It must be noted that these categories/dimensions of support are not mutually exclusive, but rather, are intertwined.

Informal Social Support Exchange Processes: Residence, Perceptions, and Support

Particularly important to this study was the informal support exchanged between former prisoners and their family members, in two different residential contexts— the family home or a recovery home—and the exchange of support and their perceptions associated with it. The insight this analysis provides is that residence in the family home elicited reports of informational support from family members who believed that the use of such information could transform former prisoners' behavior positively in society. The former prisoners, in contrast, perceived information as a form of emotional support, but failed to recognize its utility in accessing the specific resources that the family intended.

For those not residing with the family, there were similarly perceived exchanges of instrumental support as a result of family members' belief that tangible items could contribute to improving a former prisoner's life while in a recovery home. When former prisoners did not reside with family members, the family members could provide (infrequent) instrumental support— which also demonstrated their investment in the former prisoners' success. Former prisoners recognized this instrumental support because it was the basis for their interaction with their family members. This is an important point because families and former prisoners can be encouraged to use existing supports that might improve their family relationships and that provide a foundation on which to enhance the exchange of social support.

Community Context

It is important to describe the community where the participants lived because it reveals the conditions to which they are subjected and the neighborhood obstacles they encounter. North Lawndale is a community located on the west side of Chicago. As of 2000, it had a population of approximately 41,768 residents with 39.363 (94.2 percent) African Americans and 1,896 (4.5 percent) Hispanics/Latinos (Encyclopedia of Chicago 2005). In terms of unemployment, the community is at approximately 27 percent (Dighton 2002).

In terms of statistics on former prisoners in North Lawndale, it was estimated that this community held the most individuals released from prison of all the zip codes in Chicago. In particular, two zip code areas (60623 and 60624) that partially comprise North Lawndale had 6.349 former prisoners during the years 2000 and 2002 (Street 2002). Also, zip code 60624, a 98 percent black area that includes parts of North Lawndale. Garfield Park and other highly disadvantaged neighborhoods on the West Side, is the city's leading zip code for prison releases, the leading zip code for current prisoners in 2001, the second leading zip code for parole, and the third leading zip code for probation in 2000 (Street 2002, 30).

Specific to North Lawndale, there are more than 2,700 parolees who are between seventeen and thirty-five, which indicate that the community has one of the highest concentrations of individuals on parole throughout Illinois (La Vigne and Mamalian 2003).

There are other estimates as well. An employment assistance program in North Lawndale, the North Lawndale Employment Network, suggests "that more than 70 percent of all North Lawndale men between the ages of 18 and 45 have a criminal record" (Dighton 2002, 4). The sheer number and disproportionate percentage of former prisoners returning to North Lawndale has a significant impact not only on the community, but also on those released and their families, and how they perceive and exchange social support.

INFORMATIONAL SUPPORT IN THE FAMILY HOME

In cases where former prisoners resided with their family members, when queried about informational support, the former prisoners and family members gave different responses, indicating that family members and former prisoners each have certain types of support more readily available or that perceptions of support vary for each. For Jose, Henry, and Chris (pseudonyms), family members typically reported informational support and former prisoners typically reported emotional support. Family members supplied the type of support most readily available to them and that could be shared without creating undue burdens on their reserves of resources. In turn, former prisoners perceived such support as an indication of caring, not necessarily informational support with a specific intended use.

Here, we explore the significance and potential consequences of these differences in perception. One former prisoner, Jose, was single, twenty years old, of Mexican origin, and born in Chicago. He did not have any children and had two brothers and three sisters. He lived with his sister Anna, twenty-six years old. and her two children, ages three and eleven. Anna reported they exchanged informational support which emphasized education, employment, and health issues. She said:

> He has told me two different places to look for jobs for both of us to make money and put some money to buy a house together for my mom. Move out of here because it has a lot to do with the neighborhood, so we talk about that. He's gonna look for a good job, get his GED, and get a house like in a suburb or something. We do have plans.

For Anna and Jose, the exchange of information is mutually beneficial and allows them to work toward common goals. This reciprocity made Anna feel supported by Jose, which may increase the likelihood the information will be useful to both of them. Moreover, Anna realized information can lead to her brother's success in noncriminal activities. When asked specifically about whether, and on what subjects, she provided Jose with information, she responded:

> I always give him information on different things like when I went to the doctor. You know, how they have a conflict about AIDS and all that? Well, I talk to him about it and tell him, if you do have sex, protect yourself no matter what the girl tells you that she doesn't have anything. Just protect yourself. I talk to him about drugs, about drinking, I give him [phone] numbers about the GED. Like I said, he called already to this place, but they told him to call back in May. I always give him the newspaper so he can go to jobs if they're available. The thing is that the only problem he

has . . . where I work at, I tried to get him in, but the first thing they ask you is, does he have a criminal record?

Here, Anna reflected on specific instances of information that would lead her brother on a positive path. Nonetheless, she seemed to rely on providing information as a means not only to encourage Jose to avoid criminal behavior, but also to encourage him to stay occupied in activities that could enhance his mental health, social health, and general social interactions.

Jose responded to questions about his sister's general support of him, but did not mention the informational support she provided, nor did he explicitly recognize the residential support she provided. Instead, he discussed the emotional support she gave him— which she perceived as informational support. Responding to a specific question about informational support, Jose remarked, "Well, [my sister] would probably talk to me to see if I am having problems with my girlfriend. If I am having problems with my girl. . . . I would go to her and talk." It is evident that Jose relied on his sister for types of support other than just information, and that he consulted with her especially about intimate relationships. Although Anna provided him with information about safe sexual behavior, drug and alcohol use, and mentioned the mechanisms by which she provided him with information about the GED, Jose highlighted the emotional significance of his sister's support. She had gone to various lengths to encourage him to follow the information she gave him.

In these instances, former prisoners felt supported by their family members in ways that led them to believe that their family could provide support in other contexts. For family members, the constant interaction allowed them to provide the former prisoner with information. When a family member provides information to the former prisoner, he may well perceive the provision of this information as a form of emotional support. Moreover, the former prisoner may be in a position to provide family members with information, enhancing the bidirectional exchange of support.

Another former prisoner, Henry, had similar experiences. Henry, African American, single, and twenty years old was born and grew up in Chicago. He had five siblings, four sisters and a brother, Jeff, with whom he lived. Because Henry's closest relationship was with his brother, Jeff was interviewed. Jeff reported that the topic that dominated their conversations, and their daily lives, was employment. Jeff took an active role in assisting Henry by providing him with information and also by pursuing that information himself. Jeff commented on this issue.

[We] say what's been going on, what we been doing, where we gonna go try and find a job at, talk to people who already working, and see if they can try to get us on where they at. It's just really everyday things. Really, our main subject every day is getting a job. That's the main thing we really talk about or discuss is a job.

Like Jose and Anna, Henry and Jeff found that informational support could be exchanged for mutual benefit. Because both brothers were looking for employment, they had a common goal and offered each other support through the exchange of information. The information also involved the specific goal of economic advancement. Neither Jose nor Henry, however, focused on the informational aspect of the support. They, instead, interpreted it as emotional support because they perceived the information as a means to improve their relationship.

In his responses, Henry did not acknowledge the informational support his brother reported, although he was asked about it explicitly; Jeff, however, commented that Henry acknowledged the information he reported. Henry also did not openly acknowledge residence as a significant part of his support system even though the two of them had shared a residence. Henry felt that his brother provided emotional support, remarking:

"We almost make the same decisions sometimes, and then sometimes he'll make a better decision than me or I'll make a better decision than him. So I always take his input on the situation because he always had been there to help me with stuff like that."

Henry viewed this type of emotional support as providing him with help, proving to him that his brother has always "been there." Family members—in this case, Henry's brother, Jeff—again perceived that information (particularly regarding employment) was crucial to the former prisoner's well-being.

Interestingly, a number of former prisoners who resided with family members interpreted the information provided by the family members as emotional support. For former prisoners, being engaged in a relationship with family members where they felt emotionally supported signified an investment in the relationship. Therefore, regardless of the type of information provided to former prisoners, what they perceived was that the family member cared (La Vigne, Visher and Castro 2004)—which is significant in assisting former prisoners to pursue noncriminal paths. The former prisoners also implicitly understand that residence is important because it enables them to pursue other means of support, and that if they were unable to share a residence, the relationships instead might have to concentrate on securing a residence.

Although the study participants did not report similar perceptions of the exact type of support exchanged, they emphasized and acknowledged the supports that were most meaningful to them. This was the case for another former prisoner, Chris, a single, twenty-three-year-old African American former prisoner who identified his childhood residence as Chicago. In the interviews with Chris and his mother, Joan, they did not acknowledge, or comment on, similar exchanges of informational support. Nevertheless, there was a general consistency in reporting that the relationship was supportive.

Within the context of Chris's relationship with his mother, information itself—and providing information to help solve problems or overcome obstacles—strengthened Chris's relationship with his mother. Joan explained:

Before [Chris] came home, 1 had to search on the Internet and pulled up a lot of the social services that's supposed to assist inmates once they've been released, as far as placing them in jobs, assisting them with their education, furthering their education or assisting them with housing. . . . He's been home for three months and he just starting working, so none of the programs that are supposed to assist inmates when they're released have assisted him as far as housing or anything. The schooling that he was doing while he was incarcerated, he kept it up; he finished studying, sent off for the test, took the test, and he passed it. So he's done that on his own. He is working now. I think it's full time, too. So he's well on his way, but no credit goes to any state facility program that's supposed to be in place for inmates that has just been released back into society. Neither did he get any assistance . . . not to say he's not gonna get any assistance from this [program], but since he's been home, he's done all his legwork, connecting—all that he's done on his own.

As revealed in this quote, Chris's mother provided him with information on employment. His mother accessed and gave him information, but Chris also was trying to access this information on his own. When asked specifically about informational support, Chris's mother reported specific instances of her support. She previously had helped her son with social interactions and employment, which indicated that she had the resources at her disposal.

According to Joan, Chris did not use the information that she or the program provided; instead, he accessed resources through his own efforts. This corroborates the claim that informational support provided does not necessarily lead to the outcome that the "support sender" initially wanted. Former prisoners, like Chris, whose generally emotionally supportive family members provide information (within the context of a home), translate this support into motivation to pursue positive alternatives in a manner they determine for themselves. Note that Chris highlighted his mother's comments and perceptions about "stuff on my own."

'Cause now they got a lead on somebody requiring ex-cons or something like that because not all work is going through them, but the majority of it is. But I do a lot of stuff on my own to find jobs, or whatever, because I need one. . . . Always, always, always, every time I talk to my mom, I'm like, "I just talked to such and such [potential employer]."

Chris and Joan share the perceptions that he is actively seeking employment and that he receives emotional support from his mother (because he informs her partially about his progress). Once he came home, his mother provided him with information, but Chris focused on his personal efforts and that his mother was present. Although Chris resided with his mother and their relationship was close—and always had been—his mother perceived that providing information was enough, and that it was Chris's responsibility to use the information to achieve something. Despite the misperception of the exchange of informational support, Chris and Joan had similar perceptions that support—in whatever form—was present. Although they made no explicit or direct comments on residential support, it was the basis for the exchange of Joan's informational support and of Chris's ability to search for employment on his own.

For Jose, Henry, and Chris (the former prisoners who resided with family members), the family members were paying the bills and providing some of the instrumental support every day, so it simply went unnoticed. For example, they did not have to provide money for food because it was already there in the refrigerator. In the context of living in the same residence, the family members and former prisoners all agreed that support had been exchanged. Sharing the same residence may allow for frequent interaction and strengthen the tendency of the parties to support each other.

INSTRUMENTAL SUPPORT IN OTHER DWELLINGS

The second group of former prisoners in this study—Raymond, Arnold, and Johnny (pseudonyms)—did not reside with their family members, but rather lived in a recovery home. The type of support these former prisoners exchanged with their family members tended to be instrumental, and both parties had similar perceptions of that support. The significance is that when family members exchanged instrumental support, they did not have to monitor what the former prisoners did with it: the item itself, not necessarily what was done with it, was what was supportive. Moreover, the family members themselves may not have perceived mutual benefit through the exchange process.

One former prisoner, Raymond, grew up in Chicago, is African American, nineteen years old, and had two brothers and four sisters. Although he had fairly close relationships with his grandmother and one of his uncles, his twenty-four-year-old aunt, Susan, was the family member with whom he was closest. During the conversation about supportive people in his life, and in response to the questions asked about instrumental support, he remarked:

> I get the financial support [from my family].... [I]f I need cosmetics and all 1 have to do is call, or if I needed clothing or something to put in my pocket so I can just eat when I want to or anything, 1 could call them and they will bring it to me.

Raymond named cosmetics (toiletries), clothing, and money as crucial elements of instrumental support. In his commentary, he noted that his family would provide financial support when he needed it. Because Raymond did not reside with a family member, the investment from family was tangible support for a specific purpose. It is much easier to provide items (or to encourage the perception that these items would be provided) infrequently than to provide ongoing emotional support, because a family member need not feel responsible for what is done with what was given. The concept, "1 gave this to you" does not require the same investment as "I believe in and care for you," which represents a dedication to the relationship.

Although Raymond was not living with a family member, he continued to have a supportive relationship with his family. His aunt, Susan, corroborated the instrumental support that Raymond reported, and she also discussed the types of (instrumental) support that he provided to her.

The first thing he does when he comes in my house is take my garbage out. That is the first thing he do. When he get to the door, he always tells me the same thing.... "I'm not going to keep taking your garbage out," and I tell him "you take yourself out the door, you might as well take the garbage, too." He says, "Hey, you calling me garbage." I say, "Hey, whatever you see." Without me asking, I wish my thirteen-year-old son would come do it without me asking. He has to come and ask me, "Ma is there something you want me to do?" "Well, the garbage is overflowing and you asking," but [Raymond will] come and just take it out. He'll talk and say his little stuff like I said when he gets to the door, but he'll still take it out. He calls me. He is very respectful, you know? He has the key to my house, but he is not just going to come in. I told him he could come in whenever he wants to wash his clothes "cause I have a washer and dryer.... [As to money] why would I be asking him for money? I'm supposed to be able to give it to him.

Although Raymond's aunt did not provide or report the same instances of instrumental support, she did acknowledge the same category. She gave Raymond a key to her home and allowed him full access. Although money has not necessarily been exchanged, Susan trusts and supports Raymond by opening her home to him. In addition, regarding financial (instrumental) support, Raymond's aunt said:

> I mean, if he needs money, he hasn't asked me for it. He may ask me for a few dollars or something like that, and that's probably to get him some cigarettes or money in his pocket, but other than that, 1 don't ask him for none 'cause right now he doesn't really have it and I don't think I would ask for it, 'cause he is my nephew. If it is something that he needs, he will ask me for it. I never really asked him what he is expecting from me.

The matched perception of reporting similar instances of instrumental support is important to note here because Raymond and Susan have a mutual understanding that the instrumental items exchanged constitute the foundation of their support-exchange relationship.

Family members often recognized the financial support aspect in this context and realized the financial difficulty that former prisoners endured. Former prisoners do rely on their family members, but not for unlimited financial assistance. Rather, both parties recognize the exchange of minimal monetary support. Providing instrumental support, therefore, allows family members to exchange a form of support that requires minimal investment, both in giving and concerning the eventual outcome.

Arnold is a twenty-four-year-old African American born in Michigan, but whose childhood residence was in Chicago. Arnold's twenty-nine-year-old aunt, Marie, was a single parent with four children and his closest confidant. On the topic of instrumental support, Arnold described the mechanisms by which it was exchanged. This type of support was also provided indirectly; Arnold assisted his family with certain tasks, particularly for his grandmother, or on behalf of, his aunt. Arnold remarked on the kind of support he provided for his cousin on his aunt's behalf.

> I call [my aunt] sometimes, or she'll call me and tell me about what [her son] did. He out there on the streets. He caught himself not going to school today. I had to go there to check, make sure [my cousin] go to school. Right now, I be calling, waking him up, making sure he go to school in the morning because I get up early. I call to make sure he go to school. If I [am allowed to leave the adult transition center where I live], I'll go over there to make sure he goes to school. I don't want to see him. . . . I don't want him to go through what I been through. I want to see him go a different route because he's real smart. He loves the computer. He stay on the computer. He real smart. So I want to see him do something different with his life.

Arnold articulated his concern for his cousin. He monitored the boy's behavior because he was concerned that his cousin might stray from a positive path. Arnold "checked up" on his cousin and even went to his home to wake him up and walk him to school. The exchange process here is different from that of Raymond and Susan, reported earlier, but instrumental support still was exchanged. In Arnold's case, he provided specific, indirect support to his aunt because he did not want her son to pursue a path similar to his own. Arnold's efforts were focused on another family member because he wanted to repay his aunt for past support.

In another instance, Arnold voiced his viewpoint on instrumental support (money), as it pertained directly to his aunt.

> As far as financially, she knows I'm used to having money, so she knows by me not being employed, she tries to help me out. You know, give me money. But I be turning it down because I know she got kids. I be telling her, you got kids; you ain't got to give me no money. I'm gonna get through it. She's very supportive. She's very supportive. Anything I do, even if . . . she

might not agree with it, even if it was good or bad, she's been supportive.

In this context, Marie is willing to provide financial (instrumental) support, and Arnold recognizes and interprets this as an attempt to directly influence his economic (employment) situation. For many former prisoners, their family members were often willing to give financial assistance to them; however, former prisoners were cognizant of the financial burden that their family members experienced. According to Arnold, his aunt has attempted to provide him with money, but he rejected it. Although Arnold might have needed the money, he prioritized its use, saying that he was not the "highest figure on the totem pole." This instance of instrumental support was recognized, encouraged, and appreciated. Because Arnold helped his aunt with her son and because she attempted to give Arnold money, they had a mutual understanding and perception of the exchange of instrumental support.

Arnold's aunt commented about her awareness of his need and her willingness to provide support despite her inability to provide significant financial support.

> Well if he needs me . . . he'd come by and tell that he needed, um, money for a pack of cigarettes. . . . If I had the money in my pocket, I would give him some, and sometimes he would come by and if he had the money, he would give me money. If I needed something, like we'd order something from the restaurant or you know. I mean, like I said he's very generous hearted, you know. He has it, you know, sometimes I would get money from him. . . . It'll be two weeks later and he need anything: you get him a haircut, buy a pack of cigarettes or take him somewhere—Yeah, I help him.

This quote indicates that Arnold's aunt not only gave him financial support, but also discussed using money to provide other types of instrumental support. Even though funds were limited, the continuing exchange of money did not strain their relationship because both parties had the capability and desire to provide limited money to each other. The aunt, Marie, did not feel obligated to provide daily assistance because she did not see him every day. If she did, her expectations of Arnold might present a conflict.

The above excerpt reemphasizes and supports the assertion that instrumental support is more easily recognizable by former prisoners and family members alike. Because financial support has limits, however, family members are willing to provide it only temporarily. The cases of both Arnold and Raymond demonstrate intermittent instrumental support. Family members of former prisoners who did not reside with them were not present to constantly monitor their actions and therefore, showed their investment in the former prisoners' success while not feeling responsible if the support was not used positively.

Another former prisoner, Johnny, was twenty years old, African American, single, and was born in Chicago. He did not have any children and was the only former prisoner who was employed full time. Johnny's mother, Sharon, was forty-seven and single. Johnny's situation is similar to those of Raymond and Arnold, offering further evidence that instrumental support is more likely to be perceived or given when former prisoners and family members do not reside together. Johnny explained the instrumental support exchanged between him and his mother.

> Yeah. I help them sometimes, like with the phone bill or electricity bill or just putting groceries in the refrigerator. I really don't need help from them. 1 don't ask for nothing 'cause they know I can support myself, but if I do need it, if I didn't have a job and couldn't support myself, they would help mc financially.

Johnny's description of how he contributed financially to assist his family with certain bills or with food on occasion indicates that he realized he could support himself and, therefore, it was inappropriate for him to ask for financial assistance. He also suggested that if he ever needed instrumental support, his family—particularly his mother—would assist him.

The meaning of this quote, and by others in similar situations, is that money need not be actually exchanged for instrumental resources to be meaningful in the present, or even future, context. To know that the family would provide support is the important factor in the support-exchange relationship, less important to the former prisoner's perception is whether family members actually will provide, or have provided, monetary support.

Arguably, because family members are unable to monitor the former prisoners' use of the instrumental support, the appropriate use of that support is not a consideration.

DISCUSSION AND CONCLUSION

This examination of informal social support exchanges focuses on the interaction among former prisoners' residences, specific support mechanisms, and matched and unmatched former prisoner-family member perceptions of those support mechanisms. In the cases of former prisoners who resided with family members, the former prisoners did not recognize the informational support in the same detail as their family members did. although both parties recognized that their relationship was supportive. Possibly, finding information personally leads to personal responsibility: whereas, when a family member is the information source, the former prisoner's sense of self-efficacy is diminished.

Informational support perhaps is the easiest type of support that someone can offer without becoming emotionally involved and without the support reducing a family's resource base. It is argued here, however, that former prisoners interpreted the informational support as emotional support. Emotional support might be more difficult to provide without being present and observing the attendant unspoken cues. Informational support is the safest type of support as it requires, at a minimum, a superficial investment in someone. The family members in this study provided specific instances—not general occurrences—of informational support to prove that they have tried to help the former prisoner. Family members might have placed a higher priority on informational support because they perceived that the information they provided would be used as a tool to achieve success. By comparison, for the former prisoners, the specific instances of informational support were not prominent.

Despite not being asked specifically about residence, and although it was not explicitly recognized, the former prisoners seemed to interpret a residence shared with family members as an implicit form of support. They perceived that their economic advancement and non criminal pursuits were their own responsibility, not that of their family members, because the family already was providing or sharing a home. The interviews analyzed reveal that, for family members, informational support was a priority in the support relationship because they wanted to help the former prisoners avoid a criminal path and also to propel them into successful employment. For the former prisoners, the support was perceived as having family members present to consult with on various issues—and not necessarily the information given. This indicated to them that they had the support of their family members and could pursue other opportunities not related directly to the information provided by family members.

Providing information to former prisoners was important because, by residing with family members, the former prisoners realized that the family members could not afford to continuously provide instrumental support, and also that information to access resources might elevate them out of their situations. In addition, the former prisoners' resources were not depleted because they could contribute as much as they were able, or they could access information without having extensive resources or engaging in possible problematic behaviors.

For the former prisoners who did not reside with family, it is arguable that their families exchanged instrumental support and shared perceptions of the exchange because family members believed that tangible resources were most important. Because they did not live together, the family members could not—nor did they desire to—monitor whether the former prisoners used other mechanisms of support. Instrumental support enabled the family members to recognize and validate the idea that they were contributing to the former prisoner's success. Instrumental support can be disregarded or rejected, or its exchange can be denied, whereas something tangible that is exchanged is less likely to be rejected. Family members who could not monitor what the former prisoners actually did with this support, therefore, were not necessarily disappointed in the outcome—because they did not know the outcome. This did not discourage the family members from contributing, even though the instrumental support might not have been used as it originally was intended.

These findings provide useful information on working with families and former prisoners to identify and use appropriate supports for social roles for which each individual is willing to be responsible. Researchers must analyze these issues, but they have been more interested in family support in terms of its role in reducing recidivism than in how family support affects the family relationship. However, ethnographers are well suited to respond to, and uncover, these limitations. In particular, they can examine the intricacies of former prisoner-family relationships by not only uncovering and elucidating the meaning of former prisoners' family (cultural) system and interactions, but also use the findings herein to translate their experiences in such a way that brings life to this selective population (Spradley 1979). Although ethnographers should be concerned about family support as a tool to prevent recidivism and attempt to understand the family system in general, there is also a need to immerse themselves in former prisoners' and their family members' various residential contexts to link our cultural understanding of them with the needs of their communities. Such an analysis of how former prisoners and their family members interact and provide social support, admittedly, reveals that "we do not have direct access, but only that small part of it which our informants can lead us into understanding"

(Geertz 1973, 20); however, by understanding the many barriers that confront former prisoners and their family members, we can begin to conceptualize interventions that clarify the responsibilities of former prisoners and family members, and can work to create and maintain informal supports that encourage positive social roles.

The findings of this study contribute to our knowledge base to help former prisoners make the transition on their release from prison, using the available resources of the family. Undoubtedly, increasing the various types and amounts of resources is an important task for those who assist former prisoners and their families; however, of utmost importance is to understand how to direct policymakers and programs to use the existing dimensions of family support and to clarify roles and responsibilities, which can enable the existing support capacity of families to be matched with the former prisoner's capacity to support.

REFERENCES

Carlson, Bonnie, and Neil Ccrvera. 1991. Incarceration, coping, and support. *Social Work* 36 (41): 279–85.

Clear, Todd, Dina Rose, and Judith Ryder. 2001. Incarceration and the community: The problem of removing and returning offenders. *Crime & Delinquency* 47 (3): 335–51.

Cohen, Sheldon, Benjamin Gottlieb, and Lynn Underwood. 2000. Social relationships and health. In *Social support measurement and intervention: A guide for health and social scientists,* ed. Sheldon Cohen. Lynn Underwood, and *Benjamin Gottlieb.* 3–25. New York: Oxford University Press.

Dighton, Daniel. 2002. The challenge of reentry: Keeping ex-offenders free. *The Compiler*: 1–8.

Encyclopedia of Chicago. 2005. *North Lawndale.* http://www.encyclopedia.chicagohistory.org/pages/901.html (accessed April 20, 2007).

Festen, Marcia, and Sunny Fischer. 2002. *Navigating reentry: The experiences and perceptions of ex-offenders seeking employment.* Chicago: Chicago Urban League.

Fishman, Laura. 1986. Repeating the cycle of hard living and crime: Wives' accommodations to husbands' parole performance. *Federal Probation* 50 (1): 44–54.

Geertz, Clifford. 1973. Thick description: Toward an interpretive theory of culture. In *The interpretation of cultures,* ed. Clifford Geertz. New York: Basic Books.

Gottlieb, Benjamin. 2000. Selecting and planning support interventions. In *Social support measurement and intervention: A guide for health and social scientists, ed.* Sheldon Cohen, Lynn Underwood, and Benjamin Gottlieb. Oxford, UK: Oxford University Press.

Hairston, Creasie Finney. 1998. Family ties during imprisonment: Do they influence future criminal activity? *Federal Probation* 52 (11): 48–52.

Hairston, Creasie Finney. 2001. Fathers in prison: Responsible fatherhood and responsible public policies. *Marriage and Family Review* 32 (3/4): 111–35.

Hairston, Creasie Finney. 2003. Prisoners and their families: Parenting issues during incarceration. In *Prisoners once, removed: The impact of incarceration and reentry on children, families, and communities,* ed. Jeremy Travis and Michelle Waul, 259–82. Washington, DC: Urban Institute Press.

Hughes, Timothy, and Doris James Wilson. 2003. *Reentry trends in the United States: Inmates returning to the community after serving time in prison,* http://www.ojp.usdoj.gov/bjs/reentry/reentry.htm (accessed February 22, 2004).

La Vigne, Nancy, and Cynthia Mamalian (with Jeremy Travis and Christy Visher). 2003. *A portrait of prisoner reentry in Illinois.* Washington, DC: Urban Institute.

La Vigne, Nancy, Christy Visher, and Jennifer Castro. 2004. *Chicago prisoners' experiences returning home.* Washington, DC: Urban Institute.

Liker, Jeffrey. 1982. Wage and status effects of employment on affective well-being among ex-felons. *American Sociological Review* 47 (2): 264–83.

Martina, Shadd. 2001. *Making good: How ex-convicts reform and rebuild their lives.* Washington, DC: American Psychological Association.

Nelson, Marta, Perry Deess, and Charlotte Allen. 1999. *The first mouth out: Post-incarceration experiences in New York City.* New York: Vera Institute of Justice

Nurse, Anne. 2002. *Fatherhood arrested: Parenting from within the juvenile justice system.* Nashville, TN: Vanderbilt University Press.

O'Brien, Patricia. 2001. *Making it in the "free world." Women in transition from prison.* New York: State University of New York Press.

Petersilia, Joan. 2003. *When prisoners come home: Parole and prisoner reentry.* Oxford, UK: Oxford University Press.

Reis, Harry, and Nancy Collins. 2000. Measuring relationship properties and interactions relevant to social support. In *Social support measurement and intervention: A guide for health and social scientists,* ed. Sheldon Cohen. Lynn Underwood, and Benjamin Gottlieb. Oxford, UK: Oxford University Press.

Spradley, James. 1979. *The ethnographic interview.* Fort Worth, TX: Holt, Rinehart and Winston.

Street, Paul. 2002. *The vicious cycle. Race, prison, jobs, and community in Chicago, Illinois, and the nation.* Chicago: Chicago Urban League.

Wills, Thomas, and Ori Shinar. 2000 Measuring perceived and received social support. In *Social support measurement and intervention: A guide for health and social scientists,* ed. Sheldon Cohen, Lynn Underwood, and Benjamin Gottlieb. Oxford, UK: Oxford University Press.

23

Incarceration and Family Life in Urban America

Donald Braman

This article is a chapter from the book Doing Time on the Outside, *which examined the aspects of family life of those people who have a loved one incarcerated in prison. This particular chapter addresses the trials and tribulations of one husband (Derek) and wife (Londa) along with their children who simultaneously suffer the "pains of imprisonment." The realistic struggles of family members offers a rare inside portrayal of those left behind in the community when a family member is incarcerated. In this instance, the support they have provided during prior incarcerations is tested, with Derek's recent return to prison.*

Brenda's sister-in-law, Londa, is a mother of three. She broke her ankle a few weeks before we met and, worried about the impression the disarray in her apartment will give, she is quick to apologize about the mess. But, with her ankle broken and her husband, Derek, gone, She has trouble keeping the place as clean as she would like.

What really messed me up [is that] because Derek's gone he's not helping, he can't contribute anything financially, and I broke my ankle, so I'm, like, "What am I gonna do?" I don't like asking nobody for anything. Even when I had my cast on and everything, I just started hopping to the store, I started cooking myself, and doing whatever. The only thing I hate, 'cause I had the crutches, I couldn't really carry anything, so that was really hard. . . . Oh, I can't stand to ask anybody to help

me do anything, so I really hate asking my mother now, but I can't walk, I can't get around. So it's just really, really hard right now.

Londa and her three children—Pammy, who just turned eleven, Casper, who is two, and DJ, who is one—live in a small row house that is part of a housing project in central D.C. The neighborhood was devastated first by the 1968 riots, then by the heroin epidemic in the 1970s, declining public investment during the 1980s, and crack cocaine during the 1990s. Despite the efforts of numerous city and neighborhood organizations, the block she lives on is known today, as it has been for years, as a place where crack and heroin can be found on any street corner and at any hour.

Although the apartment is convenient to public transportation, Londa despises the drugs that permeate the area and has been waiting for a transfer to another Section 8 apartment in a better neighborhood for four years now.

Over the three years that I have known her, Londa has struggled with her commitment to her husband, Derek. She sees their current relationship as the culmination of fifteen years of struggle with Derek's drug addiction and incarceration, a struggle that has left Londa feeling utterly drained and Derek with years ahead of him in prison, both of them unsure of what kind of father he'll be able to be to his children. Their story is useful because, like the stories of so many families experiencing incarceration, it is neither one of flagrant injustice nor one of triumph against the odds. Instead, their story shows a family facing addiction, the criminal justice system's response to it, and the mixture of hardship and relief that incarceration brings to many families of drug offenders.

Londa and Derek grew up near one another. Londa was from a large family, with four girls and five boys; Derek's family was smaller, with two girls and two boys, but he had a large extended family in the area with whom he was close. Londa, who was shy as a teenager, was won over by Derek, her brother's bright and outgoing friend. He was spontaneous and generous, "a little over the top," but she liked that: "We use to just act silly and everybody would look at us like we crazy." Looking back on how they started, she remembers getting to know him during their long walks around the neighborhood, talking and joking. Soon they were in a full-fledged romance, and by the time they were out of high school, they were together nearly all the time.

Derek was a hard worker, making good money performing manual labor-laying carpet, working construction-any job that he could get to help them along. In many ways, Derek and Londa had a lot going for them. Despite Derek's wild streak and partying on the weekends, he kept himself in check and made it through his teens without any serious problems. Unlike many young men in the neighborhood where he grew up, Derek knew that he could earn a living if he worked at it, and he knew Londa was a good partner and would make a fine mother. Londa knew that Derek, though a little wild, cared about her and would be able to help support their children.

Londa had also developed positive relationships with Derek's mother and his two sisters, Janet and Brenda. "His family, his sisters, they're like close family to me. You know, I wouldn't call them my sisters-in-law, I would say they're my sisters." They spent a lot of time together, living the kind of family life that many people hope to be part of. They would cook for each other, watch each other's kids, help out with money in a pinch. Londa related one example:

When [Brenda's] daughter got ready to graduate she was upset—she was hurt. I know she was because you know, she had always said, "When my daughter gets ready to graduate, I'm gonna have a car waiting for her with a bow." You want to have so many things, and I understand that I want all those things too. At the time she was out of a job. You know [her boss], he didn't care. I took my car. Waxed it, washed it, did everything. And I let her use my car for her graduation. I mean there was just a lot of things we did for each other.

Derek's sisters agree that he was a great family man early on, describing how he used to take care of his sisters' kids before he had any of his own. As Derek's sister Brenda told me:

We was like a big family. He used to take the family and they'd go to the park. Derek liked to play with kids. He's better than me, I don't have the patience for it. He'd take the kids. They'll just go and hang out. I mean, it's a thrill to him. I'm like, uh-uh, not me. [But] Derek is a kid person. I mean, he just, he must have got it from our mother, our mother was like that too.

To Londa, at the time, their prospects seemed exceptionally good. As she told me, "When he first came around [I thought] it's going to be me and that person forever, you know? And I guess I've always thought that about me and Derek."

Looking back on the same time, Derek now sees that his perspective on family life was neither equal to Londa's nor what he now thinks it should have been:

Thirteen years ago, before I had my daughter, [I said,] "I want a child." I wanted a child, but I wasn't prepared for the child. I didn't save up anything. I didn't prepare a home, a stable home or anything. I didn't prepare that me and Londa go ahead and be marrying, and she have her job, and I have a nice job. I didn't prepare for none of that; I was just living life on life's terms. I was living, listening to . . . I grew up with my uncle and them, around them all the time, and I thought the way that they was living was a way of life. That you go out here and work, and you got your wife at home, then you got a girlfriend over here. Then you can go stand over there on the corner, you know, how guys hang on the little block together? Go over here, and that's where they drink at and all that. Then I figure that you can come on the block riding on your car all cool, got your girl over there. You know, I thought this was a way of life, and also going down the parks and all. I really thought this was a way of life. Now that I look at it, I was following the wrong crowd—even my own peoples now—the wrong crowd. And I see this now.

At the time, though, it seemed to Derek, Londa, and their families that they would make a good couple. Both Derek and Londa wanted a child, and it wasn't long before Londa was pregnant He was twenty-two, and she was twenty-one.

FAMILY, ADDICTION, AND INCARCERATION

Around the same time that Londa became pregnant, Derek's drug use became noticeable. By the time their daughter was born in 1987, Londa could see changes in Derek as he started covering for his growing addiction. Anyone with an addict in the family will know the litany of problems that Londa encountered: lying, erratic behavior, late night disappearances, pleading for money, and eventually stealing. Pretty soon the stealing was so bad that Londa would stay awake all night:

> As far as the drug addict, you can't really sleep around them because you're scared that when you wake up something is going to be missing. So you generally stay awake to try to keep them there or to make sure that things that you value or that you took your time out to get or spent your money on are still there when you get up in the morning.

Derek remembers this time, shaking his head. He had started selling drugs to support his habit: "I was out there at that time basically using selling in order to use. . . . I was running and staying up all the time. I'd come in the house any time of the addiction getting worse and worse."

Today, Derek makes no excuses for his behavior or his addiction. He acknowledges that his father was never around and that many of his family members—especially his male relatives—were hard drinkers and occasional drug users. But, on balance, he believes that his family was a positive influence. Given his family's stance, Derek told me, his continued drug use was a result of his being "hard-headed."

I was basically making my own decisions instead of listening to what they was trying to tell me. They always told me, "Derek, don't be going out there. Don't be doing this. Don't be. . . . I want you to stop using drugs." And they always stood a battle for me with the drugs, but I chose to do what I wanted to do.

When Londa realized how serious things had become, she tried to hold Derek accountable as a parent, something she felt like she deserved and their daughter needed. Londa was feeling more responsible now that they had a daughter, and she thought that Derek should as well:

> I felt like if I was going to grow up because I had to "be a mother" [then] he had to do it too. And I felt like that was only fair. He didn't have to be there all the time, but he just needed to grow up. And at the time he never got any help because he never felt like he had a problem. . . . I guess everybody [in his family] was upset because I wouldn't let him see our daughter. . . . But I felt like if I'm going to be sober and clean to see her, he has to be too.

When Derek did not go straight, she told him he couldn't come home and wouldn't be allowed to see their daughter until he did. "You get yourself together [and you can see her, but] I don't think she should get less from you and more from me. . . . The best you can do is to come over here like that? No. I'm sorry, she deserves more than that." And she cut him off. Shortly after that, Derek was arrested for possession and sentenced to eighteen months.

Cycling Through the System

Although Derek did not enter drug treatment while he was incarcerated, he managed to stay off of drugs and felt like he had recovered from his addiction.* Londa was surprised to see that Derek once again seemed like the person she'd fallen in love with. At the height of his addiction, she had thought that his personality had permanently changed and that they would no longer be able to relate to each other in a meaningful way. But to her

---

*While it is not impossible to get drugs while incarcerated, it is both more difficult and riskier. For these reasons, many drug offenders either get clean or significantly reduce their drug habit in prison. It is worth noting, however, that one participant in this study died of a heroin overdose while in prison. Housed in Lorton's Central Facility, he had been, after extensive discussion of his habit in court, sentenced to drug treatment while incarcerated, inpatient treatment after release, and three years' probation for robbery. He was awaiting transfer (to be sent out in the next "load" of prisoners) to a federal facility where treatment was available when he died. Just before his death, he told me he knew he needed to get help soon.

surprise, "the old Derek was back," and he was promising to reform his ways, writing long letters of regret, talking about his religious reform in prison, and suggesting that they get married on his release. †

> Right now, I'm just goin' through problems. I just wish they'd go ahead and send me on a load somewhere I can go somewhere.... They act like they don't want to send me on no load. I don't know. I'm just ... I'm just here. I have never received any type of treatment.... This is gonna be my first time, so hopefully I'll get something out of it. I need it. I need it. I really do need it.

He was survived by his sister, his son, and his son's mother.

Letter writing is part of a broader pattern of relationships that men and women enter into, however, and the moral and emotional quality of letters is colored by those patterns. Although prison is a remarkably public and social environment for men, one of the privileges afforded by incarceration is the relative privacy from female partners that men have in their correspondence and associations. The restrictions placed on when and how women can contact and visit with inmates allow incarcerated men to pursue relationships with several women at the same time, often with none of the women being the wiser. As one woman described it:

> The letters that they write you.... All of them got their jail line, their first line, it's like they teach them that line in a class or something: "How are you doing emotionally and physically?" All of this shit. But the letters that they write you and the cards that they send, I mean, if you don't know no better.... Me, in my younger days, I didn't know no better. I was, like, "Oh, this man is sure enough in love with me." And the same thing he doing to me, he doing to the next woman! And I mean, they got it. The letters and the cards, they just make you feel like you everything. But all the time, you ain't everything. The next woman ain't everything. It's all of y'all.

This kind of behavior, however, runs the risk of discovery and loss. Many people I interviewed for this study described the emotional scenes that ensued when an inmate failed to manage who visited when and more than one of the women he was pursuing showed up for the same visitation slot.

Derek's family also pressured Londa to give Derek another chance. Concerned about Derek's morale, they were worried that his isolation from Londa and his daughter could push him back into his drug use. Eventually, Londa submitted to their pleas. "His mom and everybody has always felt like I could make a difference [in Derek's recovery]. And I guess they had me at the point where I was believing that I could too." Won over, Londa accepted Derek's proposal of marriage when he was released. Looking back, she says she feels like she married two people:

> I think when I got married I was thinking, too, that I really, really wanted this person that I knew. Not necessarily he had to be the same as that person or act the same way. I didn't want that person where the demons had taken over. You know? I just wanted my Derek back.

Once Londa had seen that Derek could be responsible when clean, she wanted to help him beat his addiction, but she had little idea how hard it would be.

Trying to gain control over an addiction can be all-consuming for family members as well as for the addicts. Londa felt that in order to understand how Derek could change so much, and to help him get off drugs so that they could stay together, she needed to become an "addiction expert":

> I had to learn about drugs. I had to learn. I had to study all of that and try to figure out "Why did he do this? Why does he do that? What makes him do this? What would he do if I did this?" So I learned about it. I studied tapes, and read books, and went to the meetings, and I studied everything. I was maybe twenty-two, but I was old enough where I could be sick and tired of it myself. I could be sick and tired of being sick and tired!

During the following years of Derek's cycling through active drug abuse and recovery, Londa would work with him every time he returned to their home, accompany him to his Narcotics Anonymous meetings, and keep on him about avoiding his old friends. Derek did kick the habit each time he was incarcerated, but

---

†Prison correspondence is, perhaps, the last great stronghold of the handwritten letter. Many of the men and women with whom I spoke described letter writing as crucial to their relationships while dealing with incarceration. This is, in part, because the collect phone calls are so expensive but also because it allows men to say things they wouldn't normally say aloud. Letters are also semipermanent objects that family members collect and read over several times, whereas phone calls, while allowing a more immediate kind of communication, are ephemeral.

his recovery never lasted longer than a year after being released from prison. He would attend his meetings for a while, work hard, pay the bills, and then one day he would stop off to see some "friends" on the way home, and it was all over-another binge and another set of broken promises.

Family Aspirations

Addiction alone can strain and sour familial relationships, but incarceration adds an additional wrinkle to the problem that families struggling with addiction face. While incarceration can-and in many cases does-save addicts from losing their families or their lives, it can also extend the impact of addiction on families. Each incarceration allows the offender another chance to reestablish family relationships that had been curtailed out of frustration or anger. But because most drug offenders do not receive treatment, the likelihood of relapse is high; and because many offenders are released to their relatives, the influence on family life can be drawn out and devastating. Incarceration without treatment is, in many ways, double penalty for families of prisoners; the material and emotional costs of incarceration supplemented by the equally devastating and—in the absence of treatment—highly likely relapse of their family member. Given that most of the offenders added to the prison rolls over the last twenty-five years have been incarcerated on drug-related charges, the human costs to the parents, partners, and children of addicted criminal offenders are something that, while receiving little attention in the press or policy debates, is of tremendous consequence.

Londa coped with the cycle of incarceration, release, and relapse by learning to identify clues in Derek's behavior and to protect herself whenever she saw signs of drug use. As soon as she found him backsliding, she took away his keys, hid valuables, and kept an eye on him whenever she allowed him in the house. After Derek spent one of her paychecks, she also developed strategies for handling money. Whenever either of them got paid, she would guess at the amount of the next month's bills and send in her payments in advance.

> At first, you know, he helped me pay [the bills] and do everything. And then, you know, all of a sudden, he starts to do [drugs], and everything would just fall [apart]. I would try to keep money from him when he had it so that I could [pay my bills]. Whenever he would give me money, I would start paying everything, you know, putting more on it [than we owed]. I would do that. So it would kind of ease it a little bit by the time he starts back on drugs.

This way Londa got rid of all their money immediately and made sure the heat, electricity, and phone stayed on.

"Decent" and "Normal" Families

The pull of "normal" family life is powerfully attractive. What surprised me in my interviews was the degree to which that dream, against all odds, remained intact among families of prisoners. The assumption common in many policy circles is that few men or women in the ghetto have much interest in marriage or in what Elijah Anderson describes as "decent" living. Liberals assume that single women like Londa might not want to be dependent on a relationship with a man and that benefits will enhance the options available to poor women. Conservatives assume that single women like Londa suffer from a value deficit that prevents them from placing proper value on family life. Neither recognize what numerous studies tell us: that those who live in poor and minority communities are firmly committed to marriage arid family life but have low expectations of attaining what they hope for. Nor does either camp seem to understand just how it is to keep a family together in the inner city. Londa acknowledges that few (indeed none) of the families she knows live in this arrangement, and her dedication to her marriage raised significant difficulties for her:

> I always thought that, "Okay, we want to raise our kids together." There's not too many [families], there's not any that I can think of at this time that's not a single parent family. I never wanted that for my kids. I wanted them to have something that I didn't have. So you try to give them this and you try to give them that. But to me it is more important to have both your parents there. And I've always thought, you know, "Okay, that will happen." I always thought that would happen.

If Londa doesn't fit the stereotype of the ghetto mother, she also doesn't fit the stereotype of the often invoked selfish rational actor. In trying to decide whether or not lo stand by Derek, Londa wasn't simply evaluating him as a potential partner in an economic sense; her hope that Derek would eventually recover from his addiction was also based on their extensive history, their three children together, and the fact that both of them valued the institution of marriage itself. Divorce was not something Londa took lightly, and her adherence to that norm was something that she knew was costing her dearly.

The Last Time

The last time Derek was out of prison, Londa, his sisters, and his mother were close to cutting him off from the family altogether. His sister Brenda, recalling this time, looks down and frowns; things were worse than she had ever seen before: "He just didn't care no more. And he said he didn't care, and he wanted to die." Londa recalled that time and her daughter's reaction:

> It just really got worse. My daughter, she couldn't stand to be around him. She couldn't. She didn't want to be in the same room. And she loved her aunts, her grandmother, everybody over there. But she just didn't want him, you know. She was just having fun as long as he wasn't in her face. I know one particular time she was just hitting on him and kept saying, "Leave my mommy alone!" She was just screaming and she was hitting. All of that swinging. And she kept saying, "Leave my Mommy alone! Leave my Mommy alone! Leave my Mommy alone! I don't want my Mommy to cry no more." I . . . it just, it shocked me. It really shocked me.

Even his mother, Derek's most tireless advocate, had had enough. As Londa recounted: "I could see that his mother was really, really upset." Derek's sister Janet remembered what she thought was the tipping point, a night when Derek brought a "friend" back to the house and started smoking crack in the basement with her. "My mother, she came downstairs with a knife, and me and my sister had to hold her back and hold him back."

But just when things seemed to get so bad that Derek's family gave up hope, he finally turned a corner and decided to check into a residential treatment program. As Brenda recalled, for "the first time ever after all the years, he was just able face it. He got three kids, a wife, and he wanted to raise the kids and everything, and he seen what he was doing to us. He was tearing us apart." Derek acknowledged that the threat of destroying or losing his family, particularly his mother, was what finally turned him around. "They could just cut me off, and they won't have nothing else to do with me. It was almost to that point." For the first time, he stopped using drugs on his own and made arrangements to enter an inpatient drug treatment program.

The day before Derek was supposed to start his program, however, his mother died. Londa cries thinking back on it. Derek had just left to pick up some food that his mother had prepared for her, Derek, and the kids. Londa called to let his mother know that Derek was on his way.

> We were talking on the phone. She was telling me that he had called a drug treatment center himself and that

he was going that next day, how he finally went through with everything. She was saying, "I'm so glad," you know. And she was saying how glad she was that he was finally his old self. And it was just . . . she was so happy about that. And she passed out while I was on the phone. . . . She just collapsed.

Derek's sisters called an ambulance, and the family followed it to the hospital. Janet, the younger of the sisters, remembered it this way:

> We went back into the hospital and they put us in this special room, and that's when the nurse came in there and said that my mother had died. And then I'd say about 30 or 40 minutes later, Derek had came on the truck, and he ran in there like to bust the door in and everything. He ran in there and he asked the nurse and the doctor, and he said, "Where is my mother? Where is my mother?" And so we took Derek back there; they let us go in back there where she was after they done cleaned her up and everything. And so we went back there, and Derek, he went back there, and that's when he fell out, when he seen his mother laying up there bloated up like that, and [that was] the first time I'd ever seen Derek like that. . . . I mean, it's nothing like losing your mother.

Derek's sisters and Londa were doubly devastated. Not only had they lost their mother, but they also knew that, despite his promises the week before, their mother's death would send Derek back to the crack pipe. As Brenda put it, "Usually we'd be the ones trying to get him to a program. But this time, Derek did it because he seen that we would have. We had just had it with him. And then my mother, she died that weekend. I knew right there, forget that, it won't go nowhere." Derek abandoned treatment and went on a month-long binge that lasted through the funeral and alienated most of his family. Londa recounted a litany of outrages:

> He used drugs, lie drank alcohol. He . . . I don't even know. Come to find out he was having money wired to him from somebody—everybody—and he was spending it on drugs. I mean, I had the kids down there. It was really bad. He cursed me out. We went to stay in a hotel that my mother paid for . . . he stole my father's car that night lie borrowed money from the hotel manager. He said, "My wife and kids are stuck. They don't have gas and I don't have no money on me. Can I borrow some money so I can get them some gas?" I didn't know any of this until I was sitting in the room and the guy says, "Well he told me that um he was wailing on you to get back with the money." And I'm looking at him like,

what are you talking about? He borrowed money from his aunt [and] his uncle. They're married, but one was outside, one was on the inside, so he took from both of them. I mean it was just ... I have never seen nothing unfold like it. It was so frustrating. It was so upsetting. I mean, I have never had so many hurtful things in one time just come at me like that.

Londa knew Derek was not headed toward recovery, so again she cut him off. It was not long before Derek was back in prison, not only for violating parole but with new larceny counts in both the District and Maryland.

Cycling Through the System

Several families in this study described the cycle that drug offenders who don't receive treatment go through: the addicted family member would be incarcerated on some minor charge (usually possession or larceny), given a year or so in prison without drug treatment, and then released on parole. As was the case with Derek and Londa, the parole board would contact the family to make sure that the offender had a place to live and a supportive environment. Families, knowing full well that their loved one received little or no drug treatment and that he was thus likely to relapse, are put in a bind. If the family does not agree to take him in, they know that he will spend more time in prison or jail without treatment. If they do agree, they do so knowing that he is likely to relapse and reoffend. Unsurprisingly, most families—urged on by the pleadings of the incarcerated family member and ever hopeful that they will be able help him through recovery—agree to have him released to their care. Thus the cycle of good intentions and promises, followed by relapse, deeper addiction, and then reincarceration, goes on.

The cycle usually ends in one of two undesirable ways. The one that families fear most is death, and many drug offenders do die—victims of a drug overdose an illness secondary to their addiction, or violence. Over the three years of this study, three of the fifty offenders who participated died drug-related deaths. But most survive, and often their cycle of abuse they commit a more serious offense or wear out the patience of a judge garnering a lengthy sentence; eventually, if they do not die in prison, they are released late in life. While it is too early to say for sure, this appears to be what is likely to happen in Derek's case. After receiving several sentences for which he served less than two years apiece, Derek found himself in front of an unsympathetic judge who simply saw no reason to believe that this time would be any different from previous times.

He had had his second, third, and fourth chances, the judge told him, and now it was time to take him off the streets for a long time. What might have garnered a suspended sentence or parole for a first-time offender got him eight to twelve years.

There are also, of course, far more desirable but also far less common ways of breaking the cycle. Fortunate offenders will be sentenced to mandatory inpatient drug treatment, followed by transitional treatment in a halfway house and then outpatient services. As a number of national studies have now demonstrated, this approach is highly effective when the quality of the treatment is high and the duration is reasonably long. Despite the widely held belief that treatment must be voluntary to be successful, this same research has demonstrated that mandatory treatment is at least as successful as voluntary treatment.

One would think that mandatory drug treatment would thus be a popular sentencing option among judges and offenders alike. The chances of being sentenced to treatment, however, are slim. While some judges are perspicacious enough to sentence drug offenders to treatment, historically man) have not been. And even those judges who support treatment have to confront the practical reality that treatment—both in the correctional setting and in the community—is frustratingly scarce. As Faye Taxman, a University of Maryland professor who studies the District, observes:

> [P]robably half of the sentences for probation have drug treatment required, but probably only ten percent get any type of services, and I use the word "services" lightly. The system has been structured to provide the minimum. We provide something less than the minimum and say we are providing services

Over 40 percent of the District's offenders test positive for illegal drugs, and over 70 percent report current or recent drug use. But while it is estimated that sixty-five thousand District residents need drug treatment, well over 80 percent cannot be placed because of lack of treatment facilities.

The lack of available drug treatment also creates unintended incentives for inmates to avoid admitting to a drug problem and to submitting to drug treatment as part of their sentencing. Because inmates can wait months or even years to gain entry into a drug treatment program that is a requirement of their release, many inmates try to avoid sentencing that includes treatment even if they believe that treatment would help them. A surprising number of the inmates incarcerated on drug-related offenses in this study told me that they would rather be sentenced to "straight time" with no drug treatment and a definite release date than have their release be dependent on completing a drug program. As one inmate told me, "Then, at least, you know. This other way, you maybe get out, you maybe don't. And then even if you do get out, you have to deal with all the nonsense with your parole officer."

Although Derek was in and out of correctional institutions for over a decade on drug-related offenses, he was never sentenced to or completed a correctional drug treatment program. For the years that Derek cycled in and out of prison without serious drug treatment, Derek's family members were trying to get him into a program, but with little success. Derek resisted seeking treatment at trial both because he thought he could kick his addiction on his own and because he knew that it could add significant time to his sentence. Once he was released, he also had bills to pay. As he told me, "I just thought I could kick it on my own. I was hard-headed that way." His sister Brenda would try to talk him into going to a residential program but had no success:

> Derek is a workaholic when he's not on drugs. And he told me why he does it: to keep his mind off drugs. He wants to stay busy, because that's what he needs when he's first out. And like he told me, he also, he's scared of society. . . . He says, "It's scary out here," because he don't want to go back to jail. That's why, like I told him, I said, "Well, you need to get in a program, a real program that you can be there for a while and take care of this sickness." He said, "Yeah, I know." But the point is getting there, getting in a program.

Small People and Big People

Derek will likely spend at least another eight years in Maryland and D.C. facilities, and it could easily be as much as twenty. While he is not happy to be separated from his family, he acknowledges that there are some benefits to his being incarcerated in Maryland, where there are drug treatment and job training programs available.

> I look at [my incarceration] as taking a burden off of them and look at it as giving me back my life. . . . Because if it had not been for this incarceration, either one of two things could have happened. First of all, I could have lost them completely first. It already got to the point where I was not living with my wife and kids before I came in here. And it was almost to the point that my sister and them was ready to let go. And also, now, I could have been sleeping in the grave and be dead. But through this

incarceration . . . it's been a blessing to me. I'm not saying that I want to be here, but it was good that I came here. . . . because I never in my life want to do that again—to take my family what I took them through. And I made promises to my sister and them when my mom passed that I never held to. I promised to be there and help them, but now that I look at it, it seem like I made a promise to destroy them, because that's what I was doing.

It is hard not to agree with Derek that his current incarceration is, on the whole, better for his family than when he was out and using drugs. But Derek's sister Brenda views his predicament with less equanimity than he does, and her lament is one I heard from many family members of drug offenders. The cycle of release, relapse, and reincarceration is one that she thinks could and should have been avoided:

> It's hard when people don't have the income or know how to find people that you can talk to, to know how to get them into [a drug treatment program], because a lot of people don't want to listen to smaller people like us. And you just kneel down, and you pray, and you just ask God to lead you in the right way, and just watch over us. Well, it's hard. And you're trying to survive for yourself. And my kids, my family, take care of my income and everything with my household, and it's difficult. Then he has a wife and his kids who are on the other side of town, and they're suffering, too, you know. [Wealthy people] got people, big people, helping them, pulling them out of situations. And when people, little people, get like that, that's a different story. For them, they get thrown away in jail and locked up, while people that's on in high places, they'll take them somewhere privately to a program, and then they get clean. Then they're around positive people and live in positive areas. But they don't do the same thing for people that's small people—they just throw them away in jail instead of them trying to say, "Well, I can make a deal here. If you spend such and such time in jail, and then you go from jail to a program out somewhere, until you feel like you got it mentally together, until you prove to me that I can trust you to go from step one to step two to step three." You know? That's what I believe. That's what I see. I mean, why they don't see that? I mean, they deal with us every day. I don't know why they don't see that. It's simple. Especially if they really want to.

Clearly, the efforts of police, judges, correctional officers, wardens, state administrators, congressmen, and citizens—all of whom have produced our correctional system—are not conspiracies against poor families and communities. Yet one can see why, from the perspective of many families dealing with the criminal justice system, it seems more like part of a calculated design to destroy and injure than a collective social attempt to help or protect.

Both Derek's and Brenda's perceptions seem right. For many drug offenders, arrest and conviction *do* offer them a chance at sobriety and a chance to reestablish the family relationships that they damaged while they were free. But, as is evident from all the times that Derek went through the system, incarceration without treatment gives drug offenders yet another chance to pull their families back into the cycle of addiction. As more offenders are incarcerated on drug-related charges, the disparities in the criminal justice system become ever more tightly bound up with the disparities in drug treatment. In both cases, people get the best their money can buy, and for those without money, for "small people," that is often nothing at all.

Straining Family Ties

Despite Derek's gratitude for being alive, his family life is a mess. While he is finally in a drug treatment program, for many in his family, it is too little too late. The first time I met Londa she was worried about how the rest of the family was thinking about Derek.

> He has an aunt now that, she's at the point where she doesn't talk to him, she don't want to see him, you know. She was like, "He needs to stay where he is," and, you know, not thinking about a turnover or anything like that. She's just really, really bitter about it. And I didn't know this until I spoke with her awhile back. And I didn't know she felt like that. But she was really, really headstrong about him. "He needs to stay where he is and he better never come see me again." It's hard. Like he tells me a lot, he tries to make amends with people, and he can't. . . . And it's because most people don't understand addicts. They just know that they are addicts and they don't want to have nothing to do with them.

While she had long been a supporter of Derek, Londa's mother was very upset by Derek's behavior at his mother's funeral and would berate Londa any time she talked about Derek. "I couldn't just say, 'Well I still love him' anymore [to her]. She'd be like, 'You . . . Are you crazy?'" So Londa stopped talking about Derek to her extended family, except for Derek's sisters.

One of the hardest issues for family members to talk about is the way that children are affected by their parent's incarceration. The most obvious difficulty is simply figuring out how to help the child deal with the absence of the parent. For Derek's daughter, Pammy, that he was occasionally a good father made the times that he wasn't all the harder. Londa described their relationship as a close one that slowly deteriorated. But Londa doesn't think that her daughter has ever forgotten what it was like when Derek was sober. "She really misses that, because when she was little they were really, really close."

Beyond simply missing her father, though, Pammy has had to navigate the social world of a young girl while managing the information about her father in her encounters with friends and teachers. This, for Londa, was the hardest part and led to several arguments with Derek about how to describe his situation to their daughter. Londa wanted to keep Derek's incarceration a secret while Pammy was young and to let her know as she got older. Derek, on the other hand, initially wanted to tell Pammy, but as Pammy grew more frustrated with him he began pleading with Londa not to tell her. Londa believes that Derek's incarceration has led her daughter, already a quiet girl, to become increasingly private and withdrawn.*

> It bothers her because, you know, everybody is dealing with their fathers and school and their mothers. They come see them in shows and stuff. . . . You could see the hurt. I mean it's not more or less she's gonna come out say it. But she's real quiet like me. She's gonna keep everything in 'til she can decide, "Okay, who do I want to talk to?" You know. Other than that she really is very, she is very private. But I could see it. She has girlfriends and stuff, but they don't know.

---

*The reaction of children to incarceration is deserving of a great deal more study. One of the common responses that I found was that children generally guarded information about their incarcerated parent carefully, even when they knew that other people had full knowledge of the situation. As one aunt raising her nephew's son told me:

> He and I don't talk about it very much, but it does have an effect on him. It makes him kind of—when it comes to talking about his father—withdrawn. He has this "I don't want to talk about it" attitude. When his father calls he always talks to him on the phone, but anybody else, if you ask him, "Well, what did he say?" he won't tell you anything. It's like it's between him and his father. But otherwise he doesn't talk about his father.

He told me that he was sending her a watch or something, and I didn't tell her. And when it came in the mail, I said, "You got a package in the mail." But I wasn't really thinking about it. . . . She said, "Oh look what he got me!" She was really, really happy about it. Then her friends came along, and they were saying, "What's that?" "This is my new watch." And [her friend] said, "Oh that's cute. Where'd you get that?" She said, "My father gave it to me." [Her friend] said, "Your father gave it to you? When?" And she said, "Yeah. What you think, I don't have no father?" No father. You know?

And then her schoolwork, it showed in her schoolwork. And my daughter is a brain, you know, A's ever since she made kindergarten. She's never gotten a C. Never. Fifth grade everything just went [downhill]. He went to jail and everything just . . . she just really went down this . . . I kept talking to her. "What's going on? What's wrong." "Nothing." You know. She will not say it. Sometimes I sit and talk to her, and I try to pull it out of her. She'll say, "Yeah." Sometimes. You know. And I know that in the fifth grade year and I receive her report card and they said she had to repeat a grade, I cried, I . . . I hurt. It bothers me now. It still bothers me. You just think, you know, there is nothing that you can do. What can you do?

Londa is both exhausted from years of trying to work it out with Derek and furious with him for backsliding at his mother's funeral. She still cares for Derek but is long past putting his desires before her own, let alone the needs of their children.

I think now I'm wiser. I know a lot, a lot more than, you know, than more average thirty-three-year-olds as far as dealing with drugs and kids, and I know where to draw the line. I know how to say, "So long," [instead of] "Okay, I'll give you one more chance." I know how to say, "No, that's it. You had your chance."

After the funeral of her mother-in-law, Londa began considering filing for divorce, but still reluctantly.

We have spent eighteen years together and I'm thinking, "Okay, I can't mess up now!" . . . The only kids he has are mine, you know. I think about all of that, and I think about, you know, why did I get married?

You know, I was so blinded, and the fact that I wanted to get married that I didn't look past that he man stuff and doing drugs? Or [that] it hadn't been that long since he had stopped doing them. I mean . . . all the other times that he went back, and why did I think this was so different, you know? And I think about all of that, and sometimes I get mad at myself, because I look back, and I see all these things.

I mean, at first when we was dating, I could just walk away. But now, you know, I put a ring on my finger, and I'm married, and so it's more difficult now because I'm married to him. And I have more kids. I already had one, but I have more kids now. It would be a lot less pressure on me to stay, by me not being married to him.

Derek's Dilemma

The last time I interviewed Derek in person, he knew he was losing Londa. He was struggling to figure out how to cut his time down or to be relocated near D.C. so that he could avoid losing touch with his family altogether. Derek's sentencing judge told him he would consider reducing Derek's sentence if he completed a drug treatment program. But, as Derek notes, there are other considerations as well:

My problem now is this. I got to choose between the treatment route, the education route, and the job route. Now on the treatment route, I'll get nothing. Doing school, maybe just enough to cover cosmetics, but that's it. I go the job route, and I can send home some money and, see, that helps out Londa and keeps the family intact. The point is, though, that they ain't coming to see me here and ain't taking my calls 'cause they can't afford the collect. But if I take the job, I don't get the drug treatment. So I'm trying to focus on the family, but I'm also kinda trying to get out of here. But it's also to, I want to get back with them, even though I know I have to get the treatment first. But I just don't know. I know Londa's drifting away now.

And now I have two boys. One of them knows me but the other one was born while I was in here, and when I got out I only picked him up one time when he was a baby. And he's named after me, you know, but he don't know me from Adam. His mother may show him some pictures and things and say, "This is your father," or whatever. Maybe, I don't know. But I think my oldest son, he do know me a little bit. He's four years old now, so he may not know me as well, or maybe my face or something, you know, remember it. Well, now since I'm in here, I try to be a father to them, sending them money, you know, to be able to help the mother out. . . . I try to do that, you know. So if I keep up the job, I can send back money, keep Londa a little more happy, keep the kids knowing me. But then I just go in circles. The judge said I have to do the treatment here before I go for parole. . . . I mean, I look at it, and it would have been so easy to be a father out there. Maybe not easy, but it's like it's impossible here. You know Londa's talking about divorce.

I have often been surprised by the number of people who, while seeing their immediate world in terms of home, family, and community, shift their framework of understanding to one of radical individualism when discussing criminal justice. By conceptually stripping offenders of all their social relations, we are able to affix blame and mete out punishment. The isolated offender is a useful fiction in that regard, but a fiction that has come to so thoroughly dominate our analysis of what our criminal law should and can do that we are blind to its limitations.

Sitting in the office of a conservative congressman on Capitol Hill, I recounted an abbreviated version of Londa and Derek's story to a congressional aide. I was surprised by her response: "Why did she stay with that loser for so long? What these women need is to get out of these bad relationships." At the time, the aide's response seemed to contradict traditionally conservative "family values": here was a low-income African American woman living in one of the most drug-ridden neighborhoods in our capital city making significant sacrifices to keep her family intact against all odds— and a white, politically conservative member of the middle class wondering why she bothered. That the congressman whom the aide worked for had publicly decried the casual attitude toward divorce encouraged by our culture had led me to think that the aide would be a sympathetic advocate for this family.

Having since spoken with many policymakers (both liberal and conservative), however, I would be far less surprised today than I was then. It is not that the aide did not value family; rather, it is that Derek's status as an offender prevented the aide from seeing that Derek is part of a family and that his family feels it would be *immoral* to abandon him. "For better, for worse, in sickness and in health" are the traditional vows of marriage, and many of the wives of prisoners whom I spoke with recited them to me when I asked why they chose to stay with their husbands. The stereotype of the offender is that of an individual isolated from all social relations. The aide's suggestion stemmed from a misunderstanding of the strength and meaning of family for the rest of Derek's relatives. Had it been her own brother or husband addicted to drugs and in prison, I suspect that she would have reacted differently.

PART IX

Desistance From Crime

Participation in criminal activity does not necessarily mean that an offender will continue constantly to offend. That is, criminality oscillates throughout one's lifetime; changes vary depending on the shifting circumstances for that individual. Leaving a criminal lifestyle is very much dependent on an adherence to conventional values, with continuing association with conventional others as well as opportunities for reintegration within society. Desistance from criminal activity may be related to fear of incarceration, aging, risks involved to that person, and an introspective look at that person's life coupled with a strong desire to change. Offenders have many obstacles to face when they desire to exit from the criminal world. They have to join a conventional world, which is often reluctant to accept them, and they have to conform to a lifestyle and value system that is disdained by the criminal subculture. In addition, they experience difficulty gaining meaningful employment, especially if they are unskilled. The following article selections focus on the trials and tribulations that criminal offenders face in their attempts to join the conventional world. Their stories are real and often inspiring.

The transformation of identity for prostitutes participating in rehabilitation programs that help them transform to a more conventional self-image was evaluated by Sharon S. Oselin. Through interviews and observations of a residential program that separate these women from the outside world, the author was able to analyze how the organization's program enabled these women to transform their prior deviant identity over a period of time while actively participating in the rehabilitation program. As the former prostitutes go through the various phases of treatment, the author interviewed and observed the participants' transformation process as they transition through the stages of the program. Finally, Oselin discusses how the organizational structure facilitated their desistance from their former prostitute identity, and involvement in prostitution to a new conventional identity.

Based upon four years of ethnographic fieldwork with former prisoners released to the community, Lucia Trimbur explores how these men perceive their futures upon recovery and the obstacles they face in their attempts to desist from criminal behavior. The way these post-prisoners react is closely related to their feelings of racial oppression and social and economic exclusion. The author observes their individual responses to these obstacles and finds that their individual interpretations of their social and economic situation affect their future behavior upon reentry. Trimbur claims these ex-prisoners take several approaches to perceiving their future upon release and she discusses how they meet these challenges through interpretations of the limitations they face once back in the community.

Andrea M. Leverentz focused her research on the impact of female offenders in the community and the effects of their involvement in romantic relationships as part of the recovery process. The majority of Leverentz's sample interviewees were never married, and she examines the various differences in the types of relationships that these former female inmates were involved in, and how they helped or hindered their chances of not re-offending. Thus, the relationship could provide positive support for conventional behavior or it could be a destructive relationship. The author addresses the important issue of how these romantic relationships are not static—neither positive nor negative—but rather they are dynamic, changing throughout different periods of time.

24

LEAVING THE STREETS

Transformation of Prostitute Identity Within the Prostitution Rehabilitation Program

SHARON S. OSELIN

By participating in a rehabilitation program, former prostitutes experienced identity transformation from that of having a deviant identity to one that changes their identity to a more conventional non-deviant self. The process of transition is explored through various stages of change by these women as they leave behind their past criminal lifestyle.

INTRODUCTION

In the social science literature, there exists a broad array of studies focusing on identity, which is loosely defined as "fateful appraisals made of oneself—by oneself and by others" (Strauss 1997:9 [1959]). Identities are fluid and can change depending on one's role and social positions, thus making identity transformations commonplace. However, we know less about how individuals transition from a deviant identity to a non-deviant identity. This process may be more difficult given the stigma and labeling associated with deviant identities in general (Becker 1963; Goffman 1963).

The prostitutes at the Prostitution Rehabilitation Program (PRP) appeared to have had a deviant identity while working on the streets as they recounted stories of how they were treated poorly by others based on their occupation, their shame of "being a prostitute," and their stated desire to "do and be something different." Likewise, Sanders (2007) found street sex workers were trying to escape deviant labels as they attempted to leave the trade. Some research suggests having a deviant identity helps ease the transition from a "deviant" to "professional" identity, as in the case of substance abuse counselors (Brown 1991). However, this may in fact depend on the deviant role associated with a particular identity. While most deviant groups experience stigma, research suggests that prostitutes are among the most highly stigmatized groups, thereby making prostitution a very salient part of their identity (Chapkis 1997; Lawless et al. 1996; Pheterson 1996).

Source: Copyright © 2009. Leaving the Streets: Transformation of Prostitute Identity Within the Prostitution Rehabilitation Program. Oselin, Sharon S. *Deviant Behavior 30* (4): 379–406. Reproduced by permission of Taylor & Francis Group, LLC., http://www.taylorandfrancisgroup.com.

One of the greatest factors influencing this transformational process is the structure and regulations imposed by the prostitution rehabilitation program onto prostitutes immersed within it. Some organizational structures, such as total institutions, appear to exert a particularly strong influence over the identities of inhabitants. However, in such cases individuals still negotiated and actively constructed their identity instead of simply embracing the institutional one (Goffman 1961; McCorkle 1998; Paterniti 2000; Ponticelli 1999; Schmid and Jones 1991). Although the PRP is similar to a total institution in many ways, it also transitions to a quasi-total institutional setting over time. How do these varying organizational structures affect this process?

This article examines these neglected considerations through the ethnographic study of a residential program for women exiting prostitution in a large western American city. The PRP and its residents are an ideal setting and sample for answering these research questions because residents have recently left a deviant career and are situated within an organizational context that largely separates them from the outside world. I analyze how this organization shapes the course of identity transformation among prostitutes by examining the impact the program structure has on program clients as they leave a deviant identity and role. In doing so, I compare residents' biographical reconstruction (talk) with their role embracement (behavior) as a means to gauge identity transformation, because together these provide the most robust indicators of identity change (Snow and Machalek 1983).

THEORETICAL ISSUES

The PRP's organizational structure is unique because it contains aspects of both total and *quasi*-total institution. Past studies on quasi-total institutions conceptualize them as more "flexible" total institutions. Specifically, Armaline defines quasi-total institutions as specific organizations where "structural elements such as rules and policy are influential yet not static and impervious to challenge and reaction by residents and staff" (2005:1126). Research on quasi-total institutions and total institutions overlap because both focus on social control and the interplay that ensues between individuals and structures.

The PRP contains aspects of both total and quasi-total institutions and those dynamics are operative at different points of the resident's organizational career. The PRP displays the characteristics of total institutions particularly early on in the program, a stage when the resident's freedom and behavior are highly restricted. For example, new residents are not allowed to make unsupervised phone calls, cannot leave the premises without permission or a chaperon, cannot have contact with anyone from their past, and are expected to display dependency and submission. Alternatively, as residents progress through the program they experience a quasi-total institutional structure, which is characterized by increased physical freedom and autonomy. However, we know little about how identity transformations, particularly from a deviant to non-deviant identity, occur within changing institutional settings.

RESEARCH CONTEXT, METHODS, AND DATA

In 2002, I spent over six months collecting ethnographic data at the PRP, which is located in a large western American city, by working as a program volunteer. The PRP is a twenty-nine-year-old non-profit organization loosely affiliated with a Protestant church. The data consist of in-depth tape-recorded interviews with eight ex-prostitutes (seven were in the program and one was a graduate), and with three staff members, and approximately 140 hours of participant observation. Due to the small size of the sample population, I interviewed all the residents and staff.

Some scholars argue that researchers need to be especially sensitive and non-exploitative when studying vulnerable populations (Mishler 1986; Punch 1986). In an attempt to empower the residents, I conducted flexible semi-structured interviews that encouraged them to tell their stories. Clearly, the women seemed to feel more comfortable setting the pace and structure of the interview. I believe this strategy alleviated some of the alienating effects that interviews can produce and, in fact, created trust so that the women talked openly about their experiences and life histories with me. In these interviews, I asked them to discuss their biographies, identity, perspectives on the PRP, interactions with other residents and staff, reasons for entering PRP, future goals, and personal change. The interviews allowed the women to subjectively describe themselves, while the participant observation provided insight into their behavior, interactions with each other, and with the staff. I also observed residents at various stages of the 18-month to two-year program in order to better understand which of the PRP's different organizational characteristics were operative at different points of the program.

The PRP does not conduct outreach on the streets and the residents usually learn about the program by word of mouth from a friend, a social worker, or an attorney. Whereas many of the residents chose to enroll at PRP as an alternative to serving jail time, others came voluntarily from the streets. According to the staff and PRP manuals, the goal of the PRP is to provide street prostitutes with the resources and training necessary to re-enter society without relying on prostitution. Marie, the residential coordinator, said they consider an increased sense of self-esteem, acquired employment skills, and completion of a high school or college degree as signs of client success.

The residential setting, a two-story stucco house situated in a middle-class community, was full with six live-in clients and the program director. The residents spent most of their free time in one of three common areas: the kitchen, the living room, or the garage, which was converted into a makeshift lounge area. The PRP required residents to attend job training workshops, school, therapy sessions (both individual and group), bi-monthly one-on-one sessions with staff, house meetings, and to maintain sobriety, complete the Life Skills and Social Skills books, fulfill household chores, and eventually secure a part-time job. These requirements were structured as phases that focused on specific skills that residents should acquire while in the program, such as intimacy building or consciousness raising. Ultimately, residents must complete all these phases in order to graduate from the program.

While in the field, I took on the role of participant-observer (Junker 1960), which means that I took on an overt role (I was a known researcher) where I developed relationships with clients and staff members with a high level of contact and intimacy. My duties included being a tutor and mentor, facilitating group classes, and driving residents to and from jobs or appointments. These interactions helped to cultivate a non-threatening, non-intrusive rapport between the residents and myself, and provided ample opportunities for observation and conversational interviews. As a result, the women began confiding in me about their personal lives, feelings, frustrations, and concerns. In addition to fulfilling these duties, I was able to observe group classes and staff meetings, as well as initiate small talk and one-on-one conversations with the staff and residents while they were doing mundane activities, such as smoking, gossiping, cooking, or watching TV.

As the women moved through the program phases they also displayed different combinations of talk and behavior, which together indicated identity transformation. After conducting one to two hour semi-structured interviews with each client and staff member and reviewing my extensive field notes, I coded each individual's talk and behavior as either "resistant" or "changed" to indicate alignment with program talk and behavior and noted the most salient pattern exhibited by each client over time. Relying on the occurrences for each woman, I find women move in three main categories ("Rookies," "In-betweens," and "Experts") as they experience identity transformation. The residents' range of talk and behavior suggests that identity change is closely tied to time spent in the program and the longer women remain in the program the more they exhibit biographical reconstruction and role embracement.

Grappling With a New Identity

Many of the residents desired to leave prostitution but felt incapable of doing it on their own. With the help of the PRP, many residents adopted new talk and behaviors that helped them transition from a deviant to non-deviant identity. In other words, the PRP is the context where women learn to speak and act differently over time; however, those who do not show they are learning this process fall out of the program. In spite of the variations in program talk and behavior among clients, clear patterns emerged: The longer a client has been in the program, the more proficient she becomes at aligning her talk and behavior with those of the program, thus suggesting she has shed her old identity and embraces a new one.

Phase I: Clamp Down on the Rookies

The initial phase in the PRP lasts approximately four to five months, depending on the progress of the individual, and can be considered an adjustment period. Generally, new residents settle into the program, learn the rules, and get to know the staff members and other residents. In this introductory phase, the PRP staff creates a strict, highly structured environment that attempts to routinize the daily lives of program residents. Because of the restricted environment, the PRP is reminiscent of a total institution: residents cannot leave the premises without a chaperone, cannot have any contact with former friends, and are controlled by a strict schedule of activities including school, therapy, meetings, preparing dinner, chores, and doing homework.

The total institutional environment is accomplished primarily through the implementation of formal control mechanisms. PRP staff uses these mechanisms (e.g., program rules, staff supervision, and individual and group meetings) to help define, teach, and cultivate program talk and behaviors among residents. The staff surveillance of clients is one of the most powerful control mechanisms operating in the program. Because staff members are always on the premises, they can constantly monitor the residents in order to make sure they are adjusting to the program and abiding by program rules.

This phase, at the outset, is often characterized by resistant talk/resistant behavior from residents, partly because residents are adjusting to drastic lifestyle changes. Indeed, women in this phase spend a lot of time discussing the shame and regret they feel about working in prostitution, suggesting this identity is still very salient for them. One client, Heather, explains,

> It's degrading, especially if I don't even like the motherfucker. It's just degrading that I was sleeping with all these men. It's bad. I don't walk around telling people what I do.

Although residents at this phase express shame and remorse they have not yet learned to articulate or behave in ways that imply a new sense of identity.

Only off the streets for a short time, these residents are "rookies" in the program because they are not adept at displaying PRP aligned talk and behavior. As residents progress through this phase, staff members expect them to begin to show signs of change by exhibiting program talk and/or behavior. Accordingly, the staff considers women who are not beginning to do so "defiant" or "unwilling." Noting this resistance, they argue these women are generally doing poorly in the program.

Four months into the program, Teresa, a thirty-year-old African-American woman, provides a good example of a resident who is not adept at displaying program talk and behavior and can be considered the quintessential "rookie." Diagnosed with a bi-polar personality, she often oscillated between being outgoing and friendly or reclusive and argumentative. Because people she considered intimate had frequently betrayed her, she is particularly mistrustful of others in the program. As the following comment shows, she finds it difficult to get along with the other women:

> I hate living with the other women in competition with one another. I just avoid them and they avoid me. I don't know how to deal with them yet. They try to get my attention with new stuff. They say "oh look at this" and laugh. I say, fuck off.

Teresa not only resisted espousing PRP talk, which emphasizes speaking to other people in a respectful and friendly manner, but also failed to alter her behavior.

She began to withdraw from the other women, group conversations, and activities, and provoked arguments with both staff members and other residents. In addition to being argumentative, her interactions with others became increasingly violent and culminated in an exchange where she threatened to kill another resident because she did not like her attitude. Teresa's behavior violated the PRP rules, which promote positive social interactions and communication to solve problems rather than resorting to physical violence and bickering. At first, the staff intervened by trying to help Teresa change her talk and behavior through sit down therapy sessions and verbal reprimands, but eventually felt she needed more intense therapy than they could provide. After Teresa threatened another client with a knife, she was asked to leave the program.

Jennifer, the PRP case manager for a year and a half, offered the following account for asking Teresa to leave:

> She threatened another person. She said that she was not only suicidal, she was homicidal and had to protect herself. Yes, that was a direct threat so we asked her to leave. That's extreme. I'm sure you've seen the covenant basically it states that our purpose is to help these women. Kicking people out doesn't meet that goal. That is the last resort. She was just too far gone.

Teresa's case is an extreme example when formal control mechanisms failed to cultivate changes in talk and behavior. Nancy, a pastor and director of the PRP since 1980, described what course of action the staff typically took when they noticed a resident was not complying with PRP rules:

> Well, we do a one-on-one talk with her and discuss what we're seeing and what her take on this is. Most of the time, ninety-nine percent of the time, we are right on target—she's not dealing with something. She's hooked up with some old boyfriend or there is somebody in a meeting that she knows she used to use [drugs] with. She feels she can't possibly process all this without using. So we just put them on watch and we keep our eyes on them. And we keep telling them positive things . . .

After a talk and additional therapy sessions, the staff expects the recalcitrant resident to show attempts at change. During this period, the staff may invoke various sanctions for not following the program, ranging from revoking privileges (such as not receiving an allowance) to having "one-on-ones," to asking the resident to leave altogether. As Teresa's story suggests, they use the latter for only the most extreme cases. Residents who do not begin to exhibit PRP talk or behavior by the end of this phase typically leave the program voluntarily or, in rare instances, at the staff's request.

Although the program structure attempts to facilitate changes in talk and behavior, it is largely up to the clients' discretion to decide whether to display them. Teresa was unsuccessful at either, although it is unclear what her intentions and motivations were regarding the program. As a result she did not undergo changes typically experienced by ex-prostitutes who progressed through the PRP, such as higher educational attainment, changes in social class and personality, and an acquisition of different social networks. Indeed, identity (and role) transformations alter more than just one's identity, as identity affects many aspects of life, social standing, and interpersonal relationships (Drahota and Eitzen 1998; Ebaugh 1988).

Clearly, not all PRP residents resist learning program talk and behavior throughout this initial program phase. Some residents begin to learn and exhibit PRP talk and behavior as they progress through the program and show various combinations of program talk and behavior. After only a short time in the program, some residents begin to embrace the PRP as a home—a safe place where they can learn new ways of talking and behaving and formulate a different identity. Let us now turn to some of these cases.

Phase II: In-betweens Attempt to Transition

Clients experience this second phase, which usually lasts for about a year, for a majority of their time in the program. The most significant difference between the first two phases concerns the program structure, which changes from a total institution to a quasi-total institution, and ushers in a different milieu for program residents. Upon advancement to this phase, clients have more freedom, can leave the house without a chaperon, and receive and make phone calls to family members and other approved individuals. Client responsibilities, which accumulate the longer they remain in the program, include: enrolling in school, socializing and getting along with other residents, working a twelve-step program, completing household chores, and eventually securing part-time work and volunteering in the community. Essentially, the organization's structure grants residents more autonomy than was allotted in the previous phase and simultaneously encourages proficiency of program talk and behavior.

In this phase, residents espouse various combinations of PRP talk and behavior while living within a quasi-total institution and are therefore considered "In-betweens" or individuals who are in the process of learning PRP talk and behavior. These residents display either changed talk/ resistant behavior or resistant talk/changed behavior. Both of these patterns imply a process of change whereby women conform to or adopt certain aspects of the PRP role (such as talk or behavior), but typically do not exhibit both consistently or flawlessly. While some of the residents display signs of change others fall short and eventually leave the program.

Denise, a twenty-year-old African-American woman, exemplifies this pattern of "talking the talk but not walking the walk." She was jailed three times for prostitution charges, previously worked under a pimp, and pleaded to attend the PRP instead of serving jail time. During our conversations and those I overheard, she routinely espoused talk aligned with the PRP but her behavior contradicted her talk and did not comply with this new role. As she explained:

> The program offers a lot. And on the brochure they said, "Do you want to quit prostitution? Call us." So that really triggered me to come to PRP. And that's not what I want to do for the rest of my life, that's not what I want . . . I've wanted to be an OB/GYN since I was five years old.

On another occasion, she again expressed her desire to change by getting an education and finding employment:

> God gave me the program as a gift and it's my one chance to change my life and do something different. I need to get a job but first, I have to get my GED and ease back into things . . . it's been a long time since I was in high school and I don't remember most things . . . but I'm ready to start.

Whereas the above statements indicated Denise's longing to change and start a new life, her behaviors contradicted this stated desire. For instance, she often refused to attend her tutoring sessions with me, claimed she was too tired to complete her homework, did not need any help, and overall, avowed she was doing well in school. I soon learned this was not the case when I attended a staff meeting where Jennifer informed me Denise was barely passing her classes and was caught skipping classes by a fellow resident. Additionally, Sandra, who attended class with Denise, complained that Denise "clowned" around in class, continually distracting and disrupting the rest of the students. As a result, she incurred multiple warnings from the teacher but did not alter her behavior. A week later, I arrived at the site and learned she was no longer enrolled in the program. It became evident that Denise was juggling conflicting roles when I learned she left the house with her pimp and, in fact, had secretly called him for the past few weeks. Shortly after she left the program, staff members saw her soliciting Johns in an area rife with prostitutes. Although she became adept at program talk, she was unable to effectively master program behavior.

The second pattern exhibited among residents in this phase is resistant talk and changed behavior. Sandra, a twenty-nine-year-old African-American woman who had been in the program for thirteen months, illustrates this example well. Having worked as a prostitute for four years, Sandra claimed she left prostitution because she was tired of the lifestyle and her cocaine addiction. She was still involved with her boyfriend, the father of her four children, who visited and with whom she talked regularly on the phone. While she was doing well by the program standards, she occasionally espoused negative talk. When asked if there was anything she did not like about the program, she responded:

> I don't like the part about not having sex until two years from now. I'm being honest. Some of the rules are too strict. Especially because my boyfriend is very supportive and has stuck by me this whole time.

While Sandra openly admitted to disagreeing with PRP rules that explicitly prohibited sexual relationships while being enrolled in the program, she still respected and more importantly, upheld the no sex rule. PRP staff believes that ex-prostitutes need to "relearn" how to have a relationship (and sex) with a man. In order to accomplish this, they encourage the women to adopt a new perspective on intimate relationships by staying celibate for the duration of the program, and emphasize that sex should only occur in committed relationships.

Interestingly, a few months after this conversation, Sandra no longer complained about the no-sex rule but instead acknowledged that she played a part in being in a co-dependent relationship with her boyfriend. She explained that her involvement with men was, in part, "a power play" and she now understood that she needed to work on herself in order to be in a healthy (sexual) relationship. Accordingly, Sandra was clearly mastering both PRP talk and behavior as she advanced through the program.

Gina, eleven months into the program, is another example of an individual becoming more adept at PRP talk and behavior. Six months into the PRP, she also displayed resistant talk (no biographical reconstruction) but changed behavior (role embracement). At that time, she explained,

> I know how to please a man by being a good cook, fucking well, breeding, keeping the house clean. I'm good at it. It's really hard for me not to be with a man.

In spite of her strong orientations toward sexually pleasing and serving men, she remained in the program as a single, celibate woman who was not involved with a man.

According to PRP philosophy, these women consistently engage in unhealthy, co-dependent relationships with men, prompting them to sacrifice their desires and needs to those of their partners. Several months later, the following remark suggested that she now aligned her talk with the PRP:

> It would be nice to have a companion, a soul-mate, but fix yourself first and everything else will fall in place. That old mindset was what allowed me to sleep with anyone without thinking twice. 1 don't want to do that to myself anymore because my body is a temple.

This example captures Gina's changing orientation toward men and her increasing proficiency at program talk (biographical reconstruction) over time.

An individual entering any new role needs time to learn the appropriate talk and behaviors. Women in this phase are "trying on" the PRP role, ultimately selecting talk and behavior that upholds their burgeoning identity. Successfully learning and exhibiting program talk and behavior allows clients to remain in the program, reduces tension and conflict with staff, and garners program privileges, such as schooling and visits with family members. Although motivations for complying with the PRP vary, clients that progress through this phase enact some form of PRP talk and/ or behavior on a regular basis. By showing a willingness to change, residents temporarily appease staff and are allowed to remain in the program.

In Phase I, the PRP staff employs various techniques of formal control to facilitate changes among residents. In this phase, informal social control mechanisms, particularly mutual monitoring among residents, begin replacing formal ones to encourage residents to display PRP talk and behaviors. While the PPR staff still monitors and provides guidance for the women, support groups and intensive mutual monitoring (especially by the more advanced residents) become more important for enforcing program rules. Because the residents have more freedom, take on more responsibility, and are away from the staff for a substantial amount of time (with school, work, etc.), they "encourage" one another by monitoring and reinforcing talk and behavior that complies with their new role and identity.

Reprimanding Kelly for her attitude, Heather, a thirty-one-year-old resident, illustrates the operation of mutual monitoring:

> You need to be more positive. I always hear you talking negative about everything. Your attitude needs to change. You worry too much. How are you ever going to accomplish anything when your attitude is so bad?

This exchange suggests program internalization, particularly because Heather made this comment when no staff members were present. Although Kelly appeared irritated by Heather's comment, she subsequently stopped displaying the problematic attitude and began to exhibit increased program talk and behavior. In this way, mutual monitoring is a powerful tool residents enact on a daily basis to encourage the adoption of a new identity via changed talk and behavior.

Affective bonds and the trust these bonds engender among residents facilitate mutual monitoring. The development of these bonds is integral to conversion and identity reconstruction (Snow and Machalek 1984), and individuals rely on them to both monitor each other's behaviors and become role models (Ponticelli 1999). For example, affective bonds are found in AA groups (Denzin 1987), postpartum support groups (Taylor 1996), and in ex-gay ministries (Ponticelli 1999). They encourage a new role and identity, thus making it harder for a member to break with either. These groups thus both encourage accountability (through session attendance and progress) and also provide a venue where individuals can be monitored and assessed by peers. After experiencing and becoming accustomed to informal control mechanisms, residents begin to effectively enforce them among newer clients as they take on the self-imposed position of "role model." Although there is no specific point in time when residents become role models, PRP clients typically begin to enact this role sometime during the second program phase as they move toward becoming an expert.

Phase III: No Longer a Prostitute

Residents approaching graduation experience a further change in the organizational structure of the program. After reaching this phase, which usually lasts between three and five months, a resident lives in a predominantly "hands off" environment. Staff members allow her to make her own decisions in the hopes she will become self-reliant before moving out. A resident close to graduation is busy because she goes to school, maintains a part- or full-time job, and regularly attends outside AA/NA meetings. Due to her busy schedule and stage in the program, she is excused from most PRP planned activities and group sessions and therefore does not have as much interaction with other residents. As a result, she is less able to routinely enforce informal control mechanisms among them. Beyond basic program rules, such as sobriety and working a legal job, the PRP enforces very few formal control mechanisms among residents in this phase. The only remaining formal control mechanism imposed by staff is occasional meetings to discuss potential problems that could arise during and after the transition out of the program. These meetings function as counseling sessions, where the resident can discuss her fears and concerns, and logistical meetings that ensure she is prepared for the impending move (e.g., processing paperwork, arranging for transitional housing). The frequency of such meetings depends on a resident's desire and schedule.

In this phase, residents display talk and behavior that is closely and routinely aligned with the PRP. In other words, these individuals are "experts" at PRP talk and behavior. As a result of this mastery, formal and informal control mechanisms are replaced largely by self-monitoring. A poignant example of a resident in this phase is Susie, a thirty-nine-year-old white woman who worked as a prostitute for seventeen years, and claimed she entered prostitution because she had no positive role models when she was young. Only two months away from graduating, Susie talked about her goals in the program:

> My goals are to build myself a new foundation, which means being able to hold down a job. I want to re-establish ties with my sons. The fact that I lost communication with my children is the hardest thing for me and the thing I feel most bad about. And, my number one goal is to remain clean and sober.

Thus far, Susie has achieved all her goals, including maintaining her sobriety for over two years. She has held the same part-time job for almost a year and has been promoted twice, recently graduated from a community college, regularly attends AA and NA meetings, helps around the house, and acts as a role model by informally helping other residents. In other words, Susie has engaged in both talk and behavior that is consistently aligned with the PRP.

As Susie's case suggests, residents in this final phase are experts at program talk and behavior, and exhibit commitment to a new identity (Stryker 1980). For instance, one day shortly after I arrived at the program, Susie told me that she was really angry with another resident in the program. In the following account, she revoked a prostitute identity and claimed she was a different person:

> I was really pissed at her because she told people at school that we were all in a home for prostitutes. It's not her place to tell people that because I'm not a prostitute anymore and I don't want people thinking I am.

Another resident, Gina, also spoke as if she had internalized the program and a new identity. As she remarked near the end of my field observations:

> We tell each other that we represent the PRP when we go out in public because once we get outside we want to let our hair down but we have to tell ourselves before we get out of the van, you are what you represent. By reminding myself to remember who I am and what I represent gives me the will power to keep a straight eye towards my destination and not worry about the traffic or what's going on all around me.

Gina's words implied biographical reconstruction and role embracement as she clearly saw herself as a PRP representative. Furthermore, she also alluded to a change in identity when she explained how she looks, acts and feels differently than she used to:

> I like the respectable way I look. I get a better response from people. I could always count on a man's response before but now a woman will say hello to me on the streets. Before they would turn their heads the other way because they felt like I was being disrespectful with the outfit I had on.

Gina not only thought of herself as more respectable (personal identity change), but also perceived that other people thought so too (social identity change).

In this study, time in the program is closely associated with the routine display of PRP talk and behavior. Although the speed, consistency, and progress in biographical reconstruction and role embracement varies by client, those in or near this final phase perform both while experiencing minimum social control.

In spite of the fact that residents in this phase have extensive knowledge of program talk and behavior and consistently display it, there are still rare occasions when they solicit advice or guidance from staff members. For instance, Susie confided she was struggling with a friend (who was manic depressive and barely maintaining her sobriety) who repeatedly asked for guidance and increasingly depended on her for support. Susie was worried about her mental instability and, as a result, felt overwhelmed and reluctant to provide advice for fear of exacerbating her condition. This friend asked Susie to move in with her after graduating but Susie expressed fear she would be unable to deal with her friend's issues. Because Susie felt this situation could compromise her recovery, she decided to consult with PRP staff before continuing the conversation to ensure she would make the "healthiest and best possible decision" for maintaining her own recovery.

In this way, staff members still occasionally act as a support system for residents who are transitioning out of the program. This exchange highlights how residents experience the ongoing process of change throughout the program and even after graduation. Although PRP residents may not always graduate from the program with completely formed identities, they certainly leave bearing very different identities from the ones they presented upon their arrival.

DISCUSSION

The PRP residents move through three successive phases of change as they learn new ways of talking and behaving, that together suggest an identity transformation. Women progressing through these phases become "rookies," "in-betweens," and "experts" at PRP talk and behavior.

Upon mastery of both, residents talk and act as if they have experienced an identity transformation. For those who experience this transition, they also attain a myriad of other changes loosely connected to identity, including: personality, social standing, social networks, careers, educational attainments, and so on. While this study focuses primarily on identity changes, the overall effect encompasses far more than identity, as other scholars have noted (Drahota and Eitzen 1998; Ebaugh 1988).

I find the organizational context crucial to this process because it presents and cultivates language and behaviors among residents that are associated with a non-deviant role and identity. In order to achieve this task, the total-institutional program structure initially imposes strict formal control mechanisms on the residents by monitoring their movements and talk but also by fully immersing them into a program culture largely cut off from the outside world. As the women move through the program the organizational structure changes to a quasi-total institution.

Thus, formal control mechanisms largely subside and are replaced by informal control mechanisms, such as mutual monitoring and affective bonds. Both forms of social control appear to abate as individuals invoke self-monitoring techniques as they near graduation.

My findings suggest the process of identity change unfolds differently for individuals depending on the organizational structure in which they are immersed. More precisely, it may be a total institution's strict, overbearing milieu that fosters inhabitants' strong rejection of the organizationally imposed identity. As McCorkel summarizes, "Goffman (1961) asserts an individual's self can only emerge against something" (1998:229). Accordingly, when the PRP establishes conditions of a quasi-total institution, residents start viewing the organization in a favorable light, and subsequently reduce the utilization of secondary adjustments.

My analysis of PRP residents who experience these quasi-total institution conditions supports Goffman's claim that those who cease to display secondary adjustments also appear to adopt the organizational identity. To that end, as clients' secondary adjustments taper off, they speak as if an identity change has indeed occurred. Interestingly, as the program allots increased agency and autonomy to residents over time they still conform to and willingly embrace the program identity as they move through the phases. It may be precisely this shift in organizational structure that facilitates residents' adoption of a PRP-aligned identity because they no longer see the program as a total institution and therefore do not perceive it as something tangible to resist. However, the program structure alone cannot ensure that residents will shed a deviant identity and adopt a new one. In some cases women simply reject the program from the start and fall out, such as Teresa. In other cases, residents vacillate by espousing either PRP talk or behavior over time but not routinely or seamlessly. So, what other factors beyond organizational structures facilitate identity transformations for PRP residents?

One factor may be the intensive socialization process and importance of informal control mechanisms within the PRP culture. Residents are subjected to mutual monitoring and develop affective bonds for an extended period of time, even post graduation. As personal relationships between residents, residents and staff, and residents and sponsors solidify they become the social support that sustain and continually reify the PRP aligned identity among residents. For instance, when Susie was conflicted about moving in with her mentally unstable, drug-using friend she turned to PRP staff for guidance and support because of the affective bonds they shared.

Another possible explanation is that as residents begin to talk and act in new ways that generate positive reactions from staff, other program residents, and outsiders these interactions help ameliorate feelings of shame associated with their previous role and identity. This in turn encourages residents to continue to align their talk and behaviors with the PRP in order to perpetuate a newly acquired personal and social identity. When PRP talk and behavior is regularly enacted over time it becomes internalized and a new non-deviant identity replaces the deviant, low-status identity of prostitute. The benefits residents receive from transitioning from a deviant identity to a non-deviant one are great: they assert they feel better about themselves, they claim they get more respect from others, and they feel they are capable of achieving their lifelong goals and begin to work toward that end.

By situating individuals within a context, in which all identity transformations occur, we learn the impact organizations have on identity formation processes. This analysis can be used as a point or departure for future studies examining transformations from deviant to non-deviant identities within organizations that offer varying program structures, and the sustainability of these newly acquired identities post graduation. Although the PRP does not conduct formal follow-up studies, the staff maintained contact with many of the program graduates, most of whom still remained out of prostitution. Furthermore, future research can continue to analyze additional factors beyond organizational structures that affect the process of shedding a deviant identity and acquiring a non-deviant one.

References

Armaline, William. 2005. "Kids Need Structure: Negotiating Rules, Power, and Social Control in an Emergency Youth Shelter." *American Behavioral Scientist* 48:1124–1148.

Becker, Howard. 1963. *Outsiders: Studies in the Sociology of Deviance.* New York: Free Press.

Brown, J. David. 1991. "The Professional Ex-: An Alternative for Exiting the Deviant Career." *Sociological Quarterly* 32:219–230.

Chapkis, Wendy. 1997. *Live Sex Acts: Women Performing Erotic Labor.* New York: Routledge.

Denzin, Norman K. 1987. *The Recovering Alcoholic.* Newbury Park, CA: Sage.

Drahota, Jo Anne Tremaine, and D. Stanley Eitzen. 1988. "The Role Exit of Professional Athletes." *Sociology of Sport Journal* 15:263–278.

Ebaugh, Helen Rose Fuchs 1988. *Becoming an Ex: The Process of Role Exit.* Chicago: University of Chicago Press.

Goffman, Erving. 1961. *Asylums: Essays on the Social Situation of Mental Patients and other Inmates.* Chicago: Aldine.

———. 1963. *Stigma: Notes on the Management of Spoiled Identity.* Englewood Cliffs, NJ: Prentice Hall.

Junker, Buford H. 1960. *Field Work: An Introduction to the Social Sciences.* Chicago: University of Chicago.

Lawless, Sonia, Susan Kippax, and June Crawford. 1996. "Dirty, Diseased and Undeserving: The Positioning of HIV Positive Women." *Social Science and Medicine* 43:1370–1377.

McCorkel, Jill. 1998. "Going to the Crackhouse: Critical Space as a Form of Resistance in Total Institutions and Everyday Life." *Symbolic Interaction* 21: 227–252.

Mishler, Elliot G. 1986. *Research Interviewing: Context and Narrative.* Cambridge, MA: Harvard.

Paterniti, Debora. 2000. "The Micropolitics of Identity in Adverse Circumstance." *Journal of Contemporary Ethnography* 29:93–119.

Pheterson, Gail. 1996. *The Prostitution Prism.* Amsterdam: Amsterdam University.

Ponticelli, Christy. 1999. "Crafting Stories of Sexual Identity Reconstruction." *Social Psychology Quarterly* 62: 157–172.

Punch, Maurice. 1986. *The Politics and Ethics of Fieldwork.* Beverly Hills, CA: Sage.

Sanders, Teela. 2007. "Becoming an Ex-Sex Worker: Making Transitions Out of a Deviant Career." *Feminist Criminology* 2:74–95.

Schmid, Thomas J. and Richard S. Jones. 1991. "Suspended Identity: Identity Transformation in a Maximum Security Prison." *Symbolic Interaction* 14:415–432.

Snow, David A. and Richard Machalek. 1983. "The Convert as a Social Type." Pp. 229–289. In *Sociological Theory,* edited by Randall Collins. San Francisco, CA: Jossey-Boss.

———. 1984. "The Sociology of Conversion." *Annual Review of Sociology* 10:167–190.

Strauss, Anselm L. 1997 [1959]. *Mirrors and Masks and the Search for Identity.* New Brunswick, NJ: Transaction.

Stryker, Sheldon. 1980. *Symbolic Interactionism: A Social Structural Version.* Menlo Park, CA: Benjamin-Cummings.

Taylor, Verta. 1996. *Rock-A-By Baby.* New York: Routledge.

25

"ME AND THE LAW IS NOT FRIENDS"

How Former Prisoners Make Sense of Reentry

LUCIA TRIMBUR

This research study examines how ex-prisoners conceptualize their futures in terms of the many obstacles they encounter upon release to the community. Several approaches to reentry are discussed based upon the interpretations and experiences that confront ex-prisoners upon their returning to the community, as well as the societal and economic limitations they encounter once released.

"I'm never going back over there."

> —Aaron, several days after his release from
> a nine-month stay on Rikers Island

How to facilitate former prisoners' reintegration into the community after periods of incarceration has been the subject of significant consideration, especially over the past decade when prisoner reentry emerged as a hot topic in the sociology of crime and punishment and criminal justice studies. With two-thirds of all released prisoners rearrested in three years and over half of all released prisoners reincarcerated within three years (Hughes and Wilson 2007), recidivism has tremendous social, economic, and political consequences. Reincarceration wreaks havoc on prisoners and their families, whose lives are destabilized by episodic and chronic periods of forced confinement, as well as their communities, and costs city, state, and the federal government substantial resources. For the most part, research on prisoner reentry focuses on these consequences of reoffending as well as the factors and interventions that reduce recidivism and encourage post-prison success. With few exceptions (Burnett 2004; Richard and Jones 2004; Maruna 2001), studies have not examined how newly-released prisoners feel about their ability to reenter their communities. Fewer still have interrogated how former prisoners define success and what

Source: "Me and the Law Is Not Friends": How Former Prisoners Make Sense of Reentry by author Lucia Trimbur, *Qualitative Sociology, 32*: 259–277. © 2009. Used with kind permission from Springer Science +Business Media B.V.

successful reentry means for them; for example, whether "going straight," an assumption of much of the reentry literature, is even a goal. The studies that do consider the perspectives of ex-prisoners focus narrowly on crime desistance rather than the range of experiences related to social, economic, and political reintegration (Maruna 2001). Existing studies also rarely discuss the role of racism in reintegration processes or analyze the racialized dynamics of prisoner reentry.

This article examines how former prisoners of color conceptualize their political, social, and economic futures and how these conceptualizations relate to the social structural obstacles encountered upon reentry and decisions to reengage criminal labor. Based upon four years of ethnographic fieldwork with ex-prisoners in a New York City boxing gym, I find that, presented with similar post-prison challenges, ex-carcerated men take several approaches when reentering society. All of the men discussed in this article have faced similar *objective* conditions, such as racial oppression and attendant forms of social and economic exclusion, and yet there are a variety of *subjective* responses they have, such as the formation of both pro- and anti-crime identities as well as conflicted and ambivalent recourse to criminal reengagement. I argue that the differences among their approaches to reentry lie in their varying interpretations of how they can act as individuals against and within their social structural limitations. Their decisions are thus shaped by experiences confronting the limitations of material conditions but also emerge from their critiques of the social and economic structures into which they reenter and the ways in which they envision their possibilities for action and achievement within those structures. Understanding the experiences of these reentering men, the aspirations with which they begin the reentry process, and the relationships among experience, aspirations, critique, and social and economic structures can help both scholars and practitioners develop a fuller account of the lived experience of reintegration and, in turn, create more accurate theories and successful policies.

To argue this I begin by introducing the literature on mass incarceration, racial injustice, and prisoner reentry and presenting my methods. I then explicate some of the features of what I refer to as New York City's postindustrial landscape and its racialized social structural obstacles, which reentering men of color encounter upon their release. Finally, I analyze the various approaches reentering men take upon release from prison and conclude by suggesting how and why we should rethink processes of reentry and reintegration.

MASS INCARCERATION, RACIAL INEQUALITY, AND PRISONER REENTRY

As many have documented, American prisons, which disproportionately confine men of color with short educational histories, have expanded dramatically over the past four decades (Pager 2007; Western 2006; Mauer and Chesney-Lind 2002; Garland 2001; Mauer 1999a, 1999b). Producing a phenomenon that scholars now refer to as mass incarceration, black and Latino men were sentenced for more crimes and to longer periods of time in prison than ever before (Mauer 1999a, 1999b; Petersilia 2003). The result was an explosion in the prisoner population; between 1970 and 2003, prisons increased by a factor of seven (Western 2006) and, by the beginning of 2008, 2,319,258 men and women were incarcerated in federal and state prisons and local jails (Pew 2008). Black men made up 41% of the 2 million men in custody in 2006, and black men between the ages of 20 and 29 constituted 15.5% of all men incarcerated (Sabol et al. 2007). In addition, roughly 4.8% of all black men were forcibly confined in 2006 while more than 11% of black men between the ages of 25 and 34 were in jail or prison in the same year (Sabol et al 2007).

As prison populations increased, so too did scholarly interest in prisoner reentry. Given that 95% of the men and women incarcerated in jails and prisons are released at some point (Petersilia 2003), prisoner reentry has become an important part of criminal justice studies. Typically literature on reentry focuses on topics such as barriers to reentry, invisible punishments, post-release supervision, recidivism and desistence, and evidence-based and best practices. Travis (2005), for example, examines the loss of access to public housing, social services, student loans, employment, and voting on the reintegration of ex-prisoners. Solomon et al. (2005) and Petersilia (2004, 2003) study patterns of recidivism and post-release supervision, exploring the relationships among technical violations, new offenses, and parole practices. Jacobson (2005) and Horn (2001) offer new models of community supervision that can better facilitate successful reentry while Petersilia (2003), among others, chronicles the history of parole and advances "what works" in prisoner reintegration.

Maruna et al. lament that reintegration theory too often asks, "What works?" instead of "How?" or "Why?" (Maruna and Immarigeon 2004). The little research that has attempted to answer "how" prisoners reintegrate uses crime desistance as the criterion of success. Maruna's work (2001), for example, despite its groundbreaking psychosocial framework, understands success as the forfeiture of crime and thereby casts recidivism as irrational and preempts a number of questions, among them why men would return to criminality. Understanding reentry only through the lens of desistance misses the insight of men who are not trying to "go straight" and the complex rationale behind their analyses of legality and criminality as well as the insight of men who try to avoid reengagement with crime yet become frustrated when they crash up against the realities of their material conditions. Thus the lens of desistance obfuscates the heterogeneity of experiences of reentry and former prisoners' interactions with, understandings of, and critiques of racialized social structures.

The Urban Gym as a Site of Prisoner Reentry

Boxing gyms in the United States have a long history of helping marginalized men recover from the indignities of social and economic injury and develop new identities, social relations, and ways to achieve success (Wacquant 2004, Anasi 2002). In New York City, many young men of color join the urban boxing gym to mediate reentry processes. The gym where I conducted fieldwork is frequented by significant numbers of men who use the gym to reenter society after periods of forced confinement. It is a space where former prisoners can talk about their prison and postprison experiences especially their struggles—and receive advice from others with similar histories and without judgment, and is thus an important organic site of prisoner reentry. Although the ex-prisoners who frequent gyms are not representative of all men reentering society, the extraordinary motivation they possess and devote to their reintegration casts into the sharpest relief possible both the capabilities of and barriers presented to reentering men.

I conducted four years of ethnographic research at a boxing gym in Brooklyn to understand identity formation among amateur boxers of color, who were between the ages of 17 and 27. The majority of my research consists of participant observation. In general I spent time with roughly 40 men before, during, and after their workouts. I assisted them in various boxing-related tasks: I laced gloves, inserted mouth guards, applied grease to headgears and faces and albolene to backs, and tied the laces of cups. I video-taped spars, provided water and spit buckets in-between rounds, and occasionally was allowed to run spars. I traveled on trains and in cars with my participants when they competed in the Golden Gloves, the most prestigious amateur boxing event in New York, and in "smokers,"

unsanctioned fights held in neighborhood gyms. When asked, I assisted fighters and trainers with tasks usually associated with the completion of paperwork obtaining passports, filling out job applications, registering for tournaments, and acquiring driving directions to fights. I did some GED tutoring and a lot of babysitting for fighters' children. I worked for the gym on fight-nights: my jobs included registering fighters for the shows and tournaments, ensuring that each fighter was armed with and returned the proper ounce gloves for his or her weight division, and selling tickets at the door. I sometimes helped with tasks associated with the everyday running of the gym, such as creating and updating an amateur's USA Boxing fight book, helping with mailings, and checking members in at the door. Finally, I trained to box for two years in order to understand the bodily dimensions of the sport.

In addition to participation observation research, I conducted fifty formal, semi-structured interviews with gym members that ranged from one and a half to three hours in length. Here I draw on sixteen of these interviews, conducted with reentering men, whom I selected on the basis of the rapport and trust I had established with them over the course of several years. However, I found the most poignant insights about reentry were gleaned in informal and, one might say, more human settings than in formal interviews. That is, I learned the most about the difficulties of reentry and the hopes and vulnerabilities of reentering men by talking with them as I wrapped their hands, sat on a bench with them watching a spar, or ate lunch with them after a grueling workout. It was through these daily discussions that I learned about how reentering men conceptualize the process of reintegration and how those understandings changed over the course of four years. Also, because I could have daily discussions with my participants and see how their aspirations changed over time, I was able to witness processes of reentry as they unfolded and through a lens quite different than that of the reentry literature mentioned above. In this article, then, I draw on what I saw and heard about prisoner reentry over the course of a four-year period: over 1,000 pages of field notes, hundreds of discussions with and among former prisoners, and sixteen extensive, formal interviews with men who had recently been released from prison.

New York's Postindustrial Landscape and Its Conditions of Possibility

New York's postindustrial landscape can be characterized as the conditions produced by economic restructurings that began in the late 1960s and accompanying social policy changes, both of which disproportionately affected residents of color. First, the decline in manufacturing and acceleration of services radically reconfigured the nature of work in New York, reducing the number of manufacturing jobs available to workers of color, excluding them from the best paid positions in the new service economy, and relegating them to flexible, seasonal, part-time, and poorly paid service positions, when these positions were available at all (Baily and Waldinger 1991, p. 46; Persuad and Lusane 2000, p. 22). Anti-black racism in hiring practices made securing even low-wage employment extremely difficult for men of color (Pager and Quillan 2005; Parenti 1999, p. 43). Poverty rates skyrocketed and produced new forms of racial inequality, of which Tricia Rose writes,

> Between 1978 and 1986, the people in the bottom 20% of the income scale experienced an absolute decline in income, whereas the top 20% experienced most of the economic growth. Blacks and Hispanics disproportionately occupied this bottom fifth. During this same period. 30% of New York's Hispanic households (40% for Puerto Ricans) and 25% of black households lived at or below the poverty line. (Rose 1994, p. 28)

By 2003, only 51.8% of all black men in the city were employed while 35.1% of men between the ages of 16 and 24 could find jobs (Levitan 2004, p. 11).

Second, New York City's postindustrial conditions have been produced by significant social policy changes, such as the elimination of social welfare entitlements and the expansion of crime control, again which disproportionately burdened women and men of color. Welfare reform, which obliterated three quarters of a century of social assistance for the poor by imposing time limits on benefits, requiring clients to work in low-wage positions, and slashing compensation, dovetailed with a new focus on law and order (Neisser and Schram 1994, p. 41; Persuad and Lusanc 2000; Mauer 1999b). "Tough on crime" legislation and practices abolished, for the most part, rehabilitation, and fixated instead on an array of new penalties and policies, such as three-strike rules, truth-in-sentencing laws, victim impact statements, sentencing guidelines, and "zero tolerance." The emerging crime complex instituted longer sentences than ever before and expanded the number of nonviolent acts considered criminal, which inflated the prison population, even as crime rates dropped (Petersilia 2003, p. 22). As many scholars have noted, anti-black racism produced racial disparities at every level of criminal justice processing

and decision-making from racial profiling to prosecution to sentencing (Mauer 2007).

Today, the social and economic conditions of New York's postindustrial landscape a lack of work, a lack of social welfare entitlements, and intensified interaction with criminal justice systems among men of color—coagulate to make reintegration from prison by lawful means a tremendous challenge.

Under- and unemployment posed the greatest obstacle for the men in my study. During my fieldwork, roughly half of my 40 participants were unemployed, despite actively seeking jobs. Most of the men with whom I worked live in neighborhoods—Crown Heights, Bedford-Stuyvesant, Flatbush, East New York, Canarsic, and Bushwick in Brooklyn. Far Rockaway in Queens, and the Lower East Side of Manhattan where joblessness and rates of forced confinement among men of color are phenomenally high (Justice Mapping Center 2008; Levitan 2004). Those who can secure employment often have to settle for minimum or below living-wage positions, laboring as janitors, security guards, mechanics, restaurant workers, delivery drivers, and stockroom clerks, which, while I was doing my fieldwork, paid between $5.15 and $12 per hour. And they often have difficulty acquiring a full 40 hours of work per week (Newman 1999). Adrian, for example, found he could obtain only five to eight hours per week unloading merchandise for a department store at minimum wage, despite frequently asking for more hours. He lived with a parent and sister in a one-bedroom Bronx apartment to defray housing costs, but still found it hard to feed himself with such meager wages.

It is also not uncommon for someone to make *less* than minimum wage. Aaron was offered a dishwashing position in a neighborhood restaurant for three dollars per hour, but found it impossible to support his girlfriend and daughter with these wages on the Lower East Side of Manhattan, again, despite living with family. And finally, those who locate adequate employment find it challenging to keep, and their positions are often the first to be cut in times of economic downsizing (Levitan 2004; Newman 1999). Kenny worked as a security guard in a women's shelter, and months after being let go still could not find a job. He, too, lived with a grandmother and siblings to save on housing costs.

The practices and techniques of crime control also presented significant challenges to my participants. First, post-conviction penalties, especially those that restrict eligibility for financial aid and professional licensure, and criminal records limit the means by which former prisoners can reintegrate. Education is understood as an important ingredient of post-prison success (interestingly, both for men who want to forgo criminal labor and those who do not) yet is remarkably difficult to access. Aaron tried to enroll in a community college, but he worried that he would not get financial aid because of a drug conviction. He told me, "I want to go to college but I'm not sure about finances." Max could pay for community college while working as a drug salesman, but could not afford to pay tuition once he stopped trading heroin. When Anthony was released from prison, he immediately enrolled in several college courses, yet after learning of licensure requirements became concerned that his criminal history would affect his ability to get a professional license. He worried,

> When I came out of jail, I wanted to do that I wanted to be a pharmacist.... It came out to about eight years of school.... But the thing is that you come out and there is still the possibility that you can't get a license. You know because they need to do background checks and do little things for you to get a license.

With the possibility of spending nearly a decade in school and not becoming a pharmacist, Anthony decided that education was not the secure means by which he might succeed and terminated his schooling.

Second, managing the prison bureaucracy presented obstacles to reintegration. Technical violations and the jail and prison time they can warrant keep active a cycle of confinement that greatly affects the stability of reentering men. Jacobson (2005) points out that a significant number of people on parole are returned to prison for failing to meet the conditions of their release rather than for committing new crimes. Drawing upon a Bureau of Justice Statistics study, he demonstrates that of the 272,111 people who recidivated, 26.4% were reincarcerated for non-criminal technical violations (Jacobson 2005; Langan and Levin 2002). That is, a considerable number of former prisoners are returned to prison for social acts not considered criminal within the general population, such as breaking curfew, socializing with other former prisoners, and interacting with law enforcement regardless of the cause or outcome. These conditions of parole often produce rather than prevent criminality as well as feelings of powerlessness.

The flimsy grounds on which former prisoners feel they can be reconfined stand in sharp contrast to the magnificent energy demanded for reintegration and generate feelings of vulnerability. Omar was reincarcerated for violating a condition of his release when the police were called to his home after a domestic dispute. As a consequence, he was reimprisoned and lost both his job and car, on which he could not make payments because he was not earning an income while on Rikers Island. Losing his position in building maintenance, for which he trained in state prison, was particularly discouraging because he had worked for several years as a delivery driver while he waited to find a job in his field. Conditions of release posed significant problems for Anthony, too. Though he was not reincarcerated, he spent days consumed with worry that he would be sent back to prison after a confrontation with his sister's boyfriend, in which the police were called, even though he was never arrested or charged. He felt his parole officer had a tremendous power over his future, which was both disheartening and unnerving as he was working hard to leave behind his criminal past. Anthony lived an incredibly solitary life in order to avoid criminal reengagement. He devoted significant time and energy to his boxing, spent little to no time socializing with people outside the gym, and stayed at home reading or watching television when not in the gym.

The men with whom I worked are keenly aware of and talk openly about these obstacles and about their marginalized positions in postindustrial class and racial hierarchies. They understand the limited opportunities for lawful work for men of color in New York City and discuss with each other a racially unjust criminal justice apparatus that disproportionately confines them. To reconcile the contradictions between their subject positions and quests to achieve their goals lawful or otherwise they take several approaches to reentry and form identities that are shaped by their interactions with and interpretations of New York's racialized postindustrial landscape. Some reentering men develop pro-crime identities and undertake criminal labor immediately upon release. Others draw upon the discipline and discourses of religion and therapy in order to desist from crime, and others, still, attempt to find lawful work but reengage illegal and extra-legal economies when this proves difficult. These approaches and identities arc by no means exhaustive, or even mutually exclusive, as some former prisoners take different approaches at various points in time. But rather, these approaches are meant to characterize some of the different ways men think about and undertake reintegration.

THE POSSIBILITIES OF CRIMINAL ECONOMIES AND THE PRODUCTION OF PRO-CRIME IDENTITIES

Some men reenter society with no plans to forfeit participation in crime. They find that the status, income, and identities derived from criminal labor outweigh the potential rewards from struggling with unemployment, underemployment, and minimum-wage labor and immediately reenlist in criminal economies upon their release from jail or prison. These reentering men consider themselves talented in their lines of work and generate satisfaction, financial reward, and identities as a specialized type of laborer.

Men who reject desistance often frame their labor ontologically, that is, by providing a theory of their state of being. Lawrence, for example, discussed with me his decision not to seek lawful ways to spend his time and remarked. "I could be doing other productive things, but I think this is more me." Lawrence's reference to "other" productive things suggests he considers his labor to be, in fact, productive. His comment about illegal work being more *him* casts his labors as the generative building blocks of a career, of a vocation, or even of a Weberian "calling." Why would Lawrence struggle with the indignities and humiliations of lawful work when unlawful labor is more *him*? His insights are particularly interesting because they fuse neoliberal discourses of productivity—work for work's sake with Oprah Winfrey-esque or therapeutic quests to know oneself better. Yet Lawrence uses these discourses on his own terms and for his own purposes—to justify his participation in criminal economies. In doing so, he naturalizes his hustles as common-sensical and erases distinctions between legality and illegality.

Part of the draw of criminal labor for Lawrence is the intellectual rigor involved. He enjoys the strategizing necessary for his daily work and thinking through his work practices "play by play." That is. for Lawrence, the challenges, and even confrontations, involved in his labor provide immense satisfaction. He explained, "That what drives me." His work is also the basis for his comparison to others, and being considered as "real" is important to him. He told me, "They have a saying in the street: 'real recognize real and you looking familiar.'" He continued, "I see these dudes. They're not living like I'm living," meaning that other members of his neighborhood are not as talented and successful in their lines of work. As Sherman (2005) points out in her work on hotel laborers, such superiority comparisons help workers construct themselves as skilled. But Lawrence not only seeks to construct himself as "real" but also wants this construction to be publicly acknowledged by others. In the gym, he is recognized as "real" and is respected by members of the community on the basis of his intelligence and skill. His intelligence and skill serve as the basis of his status.

Men who never plan to leave criminal economics anticipate interactions with law enforcement and even expect episodic stints in jail and/or prison. Reincarceration

is understood as a frustrating yet nearly inescapable "occupational hazard." To cope with its likelihood, men budget for time lost in forced confinement, saving money for the loss of income, in effect creating their own unofficial unemployment insurance plans. They also put aside special amounts of money for private lawyers so that they do not need to rely on public defenders, who they believe cannot devote the same amount of time and resources to their cases. In the gym, private lawyers are often credited with helping men "beat cases."

The proportion of reentering men who immediately and deliberately reengage criminal labor after incarceration is small; in my study, only several men were adamant about continuing, over the long term, their participation in illegal and extra-legal economies. And yet their understandings, experiences, and practices tell us much about how they imagine they can and find ways to succeed after prison. That is, these men reveal that it is important to them to be challenged intellectually as well as considered skilled and talented by others, and they find ways to actualize this through illegal and extra-legal work. These understandings, experiences, and practices also illuminate, in the most practical way possible, how men conceptualize the consequences of their labors, or what prison activist George Jackson and sociologist Bruce Western have observed at different points in US history: prison time is considered a "modal experience" for young black men (Western et al. 2002, p. 170; Jackson 1994, p. 4). Men with pro-crime identities demonstrate one of the ways in which the mass incarceration of men of color has become naturalized as a feature of US urban postindustrial landscapes.

THE POWER OF REGIMENTATION AND DISCURSIVE PRACTICES

Other reentering men leave prison with the desire to terminate participation in criminal labor and are able to actualize their goals through commitments to particular disciplinary techniques and discourses. Men with therapeutic or religious loyalties take a long-term approach to achieving success and feel their day-to-day struggles build the foundation for eventual reward. They acknowledge that this reward may not come in their lifetime but achieve satisfaction and dignity and form identities by engaging in the process and through regimentation and adherence to discursive formations. Their goal is to "stay straight."

After prison, these men rigidly apply rules, restrictions, and disciplinary practices to themselves. Self-regulation is ordinary, and they do not drink alcohol, use drugs, smoke cigarettes, or socialize outside the gym. They wake up early, may limit their television consumption, and are avid readers in their search for self-improvement. And they self-impose intense dietary restrictions, such as eating vegetarian or even vegan. They also will not take over-the-counter or prescription medication. It is through and around this disciplinary process, in general, that they rebuild their lives.

Anthony, an ardent proponent of discipline, regimentation, and other forms of self-control, explicated both his definition and the importance of discipline,

> Discipline is simply, in general, instilling or imposing your rules and regulations on people so people understand your rules and regulations. . . . I think a disciplined person has something to live for. When you arc disciplined, you stand for something. . . . Right or wrong, you stand for something. . . . Without discipline, you arc a leaf in the wind.

Anthony admits that for the first several years of his sentence, he tried to resist the discipline of prison life. But after being sentenced to additional years for institutional misconduct, he decided to make a radical transformation and refrain from engaging in any form of criminal activity. His method was to exceed the disciplinary requirements of forced confinement and to self-impose additional dietary, social, and physical restrictions. He stopped hanging out with former colleagues, joined a religious group, started reading, worked out as much as he could, and avoided certain foods. When he implemented these disciplinary practices, it gave him a sense of power, control, and eventually identity. He reflected,

> It felt good. . . . It felt so good because it felt like I could overcome these things, right? It's like when you have a bad habit or anything and you tell yourself, "I'm not gonna do that anymore," and you just make up your mind, and it feels good when you tell yourself, "You win." You won over whatever it was. Even if you get a feeling that you want to do that, and you tell yourself, "For what?"

Kenny implemented similar practices when he came home from prison, reproducing, in effect, the routine of forced confinement outside the prison's walls,

> I set my curfew. On weekends, 9 o'clock 'cause I work on weekends, and I gotta get up at like 5 o'clock. And then after I go to work, I go straight to the gym. I don't have time for nobody. And I go runnin' and come home from

runnin',' and I gotta take a shower and eat. I watch the news for ten minutes, and I be sleepin.'

Regimentation is empowering for Kenny because it orders his life and provides him with structure. It helps "me to follow a plan. I know I gotta go to work, go to the gym, and go home and go running. It allows me to follow everything step by step."

Regimentation and disciplinary practices are often accompanied by narratives of self-help, recovery, and growing up, and especially by what Maruna (2001) terms redemptive self-stories. Jerry struggled with a serious crack cocaine addiction that, by his own account, led to crime, which escalated from petty theft to attempted murder. After years in Attica, he looked for help with his reentry and quickly realized that he was on his own. He had a series of relapses and eventually found his way to Damon House, a substance use rehabilitation center that he credits with giving him the tools for his "resurrection." Jerry explained how crucial engaging in this form of self-help was for him,

> I went and met this guy . . . he was the intake counselor. So he asked me questions, do I have any charges or criminal cases, and I said, "Yeah." He said "What?" and I said something. I forget what it was. Maybe a robbery charge or something like that. He said, "Why don't you go and take care of the case and after your case is over, why don't you come back?" I said, "'Man, I might be dead by then." And from there, he said that's why he let me in. Because I said that. I said, "I *might he dead by then*." I was desperate. I was at the point in my life when I would think about doing anything to stop using. I wanted to *stop* . . . I mean, I was doing anything to get help. It is like, when you're out there in that life, like, it's like you're lost in the city with maybe 10 million people and nobody reaches out and nobody helps. Nobody.

For Jerry, learning the techniques of self-help is cast a matter of life and death. And it was difficult. Utilizing this form of recovery was Jerry's responsibility: "they don't make you do nothing." Refraining from using crack cocaine was a challenge and there were temptations. He remembers his return to the Bedford-Stuyvesant section of Brooklyn, his old stomping ground, and told me, "And then it took every bit of power I had not to go out there and use again because I was determined." But to this day, Jerry's commitment to discourses of self-help and self-struggle and to his own particular narrative of "making good" (Maruna 2001) is unwavering in the midst of serious structural obstacles.

Others narrate their histories of crime as the product of a particular life-stage, such as the ignorance of youth and/or as part of the demands to establish forms of masculinity that are respected by other young men. Anthony understands his participation in criminal activities as the consequence of his "ego." In particular, he got into "trouble" because he would respond, through physical aggression, to tests of his ego. But once he "grew up," he no longer felt the need to respond to such confrontations. Like other men, Anthony utilizes discourses of life-stage and of manhood to mark the movement away from crime, carefully sequestering it as a feature of the past,

> I got caught up in the simple culture of ignorance. That's what it is. It's just ignorance. It's like being in the street you have a code to live by. It's unspoken but there are things you don't do. You don't snitch. You don't let nobody violate you. You don't let nobody cross certain lines. And there are certain things that you live by. . . . I did buy into that a lot, but you have to be ignorant. . . . You have to be ignorant to entertain it. Once you grow out of it, you realize how stupid it is. You realize somebody comes in front of you and tells you to suck their dick or disrespect you with their mouth, it doesn't change life. It doesn't hurt you. If anyone around you looks at you as smaller because of it. then it's their ignorance. That's *their* problem. You need to be the bigger person and have something better to do and not entertain whatever that person's problem is.

For Anthony, the code of the streets (Anderson 1998) and its culture is a moment in time, a stage out of which he can grow. As a consequence, he can produce alternative in this case anti-crime identities.

Men who draw upon self-help, therapy, or religion sec reintegration as their responsibility rather than looking to social structural entitlements. Change is envisioned as coming from within rather than contingent on social and economic circumstance. Jerry arrived at the conclusion that "The world don't owe me anything so what's the point walking around bitter? Every decision you made you made a conscious decision. . . . You made your own decisions in life. You just have to learn to deal with it. Accept life for what it is." Yet it is important to recall the anguish, quoted above, that was produced when Jerry recognized that in a city of "10 million," "nobody" would help him. It is also important to note that Jerry did have help, albeit limited, as he reentered. He found housing through an uncle, who owned an apartment complex in Bedford-Stuyvesant. Anthony and Kenny, too, drew on familial and communal networks: Anthony lived with a girlfriend, and Kenny lived with his grandmother.

For this group of men, interactions with law enforcement, which tend to trip up many reentering men, are discouraging, even depressing, but not overwhelming. Anthony, Kenny, and Jerry faced substantial challenges during their reentry, which could have frustrated their attempts for a lawful reintegration. Anthony experienced several run-ins with the police and worried for days on end about potential parole violations. Jerry was denied entry to Canada because of his criminal record. Kenny spent a weekend in jail after getting swept up in a police raid in his building without identification. Yet all three men remained and have remained for between seven and eleven years undeterred from their goals of desistance. Their identities of "structured," "reformed," and "grown-up" protect them from rejoining criminal economics. Their narratives echo the insights of the interviewees in Maruna's (2001) study. According to Maruna, in order to desist, ex-prisoners must construct a "coherent, prosocial identity for themselves," which is accomplished through a self-story that explains the process of reform (Maruna 2001, p. 9). This narrative works to protect desisting people from relapse by producing transformed identities (Maruna 2001).

Men who draw on disciplinary practices and discourses seem to suggest that desistance can be a matter of individual will and personal choice. However, the proportion of men who are able to actualize aspirations for crime cessation through discursive power and regimentation is very small: like men with no plans to desist, those who were able to avoid criminal reengagement could be counted on one hand. And it is important to reiterate that several of the men in this category relied on the material support of women grandmothers, mothers, and girlfriends—to help them make ends meet, either through direct financial assistance or housing. Most of the men with whom I worked fall into a third category: those who try to desist and fail, and attribute this failure to the limits of their material conditions

FROM OPTIMISM TO REENGAGEMENT

Men who take a third approach begin their post-prison lives with a desire to end participation in criminal economies. Whether tired of the ricochet between reentry and reincarceration a fatigue often expressed in the gym as "getting too old for this shit" or concerned they will miss part of their families' lives if chronically confined, these men decide to discontinue their criminal labor. They seek to achieve success through lawful, or what are generally considered "legitimate" channels, and to establish themselves in ways that conform to the norms and expectations of dominant society.

Despite the social structural barriers, these reentering men start out optimistic about their ability to earn a living and succeed in traditional ways. They try to improve their occupational, educational, and parenting skills by taking classes, accepting jobs that might be considered menial in order to gain work experience or a work history, and spending time with their children. To reconcile the contradiction between their subject position and their goals of achievement within the system, they access bootstrap ideologies to justify hardship, and they accept struggle for a period of time. That is, they accept temporarily the challenges of racial and class hierarchies and express confidence that, despite the odds, they will establish careers and generate income in lawful ways if they work hard enough.

After his release, Max decided to find a job in the official labor market. Weary of getting "locked up" and motivated by the excitement of having a baby and a commitment to fatherhood and his partner, he wanted to parent his son by example. In particular, he wanted to find ways to show his child that there are alternatives to crime. He told me, "That's what I want him to see that just 'cause you live in New York don't mean that you have to do crime. There's other things out there, and I want him to see the bigger picture." He secured a position in the stockroom of a Brooklyn retail store and lived with his mother in a social housing unit to save money. For a period of time, he could make ends meet, though the work and familial arrangement was far from ideal. He found the manager at his work unnecessarily controlling and petty and the work extremely boring. He also craved the independence of having his own apartment. Yet though he expressed frustration often, he was also quick to balance it with the assertion that short-term sacrifice was tolerable because it paved the way for future reward.

As time passes, however, optimism collides with the reality of material conditions and the difficulties of reentry. Not locating adequate employment, feeling "stuck" in poorly-paid positions with little autonomy or possibility of advancement, or dealing with racist bosses is frustrating and disheartening. Getting tripped up with parole violations produces feelings of vulnerability, which combine with negative work experiences to lead to disempowerment. This disempowerment erodes the determination to succeed through legitimate channels and, over time, changes the ways in which reentering men imagine they can succeed: the inability to achieve success and satisfaction in traditional ways and develop identities based upon lawful

employment, parenting, or education encourages some men to seek alternate channels through which to find income, identity, and satisfaction. Reengaging with criminal economies is one such channel.

Max's arrangement worked for several months, but after being laid off he could not secure comparable work. As time passed, he calculated that that the amount of money he was able to generate through illegal and extra-legal means outweighed the likelihood of generating income through lawful work. It also provided more satisfaction.

When Max discussed his decision to rejoin criminal enterprises, he vacillated between using ontological justifications and racialized social structural arguments. On the one hand, he considers himself "from the streets." He told me, "I'm a street dude. So I have a lot of trouble with the law. Me and the law is not friends." This conceptualization of an essential self justifies his decision to abort particular trajectories for success; why would someone chase the glimpse of lawful employment when one is, fundamentally, a "street dude"? That is, Max's description belies the futility of trying to be someone who one is not. It also naturalizes and works to make sense of some of the sources of frustration that he experienced while trying to "go straight." Multiple interactions with law enforcement were a source of immense frustration. The ability of the police to physically engage him and infringe upon his personal space was symbolic of their larger ability to infringe upon his life and disrupt his plans. He told me, "My big thing is 'don't touch me.'" That is, law enforcement's control over his body stands in for anticipated encounters that curtail or limit his freedom. Yet, by Max's logic, it follows that if one is a "street dude," one is, by definition, diametrically opposed to "law enforcement." By drawing upon ontology, confrontations with parole officers, the police, and other law enforcement officers can be anticipated and even structured, allowing Max to regain some of the power he felt he lost when trying to avoid such confrontations.

On the other hand, Max acknowledged that his subject position in racial and class hierarchies shaped his opportunities, experiences, and ability to embark on a conventional path. He discussed how social and economic conditions coded in his "neighborhood" structured his family and community's expectations of him and, in turn, the future he imagined for himself. He explained. "I come from a very rough neighborhood and a lot of people would like to test my patience and see if I'm a punk or not. And I was brought up I have three older brothers I was brought up by my mother to fight for mines, whatever it is." Violence is not named outright but it is subtext: we can assume that Max's response to these tests and determinations was to enact physical force and aggression. Max uses the imputation of masculine violence and its encouragement as a marker of the different type of experience that he had growing up "in the streets" and the possibilities and limitations that were structured by those experiences. Max's characterization of his "rough neighborhood" is implicitly juxtaposed with a dominant mode of operating in which violence is not sanctioned and does not help achieve success. It is this dominant mode of operating to which Max did not have access.

Max's arguments about his "very rough neighborhood" echo Anthony's critiques of the street's culture of ignorance. Yet both Max's and Anthony's comments work to justify very difference conclusions. For Anthony, the culture of ignorance is a moment in time and thus not constitutive of his identity formation. For Max, the "neighborhood" is an inescapable and defining feature of his identity, which makes him. in essence, a street dude.

Reengagement with illegal or extra-legal economics is not always as planned or as deliberate as in Max's case, and not everyone breaks so completely with aspirations for success through legitimate channels. Rather, for some, reengagement with crime is seen as a "one-time" or episodic decision motivated by the particularities of the moment's social conditions and necessities. Adrian, for example, worked in the drug trade until he was violently attacked by competitors. Concerned about future violence, he swore off criminal labor and decided to try wage labor. He worked several hours a week for a chain retail store for almost a year. Yet after he could no longer live with a family member, he became homeless and found meeting his food needs difficult. He attempted to steal food from a restaurant kitchen, was arrested, and imprisoned on Rikers Island. Immediately upon release and despite being unhoused, he vowed "never to go back" and once again was trying to find lawful work.

In the gym, the return to criminal labor after attempts to "go straight" is one that gym trainers, who are often mentors to reentering men, consider tragic but not unreasonable or unfounded. When I talked with Jay, Max's trainer, about his decisions. Jay expressed concern and even exhaustion at witnessing what he considered an inevitable boomerang between prison and reentry. At the same time, he situated decisions to reconnect with criminal networks within the particular social and economic landscape of New York City. He told me, "People don't understand that these guys don't

go out to be a drug dealer. It's financial necessity." Jay's comment shifts the inability to refrain from crime engagement from the realm of personal failure to the realm of social structural reality.

SOCIAL CRITIQUE AND RETHINKING DESISTANCE

The experiences of former prisoners in a boxing gym in Brooklyn suggest that there are at least several approaches to reentry from prison. Some men have no plans to refrain from criminal futures and immediately reengage criminal enterprises upon their release. Other reentering men are able to actualize their hopes of crime desistance by harnessing the power of self-disciplining practices and discourses. Yet another group of men finds that any aspirations for crime cessation arc defeated by the conditions of a postindustrial landscape, where racism and their subject positions as low-skill men of color limit their social and economic possibilities. These men, in particular, demonstrate that reentry processes are not always contingent on the level of internal motivation—wishes and desires but arc shaped by interactions with racial and class hierarchies.

More importantly, men who take the first two approaches—(1) developing pro-crime identities, (2) strictly regimenting their lives and drawing upon discourses valorizing self-discipline and individual uplift—suggest a distrust of the current reentry system. That is, they place little faith in the institutional encouragement to secure lawful work immediately upon release, locate housing, even if transitional in the city's infamously horrible shelter system, utilize the advice and support of parole officers and social workers, participate in support groups and fathering classes, and seek out the benevolence of charitable and non-for-profit organizations, all of which are supposed to help former prisoners reintegrate into society. Without a trust in that system, they take reentry upon themselves. That is, they draw upon resources *outside* of the system, utilizing the resources available in illegal and extra-legal spheres or discursive and disciplinary techniques. Both groups of men take a long-term approach to reintegration and create identities—both pro and anti-crime that can withstand the vicissitudes of life in postindustrial New York. This can be read as an indictment of the system. Men with both pro- and anti-crime identities reveal a shared perception that the system cannot be relied upon to aid men as they reenter and that it is so profoundly broken that only people who go at reentry alone have any chance of success The limitations of racial injustice and social conditions can be overcome, but only through acts of sheer will. In other words, where there is no support from the system, success is possible only through incredible individual action.

Ironically, men who trust the system to help them reenter fare much worse by their own estimation than those who do not. and, in a sense, remain much more vulnerable to the social injury of unmet expectations. All of the ex-prisoners with whom I worked expressed faith in some notion of American individualism: that they can succeed if they work hard at what they do, whether trading drugs, practicing discipline, or participating in lawful work. Yet the men who do not meet their own goals are usually the ones who believe that the system can help them actualize their aspirations. So an indictment of the system actually protects reentering men from "failure," and social critique is the best chance former prisoners have for long-term success, however they define it.

All of the men in my study are presented, as I have noted above, with significant obstacles to sustaining themselves lawfully in a postindustrial landscape. Of the three approaches to negotiating the obstacles discussed here, two are recidivist; one is not. But to relegate these approaches to such binary categories is to miss something significant about the lived experience of reentry and what motivates reentering men to act as they do. Reentering men reintegrate in a variety of ways despite common social structural circumstances. The differences in why and how they take various approaches lie in their interpretations of how they can act as individuals in relation to the obstacles that structure and are structured into their post-prison lives. Identity formation—the development of pro-and anti-crime identities—is thus a function of the individual's *interpretation* of his place in the social structures he is presented with upon reentry and his ability to mediate racism.

These differences in interpretation and consequent action suggest that accurate evaluation of reentry approaches cannot hinge solely on the binary criterion of what is right or wrong under the law, the criterion privileged by most literature on reentry as it stands today. Desistance, while of obvious importance, tells us little on its own about the range of ways people interpret their place in the world and the spectrum of their interpretive approaches. It also tells us little about critiques held in common by both men who recidivate and men who do not. In this case, it obscures a common distrust of the institutional networks nominally existing to aid former prisoners and skepticism about the possibilities for success within the institutions into which reentering men are encouraged to integrate.

REFERENCES

Anasi, R. (2002). *The gloves: A boxing chronicle.* New York: North Point Press.

Anderson, E. (1998). *Code of the streets: Decency, violence, and the moral life of the inner city.* New York: Knopf.

Baily, T., & Waldinger, R. (199I). The changing ethnic/racial division of labor. In J. Mollenkopf & M. Castells (Eds.), *Dual city: Restructuring New York.* New York: Russell Sage Foundation.

Burnett, R. (2004). To offend or not to reoffend: The ambivalence of convicted property offenders. In S. Maruna & R. Immarigcon (Eds.), *After crime and punishment: Pathways to offender reintegration.* Portland, Oregon: Willan Publishing.

Garland, D. (2001). *The culture of control: Crime and social order in contemporary society.* Chicago: University of Chicago Press.

Horn, M. F. (2001). Rethinking sentencing. *Corrections Management Quarterly,* 5, 34–40.

Hughes, T., & Wilson, D. J. (2007). Reentry trends in the United States. *Bureau of Justice Statistics.*

Jacobson, M. (2005). *Downsizing prisons: How to reduce crime and end mass incarceration.* New York: New York Press.

Justice Mapping Center (2008). *New York City analysis,* www.justicemapping.org.

Langan, P. A., & Levin, D. J. (2002). Recidivism of prisoners released in 1994. *Bureau of Justice Statistics Special Report.*

Levitan, M. (2004). A Crisis of black male employment: Unemployment and joblessness in New York City, 2003. *Community Service Society Annual Report.*

Maruna, S. (2001). *Making good: How ex-convicts reform and rebuild their lives.* Washington, DC: American Psychological Association.

Maruna, S., & Immarigeon, R. (Eds.). (2004). *After crime and punishment: Pathways to offender reintegration.* Portland, Oregon: Willan Publishing.

Mauer, M. (1999a). *The crisis of the young African American male and the criminal justice system.* Commission on Civil Rights: Paper prepared for U.S.

Mauer, M. (1999b). *Race to incarcerate.* New York: The New Press.

Mauer, M. (2007). Racial impact statements as a means of reducing unwarranted sentencing disparities. *Ohio State Journal of Criminal Law* 5, 19–46.

Mauer, M., & Chesney-Lind, M. (eds.). (2002). *Invisible punishment: The collateral consequences of mass imprisonment.* New York: The New Press.

Neisser, P. T., & Schram, S. F. (1994). Redoubling denial: Industrial welfare policy meets postindustrial poverty. *Social Text 41,* 41–60.

Newman, K. (1999). *No shame in my game: The working poor in the inner city.* New York: Knopf.

Pager, D. (2007). *Marked: Race, crime, and finding work in an era of mass incarceration.* Chicago: University of Chicago Press.

Pager, D., & Quillan, L. (2005). What employers say versus what they do. *American Sociological Review, 70,* 355–380.

Parenti, C. (1999). *Lockdown America: Police and prisons in the age of crisis.* New York: Verso.

Petersilia, J. (2004). What works in prisoner reentry: Reviewing and questioning the evidence. *Federal Probation, 68.*

Petersilia, J. (2003). *When prisoners come home: Parole and prisoner reentry.* New York: Oxford University Press.

Persuad, R. B., & Lusane, C. (2000). The new economy, globalisation, and the impact on African Americans. *Race and Class, 42,* 21–34.

The Pew Center on the States. (2008). One in 100: Behind bars in America in 2008. *The Pew Charitable Trusts.*

Richard, S. C., & Jones, R. S. (2004). Beating the perpetual incarceration machine: Overcoming structural impediments to re-entry. In S. Maruna & R. lmmarigeon (Eds.), *After crime and punishment: Pathways to offender reintegration.* Portland, Oregon: Willan Publishing.

Rose, T. (1994). *Black noise: Rap music and black culture in contemporary America* Middletown Connecticut: Wesleyan University Press.

Sabol, W. J., Minton. T. D., & Harrison. P. M. (2007). *Prison and jail inmates at midyear* 2006. June: *Bureau of Justice Statistics Bulletin.*

Sherman, R. (2005). Producing the superior self: Strategic comparison and symbolic boundaries among luxury hotel workers. *Ethnography,* 6, 131–158.

Solomon, A., Kachnowski, V., & Bhati, A. (2005). *Docs parole work: Analyzing the impact of postprison supervision on rearrest outcomes.* Washington, DC: Urban Institute Press.

Travis, J. (2005). *But they all come back: Facing the challenges of prisoner reentry.* Washington, DC: Urban Institute Press.

Wacquant, L. (2004). *Body and soul: Notebooks of an apprentice boxer.* New York: Oxford University Press.

Wacquant, L. (2001). Deadly Symbiosis: When Ghetto and Prison Meet and Mesh. *Punishment and Society,* 3, 95–134.

Western, B., Pettit, B., & Guetzkow, J. (2002). Black economic progress in the era of mass imprisonment. In M. Mauer & M. Chesney-Lind (Eds.), *Invisible punishment: The collateral consequences of mass imprisonment.* New York: The New Press.

Western, B. (2006). *Punishment and inequality in America.* New York: Russell Sage Foundation Publications.

26

The Love of a Good Man?

Romantic Relationships as a Source of Support or Hindrance for Female Ex-Offenders

Andrea M. Leverentz

This article analyzes the role that romantic relationships play on women's post-prison experiences. The study focuses on 49 female ex-offenders and their partners within the context of these relationships. Both negative and positive aspects of these female ex-offenders' romantic experiences are explored as they effect the women's adjustment to reentry in the community, as well as receiving support for living a pro-social lifestyle.

The impact of incarceration on communities and social relationships is increasingly a focus of research and policy. Typically, the focus of studies on crime and reentry is on male offenders or on the general offending population (which is predominantly male) and the impact of their incarcerations on their employment, civic involvement, communities, and children (see, e.g., Mauer and Chesney-Lind 2002; Nagin and Waldfogel 1998; Travis and Waul 2003; Uggen 1999, 2000; Uggen and Manza 2002). Women often play a tangential role in these studies, in that they are affected by high rates of male incarceration in some communities and by the incarceration of their loved ones. For example, partners of male inmates (or the parents of their children) are solely responsible for child rearing and family finances. In addition, women in

neighborhoods with high concentrations of incarceration experience a dearth of "marriageable" men (Wilson 1987). Less often is the focus on female offenders.

In addition to those areas listed above, another collateral consequence is the impact of incarceration on romantic relationships or, alternatively, the impact of romantic relationships on future offending. Women play a significant role in our understanding of male desistance. They (specifically wives) are a stabilizing force in male offenders' lives, and these relationships contribute to desistance from offending (Horney, Osgood, and Marshall 1995; Laub and Sampson 2003; Sampson and Laub 1993; Shover 1996; Warr 1998). The relationships that men develop are usually with prosocial women; in other words, men form relationships with women without current or former involvement in

Source: The Love of a Good Man? Romantic Relationships as a Source of Support or Hindrance for Female Ex-Offenders by Leverentz, Andrea M., *Journal of Research in Crime and Delinquency, 43* (4), November, 2006, pp. 459–488. Reprinted with permission.

offending or incarceration. These women provide direct control and a stake in conformity, and these relationships lead to changes in men's routine activities. They spend less time with their peers, especially those involved in delinquent activities, and more time at home (Laub and Sampson 2003; Warr 1998). In contrast, when men are implicated in female criminality, it is typically in terms of the role that men play in female offending, not desistance.

Despite the lack of attention, there is ample reason to suspect that men may play a significantly different role in female desistance than women play in male desistance. One reason is the differential rates of male and female offending and incarceration. The vast majority of incarcerated populations are men, and when released, they are heavily concentrated in a fairly small number of neighborhoods. Thus, the likelihood of a female offender, especially when she also is returning to a neighborhood with a high number of ex-felons, becoming romantically involved with a man with no history of offending or incarceration is much lower than the likelihood of a male offender becoming involved with a woman without this history.

Given the differences in the offending patterns between men and women, Laub and Sampson (2003:46) questioned the applicability of their own argument that marriage contributes to desistance: They rightfully asked, marriage is "good for whom?" In their sample, the men married prosocial women who had no involvement with illegal activity and so served as bonds to conventional life (when the marriages themselves were quality bonds). For men, marriage creates an interdependent system of obligation and restraint that constrains involvement in criminal activity (Laub and Sampson 2003). For women, finding prosocial spouses who may foster that interdependence is more difficult, especially when they are coming from, and returning to, high-crime neighborhoods with high proportions of male ex-felons. For example, in the United States, 22.3 percent of Black men born between 1965 and 1969 had been incarcerated by 1999 (Western, Pettit, and Guetzkow 2002). For those without high school diplomas, the percentage rises to 52.1 (Western et al. 2002). In Illinois, half of all prison inmates are released to Chicago, and a third go to just six neighborhoods (Austin, Humboldt Park, North Lawndale, Englewood, West Englewood, and East Garfield Park (La Vigne, Visher, and Castro 2004). These neighborhoods are all poor and largely African American. This concentration of releasees in poor, African American neighborhoods contributes to the limited "marriage pool" for inner-city African American women, if a felony record is seen as a strike against a potential partner (Wilson 1987). Again, if this is the case, female ex-offenders would have even less likelihood than nonoffenders of marrying, or having, relationships with men without criminal records themselves.

In this article, I focus on women's romantic relationships following periods of incarceration. Only 8.1 percent of the women interviewed in this study were married at the time of the interviews, and nearly two-thirds had never been married. This is consistent with the overall female Illinois Department of Corrections (IDOC) population (11 percent married, 67.7 percent never married). To the extent possible, I discuss possible differences in types of relationship (marriage, cohabitation, noncohabiting boyfriend or girlfriend, no relationship) and the roles they play in the women's desistance.

This distinction between all romantic relationships and marriage is significant. For example, among male offenders, marriage and cohabitation seem to have very different impacts on offending. Much of the previous literature on the romantic relationships of male offenders has focused specifically on the benefits of quality bonds with wives (Horney et al. 1995; Laub, Nagin, and Sampson 1998; Laub and Sampson 2003; Sampson and Laub 1993; Warr 1998). These authors argued that the mere existence of a marital relationship is not enough to lead to desistance; the bond must be a strong one. In contrast, the role of non spousal relationships for men has the opposite effect on offending. For example, Warr (1998) concluded that there is something about marriage itself that affects the routine activities of men, because unmarried men who live with parents, live alone, or cohabit all spend more time with friends than do married men. This decrease in time spent with peers, then, contributes to lower rates of offending.

SOCIAL BONDS, HUMAN AGENCY, AND GENDER

This article explores how one type of social bond functions for female offenders. Social-bond theorists argue that social ties to family and employment provide a disincentive to commit crime (Hirschi 1969; Kornhauser 1978; Laub and Sampson 2003; Sampson and Laub 1993). These bonds raise the cost of engaging in illegal activity, and thus it is those without these strong (quality) bonds who are most likely to continue to offend. These social bonds are dynamic and likely to grow or change over time (Laub and Sampson 2003; Maruna 2001). In Shover's (1996) study of persistent thieves, he found that among young men, romantic relationships are often exploitative. As the men age, their relationships change, along with their personal resolve to desist from offending. Among older, desisting offenders, relationships with girlfriends and wives become a prosocial force. This depends on the quality of the bonds (Sampson and Laub 1993) and the prosocial orientation of the partners (Giordano, Cernkovich, and Rudolph 2002). Laub and Sampson (2003) added that "because investment in social relationships is gradual and cumulative, resulting desistance will be gradual and cumulative" (p. 137; see also Laub et al. 1998).

The social-bond theory can be summarized as the "love of a good woman" argument, though other bonds, such as those to employment or religious involvement, can serve the same function, and multiple quality bonds will be more effective than a single tie or type of tie (Laub and Sampson 2003). Social bonds may foster desistance in several ways. Spouses may provide a direct social control function, monitoring the behavior of offenders (Laub and Sampson 2003). Marriage also may lead to a change in routine activities, with more time spent at home and less time spent with delinquent peers (Laub and Sampson 2003; Warr 1998). Thus, in addition to raising the cost of offending, these ties also lead to more conventional activities. These activities in turn have conventional rewards and contribute to a corresponding non criminal identity (Giordano et al. 2002; Laub and Sampson 2003: Shover 1996; Sommers, Baskin, and Fagan 1994). In addition, "marrying up" may provide tangible material rewards, such as housing or employment (Laub and Sampson 2003).

In sum, male offenders who form heterosexual relationships are much more likely to be able to form bonds with women with no histories of offending than women offenders are to form relationships with such men. Because of the different roles that romantic partners play in offending for men and women, it is likely that they will likewise play different roles in desistance. Factors such as race and the type of offending background (e.g., drug use) also may affect the importance and role of such relationships. Given declining rates of marriage and the differential effects of marriage compared with other types of relationships among men, it is important to consider non-marital romantic relationships as well. Female ex-offenders, like everyone, will form romantic partnerships that are dynamic and therefore are best looked at over a period of time.

METHOD

This article is based on a series of up to four interviews over the course of a year with 49 women who had been involved with the criminal justice system. All the women were recruited through their current or past involvement with a 14-bed halfway house for female ex-offenders in Chicago. Although many of the respondents were on parole or probation at the time of the interviews, their stay at the halfway house was never a requirement: all women go there voluntarily. Most often, women go to the halfway house immediately on release from prison, though a few women come from inpatient drug treatment and typically stay for six months to a year. Although there is an application and interview process, there are few formal criteria for entry, beyond a desire to change one's life. At the time I began interviewing them, the women had been out of prison for between a few days and nine years and were both current and former halfway house residents. By the last interview, all of the women had moved out of the halfway house. This meant also that they were at different stages of their reentry processes. Some women were newly released and experiencing related changes and confusion; others were much more established in their lives and looked back at these stages in their lives.

I used a methodologically inductive approach, learning from the respondents issues that were important in their lives and adding these questions to subsequent interview guides. By later interviews, I had established more rapport and trust, making the women more open to discussing sensitive or painful issues. I also could witness and hear about important changes in the women's lives and relationships over the course of the year. In addition to hearing about past evolutions of relationships, I heard about currently evolving relationships and evolving attitudes about relationships as they happened. Their experiences also reflected the different lengths of time they had been out of prison. Although this design was limited in that interviews took place over only one year, there was substantial benefit over a purely cross-sectional design because of both the multiple interviews and the different stages of reentry.

In addition to the interviews with the women, I invited the participation of members of the women's social networks. The women suggested people they would be comfortable having me interview and invited their participation. 1 then interviewed those who contacted me. In this article, I draw on the interviews with all women and also on the interviews with the romantic partners of the women. I interviewed two boyfriends, one husband, and one fiancé. In addition, two pairs of women became romantically involved with each other during the course of the interviews. In these cases, I talked with them about their relationships in the regular interviews.

Respondent Characteristics

In many ways, the women interviewed are comparable with the IDOC population, though they were more likely to be African American, were older, and had more extensive incarceration. A vast majority (87.5 percent) of the women in the sample had at least one child, though only a small number (12 percent) were living with their children at the time of the interviews. In a few cases, they had given their children up for adoption or had permanently lost custody. More often, however, the minor children were living with family or friends: the mothers had not lost custody and hoped to live with their children again once they were more established and financially stable. About half of the women in this study lived in some type of subsidized housing, only two with their children; the rest lived in private housing, either with family or alone.

About half the women lived in the neighborhoods in Illinois with the greatest concentrations of ex-offenders (La Vigne et al. 2004). Few of the women received financial support from romantic partners, and few aspired to a "gendered respectability package" (Giordano et al. 2002). Nearly all of them had achieved, or aspired to achieve, personal financial independence. Although it is hard to generalize, on the basis of the limited numbers of women in this sample who were not African American, drug users, or living in neighborhoods of concentrated disadvantage, there were no clear differences in the types of relationships or partners on the basis of these characteristics.

Halfway house staff members strongly discourage the women from having romantic relationships. They encourage them to focus on their own recovery, and this mind-set is evident in the way many women talked about their relationships, past and present. In addition, the women were steeped in the recovery language of self-help programs such as Alcoholics Anonymous and Narcotics Anonymous, which encouraged them to stay away from "people, places, and things" that were related to their drug and/or alcohol use. In addition, their halfway house stays provided them with positive social relationships (with both residents and staff members, many of whom had offending backgrounds themselves) and gave them a (temporary) place to live removed from their offending. Both of these factors can help them wean themselves from some of their offending peers.

These resources make them fairly unique among the overall ex-offending population.

Over the course of the year, nine of the women (18 percent) lived with romantic partners for at least part of the year. Three women moved out of the halfway house into apartments with romantic partners (in these cases, the partners were all women), three former residents were living with boyfriends or fiancés, and three former residents were living with husbands. In one of these cases, the woman left the apartment when her boyfriend asked her (and her mother) to leave when she began using drugs. In another case, a woman's husband was arrested and jailed for part of the year.

Although the focus of this article is romantic relationships and desistance from offending, I first contextualize the women's experiences by describing their relationships before and during their addictions and/or periods of offending. These early relationships were important in the lives of these women because often they were central to the origins of their offending and shaped their current attitudes toward relationships. Although many of the women fit the pattern of offending with or for men, this was often a secondary stage, after exposure to drugs, crime, and violence in their childhoods.

ORIGINS OF DRUG USE AND OFFENDING

Drug addiction factored strongly into the offending backgrounds of most of the women in this study. Much of their offending was directly related to drug use, in terms of either drug-related offenses or offenses committed to support drug habits. In addition, their drug use played heavily into their relationships with others. These women were more likely to be first exposed to drugs through family or friends and less likely to have initial exposure through romantic partners. Twenty-two percent of the women reported initial drug exposure via romantic partners. In contrast, roughly a third of the respondents (30.6 percent) reported being exposed to drugs through their friends. Often, the women reported frequent drug use among their peer groups and a resulting curiosity. The most common initiation into drug use was exposure through family members. Nearly half (n = 22, 45 percent) reported drug or alcohol use among their family members. Often, these were their parents, and it was fairly equally likely that either their mothers or fathers were drinking, using, or selling. Second to exposure through parents was exposure through members of the women's own generations, either siblings or cousins.

In addition to drug use, about 30 percent of the respondents reported physical and/or sexual abuse by family members while they were growing up. Most often, this was abuse by fathers or stepfathers. Typically, the abuse was at the hands of men, though one woman reported being molested by her older sister. An additional 15 percent witnessed the abuse of their mothers by their fathers or stepfathers, though they themselves were not abused. Fifteen percent reported having little to no contact with their fathers throughout their lives, either not knowing who they were or meeting them briefly later in life. Several of their fathers were imprisoned for long periods.

Drug use, especially addiction, often was preceded by some traumatic incident or series of events. Many of the women had troubled family lives.

Others grew up in stable homes but were raped or assaulted as children or teens by strangers. In several cases, the women reported these stranger incidents as being "the beginning of the end" for them. In some instances, happy homes were disrupted by tragedies, such as the death or illness of a parent. Often, the women turned to drug use (either initially or increasing their use) as a form of escape. Some women escaped their childhood homes for the street, and others escaped romantic partners later in life. Some women also were responding to particular traumas, such as the breakup of a romantic relationship or the death of a significant person, such as a parent or romantic partner.

A second pathway to addiction for these women, however, was experimentation. Although many of the women experienced trauma in childhood or adulthood, this was not true for all. Some women began experimenting with drug use, often in adulthood, out of curiosity or for recreation, but it eventually became more serious and led to additional problems such as job loss and criminal activity. For most of the women who reported drug abuse, their drug use often began casually and continued for significant periods of time before it became disruptive in their lives. The women often could not pinpoint when their drug use went from recreational use to addiction. For many women, their use of "heavy" drugs (e.g., heroin, cocaine) did not start until well into adulthood.

In most cases, regardless of the actual charge, drug use was directly related to the offenses leading to incarceration. Although romantic relationships were often not the source of the drug problems, they were heavily implicated by drug use. The next section focuses on the relationships that the women developed once they were engaging in drug use and offending behaviors.

OFFENDING, DESISTANCE, AND ROMANTIC RELATIONSHIPS

Relationships and Addiction

Although romantic partners often were not the initial source of exposure to drug use, they did play an important role in the women's addictions. Fifty-one percent of the women reported being in abusive relationships with romantic partners at some point (five women [10 percent] were abused by both romantic partners and parents or relatives). Often, the abuse was directly tied to drug use, and often, it was mutual. Several of the women described these relationships as "kill or be killed." The father of one of Danielle's children abused Danielle and later served a long-term prison sentence for beating another woman. Sheila believed that if she had killed her husband of 26 years, there was no way she would have been sent to prison, because of the severity of the abuse she endured. Still, she said that she had never thought of leaving him. Erma said that she had been abused by her husband "whenever he felt like it," until she finally did leave him. Sugar's abusive relationship ended when both she and her boyfriend went to jail. Abra told me about several instances in which a girlfriend physically assaulted her, and vice versa. Shorty D said that although she never endured abusive situations for long, they "come with getting high."

The abuse the women endured ranged from single incidents to long-term physical and emotional abuse. Many of the women stayed in these relationships for long periods, and often the relationships were with the fathers of their children. In addition, the women were often violent in these relationships. Mary, for example, had several abusive relationships during her addiction, but she also said, "I did a whole lot of being abusive myself. I used to like to fight." For those women who continued the relationships they had had during their addiction (a subject to which I return later), the abuse largely abated when both partners stopped using drugs.

Relationships and Desistance

All of the women in this sample voluntarily went to recovery homes after their release from prison. They all expressed an interest in changing their lives and ceasing their offending and drug use. In doing so, they were all consistent with at least the first two components (openness to change and exposure to a set of hooks for change) of Giordano et al.'s (2002) cognitive-change model and Baskin and Sommers's (1998) and Sommers et al.'s (1994) process of change.

However, even when people decide to stop using drugs and offending, this is often a process that includes several attempts. Although the halfway house strongly discouraged romantic relationships and created an environment in which the women could create new friendships, some of the women were reluctant to give up their connections to old romantic partners or friends. Even when they exited prison with a desire to desist from drug use and offending, their relationships with abusive and/or addicted men (or women) often continued. As of the last interview, six women were involved with men who were then using drugs, involved with illegal activities, or incarcerated.

Ongoing relationships. There were three likely and common outcomes to these relationships. Some women relapsed into addiction and/or street life themselves in part as a result of these relationships. Over a quarter (29 percent) of the women directly attributed their (current or former) drug use, relapses, or offending to relationships with romantic partners. Another possibility was that the women cut ties with these men to foster their own recovery. Often, this happened while they were at the halfway house. Caprice, for example, said that she ended an 11-year relationship while at the halfway house because "'it was time to move on.'" The women may have held on to relationships for a period but realized that they could not move forward in their own lives while the men continued to use drugs and/or offend. In addition, they tended to grow apart, because drug use was their primary, or an important, bond. Once they lost this, they had little in common and little reason to stay together.

Although on the surface, this seems to be the best path for the women to take, staying together also can have a positive long-term outcome. A third pattern was that both of the partners went into recovery, and their relationship continued. This is an important twist on the idea of social bonds and prosocial partners. Although according to much conventional wisdom and the messages they heard in recovery settings, the women should have ended these relationships, over time they can develop into strong, supportive, and prosocial ties. Here, a couple redefines itself, both independently and together, as law-abiding and in recover). One example of this is Bennie and Joe. When they first met, both were using drugs. Bennie said that she was originally introduced to crime and drugs by her oldest child's father. She was "looking for love in all the wrong places—or what I interpreted to be love." At the time, she said that she "thought it was the thing to do . . . I didn't know any different, I didn't want any different." When her boyfriend was incarcerated, she "was an outlaw by myself. I discovered I didn't need anybody. I could do it alone. I did for some years. Then I met Joe."

In the following passage, Joe describes how he met Bennie and the inauspicious start to their relationship:

> Oh, well, I met her. I was having, I was in a situation with two other women. My wife, and another lady. . . . So, I got five kids with my wife, and three kids by her. And I was living in two houses, a situation. And I didn't know Bennie. And, one of the girls called my father and told her that uh, she needed him to come get me one night. I was high, I was using. I was getting high, and the girl had stopped getting high. She was trying to straighten her life up, and so he came by, picked me up.
>
> I think I was 35 years old at the time. . . . So, I went, so he took me over to my sister's house. So, when he left, I went on out. I went on 47th Street and went back, I was using at the time, right. So I went out, I had some money and whatever, and I went to this place to shoot some dope. And I had no place to get high, I bought some dope, now I got no place to get off. So, they was telling me where to go. So I went around this place on 47th and Michigan, and they told me to go in there, so I'm hearing on the third floor there's a shooting gallery. So, I went up there, and while I was here, there was a few guys in there that I knew. And, so they telling me about some of the girls that was around there, whatever, they was telling me about Bennie.
>
> So they said yeah, when she come back, she ain't got nobody, you should hit on her man, whatever. So when she came back, um, she liked me. She told the girl, I didn't know, but she told the girl, "Who is that?" I'm not from, I'm not around there. I was like the new guy up there, and she was telling them, "'Oh, he's fine, he's real clean," you know. . . . And then the next day, we was all still there, because it was right before the 4th of July, so everybody was getting high or whatever. And, uh, I talked to her. I called her over there and started talking with her and stuff like that. . . . And that's how we started going together. And it was hers, come to find out, the place was hers. And, so after that, we, I . . . So, I stayed. What happened is I sort of stayed right there. I didn't go back to where I lived. I had two places where I was living, but I was like, I had sort of messed that up, being in a situation with women, or whatever. . . . A couple weeks went by, and she started telling me, "Look, we can't be together if you can't, you know, let me know if you're a man or a woman, or whatever." We had kissed a couple times, but we hadn't really done nothing, and so we had sex, and that's when we started being real close. We got real close. She liked it, and later on she got pregnant by me. I think it was during that same summer. So, we had our first child about nine months later, something. So, that was how we got together, and then we sort of stuck together pretty good.

They have been together ever since, married for 25 years, with 11 children between the two of them (2 together) and living together again (after recovery) for 6.5 years. They stayed together through two prison incarcerations each and two attempts at recovery. Their latest attempt at recovery has lasted for close to 10 years, and both are confident that it will continue. Bennie said, "God and my husband, those are where my loyalties lie" and described Joe as wanting "to be the right side of my brain. He wants to finish my sentences and my thoughts. I need to put him in a box and sell him—he's a genius. . . . We're closer than close." Bennie attributed her incarcerations (and subsequent sobriety) to "God doing for me what I couldn't do for myself." Their last relapse was a result, according to both of them, of the death of her mother. Since then, they have endured the death of Joe's brother without relapse.

Both Bennie and Joe spent time in halfway houses after their last incarcerations. Joe thought that the time apart during their incarcerations and halfway house stays may have helped their relationship. Bennie was the first to move out of the halfway house into her own apartment. Joe then joined her when he was ready to leave the halfway house and transitional housing. Joe described their relationship as a success because of "my maturity, basically being humble, allowing her ideas to come in without resentment." Although Joe also attributed their success to God and the church, he considered himself an inspiration for Bennie. According to him, she "did a copy of what I did. What I do. I relate it to her, she do the same thing." and they have supported each other in transforming their lives. At the same time, he saw her as an independent, strong, and intelligent woman with her "own mind" and survival skills. Joe said that he has helped Bennie by "staying clean myself. I am not doing it for her, but it may help her. It's an individual situation. It's on you, not me."

Although the origins of their relationship do not sound conducive to a desisting lifestyle together, they both became clean, law-abiding, and supportive of each other's recovery. Although their lives and experiences paralleled each other, ultimately, both made independent decisions and independent steps to stop using drugs and stop offending. In addition, because both had similar experiences, they were equals, and one could not hold his or her past over the other. Here, their shared background led to additional understanding and empathy, and their relationship was on a more equal playing field. Thus, they each provided a hook for change (through their marriage) and reinforced the cognitive transformations in the other (Giordano et al. 2002; Sommers et al. 1994).

Obviously, this can be a difficult transition. It is also a process, which often does not succeed at the first attempt. Bennie and Joe went through one relapse together, and they and their relationship survived. Angela was struggling with her husband's relapse and reincarceration. She described herself and her husband as "partners in crime." They had known each other for 20 years, entered into addiction together, and were twice incarcerated on the same cases. At the time of the interviews, they had been married for just under 2 years. Over the summer, he was jailed for driving without a license while visiting friends in their hometown. In addition, he had used drugs. When she found this out, she would not let him come home. She was frustrated and angry, because she "thought we were working towards the same goals." She was doing very well on her own, working for a nonprofit agency and getting involved in her church and school. She did not know whether she should stick by him or leave him: she feared that his addiction could lead to her own relapse. In many ways, this parallels Bennie and Joe's experience, when Bennie relapsed following the death of her mother. Ultimately, in both situations, both partners made individual decisions as to whether to use drugs, though the drug use of a romantic partner can be too great a temptation for the other.

In a similar example, Melvina struggled throughout the year with her on-again, off-again boyfriend of 17 years, who was also struggling with drug addiction. In the first interview, she said that she was single, but she went on to talk about how she had changed since she had been at the halfway house:

Melvina: I don't go to the old places, because I've been here for like 10 months and for maybe like 8 of those months I was still going around the same stuff and I haven't been there in about a month. I've met quite a few people that's sober.

Author: What made you stop going over to the old places'?

Melvina: Because I kept feeling stuck; I wasn't moving nowhere. Now I go to school. I have a lot of homework so I don't want to stay focused on that no more.

Author: And where are the old places?

Melvina: I used to go up to my boyfriend's house.

Author: And he's not still your boyfriend or he is?

Melvina: Oh, he probably is but I'm not with him right now because he's still using.

The second time I interviewed Melvina, she was back together with her boyfriend (though not living with him). He had been clean for 6 months, after his mother moved and could no longer take care of him. She said then, "It's the first time I've been with him sober. I see the difference; he's nicer, gentler. I like it." The last time I met with her, the two of them had relapsed together. She said, "We do good till we get high; then it always ends in an argument."

In addition to demonstrating the difficulty of being in a relationship with an addict or recovering addict, especially one with whom one has a shared history of addiction, these examples also show how these social bonds can change over the course of several months or years. If they were looked at purely cross-sectionally, they may look strongly prosocial or antisocial, depending on when they are considered. Although clearly these are complicated relationships with many difficulties, examples such as that of Bennie and Joe suggest that they can be successful in the long run, even if they go through difficult and destructive stages. Although one conclusion is that these interviews reveal inherently unstable relationships, another interpretation is that these relationships reveal a recovery and desistance process that is just that: a process (Maruna 2001). Much as Shover (1996) discussed men who go from having exploitative relationships with women when they are offending to having relationships that serve as sources of social control later in their lives, these women had relationships that were tied to their offending at one point in their lives and to desistance at a later point, though in some cases, they were relationships with the same men. By looking at these relationships over even a fairly short period of time, they clearly become processes. Melvina and Angela's relationships, for example, both changed drastically over the course of the interviews. Although we do not know the "final" outcome, we clearly see the problem with looking at them dichotomously or statically.

In this sense, the relationships reflect the inherent instability of the desistance process. Both desistance and the development and effect of quality social bonds are cumulative (Laub et al. 1998; Laub and Sampson 2003; Maruna 2001; Sampson and Laub 1993). In terms of cognitive change, these relationships also support changing self-conceptions. In these relationships, the women made independent decisions to stop offending, and if their romantic partners did likewise, the relationships helped maintain new behaviors and self-concepts (Baskin and Sommers 1998; Giordano et al. 2002; Sommers et al. 1994).

New relationships. In addition to ongoing long-term relationships, many women established new relationships through the halfway house or other recovery settings. About a third of the women were romantically involved with people who at the time were not involved with drugs; however, almost all of them had histories of addiction. This is not surprising, given the social circles of which the women were part. Many of the women were heavily involved in the recovery community and had met their partners in this way. Many others met in daily life, at work or in their neighborhoods, but these were likely to be in populations with high rates of ex-offenders. These relationships often began with common bonds and experiences, and they supported each other in their recovery.

One example of this scenario is that of Linette and Chad. Linette met her fiancé Chad when she was in a work-release program. During the interviews, they were living together in his mother's house. She described him as "a big help. He's always trying to understand what's going on. He's a caretaker." Chad said,

> I've been into stuff myself. We both had done bad things . . . I'm getting too old; I woke up and realized it ain't a place to be. Now, I go to work and I come home. If I go out, we both go.

He described Linette as "a beautiful person, she's kind and honest. She's never told me a lie, as far as I know." In talking to each of them and watching them interact with each other, they did seem to have a strong and positive relationship. Linette may have served as a direct source of social control for Chad: He did not go out, other than to go to work, without her. Chad was a source of emotional and financial support for Linette. To a certain extent, he also may have served as a source of direct social control, but because she was unemployed and therefore home alone during the day, she had more opportunities to go out without him (if she chose to do so). If prosocial is defined only in terms of current behavior rather than total behavior, this relationship was a typical example of a prosocial, bonding relationship. They each provided a stake in conformity, as they struggled to get their lives in order, get their own apartment, and regain custody of the child they shared. Yet by the more narrow definitions of prosocial partners, Chad and Linette may be seen as negative partners because of their histories of offending.

These examples demonstrate that the positive effect of relationships need not be limited to purely prosocial partners. As Giordano and others (Giordano, Cernkovich, and Pugh 1986; Giordano et al. 1998; Giordano et al. 2002) have argued, the normative orientation of a partner does matter, but this orientation may change over time. This is an interesting twist on the positive relationship effects among male offenders (Homey et al. 1995; Laub et al. 1998; Laub and Sampson 2003; Shover 1996; Wan 1998). In this case, the women clearly demonstrated publicly declared commitments to desistance and recovery through their participation in the halfway house and the recovery community. In addition, they maintained these lifestyle changes by integrating themselves into new social networks, again, often closely tied to recovery situations (Baskin and Sommers 1998; Giordano et al. 2002; Sommers et al. 1994).

As with long-term relationships with offending partners, these new relationships can lead to both positive and negative results. Although relationships with ex-offenders or former drug users can provide support, empathy, and equality, they can also be the source of strain and can lead to relapse or reoffending. Wanda also met her fiancé while they were both in recovery homes. They were living together, along with her mother. She said, "I still have dope tendencies; he doesn't understand." I later heard from her downstairs neighbor (another respondent) that her fiancé had asked her and her mother to leave the apartment they had all shared because she had relapsed back into drug use. Although I never heard from Wanda again, I heard from her neighbors that her mother was in a nursing home, and she was back on the streets and not doing well. Shorty D experienced both destructive and supportive relationships with (formerly) drug-addicted men. Her first boyfriend, whom she met in recovery meetings, relapsed and began using again, including bringing the drugs around her. She also then relapsed. She said that although she may have relapsed otherwise, it would not have happened when it did without his influence. Her second relationship was with Greg, whom she met at a Laundromat. Greg also had a history of drug use. He said that the day he realized that he was an addict was "the day I wanted to quit. It was the worst thing I ever fought in my life." He thought that it was very likely that Shorty D would stay off drugs in the future, because "she's got me. She's not satisfied with that type of lifestyle; she's been through it already." When asked what he would do if she did relapse, he said "I'd snap. I wouldn't want it to be around. I am dead against it myself."

At least in the time that I knew the women, it looked as though these relationships were less likely than the long-term relationships to continue if one partner relapsed. This may be merely a reflection of the short amount of time I knew the women; it is possible that one or more of these relationships will go through the same tips, downs, and separations of Bennie and Joe's long-lasting relationship. This also may depend on the nature of the relationship. Shorty D, who lived alone in a single-room-occupancy building, may have been less invested in her relationships (both of which were short term). On the other hand, Linette and Chad and Wanda and her fiancé lived together, and both pairs planned to marry. Linette and Chad had been together for two years and living together for five months when we first met. They were doing well, despite some significant hardships (such as a miscarriage and Linette's subsequent depression). In contrast, the relationship between Wanda and her fiancé ended after close to two years together. Again, in just one year, it is impossible to know the ultimate outcomes of these relationships. At a minimum, however, we begin to see their complexity.

Same-sex relationships. In addition to establishing relationships with outsiders, the halfway house itself has also fostered several romantic relationships. Romantic relationships are discouraged by the staff, and in at least one case, a couple was asked to leave (they believed) because they had entered into a relationship with each other. A total of 12 percent of the women told me about romantic relationships they had with other residents, though often they did not begin (or were kept sufficiently under wraps) until one or both of them had moved out. Although close to half of the women (43 percent) identified themselves as purely heterosexual, the rest had some type of romantic or physical relationship with women. Ten percent of the women I interviewed identified themselves as lesbians; 27 percent had relationships with both men and women (they identified themselves in terms of the sex of their current partners, as bisexual, or by saying "I don't put a label on it"); and 20 percent said that they had engaged in physical relationships with women, but in a utilitarian way, and often during their addiction. Dee Dee said,

> In my addiction I did [have physical relationships with women]; when I got straight, I left all that alone. These things go hand in hand. . . . When I was using, I was drawn to women when it wasn't going good with men. . . . They served a purpose, but were unnatural.

Same-sex relationships function just as heterosexual relationships did, both positively and negatively. When both partners succeed in staying clean and avoiding criminal activity, they provide support and empathy for each other. Sugar and Sasha, the couple who were asked to leave the halfway house, left and moved together to another city to live with the father of Sugar's baby. They both cited their relationship with each other as the most significant and meaningful of their lives. Although Sasha had always considered herself a lesbian, this was Sugar's first serious relationship with a woman. Much as these relationships function positively in the same way as heterosexual relationships, they likewise can be destructive when one or both partners relapse. For example, Vivian was involved with Sunshine, who also was in her first romantic relationship with a woman. Vivian then relapsed after they broke up and tried to persuade Sunshine (who did not have a history of drug use herself) to get back together with her, to "save" Vivian. Although Sunshine was concerned for Vivian, she did not believe that she could save her; rather, Vivian would have to recover herself.

Presumably, women who are interested in relationships with other women have a greater chance of meeting partners without histories of drug use, offending, or incarceration (again because of differences in rates of offending), but this did not happen among this group. These women met their girlfriends in the same ways that women met boyfriends or husbands. Sugar and Sasha and Vivian and Sunshine met at the halfway house. Starr met her girlfriend at work. These examples are consistent with the heterosexual couples, who met in recovery or educational settings, at work, or in the neighborhood. In addition, although a few women did cite long-term relationships with women, in no case was the relationship always a romantic or physical one. For example, Dee Dee had a 10-year on-again, off-again relationship with another woman. Although she still loved her, she kept her distance because the woman was still using drugs. She also said that the physical aspect of their relationship was "the devil's work" and now considered her only a friend. Much more common were same-sex relationships that started while the women were at the halfway house or afterward. Two same-sex couples (Sugar and Sasha and Starr and her girlfriend) lived together once they moved out of the halfway house.

Again, relationships with other former offenders or drug addicts (male or female) provide an interesting and important twist to the importance of strong social bonds. Recovering addicts are often very committed to the idea of reshaping their lives and staying away from drugs. They could provide a support network for each other. However, there is also a strong likelihood that one or both will relapse. Given the social networks most of the women were in, they were much more likely to meet other people in recovery. Some women purposely stayed away from Alcoholics Anonymous and Narcotics Anonymous meetings for this reason, because some of the meetings seemed to the women to be more about dating than about recovery. Aside from meetings, the women also often were living in neighborhoods with extremely high rates of ex-offenders in the population, most of whom were men. Many of the potential romantic partners they met, through recovery communities or through everyday life, had histories of incarceration or addiction.

However, as with continuing relationships, a history of drug use or criminal involvement is not necessarily bad, because it can provide a basis of understanding and mutual support. These examples also point to the dynamic nature of romantic relationships and the role they may serve in the women's desistance and recovery. Although in some cases, these relationship changes may reflect an inherent instability in the relationship, they also may reflect relationships that are "probably better understood as social constructions or processes than as stable conditions or events" (Maruna 2001:31). Of course, only by looking at these relationships over time can this distinction be made.

Relationship avoidance. A final, and significant, common response that the women took was to stay away from romantic relationships altogether. At the time of the interviews, 41 percent of the women were not in relationships, and another 10 percent were "just friends" with someone and did not want serious relationships. Some women saw this as a permanent state, and others saw it as temporary until they were ready to move on and form solid relationships. Some realized that even when in new relationships, they were based on old behaviors, which they were trying to shed. In many ways, this seems like a clearly positive step. The women had histories of abusive relationships and often offended directly or indirectly because of relationships they had with men; avoiding relationships may be a way to avoid such sources of strain (Agnew 1992; Broidy and Agnew 1997). On the other hand, staying away from all romantic relationships seems counter to relational theorists' admonition that women need connection and relationships (Covington 2003) and social-bond and differential-association theorists who argue that marriage is an important tie to conventional society (Laub et al. 1998; Warr 1998). For some, this meant that they formed these connections with nonromantic friends, often through recovery communities. Thus, they still clearly fit in the motivation-declaration-maintenance model of desistance (Sommers et al. 1994). They had both the cognitive changes necessary for desistance and the social network support of it (Giordano et al. 2002; Martina 2001; Sommers et al. 1994). Others, however, distanced themselves more completely.

Although a few of these women wanted romantic relationships, most were consciously single. Sunshine, after having both a girlfriend and a boyfriend relapse and another man "'smother" her, decided that she would rather be by herself. She planned to move back to her home state when she completed parole, to be closer to her children. Sandra also had a relationship but ended it because she decided that she could not do it and "'focus on the program" at the same time.

Lisa D. said that she was "in a romantic relationship with her books," referring to her need to focus on her schooling.

As with those who did have romantic relationships, these decisions reflect a process and their particular stages of recovery and desistance. Because men were heavily implicated in many of their drug addictions and offending, the women felt the need to be by themselves, at least for a time, to establish prosocial, drug-free, and independent lives. Erica ended a relationship "because of my self-esteem. It's not healthy right now; it doesn't make any sense to me." Likewise, Lisa S., who wanted to remarry eventually, said, "I would like to [have a relationship], but there's no room now. I have to prioritize [work, school, and her last child at home]." The women were also less tolerant than they had been in the past of men's behavior. For example, Dee Dee ended one relationship because the man was in a relationship with someone else at the same time. She said, "I can't keep doing the same thing expecting a different result." She broke up with her next boyfriend because he was "jealous and insecure. . . . If he's miserable, he wants everyone to be miserable. He wants submissive women; I'm not submissive."

Again, this is an important difference from the roles of romantic relationships in men's lives. Women are often tangential to men's offending (though certainly not to their lives or their self-perceptions, often in an exploitative way), and then central to the desistance process, serving then as sources of control (Laub and Sampson 2003; Sampson and Laub 1993; Shover 1996). Although surely not all desisting men can attribute their changes in behavior to successful romantic relationships with prosocial partners, researchers do not describe avoiding such relationships as a conscious and productive choice that men make. For these women, on the other hand, men are often central to their offending and tangential to their desistance. Because men often played a central role in the history of a women's offending, some women purposely avoided relationships to successfully desist from offending. This is also surely an artifact of the women's experience with the halfway house and recovery communities, in which they were repeatedly taught to avoid people, places, and things and to avoid romantic relationships, at least in the early stages of recovery. It can also be seen as an attempt to avoid or manage the strain of which men had been the source in the past (Agnew 1992; Broidy and Agnew 1997).

In sum, few women in this sample established romantic relationships with traditionally defined prosocial partners. However, many of the women did establish prosocial relationships with others (men and women) who had similar histories as themselves, and these relationships evolved into supportive and mutually reinforcing bonds. Thus prosocial relationships need not be limited to those with no histories of antisocial behavior but also can include those who are desisting or in recovery themselves. Also important for many women, however, is an absence of romantic relationships. These women feel a need to establish their own independence and successes before (if ever) they form attachments to romantic partners. This is an outgrowth of their histories of abuse, the roles men played in their own offending, and the messages they receive in recovery communities.

DISCUSSION AND CONCLUSIONS

This research raises several important issues related to social-bond theories of desistance. First, in previous research, a logical assumption has been made that women are less likely than men to be able to form attachments to prosocial spouses or partners. The assumption of a small pool of purely prosocial romantic partners is supported with this sample of female ex-offenders. However, many of these women did form supportive, mutually beneficial relationships with men and women with histories of offending and/or drug use who in many studies would be described as antisocial partners. This suggests the need to more carefully define prosocial and antisocial partners and bonds. We may be well advised to expand our notions of "marriageable men" (or women) beyond those who have no histories of involvement with drug use or the criminal justice system (Wilson 1987).

This study was limited to a group of female offenders who lived at a halfway house after their release from prison. The findings are thus not generalizable to the entire offending population, and future research should test the ideas developed here with additional samples. There were no clear differences in the experiences of these women because of racial background or drug-use history. However, there was limited variation in these characteristics among this group, and more exploration is warranted. Although this article has focused on the role of social bonds for women, there are possible applications to male offenders as well. Some of the differences between the experiences of these women and the men in Sampson and Laub's (1993) (Laub et al. 1998; Laub and Sampson 2003) work may be attributed to changes in social-historical context. Today, men in recovery settings receive the same messages as women to avoid people, places, and things. Do they then receive these messages in similar ways that these women do? In addition, these women are a select group of ex-offenders in that they are receiving a fairly high level of services. They are provided with financial and emotional support in the early stages of their reentry that most ex-offenders do not receive. The ideas in this article should be tested with a broader group of ex-offenders. Do they also feel a need to avoid relationships? If so, is it realizable? Are they exposed to an ex-offender population, or are their networks qualitatively different, and how does this influence their experiences?

This research supports the idea that relationships, like desistance, are social processes, not static facts. There is evidence that romantic relationships function differently for female and male ex-offenders, but this study also raises questions about possible applications to male desistance in contemporary groups. This study, then, provides a starting point for additional research on the role of romantic relationships in the desistance of both men and women.

REFERENCES

Agnew, Robert. 1992. "Foundations for a General Strain Theory of Crime and Delinquency." *Criminology* 30:47–87.

Baskin, Deborah R. and Ira B. Sommers. 1998. *Casualties of Community-Disorder: Women's Careers in Violent Crime.* Boulder, CO: Westview.

Broidy, Lisa and Robert Agnew. 1997. "Gender and Crime: A General Strain Theory Perspective." *Journal of Research in Crime and Delinquency* 34 (3): 275–306.

Covington, Jean Lte. 1985. "Gender Differences in Criminality among Heroin Users." *Journal of Research in Crime and Delinquency* 22 (4): 329–54.

Covington, Stephanie. 2003. "A Woman's Journey Home: Challenges for Female Ex-Offenders." Pp. 67–104, in *Prisoners Once Removed: The Impact of Incarceration and Reentry on Children, Families; and Communities,* edited by J. Travis and M. Waul. Washington, DC: Urban Institute.

Giordano, Peggy C., Stephen A. Cernkovich, H. Theodore Groat, M. D. Pugh, and Steven P. Swinford. 1998. "The Quality of Adolescent Friendships: Long Term Effects?" *Journal of Health and Social Behavior* 39 (1): 55–71.

Giordano, Peggy C., Stephen A. Cernkovich, and M. D. Pugh. 1986. "Friendships and Delinquency." *American Journal of Sociolog)* 91 (5): 1170–1202.

Giordano, Peggy C., Stephen A. Cernkovich, and Jennifer L. Rudolph. 2002. "Gender, Crime, and Desistance: Towards a Theory of Cognitive Transformation." *American Journal of Sociology* 107 (4): 990–1064.

Horney, Julie, D., Wayne Osgood, and Ineke Haen Marshall. 1995. "Criminal Careers in the Short-Term: Intra-Individual Variability in Crime and Its Relation to Local Life Circumstances." *American Sociological Review* 60 (5): 655–73.

Laub, John H., Daniel S. Nagin, and Robert J. Sampson. 1998. "Trajectories of Change in Criminal Offending: Good Marriages and the Desistance Process." *American Sociological Review* 63 (2): 225–38.

Laub, John H. and Robert J. Sampson. 2003. *Shared Beginnings, Divergent Lives: Delinquent Boys to Age 70.* Cambridge, MA: Harvard University Press.

La Vigne, Nancy, Christy Visher, and Jennifer Castro. 2004. *Chicago Prisoners' Experiences Returning Home.* Washington, DC: Urban Institute.

Maruna, Shadd. 2001. *Making Good: How Ex-Convicts Reform and Rebuild Their Lives.* Washington, DC: American Psychological Association.

Mauer, Marc and Meda Chesney-Lind. eds. 2002. *Invisible Punishment: The Consequences of Mass Imprisonment.* New York: Free Press.

Nagin, Daniel and Daniel Waldfogel. 1998. 'The Effect of Conviction on Income through the Life Cycle." *International Review of Law and Economics* 18 (11): 25–40.

Sampson, Robert J. and John H. Laub. 1993. *Crime in the Making: Pathways and Turning Points through Life.* Cambridge, MA: Harvard University Press.

Shover, Neal. 1996. *Great Pretenders: Pursuits and Careers of Persistent Thieves.* Boulder, CO: Westview.

Sommers, Ira, Deborah Baskin, and Jeffrey Fagan. 1994. "Getting out of the Life: Crime Desistance by Female Street Offenders." *Deviant Behavior* 15:125–49.

Travis, Jeremy and Michelle Waul. eds. 2003 *Prisoners Once Removed: The Impact of Incarceration and Reentry on Children, Families, and Communities.* Washington, DC: Urban Institute.

Uggen, Christopher. 1999. "Ex-Offenders and the Conformist Alternative: A Job Quality Model of Work and Crime." *Social Problems* 46 (1): 127–51.

———. 2000. "Work as a Turning Point in the Life Course of Criminals: A Duration Model of Age, Employment, and Recidivism." *American Sociological Review* 65 (4): 529–46.

Uggen, Christopher and Jeff Manza. 2002. "Democratic Contraction? Political Consequences of Felon Disenfranchisement in the United States." *American Sociological Review* 67 (6): 777–803.

Warr, Mark. 1998. "Life-Course Transitions and Desistance from Crime." *Criminology* 36 (2): 183–216.

Warr, Mark and Mark Stafford. 1991. "The Influence of Delinquent Peers: What They Think or What They Do?" *Criminology* 29:851–66.

Western, Bruce, Becky Pettit, and Josh Guctzkow. 2002. "Black Economic Progress in the Era of Mass Imprisonment." Pp. 165–80 in *Invisible Punishment: The Collateral Consequences of Mass Imprisonment,* edited by Marc Mauer and Meda Chesney-Lind. New York: Free Press.

Wilson, William Julius. 1987. *The Truly Disadvantaged: The Inner City, the Underclass, and Public Policy.* Chicago: University of Chicago Press.

REVIEW QUESTIONS

PART I. PROPERTY CRIMES

1. Understanding Adolescent Property Crime Using a Delinquent Events Perspective

1. What were the motivating factors that adolescent property offenders gave for their involvement in this offense?

2. The author discusses the offending youths' interpretive process while they were actively engaged in the crime. What meaning is the researcher attempting to discover by trying to understand this process?

3. This study uses a "criminal events" perspective according to Lopez. What is its purpose and how is this perspective operationalized in this research?

2. Streetlife and the Rewards of Auto Theft

1. What does Copes mean when he states that he is interested in relating the auto thieves' perceptions of rewards within the sociocultural context of street life?

2. What methods do auto thieves use to benefit financially from stealing cars?

3. Auto thieves have multiple motivations over their careers. What are they?

3. Gender, Social Networks, and Residential Burglary

1. How does gender affect access to participate in the criminal activity of residential burglary?

2. What are the expectations of male co-offenders when committing burglary with females?

3. The powerful sexism that structures street life in poor urban neighborhoods serves to constrain the criminal opportunities available to engage in burglary. What role doesit play when involved in this property offense?

PART II. VIOLENT CRIMES

4. Retrospective Accounts of Violent Events by Gun Offenders

1. Why did the convicted gun offenders use accounts to explain their violent acts to the researchers?

2. In what ways did the offenders justify the denial of a victim in their violent act?

3. The women who participated in violent crimes using a firearm provided multiple rationales for committing a violent crime. Did they portray themselves differently than the men did in this study?

5. Dubs and Dees, Beats and Rims: Carjackers and Urban Violence

1. Carjackers indicate that their offenses occur where opportunities and situational inducements overlap. What is meant by those motivating factors?

2. How do carjackers profit economically from committing this violent offense?

3. In what carjacking situations are the risks low and the rewards very high?

6. **Gangstas, Thugs, and Hustlas: Identity and the Code of the Street in Rap Music**

   1. What is meant by the "code of the street" in inner-city communities?

   2. Portrayals of violence in the lyrics of rap music serve as functions of social identity and reputation. Explain this relationship.

   3. How does "gangsta-rap" relate to the culture of violence in the inner-city neighborhoods?

Part III. Sex Crimes

7. **Street Smarts and Urban Myths: Women, Sex Work, and the Role of Storytelling in Risk Reduction and Rationalization**

   1. What was the purpose of the narratives in the tales of extreme risk told by women involved in street-based sex work?

   2. What are differences between street smarts and urban myths in storytelling?

   3. Very few of the drug-using sex workers capitalized on the risks the stories pointed out. Why?

8. **Accounts of Professional Misdeeds: The Sexual Exploitation of Clients by Psychotherapists**

   1. Why is the therapeutic relationship between a therapist and a client considered problematic?

   2. What types of accounts did therapists offer for having sexual relations with clients?

   3. Should professional practitioners in any position of trust face criminal charges for engaging in sexual relations with people under their care?

9. **Constructing Coercion: The Organization of Sexual Assault**

   1. What is meant by having rape events be organized by the offenders?

   2. The men who raped reported lives filled with a sense of futility and emotional turmoil. How did these life experiences relate to the women in their lives?

   3. Restoring a sense of control and respect were two factors these offenders claimed were explanations for committing sexual assault. What did the rapists mean by this statement?

Part IV. Gangs and Crime

10. **From Punk Kids to Public Enemy Number One**

    1. What tensions exist among members of the Public Enemy Number One gang, having to do with their commitments to racial politics and their involvement in crime?

    2. Conflicts surrounding drugs and crime serve to illustrate the racist skinhead scene. Why does this conflict exist?

    3. What is the relationship between the Public Enemy Number One gang and other gangs?

11. **Gang-Related Gun Violence: Socialization, Identity, and Self**

    1. How is socialization into a gang related to issues of identity and self?

    2. What role do guns play, and why does gang membership increase the chances of carrying them?

    3. What roles to masculinity, reputation, and respect play in gang affiliation?

12. **Young Mother (in the) Hood: Gang Girls' Negotiation of New Identities**

    1. Explain how the transition from gang member to motherhood changes the lifestyle of gang girls.

    2. How does the important factor of respectability shift for gang girls as they move into motherhood?

    3. How does being a parent and becoming dependent on their families for support lessen the gang girl-mother's autonomy?

PART V. WHITE-COLLAR OCCUPATIONAL CRIME

13. Dialing for Dollars: Opportunities, Justifications, and Telemarketing Fraud

1. Contemporary fraud is nonconfrontational, violates trust and can be carried out over a long distance. How does telemarketing fraud follow this pattern?

2. What part do family backgrounds of telemarketing fraud offenders play in preparing them for this deviant occupation?

3. How did telemarketing fraud allow these offenders to experience a strong sense of themselves as having power?

14. Understanding Identity Theft: Offenders' Accounts of Their Lives and Crimes

1. Why does the author find that identity theft is difficult to classify as a white-collar crime?

2. What types of identity theft offenses are there?

3. When seeking out identifying information from victims, what methods did these offenders utilize?

15. Transferring Subcultural Knowledge On-Line: Practices and Beliefs of Persistent Digital Pirates

1. How do digital pirates learn the norms and values of digital piracy?

2. Do you think a digital piracy subculture exists? Explain.

3. How did pirates learn to recognize and avoid the risks associated with their piracy?

PART VI. DRUGS AND CRIME

16. "Cooks Are Like Gods": Hierarchies in Methamphetamine-Producing Groups

1. What are some of the statuses that exist in methamphetamine-producing groups?

2. Why do women who move up in the hierarchy of the methamphetamine production process perceive themselves to be equal to their male counterparts?

3. Unlike the domestic production of marijuana and crack cocaine, methamphetamine production benefits from group involvement. How?

17. "We Weren't Like No Regular Dope Fiends": Negotiating Hustler and Crackhead Identities

1. How did participants in the street economy of crack cocaine construct a hustler identity?

2. What street status did crackheads have?

3. What is the biggest fear of crack cocaine dealers that could affect their street status?

18. Writing Against the Image of the Monstrous Crack Mother

1. What are some of the ways culture is represented in personal stories as this article illustrates?

2. The recovering drug addict applied both a twelve-step and a spiritual approach to contend with the stereotype of the monstrous crack mother. Explain how this occurred?

3. What is the meaning of the monstrous crack mother? Describe this deviant status from a societal point of view.

PART VII. GENDER AND CRIME

19. Moving Beyond the Stereotypes: Women's Subjective Accounts of Their Violent Crime

1. The study found five main motives for violence that the incarcerated women recounted. What were they?

2. What part did race play in women's violent offenses?

3. What is meant by private and public violent incidents?

20. **The Work of Sex Work: Elite Prostitutes' Vocational Orientations and Experiences**

   1. How do elite prostitutes view sexual labor in the context of an occupation?

   2. What factors influenced their decision to enter the work of prostitution?

   3. How do elite sex workers define the meaning of honor in the context of their trade?

21. **Mothering, Crime, and Incarceration**

   1. Why do incarcerated women feel more remorseful about the impact of their crimes as it affects their children than they do about committing the crime(s) they are being punished for?

   2. How does being a female single parent, living in an environment of scarce resources, play a role that leads to incarceration?

   3. The authors note that for many women offenders, life was so difficult and precarious that being locked up was actually perceived as an improvement. What criteria did the researchers use to substantiate this comment?

PART VIII. SUPPORT SYSTEMS AND CRIME

22. **The Familial Relationships of Former Prisoners: Examining the Link Between Residence and Informal Support Mechanisms**

   1. Why is family support for released prisoners considered so important?

   2. What are the five types of support used in this study?

   3. What part did an ex-prisoner's residence play in determining a family support system?

23. **Incarceration and Family Life in Urban America**

   1. Incarceration without treatment for drug addicts can be a double penalty for families of prisoners. Why?

   2. From the perspective of many families dealing with the criminal justice system, it seems like the system is a calculated design to insure them rather than to help or protect. Explain why these citizens perceive this to be true?

   3. The effect on the children of a parent's imprisonment is one of the most difficult issues for family members to talk about. Explain why this subject is so painful to discuss.

PART IX. DESISTANCE FROM CRIME

24. **Leaving the Streets: Transformation of Prostitute Identity Within the Prostitution Rehabilitation Program**

   1. What are the three successive phases of change former prostitutes move through as they rid themselves of their deviant identity?

   2. What was the purpose of the prostitution rehabilitation program having such strict formal social control mechanisms on the residents?

   3. What factors facilitated identity transformation for the program residents?

25. **"Me and the Law Is Not Friends": How Former Prisoners Make Sense of Reentry**

   1. How does the racism and the ability of low-skilled men of color limit their social and economic possibilities for successful recovery?

   2. Reentering men reintegrate in a variety of ways despite common social-economic circumstances. Discuss some of the ways they attempt to reintegrate.

   3. Desistance from crime offers little explanation on its own about the range of ways these ex-prisoners interpret their place in the world and their skepticism about the possibilities for success. Why would it be important to know these perceptions?

26. **The Love of a Good Man? Romantic Relationships as a Source of Support or Hindrance for Female Ex-Offenders**

   1. How can romantic relationships for reentering women ex-offenders prove to have a positive or negative effect on their desistance from crime?

   2. Some female ex-prisoners avoid romantic relationships for personal growth reasons. Explain why these women choose not to become involved in a romantic relationship for a period of time.

   3. This research supports the idea that relationships, like desistance, are social processes, not static facts. How does the idea of social process explain the relationships these ex-offenders were involved in?

INDEX

ABOUT THE CONTRIBUTORS

Donald Braman is an Associate Professor of Law at The George Washington University.

David G. Bromley is a Professor of Sociology at Virginia Commonwealth University.

Kristin Carbone-Lopez is an Assistant Professor of Criminology and Criminal Justice at University of Missouri St. Louis.

Johnna Christian is a Professor of Criminal Justice at Rutgers University.

Glenn S. Coffey is an instructor at L. Douglas Wilder School of Government and Public Affairs.

Heith Copes is an Associate Professor of Criminal Justice and also has a faculty appointment in the Department of Sociology at the University of Alabama at Birmingham.

Kathleen J. Ferraro is a Professor of Sociology at Northern Arizona University.

Aline Gubrium is an Assistant Professor of Public Health at the University of Massachusetts-Amherst.

Andy Hochstetler is an Associate Professor of Sociology at Iowa State University.

Thomas J. Holt is an Assistant Professor of Criminal Justice at Michigan State University.

Geoffrey P. Hunt is a senior research scientist at the U.S. Institute for Scientific Analysis and the Principal Investigator on three U.S. National Institute of Health projects.

Robert Jenkot is a Professor of Sociology at Coastal Carolina University.

Karen Joe-Laidler is a Professor of Sociology at the University of Hong Kong.

Candace Kruttschnitt is a Professor of Sociology at the University of Minnesota.

Charis E. Kubrin is Associate Professor of Sociology at George Washington University.

Andrea M. Leverentz is an Assistant Professor of Sociology and Director of Graduate Certificate in Forensic Services at the University of Massachusetts at Boston.

Vera Lopez is an Associate Professor of Justice and Social Inquiry at Arizona State University.

Ann M. Lucas is a Professor of Law and Justice at San Jose State University.

Kathleen MacKenzie is a senior research associate at the Institute for Scientific Analysis.

Joseph A. Marolla is the Vice Provost for Instruction at Virginia Commonwealth University.

Amos Martinez is Program Administrator for the Mental Health Licensing Section, Colorado Department of Regulatory Agencies.

Damian J. Martinez is an Assistant Professor in the School of Criminology and Criminal Justice at Arizona State University.

Maureen Miller is an Adjust Associate Professor of Epidemiology at Columbia University.

Angela M. Moe is an Associate Professor of Sociology at Western Michigan University.

Molly Moloney is a senior research associate at the Institute for Scientific Analysis.

Brian A. Monahan is Assistant Professor of Sociology at Iowa State University.

Christopher W. Mullins is an Assistant Professor and Undergraduate Program Director of Criminology and Criminal Justice at Southern Illinois University Carbondale.

Alan Neaigus is Director of Research in the HIV Epidemiology and Field Services Program at the

New York City Department of Health and Mental Hygiene and an Adjunct Associate Professor of Epidemiology at Columbia University.

Sharon S. Oselin is an Associate Professor of Criminology and Social Psychology at California State University.

Mark R. Pogrebin is a Professor of Criminal Justice and Director of the Criminal Justice Program in the Graduate School of Public Affairs at the University of Colorado at Denver.

Eric D. Poole is a Professor of Criminal Justice in the Graduate School of Public Affairs at the University of Colorado at Denver.

Ann M. S. Reeser is a Professor of Criminology and Criminal Justice at the University of Nebraska, Omaha.

Brenda Roche is Director of Community-Based Research at the Wellesley Institute.

Clinton R. Sanders is a Professor of Sociology at the University of Connecticut.

Neal Shover is a Professor of Sociology at the University of Tennessee Knoxville.

Pete Simi is Assistant Professor of Criminology and Criminal Justice at the University of Nebraska Omaha.

Lowell Smith is Deputy Probation Officer at the Intensive Unit of Orange Country Parole and Probation in Santa Ana, California.

Paul B. Stretesky is an Associate Professor of Public Affairs at the University of Colorado at Denver.

Volkan Topalli is Associate Professor of Criminal Justice and Faculty Associate of Partnership for Urban Health at Georgia State University.

Lucia Trimbur is an Assistant Professor of Sociology at John Jay College of Criminal Justice.

N. Prabha Unnithan is Professor of Sociology and Director of the Center for the Study of Crime and Justice at Colorado State University.

Gerald Venor is a Professor of Sociology at Colorado State University.

Lynne M. Vieraitis is a faculty member in the School of Economic, Political and Policy Sciences at the University of Texas at Dallas.

J. Patrick Williams is a Professor of Sociology in the Division of Sociology, School of Humanities and Social Sciences at Nanyang Technological University in Singapore.

Richard Wright is Curators' Professor of Criminology and Criminal Justice at the University of Missouri St. Louis.